KU-481-770

A History of Germany
1815–1985
Third Edition

William Carr
Professor of History, University of Sheffield

Edward Arnold

© William Carr 1969, 1979, 1987

This edition first published in Great Britain 1987 by Edward Arnold (Publishers) Ltd, 41 Bedford Square, London WC1B 3DQ

Edward Arnold (Australia) Pty Ltd, 80 Waverley Road, Caulfield East, Victoria 3145, Australia

Edward Arnold, 3 East Read Street, Baltimore, Maryland 21202, U.S.A.

First edition 1969
Second edition 1979
Third edition 1987

British Library Cataloguing in Publication Data

Carr, William, *1921–*
  A history of Germany, 1815–1985.——3rd ed.
  1. Germany——History——1789–1900
  2. Germany——History——20th century
  I. Title
  943′.07   DD203

  ISBN 0-7131-6495-6

All rights reserved. No part of this publication may be reproduced, stored in a retrieval system, or transmitted in any form or by any means, electronic, photocopying, recording, or otherwise, without the prior permission of Edward Arnold (Publishers) Ltd.

Text set in 11/12 pt Compugraphic Plantin
by Colset Private Limited Singapore
Printed and bound in Great Britain by Billings & Sons Ltd, Worcester

Contents

Maps

Preface

The history of Germany has fascinated me for many more years than I care to remember. That was not the only reason why I embarked on the task of writing this book. Teaching German history to undergraduates and discussing aspects of contemporary history with Extramural audiences in Yorkshire, Derbyshire and Lincolnshire over the years convinced me that there was room for a history of Modern Germany, surveying in some detail the period between the Congress of Vienna and the collapse of Hitler's *Reich* in 1945. The present volume is an attempt to meet this need. I hope that students of European history will find it useful and that it may help them and all readers who are interested in contemporary history to understand something of the historical background of what was for over a hundred years the most intractable problem facing Europe.

The absence of clear-cut geographical boundaries and the movement of German-speaking people into Eastern and Central Europe over the centuries have made it difficult to define the frontiers of Germany with any precision. A further complication arises from the fact that when the barbarian kingdoms donned the trappings of imperial Rome in early medieval times, they conferred a universal character on themselves which was preserved for centuries in the form of the Holy Roman Empire of the German Nation. This spirit of universalism lingered on long after the empire came to an end in 1806. During the War of Liberation in 1813 Jahn, one of the most popular writers and patriots of his day, dreamt of a *Reich* still ruled by the Habsburgs but extended to include the Dutch, the Flemings, the Danes and the Swiss on the ground that these peoples were as German as the Prussians and the Austrians. A century later during the First World War the phenomenal success of Friedrich Naumann's book, *Mitteleuropa*, a work which advocated a close union with Austria-Hungary, was a further manifestation of the deep longing for a greater *Reich*, in this case an extension of the *Grossdeutschland* ideal of 1848. When German army officers between the world wars boasted of their loyalty to the 'imperishable *Reich*' rather than to the 'transitory republic', they, too, were elaborating on a theme which runs throughout the whole of Germany history. And more recently still the fanatical followers of Hitler dreamt of a new *Reich* extending eastwards to the Urals with the Teutonic race lording it over the subject Slav peoples. I do not mean to imply by these examples that liberal humanitarians such as Jahn and Naumann, or even conservative soldiers such as Seeckt had much in common with the nihilist Hitler. The point is that these representative Germans[1] were all groping for a new imperial concept commensurate with the dominant role they expected Germany to play in Europe.

In fact the decisive turn taken by German history in the middle of the nineteenth century owed much less to Romantic dreams of universal empire than to the earth-bound concept of Little Germany, that is, a state built around the solid nucleus of Prussian power from which Austria, the power-house of universalism, was completely excluded. Of course, no history of Germany can ignore the influence of Austria. Metternich and Schwarzenberg in the first half of the nineteenth century, Aehrenthal and Berchtold in the early twentieth century, and Dollfuss and Schuschnigg between the world wars; all left their mark on the course of German history. But it is a fact that Prussia, not Austria, took the lead in transforming Germany from a quiet pastoral country, the home of poets and philosophers, into the highly industrialised empire of Bismarck and William II, a mighty state feared and respected by other powers. For that reason the history of Prussia looms large in this book, and references to the Habsburg Monarchy are made only where it is necessary for an understanding of the main theme.

The Congress of Vienna is a natural starting-point for a history of Little Germany. Germany emerged from the maelstrom of the French Revolution purged of many of the weaknesses which beset the Holy Roman Empire. Napoleon is rightly regarded as one of the makers of Modern Germany. The Revolution, of which he was the embodiment, dealt a mortal blow to medievalism and thrust Germany head first into the modern world. The colourful but chaotic mosaic of the empire was shattered to pieces. Most of the states which survived this ordeal were sounder in wind and limb and more capable of an independent existence that the free cities and tiny principalities of the imperial knights had been. Many of the new states adopted the modern administrative techniques which the French carried with them wherever they went in Europe. Finally, the presence of French soldiers on German soil helped to produce the first faint stirrings of nationalism, the ideological force which welded Germany into a nation in the middle of the nineteenth century. Despite its faults, the German Confederation of 1815 represented the first faltering step forward on the road to political unification which culminated in the proclamation of the German Empire in the Hall of Mirrors at Versailles in January 1871.

---

[1] Hitler remained an Austrian citizen until 1925 and was thereafter stateless until he acquired German citizenship in 1932.

In this third edition it seemed only right and proper to take account in a final chapter of the important developments in Central Europe in the forty years since the collapse of Hitler's Reich. Bismarck's Germany survived the defeat of 1918 and within a few years had regained most of its old power and prestige. The defeat of 1945 was different in kind. Foreign armies invaded Germany for the first time since the days of Napoleon, and when Russian soldiers established themselves on the line of the river Elbe the balance of power in Europe was altered decisively. Germany soon became a casualty of the 'Cold War'. By 1949 the Russian and the Anglo-American zones of occupation hardened into separate states: the Federal Republic of Germany and the German Democratic Republic which in the early 1960s glared at each other over the Berlin Wall. It was difficult at that time, when this book was originally conceived, for my generation, which fought against Nazi Germany, to believe that the vigorous and inventive people who live between the Rhine and the Oder would tolerate the division of their country indefinitely. But now in the last quarter of the twentieth century it looks as if the fires of nationalism have at last burned themselves out in Europe. The two Germanies, together with the independent Austrian Republic, co-exist peacefully and the possibility of political reunification has receded into the very distant future. The configuration of political, cultural and socio-economic forces which made possible the *Reich* that Bismarck created, William II inherited and Hitler destroyed was peculiar to a historic epoch when Europe was still the centre of the universe and when war was not synonymous with nuclear annihilation. The shift in the balance of world power and changes in the nature of modern warfare have between them made wars of unification a historical anachronism in Europe today and completely transformed the nature of the German problem.

Books are not written – or revised – in a vacuum. They are the product of a fruitful interplay between the material and the opinions of the author. To my friends at the University and in the City of Sheffield I am deeply indebted for experiences which have enriched the mind and given me some insight into the mainsprings of human conduct. A special word of thanks is due to the late Professor G.R. Potter, formerly head of the Department of Modern History in this University, for his unfailing interest in my work and his constant encouragement of my efforts when I was a young lecturer. Finally, no words can express my deep sense of gratitude to my wife for her patience and tolerance during the writing of this and other books.

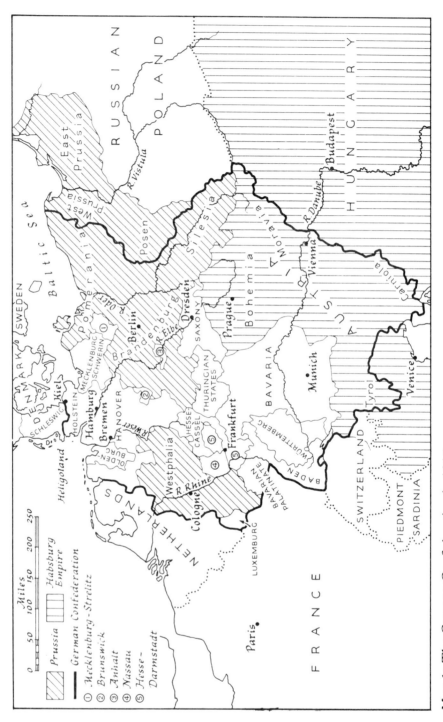

Map 1: The German Confederation in 1815

1

Restoration Germany 1815–1847

Europe in 1815 was in a state of mental and physical exhaustion after the tremendous upheaval of the Revolutionary and Napoleonic Wars. Men longed for peace and order and turned away from the liberal philosophy of a revolution which had ended in tyranny and bloodshed. Edmund Burke in England, Joseph de Maistre and Louis de Bonald in France and Novalis (Friedrich von Hardenberg) in Germany expressed the essence of the Restoration era in their writings when they poured scorn on the rationalism of the Enlightenment and Revolution, and declared that obedience to princely authority, respect for the legitimate rights of rulers and maintenance of the Christian religion were the only foundations for a healthy and durable social order.

At an international level Austria, Britain, Prussia, and Russia the four great allied powers who had played the major single role in the defeat of France, took upon themselves the task of recapturing the calm and stability of that lost age for which the kings and princes of Europe yearned. The victorious allies tried to do this by creating a new balance of power favourable to the forces of conservatism. Germany played a vital role in their scheme of things. For clearly the peace of Europe would depend upon the existence of a strong and stable Germany capable of acting as a barrier to French imperialism in the future. This raised awkward questions at the very outset of their deliberations. Respect for legitimate rights was perfectly compatible with a viable balance of power in Italy and Spain but not in Germany. If Germany was to be an effective link in the *cordon sanitaire* around France, then the ramshackle and militarily indefensible Holy Roman Empire could not possibly be restored in its entirety. Security won the battle against legitimacy in the councils of the Great Powers. Napoleon's drastic reorganisation of Germany was allowed to stand, and the powers turned a deaf ear to the clamour of the petty princelings for the restoration of their tiny principalities on the left bank of the Rhine; all these rulers retained after 1815 were their titles and social privileges. Strategic considerations were reinforced by political commitments. In 1813, when the outcome of the final struggle against Napoleon was far from certain, the allied powers succeeded in detaching the *Rheinbund* princes from their French protector; in return the allies were obliged to guarantee the territorial integrity and sovereignty of the new South-German states which had grown great at the expense of the smaller ecclesiastical and secular principalities.

The peace settlement of 1815, of which the German settlement was an integral part, was deeply influenced by Prince Metternich, foreign minister of Austria from 1809 to 1848 and chancellor from 1821. Contemporaries regarded Metternich as the embodiment of the spirit of the Restoration Era, a legend which lingered on well into the twentieth century. In fact he belonged to the eighteenth rather than the nineteenth century; at heart he was a rationalist out of sympathy with the new theories of legitimacy and divine right and somewhat suspicious of the pretensions of the Restoration Church; he was a manipulator of men not of theories, an admirer of benevolent despotism and above all a devoted and loyal servant of the house of Habsburg. His aim was quite simply the maintenance of Austrian power, the means skilful diplomacy which by 1814 had already won for Austria a position of great influence in international affairs, out of all proportion to her military strength, and one which she retained for the next thirty-four years. Curiously enough, despite his success in maintaining the illusion of Austrian greatness for so long, Metternich was full of pessimism about the future. He had too acute a sense of power realities not to appreciate how impermanent the foundations were on which his life's work rested. In public he delighted in the title *rocher de l'ordre politique et sociale*; in private he sadly compared himself with a physician who correctly diagnosed an illness but could not cure his patient; at most he could only prolong the patient's life.

Equilibrium, or balance, was the key to Metternich's 'system'. He was firmly convinced that monarchs could sit securely on their thrones only when the balance of forces inside society favoured the established order, and when the balance of power between states was sufficiently durable to deter potential aggressors. To preserve a happy equilibrium, Metternich fostered close co-operation between rulers after 1815 and encouraged them to interfere in the affairs of neighbouring states whenever revolution threatened the established order. He was one of the first to appreciate that the first faint stirrings of liberalism and nationalism represented a fundamental challenge to all Restoration Europe stood for. He had no doubt that the victory of the new ideologies in Germany and Italy would lead inevitably to the destruction of the precarious foundations of Habsburg ascendancy, and the disruption of the European balance of power, and would plunge the peoples of Europe into a disastrous series of wars between new and unstable national states. To keep the dark forces at bay in Central Europe, Metternich relied on the prestige of Austria and on the goodwill and co-operation of the German princes, all of whom had a vested interest in the permanence of the existing social order. In the interests of European peace the princes would have to relinquish the right to wage war on each other and agree to live together in a loose association or confederation of states. At the same time the fact that the princes would remain rulers of virtually sovereign states was the best possible insurance against the creation of a united Germany.

Thus before the Congress of Vienna assembled in the autumn of 1814 the Great Powers had already decided upon the creation of a German Confederation. A committee composed of Austria, Prussia, Württemberg, Bavaria and Hanover was set up to draft a constitution for the Confederation. The deliberations soon ended in deadlock. Bavaria and Württemberg were determined to restrict the scope of the Confederation as much as possible, and were particularly incensed by Austrian and Prussian proposals that these powers be accorded privileged positions in Germany. At the end of 1814 the attention of the Great Powers was distracted by the Polish-Saxon dispute, which threatened to disrupt the wartime coalition. For a time it looked as if Britain, Austria and France might go to war to prevent Prussia absorbing the whole of Saxony as compensation for the loss of most of her former Polish territories. In the end Prussia settled for part of Saxony, and the crisis died away. Austria and Prussia turned back to the German settlement and reactivated the German Committee. At long last they acceded to the request of the twenty-nine minor German states and admitted them to the deliberations of the committee. Not that this greatly affected the issue. Austria and Prussia still made the running. In a series of hurried conferences in May and June 1815 the enlarged committee agreed to a draft constitution based on Austrian proposals. The German constitution, or Federal Act, as it was called, was included in the Final Act of Congress signed by the powers in June 1815. This was Metternich's idea; like Litvinov a century later, Metternich believed that peace was indivisible and cherished the hope that once the Great Powers had set the seal of approval on the Act they would feel committed to the maintenance of its provisions should Germany be threatened by the forces of revolution.[1]

The German Confederation of 1815 was essentially a more rational version of the Holy Roman Empire. It resembled the latter in territorial extent, the most important difference being that the former Austrian Netherlands were now an integral part of the kingdom of the United Netherlands. But the face of Germany had changed out of all recognition. The colourful mosaic of the old empire, which embraced several hundred sovereign territories ranging from the great kingdom of Prussia to the tiny principalities of the imperial knights had gone for ever, swept away by

---

[1]Strictly speaking there was no formal guarantee of the German settlement. All that could be argued was that the signatories had assumed some kind of moral obligation towards Germany.

Napoleon. Very few of the thirty-nine states[2] in the Confederation of 1815 were restorations, and the exceptions were only small states, notably Saxe-Weimar and Brunswick.

The Federal Act declared that one of the objects of confederation was the defence of the independence of member-states. For the German princes this was its primary purpose and they saw to it that very few restrictions were placed on their sovereign powers. The Federal Diet or Bundestag at Frankfurt (modelled on the Diet of the *Rheinbund*) was little more than a congress of ambassadors whose function it was to protect the interests of their rulers. Constitutional amendments were virtually impossible, as they required the consent of all the states meeting in plenary session. Many other measures, including declarations of war, required a two-thirds majority in that body. In fact there were only sixteen plenary sessions in the entire history of the Confederation. Day-to-day business was conducted on the basis of simple majority decisions in an inner committee (*engerer Rat*) in which the eleven large states had one vote each while the other states shared six votes between them. Austria and Prussia possessed only one vote each, an arrangement designed to neutralise their power. However, in practice these states were usually able to get their own way in the inner committee by virtue of the indirect pressures they could exert on the smaller states.

The lingering hope in progressive circles that the Diet might develop a corporate spirit of its own and pursue policies conducive to national unification was quickly dispelled at the first meeting in 1816. It was soon apparent that the Diet preferred to avoid positive action whenever possible. Nothing was ever done to devise national policies on trade and communications. The establishment of a federal court was frustrated by opposition from Bavaria and Württemberg. The task of defining the personal liberties of German citizens was left to the discretion of member-states. A similar fate overtook clause thirteen of the Federal Act which stated that constitutions based on estates should be set up in each state – a concession to the spirit of an age which gave France a charter and Poland a constitution. Once again the Diet evaded the issue and decided that the implementation of this clause must be left to the discretion of individual rulers. Arrangements for the defence of Germany, although a considerable improvement on what had existed before, were still inadequate. The Diet finally agreed in 1821 to establish a federal army of ten corps, three from Austria, three from Prussia, one from Bavaria, and three from the other states. From the start the army was seriously weakened by the refusal of the smaller states to allow the Diet any jurisdiction over their contingents; the smaller the state the more insistent was the ruler upon complete control of his soldiers. Nor was the vital question of the supreme command

---

[2]There were only thirty-eight in 1815; Hesse-Homburg, the only mediatised principality to be restored, did not join until 1817.

of this army ever satisfactorily resolved; the Diet merely stated that it would choose a commander-in-chief in the event of war. In effect the defence of the German Confederation was dependent upon continued co-operation between Austria and Prussia; once their relations became less amicable, as they did after 1850, the Confederation was virtually unable to defend its members against external attack.

Despite its name, the German Confederation was no more a national state than the old empire had been. There were important non-German minorities; the Czechs in Bohemia and Moravia, Slovenes in Styria and Carniola, and Italians in South Tyrol. On the other hand, the Confederation excluded considerable German minorities living in Schleswig, West Prussia and Posen, as well as a German majority in East Prussia; the exclusion of the latter territory resulted from the anomalous circumstances that only that part of the Prussian kingdom which had been in the Holy Roman Empire was allowed to enter the Confederation. Similarly half the Habsburg Empire, namely the Hungarian territories, lay outside the Confederation. A further anomaly was that some states were ruled by foreign princes, as they had been in the Empire. The king of England continued to rule Hanover until 1837. The king of Denmark remained duke of Holstein until 1864 as well as duke of Lauenburg, a small territory adjoining Holstein and previously ruled by Hanover but transferred to Denmark in 1815. A newcomer was the king of Holland who became grand duke of Luxemburg in 1815 to compensate him for the loss of his estates in Nassau which were taken by Prussia.

Nineteenth-century historians were often bitterly critical of the Confederation on the grounds that it did pathetically little to promote the unification of Germany. This is a harsh judgement. The German Confederation must be seen in context like any other historical phenomenon. The fact of the matter was that no viable alternative to confederation existed in 1815; the Great Powers had no wish to see the delicate balance of power they had constructed at the Congress of Vienna upset by the emergence of a united Germany; and powerful states such as Bavaria, Baden and Württemberg, all of which had expanded under French patronage, had no interest in unification, and were in any case too firmly rooted in the affection of their subjects for their wishes to be ignored.

The Confederation had some positive merit. It represented a step forward on the road to nationhood, away from the chaotic administrative tangle of the Empire. It did at least give Germany peace for half a century after the upheaval of the Napoleonic Wars. Given time, it is possible that the latent powers of the Federal Diet might have developed at the expense of member-states, leading Germany slowly but surely towards the goal of final unification. What is certain is that most Germans were perfectly satisfied with the new Confederation; the national feeling which burnt so fiercely in 1813 soon died out; it had been restricted largely to Prussia; only after the battle of Leipzig did other parts of Germany share in it and then only to a limited extent. Once the French armies had departed, interest in public affairs declined sharply. Most Germans felt a deep sense of devotion to the ruling dynasties, a not unusual phenomenon in a patriarchal society where seventy-five per cent of the population lived in the countryside and only fourteen towns had more than 100,000 inhabitants. This feeling was shared, too, by the middle class; when the elector of Hesse-Cassel, a member of a princely house notorious for tyrannical and oppressive rule, returned to his principality, the brothers Grimm, philologists who won immortal fame for their collections of folk tales, ran alongside his coach shouting greetings.

It is true that important social changes were taking place in Restoration Germany. Legal serfdom, which the French had abolished, was not restored after the war, while the process of transforming feudal obligations into monetary payments continued in West and South Germany after 1815. However, change is a slow and uncertain process in a pre-industrial society where the organic ties of family and corporate life are very strong and local loyalities are tenaciously preserved. Socially and politically Restoration Germany was still dominated by the landed aristocracy, whose real power survived the revolutionary era virtually unbroken. No attempt had been made to abolish the judicial powers of landowners, and, as they frequently withheld consent to commutation of feudal services, the basis of their economic power remained unimpaired. In 1815 the middle class was again excluded from court functions, the front seats in theatres were reserved for the nobility and the old hunting rights restored. The middle class bitterly resented social demotion; for during the period of French ascendancy in Germany they had experienced their first taste of freedom. The accumulated lumber of centuries had been swept away in many states, notably in the Rhineland and in South Germany. Social privilege was abolished; the equality of all citizens before the law and the *carrière ouverte aux talents* became accepted principles; and irksome restrictions on trade and industry were removed. Yet, however much the restoration of the social order was resented, the state officals and shopkeepers who formed the bulk of the middle class were far too weak in numbers, and too dependent on princely courts for their livelihood, to make any effective protest.

The dominant power in the Confederation was Austria, a fact recognised at Frankfurt where her representative presided over the Diet. Appearances were deceptive; Austria was in many ways a backward state and something of a anachronism in the modern world. The ideas of the French Revolution passed her by, and during the unenlightened reigns of Emperor Francis I, *der gute Kaiser Franz* (1804–1835), and his weak minded-successor, Ferdinand I (1835–49) little was done to reform the antiquated and cumbersome bureaucratic machine which held the empire together. Press censorship and a ubiquitous secret police repressed what interest there was in political change. True, the old provincial estates were revived at Metternich's suggestion, but only as a means of preserving the established social order; to truly representative institutions Metternich was as implacably opposed as was his imperial master. In his treatment of the non-German peoples of the Habsburg monarchy Metternich was more enlightened. He studiously avoided the centralist policy of Emperor Joseph II which had aroused much opposition at the close of the eighteenth century. Instead, Metternich allowed Magyars and Slavs to go their own way with a minimum of interference from Vienna in the hope that loyalty to the Habsburgs and the existence of divisions among the non-German peoples would between them neutralise the power of centrifugal forces. Perhaps masterly inactivity was the only hope for the survival of the dynasty. However that may be, time showed that the forces of history were too strong for Metternich; he could do little to prevent the cultural renaissance, which he encouraged in Bohemia, Illyria and Hungary, from developing into an aggressive political nationalism which gradually destroyed the equilibrium on which the empire rested and eventually shook it to pieces in the twentieth century.

Prussia, the second major state in the Confederation, had become a more German power as a result of the Congress of Vienna. She had been obliged, reluctantly, to abandon most of her Polish territories to Russia and to content herself with only the northern part of Saxony. In return for this sacrifice Prussia received the Rhineland and the duchy of Westphalia. The exchange had profound effects on the course of German history. At a stroke of the pen the population of Prussia doubled, the centre of gravity of the kingdom moved from Poland to Germany, and Prussia became the guardian of Western Germany against France. Prussian policy changed direction accordingly; it now became a primary objective in Berlin to extend Prussian influence over the territories separating Brandenburg from the Rhineland; in short, the unification of North Germany was thrust upon this powerful and restless state by the facts of her political geography.

Prussia was a better organised state in 1815 than she had been in 1806 when she suffered humiliating defeat at the hands of the French. The change was due in large measure to the work of the Prussian Reformers, a small group of high officials (most of them not Prussian by birth) who began to modernise Prussia between 1807 and 1814. The reforms started when Freiherr Karl vom Stein, son of an imperial knight and a fervent admirer of Edmund Burke, was appointed chief adviser to the king in 1807. He abolished serfdom (1807) and reorganised the system of municipal government (1808) before being dismissed at the insistence of the French who suspected that he was preparing Prussia for war. The reforms continued under the auspices of Prince Karl August von Hardenberg, who was appointed chancellor in 1810; the army was reorganised by the soldiers

Scharnhorst, Gneisenau, Boyen and Clausewitz and educational reforms were carried out by Humboldt, former Prussian resident in Rome and a friend of Goethe and Schiller. After 1815 the tradition of reform was kept alive in the provinces of Westphalia, the Rhineland, Silesia and Prussia by dedicated civil servants who strove to rationalise the apparatus of government and promote the economic well-being of the people. But at national level the era of reform came to an abrupt end. Once the French were defeated, King Frederick William III lost interest in reform and turned for support to his natural allies, the conservative landowners of East Prussia. They had in fact survived the reforms without loss of real power; indeed their power was enormously strengthened by the edict of 1816, which restricted commutation to the larger farmers and made it dependent on the payment of heavy compensation. Hardenberg remained the king's chief minister until his death in 1822, but, now an old man, he showed little of his earlier radicalism. The greater disappointment came over the constitution. The king delayed for several years before attempting to fulfil the promise made in 1815 at Hardenberg's suggestion to give Prussia a representative constitution. And in 1823 he only set up provincial estates with limited advisory powers and completely dominated by the landowners; Stein's plan for a national assembly elected by the estates had been abandoned. Consequently the political education of Prussia was seriously retarded, and she forfeited much of the moral authority she had enjoyed in liberal circles in 1813. But in the things of the spirit Prussia continued to enjoy a considerable reputation during the Restoration period. When the French philosopher Victor Cousin visited Berlin in 1830, he was surprised to discover that Prussia was a classic land of schools as well as barracks; the Prussian system of secondary education was a model for other states, and the new universities of Berlin, Breslau and Bonn attracted students from all over Germany eager to sit at the feet of the great philosopher Hegel, the brilliant historian Ranke and the eminent philologist Lachmann.

The old rivalry between Austria and Prussia, which had caused two major wars between 1740 and 1763, was temporarily muted in Restoration Germany. Chastened by the traumatic experience of the Revolution, these powers discovered a common interest in the preservation of the *status quo*. Thus after 1815 the Prussian king and his advisers were eager to work as closely as possible with Metternich in their anxiety to keep liberalism and nationalism, the universal enemies of monarchy, at bay. Metternich for his part valued good relations with Prussia, being quick to appreciate that continuous cooperation and consultation between the two most powerful states in the Confederation was the best guarantee of the permanence of the conservative order of things in Central Europe. He took great care to keep Prussia informed about Austrian intentions and went through the motions of consultation on all important issues. In return he could always rely on loyal support from Prussia in the Federal Diet, an amicable arrangement which made Austria's task an easier one and had the additional advantage that it excluded the other states from an effective voice in German affairs.

The calm and stability of Restoration Europe was illusory. Behind the peaceful façade the new social forces liberated by the Great Revolution were stirring. Nationalism and liberalism, the ideological solvents of Metternich's Europe, were emerging in embryonic form in Germany as in other countries after 1815, and challenging the assumptions on which the conservative order rested.

German nationalism was a somewhat vague and open-ended concept. For most ordinary Germans it amounted to little more than resentment of French rule and a fervent desire to be rid of an invader who had burdened the people with heavy taxes, interfered with trade and commerce, and taken their sons off to fight in interminable wars. Only a handful of educated Germans had advanced beyond this negative attitude and this largely as a result of the influence of the German Romantics. Just before the beginning of the nineteenth century writers such as Müller, Schelling and the Schlegel brothers started to proclaim the virtues of the Middle Ages, a period which had been dismissed as 'Gothic' and 'barbarian' by eighteenth-century historians. The Romantics revelled in the colour and magic of the medieval empire, when knights, estates and emperor were allegedly inspired by a truly 'national' spirit, and dreamt of a new *Reich*, freed from the French yoke, with frontiers extended in the west to include the lands lost in the Middle Ages. Thus Arndt, one of the best known patriotic writers during the War of Liberation (1813–14), declared in his poem *Was ist des deutschen Vaterland* that Germany's new frontiers should extend

> So weit die deutsche Zunge klingt
> Und Gott im Himmel Lieder singt.[3]

Measured by this yardstick, Switzerland and Styria were as much part of Germany as Prussia and Bavaria. *Turnvater* Jahn,[4] another well-known patriotic writer of 1813, went even further and laid claim to Denmark and the Low Countries as well as Switzerland. However, most Germans resisted these unhealthy dreams of imperial grandeur and were perfectly content with the frontiers of the Confederation which were substantially those of the Empire in decline.

Nationalists wanted more than a mere restoration of the old imperial

[3] As far as the German tongue is heard, and sings songs to God in heaven.
[4] Jahn founded the first *Turnverein*, or gymnastic society, in Berlin to train young men for the war against the French.

trappings. Painful memories of the humiliating occupation of their country aroused in them a firm determination to make the new Germany stronger and able to hold its own in the world. To achieve this the emperor would have to be given real power over the princes for the first time in history. Nationalists believed it equally important to give the German people a vested interest in the defence of the new *Reich* by associating them with the work of government through an elected imperial diet. Curiously enough, nationalist critics of the settlement of 1815 did not think that the continued existence of thirty-nine sovereign states was in any way incompatible with the creation of a strong German *Reich*. Flying in the face of the lessons of medieval history, they assumed that the changes they advocated could be brought about by amicable agreement with the German princes. Only in 1848 was this naïve illusion shattered.

There was nothing narrow or exclusive about German nationalism after 1815; on the contrary, it was inextricably interwoven with supranational threads. Educated Germans were firmly convinced that a strong Germany, far from disturbing the peace of Europe, would act as a stabilising factor. Germany had a universal mission to perform: as custodian of the cultural treasures of Europe and standardbearer of humanistic values in the modern world, she would draw all the people of Europe to her. In a sense this belief rendered political unification superfluous; indeed many German writers made a virtue of necessity and praised the 'God-given diversity' of the states in which they professed to see an enrichment of the human personality and an incontrovertible proof of the universality of the German way of life. Dahlmann and Welcker, eminent academics who played a leading role in the North-German liberal movement, even argued that the presence of foreign rulers in the Confederation did not retard national development but actually enhanced it, because it underlined the supranational character of Germany and helped to make her the nucleus around which the unification of Europe would one day take place. Those extremists who were constantly harping on peculiarly German qualities or characteristics were, according to these writers, behaving in a thoroughly 'un-German' manner and failing to appreciate Germany's true vocation in Europe. Behind this vague, inconsistent and open-ended cosmopolitanism lay a belief, consciously or subconsciously held, that the pre-eminence of Germany in philosophy and literature would, in the natural order of events, confer on her the moral and perhaps the political primacy of Europe.

German liberalism was a much clearer cut concept. It was part of the wider European movement which had its origins in the Enlightenment of the eighteenth century and in the French Revolution. German, French, Italian and Belgian liberals were opposed to the growing power of the post-Napoleonic state, and were seeking to maximise the freedom of the individual by restricting the activities of governments to an irreducible minimum. They wanted to place constitutional limitations on the power of the rulers, establish the rule of law in society, sweep away all restrictions on individual enterprise and give to men of property a voice in the government of their country without sliding down the slippery slope of democracy into 'mob rule'.

Several indigenous factors fortified these universal trends in the case of Germany. The memory of the Prussian Reformers still burned bright in North Germany. In addition, there was a reforming tradition in states, such as Baden, where enlightened rulers in the second half of the eighteenth century had started to introduce a note of uniformity and order into bumbling and inefficient administrative systems, work which continued at an increased tempo in the first decade of the nineteenth century under French guidance. Finally, the writings of classical humanists and Romantics, with their emphasis on the freedom of the human personality, favoured the spread of liberal ideas. On the other hand, the existence of separate states with their own traditions and loyalties undoubtedly narrowed the focus of German liberalism. Critics of the Federal Act, once they realised how powerless they were to realise their ambitions at national level, turned their attention to the task of obtaining constitutions at home. The paradoxical outcome was that, in so far as their efforts to revitalise the inner life of their own states succeeded, liberals were making the task of unification infinitely more difficult, as the events of 1848 proved.

The size of Germany, the variety of cultural influences and historical experience and the diverse personalities of liberal leaders militated against the growth of a uniform liberal movement. Liberalism was localised in character, and liberals for the most part had little knowledge of, or interest in, the activity of their colleagues in other states. The result was that disparate elements, which would have crystallised into separate parties in lands where political movements were nationally based, continued to co-exist uneasily in Germany almost to the eve of the 1848 Revolution. Nevertheless, it is possible to detect two main streams of liberal thought in Germany between 1815 and 1848: historical liberalism and theoretical liberalism, as they are sometimes called.

Historical liberalism was strongest in North Germany. Liberty, Equality and Fraternity, the watchwords of the Great Revolution, were thoroughly repugnant to North-German liberals who had a hearty dislike of the French. This antipathy to France was in part a legacy of the War of Liberation, which aroused most enthusiasm in the north. It was also a reflection of the very profound influence exerted by German Romanticism on the political thinking of North-German liberals. From the Romantics came their belief that constitutions were not mere legal abstractions which could be imported ready-made from abroad, but living organisms evolving slowly and painfully as part of a complex historical pattern. England was greatly admired by these liberals, who confidently asserted that it was a perfect example of a truly 'organic' society where all estates or classes played a part in the constitutional life of the nation. Like all Romantics, they were fascinated by the history of medieval Germany and attached an exaggerated importance to the remnants of medieval estates which lingered on in some places. Their liberalism took the form of a demand for the restoration and transformation of these historical relics into two-chamber legislatures with limited legislative and financial powers. They had no wish to turn the king into a mere figurehead. On the contrary, they were filled with a deep respect and reverence for the crown and invariably insisted that the king must have veto power over all legislation; as Dahlmann expressed it: 'A king must not be able to do everything he wants to, but he must not be compelled to do anything he does not want to.' They were also respectful towards the landed aristocracy, not on account of rank but rather because noblemen had a considerable stake in the country and must play a role of corresponding importance in affairs of state. The upper chamber was reserved, in their scheme of things, for the aristocracy, while the upper middle class would control the lower chamber, which would be elected on a restricted franchise heavily weighted in favour of property.

The old provincial estates did come into favour again in Restoration Germany. In Saxony, Hanover and the Mecklenburgs estates which had lingered on throughout the Napoleonic period were kept in being after 1815. In Prussia, where the local estates had withered away, new estates were created in 1823. This was not a tribute to the attraction of historical liberalism. It occurred simply because the rulers in question wished to bolster up the conservative order of things. Restorations of this kind did not please the liberals, because the new estates possessed only a consultative function and were completely dominated by the aristocracy to the exclusion of the middle class.

On the rare occasions when liberals tried to badger rulers into granting constitutions, they failed completely. Such was the case in Schleswig-Holstein. By and large the German aristocracy remained loyal to the ruling dynasties, thankful for the restoration of social privilege. But in Schleswig-Holstein dissident members of the local aristocracy came into conflict with the Danish king over tax arrears. In an attempt to preserve their financial privilege they demanded the restoration of the old estates. The local liberals led by Dahlmann, then a professor of history at Kiel University, sprang to the defence of the aristocracy and in the pages of the *Kieler Blätter* called for a more modern version of the defunct medieval estates; they carefully pointed out that a constitution of this kind would be truly 'German' and not a detestable 'French' innovation. The agitation ended in failure. The local aristocracy was uninterested in the wider issue of constitutional freedom, and the academics and officials who consorted with the aristocracy lacked public support and would have been extremely embarrassed to receive any. The Federal Diet was asked to intervene in the dispute but it declared in 1823 that it had no competence to interfere in Schleswig, which was outside the Confederation, and that in any case it could only recognise estates still in existence, which was manifestly not the position in Schleswig-Holstein.

The second main stream of liberal thought, theoretical liberalism, derived most of its support from the south and west of Germany. Although not completely unmindful of historical factors, these liberals were primarily influenced by the constitutional theory and practice of France. They did not employ cumbersome historical and legal arguments to justify constitutional liberties but boldly invoked the Declaration of the Rights of Man and Citizen adopted by the French National Assembly in 1789. The French constitution of 1791 represented for them the summit of political wisdom and was a model to be copied as widely as possible. Northern liberalism was always a weak growth dependent almost exclusively on the upper middle class. Liberalism in the south, on the other hand, was much more virile and vigorous because it enjoyed wider support especially from lower-middle-class *Handwerker*[5] in the towns. And this, in its turn, was due in part at least to the fortunate circumstances that between 1814 and 1820 several rulers in South Germany had given constitutions to their subjects.

This was no sudden conversion to liberalism but simply a matter of practical politics. South-German rulers saw in constitutions a convenient instrument for the consolidation of newly acquired dominions; this was a means of binding subjects more closely to the ruler and of giving the more articulate citizens a positive interest in the preservation of the state. In the case of the duchy of Nassau and the tiny grand duchy of Saxe-Weimar the constitutions were still based on the old estates with some modifications; incidentally, Saxe-Weimar enjoyed a high reputation with liberals before 1848 not on account of its constitution (which was certainly not the most progressive in Germany), but because during the reign of Grand Duke Karl August, a friend of Goethe and a patron of the arts, the administration of the grand duchy was exceptionally enlightened and the press the most free in Germany.

In Württemberg, Bavaria, Baden and Hesse-Darmstadt constitutions were much more advanced, being modelled on the French Charter of 1814. Citizens enjoyed the fundamental liberal rights of a free press, freedom of association, religious toleration and equality before the law. The elected lower houses established in all these states made full use of the right to approve or reject legislation, and quickly became focal points in the political life of South Germany. The deputies, who were usually academics or officials, profited from the opportunity of learning parliamentary techniques, and their readiness to criticise the administration

[5]Skilled artisans or craftsmen.

helped to create a rudimentary public opinion in Germany. In Baden, a state more open to western liberal influence through its proximity to Switzerland and France, an exceptionally progressive franchise produced a virile liberalism, the most advanced in Restoration Germany. At the first meeting of the Karlsruhe estates in 1819 there was a sharp clash between the government and the lower house; the latter refused to approve military expenditure and compelled the former to withdraw an edict which would have restored financial and judicial privileges to the aristocracy.

Admittedly the power of the crown remained virtually unbroken in most states. The constitution was a free gift from the monarch who remained the source of sovereignty;[6] care was taken to establish a nominated upper house invariably dominated by the aristocracy; this acted as a brake on the activities of the lower house, which in any case could not initiate legislation, had limited budgetary control and was elected on a highly restricted franchise. For all that, the states south of the river Main compared favourably with the rest of the Confederation. In Austria all that existed were provincial estates dominated by the local aristocracy; Metternich's modest plan for an imperial council, or *Reichsrat*, nominated by the estates and endowed with advisory functions was never implemented owing to the stubborn opposition of Emperor Francis I. And in the rest of Germany, as indicated already, rulers merely allowed the old unreformed estates to continue in existence; in Brunswick and Hesse-Cassel the rulers soon abandoned any pretence of working with their estates and behaved in a thoroughly tyrannical fashion reminiscent of the worst days of the *ancien régime*.

It would be quite wrong to suppose that most Germans cared about constitutional liberties in the post-war years. Those who did formed a very small minority even among the middle classes and were completely isolated from the mass of the people. There were a few pamphleteers such as Görres, the Catholic journalist who openly criticised the Federal Act of 1815 in the *Rheinischer Merkur* until the paper was suppressed at the request of the Russians; poets such as the Swabian Ludwig Uhland, author of the famous ballad *Ich hatt' einen Kameraden*, who staunchly defended '*das gute alte Recht*'[7] in Württemberg when the old estates came into conflict with the king over constitutional problems; a few Rhineland merchants and lawyers brought up on the *Code Napoléon*; and, lastly, a number of university teachers. The last-named were the most influential group because only in secluded university circles was there any sustained political discussion. Professors such as Dahlmann, Rotteck, Welcker, Grimm, Mohl and Gervinus turned their backs on the long academic tradition of political disengagement and threw themselves whole-heartedly into the struggle for constitutional freedom. The 'political professors', as

[6]Württemberg was an exception; the constitution was agreed between the king and the estates.
[7]The good old laws.

they are called, supplied the liberal movement with most of its ideas and its leaders between 1815 and 1848.

The professors usually enjoyed the enthusiastic support of their students, who were busily organising themselves in the *Burschenschaften*. The term was first used by *Turnvater* Jahn when he proposed in 1811 that Berlin university should establish one student body to supersede the old *Landmannschaften*; the latter had restricted membership to students from particular provinces, an arrangement which obviously militated against the notion of a common German fatherland. Nothing came of the plan. In 1815 the first *Burschenschaft* was founded at Jena university by students who had known Jahn and had fought in the Free Corps founded by Major von Lützow in 1813. Other universities in Central and South Germany followed suit. Progress was, however, slow in North Germany, while Bavaria and Austria, the Catholic parts of Germany, were little affected by the movement. The *Burschenschaften* represented a new style of student association. In the old *Landmannschaften* students spent their time rioting, drinking and duelling, the normal pastimes of German students since the Thirty Years War; indeed Jena was notorious at the end of the eighteenth century for the moral degeneracy of its students. The *Burschenschaften* were permeated with the new spirit of patriotism and elevated by a sense of moral responsibility; the Jena *Burschenschaft* took for its motto the words 'Honour, Freedom and Fatherland' and set to work at once to reform student morals. In an attempt to underline the need for solidarity among students, the Jena *Burschenschaft* organised a general meeting at the Wartburg castle in Saxe-Weimar in October 1817. Five hundred students from many parts of Germany assembled there on the three-hundredth anniversary of the Reformation and the fourth anniversary of the battle of Leipzig, and gave voice to the nebulous, noisy and colourful nationalism which lingered on in student circles long after it had died out elsewhere. At the end of the formal celebrations a high-spirited group of *Turnvater* Jahn's followers from Berlin burnt in effigy the works of some anti-liberal writers in imitation of the burning of the papal bull by Luther in 1521. A juvenile but dramatic gesture and one which caused concern in ruling circles. Austria and Prussia took the Grand Duke Karl to task for allowing the Wartburg festival to take place. The grand duke resisted these external pressures and allowed the *Allgemeiner Burschentag* to meet in Jena in October 1818. At this meeting representatives from fourteen universities founded the *Allgemeine deutsche Burschenschaft*, the first all-German student organisation. They adopted the black, red and gold colours of the Jena *Burschenschaft* as the national colours of German students; it was alleged that these were the old imperial colours; in fact they were the colours of the uniform first worn by the Lützow Free Corps and then by Jena students.

These manifestations of student activity increased the feeling of alarm and unease in German ruling circles. These were troubled years in Europe; between 1819 and 1821 the first earth tremors shook the calm of Restoration Europe. Frightened governments reacted sharply to any sign of discontent; in Britain Parliament passed the Six Acts after the Peterloo disturbances; in France reactionary Ultra-Royalists were attempting to restore the *ancien régime,* and in Italy minor disturbances were savagely suppressed by Austrian soldiers. In March 1819 Karl Sand, a mentally unbalanced theology student who was a member of the Jena *Burschenschaft,* murdered Kotzebue, a dramatist who had been in the tsar's service and was especially detested by students for his anti-liberal writings. His murder was followed in July by an abortive attempt on the life of a Nassau official.

The assassins delivered Germany into the arms of political reaction. For Metternich this was a golden opportunity to stamp out the revolutionary spirit before it overwhelmed the existing order. He could rely on the eager support of horrified princes who readily believed in the existence of some deep-laid subterranean plot to destroy monarchy and looked to Austria for salvation. Metternich, eager to strike at once, by-passed the cumbersome Diet and came to terms with Prussia. At the Teplitz meeting King Frederick William III agreed with Metternich on the need for stern measures. In August Metternich called a secret conference at Carlsbad where the representatives of nine states, on whom Austria could rely, worked out the details of the repressive measures. In September 1819 the Carlsbad Decrees were passed unanimously by a secret session of the Diet. A rigid censorship was imposed on newspapers and periodicals for the next five years; universities and high schools were subjected to close supervision; and a central investigation committee of jurists was set up at Mainz to investigate revolutionary activities and report on them to the Diet. A further conference, attended by the eleven members of the *engerer Rat,* was held in Vienna to devise more permanent methods of combating revolution. It produced the Vienna Final Act, which was passed unanimously by the Diet in 1820. *Inter alia* the Final Act charged the Diet with the task of supervising the implementation of clause thirteen, and declared that existing constitutions could only be amended in a constitutional manner. Most states were only too willing to implement these measures fully; many teachers were dismissed for propagating subversive ideas, many were imprisoned, some newspapers were suppressed and the *Burschenschaften* were dissolved although many did, in fact, survive as underground organisations.

In its unreasoning panic the German ruling class grossly exaggerated the importance of student societies. Karl Sand was a most untypical *Burschenschaftler.* Most students took no active part in politics. They were certainly more serious-minded than previous generations; there was less drinking and duelling and a greater sense of responsibility among them;

they were filled with patriotic enthusiasm; they wore long hair and beards in the old 'German' style, refused to use French words and talked nostalgically about the medieval splendour of the 'Christian-German' fatherland. But there it ended, so that the immediate political significance of the *Burschenschaften* was slight; indeed, once the war-time students had left university, some of the bad habits of the *Landmannschaften* crept back again into student life. What matters most is their historical significance; in these student bodies a whole generation of young men, who later occupied leading positions in German society, experienced for the first time the spell of an idealistic nationalism which transcended local loyalties and bound together students of all classes in a spirit of genuine comradeship.

The Carlsbad Decrees succeeded in keeping Germany quiet for a decade. Metternich's influence was now at its zenith, the Diet was a fairly obedient tool of Austrian policy, and German political development was seriously retarded; there was so little work for the Diet to do that it actually stopped publication of its proceedings in 1828. No new constitutions were conceded after 1820. King Frederick William III of Prussia finally abandoned the idea of a representative constitution at the Teplitz meeting and in some states restrictions were placed on existing constitutions.

Yet even in 1820 there were limits to Austrian influence. It is significant that Metternich's determined attempts at the Carlsbad and Vienna conferences to persuade the southern states to replace their representative constitutions with provincial estates failed completely; the Württemberg and Hesse-Darmstadt constitutions were actually promulgated after the Diet had approved the Carlsbad Decrees; Metternich consoled himself with the tart comment that Württemberg could keep her constitution as a punishment. The fact of the matter was that however much the South-German princes might be alarmed by the unruly behaviour of their lower houses, they were not prepared to dispense with institutional aids which were proving a most efficacious means of welding their dominions together. And in any case the lower houses were brought to heel in the early 1820s; the Carlsbad Decrees were enforced in the south, and in Baden and Bavaria the governments used their influence at election time to secure the return of amenable lower chambers.

The Carlsbad Decrees were not the only cause of the political apathy characteristic of the 1820s. Economic depression was an important contributory factor. Bad harvests in 1816–17 caused very severe food shortages throughout Germany. This was followed by a serious economic crisis. During the Napoleonic period there was some industrial development in the Rhineland and in Saxony. After the war, deprived of the protection afforded by the Continental System, German merchants and manufacturers were unable to face competition from cheaper British goods. At the same time agriculture experienced a depression owing to the English Corn Law of 1815 which restricted the external market for German wheat; the price of wheat fell sharply and the brief period of post-war prosperity ended. For the next few years the Germans were too preoccupied with the problems of economic survival to bother much about politics.

The relative peace and calm of the 1820s came to an abrupt end in 1830. In July the Bourbons were overthrown by an uprising in Paris, and Louis Philippe, the Citizen King, ascended the throne. The tremors of the July Revolution were felt throughout Europe. In August the Belgians rose in revolt and by October had declared their independence; in mid-November the Polish insurrection commenced; and in the winter of 1830–31 there were risings in several parts of Central Italy. Germany was affected by the wave of unrest, but only to a very limited extent; Austria and Prussia remained quiet. Only the smaller states of Brunswick, Hesse-Cassel and Saxony and the kingdom of Hanover were affected, and only in Brunswick did a real revolution occur. Duke Karl II had misruled Brunswick for several years like a tyrant of the old school; he refused to summon the provincial estates, surrounded himself with corrupt time-servers and squandered resources on his pleasures; even the Federal Diet sympathised with the complaints laid in Frankfurt by members of the Brunswick estates. Early in September there was an uprising, the royal palace went up in flames, the duke and his mistress fled, and the estates summoned Duke William to the throne. Eventually he accepted the offer and in 1832 gave the people of Brunswick a constitution. In the other states the disturbances were less serious and only led to the introduction of constitutions because high officials persuaded their rulers to agree to timely political changes. The new constitutions in Saxony, Hanover and Brunswick resembled those already in being in South Germany. Only in Hesse-Cassel were the new estates allowed to meet as one chamber and given full legislative and financial power; this was the most advanced constitution in any pre-1848 state, though in practice it was largely nullified by the obstructionist tactics of the Electoral Prince Frederick William who acted as co-regent during the long absence of his father.

The basic political structure of Restoration Germany survived the 1830 Revolution intact. But the psychological effects of the Revolution were profound. The external fabric of Restoration Europe was beginning to crumble at last with the emergence of an independent Belgium ruled by a prince from the tiny duchy of Saxe-Coburg-Gotha. The solidarity of the Holy Alliance was broken for ever; throughout the 1830s the liberal monarchies, Great Britain and France, boldly challenged the conservative policies of Austria, Prussia and Russia. All over Europe the complacent belief in the permanence of Restoration values began to falter; in Germany contemporaries such as Goethe sensed that they were moving into a new period of storm and stress.

The political and intellectual life of Germany quickened after 1830. Liberalism revived rapidly especially in South-West Germany, where Baden and the Palatinate were the main centres of activity. A number of short-lived liberal papers flourished in the early 1830s. Between 1834 and 1844 Rotteck and Welcker, professors at Freiburg University and members of the Baden lower house, published their *Staatslexikon*,[8] a monumental work which soon became the bible of theoretical liberalism. In 1835 a classic exposition of the views of the historical liberal school appeared in the shape of Dahlmann's *Politik*.[9]

The death of Goethe in 1832 brought a great literary epoch to a close. New intellectual currents were flowing in the 1830s. The Young Hegelians, a group of radical philosophers led by Ruge, an ex-*Burschenschaftler*, were applying the principles of the master to contemporary problems starting with religion; the first fruit of their work was the life of Jesus published by Strauss in 1835, which caused a sensation in Germany. Between 1838 and 1843 Ruge and his colleagues Feuerbach and Bauer expounded their philosophical radicalism in the influential *Hallische Jahrbücher für Wissenschaft und Kunst* and attacked political reaction as well as religious orthodoxy.

Restoration Germany also came under fire from Young Germany, a school of writers and journalists the most notable of whom were Gutzkow, Mundt, Laube, Herwegh and Freiligrath. Associated with them were Ludwig Börne and the great lyrical poet Heinrich Heine, both living in exile in Paris but still bitter and perceptive critics of conditions in Germany. Like young writers in other lands, Young Germany was in revolt against the established order and bitterly critical of Romanticism which had dominated the literature, art and politics of Restoration Germany. In sober, realistic prose Young Germany denounced Romanticism as the ally of political reaction, paralysing the will of the people for political change. They looked to France and Belgium for political inspiration: 'Paris is the new Jerusalem', wrote Heine, 'and the Rhine is the Jordan which divides the land of freedom from the country of the Philistines'. These angry young men dismissed with contempt the belief of the older generation that political change should take place only when rulers were willing. Men of lower-middle-class origins themselves, they declared war on princely houses, insisting that constitutions were the product not of agreement but of conflict between peoples and rulers and had to be wrung out of tyrants by a determined show of force. Young Germany did not secure a wide following in Germany; their ideas were unpopular in this orthodox and traditionalist society; all the same, the angry iconoclasm of these young

[8] *Staatslexikon oder Encyklopädie der Staatswissenschaft*, 15 vols. and 3 supplementary vols. Altona, 1834–43.
[9] *Die Politik auf den Grund und das Mass der gegebenen Zustände zurückgeführt*, Leipzig, 1847.

writers had a profoundly disturbing effect on the values of Restoration Germany.

The radical and democratic note characteristic of politics in the 1830s was much in evidence at the Hambach festival in May 1832. This was the culmination of a series of popular demonstrations in the Palatinate. It was organised by the local radical leaders, Wirth and Siebenpfeiffer, and attended by 2500 people, including some Frenchmen and a number of Polish refugees from the 1831 uprising, who were given a sympathetic reception as they passed through Germany. Students were well repre- sented, for the *Burschenschaften* had been encouraged by the 1830 Revolu- tion to come into the open once more and decided at the Frankfurt and Stuttgart *Burschentage* of 1831 to give active support to popular move- ments. The atmosphere was very different from the Wartburg festival; instead of sentimental talk about a fictitious Christian-German past, there were trenchant demands for a *Rechtsstaat* in which Germans would enjoy the personal freedom already won by Frenchmen and Belgians; other speakers called enthusiastically for a German republic based on popular sovereignty. A somewhat naïve cosmopolitanism pervaded the proceedings; most speakers expressed boundless confidence in the goodwill and peace- ful intentions of all peoples, demanded justice for Poland – a popular cause in the 1830s – and looked forward to the creation of a united states of Europe organised on republican lines.

The German princes were thoroughly alarmed by the radicalism of the Hambach festival. Metternich, with the support of Prussia and other large states, had little difficulty in securing the agreement of the Diet to the Six Articles in June 1832. The new measures forbade political associations and popular meetings and condemned the 'revolutionary agitation' of the popular press. In May 1833 the Frankfurt incident increased the appre- hension in ruling circles. A small group of young men, mostly radical- minded *Burschenschaftler*, stormed the guard-house at Frankfurt with the intention of arming the people and proclaiming a republic. To their cha- grin they found the people reluctant to play the part expected of them; the soldiers quickly recaptured the guard-house and the conspiracy collapsed.

The frightened Diet agreed in June 1833 to set up a new central com- mission to supervise constitutions in member states. In 1834 Metternich summoned a new Vienna conference, hopeful that he might at last succeed in snuffing the life out of representative institutions. Once again he was disappointed; Bavaria, Württemberg and Baden resisted interference in their internal affairs and were supported in this by Saxony and Hanover. However, the conference did agree on further repressive measures; the press censorship was intensified, fresh controls were placed on university teachers and students, estates were commanded to accept decisions of the Diet without question and an arbitration tribunal was to be established to adjudicate in all disputes arising out of existing constitutions.

Compared with the Carlsbad Decrees, the new measures proved ineffectual. Most liberal newspapers were suppressed by the Diet, but the arbitration tribunal did not meet before 1848 and – contrary to Metternich's expectations – the new measures did nothing to strengthen either the Diet or the states in respect of existing constitutions. It was not easy to contain the lively liberalism of the 1830s; for example, when the law guaranteeing freedom of the press was revoked in Baden, there were vigorous protests from the lower house; in the end the government removed the leaders Rotteck and Welcker from their teaching posts and closed Freiburg University. In Württemberg the estates protested against the actions of the Federal Diet and were dissolved for their pains in 1833. Liberalism received unexpected support from abroad. Britain and France turned the tables on Metternich in 1832 by claiming the right, as signatories of the Vienna treaties, to intervene in Germany on behalf of liberalism; when they renewed their claim in 1834 it was summarily rejected by the Diet.

In an age when the paternalist pattern of government was crumbling all over Western Europe, repressive measures of this kind were bound to be ineffectual. On the other hand, the readiness of rulers to resort to repression confirmed and deepened the feelings of animosity which the princely dynasties aroused in every radical breast. This had a curious side effect; it impeded the growth of German nationalism. Under the spell of the Pan-European spirit so much in evidence at Hambach, radicals became deeply conscious of their solidarity with liberals in other lands, all allies together in the universal struggle against tyranny. Most radicals regarded nationalism as an anachronistic and retrograde force, heavily tainted with Romanticism and certain to weaken the solidarity of progressive forces through the erection of completely artificial barriers between nations. The Young Hegelian Ruge scorned the thought of a recrudescence of the spirit of 1813 and denounced it as 'a dangerous reaction against reason and history'. His colleague Laube, writing the first part of *Das junge Europa* in 1833, prophesied the disappearance of all nationalities and the establishment of a world republic dedicated to the service of humanity. But five years later in the second part of the book Laube changed his mind; he abandoned the notion of a world republic and openly declared his allegiance to the national cause. This change of heart was typical of German liberalism at the close of the 1830s, and was due in large measures to the growing economic power of Germany. The 1830s were a period of economic as well as political change. In the early decades of the nineteenth century Germany was a predominantly agrarian society. Industrial activity was scattered and small-scale in nature; it was based very largely on the handicraft system and suffered from a chronic shortage of capital. After 1835 there was a modest but perceptible increase in the tempo of industrial activity. The leading industry, textiles, grew steadily in importance in Saxony, and an iron and steel industry began to flourish in West Germany, using coal from the Saar, Ruhr and Aachen mines.

This general economic revival was due partly to improved communications. German roads had improved steadily since the days of Napoleon. After 1815 Prussia embarked on a road-building programme to consolidate her newly acquired dominions; by 1828 she had built over 2,800 miles of new road. In the 1820s steamships speeded up traffic on the Rhine, and by 1845 the rivers Rhine, Main and Danube had been joined by canal. But the real revolution in communications came with the railway; the first line was opened in 1835 between Nuremberg and Fürth; in 1837 work commenced on the first freight line in Saxony between Leipzig and Dresden, thanks to the tireless efforts of the economist Friedrich List, who, since his return in 1832 from exile spent in North America, devoted his considerable energies to the promotion of railways.

The second major cause of the economic revival was the gradual destruction of customs barriers. One of the most serious obstacles to economic growth in Germany was the existence of numerous customs barriers not only between states but, in the case of the larger states, between provinces as well. Clause nineteen of the Federal Act laid upon the Diet responsibility for devising a common policy on trade and navigation. The Diet failed to act in this matter, leaving it instead to individual German princes who did nothing about it. In 1819, List acting as spokesman for the newly founded *Deutscher Handels- und Gewerbeverein*, tried in vain to interest the Vienna ministerial conference in a unified customs system to protect German industry against British competition; Metternich believed that this would infringe the sovereignty of rulers, and in any case Austria could see little benefit in it for herself. All the Vienna conference could agree upon was the condemnation of the recent Prussian tariff law as a selfish measure likely to hinder a more general customs union.

With the tariff law of 1818 Prussia had taken a step of momentous significance. Her general development was severely handicapped by the existence of sixty-seven internal tariffs, plus Swedish tariffs in Pomerania and French tariffs in the Rhineland; consequently the collection of customs dues was most difficult, there was much smuggling across the long, straggling frontiers, and the consolidation of Prussia's new territories was seriously impeded. The law of 1818 was in large measure the work of Maassen, a Rhineland administrator and pupil of Adam Smith and one of the many liberal-minded civil servants who served Prussia so well in the early nineteenth century. The new law was a victory for the principles of free trade; it was, incidentally, a victory for Prussian landowners over Rhineland industrialists who had clamoured for high tariffs to protect them against British competition. The law abolished most internal customs barriers, allowed most raw materials into Prussia duty-free, imposed only ten per cent *ad valorem* duty on manufactured goods, but placed a quite substantial transit duty, calculated by weight, on goods passing through Prussia; the latter provision supplied Prussia with a powerful means of coercion which she used to extend her customs system to other states.

The new tariff had no immediate effects on Prussian industry and agriculture but in the long run it made large-scale economic expansion possible. Prussia quickly absorbed a number of tiny enclaves, parts of the Thuringian territories, into her system as well as the three Anhalt principalities. In 1819 Prussia concluded a treaty with Schwarzburg-Sonderhausen whereby this tiny state accepted Prussian tariffs administered by Prussian officials, in return for a proportionate share of the joint customs receipts. Under the firm hand of Motz, Prussian finance minister from 1825 to 1830, a determined attempt was made to extend the scope of these arrangements. By 1831 nine small states, whose territories adjoined Prussia, had followed the example of Schwarzburg-Sonderhausen. But only in 1828 did the Prussian Customs Union really begin with the conclusion of a treaty between Prussia and Hesse-Darmstadt, a large state whose frontiers did not adjoin Prussia; under this treaty Hesse-Darmstadt received a share of the customs revenue but retained her own customs officials.

Prussia was not alone in her attempts to create a viable customs union. In 1828 Bavaria and Württemberg formed a customs union. The same year the Mid-German Commercial Union was formed by Saxony, Hanover, Brunswick and several small Central-German states. This union was potentially a serious threat to Prussia; it commanded the North Sea coast and controlled parts of the Rhine, Elbe, Weser and Main rivers, and its avowed aim was to divert the lucrative transit trade away from the Prussian-Darmstadt union. The Mid-German Union had the support of liberals in Central and South-West Germany and was encouraged by Metternich, who had no desire to see Prussia become too powerful in North Germany. However, Prussia soon won the economic battle with the Mid-German Union, which for one thing lacked the cohesion of the Prussian system; and Prussia was able to outflank this union by building a new road linking Prussian Saxony with South Germany, and by securing Dutch agreement in 1829 to a considerable reduction of the tolls levied on Rhine shipping. The Mid-German Union disintegrated. At the same time Bavaria and Württemberg, realising that a larger South-German customs union could not be created, decided to come to terms with Prussia. The negotiations, which were skilfully conducted by Maassen, who had succeeded Motz as finance minister in 1830, resulted in the formation of the *Deutscher Zollverein* or German Customs Union. When it came into being on 1 January 1834, the Customs Union embraced eighteen states with a population of twenty-three millions and covered a total area of 112,000 square miles.

This was an epoch-making event. The Customs Union led eventually to a considerable increase in the volume of trade, for German import duties were lower than those in most West-European states. The financial advantages of membership were so evident that the remaining states joined within the next few years. The political consequences were even greater. Certainly Prussia was not thinking in terms of political unification when she founded the Customs Union. Nor had the states joined it out of love for Prussia but simply and solely to escape from the financial and economic difficulties which beset them. Political rivalries were not in any way diminished by the success of the Customs Union; the members continued to eye Prussia with suspicion and they guarded their own independence jealously even in purely commercial matters.

All the same, the Customs Union was an object lesson for the German people. Eighteen states had voluntarily restricted their sovereignty in the common interest, an action without precedent in the history of the Confederation. This was a step towards a wider political union, as German liberals were at last beginning to realise at the close of the 1830s. Their feelings were expressed in the lines written by the poet Fallersleben in 1840:

> Denn ihr habt ein Band gewunden
> Um das deutsche Vaterland
> Und die Herzen hat verbunden
> Mehr als unser Bund das Band.[10]

Liberal interest in the unification of Germany was quickened and deepened by the events of 1840. This was the year of the War Scare on the Rhine, a crisis which evoked an upsurge of national feeling in Germany comparable in intensity to that of 1813. France was out-manouvered by Britain over the Egyptian question in the summer of 1840. The French, irritated by their isolation in the Near East, sought to retrieve their prestige by pursuing an active foreign policy in Europe. Thiers, the new foreign minister, prepared the army for war, while the Paris press denounced the treaties of 1815 and called with enthusiasm for the immediate reconquest of the Rhineland which had been an integral part of France from 1792 to 1814. Once again events in France gave a decisive twist to the course of German history. After the 1830 Revolution liberals in South and West Germany had been filled with admiration for France; overnight these friendly sentiments waned and were replaced by a mood of sharp hostility, expressed so forcibly in the *Rheinlied*:

> Sie sollen ihn nicht haben,
> den freien deutschen Rhein,

[10]For you have wound a bond around the German fatherland, and this bond has done much more than the Confederation to bind our hearts together.

ob sie gleich gier'gen Raben
sich heiser danach schrei'n.[11]

The poem attained enormous popularity and won for its author, Becker, the patronage of the kings of Prussia and Bavaria. The German princes did not try to oppose nationalism as they had opposed liberalism, perhaps because they sensed for the first time the power of the elemental forces which nationalism could conjure up out of the grass-roots of a people. Even Metternich approved of the popular outburst, noting with his customary perception that nationalism had at last freed itself from the taint of revolutionary liberalism. Passions died down on both sides of the Rhine by the end of 1840. But the crisis left its mark on Germany; cosmopolitan liberalism was dead; the unification of Germany, not the universal struggle against political tyranny, was the burning issue throughout the 1840s.

In the new decade liberals north of the river Main looked increasingly to Prussia for leadership. The Customs Union had conferred a new importance on her; under the aegis of Prussia Germany was at last enjoying some of the benefits which flowed from economic unification. The events of 1840 had underlined the military role of Prussia as well. As popular indignation mounted against the French in the summer of 1840, Prussia hastily negotiated a treaty with Austria in which it was agreed that in the event of war Prussia would take command of the North-German contingents to the federal army, and would help defend Austria's possessions in Italy. The crisis died away without war when Louis Philippe, who had never wanted war, dismissed the bellicose Thiers in October 1840. But the episode had made the liberals of North and West Germany aware for the first time of their dependence on Prussia for protection in the hour of need.

There was another reason why liberals looked with confidence to Prussia. In June 1840 King Frederick William III died. The new monarch Frederick William IV was very different from the normal run of Hohenzollern rulers; a gifted and intelligent prince, he was a great lover of art and literature, a charming personality and a fluent conversationalist, who spoke often and enthusiastically of his pride in the 'German nation'. Prussian liberals were filled with hope by his first acts as king. A political amnesty was proclaimed, Arndt was restored to his professorial chair at Bonn, *Turnvater* Jahn received the Iron Cross, the brothers Grimm, dismissed from Göttingen in 1837, were given posts in Berlin, and Boyen, who had been driven from office in 1819, became minister of war in 1841. The censorship of the press was relaxed; provincial estates were again summoned regularly; the estates were allowed to set up committees to consult the king on matters concerning the general welfare of the various provinces; and in 1842 the king convened a general meeting of these committees in Berlin.

[11]They shall not have the free German Rhine, even though they cry for it like greedy ravens until they are hoarse.

In fact liberal hopes of real constitutional progress under the new ruler were sadly misplaced. Frederick William was an archaic figure of pseudo-Gothic proportions, a romantic who lived in the unreal world of the *Burschenschaften* and dreamt of a 'Christian-German' *Reich*, ruled by the Habsburgs but with the Prussian monarch as his second-in-command responsible for the defence of the German fatherland. In short, Frederick William was totally out of sympathy with modern liberalism. By inclination and conviction he was a paternalist whose political ideal was the Christian *Ständestaat* as expounded in the writings of Haller, the Swiss historian and jurist.[12] It was not long before liberals were disillusioned with the new ruler. Nevertheless, the hesitant steps Frederick William had taken to extend the activity of the provincial estates did something to maintain interest in the political evolution of Prussia in the 1840s.

National liberalism was the dominant political posture of the 1840s. It was nurtured and sustained by the growing political awareness of the German people, a development made possible in large measure by the growth of the press. The spread of railways and the introduction of the telegraph drew Germany closer together, facilitating the collection and distribution of news. New techniques reduced the cost of printing and encouraged the growth of local newspapers and periodicals. Popular journalism now played a role of crucial importance both in arousing interest in affairs of state, and in helping to create – within the limits of the press censorship – an informed public opinion, the life-blood of any active political movement.

There were already signs of a wider interest in politics at the close of the 1830s. In 1837 the new king of Hanover, Ernst August, formerly the duke of Cumberland and uncle of Queen Victoria, abrogated the constitution of 1833 and announced his intention of restoring the old estates. Seven professors at Göttingen University, all eminent scholars with national reputations, led by Dahlmann, declared that as state officials they must respect the oath of allegiance they had sworn to the 1833 constitution. The king summarily dismissed them from their teaching posts. Three of them were ordered to leave Hanover within three days. This 'protest of conscience', as Dahlmann called it, aroused nation-wide interest. The seven professors became popular heroes; in several towns societies were formed to raise funds to pay the professorial salaries of the seven; and in Baden the lower house petitioned the Federal Diet to secure the restoration of constitutional liberties in Hanover. True, Ernst August won in the end when the Diet, under pressure from Austria and Prussia, refused to intervene in Hanover. But it was a significant episode; for the first time a local issue had aroused general interest in Germany and helped to bring liberals from north and south into closer contact with each other.

---

[12]Restoration Europe took its name from Haller's six-volume *Restauration der Staatswissenschaft* etc., Winterthür, 1820–34.

The issue which did most to nurture and mould national liberalism in the 1840s was the Schleswig-Holstein question. Schleswig and Holstein were two small, sparsely populated and inaccessible duchies on the shores of the Baltic which had been ruled by Denmark since 1460. Holstein was wholly German-speaking and a member of the German Confederation. Schleswig, half-Danish- and half-German-speaking, was not a member of the Confederation but had been closely associated with Holstein since medieval times.

At the beginning of the nineteenth century it seemed possible that the male line of the Danish royal house would soon become extinct. According to the Germans in Schleswig-Holstein, the duchies would then revert in their entirety to a cadet branch of the royal line, the Augustenburgs, and all ties with Denmark would be severed. The Danes dissented sharply from this view, and maintained that Schleswig at least, by virtue of its Danish origins and associations, would remain under Danish rule.

When Christian VIII became king of Denmark and duke of Schleswig-Holstein in 1839, he was naturally anxious to preserve his dominions intact. After failing to persuade the duke of Augustenburg to abandon his claims to the duchies, King Christian toyed with the possibility of introducing the Danish succession law into Schleswig-Holstein; this law permitted females to pass on the crown to males and so would enable Denmark to maintain the connection with the duchies. In 1844, when the Danish estates petitioned the king to do this, there were loud protests in the duchies, where it was widely believed that the king sympathised with the Eider Danes, the name given to the nationalists who were working for the annexation of Schleswig by Denmark. Echoes of the controversy were heard in Germany, where the dispute between German and Dane was beginning to assume national significance. Hecker, a leading South-German liberal, speaking in the Baden second chamber in 1845, referred to Schleswig-Holstein as 'a bulwark of the German empire', and declared that 'anyone whose heart burns for the German fatherland . . . must do what he can by word and deed and if need be by the sword to make certain that not one inch of German soil is alienated from Germany.'

In July 1846 King Christian issued an open letter which declared that the female-succession law applied without doubt to Schleswig and even to parts of Holstein. There was an immediate storm of protest in the duchies, the Germans walked out of the local estates, and several prominent German officials resigned. Germany was swept by a new wave of national feeling reminiscent of 1840; in 1840 France had been the enemy; in 1846 it was Denmark. Universities, learned societies and several estates added their voices to the chorus of protest, demanding action from the Diet in support of the duchies in their struggle to defend 'ancient rights' against 'Danish aggression'. The German princes were swept along with the tide. The king of Bavaria openly declared his sympathy with the house of

Augustenburg, the king of Prussia spoke with disapproval of the Open Letter; and Metternich, the champion of legitimacy, thought it necessary to remind the Danish ruler of his duty to respect the well-established succession rights of the Augustenburgs. When the Diet expressed the cautious hope that the rights of all parties would be respected but went on to urge member-states to repress popular demonstrations, it was denounced by the liberals for excessive timidity. At a popular level the spirit of 1846 was expressed in the well-known lines of a contemporary writer:

> Wir rufen Nein! und aber Nein
> zu solchem Einverleiben
> Wir wollen keine Dänen sein
> Wir wollen Deutsche bleiben.[13]

The growing desire in Germany for national unification found at once a safety valve and a focal point in the emotional commitment to Schleswig-Holstein, a remote territory on the periphery of the Teutonic world. No popular demonstration was complete in these years without the red, white and blue flag of Schleswig-Holstein, several renderings of the Schleswig-Holstein song and a few anti-Danish speeches. Popular enthusiasm for Schleswig-Holstein kept the issue of unification firmly in the forefront of German politics in the late 1840s and indeed for the next twenty years.

The growth of national liberalism was a reflection, too, of the continuing economic expansion of Germany. The Customs Union gathered momentum in this decade; Baden and Nassau joined in 1835, Frankfurt-on-Main in 1836, the Brunswick lands between 1841 and 1844, Luxemburg in 1842, Hanover in 1851 and Oldenburg in 1852. Only the two Mecklenburgs, the Hansa towns and Holstein remained outside. A railway network was spreading out all over Germany in the 1840s; by 1846 2,000 kilometers of line had been laid. Railways were of great political significance. They helped to break down provincial barriers, brought town and country nearer together and underlined the need for national unification. List described them in a happy phrase as 'the firm girdle around the loins of Germany binding her limbs together into a forceful and powerful body'. Railways started a new era in heavy industry. Coal and iron production increased to supply the demand for fuel, lines, sleepers and rolling stock. In the 1830s Germany bought her locomotives from Britain. In the 1840s Germany broke the British monopoly and began to supply her own needs; in 1841 the engineer Borsig constructed his first locomotive in a Berlin workshop; in 1848 he supplied sixty-seven of sixty-nine locomotives ordered by Prussian railways in that year, and by 1854 he

---

[13]We cry no! and no again to any annexation. We don't want to be Danes, we want to remain Germans.

was known in international markets. Textiles expanded in the 1840s; cotton rapidly overtook woollens and linen, and machinery began at last to supersede the hand-looms and spinning-wheels. The appearance of a few large-scale concerns, employing hundreds of workers, in the textile, iron, steel and engineering industries already pointed the way ahead to a new pattern of industrial development.

As the economic structure of Germany changed, the outlines of a new social structure were dimly visible. In the towns which were increasing in size in this decade (Berlin grew by 100,000 between 1840 and 1850) an industrial proletariat appeared, very weak in numbers – there were only 600,000 industrial workers in the whole of Germany in 1848 – politically apathetic, but living and working in conditions which made this new working class a potential source of social discontent.

The middle class, too, was changing in complexion in the 1840s with the rise of a prosperous class of merchants, bankers and industrialists, organised in chambers of commerce in the larger towns. This was a factor of some political importance. The new captains of commerce and industry, men such as Camphausen and Mevissen of Cologne, Hansemann of Aachen and Borsig of Berlin, were not defenders of the *status quo*; on the contrary, they were in favour of political change. For as the economy expanded it came increasingly into conflict with the obsolete political structure of Restoration Germany; a multiplicity of monetary systems and commercial codes, different systems of weights and measures, and the restrictive practices of guilds and corporations impeded the free flow of trade.

It would be wrong to over-estimate the degree of political consciousness attained by the German people on the eve of the 1848 Revolution. Traditional attitudes were deeply rooted in what was still very largely an agrarian society; industrialisation affected only the fringes of the economy – in this respect Germany lagged far behind Britain and Belgium. Only in the towns was there any sustained political interest, and even in the middle classes only a small minority was politically active. The liberal movement was still dominated by the universities, although even here only a small minority of professors were liberal-minded.

Liberalism was not a mass movement; only on rare occasions, as in 1846, did liberals enjoy a wide measure of support. But there were significant signs that the age of elegance, when politics concerned only a handful of people, was coming to an end at last. The ordinary people of Germany were emerging from the shadows of history in the 1840s. This was the age of the political lyric. Young Germany in the 1830s had written for the educated minority; the lyrical poets, Fallersleben, Prutz, Dinglestedt and Herwegh, spoke directly to the masses. In passionate and prophetic tones they attacked the old order and wrote about the social problems which beset ordinary Germans. By their writings they did much to keep the spirit of patriotism burning bright; the most famous of all German patriotic songs were written in these years: *Die Wacht am Rhein* by Schneckenburger in 1840 and the *Deutschlandlied* by Fallersleben in 1841, the latter composed, curiously enough, on the island of Heligoland then ruled by Britain.

It was also an age of intense social activity. Professional men started to meet regularly at national congresses to discuss vocational problems. Typical of these gatherings were the *Germanistentage* held at Frankfurt in 1846 and Lübeck in 1847 and attended by philologists from all parts of Germany. These were 'intellectual *Landtage*', as the German historian Treitschke called them, where liberal-minded academics were able to establish closer contact than ever before with their colleagues and discuss politics as well as vocational matters. Unification was the issue uppermost in their minds, and it is not without significance that the Lübeck congress, before it dispersed, passed a resolution upholding the German nationalists in Schleswig-Holstein. In most towns in the 1840s choral societies and shooting-clubs flourished, being patronised largely by the middle class. But when the choral societies organised local festivals or national festivals, such as the *Allgemeines Deutsches Sängerfest* at Lübeck in 1847, they were able to draw on a much wider audience than the middle class. Popular musical festivals, which were often attended by tens of thousands of people, played a role of some importance in the growth of national feeling. These were important political as well as social occasions. For in addition to the entertainments, fireworks and patriotic songs, there were many political speeches delivered by liberal leaders, who could in this way establish some contact with the masses of the people and explain the rudiments of national liberalism to them.

But there it ended. The liberals were not seeking to take the people into partnership with them; their only concern was to make sure that the people would support them when the old order finally fell to pieces. But the people were expected to leave the formulation of policy and the strategy of battle to their betters. This was not peculiar to Germany but simply a reflection of the predominantly upper-middle-class character of European liberalism in the first half of the nineteenth century.

There were no political parties at this time. Only on the eve of the 1848 Revolution did 'moderate' and 'radical' liberals begin to organise separately, and that largely by accident. Liberalism was reviving in South Germany in the 1840s, especially in Baden after 1842. In 1846 Bassermann and Mathy, the liberal leaders in Baden, became ministers, and in 1847 the liberals obtained a majority in the lower house. Most liberals were prepared to support the ministry which had started to modify the press censorship and to tackle the reform of justice. However, a handful of radical deputies led by Hecker and Struve refused to compromise their principles. They met at Offenburg in September 1847 and drafted a radical democratic programme which called for a free press, freedom of conscience, trial by jury, the summoning of an elected German parliament, the formation of a people's militia to replace standing armies, the abolition of all feudal privileges and the introduction of a progressive income tax. A month later moderate liberals from South and West Germany including Heinrich von Gagern, the liberal leader in Hesse-Darmstadt, Hansemann and Mevissen from Prussia, and Bassermann and Mathy from Baden, met at Heppenheim to draw up a counter-declaration. This restated much of the radical programme, though couched in more moderate tones and without the republican and social undertones of the Offenburg programme. Despite this, there was still no very clear distinction between moderates and radicals. Most radicals mistrusted the masses as much as the moderates did. They also disliked revolution, for at heart they agreed with the moderates that constitutions should be the product of understanding between ruler and people. And although committed to the revolutionary principle of universal suffrage, when they spoke of the 'people' the radicals were thinking for the most part of men of property and education. In short, the great majority of liberals, whether moderate or radical in outlook, failed to comprehend the immense historical significance of the entry of the masses into the political arena. It required a revolution to bring home the full significance of this epoch-making phenomenon. As the 1840s drew to a close there were many portents that revolution in Europe would not be long delayed.

2

The Revolution of 1848–1849

Contemporaries were not surprised when the hurricane of revolution swept through Europe in the spring of 1848; as the Pre-March period moved to a close the foundations of Restoration Europe were obviously crumbling away. In France, Italy and Poland there were unmistakable signs of political and social tension which could no longer be contained within the straitjacket of the absolutist state. Similarly in Germany, events were clearly moving to a crisis; several significant developments in 1847 accelerated the growth of a revolutionary situation.

In February 1847 King Frederick William IV finally decided – against the advice of Metternich – to allow the eight provincial estates to meet together in Berlin as a united estates. Prussian liberals were not greatly impressed by the offer; the royal patent limited the power of the estates to the approval of new taxation and state loans, and made provision for an upper house of nominated peers which would act as an additional brake on the lower chamber. However, the opening of the estates was a major event and liberal observers came from all over Germany to Berlin in a mood of high expectancy. Hopes of real constitutional advance were, however, soon dashed by the king's categorical but characteristic declaration that he would never permit a written constitution to come between him and his people. Efforts to persuade the king to promise to summon the estates regularly and to extend their powers failed completely. In retaliation the liberals persuaded the estates to withhold approval from various financial measures, including a twenty-five million talers loan for the building of the *Ostbahn*, a railway linking Königsberg to Berlin. The incensed monarch stopped the work which had already begun on the line and dissolved the estates in June 1847. The immediate failure of the Prussian liberals to attain their objectives. was far outweighed by the general encouragement the meeting of the estates gave to liberalism in North Germany. For the first time liberals from the Rhineland and Westphalian estates, led by the industrialists Camphausen and Hansemann, had worked closely with East Prussian liberals led by the landowner Auerswald. Revolution was far from their minds. They all dispersed quietly enough when the king dissolved the estates. But the wide publicity given to the sharp conflict between the crown and the estates helped to weaken the basis of Prussian absolutism.

At the close of 1847 events in Switzerland aroused great public interest in South Germany. In November civil war broke out between the conservative-Catholic cantons in the *Sonderbund* and the liberal-Protestant cantons who were fighting to transform the Swiss Confederation into a federal state. Within a month the *Sonderbund* collapsed. This was an open defeat for conservatism and for Metternich, who had tried – and failed – to organise intervention on its behalf. Liberals in South Germany drew fresh inspiration from the victory of their Swiss colleagues. In Baden liberalism was now a formidable force. The liberals dominated the lower house and in February 1848 through their leader, the Mannheim merchant, Bassermann, they demanded the immediate summoning of a German national parliament.

In Bavaria the Lola Montez scandal caused great unrest on the eve of the Revolution. In 1846 King Ludwig I became infatuated with an Irish-born dancer called Lola Montez. Early in 1847 he asked the conservative-Catholic Abel ministry to make her a Bavarian citizen so that the title of countess might be conferred on her. The ministers refused and resigned. A new liberal-minded ministry agreed to the king's request. Disturbances in Munich were put down by the military. Early in February 1848 the tactless behaviour of the new countess provoked fresh disturbances led by the students. The king closed the university. Renewed rioting occurred and reports came in of general unrest in Bavaria. Finally the king agreed to reopen the university, summon the Bavarian diet and banish Lola Montez from Munich. The affair was not yet over, but already it had wrought unbelievable harm to the prestige of monarchy in South Germany.

Yet these dramatic events on their own would not have led to revolution. Behind every revolt against the established order there lies a story of social discontent, and in this respect the 1848 Revolution was no exception.

The 1840s were a period of rapid social change. Industrialisation was making an impact on the conservative structure of German society. However, it was not the small industrial proletariat in the towns which supplied the dynamic for social revolution in 1848. Working conditions in the factories were admittedly bad and living conditions in the new urban slums were appalling. On the other hand, cheap factory labour was in short supply, therefore wages were relatively high and conditions better than those in the countryside, at least until the depression in the late 1840s. In fact industrial workers formed a labour aristocracy and for that reason stood largely on the side lines during the 1848 Revolution. They had no sense of class solidarity; factory owners were not rich absentee magnates but often *Handwerker* made good; and many workers were not true proletarians at all, but part-time workers who still cultivated their small holdings.

Urban discontent in the 1840s centred round the *Handwerker*, a far more numerous class than factory workers. Since the close of the 1830s these craftsmen had been fighting a desperate rearguard action in the guilds against the advance of modern technology which was gradually undermining the basis of small-scale industry. They fought without government protection because economic liberalism was practised in many states; laws terminating compulsory membership of guilds for journeymen and apprentices were passed by Prussia in 1845 and in Hanover in 1847. The status of the craftsmen declined slowly but surely, and unemployment and poverty became their lot as markets for their products contracted. The movement of people away from the countryside and into the towns overcrowded the trades, depressing the living-standards of the *Handwerker*. There were ominous signs of discontent. Disturbances occurred in Hesse-Cassel and the Palatinate as early as 1832; the most spectacular protest occurred in 1844 when the Silesian weavers rose in revolt, driven to desperate measures by the decline of the linen industry. At the close of the 1840s out-of-work journeymen and apprentices joined with ruined masters to form *Handwerkerverbindungen* in the towns in a despairing attempt to arrest the continuing decline in their status. These frustrated and resentful men, crowded together in the new towns, were the standard-bearers of social revolution in 1848.

There was much discontent in the countryside at the close of the 1840s. Agrarian conditions varied a great deal in Germany. In Schleswig-Holstein, Oldenburg and Hanover a semi-independent peasantry enjoyed tolerable conditions. Elsewhere the lot of the peasant was an unhappy one. East of the Elbe large estates run by efficient Junker landowners growing wheat for export were the dominant feature of the rural landscape. In the first half of the nineteenth century these estates were expanding rapidly at the expense of the peasants. In Pomerania, Silesia and the Mecklenburgs peasants could not survive on the remaining land and were reduced to the status of landless labourers working for their old masters on less favourable terms.

In West and South Germany there were few large estates. Small holdings predominated, and here feudal dues were being commuted into monetary dues or extinguished by final payments. But commutation was a painfully slow process when most peasants lacked the capital to become independent farmers. The rapid growth of population added to their difficulties. Between 1816 and 1848 the population of Germany increased from twenty-four to thirty-six millions. In the north the increase was easily absorbed, but in the south and west an intolerable burden was placed on small holdings. In a vain attempt to survive, the peasant further subdivided his land but only succeeded in making it too small for efficient farming. As living standards declined, the burden of feudal dues became increasingly onerous and the peasant grew restless and resentful of the power of the landowner.

Conditions in town and country deteriorated quite sharply on the eve of the 1848 Revolution. In 1847 the last major famine occurred in Europe. The potato harvests of 1845 and 1846 were ruined by blight, and peasants all over Europe were deprived of their staple food; the next year a sudden drought destroyed the grain harvest. Prices were driven up, and fearful hunger gripped Germany. Then came a cholera epidemic in Upper Silesia, which carried off hundreds of souls. Many peasants, quite unable to carry the double burden of commutation payments and taxation any longer, were forced off the land. Some emigrated but most drifted to the towns where they augmented the growing army of the unemployed.

The agrarian crisis coincided with industrial crisis. The demand for manufactured goods declined after 1846. As credit facilities dried up, factories closed and unemployment grew in the towns. Hastily improvised relief measures proved completely inadequate to cope with the accumulated human misery, and in the winter of 1846–47 disturbances occurred in several towns. The most serious occurred in Berlin; during the so-called 'potato revolution' barricades were erected, shops looted and the crown prince's palace was stormed before soldiers managed to restore order. These outbursts of popular violence were an ominous portent of impending revolution.

Social discontent played a vital role in the outbreak of the 1848 Revolution. Political unrest and social discontent are the twin sisters of revolution, the one as indispensable as the other. The mass of the people would never have risen in revolt to secure constitutional liberties on their own. But, overwhelmed by social misery, they willingly followed the lead given them by the liberals in the spring of 1848.

Once again the signal for revolt came from Paris. At the end of February 1848 Louis Philippe fled from the capital, a republic was proclaimed and the Year of Revolution had begun.

There were immediate repercussions in Baden, the home of radicalism. On 27 February a mass meeting in Mannheim formulated the major demands of the 1848 revolutionaries: freedom of the press, formation of a peoples' militia, trial by jury, responsible government in all states and the summoning of a German parliament. Similar resolutions were passed by meetings in other towns. Two days later the grand duke agreed to the demands, much to the relief of moderate liberals who were anxious to forestall more radical action by the followers of Struve.

Baden set the pattern for the rest of Germany. The March Revolution was bloodless in most states; mass meetings and monster petitions were sufficient to force the hands of frightened princes. The old order capitulated without resistance, as it was to do again in 1918. Only in Bavaria did a monarch lose his crown and this because of fresh disturbances over Lola Montez.[1] Elsewhere princes kept their crowns and hurriedly conceded constitutions or remodelled existing constitutions on the Belgian model of 1831. Popular sovereignty superseded monarchical power, and the lower house became the centre of political gravity in all states. From the south-west the revolutionary tide swept northwards carrying all before it.

With liberals at the head of affairs in most states, the complexion of the Federal Diet quickly altered. On 1 March the Diet issued a patriotic appeal to the nation. Shortly afterwards it authorised the abolition of press censorship in all states and recognised the black, red and gold colours as the emblems of national unity. A committee of seventeen, including many famous academics under the chairmanship of Dahlmann, was set up to draft a revised constitution for the Confederation.

But liberals had long lost faith in the ability of the Diet to solve Germany's problems. The impetus to national unification came from elsewhere. On 5 March fifty-one leading liberals from South-West Germany met at Heidelberg and decided to convene a large meeting to discuss the German problem and prepare the way for the calling of a national parliament.[2] Before dispersing they set up a committee of seven to make the necessary arrangements.

The Revolution had made very rapid progress in the early days of March. But revolutionary exuberance on its own was unfortunately no guarantee of the permanence of the liberal gains. Clearly little progress could be made towards the unification of Germany without the active co-operation of the major powers, Austria and Prussia. In a very real sense the future of the German Revolution depended on events in Berlin and Vienna.

Austria was in the grip of revolution by the middle of March. There were ominous signs of restlessness among the non-German peoples; in Italy revolution was imminent; on 3 March Kossuth demanded a constitution for Hungary, and on 6 March petitions were circulating in Vienna demanding a free press and representative institutions. When the estates of Lower Austria met on 13 March, there were disturbances in Vienna led by students supported by *Handwerker* who were suffering severe economic hardship. Then on the evening of 13 March Metternich, recognising with his customary perception the inevitability of change, resigned and fled to England. The disappearance of the man who had embodied the spirit of European conservatism for three decades had profound psychological effects. The revolution triumphed in Vienna; on 15 March the emperor promised Austria a constitution and steps were taken to summon a

[1] King Ludwig I was succeeded by his son Maximilian II.
[2] Twenty came from Baden, nine from Württemberg, only two from Prussia and one from Austria.

constituent assembly. Austria was for the time being too engrossed in her own affairs to exert her customary influence on Germany.

Events in Prussia had a more direct bearing on the course of the Revolution. A city like Berlin, where a quarter of the population was working-class, was especially vulnerable to economic depression. Early in March 400 workers were dismissed from the engineering works of Borsig. Soon thousands more had joined the growing army of the unemployed who whiled their time away at mass meetings addressed by radical agitators. The king's announcement on 14 March that the united estates would be recalled at the end of April had little effect. When news arrived from Vienna the next day, the tension mounted, and serious clashes occurred between the crowds and the soldiers. At this point the king's advisers persuaded Frederick William to take the initiative. On the eve of the Revolution Austria and Prussia exchanged views on the reform of the Confederation and agreed on 10 March to summon a congress of princes to discuss the question further. Emboldened by Austria's difficulties, the king's advisers now urged him to make a bold bid for leadership in Germany. The result was a patent issued on 18 March in which Frederick William IV announced Prussia's intention of playing an active role in the creation of a German federal state; a German parliament would be summoned; constitutions would be granted in all states including Prussia; the united estates would meet on 2 April and a new ministry would be appointed. As the king remarked afterwards to a conservative friend, 'we had to recognise constitutionalism for the sake of Germany'.

Rumours of the royal concessions brought the crowds together in the palace yard, where they cheered the king. His triumph was short-lived. When the soldiers began to clear the crowds away two shots were accidentally fired. So tense was the atmosphere in Berlin that the crowds immediately concluded that the king was betraying them; barricades were hastily erected by the *Handwerker* and factory workers, and fierce street fighting broke out when the soldiers attempted to dismantle them.

The soldiers had, in fact, almost succeeded in crushing the revolt when the king decided to end the bloodshed. Horrified and depressed by the street fighting, which diverted attention from his lofty dreams of uniting Germany, Frederick William ordered his soldiers to withdraw from the streets. Reluctantly the soldiers obeyed. Then, as a result of ambiguous orders and misunderstanding between the king and his commanders, the troops were withdrawn entirely from Berlin leaving Frederick William at the mercy of his subjects. On 19 March the king received a mass demonstration in the palace yard and was forced to doff his hat as the corpses of the fallen were carried past on a furniture-waggon. The king's brother, Prince William of Prussia, who was regarded as the embodiment of militarism, fled to England. On 21 March, surrounded by some of his generals and ministers and wearing the black, red and gold colours of the Revolution, the king rode in theatrical style through the streets of Berlin. Being anxious to focus attention once more on the unification of Germany, Frederick William issued a new proclamation, in which he declared his intention of leading Germany in her hour of need and defending her if need be against all external foes. When the united estates met, they would be transformed into a German parliament by agreement with the princes, and a new Germany would be born. The document ended with the resonant phrase '*Preussen geht fortan in Deutschland auf*'.[3] A cry of despair to conservative ears, it was interpreted by liberals as a pledge that Prussia would sacrifice her particularism in the interests of a wider unity. Speaking to his officers at Potsdam on 25 March, the king assured them that he was perfectly safe in Berlin, and urged his audience, for the sake of the great German fatherland, to forget the humiliating experience they had just suffered.

The revolution had apparently triumphed in Berlin – or so it seemed on the surface. Militarism had been defeated; on 29 March the new ministry was further strengthened by the appointment of the liberal leaders Camphausen and Hansemann as minister-president and finance minister respectively; and it was also announced that a constituent assembly elected by universal suffrage would soon be called to draft a constitution for Prussia.[4] The reality was rather different. The army was unbeaten and under the control of officers determined to have their revenge. As for the king, he privately mistrusted his ministers – he could not believe that merchants were fitting people to conduct the affairs of a great kingdom. Nor could a Hohenzollern tolerate for long the idea that a mere minister of war should come between a king and his army. Characteristically Frederick William could not bring himself to regain power by *coup d'état* as hot-headed conservatives, notably young Otto von Bismarck, urged him to. Instead he relied increasingly on conservative officials and soldiers for advice. As the months passed his court *camarilla* became the real power behind the throne.

In fact Frederick William had no real cause to fear his liberal ministers. They were greatly alarmed by the victory which the workers had won – or seemed to have won – on the barricades. For men of property the street fighting on 18 March was the lightning flash which lit up the horizon. Street violence was a threat to social order and the high road to mob rule. Faced with these new perils, liberal ministers were concerned to preserve the power of the crown, the army, and the civil service, as essential bastions of social order; by the end of the month several infantry regiments had been called back to Berlin to protect the new government.

In the spring of 1848 a wave of popular unrest swept through Germany. In March and April serious disorders occurred in many places when

---

[3]From henceforth Prussia is merged in Germany.
[4]The elections were,however, to be indirect.

sections of the people resorted to direct action to redress their grievances. The *Handwerker* indulged in a violent orgy of machine-breaking in an attempt to dragoon governments into restoring the old restrictive guild system, which it was supposed would insulate the craftsmen against the effects of industrialisation. In Nassau teamsters put out of work by railways in the 1840s took their revenge by wrecking sections of railway lines. Sailors made redundant by the growth of big steamship companies retaliated by attacking company vessels. Business confidence was shaken by the disorders and share prices fell sharply. The disturbances in the countryside in West and South Germany were much more widespread and serious, especially in Baden and Württemberg, where castles were looted and burnt down and manorial records destroyed. Disturbances were less severe east of the Elbe, but a rudimentary agrarian socialism made some headway amongst the landless labourers, and in Pomerania and Brandenburg there was talk of land redistribution.

Faced with a popular movement which threatened to shake the social order to its foundations, liberals felt that their first duty, as responsible ministers, was to restore law and order. In the towns they were assisted by the willingness of industrialists to make concessions to revolutionary *Handwerker* in order to forestall further violence; thus the weavers in Krefeld and Elberfeld were able to force important concessions out of their employers, including the recognition of guilds as negotiating agencies and the imposition of restrictions on the use of machinery. Business confidence was restored in Prussia by prompt government intervention; a bank of issue backed by state funds was established to offer credit facilities to merchants. Liberal administrations all over Germany issued proclamations exhorting citizens to refrain from violence. Prussia, Hesse-Darmstadt, Baden and Württemberg promised prompt action to remove rural grievances, and municipalities hurriedly embarked on programmes of public works to provide employment. Last, but not least, civic guards, solidly middle-class in complexion, were formed to protect property, disperse demonstrators in the towns and put down peasant revolts. This mixture of conciliation and coercion proved successful in restoring law and order; the *Handwerker* and the peasantry abandoned direct-action techniques, and relied in future on congresses and petitions to draw the attention of parliamentary bodies to their grievances. At the same time, because their demands had been partially satisfied and because liberal administrations had firmly resisted radical pressures, the revolutionary enthusiasm of the masses began to ebb away in the early summer of 1848.

The liberals could now turn their attention to the Herculean task of creating a united Germany. On 31 March the Pre-Parliament (or *Vorparlament*) met in the Paulskirche at Frankfurt. This was not an elected body; in the main it consisted of members of local estates together with other prominent liberals summoned by the committee of seven. The overwhelming majority of the 521 members were from South and West Germany.[5] Only two Austrians attended, and 100 of the 141 Prussian representatives were from the Rhineland with its strong liberal tradition.

The Pre-Parliament had no popular mandate. It simply assumed the right to speak for the German people and arrange the calling of an elected national parliament to decide Germany's future. So strong was the revolutionary spirit in the spring of 1848 that this assembly, composed very largely of moderate liberals, agreed without question to universal suffrage as the basis for the elections. Of course this did not mean that the moderates wanted the national parliament to act on its own initiative in solving Germany's problems; these could only be solved, in their opinion, by agreement with the princes.

This view was not shared by a large radical minority of some 150 members led by Hecker and Struve. The radicals favoured the abolition of hereditary monarchy and standing armies and the introduction of a federal constitution modelled on North American lines. At all costs they wanted to keep the flame of popular revolution burning; so they tried to transform the Pre-Parliament into a permanent revolutionary executive armed with plenary powers to decide the future of Germany without reference to the princes or the Federal Diet. The attempt failed. The Pre-Parliament dispersed on 3 April having first appointed a committee of fifty – from which Hecker and Struve were excluded – to work out the election details and to act as an executive until the national parliaments met.

Bitterly disappointed over their rebuff in the Pre-Parliament, a few of the radicals resorted to direct action. The impulsive Hecker, then at the height of his popularity as an orator, was so intoxicated by the radical spirit in Baden that he proclaimed a German republic on 12 April. The so-called *Heckerputsch* was a miserable failure. Inadequately prepared, it collapsed within a week. Hecker's followers, a mere thousand peasants armed with scythes, were quickly dispersed by the military. The German Legion, some 800 exiles recruited in Paris by the poet Herwegh, met a similar fate when it crossed the Rhine later in April. Hecker escaped to Switzerland and eventually became a farmer in the United States, then a recognised haven for persecuted radicals from Europe.

No doubt moderate liberals, believing passionately as they did in the power of reason to change men's minds, were deeply offended and frightened by the readiness of a radical minority to use violence to accomplish its political ends. But it would be wrong to suppose that the ill-advised *Heckerputsch* drove the moderates into the arms of the princes. The fact is that from the start the moderates, being instinctive anti-revolutionaries, hankered after a junior partnership with the aristocracy. All the radical bogey did was to emphasise the need for such an understanding.

[5] Eighty-four were from Hesse-Darmstadt, seventy-two from Baden, fifty-two from Württemberg and forty-four from Bavaria.

On 1 May 1848 the election of the National Assembly took place. On 18 May the members walked in solemn procession to the Paulskirche in Frankfurt amidst the roar of cannon and the ringing of bells. This was a great moment in the history of German liberalism. A galaxy of brilliant and talented personalities sat in this first German parliament. All the leading figures in German politics for the last three decades were there: the political professors Dahlmann, Droysen and Waitz, the veteran patriots of 1813 Arndt and *Turnvater* Jahn, prominent radicals such as Blum and Ruge, and the Catholic leader Bishop Ketteler.

The Frankfurt Parliament was more representative of the liberal middle class than the people as a whole. This was hardly surprising for although the Pre-Parliament decided to give the vote to every independent citizen who had attained his majority, it was left to the various states to define the conditions of 'independence'. A few states, including Austria, Prussia and Schleswig-Holstein, imposed no restrictions on their citizens; in Bavaria only those paying direct taxation had the vote; in Baden and Saxony farm hands had no vote, and in Bavaria and Württemberg domestic servants and workers were excluded. The ballot was not secret, and despite the recommendation of the Pre-Parliament indirect election was adopted in most states. Consequently the great majority of the 585 members were middle-class in social origin. One hundred and fifty-seven judges and lawyers, 138 higher officials, over 100 teachers from university and high schools and some forty merchants and industrialists sat in the parliament; but only one peasant and four *Handwerker*; and of the ninety members of the nobility most were members of learned professions.

At first the Parliament hoped to establish a provisional central government for Germany by agreement with the larger states. Only when negotiations deadlocked, did the Parliament act on its own initiative – largely at the bidding of its president Heinrich von Gagern – and proceed to elect a *Reichsverweser*.[6]

The king of Prussia was far too unpopular a figure to be elected to this office; he very quickly regretted the proclamation of 21 March and refused to take any fresh initiative in the German question. So in June the post of *Reichsverweser* was offered to Archduke John, the brother of Emperor Ferdinand and a man of liberal views, who had married a postmaster's daughter. The Frankfurt Parliament was held in such high esteem in the summer of 1848 that the states had no alternative but to accept the new appointment. In July the Federal Diet handed over its functions to Archduke John, who set about the task of creating a central government. To head it he chose Prince Leiningen, a high-minded Bavarian aristocrat who was elder half-brother to Queen Victoria and cousin and brother-in-law to Prince Albert.

---

[6]Imperial administrator.

On paper the new ministry looked most impressive. In practice its authority was strictly limited and depended entirely on the willingness of individual states to co-operate with the Frankfurt government. The first intimation of this unpleasant truth was the resistance encountered by the minister of war when he attempted to exercise some control over the armies of the princes. Most small states allowed their soldiers to swear an oath of allegiance to the *Reichsverweser*. The larger states, notably Austria, Prussia and Hanover, refused to comply with the request and nothing could be done to coerce them. Similarly in financial matters the government was completely dependent on the states once the resources of the Federal Diet had been used up. Unfortunately these power realities were temporarily obscured by the revolutionary fervour which gripped Germany in the early months of 1848.

It was not long before the veil was torn rudely aside. The occasion was the Schleswig-Holstein question. At the close of the 1840s Schleswig became the battle-ground of rival national movements. German nationalists claimed that Schleswig was an indisputably German land, intimately associated with German Holstein for centuries, and ought to be a member of the Confederation. Their opponents, the Danish nationalists, maintained that Schleswig was a Danish land and must become an integral part of a Danish national state. Towards the end of March 1848 news was received in the duchies of revolution in Copenhagen and of the inclusion of prominent Eider Danes in a new ministry. The Germans immediately set up a provisional government in Kiel to defend the duchies and appealed to the Federal Diet for assistance against the Danes.

The Federal Diet recognised the Kiel government and asked Prussia to intervene in the duchies. King Frederick William needed no prompting; he had already assured the duke of Augustenburg that Prussia would defend Schleswig-Holstein against external attack. In April Prussian troops entered the duchies, and in early in May General Wrangel, commander of the Prussian forces and federal contingents, drove the Danes out of South Jutland.

Then the king of Prussia began to regret his hasty intervention. Austria had not supported Prussia in Schleswig-Holstein; little assistance had been given by the Central and Southern states; the Danish blockade of the North-German coastline was affecting Prussian commerce; and the Great Powers had expressed strong disapproval of Prussian policy. There seemed little point in continuing a war which pleased only the Berlin radicals. At the end of May Wrangel was ordered to evacuate South Jutland. The Frankfurt Parliament protested and demanded that Prussia prosecute the war energetically. Prussia paid little attention. In July Wrangel was ordered to negotiate an armistice with Denmark. This was eventually signed on 26 August at Malmö in Sweden. Under the terms of this armistice Prussia was to evacuate the duchies.

The moment of truth had arrived for the Frankfurt Parliament. Although Prussia had obtained authorisation from the central government to conclude an armistice on certain conditions, she had ignored these and in effect contracted out of a war approved by the Frankfurt Parliament. The Paulskirche seethed with indignation. Dahlmann, a man of the political centre but a veteran campaigner for Schleswig-Holstein, was widely applauded when he declared: 'If we submit in this first trial with the Great Powers, if we show ourselves faint-hearted at the first onset of danger, then, gentlemen, you will never raise your proud heads again.' The radicals put the same point more strongly still. Convinced that the defeat of the Paris workers in June had endangered the cause of revolution all over Europe, the extreme left, taking Jacobin France as their model, favoured a militant foreign policy to halt the progress of counter-revolution and bring about radical political change in Germany. After heated debate the armistice was indeed rejected by a narrow margin. The Leiningen ministry, which had counselled caution, resigned. Dahlmann tried in vain to form a new ministry. On 16 September after a tense three-day debate the Parliament reversed its previous decision by a narrow majority; fear of a clash with Prussia and fear of radicalism getting the upper hand tipped the scales in favour of acceptance of the armistice.

There was bitter opposition to the armistice on the left wing, where the compliant attitude of the Parliament was denounced as a betrayal of the national honour of Germany. *Turnvater* Jahn, one of the offending majority, had to hide from the crowds. A mass demonstration in Frankfurt on 18 September, attended by thousands of *Handwerker*, demanded that left-wing members leave the traitorous Parliament, set up a national convention and continue the war. The parliamentary left, however, declined the invitation; Robert Blum warned against hasty action likely to damage the radical cause still further, and in the end only nineteen members withdrew. The central government, now led by the Austrian Schmerling, called in Austrian and Prussian troops to defend the Parliament. On 18 September an attack on the Paulskirche was repulsed, artillery from Darmstadt quickly destroyed barricades erected in the vicinity, martial law was proclaimed and all political clubs suspended. During the disorders two conservative members of parliament were murdered by the mob. On 21 September Struve staged another rising in Baden; he proclaimed a German republic and announced the abolition without compensation of all feudal dues and the nationalisation of all land owned by Church and State. The authorities dispersed Struve's followers with ease, and he followed Hecker into permanent exile. Minor disturbances in Württemberg and in Cologne were quickly suppressed.

The ill-fated Malmö armistice dealt a very serious blow to the authority of the Frankfurt Parliament. The attempts of the central government to pursue an independent foreign policy, always fraught with difficulty, were now completely discounted abroad. The Great Powers realised that power still resided in Berlin and Vienna. Consequently the central government failed to establish full diplomatic relations with any Great Power except the United States.

In Germany the popularity of the Parliament began rapidly to wane. Ardent nationalists did not lightly forgive the miserable failure to protect the Germans in Schleswig-Holstein. The fact that soldiers acting in the name of the Parliament had opened fire on the people who were the real source of the Parliament's moral authority alienated opinion on the left. The September disorders had a wider significance; they were the German counterpart of the June Days, an outburst of violence in Paris which had frightened the middle classes all over Europe. Terrified by the spectre of 'red revolution' and understandably horrified by the murder of two of its members, the Frankfurt Parliament moved steadily to the right and placed increasing reliance on princely armies for the speedy restoration of law and order. With the radical left weakened by internal dissensions, this right-ward movement of opinion encouraged the forces of counter-revolution. It must also be remembered that popular discontent was less acute by the autumn of 1848; the economic depression reached a nadir in the summer of 1847; and Germany was already recovering in the spring of 1848, a fact which helped to damp the revolutionary enthusiasm of the people.

It was an article of faith with European liberals that all peoples would live in peace and harmony with each other once they had thrown off the yoke of foreign oppression. The years 1848–49 destroyed this naïve illusion. The relations between the peoples of Central Europe deteriorated as national conflicts blazed up between Magyars and Slavs and between Germans and their neighbours. This was perhaps the most ominous legacy of the Revolution; for the first time Germany was brought up against intractable national problems to which no lasting solution has been found.

These problems arose in an acute form for Germany when the Frankfurt Parliament attempted to define the frontiers of the new German state. A few members, notably Arndt and Jahn, demanded the inclusion of all German-speaking areas. The overwhelming majority was satisfied with the existing frontiers of the Confederation extended to take in Schleswig and East and West Prussia. Thus from the beginning the Frankfurt Parliament expected the new Germany to include large non-German minorities: the Czechs of Bohemia, the Danes of Schleswig and Polish minorities in East and West Prussia.

German liberals did not consider the presence of these minorities incompatible with the creation of a national state. The language of uneducated people – whether Danes, Poles or Czechs – had little bearing, in their view, on the national character of border regions. National affiliation did not depend on the will of the majority – although if the majority spoke German this was a useful ancillary argument. The decisive factor was the character of the institutional framework of an area; if German was spoken in church, in the schools – at least in the institutions of higher education – in the law courts, and in the administration and if it was the language of polite society, then the area was German. The language of pastors, officials and teachers was considered a more significant yardstick than the language of peasants and workers because the Germans tacitly assumed that their language was a superior cultural medium. In short, the Germans thought not in terms of nationality but of the historic frontiers of the *Reich* extended to include East and West Prussia and Schleswig, all of which had close historical ties with Germany. The Germans did not attempt to prohibit the use of non-German 'dialects' in everyday life; on the contrary, clause thirteen of the Fundamental Rights of the German People guaranteed equal treatment of all minorities; they would have the right to use their own tongue in church and school and in the local administration provided that German remained 'the language of state'.

It is important to realise that the Germans were no worse than other peoples in their attitude to minorities. Curiously enough, nationality was often a secondary consideration in this nationally conscious age; history and strategic necessity were the prime determinants of national boundaries in Europe in 1848 and for long after.

There were many examples of this. The Magyar 'national' state included several non-Magyar minorities simply because they happened to form part of the historic complex known as the crown lands of St. Stephen ruled by the Magyars. Similarly the Czechs laid claim not only to areas inhabited by Czech-speaking people, but to the historic area known as the crown lands of St. Wenceslaus, which included a sizeable German minority. Polish nationalists did not hesitate to demand the inclusion of the historic kingdom of Galicia in a Polish 'national' state despite the presence of a large Ruthenian minority. Danish nationalists, or Eider Danes as they were called, demanded the inclusion of Schleswig in their 'national' state regardless of the fact that South Schleswig was wholly German; they claimed that the Eider river, which separated Schleswig from Holstein, was the historic frontier between Denmark and Germany, and that in any case its retention by Denmark was a military necessity.

During the Revolution relations between the Germans and their neighbours the Danes, the Poles and the Czechs deteriorated sharply. In the north the outbreak of war with Denmark exacerbated relations between Germans and Danes. In April 1848 the Kiel government attempted to conciliate the Danes of Schleswig by offering them the right of self-determination. But once Kiel was assured of German military support the offer was withdrawn. During the war heavy taxation and attempts to levy recruits in Danish-speaking districts alienated the Danes from Germany. National passions deepened on both sides, and the scars of war were never eradicated from the duchy.

In the east relations with the Poles worsened after a brief honeymoon in the early days of the Revolution. The liberation of Poland was a popular radical cause; 'No free Germany without a free Poland; no free Poland without a free Germany' wrote Herwegh in the spring of 1848. There were also practical considerations. Many Germans believed that war between autocratic Russia and liberal Europe was inevitable; the Poles would be welcome allies in a popular anti-Russian crusade which would unite the German people and help to heal internal divisions.

The Pre-Parliament sympathised with Polish national aspirations. It denounced the eighteenth-century partitions as a shameful injustice and declared that the Germans had a sacred duty to assist in the resurrection of Poland. East and West Prussia would become part of the new Germany but the future of Posen, the grand duchy acquired by Prussia in 1793 and inhabited by 800,000 Poles and 500,000 Germans, would be decided by the Frankfurt Parliament. Meanwhile, under liberal pressure, the king of Prussia promised Posen greater autonomy as a gesture to redress past injustices.

However, friction soon developed between the Germans and the Poles when the latter attempted to make Posen the nucleus of a fully-restored Polish Kingdom. The Germans in the grand duchy, abandoning the historical-territorial principle upheld so zealously elsewhere, clamoured for partition. In April Prussia, anxious to preserve her power base in the east, came out in favour of this solution and incorporated the largest part of the duchy. Eventually after an abortive uprising, the Poles appealed to the Frankfurt Parliament. But when the radical left spoke in support of Poland during the debate on Posen in July, it suffered a crushing defeat. Jordan, a Berlin radical, was applauded for a chauvinistic speech asserting the superiority of the Germans over the Slavs. By a huge majority the Frankfurt Parliament approved Prussia's action and rejected a motion condemning the eighteenth-century partitions; the truth was that as the prospect of a general war against Russia receded, the German liberals lost interest in the resurrection of Poland. Finally, in 1849 Prussia decided to keep the whole of Posen.

In the south-east relations between Czechs and Germans quickly deteriorated. The Germans expected the Czechs to elect members to the Frankfurt Parliament. In April Palacky, the Czech leader, refused to accept representation on the committee of fifty; in a famous letter he declared that the Czechs had a right to determine their own future; they preferred to remain under Habsburg rule but would seek to transform the empire into a federal state in which Czechs and Germans would enjoy equal rights. When most Bohemian constituencies failed to send representatives to Frankfurt, the Parliament was deeply offended. Liberals and radicals were in complete agreement on the Czech question; both were equally blind in their stubborn refusal to recognise that Czech nationalism was as genuine a phenomenon as German nationalism. Instead they insisted that Bohemia was a historic German land which must remain part of Germany, and they denounced Czech nationalism as a reactionary anomaly. When clashes occurred in Prague between Germans and Czechs, the liberals called for Austrian intervention. They looked on approvingly when Windischgrätz bombarded Prague in June and crushed the Czech revolt. The liberals completely failed to appreciate the cosmic significance of the imperial commander's victory, and in July naïvely requested the Austrians to compel the defeated Czechs to send representatives to Frankfurt.

Initially the German liberals anticipated little difficulty in securing suitable frontiers for a united Germany. The break-up of the Habsburg empire seemed imminent in the spring of 1848. In accordance with the principle of nationality, Austria's Italian possessions, would then become part of a united Italy, Galicia would join a united Poland, and the crown lands of St. Stephen would become independent Hungary, leaving Bohemia and Austria to gravitate towards Germany.

The Habsburg empire proved much more resilient than the liberals imagined. It became apparent that neither the Czechs nor the South Slavs wanted to see the empire disrupted; they felt instinctively – and correctly, as subsequent history showed – that without the Habsburgs the Slav peoples would find it impossible to avoid absorption by either Germany or Russia. In the summer of 1848 the Austrian government began to recover its old power. The bombardment of Prague was followed in July by Radetsky's defeat of the Piedmontese army at Custozza. The tide had turned, and by the early autumn the counter-revolution was in full swing. Military operations were started against the Magyars, who promptly declared themselves completely independent. In October a radical rising occurred in Vienna in protest against the attack on Hungary, and the emperor was obliged to fly once more from his capital city. But imperial forces commanded by Windischgrätz, the conqueror of Prague, were soon advancing on Vienna.

At this critical moment in the Austrian revolution the Frankfurt Parliament stood helplessly by. The radicals wanted to help their Viennese colleagues. But the moderate-minded majority saw no point in offending the Austrian authorities for the sake of Viennese radicals. In any case, as the Parliament disposed of no armed forces it could not give assistance to anyone. Finally Frankfurt dispatched two peace emissaries to Austria. They were coldly received at Windischgrätz's headquarters and decided not to proceed to Vienna. By the end of October Windischgrätz had crushed the rising and re-entered Vienna. Blum, a prominent radical in the

Frankfurt Parliament who had conveyed the greetings of the left to the Viennese insurgents and had later taken part in the street fighting, was summarily shot by the Austrians. The execution was an act calculated to humiliate the Frankfurt Parliament. The members protested indignantly and called on the central government to punish those guilty of this deed. The Austrians blandly ignored all protests; once again the Frankfurt Parliament was forced to recognise the harsh reality of power.

Against this gloomy back-cloth the Frankfurt liberals began to debate the first part of the German constitution almost five months to the day since they had first assembled in the Paulskirche – a fatal delay as events quickly proved.

Under the influence of Dahlmann and Droysen the committee responsible for drafting the constitution grasped the Austrian nettle firmly and boldly. Germany, it declared, would have the frontiers of the old Confederation; the constitutional position of Schleswig and the precise delineation of the frontier in Posen were details which could be decided later. The vital principle was enunciated that German and non-German territories could not be united in one state. Where German and non-German territories had the same ruler the dynastic ties could be maintained. But in all other respects the German territories would be an integral part of the German fatherland. These recommendations, which were accepted by a large majority on 27 October, reflected the belief of members that Austria and Bohemia would remain – and Schleswig would become – part of the new German state.

The optimism was ill-founded and short-lived. Neither the Danish king nor the Austrian emperor intended to dismember his dominions to please Frankfurt. The new Austrian premier, Prince Felix Schwarzenberg, was a soldier and diplomat by training who believed firmly in the mission of the Habsburg monarchy in Central Europe. On 27 November, shortly after his appointment, he declared that the preservation of the empire was essential in the interests both of Germany and of Europe. There could be no loosening of the ties between Austria and Bohemia and the rest of the Habsburg dominions. On 2 December the feeble-minded Emperor Ferdinand was at last forced to abdicate. He was succeeded by his nephew Francis Joseph, a boy of eighteen who was destined to rule the empire for the next sixty-eight years.

As the Frankfurt Parliament continued throughout the winter of 1848–49 to wrestle with the knotty problem of relations with Austria, two distinct schools of thought emerged in the Paulskirche. A growing body of opinion, labelled Little-German by its opponents, favoured the complete exclusion of Austria and Bohemia from Germany, and the union of the remaining states under Prussia. These views were supported by many members from North and Central Germany who had long believed that Prussia was destined to rule Germany. Heinrich von Gagern, the leading exponent of Little Germanism, tried to mitigate the effects of the exclusion of Austria from Germany by advocating a loose association (or *weiterer Bund*) between a united Little Germany and the Habsburg empire on matters of common interest including foreign policy, defence and customs. In mid-December the Parliament authorised von Gagern, who had succeeded Schmerling as head of the central government, to negotiate with Austria on these lines – but only because he had mollified his opponents by promising not to exclude the possibility of integrating Austria and Bohemia in Germany. In January 1849 the Prussian government, with the reluctant consent of the king, cautiously expressed sympathy with Gagern's proposals in a circular letter to all German states.

The Little Germans were vigorously opposed by the Greater Germans led by Schmerling. The Greater Germans worked to maintain the traditional ties between Austria and Germany, and insisted that Austria and Bohemia must remain part of the new German state – an attitude aptly summarised in Arndt's phrase '*Das ganze Deutschland soll es sein*'.[7] Greater Germanism was supported by a heterogeneous and uneasy alliance of radicals who wanted a unitary republic, particularists who hoped to preserve the power of the states, and Catholics suspicious of Protestant Prussia.

In the early days most Austrian members at Frankfurt had been Greater Germans. By the end of 1848 many had changed their minds. They still voted with the Greater Germans against Little Germany but they were equally opposed to Greater Germany. They had in fact become Greater Austrians, intent on preserving the Habsburg dominions for their own sake. Some Austrians were dreaming of a great political and economic union between the empire and the German Confederation, a mid-European union centred on Vienna and capable of defending Europe against Russian Panslavism. These views received some support in Bavaria from South-German manufacturers seeking to enter the markets of the Danubian basin.

In the end the Habsburgs forced the hand of the Frankfurt Parliament. On 4 March 1849 Francis Joseph dissolved the Kremsier constituent assembly and promulgated a new constitution which subjected all parts of the empire to rigid control from Vienna. The door had closed on all hopes of uniting Austria with Germany. On 9 March Schwarzenberg made the dramatic proposal that the whole of the Habsburg dominions, a total of thirty-eight million people, should be united with the German Confederation with its thirty-two million inhabitants to form a great empire of seventy million people. The empire would be administered by a directory of seven, headed alternately by Austria and Prussia, and assisted by a chamber of estates consisting of thirty-eight Austrian members and thirty-

[7] It must be the whole of Germany.

two Germans. Following in the footsteps of Metternich, Schwarzenberg was making a determined bid to restore Austria to a position of primacy in Central Europe. To him Germany, Italy and Hungary were merely pieces to be moved across the chess board in the interests of Greater Austria.

The Frankfurt Parliament was now faced with a stark choice between a Little Germany and a mid-European union which represented the negation of national aspirations. Some of the opponents of Little Germany now changed their minds; in particular a group of democrats led by Simon was won over in return for constitutional concessions. As a further sop to Greater Germanism the constitution in its final form still declared that Germany should have the frontiers of the old Confederation. Eventually on 27 March it was decided by a majority of twenty-four to offer the crown of Little Germany to a reigning prince, and by a bare majority of four to make the crown hereditary. Five days later the king of Prussia was elected German emperor by 290 votes with 248 abstentions. As the bells pealed and the cannon roared in celebration, it looked as if the Frankfurt Parliament was at last in sight of the promised land.

By the end of March the details of the constitution had been worked out. In accordance with the wishes of the moderate majority, Germany was to become a constitutional monarchy. In order to win support for Little Germany, the 1849 constitution was made more democratic than was originally intended. The emperor still possessed a power to delay legislation, but it was no longer an absolute veto, and the primacy of parliament was now firmly asserted; the ministers were made responsible to parliament, not to the emperor, and all proclamations required ministerial counter-signature. Parliament was to consist of two chambers, an upper house partly nominated by the state governments and partly elected by state legislatures, and a lower house elected by universal suffrage and armed with budgetary powers.

The new *Reich* was to be a federal state. Foreign policy, defence and transport were reserved to the federal government while residual powers remained with the states. No other solution was possible as long as the thirty-nine states remained in being; they could not be conjured out of existence by the Frankfurt Parliament, nor did the liberals wish to strip them of all their power. But it was laid down that federal legislation took precedence over state laws. The federal government would be financed from customs revenue and from indirect taxation, but in special cases it could levy direct taxation. Finally, an imperial court would adjudicate in all disputes between states and the imperial government. In the last days of March 1849 a deputation representing all the states except Austria and led by Simson, president of the Frankfurt Parliament, set off for Berlin to offer the crown of Little Germany to Frederick William IV.

The situation in Prussia had changed completely since March 1848. In May the Prussian assembly met in Berlin to help in the drafting of a new constitution. The assembly was a much more radical body than the Frankfurt Parliament; landed property and industry were poorly represented; consequently the 120 members on the left, led by the radicals Jacoby and Waldeck, were able to exert great influence over the proceedings. They wanted to turn the parliament into a constituent assembly armed with plenary powers and could rely on the support of the *Handwerker* and proletariat in Berlin, a formidable pressure group and a constant source of embarrassment to the Camphausen ministry. In June 1848 the Berlin arsenal was stormed by a mob. This event confirmed the growing fear of radicalism in middle-class circles and made the liberals more dependent than ever before on the forces of law and order.

The news that the new Hansemann ministry was preparing to end the tax exemptions of the nobility and abolish the manorial obligations of the peasantry alarmed landowners and encouraged the forces of counter-revolution to venture into the open. While the national assembly was moving further to the left in the high summer, landowners and noblemen were forming local associations to defend their interests. In August the League for the Protection of Landed Property met in Berlin; the 'Junker Parliament', as it was dubbed by the radicals, pledged itself to work for the abolition of the assembly and the dismissal of the liberal ministry. Caught in the cross-fire from radicals and conservatives Prussian liberalism was mortally wounded.

In October the crisis deepened. The assembly deleted the phrase 'by the grace of God' from the royal title, an action which deeply offended the pious monarch. In August the assembly had abolished the judicial and financial privileges of the nobility; in October it was preparing far-reaching agrarian reforms, for – in sharp contrast to the Frankfurt Parliament – sixty-eight peasants sat in the Berlin assembly. When news arrived of the fall of Vienna the king decided to act. The old ministry was dismissed and Count Brandenburg, a conservative landowner, was appointed prime minister on 2 November. On 9 November – 18 Brumaire in the French calendar – Brandenburg ordered the assembly out of Berlin. The assembly refused. The next day Berlin was in the hands of the army, martial law was proclaimed, all political clubs were closed and demonstrations forbidden. A remnant of the assembly met later in November in Brandenburg but was abruptly dissolved by the king on 5 December.

The counter-revolution had triumphed in Prussia. It was significant that even at the height of the crisis, the radicals declined offers from the Berlin workers to resist the *coup d'état* by force. They preferred to rely on passive resistance to vindicate their cause, declaring before leaving Berlin that Count Brandenburg had no authority to raise taxes unless the assembly stayed in being. When Karl Marx and his associates urged the people to resist the collection of taxes, their appeals fell on stony ground. Minor disturbances in several cities were easily suppressed.

On 3 April 1848 Simson's deputation met the king. Surrounded by ministers and generals, Frederick William thanked the Frankfurt Parliament for its confidence in him and promised once more to defend Germany against external foes. But he made it clear that he could not reach a decision about the crown of Little Germany without the full agreement of the princes. It was obvious that the king had virtually rejected the crown, and the deputation returned to Frankfurt in a mood of deep despair.

Why had Frederick William rejected the primacy of Germany which his brother William was to accept twenty-two years later?

The simple truth is that the king was completely out of sympathy with the Revolution. The conservative *Ständestaat* was still his political ideal; events since March 1848 merely confirmed his detestation of constitutional liberalism. He was bitterly contemptuous of the 'imaginary little crown baked from mud and clay' offered him by the Frankfurt Parliament; only with reluctance did he even agree to receive Simson's deputation. He was deeply suspicious of Little Germany; 'Germany without the Tyrol, Trieste and the Archduchy [Austria] would be worse than a nose without a face' he exclaimed. To the end of his days he remained faithful to his adolescent dream of a Christian-German empire ruled by the Habsburgs, with the Prussian monarch as *Reichserzfeldherr*[8] holding the emperor's stirrup.

The foreign political situation confirmed Frederick William's instincts. The German question was a European question in 1848–49 as it had been in 1815. And the unpleasant truth was that the Great Powers were not particularly well-disposed towards Germany. There was some sympathy for German national aspirations among English liberals; Palmerston welcomed the prospect of a strong Prussia keeping France and Russia at bay; but the attempts of the Frankfurt Parliament to build a navy and Prussia's intervention in Schleswig-Holstein aroused his displeasure. Franco-German relations deteriorated after a brief honeymoon in March 1848; Bastide, the French foreign minister, took the side of the German princes against the Frankfurt Parliament. Austrian hostility to Little Germany was evident, and behind Austria stood the tsar who dismissed German unification as a utopian dream. In these circumstances Frederick William felt justified in assuming that acceptance of the crown would lead to serious complications and possibly to war with Austria and Russia. And he was not the man to lead Germany through the storm of war; when an emissary from Frankfurt pleaded with him to accept the crown, he replied in a perceptive moment that it was a pity Frederick the Great could not hear these words – 'He would have been your man. But I am no great regent.'

Faced with the destruction of all its hopes, the Frankfurt Parliament did

8Commander-in-chief of the imperial army.

not waver, but reaffirmed its faith in the new constitution and in Little Germany. Under growing popular pressure the plenipotentiaries of twenty-eight states hurriedly declared their support for the constitution, and the Prussian assembly decided by a small majority that the constitution was legally binding on Prussia. Then on 28 April 1849 the Prussian government informed Frankfurt that the king would not accept the crown of Little Germany. The lingering hopes of the Little Germans that Frederick William might change his mind were destroyed and the death knell sounded for the Frankfurt Parliament. Austria had already ordered her members to leave Frankfurt. Several states, including Saxony, Hanover and Bavaria, plucked up courage and repudiated the new constitution. The Parliament struggled on, discussing the details of elections for the new Reichstag and agreeing to appoint a *Statthalter* to take charge of the new *Reich*. All in vain; on 14 May Prussia ordered her representatives to leave Frankfurt. This was the signal for moderate liberals – already seriously alarmed by disturbances in several parts of Germany – to abandon ship. By the end of May only the radical left remained in Frankfurt. They kept up the pretence a little longer. They appealed to the people to rally in support of the constitution and moved to more congenial surroundings in Stuttgart, where they set up an imperial regency consisting of five members. The end came when the regency called on the Württemberg authorities for men and money. On 18 June the king sent troops to occupy the town hall where the 'Rump Parliament' was meeting, and cavalry dispersed the hundred-odd members when they tried to take their seats. On that ignominious note a parliament which had caught the imagination of the German people a year before came to an abrupt end.

This was not quite the end of the 1848–49 Revolution. The demise of the Frankfurt Parliament was quite overshadowed by the wave of disorder which swept through Germany in May, June and July 1849. This was in effect a second revolution, in defence of the federal constitution. Its outbreak was an impressive tribute to the strength of revolutionary feeling even though popular support was very limited outside South-West Germany.

In Berlin and Breslau there were bloody clashes between the crowds and the military. In the Rhineland abortive republican risings occurred in several towns. In Saxony the disturbances were more serious; a rising occurred in Dresden in early May following the dissolution of the lower house; the king fled and a provisional government, which immediately recognised the federal constitution, was formed. However, the rising was confined to Dresden, and within a few days Saxon and Prussian soldiers had completely crushed it.

The storm centre of the disturbances lay in the Bavarian Palatinate and in Baden, where radicalism had deep popular roots among the *Handwerker* and lower middle class generally. On 18 May a provisional government was established at Kaiserlautern in the Palatinate. In Baden the garrisons at Rastadt and Karlsruhe had already mutinied. Grand Duke Leopold fled, an executive committee assumed power, a constituent assembly was convened and a free corps for the defence of Baden was formed under the command of the Polish soldier Microwslawski. The grand duke turned to Prussia for assistance and two army corps commanded by Crown Prince William advanced on Baden. Despite heroic resistance by the free corps, Prussian troops soon occupied the whole of Baden. The revolt ended on 23 July with the capitulation of Rastadt, where several revolutionary leaders were executed after summary court martial. With the collapse of the Baden insurrection the 1848–49 Revolution came to an end in Germany. When the Hungarian army surrendered at Vilagos on 13 August 1849, the revolution had ended generally in Central Europe.

National liberal historians in their eagerness to glorify the achievements of Prussia brought up a whole generation of Germans in the belief that the Revolution of 1848–49 was an irrelevant comment on the margin of German history. According to these historians the liberals of 1848–49 were unpractical doctrinaires who wasted valuable time discussing the Fundamental Rights of the German People for six months where men of action would have boldly cut the Gordian knot of the German problem.

This view does less than justice to the men of 1848–49. All European liberals attached immense importance to the precise definition of the basic freedoms of speech, assembly and thought in order to protect citizens from arbitrary treatment at the hands of rulers. This is not to deny that liberals were inclined to attach too much importance to the spoken word; expert though they were in the techniques of debate, they lacked executive experience, a situation which encourages a certain dichotomy to arise between the constitutional theorist and the practising politician. Still, many members of the Parliament were well aware of their limitations.

The basic weakness of the liberal experiment was insurmountable, given liberal premises. The Frankfurt Parliament enjoyed a purely moral authority; material power lay with the princes, as the Schleswig-Holstein affair revealed so vividly. Moderate liberals accepted the German princes as fixed points in the political landscape, and relied on their bureaucracies and armies to implement the decisions of the central government. For it was not the business of liberals to force rulers to abandon absolutism against their will, but rather to persuade them to share power with the upper middle class. For the most part the rulers indulged them, feeling the need for liberal support against the masses. It was the refusal of the more powerful states, especially Austria and Prussia, to do the bidding of the liberals that finally revealed the fundamental naïveté of the belief that Germany could be united by agreement with the princes.

At the same time, once radicalism had emerged as a major threat, the liberals became increasingly dependent on the princes and quite unable to exploit the unrivalled moral authority enjoyed by the Frankfurt Parliament in the spring and early summer of 1848. Of course, far from overestimating their standing with the masses of the people, liberals consistently underestimated it. But they had no wish to appeal over the heads of the princes to the people at large and enlist their support for the building of a new Germany. When liberals spoke of 'the people', they were thinking of the educated minority which had monopolised politics for half a century and which sought to alter the structure of politics, not the structure of society.

The radicals, on the other hand, being dependent on the *Handwerker* for support, often displayed a considerable interest in social problems. But the appeal of radicalism was limited; it was essentially an urban product, and radicals made no attempt to forge that alliance between *Handwerker* and peasantry which enabled the French revolutionaries to transform the social structure of their country. It is significant that Hecker and Struve were greatly alarmed by the peasant uprising in Baden in 1848. Even in the summer of 1849, when fighting for their very existence, radical leaders rejected Friedrich Engels's advice and urged their followers to respect property and not to turn the struggle into a class war. Despite a network of local clubs, the radicals never succeeded in building up a mass following outside Baden. In fact radicals lacked mass appeal almost as much as moderate liberals. Marx correctly observed that the Revolution had staff officers and non-commissioned officers but no rank and file. Besides, the direct-action techniques advocated by some radicals did not make them popular with the mass of the people.

The truth was that Germany, a semi-feudal society, was deeply conservative in structure and outlook. Local patriotism was a virile force and obedience to princely houses a deeply rooted instinct with most people. German liberalism was not the ideological expression of dynamic forces; it lacked those material foundations which made it triumphant in Britain or Belgium. Industrialisation was in its infancy. The middle class was weak and divided; in the upper echelons it consisted of officials and academics, in the intermediate ranges of tradespeople and shopkeepers, and it rested on a broad base of *Handwerker* whose interests separated them from the industrial proletariat. That is the reason why, compared with France, there were few signs of class consciousness in Germany in 1848–49.

In a society where most people lived in the countryside – in Prussia sixty-four per cent of the whole population did so in 1849 – the reaction of the peasant was a decisive factor in 1848–49. That the peasant had obtained some redress for his grievances at an early stage made him less interested in the later stages of the revolution. The liberals had been obliged to yield to popular pressure in the countryside. Several governments – especially in the south, where discontent was more vocal – abolished some feudal dues or commuted them into monetary payments; in Baden the peasants scored their greatest success when all feudal dues were abolished in April 1848. Feudal dues were abolished in principle by the Frankfurt Parliament. But out of respect for property the liberals only abolished certain dues outright, the remainder being transformed into contractual rents.

It is important to realise that the successful counter-revolution at the close of 1848 did not reverse these advances. Conservatives recognised the inevitability of economic change in the countryside. They saw the need for liberal policies and even accelerated the rate of change in order to win peasant support. Before the elections to the Prussian assembly in January 1849, Prussian Conservatives promised to deal with peasant grievances, and in April the necessary legislation was introduced. Other states acted in like manner. Therefore when the second revolution occurred rank-and-file peasants in the Prussian army willingly suppressed the uprisings.

Conservatives showed equal skill in handling the *Handwerker*. After playing a crucial role in the early stages of the Revolution, the *Handwerker* lost faith in liberalism; the liberal belief in economic freedom conflicted sharply with the desire of the *Handwerker* – an economically backward pressure-group – for a revitalised guild system to protect their members against factory competition. Rebuffed by the liberals – and by the radicals who were suspicious of guilds – the *Handwerker* found conservatives more sympathetic. The 'Junker Parliament' supported the *Handwerker* against the factory owners, and in February 1849 Prussia introduced legislation restoring the guild system, thereby reversing the broad trend towards economic freedom initiated by Stein. Other states followed suit. Consequently support for liberalism declined steadily throughout 1849.

The failure of the 1849–49 Revolution represented a severe set-back, if not a mortal blow, for liberalism. Counter-revolution triumphed everywhere; the idealism of 1848 evaporated and the democratic left was seriously weakened when many of the more able radicals emigrated, seeking a new life in the United States. After 1849 the upper middle classes, the mainstay of the Frankfurt Parliament, never fully recovered their political self-confidence; significantly enough many of them now sought outlets for their energy in fields other than politics. At the same time, out of fear of the masses, they were moving closer to the feudal aristocracy precisely when many landowners were beginning, from sheer economic necessity, to jettison feudal privilege and transform themselves into efficient farmers, overcoming in the process their traditional mistrust of industrial wealth; in short, the future alliance between landed and industrial wealth, which underpinned the social order in William II's Germany, was already taking shape in the aftermath of the Revolution.

The tragedy of the German Revolution must be seen against the

European background of which it was an integral part. The revolution of 1848 had failed not only in Germany, but all over Europe; Italy remained divided, Poland failed to achieve her independence, the Habsburgs had forced the subject peoples into submission again, and in France a democratic republic had succumbed to popular imperialism.

On the other hand, the Revolution in Germany had positive as well as negative aspects. It marked the entry of the German people into the political life of the nation, confirming the trends discernible in the 1840s. True, the men of 1848 did not attempt to build up a mass following. Nevertheless, wider circles of the population began to take an interest in politics. Public discussion of constitutional and national problems acted as a catalyst destroying political apathy. Before 1848 only a small section of the German middle class was politically conscious; after the Revolution the whole of the middle class was politically and nationally conscious. This development was crucially important; it was to alter profoundly the structure of politics in Germany as in other European countries; furthermore, without the ground swell of public opinion favourable to unification which the Revolution had created, the achievements of Bismarck in the 1860s would hardly have been possible.

The Revolution also helped to clarify political attitudes and encouraged the formation of political associations, the forerunners of modern political parties.

In the case of liberalism, the dominant ideology of the Revolution, centrifugal tendencies were soon at work. All over Germany in political clubs and state legislatures as well as in the Frankfurt Parliament, liberalism crystallised out into three distinct groupings; a large moderate liberal centre, flanked by an active radical left and a smaller neo-conservative right; three future political parties were present here in embryonic form.

National liberalism emerged from the debates of these years a more precisely defined concept. The 1849 constitution represented the essence of national liberalism, and was a significant pointer to future development. The men of 1848 had little in common with Bismarck; all the same, Bismarck did not destroy the work of the Frankfurt Parliament, but carried it forward to a successful conclusion. When Germany was united in 1871 the king of Prussia became emperor of a Germany from which Austria was excluded. Even the Fundamental Rights of the German People, for which the Parliament was often taken to task by its critics, were of importance later on; they were incorporated in the Weimar constitution of 1919 and influenced the constitution of the German Federal Republic in 1949.

German conservatism emerged as a significant political force during the Revolution. The famous conservative newspaper, *Kreuzeitung*,[9] edited by

[9]Officially called the *Neue Preussische Zeitung*. The name *Kreuzeitung* was derived from the cross displayed on the title page.

Wagener, first appeared in July 1848. Landowners, army officers and higher civil servants joined forces to found numerous local associations including the League for the Protection of Landed Property and for the Promotion of the Well-being of all Classes of the People. The second half of the title was most significant. The more perceptive conservatives, among them Radowitz, the friend and admirer of Frederick William IV, had begun to appreciate the political consequences of universal suffrage. It seemed clear that reactionary conservatism could not survive under the new dispensation. Only if conservatives were prepared to show some interest in the social problems of the lower orders, could they hope to win mass support for their policies. Their intuition proved correct. By pursuing enlightened social policies the conservatives built up a considerable following in the rural areas during the Revolution, and, as indicated above, their readiness to make concessions to peasants and *Handwerker* was a factor of some importance in bringing the Revolution to an end.

The years 1848–49 witnessed the emergence of another ideology, political Catholicism, which, like conservatism, was much more successful than liberalism in securing mass support.

Catholicism was a growing force in the first half of the century. The Church had emerged from the Napoleonic period sounder in wind and limb, stripped of her landed property and less dependent on secular governments. As a result of the extensive territorial adjustments in Germany, nearly all the larger states were mixed in religion. Disputes arose between the state authorities and religious minorities, especially where the latter lived in recently acquired territories. A classic example of this occurred in 1837, when the Catholic Church came into collision with Prussia over mixed-marriage regulations in the Rhineland. The Prussian authorities insisted that the father should determine the religion of the child except where both parents wished otherwise. The new archbishop of Cologne refused to sanction mixed marriages unless the children were brought up as Catholics. The archbishop and his colleague, the archbishop of Posen, were imprisoned by the authorities. The dispute aroused wide interest in Germany; for the first time since the days of Napoleon prelates had fallen seriously foul of the state. Liberals sympathised with the Church and denounced Prussian high-handedness. Catholics began to feel the need for a popular organisation to rally the faithful in defence of the Church against the State – and a Protestant state at that; in short, political Catholicism was born. The position of Rhineland Catholics eased when Frederick William IV came to the throne. But the 1848 Revolution confirmed the general trend; popular Catholic organisations like the *Piusverein* proliferated, Catholic newspapers were founded and Catholic intellectuals developed an interest in social problems which later proved invaluable in enabling the Church to keep contact with the toiling masses. On the debit side were signs of deepening religious animosity between Catholic and Protestant.

Religious affiliations intruded into neutral political issues; it was no coincidence that Little Germans were solidly Protestant whereas Catholics invariably sided with the Greater Germans.

The Revolution also witnessed the first attempts of the industrial proletariat to organise politically. In Berlin, where 100,000 workers lived, an active and rich working-class movement emerged in the spring of 1848. One of the most important groups was the Central Committee of Workers founded by Born, a bookbinder and editor of *Das Volk*. Born was acquainted with the works of Marx and Engels but soon realised that the Communist Manifesto was unrealistic in its expectation of a socialist revolution following quickly on the heels of a bourgeois revolution in Germany. The Manifesto was little read or understood by German workers, who were concerned primarily with the improvement of working conditions. The Central Committee, which was supported mainly by *Handwerker*, put forward a radical programme demanding minimum wage rights, the right of association, and introduction of a progressive income tax, free education, state intervention to aid the unemployed and measures to protect small-scale industry. In August 1848 Born convened the first Worker's Congress in Berlin, which was attended by forty representatives from organisations in several towns. The Congress founded a new organisation, the first all-German worker's association, *die Arbeiterverbrüderung*, with headquarters in Leipzig. The membership, however, never exceeded 12,000.

Marx and Engels played in fact a very minor role in the Revolution. In 1847 they founded the Communist League in Brussels and drafted its political programme, the Communist Manifesto, published in February 1848. Once the Revolution started, they hastened back to Germany like hundreds of other revolutionaries. At first they dreamed of an alliance between the new working-class associations and the radical left in order to complete the bourgeois revolution but quickly abandoned their plan because of working-class apathy. Instead they concentrated their efforts on encouraging the radical left to continue the struggle against feudalism and establish bourgeois democracy on firm foundations. In the months that followed Marx harried the liberals and defended the radicals in the columns of the *Neue Rheinische Zeitung*, of which he was editor. Tactical support of radicalism led Marx and Engels down strange paths. They supported the radical demand for war against Russia, opted for Greater Germany, supported the Germans in Schleswig-Holstein and condemned Czech nationalism, not so much because they were attracted by the xenophobic nationalism of the radicals, who were more eager than most to use 'the sharp German sword' to defend Germany's honour, but out of a belief that only a national crisis could radicalise the German Revolution as foreign invasion had radicalised the French Revolution in 1792. But by the spring of 1849 Marx lost faith in the radicals and turned to the working class. Too late; the leaders of the second revolution paid scant attention to the advice pressed on them by Marx and Engels. When the *Neue Rheinische Zeitung* was suppressed in 1849, Marx left Germany never to return. Many years elapsed before his philosophy exerted any significant influence on the German working class.

Finally, important economic changes were brought about by the Revolution. The process of liberating the peasant from the feudal system, begun at the end of the eighteenth century, was greatly accelerated. In Central and West Germany the manorial system was practically destroyed. In other parts, especially in Prussia, the liberation process continued throughout the 1850s; under conservative auspices feudal jurisdictions were cancelled, some dues abolished and others commuted. Many landowners, especially in East Prussia, derived substantial benefits from the destruction of feudalism; they used the capital received as compensation to make their estates economically viable. But for the mass of the rural population the benefits were marginal; the paternalism of village life persisted; basic agrarian problems remained unsolved; landless labourers in East Germany received no land; population pressure on land in West and South Germany increased; the burden of rent payments proved too great for many peasants and the general drift to the towns continued. In general, the Revolution helped to sever the ties binding peasants to the land but relied upon the untrammelled operation of market forces to solve the problem of their future.

3

Germany in the 1850s

The story of the 1850s commences with a postscript to the Revolution of 1848–49; the Erfurt Union. Although King Frederick William IV rejected the crown of Little Germany offered him by the Frankfurt Parliament, he still hoped to unite Germany by agreement with the princes, his equals. With Austria fully extended in Northern Italy and Hungary, conditions seemed favourable for a fresh Prussian initiative. This was the view of the gifted and energetic Radowitz, a Catholic aristocrat of Hungarian extraction and a close friend of the king when the latter was crown prince. Called to Berlin by the king, Radowitz revived von Gagern's plan for a federal state excluding Austria from Germany, but supplemented by a loose association based on a common foreign and commercial policy. Radowitz was seeking the best of both worlds; Prussia would dominate Little Germany and still retain the advantages of association with conservative Austria. That the plan was wildly utopian in its appraisal of Austrian policy was quickly apparent. In May 1849 Radowitz, now virtually in charge of the foreign ministry, persuaded the king to offer Schwarzenberg assistance against Hungary on condition that Austria accepted Gagern's plan, and allowed Prussia to take over provisionally the duties of *Reichsverweser* from Archduke John. Schwarzenberg bluntly refused. He saw no need to submit to Prussian blackmail as long as Austria could rely on the tsar's unconditional support against the Hungarian insurgents.

Undeterred by Austria's refusal, Radowitz formed the League of the Three Kings (*Dreikönigsbündnis*) with Saxony and Hanover in May 1849. The League did not really amount to much; Saxony made her adherence conditional on Bavaria's joining and Hanover consented only on condition that Austria was included in the federal state, conditions which Radowitz weakly accepted. Some seventeen states joined the league simply because in Austria's absence Prussia exerted decisive influence in Germany; in the summer of 1849 her soldiers were busily suppressing disturbances in several states. In June 150 members of the former Frankfurt Parliament, mostly men of the right and centre, met at Gotha to discuss the Prussian initiative. One hundred and thirty of them signed a statement declaring that, as the constitution approved by the Frankfurt Parliament could not be implemented, all states should adopt the constitution sponsored by the league. This provided for an imperial directory (*Reichsvorstand*), which would be closely associated with Prussia, and a college of princes armed with an absolute veto and sharing legislative power with a two-chamber Reichstag; the powers of the lower house were very limited, and it was to be elected, not by universal suffrage, but on a three-class system heavily weighted in favour of wealth and property.

By August Hungary was subdued and Austria turned her attention to Germany. Schwarzenberg's first instinct was to demand immediate abandonment of the Prussian plan. But out of deference to the Austrian emperor and tsar, both of whom sought a peaceful settlement of the Austro-Prussian dispute, Schwarzenberg signed an interim agreement with Prussia in September 1849. In the so-called interim Austria and Prussia agreed to administer Germany jointly until May 1850. In December 1849 Archduke John surrendered his executive power to them. For Schwarzenberg the interim was merely a delaying tactic, to be abandoned as soon as Austria was free to take a stronger line. Radowitz, unaware that he had seriously weakened Prussia's standing in Germany by signing this agreement, naïvely hoped for genuine co-operation from Austria.

Heartened by the renewed interest Austria was showing in Germany, the larger states recovered their nerve. Bavaria and Württemberg decided finally against the Union. In October Saxony and Hanover virtually seceded, relying upon Austria to save them from this or indeed from any solution of the German problem which threatened to diminish their sovereignty. This was a serious blow for Radowitz, who was now encountering formidable opposition from Prussian conservatives, for whom good relations with Austria and Russia were axiomatic in the interests of social order. Under their influence the king was beginning to waver. Even the 'Gothaers' were losing heart; in March 1850 the union parliament met at Erfurt in the Prussian province of Saxony, its lower house packed with enthusiastic 'Gothaers'. They were quickly disillusioned by the Prussian king's wish to restrict the union constitution still further and by his reluctance to swear an oath of allegiance to it.

In May 1850, when the interim lapsed, Schwarzenberg revived the old Diet at Frankfurt under Austrian presidency, and invited all states to send representatives to discuss revision of the old Confederation and the establishment of a central authority for Germany. Ten states attended, with Prussia a conspicuous absentee. All attempts at compromise failed. Prussia clung to the remnants of the Erfurt Union, and war with Austria suddenly loomed on the horizon.

The affairs of Schleswig-Holstein added to the growing tension. War had broken out again between Denmark and Germany in 1849. Under strong Russian pressure Prussia made peace in July 1850 on terms favourable to Denmark. The treaty authorised the Danish king to request the Confederation's assistance in restoring order in Holstein, last refuge of the German insurgents. Schwarzenberg, realising that this was Prussia's Achilles heel, promised to support the Danish king in his request to the newly restored *engerer Rat* of the Diet for federal execution. The danger of conflict grew, for if federal execution was carried out by Austrian soldiers in an area where Prussia had vital interests, hostilities seemed unavoidable.

In fact, the affairs of Hesse-Cassel precipitated the final crisis. The elector was, as usual, at loggerheads with his subjects, who were opposing his attempts to revoke the financial powers given to the estates in 1831. A state of siege existed in Hesse-Cassel, the estates had been dissolved, the civil servants refused to collect taxes, and most army officers had resigned rather than use force against the people. The elector, once a member of the Erfurt Union, fled to Frankfurt and appealed to the Diet for assistance. Schwarzenberg persuaded the Diet to invoke federal execution against Hesse-Cassel. A war alliance was signed by Austria, Bavaria and Württemberg, and a powerful Austrian army, supplemented by contingents from Bavaria and Württemberg, marched northwards. This was a direct challenge to Prussia; she could hardly allow Austrian troops to occupy Hesse-Cassel when vital strategic roads linking the Rhineland and Brandenburg ran through the small electorate.

At this critical moment Prussian policy wavered. Radowitz, recently appointed foreign minister, failed to persuade the council of ministers to mobilise the army; a majority was firmly opposed to conflict with Austria. Russian influence was the decisive factor. In October 1850 the tsar promised moral support to Austria if Prussia opposed federal execution in Hesse-Cassel. At the same time he informed Prussia that Russia would regard obstructionism over federal execution in Holstein as a *casus belli*. Radowitz resigned; Bismarck celebrated the news with a bottle of champagne. Then at the last moment the king, feeling that a defiant gesture might make surrender more palatable to his people, ordered mobilisation. A slight skirmish occurred at Bronzell when advance units of the federal army came into conflict with Prussian troops guarding the military roads in Hesse-Cassel; a few Austrian soldiers and a Prussian horse were wounded. Frederick William drew back from the brink. He had never intended to fight a brother sovereign for the sake of the Erfurt Union. Faced with an Austrian ultimatum, which demanded Prussian consent within forty-eight hours to the occupation of Hesse-Cassel by federal troops, the king capitulated.

The new foreign minister, Otto von Manteuffel, signed an agreement with Schwarzenberg at Olmütz in Moravia on 29 November. In the Olmütz Punctation Prussia abandoned the Erfurt Union and agreed to the restoration of the Confederation. Both powers would demobilise, Prussia first and fully, Austria later and partially. A final settlement of Hesse-Cassel and Holstein was reserved to the Confederation, but Prussia in effect accepted federal execution in both states.

Schwarzenberg had won a great victory. Then at the Dresden Conference which met early in 1851 to discuss reform of the Confederation, he suffered a sudden reverse. His ambitious scheme for the inclusion of the Habsburg empire in the Confederation was firmly opposed by Prussia, who demanded a *quid pro quo* in the shape of parity of status with Austria in Germany. Schwarzenberg refused to give way. External powers came to Prussia's aid; Russia was unwilling to force the scheme on Germany, and Britain and France added their warnings. Reluctantly Schwarzenberg abandoned the plan. He was no more successful in securing a revision of the machinery of the Confederation in Austria's interest. In the end the Confederation was restored unaltered in May 1851; for as Schwarzenberg ruefully observed 'a threadbare and torn coat is still better than no coat at all'. The only consolation prize was a three-year alliance with Prussia in which the signatories promised to defend each other's territory whether inside or outside of the Confederation. The initiative came from Prussia; for Frederick William this was a new Holy Alliance, an impressive gesture to reassure conservatives that Austria and Prussia were still the enemies of revolution.

This could not alter the fact that for the first time in sixty years a serious crisis darkened Austro-Prussian relations. Prussia had suffered a serious defeat – not because of inherent military weakness but because her king and advisers lacked the will to fight – and Austrian power in Germany was greater than in the days of Metternich. Of course, Austria's victory could only be of temporary duration. For Prussia was now bent on securing parity of status with Austria and recognition of her dominant position in Germany. The haughty and self-confident Schwarzenberg was not prepared to pay this price to keep Prussia as an ally. Prussia was a loyal follower of Austria between 1815 and 1848 partly because a common fear of revolution obscured the latent power conflict, but mainly because Metternich handled Prussia skilfully and never failed to consult her on vital issues. Schwarzenberg, on the other hand, lacked Metternich's power of simulation. Once he had made his mind up that Prussia was a serious rival standing in the way of his ambitious plans for Austria, Schwarzenberg was perfectly prepared to put her in her place by force of arms if need be. It would be wrong to suppose that Austria and Prussia were now set on a collision course ending inevitably in the war of 1866. Nevertheless, the seeds of conflict were present for all to see after 1850. Close co-operation between Austria and Prussia in the Diet was a thing of the past; Austria did not hesitate to outmanoeuvre and isolate Prussia whenever she could. An uneasy truce was the most that could be hoped for, with war a distinct possibility as the power conflict came increasingly into the open. In short, the old political and military dualism of the eighteenth century had reappeared in Germany.

With the Confederation restored, the heavy hand of autocracy descended on Germany once more. The Federal Diet, at the instigation of Austria and Prussia, declared the Fundamental Rights of the German People null and void and sold the federal navy by auction. The princes restricted the constitutional liberties so readily conceded in 1848. In Austria the emperor suspended the 1849 constitution and ruled his dominions absolutely for the next few years. In Prussia the landed aristocracy reasserted itself in the army, in the administration, at court and in the countryside, where the landowners' police powers – but not their judicial functions or hunting rights – were restored. Press censorship was restored; schools were placed under Church control; local government was restricted, and the king recovered his old powers. On the day he dissolved the Prussian assembly in December 1848, the king, for tactical reasons, promulgated a new constitution based on the Belgian constitution of 1831. Its wings were soon clipped; in 1849 universal suffrage was replaced by the plutocratic three-class system as the basis for elections to the lower house, and in 1854 the elected second chamber became a nominated house of peers. The budgetary powers of the lower house survived in the amended constitution of 1850 simply because the king's advisers saw the need for a constitutional façade in order to secure the loans without which Prussia would be bankrupt. In North Germany aristocracy came into its own, and the *Ständestaat* blossomed briefly in Mecklenburg, Saxony and Hanover. In the south most rulers restored the pre-1848 constitutions. But there were limits to the effectiveness of political reaction in the 1850s. The Federal Diet set up a central committee – 'the committee of reaction', as it proudly called itself – with a watching brief over the states; in fact its recommendations for suppressing political societies and censoring the press were not implemented in all states; only in Hesse-Cassel did the Diet intervene energetically on the side of reaction and abolish the 1831 constitution.

Political reaction in the 1850s, unlike that of the 1820s, was accompanied by social policies designed to win mass support for the old order. The dismemberment of feudalism continued after the Revolution; between 1850 and 1865 640,000 Prussian peasants terminated their feudal obligations with the aid of loans from government-sponsored banks established for this purpose. In several states, notably Prussia, efforts were made to halt the decline in status of the *Handwerker*. The guild system was protected and encouraged; guild membership was made compulsory, working conditions were carefully regulated and industrial courts set up to assist in the settlement of trade disputes. This was the Indian summer of a doomed way of life. For despite government legislation the *Handwerker* continued to decline in the 1850s and 1860s as the industrial expansion of Germany got under way.

It is no exaggeration to say that industrialisation completely transformed the face of mid-nineteenth-century Germany. It was, of course, part of a more general phenomenon. All over Western Europe trade and industry expanded rapidly in the 1850s and 1860s as banking facilities and communications improved and governments bestowed their benediction on the spirit of free enterprise.

In Germany industrial activity proceeded at a leisurely pace before 1850. Traditional social values and institutions remained virtually intact; there was little large-scale industry; domestic industry and the handicraft system predominated almost everywhere. In the 1850s and 1860s – the period of industrial 'take-off' – the pattern altered abruptly. The handicraft system was superseded by large-scale concerns in the basic sectors of the economy; Krupp of Essen and Borsig of Berlin were world-renowned by 1860. The growth of the basic industries, coal, iron, metals and textiles, was engendered by the expansion of Germany's railway network. In 1846 Germany produced 3.2 million tons of coal; by 1860 she produced 12.3 million tons and by 1871 this had risen to 29.4 million tons, a total exceeding the combined output of France and Belgium. The demand for railway equipment and the increased use of coke for smelting inaugurated a new era in the iron and steel industry; in 1850 Germany produced 529,000 tons of pig iron; by 1875 she was producing 2 million tons compared with 1.4 million tons in France. Comparable expansion occurred in textiles, chemicals and the electrical industry.

Several factors contributed to the upsurge of the German economy. The growth of population from thirty-five millions in 1850 to forty millions in 1870 made available the labour force needed for rapid industrialisation. Large-scale industry required capital sums beyond the resources of individual entrepreneurs. The necessary capital was supplied either by foreign investors or by large joint-stock banks mobilising capital for investment. The first of these banks was founded by the Rhineland liberal Mevissen in 1848. It was followed by the *Disconto-Gesellschaft* (1851), the *Darmstädter und Nationalbank* (1853), the Austrian *Kreditanstalt* (1855) and the Berlin *Handelsgesellschaft* (1856).

Important, too, was the gradual liberalisation of the social structure of Germany, for without this a free-enterprise system could not function properly. In the countryside the end of the manorial system accelerated the drift to the towns where labour forces were needed. The guilds were declining rapidly, handicapped by the high prices and limited range of their products and by their general backwardness. In the late 1850s the reviving liberal movement condemned guilds as impediments to economic growth. The turning-point came in 1859 when Austria, defeated in war and anxious for middle-class support at home, abolished all restrictions on entry into trades. The example proved infectious; within five years sixteen states followed suit and by 1869 thirty had done so, dealing a death-blow to the restrictive guild system.

By an accident of geography German industrial expansion occurred largely in Prussian territory in the Ruhr, Silesia and the Saarland – Saxony was the only significant exception. Consequently the economic balance of power was moving slowly but surely in favour of Prussia in Germany and in Europe throughout the 1850s and 1860s; long before the battles of Sadowa and Sedan were fought, Prussia had drawn ahead of Austria and France in the industrial race, with all that this implied for the political future of Germany.

The Prussian state played an important role in the industrial field. The fact that support was given to the *Handwerker* in the interests of conservatism did not prevent liberal-minded officials, who believed firmly in free enterprise, from encouraging the growth of industry. In the case of coal, legislation between 1851 and 1865 freed the Ruhr from all controls and resulted in rapid expansion. On the other hand, in Saarbrücken the state established a mining monopoly making the industrial complex dependent on state-owned mines. Through its control of the Saarbrücken and Upper Silesian mines the Prussian state became the greatest coal producer in Germany and was able to exert considerable influence over Prussian industry. The Prussian general staff was alert to the implications of industrial expansion; by their intervention the generals ensured that strategic needs were not neglected when railways were constructed. Meanwhile the heavy industries of the Ruhr were producing the artillery which was to revolutionise warfare in the 1860s.

Diplomatically, Austria and Prussia remained on lukewarm terms throughout the 1850s. The growing divergence between them was underlined by the Crimean War. Austria was moving towards conflict with Russia in the Balkans; in the summer of 1854 she forced Russian troops out of the Danubian provinces, and in December allied herself with Britain and France. At first Prussia followed Austria and renewed the alliance of 1851 largely because Frederick William IV still believed in the alliance against 'revolution'. But he certainly did not want war with Russia, despite the intrigues of the so-called *Wochenblatt*[1] party, a group of high officials and diplomats patronised by Crown Prince William, who were anxious to avenge Olmütz by allying with the western powers against Russia. When Austria asked the Diet to mobilise half the federal army in January 1855 in preparation for armed intervention in the Crimea, the request was vigorously opposed by Bismarck, then Prussian minister at Frankfurt. He persuaded the Diet that Germany should keep out of a war which did not affect her vital interests. In the end the Diet endorsed the

[1]The organ of this group was *Das preussische Wochenblatt* founded in 1851.

principle of armed neutrality, declaring – much to Austria's annoyance – that there was no cause for mobilisation against Russia; for the first time Austria found herself outmanoeuvred and isolated at Frankfurt.

In the economic sphere the conflict of interest between Austria and Prussia was even clearer. Schwarzenberg, who died in 1852, was not alone in his desire to establish Austrian primacy in Central Europe. The seventy-million-strong *Reich* originated with Bruck, a Rhineland merchant appointed minister of commerce by Schwarzenberg in 1848. Bruck, who was deeply influenced by the liberal philosophy of List, planned to abolish the customs barrier between Austria and Hungary, overhaul the antiquated tariff system in the Habsburg dominions and negotiate a customs union with the German Customs Union. His scheme for a huge Central-European customs union stretching from the Black Sea to the Baltic supplied the economic base for Schwarzenberg's political plans. Bruck dreamt of a huge social and economic axis revolving around Vienna, a huge common market rivalling in time the economic power of the United States and assuring the future of the Habsburgs. Magyar landowners seeking new markets for their wheat, and some of the influential industrialists in Austria, welcomed Bruck's scheme. South German industrialists interested in Danubian markets were also well-disposed towards it.

From the beginning Prussia set her face against the scheme, seeing in it a challenge to her dominant position in North and Central Germany. Delbrück, a brilliant young official in the Prussian ministry of commerce, outmanoeuvred Bruck. Fearing that Austria and her friends would try to force damaging concessions out of Prussia when the German Customs Union was due for renewal in 1854, Delbrück looked around for new allies. By offering very favourable terms to Hanover and Oldenburg he persuaded them to join the Customs Union in 1851, thereby consolidating Prussia's position. The southern states were offended by these concessions to Hanover, and, assiduously courted by Austria, they gave serious consideration to a fiscal union with her. In the end Prussian diplomatic pressure, together with the realisation that their economic well-being was bound up with the German Customs Union, made them renew it for a further twelve years in 1853. There was no Austro-German customs union; only a commercial treaty with Prussia in 1853 conferring some benefits on Austria but only on condition that negotiations for a customs union were postponed until 1860. For the first time since Olmütz Prussia had won a decisive victory over Austria.

Austria never succeeded in her attempts to transform the German Customs Union into a Mid-European union. After the economic crisis of 1857 there were demands in Austria for greater tariff protection, whereas in Germany, especially in Prussia, great wheat-exporting landowners, middle-class merchants and some industrialists continued to benefit considerably from free trade. In 1859 Austria was weakened by war, and in 1860

Bruck, her ablest economist, died. In 1862 Prussia placed a formidable obstacle in Austria's path when she signed a commercial treaty with France lowering tariffs still further. At first Bavaria and Württemberg objected to the treaty, partly because South-German manufacturers wanted protective tariffs, but also because these states were suspicious of Prussian designs in Germany. For most states the alternative to the German Customs Union – inclusion in a highly protected Danubian union – spelt economic ruin. Prussia made it plain that she would not compromise over the French treaty, and eventually Bavaria and Württemberg accepted it. When the Customs Union was renewed in May 1865, it was on Prussian terms. This was a great victory for Prussia; she had won economic mastery in Little Germany long before the war of 1866. All that Austria secured was a customs and trade treaty with Prussia. The idea of an Austro-German customs union was postponed for future discussion and in fact virtually buried.

As the industrialisation process gathered momentum at the close of the 1850s, the dichotomy between the obsolete economic and political structure and the evolving pattern of modern Germany deepened. At last the grip of reaction loosened. In October 1858 the 'New Era' began in Prussia when Crown Prince William became regent on behalf of his brother King Frederick William IV, now totally incapacitated by a stroke. The regent was a man of sixty-one, a pious, sober-minded and deeply conservative ruler, typically Hohenzollern in his belief that strong government and military power were the twin bases of the Prussian state. A soldier by training, William was deeply suspicious of Austria and longed to avenge the Olmütz humiliation. He was the hope of the liberals in the 1850s, as his brother had been in 1840; William's wife, Augusta, had liberal sympathies, his son was engaged to Queen Victoria's eldest daughter, and his own daughter married the liberal-minded grand duke of Baden; in the 1850s William had been associated with the *Wochenblatt* party; he was temporarily disgraced for anti-Russian views during the Crimean War, and made no secret of his distaste for the ultra-conservative court *camarilla*.

At first William lived up to expectations. He preserved the constitution despite Frederick William's death-bed wish that it be revoked. He dismissed the Manteuffel ministry and appointed men of moderate liberal persuasions drawn largely from the *Wochenblatt* party. The new government's programme promised a more progressive domestic policy, and spoke of a policy of 'moral conquests' which would give Prussia a dominant position in Germany. The liberals were encouraged by this wind of change and resumed their political activity, albeit cautiously out of respect for the regent. They did not demand parliamentary government; indeed they were perfectly satisfied with the 1850 constitution; all they wanted was the end of bureaucratic paternalism and the passage of supplementary legislation to guarantee basic freedoms, objectives which now seemed realisable. Nor did they seek mass support; Hansemann, Camphausen and Mevissen were all opposed to universal suffrage, not so much because it was a radical demand – radicalism was an extremely weak force in the 1850s – but because they were beginning to appreciate that universal suffrage was 'counter-revolution'; the enfranchised masses were more likely to favour conservatism than liberalism. The three-class system, on the other hand, suited these upper-middle-class liberals admirably; they were now wealthy enough to benefit from it, and now that the regent had discouraged the civil service from interfering at election time in the conservative interest, the liberals swept the board in 1858, winning over 260 seats in the lower house.

The Prussian liberal revival was followed in the summer of 1859 by a resurgence of German nationalism. The Germans were stirred by the Italian struggle for independence but alarmed by its international repercussions. Napoleon III had long been suspect in German eyes on account of his supposed designs on the Rhineland; it was widely believed in 1859 that Napoleon had an understanding with Russia which would free his hands for an attack in the west as soon as he had defeated Austria in Italy. A wave of anti-French feeling swept through Germany; disputes between liberals and conservatives and between Little Germans and Greater Germans paled into insignificance; at this moment of crisis the Germans expected Austria and Prussia to stand shoulder to shoulder in defence of German soil against the 'hereditary foe' France. This was a decisive moment in Franco-German relations. Napoleon's annexation of Savoy and Nice in 1860 confirmed the growing fear of French imperialism. By 1861 the German people were united in their hatred of France, an enmity which lasted well into the twentieth century.

A few Germans held out against the popular tide; veteran radicals such as Ruge still denounced Austria as the arch-enemy of liberty. Another odd man out was Bismarck, now an influential figure in Prussia. He had urged the government to seize a unique opportunity of expanding at Austria's expense; if Prussia struck swiftly, he wrote, her soldiers could carry boundary posts in their knapsacks and plant them on Lake Constance. Prince William did not follow this daring and eccentric advice. But in a muddled fashion he tried to exploit the situation by making his military support conditional on Austria's allowing Prussia to be commander-in-chief of the federal forces should France attack in the west. Austria refused; rather than recognise Prussian hegemony in North Germany, she preferred to lose Lombardy – which she did in July 1859. The rivalry between Austria and Prussia was accentuated by the war; Austria did not hesitate to blame her defeat on Prussia's failure to help an ally in distress, and many Germans roundly condemned Prussia's dilatory and ambiguous policy. The policy of 'moral conquests' had got off to a bad start.

The events of 1859, particularly the threat of war with France, revealed the military weakness of Germany and underlined the urgent need for radical reform of the Confederation. At separate meetings in July Thuringian democrats and Prussian liberals called for a German Parliament and the replacement of the Federal Diet by a strong central authority associated with Prussia. In August leading liberals from several states met at Eisenach and issued an appeal for the foundation of a party to work for unification. In September 1859 the *Nationalverein* was founded with the Hanoverian liberal leader Bennigsen as its first president. This was the first national organisation to transcend the frontiers of the German states and bring liberals and radicals together under one roof. A pressure group rather than a political party, the *Nationalverein* was modelled on the Italian *Società Nazionale*. However, the *Nationalverein* played a less important role in German history than the *Società* did in Italy. Lack of official support was a serious handicap; most states restricted the *Nationalverein's* activities, and even Prussia was reserved in her attitude; moderate liberals, the men of the New Era, stayed aloof from it, not wishing to offend the regent. The *Nationalverein* was not, of course, a mass organisation; at the height of its fame it numbered only 25,000 members, drawn mostly from the professional and official classes in North Germany; in 1863 it categorically rejected the appeal of Leipzig workers that membership be opened to a wider section of the public. Nevertheless, the *Nationalverein* exerted considerable influence through other organisations, helping to mobilise public opinion behind the national cause. At the close of the 1850s there was a great revival of popular festivals, *Turnfeste*, *Sängerfeste* and *Schützenfeste*, all of which were attended by thousands of people, especially from the lower middle classes. The political speeches at these functions were invariably delivered by *Nationalverein* orators, who helped in this way to keep the flame of nationalism burning in the German middle classes.

The *Nationalverein* was Little-German in outlook. Its leaders longed for a national lead from Prussia, confident that Prussia would then turn to the liberal movement for support and become a more liberal state in the process. But for fear of alienating southern support the *Nationalverein* trod warily. In 1860 it faced both ways, declaring that Austria and Bohemia were part of the German fatherland and would one day be united with Germany, but adding that this must not delay the union of Germany under Prussia in the near future. There was some competition with the *Nationalverein* when the *Deutscher Reformverein* was founded in October 1862 by South-German radicals hostile to Prussia. However, the new association was never able to equal the influence of the *Nationalverein*.

National liberalism had changed in character since 1848. The romantic idealism of the year of revolution had been replaced by a colder, more realistic spirit. This was only to be expected, for the generation in power in the 1860s had been brought up on the anti-Romantic and materialist philosophy of the 1830s. The new mood was a deliberate reaction against the spirit of 1848. The men of 1848 had overestimated the power of ideas and underestimated the importance of material power; mid-century liberals tended to be sceptical of ideas and respectful of material power. This attitude was expressed in somewhat exaggerated fashion by Fröbel, a one-time radical member of the Frankfurt Parliament; writing in 1859 he declared that 'the German nation is sick of principles and doctrines, literary existence and theoretical greatness. What it wants is power, power, power and whoever gives it power, to him will it give honour, more honour than he can imagine'. This preoccupation with power made it easier for liberals to co-operate with the forces of tradition and monarchy in German society. It also helped to loosen the links between nationalism and supranationalism forged by the Romantic writers; the concept of the amoral *Machtstaat* at last broke away from the supranational anchorage which held it fast in the early nineteenth century.

The intellectual content of national liberalism in the 1860s was supplied by writers such as Sybel, Droysen and Treitschke, the political professors who used their powerful pens to mobilise public opinion behind Prussia. Historians, and pupils of Ranke, they were deeply influenced by Hegelian philosophy. They saw in History the progressive revelation of Freedom working itself out in states and institutions and finding fulfilment in national unity. They carried their political commitment to Little Germany into the study, believing that History demonstrated beyond all doubt that Prussia was destined to rule Germany. The message was spelt out in detail in great partisan works such as Droysen's *Geschichte der preussischen Politik*, a work full of praise for Prussia, hostile to Austria and critical of the smaller states which Droysen regarded merely as an obstacle to unification. As liberals they belonged in the mainstream of historical liberalism; they rejected 'quasi-democratic' theories from France and insisted that German constitutions must be in tune with the *Volksgeist* – in practice this meant that they could settle for much less than a full-blooded parliamentary system in 1867. They believed sincerely in the rule of law and the preservation of individual liberties but maintained that only in a powerful and mighty state like Prussia could freedom be a reality and a worthwhile cultural life flourish. In international affairs they saw only a struggle for power; states were autonomous personalities pursuing their own interests ruthlessly; Droysen, for example, spurned the concept of a concert of powers and boldly asserted that Prussia had a moral obligation to seize the leadership of Germany by force. This Darwinian view of the state was not peculiar to Germany. Nineteenth-century nationalists all over Europe attached supreme importance to the attainment of national unity and paid scant respect to the strands binding the peoples of Europe together.

National liberalism was vigorously challenged from a conservative tra-ditionalist standpoint by historians such as Klopp of Hanover, Jörg of Munich and Ficker of Innsbruck. These scholars were deeply hostile to nationalism and critical of the Little-German outlook of Prussian liber-alism. Prussia they regarded as an illiberal and aggressive state whose history proved that she was bent on the conquest of Germany. A Germany dominated by Prussia, imbued with the martial spirit of that state and organised on centralised bureaucratic lines, would be a travesty of the German *Volksgeist*. Some of their comments have an uncannily modern ring about them; for they were already looking beyond the narrow con-fines of Europe, and had realised that Russia and the United States of America were the great powers of the future; Europe could not survive as a third force between east and west if she insisted on exaggerating the dissimilarities between peoples – that was the error of the Little Germans – but only by promoting those values common to all European peoples.

The traditionalists believed in the unity of Europe but did not on that account cease to be Germans. Like the Romantics half a century before, they maintained that universalism was the special vocation of the Germans. Konstantin Frantz, the best-known of the traditionalist writers, argued that the creation of a highly centralised Little-German state in the heart of Europe would not assist Germany to fulfil her great mission of being the intermediary between the peoples of Europe; she could only play her true role in a loosely organised federal system, similar to the Holy Roman Empire, drawing the peoples of Europe closer to Germany and reconciling them with each other. Frantz dreamt of an association of 'German' states – Britain, the Netherlands and Scandinavia – grouped around a German Confederation dominated by multi-national Austria. This grand alliance of Christian states would keep atheistic France and Panslav Orthodox Russia at bay – Frantz believed in preventive war to roll Russia back – and in the fullness of time would blossom into a great European federation, a renewal of Charlemagne's empire. All this would be impossible if the Little Germans had their way; fresh enmities would be generated in the heart of Europe, and the continent would gradually decline and be overshadowed by Russia and the U.S.A.

Prophetic words, but hardly practical politics. Austria, on whom the federalists pinned their hopes, was too preoccupied with internal problems to take the initiative in the creation of a supranational Europe. In any case the tides of history were flowing against supranationalism; nationalism was on the march in Italy and stirring in Eastern Europe and the Balkans. The Greater Germans, who sympathised with the ideas of Frantz and Jörg, were weak and divided, whilst their opponents, the Little Germans, had a powerful press, influential periodicals, such as the *Preussische Jahrbücher*, and superior organisation on their side in the battle for the soul of Germany.

The *Nationalverein* was not supported only by academics and high officials, the backbone of the 1848 liberal movement. It attracted much support from financiers and industrialists, from men such as Siemens, inventor of the electric dynamo, and Meier, founder of the North German Lloyd Shipping Company. This was no accident. As the middle classes grew in economic and social power, they became increasingly vocal in their demands for unification. Middle-class people in many countries were forming professional associations in the 1850s and 1860s to discuss their problems at national level. The German Economists' Congress was founded in 1858 and set to work for the promotion of free trade and a uniform coinage. Through its endeavours the *Deutscher Handelstag* was founded in 1861. German lawyers founded an association in 1860 to work for a unified legal code. Liberal members of local parliaments met regularly from 1862 at the *Deutsche Abgeordnetentage*. The impact of industrialisation, the spread of the railway system and the growth of an increasingly complex financial and commercial network were drawing all parts of Germany into ever closer association, stimulating and sustaining the demand for political unification to crown the edifice of economic unity. As John Maynard Keynes commented with some justification: 'The German Empire was built more truly on coal and iron than on blood and iron.'

The Prussian liberal revival referred to above was part of a general European phenomenon. Absolutism was crumbling all over Europe. In France Napoleon III was taking the first tentative steps towards the Liberal Empire. In Italy the Risorgimento liberals had virtually completed unification by 1861. In Austria after 1859 Emperor Francis Joseph was forced by financial pressures to experiment with constitutional forms; the October Diploma of 1860, and the February Patent of 1861, were steps on the way to the Ausgleich of 1867 which radically transformed the monarchy. In Britain pressure for parliamentary reform led to the 1867 Reform Bill. It was symptomatic of the changing political climate in Germany that Austria and Prussia co-operated over the affairs of Hesse-Cassel, the issue which had brought them to the brink of war in 1850. The elector was still attempting to rule absolutely in the face of bitter opposition from his subjects. In 1859, pursuing her policy of 'moral conquests', Prussia proposed the restoration of the 1831 constitution in Hesse-Cassel, an initiative which heartened liberals all over Germany. In 1862 Austria sided with Prussia, and together they persuaded the Diet to order restoration of the constitution. Prince William – King William I since 1861 – broke off diplomatic relations with Hesse-Cassel, ordered the elector to dismiss his reactionary advisers and mobilised two army corps. When Austria warned the elector not to expect assistance, he capitulated and restored the 1831 constitution.

Prussia's moral victory was short lived. In the autumn of 1862 she was plunged into a serious political crisis which quickly tarnished her newly won liberal reputation. The crisis arose over reform of the Prussian army. Military efficiency was dear to the regent's heart. He firmly believed in a strong army as the only sure guarantee of a strong monarchy, and he realised that without a strong army Prussia could not play the great role in Germany which he expected of her; William never forgot the humiliation of 1850 when he had to listen to the minister of war informing a Prussian cabinet that Prussia was too weak to fight Austria. When Prussia mobilised in 1859, glaring defects were revealed in her defences. William determined to remedy these and appointed Count Albrecht von Roon, an administrative genius and extreme conservative, minister of war to effect major reforms.

The population of Prussia had increased from ten millions to eighteen millions since 1820, yet for reasons of economy the annual army intake remained at 40,000. Consequently each year 25,000 young Prussians escaped military service. To remedy this defect and make universal service a reality, Roon proposed to increase the intake to 63,000. In the past soldiers served three years with a line regiment (in practice being released after two and a half years), two years in the reserve, seven years with the first levy of the *Landwehr* and finally seven years with the second levy. In war-time the first levy of the *Landwehr* was used in the line. The latter arrangement was unsatisfactory for *Landwehr* soldiers were older men, half of them burdened with family commitments, and many were unfit for battle. Roon decided to change the system so that a man would serve a full three years with a line regiment, followed by four years in the reserve and eleven with the *Landwehr*. Intensive military training in the first seven years would raise the general standard of efficiency. The *Landwehr* would no longer be called upon for front-line service; in future it would play a subordinate role as rear echelon or garrison troops. To accommodate this vastly increased army, thirty-nine new infantry regiments and ten cavalry regiments – nearly double the existing number – would be created.

A bill embodying the proposals was placed before the lower house of the Prussian Landtag in February 1860. The liberals were critical of increased military expenditure so soon after the 1857 crisis. More fundamental was their opposition to the demotion of the *Landwehr*. Since the days of Scharnhorst and Gneisenau liberals had attached great importance to the *Landwehr*; under middle-class officers it had become a symbol of the people in arms and was regarded as a civilising influence and a welcome antidote to the spirit of 'cadaver obedience' characteristic of the old Frederician army. Liberals suspected, quite rightly, that political considerations lay behind Roon's proposal. King William and Roon were certainly highly critical of the military shortcomings of the *Landwehr*. But basically they were frightened of a body which represented a potential threat to absolute control of the army by the crown.

The liberals were not pacifists; on the contrary, they knew that Prussia must have a strong army if she was to take the lead in creating Little Germany. They gladly assented to the increased army intake but rejected the proposals for the *Landwehr*, and in their anxiety to save money demanded a reduction in the period of service from three to two years. The government outmanoeuvred the liberals by suddenly withdrawing the bill. Roon decided that the army laws of 1814–15 gave him sufficient authority to carry through the reforms by using the powers vested in the king as supreme commander; the lower house need only be asked to provide the necessary funds. The liberals, anxious not to endanger the 'New Era', voted nine-and-a-half-million talers for additional military expenditure for one year in May 1860, but on the verbal understanding that those reforms to which the liberals objected would not be implemented. The regent and his military advisers, however, assumed that the lower house had given them *carte blanche*. The new regiments were created, and in January 1861 the flags were dedicated by the king over the tomb of Frederick the Great. The liberals were incensed by this sharp practice. Nevertheless, they approved a second provisional appropriation, although only by a majority of three and on condition that legislation be introduced to reduce the period of service to two years.

By this time there was mounting dissatisfaction on the left wing of the liberal party. Very slow progress had been made since 1858 towards administrative reform; vested interests were deeply entrenched in Prussia; permanent officials, particularly the influential *Landräte,*[2] and the upper chamber of the Landtag had successfully sabotaged most reforms. The compliant attitude of the liberal leaders over army reform was the last straw. The left wing demanded real progress towards the *Rechtsstaat* and more positive steps towards unification. Full of determination to achieve these objectives, the left-wingers broke away and founded the German Progressive Party (*Deutsche Fortschrittspartei*) in June 1861. At the elections in December the Progressives gained 110 seats, becoming the largest group in the house.

The Progressives wanted a strong army as much as the liberals. But unlike the older liberals the Progressives intended to use the army question as a lever for constitutional reform, in particular for a reduction in the powers of the upper chamber. To prevent further army reorganisation without parliamentary consent, the Progressives persuaded the lower house to insist on a detailed budget analysis – a step intended to prevent cuts from being imposed on other departments for the sake of the army. The king was persuaded by his advisers to dissolve the house. The liberal ministers, trapped at last between reactionary military chiefs and impatient Progressives, resigned. When they were replaced by conservative ministers, the New Era was seen to be over.

---

[2] Administrative heads of *Kreise* or districts.

In May the Progressives won a resounding victory at the polls. With 135 seats and the support of other opposition groups, they had overall control in the lower house. An agreed settlement was still possible. Some Progressives were ready to accept a two-year service period. Roon was agreeable; the generals thought two years perfectly adequate for military training; the third year was important only because it afforded an opportunity for indoctrinating the rank-and-file with the virtues of obedience and loyalty to the monarchy. The stumbling-block was the king. On no account would he give in to a parliamentary majority on military matters. In August the lower house refused to vote for further sums for any reorganisation. At last king and Landtag faced a clear constitutional issue – was the king or the parliament to rule in Prussia? The crisis deepened. Crown Prince Frederick advised surrender. In despair William considered abdication while Manteuffel pressed for the implementation of plans for a dictatorship drawn up months ago by the military cabinet. At this critical moment Roon at last persuaded the king to summon Otto von Bismarck-Schönhausen to Berlin.

Bismarck, who had watched the crisis with mounting concern from France, where he was Prussian minister, hurried back home when he received his friend Roon's cryptic telegram: *'Periculum in mora. Dépêchez vous'*. The king received Bismarck with some apprehension, for he harboured grave doubts about his brilliant but erratic servant, 'who wanted to turn everything upside down'. Bismarck played cleverly upon the king's feelings, presenting himself as a loyal vassal come to rescue his lord from the horrors of parliamentary government, even if it meant a period of dictatorship. By promising to stand by the king to the bitter end Bismarck overcame Williams's lingering doubts. On 22 September Bismarck was appointed minister-president; in an atmosphere of *coup d'état* he assumed office, not as a constitutional minister but simply as the king's servant.

Now forty-seven years old, Bismarck was a restless, ambitious and dynamic personality. The son of a Pomeranian Junker, he was born in 1815 at Schönhausen in the Altmark in the very heart of the old mark of Brandenburg. He had the landowner's love of nature and forests, and possessed the physical stamina, gargantuan appetite and zest for living of a typical Junker. But he was also a highly intelligent and cultured man of the world, having inherited considerable intellectual qualities from his mother, the daughter of a high official. He was educated in the style of the well-to-do middle class at schools in Berlin and later at Göttingen University. After a brief and unsuccessful interlude as an official, Bismarck retired to the countryside and became a landowner first at Kniephof and then at Schönhausen. He remained restless and dissatisfied, longing to play a great role in public affairs. His first encounter with public life was accidental; the united estates were meeting in Berlin in 1847 when the member for the Altmark was taken ill and Bismarck was asked to replace him. Although an indifferent public speaker, Bismarck soon established a reputation as an extreme conservative and an outspoken enemy of liberalism. During the 1848 Revolution he tried in vain to talk King Frederick William into a *coup d'état*, then continued to advocate extreme courses of action through the influential circle presided over by the Gerlach brothers, Leopold and Ludwig. He was elected to the Prussian Landtag in 1849, and in 1850 made a name for himself by defending the Olmütz agreement as a victory for conservative principles over the forces of revolution. The king's advisers persuaded him to reward Bismarck. In 1851 he commenced a diplomatic career as minister in Frankfurt, where he spent eight years before being transferred to St. Petersburg in 1858 and then to Paris in 1862.

Bismarck had pledged unflinching support to William in the struggle against parliament. All the same, the new minister-president saw no advantage in having a serious domestic crisis on his hands when he wished to concentrate on foreign affairs. So, as a conciliatory gesture, he withdrew the budget proposals for 1863, and negotiated secretly with the liberal leaders, hinting that he could win the king for a two-year period of service; in fact the king was immovable on this point.

Even the celebrated remarks during Bismarck's speech to the budget commission on 30 September 1862 were conciliatory in intent. 'The position of Prussia in Germany', he declared in an aside, 'will be decided not by its liberalism but by its power . . . not through speeches and majority decisions are the great questions of the day decided – that was the great mistake of 1848–49 – but by blood and iron'. The words raised a storm of disapproval from the liberals and confirmed the popular image of Bismarck as the blood-thirsty and irresponsible Junker forever itching to let slip the dogs of war. In fact this was not so much an indiscretion as a rather clumsy attempt to win over the liberals by hinting that he had great plans for Prussia if only they would allow army reform to proceed unhindered.

Hopes of compromise faded when the Progressives rejected Bismarck's olive branch and declared once again that expenditure without the lower house's consent was illegal. Bismarck resorted to sterner tactics. In October at his suggestion the upper chamber rejected the amended budget sent from the lower house and voted for the original budget. Bismarck immediately prorogued parliament and commenced to rule without a budget. Tongue in cheek, he justified his policy on the basis of a sophisticated conservative gloss on the 1850 constitution. The constitution required the passage of an annual budget but made no provision for failure to reach agreement on this item. Prussia was not England, argued Bismarck; there was no question of the ministry's being responsible to parliament; only the crown possessed residual powers to govern in a constitutional deadlock. Furthermore, the constitution stipulated that the consent of the king and both houses was necessary for legislation. As the upper chamber agreed with the king over the budget, it could be argued that the lower house was demanding a monopoly of government in trying to force its will on the king. Such behaviour destroyed the compromise or balance of forces on which all constitutions rest. The question in Bismarck's mind simply resolved itself into a naked struggle for power between the lower house and the forces of law and order, all of which were ranged on the king's side.

Bismarck embarked upon the struggle against liberalism with zest and enthusiasm. Heavy pressure was brought to bear on liberal-minded civil servants and judges, and freedom of the press was curtailed more drastically than in Napoleon III's France. The liberal intellectuals, notably Droysen and Sybel, were horrified by Bismarck's ruthlessness. Crown Prince Frederick ostentatiously dissociated himself from repressive measures. Bismarck remained unmoved. When fresh elections were held in September – against Bismarck's advice – the minister-president intervened actively in the campaign in an attempt to whip up support for the government. But the opposition remained in control of the lower house though reduced in strength. Bismarck brushed aside renewed accusations of unconstitutional action and criticism of his foreign policy, which it was claimed had as its objective Prussian aggrandisement, not German unification. Meanwhile the government calmly continued to collect taxes without reference to the lower house.

Face to face with a resolute government, the Progressives were virtually helpless. Even if they had believed in the use of force – and they did not – their leaders realised that successful resistance was impossible in a state with strong authoritarian traditions; the king had a well-trained army of 200,000 men and an obedient civil service behind him, and could rely on the traditional loyalty of his people in time of crisis. The Progressives were also anxious to avoid precipitate action likely to offend the sympathetic crown prince who might soon ascend the throne. Hence efforts to organise a tax boycott came to nothing. Even a proposal to adjourn the house indefinitely until the government capitulated was supported by only a single deputy. Furthermore, the Progressives were well aware of structural weaknesses in their party. Their strength in the lower house was illusory; relatively few of those entitled to vote did so.[3] Most of the influential upper middle class did not support the Progressives. Nor did they have a broad popular following outside the middle class. The peasantry, still a majority of the population even in Prussia, the most industrialised state, was not attracted by liberalism. And the Progressives made little attempt to mobilise the new urban working class.

True, the Progressives dimly perceived the need for some contact with

---

[3]Only thirty-five per cent in 1862 and only thirty per cent in 1863. Examination of individual classes in 1863 reveals that fifty-seven per cent of class I voted but only twenty-seven per cent of the more numerous class III.

the working class, fearing that otherwise the workers would easily fall victim not to Marxism, a practically non-existent force in the 1850s, but to conservatism. Educational societies (*Arbeiterbildungsvereine*) were founded to elevate the moral and cultural level of the working classes whilst carefully avoiding all reference to their social and political aspirations. The working class did not remain in leading-strings for long. A workers' delegation came back from the London Exhibition of 1862 deeply impressed by English trade unionism. Workers in Leipzig and Berlin planned to call a German workers' congress to found a separate working-class organisation. The ideas was strongly opposed by the Progressives, who feared that a working-class party would quickly fall under conservative influence. In January 1863 a deputation of Leipzig workers demanded the right of admission to the *Nationalverein*, from which they had hitherto been excluded. They also asked the Progressive party to adopt the principle of universal suffrage. Both requests were rejected.

The German working class had arrived at the parting of the ways. The Leipzig workers turned to Ferdinand Lassalle for advice; his open letter in March 1863 was one of the foundation-stones of German socialism. Lassalle, the son of a Jewish merchant, was a man of great intellectual power and determination. Though rejected by Marx and Engels, he devoted his life to the radical cause. Imprisoned for his part in the 1848 Revolution, he was active again in the 1850s in Berlin as a pamphleteer and journalist. A bitter critic of liberal tactics during the constitutional crisis, he turned away from the Progressives when they rejected his advice to break completely with the government. As Lassalle had spoken and written in defence of the working class, the Leipzig workers' committee naturally approached him. In his reply Lassalle declared that the working class must form their own political party and fight for the introduction of universal suffrage. This was a truly revolutionary weapon, which would enable the workers to conquer the state and use its power to alleviate their sufferings. Social legislation would not help the working class. Nor would 'self-help' co-operatives which originated with the radical liberal Schulze-Delitzsch in 1849. Lassalle realised that Schulze's privately financed co-operatives were intended to help lower-middle-class *Handwerker*; they were of no use to an industrial proletariat ground down by the 'iron law' of wages and unable to accumulate the capital required for membership. State intervention was Lassalle's answer. Producers' associations financed by the state would make the worker economically independent and free from exploitation.

In May 1863 workers' representatives from eleven towns met in Leipzig and founded the General German Workers' Association (*Allgemeiner Deutscher Arbeiterverein*) to agitate for universal suffrage, with Lassalle as its president. This, and the rival Union of German Workers' Associations (*Vereinstag deutscher Arbeitervereine*), were the first political associations of

the German working class and forerunners of the German Social Democratic Party. Lassalle's hopes proved over-sanguine. At the time of his
death there were only 4,600 members in the *Arbeiterverein*. It was bitterly
opposed by employers and by most workers in the *Bildungsvereine*, who
remained loyal to the liberals. Even if the working class had been united it
was still far too weak in the 1860s to compel governments to do its bidding.
Lassalle's belief in universal suffrage as an infallible instrument of social
change was really an act of faith in the future; the Progressives attacked him
bitterly, seeing in him nothing more than a tool of the reactionaries bent on
the destruction of liberalism. Marx and Engels both mistrusted him for
they believed like most middle-class people that universal suffrage would
probably put another Napoleon in power. They remained dedicated to the
proposition that the working class could only storm the citadels of power
by violent revolution. Their suspicions of Lassalle were to some extent
justified, for he undoubtedly toyed with the thesis that the working class
would willingly support a dictator provided he pursued a radical social
policy. Unlike Marx, Lassalle was deeply impressed by the power of the
Prussian state. He even believed in the possibility of an alliance between
monarchy and working class to encompass the destruction of his chief
enemy – the liberal middle class. Here he differed sharply from Marx,
who saw in the alliance of middle class and working class one of the
indispensable steps on the road to socialism.

Lassalle's brief friendship with Bismarck is a fascinating episode on the
margin of events. Bismarck asked Lassalle to meet him secretly in May
1863. They conferred together on several occasions down to February
1864, when Bismarck terminated the relationship. The minister-president
was greatly attracted by the charming, intellectually gifted Lassalle, and
listened enthralled to his defence of producers' associations and universal
suffrage. Lassalle greatly admired Bismarck's achievements and shared his
understanding of the importance of power in politics. But there was no
basis for political agreement between them. Much as Lassalle longed to
harness Bismarck to his cause, he had nothing tangible to offer the minister-president in return. In August 1864 he died prematurely in a duel. A
proud, arrogant and ambitious man, a natural power-seeker but also a
humanitarian, genuinely concerned to promote working-class interests,
Lassalle will always be remembered as one of the great founder figures of
the German Socialist movement.

In the autumn of 1863 Prussian liberalism was losing the struggle against
Bismarck. Timidly led and conscious of their lack of mass support, the
Progressives were no match for the ruthless minister-president. Curiously
enough, they did not despair of the future. On the contrary; the onset of
the Schleswig-Holstein crisis filled them with new hope. Liberals felt

confident that once Prussia was swept forward on a tidal wave of national feeling over Schleswig-Holstein, Bismarck would be compelled to abandon his reactionary policies and seek popular support, delivering himself into their hands. They consoled themselves with the thought that the initiative which they had lost at home would be easily regained abroad. Nationalism and liberalism were closely identified in their minds as they had been in 1848; the victory of nationalism predicated the victory of liberalism. So, as the external crisis deepened, liberals believed that Bismarck's days in office were numbered. This naïve analysis was rapidly overtaken by events. The Schleswig-Holstein question was to put Prussia on the high road to German unification. but the triumph of nationalism did not lead to an era of liberalism at home; instead it renewed and consolidated the traditional conservative forces in Prussian society at the expense of liberalism.

4

The Unification of Germany
1862–1870

'I shall soon be compelled to undertake the leadership of the Prussian Government. My first care will be, with or without the help of Parliament, to reorganise the army. The King has rightly set himself this task; he cannot, however, carry it through with his present councillors. When the army has been brought to such a state as to command respect, then I will take the first opportunity to declare war with Austria, burst asunder the German Confederation, bring the middle and smaller states into subjection, and give Germany a national union under the leadership of Prussia. I have come here to tell this to the Queen's ministers.' Bismarck, attracted to London by the international exhibition in 1862, is alleged to have made these remarks to Disraeli, leader of the Opposition, during dinner at the Russian embassy. According to the Saxon ambassador, Count von Eckstadt, the source of the story, Disraeli added: 'Take care of the man; he means what he says.'

These frank revelations over the port which so shocked and impressed Disraeli did not mean that Bismarck had suddenly been converted to the cause of national liberalism. At bottom a loyal servant of his monarch, Bismarck simply intended like Frederick the Great to seize opportunities as and when they arose to make the kingdom of Prussia the dominant power in the geographical area bounded by the North Sea, the Rhine, the Alps, the Bohemian Forest and the river Vistula. But although Bismarck was utterly opposed to the liberal connotations of national liberalism, like other Prussian conservatives he was a nationalist in the sense that he believed those larger German states with their own sense of identity such as Prussia, Austria and Bavaria to be truly 'German' because all shared in a common *Volksgeist*. Thus while advancing the power interests of Prussia Bismarck was able to square the circle by claiming to be furthering the cause of German nationalism as well. As he once remarked in 1858: 'there is, in fact, nothing more German than the growth of Prussia's particular interests properly understood.'

His appointment as minister-president of Prussia in 1862 aroused alarm and misgivings in liberal circles. For the general public saw in him a reactionary and bigoted conservative of the old school, full of fire and brimstone, the staunch friend of Austria and the dedicated enemy of liberalism and nationalism in 1848. Since then he had served a political apprenticeship as Prussian minister to the Confederation, eight momentous years between 1851 and 1858 which turned him into a con-summate master of the diplomatic arts. It had been a traumatic experience for the 'Mark Junker'. At Frankfurt he gained first-hand experience of the deep-seated rivalry between Austria and Prussia. An irascible and sensitive man by temperament, Bismarck resented the grand-seigneurial airs of Count Thun, Austria's representative, and never missed an opportunity of emphasising Prussia's parity of status, even in the most trivial matters. Greeted by the count in shirt-sleeves, Bismarck at once removed his own jacket. In the federal military commission, where previously only the Austrian president smoked, the new ambassador ostentatiously opened his cigar-case, adding insult to injury by asking Count Thun for a light. Obliged to wait for a few minutes in the president's ante-chamber, Bismarck impatiently walked away. As a matter of course he opposed most Austrian proposals in the Diet, trying – generally with little success – to win the support of the smaller states. This aggressive policy of pinpricks and obstructionism was designed to force Austria's hand and make her accept Prussia as an equal, and consult her on major matters before approaching the Diet as she had done before 1848.

However, co-operation with Austria, or with any other power for that matter, would in future depend entirely upon the benefit Prussia derived from such arrangements. Gone were the days when Bismarck believed that the traditional conservative powers, Austria, Prussia and Russia, must always co-operate blindly in defence of monarchy and the *status quo*. Once the spectre of revolution had disappeared and radicalism was no longer a serious force in German politics, Bismarck ceased to believe that ideology should be the mainspring of foreign policy. As early as 1850 he remarked that the 'only healthy basis for a great state and one which differentiates it fundamentally from the policy of a small state is political egoism, not romanticism. It is not worthy of a great state to quarrel about matters which do not appertain to its own interests.'

In many ways Bismarck was an anachronistic figure in an age when industrialism was drawing peoples closer together and increasing their interdependence. For him politics, whether national or international, were little more than a naked struggle for power; the ruthless pursuit of self-interest was the only possible policy for a great state; treaties were tempo-rary expedients entered into as circumstances dictated, and discarded once they had outlived their usefulness; ideology and sentiment had no part in this world of *Realpolitik*.[1] Orthodox conservatives were blinded by their

[1] The word was coined in 1859, significantly enough by the liberal journalist and historian Rochau.

loathing and detestation of France, the *fons et origo* of revolution, whereas the unblinkered Bismarck saw in Napoleon a valuable piece on the diplomatic chessboard which could be pressed into service to coerce Austria and bring her to her senses.

The new minister-president was not bent on war with Austria. His diplomacy was much more subtle, flexible and many-sided than his utterances sometimes suggest. War was obviously one solution to the rivalry with Austria – and probably the most likely outcome in his estimation. Yet this was no blood-thirsty and frivolous Junker eager to commit Prussia to war to satisfy personal vanity. On the contrary, he firmly believed that war should be resorted to only as a last expedient when all hope of a peaceful solution had been abandoned; speaking to Friedjung, the Austrian historian, in 1890, he remarked that 'a statesman is like a man wandering in a forest who knows his general direction but not the exact point at which he will emerge from the wood. It was difficult to avoid war with Austria, but he who is responsible for the lives of millions will shrink from war until all other means have been exhausted.'

The natural sense of restraint of the experienced diplomat was reinforced by religious conviction. After a wild and undisciplined youth Bismarck was converted to a pietistic brand of Christianity in the 1840s. His God was a rather remote and severe Old-Testament character. Significantly enough Bismarck always maintained that the perfect law of Christ had no direct relevance to political life; the politican must not hesitate to use force, one of the basic ingredients in the politics of a sinful world; to apply the teaching of the Sermon on the Mount literally would simply deliver the just into the hands of the ungodly, hardly a Christian objective. But politics and religion were not completely divorced in Bismarck's world. He believed that the devout Christian had at all times to do the Will of God, ever conscious of his personal responsibility for all his actions. There was no doubt a strong element of self-deception in all this. All the same, Bismarck was constantly scanning the horizon for signs of the Divine Will. He once declared that a statesman could achieve absolutely nothing of himself but could only wait 'until he hears the footsteps of God sounding through events and then spring forward to seize the hem of His Garment'.

There was in fact no change of direction in Prussian policy when Bismarck assumed power. In foreign affairs he continued the policy pursued by Count Bernstorff, Prussian foreign minister since 1861. There was nothing new in the skirmishing with Austria, the flirtation with France or the attempts to cultivate the friendship of Russia. The basic difference between Bismarck and his predecessor was simply that the constitutional crisis made the king much more dependent on his new minister-president. Because of this, William had appointed Bismarck without even bothering to commit the minister-president to a political programme. These circumstances opened the door for Bismarck to pursue policies with which his sovereign might not wholly agree.

His first major excursion into the realm of foreign policy did not augur particularly well for the future. In January 1863 liberal sympathies were aroused by the Polish revolt. Bismarck at once sent troops into Prussian Poland and dispatched General Alvensleben to St. Petersburg to discuss military co-operation with Russia. The general signed a convention in February 1863 providing for joint military action to seal off the disaffected frontier districts. There were several reasons for Bismarck's action. Always violently antagonistic to the Poles, he was gravely alarmed by the possible repercussions of a Polish success on Prussia's Polish subjects; 'the suppression of the revolt is for us a matter of life and death,' he informed the British ambassador. He also wanted to strengthen the hand of Russian conservatives against the Gortschakov faction, which, so it was rumoured, favoured a liberal Polish policy – Bismarck feared a complete Russian withdrawal which would oblige Prussia to annex Congress Poland. Finally, the convention might weaken the *entente* between France and Russia and re-establish Prussia as the true friend of Russia. There were bitter protests from the Prussian liberals who hated autocratic Russia. Nor was the convention welcomed by the Russians, who felt quite capable of suppressing the revolt unaided. International repercussions arose when the French foreign minister, Drouyn de Lhuys, anxious to put Bismarck in his place, proposed to Britain and Austria that they join with France in making a protest in Berlin. Bismarck discovered that Russia would not support Prussia against the other powers, and he reluctantly dropped the convention. This was not the great diplomatic success Bismarck pretended in later years; it did little to improve relations with Russia; on the other hand, the danger of a more liberal Russian policy in Poland was averted, and the Franco-Russian *entente* foundered over Poland later in 1863.

Before Bismarck came to power relations with Austria were entering a new and more critical phase. For some months after King William and Emperor Francis Joseph met at Teplitz in July 1860, Austria had shown interest in a Prussian alliance to help recover Lombardy and protect Venetia. Prussia would only defend Venetia in return for control of the federal army. As always the price was too high for Austria to pay. By the spring of 1861 negotiations were broken off, and the latent rivalry between them burst into the open once more. With liberalism in the air in the early 1860s the rivalry was centred on the military and political reorganisation of the Confederation. In 1859 Prince William proposed that Austria and Prussia share supreme command in war-time of a remodelled federal army. The proposal was defeated in the Diet by Austria with the support of the small states, who clung pathetically to the fiction of military independence.

Nor did anything come of several schemes for political reform of the

Confederation. In October 1861 Saxony proposed a tripartite reorganisation between Austria, Prussia and the smaller states. In December Prussia rejected the scheme and declared that the Confederation could not be reformed; the popular demand for unification could be satisfied only by the creation of a federal state under Prussian leadership within the existing Confederation. Austria was shocked by this blunt intimation that Prussia had revived Radowitz's plan for an Erfurt Union. Schmerling, Francis Joseph's new minister of state, was eager to win wider German support for his liberal reforms in Austria – reforms which favoured the Germans at the expense of both Czechs and Magyars – and succeeded in persuading the Ballplatz to take up this Prussian challenge. In February 1862 Austria put forward a modified version of the Saxon scheme which won the support of Hanover, Saxony, Württemberg and Bavaria. Again Prussia rejected it. Bernstorff, who greatly admired Radowitz's defiance of Austria in 1850, added a warning to the effect that if war was forced on her over the reform question, Prussia would not give way this time. Relations deteriorated still further in the summer of 1862 when Prussia ratified the commercial treaty with France, a step which made Austrian entry into the Customs Union infinitely more difficult.

So when Bismarck came to power, relations with Austria were already severely strained, and war seemed a distinct possibility. Early in December 1862 Bismarck warned Austria that unless she recognised Prussia as an equal in Germany, she was inviting catastrophe. A few days later he attempted, unsuccessfully, to obtain a promise of neutrality from France in the event of war. The crisis subsided in January 1863 when the Austrian proposals were finally defeated in the Diet by a narrow margin after Prussia had threatened to walk out in the event of acceptance.

In the summer of 1863 Austria made a last determined bid to seize the initiative in Germany. The situation seemed to favour a policy of 'moral conquests' by Austria; the New Era was over in Prussia; the *Nationalverein*, now coming increasingly under radical influence, was bitterly critical of Bismarck's domestic and foreign policy and looked hopefully to Vienna, where Schmerling's liberalism was putting new life into Greater Germanism. In August Austria summoned the German princes to meet in Frankfurt and discuss a new reform plan; the main points included periodic congresses of the princes, the establishment of a directory of five armed with executive powers and, as a sop to nationalist feeling, the creation of a consultative assembly of 300 chosen from local parliaments. This attempt to unite Germany by consent aroused deep interest. All the rulers with a few minor exceptions attended the Congress of Princes, a last glittering display of the old order held under the presidency of Francis Joseph. At first the King of Prussia, advised by Bismarck, declined to attend, but on receiving a second summons from the assembled princes his resolve weakened.

This was a critical moment for Bismarck who argued vehemently against attendance on the grounds that Prussia would be outvoted and committed to an ill-considered scheme designed to perpetuate Austrian ascendancy in Germany. His strongest weapon was the threat of resignation, which would leave William face-to-face with the intransigent lower house. After a nerve-racking interview Bismarck emerged exhausted but triumphant, leaving his sovereign sobbing on the bed. Never again did the king seriously oppose his minister-president. The Prussian chair at Frankfurt remained vacant. The Congress of Princes continued its deliberations and eventually endorsed the essentials of the Austrian proposals. But it was a hollow victory, for without Prussia nothing could be done. Perhaps the smaller states were rather relieved at this outcome; Prussia had saved them from Austrian domination much as Austria saved them from Prussian domination in 1850; the 'Third Germany', of which there was much talk in the 1850s and 1860s, could only survive by balancing precariously between the two great powers.

There was a significant postscript to the Congress. When Prussia was invited to endorse the work of the princes, Bismarck imposed conditions which spotlighted the basic rivalry with Austria, glossed over by the Congress; Austria and Prussia must possess veto rights over declarations of war by the reformed Diet; Prussia must have parity with Austria in the presidency; and in place of a meeting of delegates there should be an assembly elected by the whole nation. The conditions were quite unacceptable to Austria, and the last chance of an agreed solution of the German problem passed. Bismarck's last proposal aroused great surprise in Germany. The *Nationalverein* dismissed it as an irresponsible ploy. Bismarck was in earnest. Always receptive to new ideas, he had toyed with the idea of a popularly elected assembly since 1858. His detailed knowledge of the French electoral system convinced him that conservatives had little to fear from universal suffrage; by posing as the champion of the masses and paying some attention to their material needs, Napoleon had shown that an autocratic system could rest on popular support. During their conversations Lassalle enthralled Bismarck with his vision of the urban proletariat conquering the state; Bismarck inverted the process, sensing that the loyal German peasantry, harnessed to the Prussian cause, could preserve the conservative order in Germany; in carefully stage-managed elections the power of the rural masses could be mobilised to destroy middle-class liberalism and inaugurate an era of popular 'social monarchy'. However, this was all speculation, an excursion into the shrouded mists of the future. The fact remained that in the early autumn of 1863, on the eve of his greatest triumph over Schleswig-Holstein, the Prussian minister-president was an unpopular and derided figure.

*   *   *

After the Revolution the *status quo* had been restored in Schleswig-Holstein. Under the Olmütz agreement Austrian troops entered Holstein at the Diet's request, dissolved the rebel government and handed the duchy back to Denmark. In August 1850, in the London Protocol, the Great Powers expressed their interest in seeing the Danish monarchy preserved intact – it was a familiar landmark and a reassuring sign that the old order was restored – and approved the efforts the king of Denmark was making to prepare a new order of succession. After arduous negotiations the duke of Augustenburg renounced his dynastic claims and those of his family, for a cash payment in favour of Prince Christian, head of the Schleswig-Holstein-Sonderburg-Glücksburg line. Meeting in concert in London in May 1852, the Great Powers set their seal to this arrangement and expressed their earnest conviction that the preservation of the Danish monarchy – like the Habsburg dominions – was a European necessity. In December 1851 Denmark promised Austria and Prussia that a common constitution for the whole monarchy would be drawn up in consultation with the duchies; Schleswig and Holstein would have their own local constitutions; Schleswig would not be incorporated in Denmark, and Germans and Danes would enjoy equal rights in the duchy. The Federal Diet expressed its approval of a royal proclamation of January 1852 confirming these promises, and withdrew the remaining forces from Holstein.

The Great Powers had restored the external fabric of the Danish monarchy in the interests of the balance of power. They could not revitalise the monarchy: three years of war had destroyed the old amity between Germans and Danes; Danish measures such as the removal of disloyal officials, the ban on public meetings and the introduction of Danish into the schools in parts of Schleswig, made matters worse.

Difficulties arose over both the local constitutions and the common constitution. In 1855 the Danes produced a common constitution which established a council of state (*Rigsraad*) to handle foreign policy, defence and trade; of the eighty members forty-seven were from Denmark and thirty-three from the duchies, a natural reflection of the numerical superiority of the Danes. The Germans objected, fearing assimilation in a monarchy which was becoming a viable and prosperous economic unit in the 1850s; instead, the Germans insisted on absolute parity with the Danes in keeping with the essential tenet of Schleswig-Holsteinism, i.e. that the duchies were a state equal in all respects to Denmark. In the interminable disputes which followed the duchies looked to Germany for support. Austria and Prussia made diplomatic representations in Copenhagen, and in 1858 the Diet threatened federal execution unless Holstein was given the independent status promised her in 1852. At the close of the 1850s Schleswig-Holstein was again capturing the imagination of the German people as the national revival gathered momentum. At the great popular festivals in the early 1860s the duchies were once more a mystic symbol of national aspirations. No gathering was complete without fiery anti-Danish speeches and resolutions of sympathy for the 'gallant Schleswig-Holsteiner' resisting Danish 'aggression' and 'tyranny'.

Negotiations about the common constitution were virtually deadlocked. Emboldened by the growing support from Germany, the Holstein estates rejected the Danish plans in 1859 and proposed a reversion to the pre-1848 situation of four separate assemblies, two Danish and two German. This was completely unacceptable in Copenhagen, where nationalist pressures were equally pronounced; Eider-Danism was on the march, committed to the union of Schleswig and Denmark; in 1861 Orla Lehmann, the *bête noire* of the German nationalists, was appointed a minister as a sop to the Eider Danes. Behind the Eider Danes stood the Scandinavian movement. At the close of the 1850s there was a significant revival of interest in Pan-Scandinavianism; in 1859 Karl XV, a convinced Pan-Scandinavian, became king of Norway-Sweden. He gave active support to Denmark, even proposing a formal alliance against Germany. Nothing came of it, because Pan-Scandinavianism was an insubstantial movement. When war came in 1864 there was no official help from Norway-Sweden, only volunteers who fought alongside the Danes as they had done in 1848.

Eider-Dane pressure forced the King of Denmark's hand in 1863. In January the lower house of the Danish parliament demanded the union of Schleswig and Denmark. The international situation looked promising; Austria and Prussia were at loggerheads over reform in Germany, and the attention of the Great Powers was distracted by the Polish revolt. The Danes hesitated no longer. On 30 March 1863 the king issued a royal patent offering Holstein a new constitution but practically excluding it from the council of state. This was intended as a first step towards the dissolution of the ties between Holstein and Denmark. When the king opened the Danish parliament in April, he confirmed that Danish law was binding on Schleswig.

Austria and Prussia protested. The Diet demanded withdrawal of the patent under pain of federal execution and called on Denmark to devise a new constitution based either on the promises made in 1852 or on the British mediation proposals of 1862. The Danes ignored the protests, encouraged still further by the international situation; German opinion was distracted by the Congress of Princes, Sweden had promised to support Denmark, and Palmerston had hinted in the House of Commons that Britain might be on Denmark's side in the event of war. The Danes bluntly declared that federal execution would be regarded as a *casus belli*, and in September produced a common constitution for Denmark-Schleswig. The Diet immediately ordered Austria, Prussia, Saxony and Hanover to impose federal execution on Denmark. The Danes were still unimpressed; they discounted Austrian support for federal execution as a face-saving strategem after the Congress of Princes' *débâcle*; they noted that Prussia was still most conciliatory in her attitude despite her formal commitment to federal execution. On 13 November 1863 the council of state approved the constitution for Schleswig. The premier hurried off to obtain his king's signature. He found King Frederick dangerously ill and in his lucid moments unwilling to sign. On 15 November the king was dead. The male line had died out. In accordance with the Treaty of London Prince Christian of Glücksburg – 'The Protocol Prince' as German nationalists dubbed him – became King Christian IX. On 18 November, under heavy pressure from the Eider Danes and against his better judgement, he signed the constitution. Next day Frederick of Augustenburg, liberal-minded son of the old duke, proclaimed himself duke of Schleswig-Holstein. He maintained that with the death of King Frederick the duchies' connection with Denmark had finally ended, making Schleswig-Holstein an independent state. Officials in Holstein refused to swear allegiance to King Christian, and the Holstein estates, supported by the local *Ritterschaft*, appealed to the Diet to recognise Duke Frederick.

These events were the signal for a massive outburst of national feeling which swept through Germany like a tidal wave carrying all before it. The Diet received innumerable addresses from local parliaments, learned societies and popular meetings usually organised by the *Nationalverein*, all demanding immediate recognition of Duke Frederick and the speedy admission of Schleswig-Holstein into the Confederation. The German princes did not dare resist the popular mood; many of them, like the grand duke of Baden, recognised Duke Frederick at once. Volunteers enlisted for war with Denmark, and historians and journalists vied with each other in demonstrating that the sacred voice of nationality took precedence over the paper clauses of the Treaty of London, a document imposed on a reluctant and impotent Germany by jealous foreign powers. Overnight the Augustenburg prince became the most popular figure in Germany, a symbol of the national will to live. Once again, as in 1848, the dynastic claims of the duke coincided with the national aspirations of the people, a fortuitous circumstance which united conservatives and liberals in his defence. On 18 November the Diet refused admittance to Christian IX's envoy and suspended the vote of Holstein and Lauenburg, a step which did not go far enough for ardent nationalists but too far for Austria and Prussia; acting together for the first time in recent years, they opposed the motion. In Berlin the opposition waited expectantly for Bismarck to take the initiative as Frederick William IV had done in 1848; for it was well known that the crown prince was a personal friend of Duke Frederick, and that the king himself favoured the duke's recognition.

The sequence of 1848 was not repeated. Bismarck remained unmoved by popular demonstrations. He had only contempt for those who 'chased after the phantom of popularity'. Cabinets, not peoples, made policy in his world, and self-interest, not sentiment, was the foundation of his Schleswig-Holstein policy: would Prussian interests be served by the creation of another independent state in North Germany likely to become a centre of pro-Austrian intrigue? The answer was emphatically no. The most desirable solution for Prussia would be annexation; Schleswig-Holstein with its excellent naval base at Kiel would enable Prussia to dominate the North Sea and Baltic. Therefore, as Bismarck admitted later, annexation was in his mind from the very beginning. But he was too much of a realist to exclude other solutions, such as personal union with Denmark; after all annexation seemed a rather remote possibility with public opinion so firmly in favour of the Augustenburgs; when Bismarck referred to annexation in the crown council in February 1864, the crown prince raised his hands in horror while King William assumed that his eccentric minister-president had been drinking too heavily at lunch.

German nationalists paid scant attention to the international aspects of the Schleswig-Holstein affair; they assumed that the cause of nationalism must inevitably triumph over the machinations of reactionary powers seeking to preserve the Danish monarchy. Bismarck, the practised diplomat, kept the Great Powers constantly in mind; as he remarked to a colleague, he was not concerned 'with the politics of the chamber and the press but only with the politics of Great Powers carried on by arms'. However much the Prussian liberals supported Duke Frederick, there could be no doubt that in point of law Christian IX was indisputably king of Denmark and duke of Schleswig-Holstein by the will of the Great Powers (including Prussia) who had signed the London treaty. At the same time Bismarck pointed out that Denmark had assumed certain obligations towards Austria and Prussia in respect of the duchies in 1851–52. By treating the arrangements of 1852 as a whole, Bismarck in fact established a conditional relationship between separate agreements; Prussia would only respect the London treaty as long as Denmark kept her promise; if Denmark broke her word, Prussia would feel free to act independently. However, the timing of this operation, as he warned the Prussian lower house in December, was a matter to be decided by the governments of Austria and Prussia, not by opposition liberals.

Austria's attitude to Schleswig-Holstein was of crucial importance. In fact there was little she could do to turn the affair to her advantage. The instinct of self-preservation made her oppose nationalism in Germany as she opposed it in Italy. What she now had to do was prevent Bismarck from allying Prussia with the forces of nationalism. When Bismarck behaved in a reassuringly conservative fashion by upholding the Treaty of London, Austrian fears abated. Disheartened by the failure of the Congress of Princes and disillusioned with liberalism at home, Austria was prepared psychologically for the alliance of January 1864. This alliance committed Austria and Prussia to joint military action against Denmark and stated that they would decide the future of the duchies by mutual agreement. Austria congratulated herself that she had taken Prussia prisoner, pinning the adventurous Bismarck down to a conservative policy. Bismarck was nearer the truth when he remarked that Prussia had hired Austria and that she was now working for the king of Prussia. King William, ever mistrustful of Austria, disliked the alliance; a threat of resignation as usual forced his hand. The Austrian alliance was a great stroke of good fortune for Bismarck; without it the conquest of Schleswig-Holstein might have been impossible. At a stroke of the pen he had put Austria in Prussian leading-strings and excluded the possibility of an understanding between France and Austria directed against Prussia.

Meanwhile the Diet was debating a most crucial issue; should its protest against Denmark be restricted to federal execution, an action implying recognition of the legality of Christian IX's title as duke of Holstein, or should it throw caution to the winds and order occupation, an action which implied that Christian was not the lawful duke and which would leave the door open for recognition of Duke Frederick? Austria and Prussia strongly opposed occupation as an infringement of the London treaty. For years Austria had led the smaller states against Prussia; now Austria had sided with Prussia against them, a *volte-face* which completely undermined her standing with them. The Diet, intimidated by this united front, settled reluctantly on 7 December, by eight votes to seven, for federal execution. There was a storm of protest from the liberals; Bismarck was denounced as a 'traitor to the national cause'. Conservatives were equally critical; King William was deeply incensed by Bismarck's refusal to recognise Duke Frederick and doubted whether his minister-president cared about Germany at all. A meeting, attended by 500 members of local parliaments and sponsored by the *Nationalverein*, met in Frankfurt. Full support was pledged for Duke Frederick, and a committee of thirty-six was set up to assume guidance of the national campaign. On Christmas Eve 1863, in accordance with the Diet's decision, Saxon and Hanoverian troops entered Holstein, the Danish forces having withdrawn without resistance. Duke Frederick at once set up court in Kiel and was enthusiastically acclaimed by his 'subjects'.

As the excitement mounted in Germany, Bismarck feared that the pressure of public opinion might sweep the Diet into precipitate action. There were already disturbing signs that the Diet might not hold back much longer. On 23 December Hesse-Darmstadt tabled a motion demanding the occupation of Schleswig. Bismarck sensed danger. Occupation, followed – as it assuredly would be – by recognition of Duke Frederick, might well provoke the Great Powers and lead to serious complications reducing Prussia's chances of annexing the duchies. On the other hand, if the Diet successfully defied the powers over Schleswig, liberalism would triumph in Germany. To keep the liberals as well as the Great Powers at bay, and to retain control of the situation, Bismarck decided to act independently of the Diet if need be. He had found a perfectly legitimate pretext for intervention; the November constitution uniting Schleswig with Denmark violated the promises made to Austria and Prussia in 1851–52.

At first Bismarck tried to persuade the Diet to follow the Austro-Prussian lead. On 28 December Austria and Prussia called for the occupation of Schleswig by federal forces but only until Denmark withdrew the offending constitution. The motion, which implied recognition of Christian IX, stood no chance of acceptance; the 'Third Germany' was already bitterly critical of Austro-Prussian attempts to suppress the committee of thirty-six and expel Duke Frederick from Holstein. There were scenes of uproar when, after the defeat of the motion on 14 January 1864, Austria and Prussia announced their intention of taking whatever action was deemed necessary without further reference to the Diet. On 16 January the Austro-Prussian alliance was signed, and an ultimatum dispatched to Denmark threatening her with the occupation of Schleswig unless she withdrew the constitution within forty-eight hours.

Untenable as their position was in international law, the Danes refused to submit. Britain, despite Palmerston's remarks in the House of Commons, did not come to their assistance, once it was clear that no continental power would support her. Russia added her voice to that of Britain in urging compliance with the ultimatum. King Christian was willing enough; the Eider Danes were not. So Denmark rejected the ultimatum, and on 1 February 1864 Austrian and Prussian forces crossed the Eider river. Within two weeks they had occupied the whole of Schleswig.

The Great Powers were naturally anxious to end the Danish war as quickly as possible. Britain took the initiative in proposing a conference of the Treaty-of-London powers in London in April, and a month's armistice was signed by the belligerents. It seemed to the German liberals that Bismarck had at last over-reached himself; he had gone to war as a conservative upholding international agreements; but a week before the conference met, Prussia inflicted a decisive defeat on the Danes at Düppel. This victory, coming after an indifferent campaign, confirmed Prussia's power and made it unlikely that the *status quo* could now be maintained. Liberal opinion was confident that Duke Frederick would be recognised by the powers whether Bismarck liked it or not.

Events proved them wrong. Bismarck, who did not come in person to London, stage-managed a great Prussian victory at the conference table. When the conference opened, Austria and Prussia at once declared that in the changed circumstances they could no longer abide by the London treaty, but left open the possibility of personal union, i.e. independent status for the duchies though they would retain their dynastic ties with Denmark. Bismarck could not openly oppose personal union, for ostensibly it had been the object of Prussian intervention. Still less did he favour it, as it brought annexation no nearer. Manoeuvring with incredible dexterity, he mobilised the German public opinion he despised against this solution. The powers were impressed by the evidence of widespread German support for Duke Frederick. France also came to Prussia's assistance, because Napoleon believed that the future of the duchies should be determined in accordance with the nationality principle. In the end the Danes rejected personal union, and the Great Powers tore up the London treaty, which, as far as Bismarck was concerned, had served its purpose of shielding a Prussian advance into Schleswig. Austria, frightened by Bismarck's talk of annexation, suddenly changed horses, making the daring proposal that the duchies be completely independent under Duke Frederick, a proposal which won them belated liberal support. Bismarck was taken by surprise but tagged along behind Austria, hoping somehow to turn the unwelcome proposal to his advantage by loosening the ties between the duchies and Denmark; he brought heavy pressure to bear on the duke, making it clear that Prussia could tolerate an independent Schleswig-Holstein only if Frederick turned himself into an obedient Prussian satellite (which he would not do). Again the Danes rescued Bismarck by rejecting this solution. Finally, the conference deadlocked over a French proposal to partition Schleswig on national lines. Bismarck favoured a line approximating roughly to the present frontier between West Germany and Denmark; the Danes insisted on a line further south. No compromise was possible and the conference ended on 25 June. As the Great Powers had destroyed the Treaty of London without agreeing on an alternative solution, the Schleswig-Holstein affair ceased to be an international problem and became a domestic German problem, the responsibility of Austria and Prussia. As Clarendon, the British representative, remarked to his Prussian colleague: 'You came to the conference masters of the situation and you leave it masters of the situation.'

The war continued and by July 1864 Denmark was defeated. Bismarck now attempted to secure the duchies for Prussia in return for a vague promise to help Austria in Northern Italy. Neither King William nor Emperor Francis Joseph was agreeable; the king felt he had no right to take the duchies and would only fight in Italy if Austria recognised Prussian hegemony in Germany; whilst the emperor would only agree to annexation if Austria received part of Silesia as compensation. The deadlock was broken only when Bismarck reluctantly agreed to joint ownership of the duchies, which were formally surrendered to Austria and Prussia in the Treaty of Vienna in October 1864. The victorious powers agreed privately to decide on the future of the duchies without reference to the Confederation.

Skilful as Bismarck's diplomacy was over Schleswig-Holstein, he owed almost as much to an exceptionally favourable international situation.

Germany was not surrounded by hostile powers, as the men of 1848 had been. No Great Power was prepared to fight for Denmark in 1864. France, the traditional friend of Denmark, would not help her; having lost Russia's friendship over Poland, Napoleon wanted to be Prussia's friend; he believed the duchies were German and ought to be annexed by Prussia in accordance with the nationality principle; in any case with Austria and Prussia united over Schleswig-Holstein, he could not move in Germany. Russia, it is true, was concerned about the strategic implications of changes in the Baltic, but had no objection to control passing from Danish to Prussian hands; as far as Russia could see this would not harm her – after all, conservative Prussia was not the radical parliament of 1848, and besides, Russia positively disliked the democratic nationalism of the Eider Danes. As for Britain, Palmerston finally decided that Prussian expansion in North Germany did not threaten her; France and Russia were her main enemies not Prussia; accordingly the British cabinet decided in June 1864 not to go to war to uphold the Treaty of London. Finally, the Danes, through misguided intransigence, played a not inconsiderable part in enabling Bismarck to detach the duchies from Denmark without facing a coalition of hostile powers.

By the autumn of 1864 it had dawned on Rechberg, Austrian foreign minister and architect of the pro-Prussian policy, that he had blundered; Austria had gained nothing by supporting Bismarck in Schleswig-Holstein. Nor had she succeeded in entering the German Customs Union when the members agreed in October to renew it the following year. She even failed to extract from Prussia a promise to consider Austrian membership. Rechberg, his policy completely discredited, resigned in October. His successor, Count Mensdorff, was an easy-going cavalry general unversed in foreign affairs, who relied for advice on Biegeleben, a foreign-office official, and on the conservative statesman Count Esterhazy, both bitter opponents of Bismarck. Under their influence Mensdorff made a despairing effort to revive Austria's prestige, sunk disastrously low in Germany. To demonstrate his independence of Berlin, Mensdorff took Duke Frederick under his wing and started to advocate recognition of the duke's claim to Schleswig-Holstein.

Bismarck had no intention of allowing the duchies to slip through his fingers. He was already tightening Prussia's grip over them, confident that Austria would soon lose interest in an area which did not directly concern her. In November 1864 Bismarck bullied a reluctant Diet into withdrawing federal forces from Holstein, leaving Austria and Prussia in complete control. In February 1865 Bismarck at last revealed to Austria the only terms on which Prussia could recognise Duke Frederick. They were even more onerous than those offered Frederick in June 1864. The duke stoutly refused to become a Prussian puppet, and Austria agreed with him that the terms were totally unacceptable. Despite her promise not to consult the Confederation over Schleswig-Holstein, Austria turned to the Diet in March and supported a Bavarian-Saxon motion calling for recognition of Duke Frederick. Prussia retaliated by moving her Baltic naval station from Danzig to Kiel. In April the Bavarian motion was carried, with Austria and Prussia on different sides. This was a turning-point; '. . . our tickets are on diverging lines', Bismarck observed ominously. Friction developed quickly over the administration of the duchies, and relations between the two powers deteriorated sharply. In the Prussian crown council in May 1865 the generals and the ministers pressed for annexation even at the risk of war; the king's opposition to war was weakening; only the crown prince held out against fratricidal war. Oddly enough, Bismarck now pleaded for moderation, feeling that he had not exhausted the possibilities of an understanding with Austria. As the tension mounted in the high summer, with Prussia insisting on the expulsion of Duke Frederick from Holstein, King William, accompanied by Bismarck, met Emperor Francis Joseph at Bad Gastein. Francis Joseph, distracted by serious domestic problems, proposed a compromise settlement which the king gratefully accepted. Under the terms of the Gastein Convention of August 1865 Austria was to administer Holstein and Prussia Schleswig. The duchy of Lauenburg was bought by Prussia, who was also given military and naval bases in Holstein. German liberals roundly condemned this agreement as a cynical division of the spoils which completely ignored the historic ties between the duchies and the claims of the Augustenburgs to rule over them.

Why did Bismarck agree to the Gastein Convention? Was it merely a postponement of the inevitable trial by battle – 'a stopping up of the cracks in the building', as Bismarck described it – because he was as yet unsure of France and Italy? Or was it a last attempt, as some historians suggest, to find a basis for a general *détente* which would allow these conservative powers to turn their attention once more to the real struggle against the forces of liberalism and democracy? The truth is that Bismarck was surprised by Austria's willingness to compromise and simply accepted a favourable offer which loosened Austria's hold over the duchies and avoided all reference to Duke Frederick. Bismarck's determination to force Austria out of Holstein and dominate Germany remained unchanged. At most Austria's willingness to agree to the convention suggested that she might even abandon the duchies to Prussia without war if sufficient pressure was brought to bear on her. But a general *détente* with Austria, based on a division of power in Germany, was now a remote possibility, as Bismarck was well aware.

Bismarck had to be certain of France in the event of war. In October 1865 he visited Napoleon at Biarritz. His opponents immediately accused him of wanting to surrender the Rhineland against a promise of French neutrality when war came. There were no firm offers at Biarritz, only innuendoes and insinuations. Bismarck successfully allayed French fears about the Gastein Convention and encouraged Napoleon to believe that war was inevitable between Austria and Prussia; the emperor was delighted by the prospect of what he assumed would be a long war; and he dreamt of imposing terms on the exhausted belligerents in the manner of his uncle half a century before. Bismarck's major objective at Biarritz was simply to prevent a Franco-Austrian alliance. This he sought to do by assuring Napoleon that Prussia would not support Austrian attempts to hold on to Venetia. Once Napoleon had been assured on this score, he readily repudiated the thought of an Austrian alliance. Beyond this there were some vague hints of compensation for France, should Prussia expand in Germany. Bismarck returned to Berlin reasonably certain that he need not fear French intervention as the crisis deepened in Germany in 1866.

The improvement in Austro-Prussian relations following the Gastein Convention was short-lived. By the end of 1865 there was renewed friction over the duchies. In January 1866 Austria allowed a mass meeting to be held in Altona, outside Hamburg, in support of Duke Frederick. Bismarck denounced Austria's action and threatened to end the Austro-Prussian alliance. Austria coolly retorted that Holstein was no concern of Prussia's. The alliance had in effect broken down and the drift to war had started. On 28 February 1866 the Prussian crown council decided to take up the Austrian challenge even at the risk of war. A few days later Biegeleben and Esterhazy persuaded Francis Joseph to strengthen his forces in Bohemia.

The international situation was again favourable for Prussia. Britain and Russia could be relied upon not to intervene in the war. France would probably stay out of it. Only Italy remained doubtful. Encouraged by Napoleon, Italy allied with Prussia in April. Strictly speaking this was a breach of the confederate constitution which forbade alliances with foreign powers. Military considerations were involved in the Italian alliance; Helmuth von Moltke, chief of the Prussian general staff, wanted to attack Austria on two fronts to be certain of victory. Political considerations were, as usual, uppermost in Bismarck's mind; if Prussia promised to help Italy obtain Venetia, Napoleon would certainly remain neutral. In an age when public opinion was beginning to count, a war fought to unify Italy would have a better press than an old-fashioned war of expansion in North Germany. As usual, Bismarck was cautious to the very last, leaving escape routes open; the alliance merely stated that if Prussia went to war with Austria within the next three months Italy would join in and take Venetia.

By the end of April military preparations were under way in Austria and Prussia. Austria was anxious not to incur the odium of aggression by mobilising first. In April she offered to stop her military preparations if Prussia did the same. At the king's request Bismarck reluctantly agreed; the most he could do in the official reply was make Prussian disarmament dependent on Austria. Then on 21 April the situation was suddenly transformed; hearing rumours of Italian troop movements, Austria mobilised her southern armies. The king's scruples were overcome at last; convinced that Austria had never been in earnest, William ordered mobilisation.

With war a near certainty, Bismarck was anxious to win general support for Prussia in Germany. Much as he despised nationalism and democracy he never hesitated to exploit them shamelessly in Prussia's interests. On 9 April, the day after the Italian treaty, Prussia proposed in the Diet that a directly elected parliament based on universal suffrage be called to discuss reform of the Confederation. Governments inside and outside of Germany were amazed. 'This is revolution', cried King William in horror; 'What can that matter to Your Majesty', enquired Bismarck, 'if universal suffrage puts you on a rock where the waters can never reach you' . . .? In fact the stratagem misfired; most Germans were unimpressed by Bismarck's resurrection of the 1849 franchise, seeing in it yet another tactical manoeuvre by an inveterate political gambler. Bismarck was equally unorthodox in the use he made of national discontents. Since 1862 he had been in touch with underground agents of Kossuth, the Hungarian nationalist leader, now in exile in Italy; on the eve of war Bismarck encouraged the formation of a Magyar legion to fight Austria and supported attempts in Serbia and Rumania to exploit national feeling against the Habsburgs.

Austria made a last attempt to win the support of the smaller states in the coming struggle. On 1 June 1866 she asked the Diet to decide the future of Schleswig-Holstein and announced that the Holstein estates would be called to express their views. As Austria's proposal was a breach of the 1864 alliance, Bismarck at once terminated the Gastein Convention. Consequently the *condominium* established by the Treaty of Vienna (1864) came into force once more; this entitled Prussia to send troops into Holstein which she did on 7 June. Austria obligingly withdrew, much to Bismarck's annoyance, for he had expected Austria to resist and provide him with a pretext for war. Unfortunately the local commanders continued to act like gentlemen long after their governments had ceased to. On 10 June Prussia outlined her plans for a new state which would exclude Austria from Germany. On 11 June Austria replied to the occupation of Holstein by moving in the Diet that the federal army be mobilised against Prussia on the grounds that she had violated the Gastein Convention. Strictly speaking, the motion was out of order, as the Diet had not been a party to the convention. King William's moral scruples against war were overcome at last. Prussia warned all states that a vote for the Austrian motion would be regarded in Berlin as a declaration of war on Prussia. On 12 June Austria and Prussia severed diplomatic relations. The final scene in the drama was enacted on 14 June, when a modified version of the Austrian motion was carried by nine votes to six with one abstention.[2] The Prussian representatives at once declared the Confederation dissolved and called upon the states to follow the Prussian lead and found a new German state. On 15 June Prussia delivered ultimatums to Saxony, Hanover and Hesse-Cassel, ordering them to demobilise and accept the Prussian reform proposals. As satisfactory replies were not received from these states, Prussian forces invaded them on 16 June 1866. The German war had begun.

Contemporaries expected a long war ending in an Austrian victory. In Paris the betting odds were four to one in her favour. Austria had the active military support of the larger German states, whilst Prussia had only one ally of consequence, Italy, and she was heavily defeated on land at Custozza and at sea in the battle of Lissa. Moltke thought a hard fight certain and Bismarck talked of falling in battle. Public opinion was overwhelmingly hostile to Prussia and especially to Bismarck, who was condemned for deliberately plunging Germany into fratricidal strife to further Prussian interests. Contemporaries were wrong about the war; within seven weeks it was all over. Within the first three days Saxony, Hanover and Hesse-Cassel were occupied, giving Prussia complete mastery of North and Central Germany. The Hanoverians won a victory at Langensalza, but by the end of June their army had capitulated. The decisive battle of the war took place on 3 July at Königgrätz (Sadowa), when the Austrian armies in Bohemia were routed by three Prussian armies. Resistance in South Germany crumbled away after Sadowa and ceased by the end of July. The Prussian victory was due not to great numerical superiority – in Bohemia 221,000 Prussians faced a combined Austrian and Saxon army of 215,000 – but to the meticulous planning of Moltke and to the superior fire-power of the new needle-gun.

Napoleon was as surprised as anyone else by the news of Sadowa. He recovered quickly when Austria offered Venetia to him and requested his assistance in restoring peace. On 5 July he announced his intention of acting as mediator. Bismarck reluctantly accepted, feeling that if he refused, French military intervention was possible, and that Russia, alarmed by the collapse of Austria, might then be drawn into the war. In fact it was not difficult to persuade Napoleon, already a sick man, to endorse the terms offered to Austria in the Nikolsburg preliminary peace; the Confederation was dissolved and superseded by the North German Confederation from which Austria was excluded; Prussia, now the dominant military power north of the river Main, annexed Schleswig-Holstein, Hanover, Hesse-Cassel, Frankfurt and Nassau; the addition of four-and-a-half million inhabitants helped to make Prussia a more German power although this wholesale violation of the legitimacy principle caused consternation in conservative circles and distressed the king. Napoleon

[2]Prussia abstained; Brunswick, the Free Cities, Luxemburg, the Mecklenburgs, Oldenburg and the grand-ducal and ducal Saxon houses voted against the motion.

appreciated that the creation of Little Germany altered power relationships in Northern Europe decisively in Prussia's favour; to preserve some semblance of a balance of power he insisted that Prussia respect the independence of the four southern states, Bavaria, Baden, Württemberg and Hesse-Darmstadt. For the time being this was perfectly acceptable to Bismarck. It was also agreed that the states remain outside the North German Confederation with the option of forming their own union. Napoleon naturally hoped that these states would look to Paris for protection, giving him a pretext for unlimited interference in Germany. Finally, Bismarck agreed to a plebiscite in North Schleswig to allow those Danes who wished to do so to join Denmark. Napoleon was reasonably satisfied. The principle of nationality had been recognised; Italy had Venetia, Denmark would have North Schleswig, and Germany was partially united – that all Germans were not united pleased him, for neither in Italy nor Germany did Napoleon wish to see strong states arising. In addition to this, hints made during the negotiations with Prussia encouraged Napoleon to believe that he would receive territorial compensation in the near future.

Bismarck's most difficult task in the summer of 1866 was not to placate France or reassure Russia but simply to restrain the Prussian monarch and his generals. King William had opposed war to the very last; once it started he worked himself into a fury of moral indignation against Austria and, supported by his generals, demanded that Austria be severely punished for her misdeeds. For Bismarck the war had served its purpose. Why then needlessly humiliate Austria by taking territories off her and parading Prussian troops through the streets of Vienna? His task, as he remarked to his wife in these critical days, was that of 'pouring water into sparkling wine and making it understood that Prussia doesn't live alone in Europe but with three nations who hate and envy her.' He had the crown prince on his side, but only with great difficulty and by reducing himself to a state of nervous exhaustion did he finally persuade King William to leave Austria intact.

The signature of the preliminary Peace of Nikolsburg on 26 July and the definitive Peace of Prague on 23 August 1866 was a turning-point in German and European history. This was, as the Swiss historian Jakob Burckhardt remarked, 'the great German revolution'. The war had not united Germany but divided it. The German Confederation, like the old Holy Roman Empire, included all the lands historically associated with the German people from the Tyrol to the Baltic. The war of 1866 destroyed this unity. Germany was divided into three: the area north of the river Main under Prussian domination, four Southern states enjoying a precarious independence, and Austria, soon to become part of the new state of Austria-Hungary. These arrangements were in fact provisional. By 1871 the southern states were united with the North German

Confederation. But Austria and Germany were divided for ever.[3] German political influence no longer extended to the Adriatic but ended at the Austrian frontier posts. Conservatives such as Frantz mourned the passing of the old Confederation and looked into the future with trepidation. Some writers have seen in the collapse of Germany and Austria-Hungary in 1918, the fragmentation of Central Europe between the two world wars, and the new division of Europe in 1945, ample confirmation of the gloomy conservative prognostications of 1866. Nostalgia for a lost order must not blind one to hard historical realities. In 1866, when the nation state was reaching the height of its potency as a political ideal, Little Germany was the only possible solution to the German problem once the Habsburgs made their understandable but fatal decision not to allow Austria and Bohemia to become part of Greater Germany.

Once Bismarck had settled accounts with Austria, he quickly abandoned his attempts to disrupt the empire by encouraging national discontents; henceforth he sought to maintain Austria as a Great Power, a conservative barrier against revolution, as she had been in Metternich's day. But Austria was more profoundly affected by her defeat than Bismarck realised. Thrust out of Germany and Italy, her centre of gravity moved to South-Eastern Europe; she began to look down the Danube to the Balkans with all that this implied for the peace of Europe in the next fifty years. Furthermore the termination of the German connexion weakened irreparably the position of the Germans in the empire. The Habsburgs were obliged at last to share power with non-Germans; the *Ausgleich* of 1867 which created Austria-Hungary was a direct result of the defeat in Bohemia.

The Peace of Prague aroused serious misgivings in France. Influential political circles felt that France had been defeated at Sadowa just as much as Austria; the balance of power in Europe was moving in favour of Prussia, and to even it up again it was imperative that France obtain territorial compensation. Napoleon was at first satisfied with the peace settlement. But he easily succumbed to the pressure of advisers, and early in August he demanded the cession of the Saarland and the Bavarian and Hessian territory on the left bank of the Rhine as well as a Prussian withdrawal from the frontiers of Luxemburg. A month earlier Bismarck might have sacrificed the Rhineland to make certain of victory over Austria. Now he threatened to call up the demon of a nationalist uprising against France. He also put the French demands to good use in Germany, where he was currently negotiating separate peace treaties with the four southern states. By revealing these demands to them he stampeded the alarmed states into signing secret offensive-defensive alliances with Prussia (*Schutz- und Trutzbündnisse*) which required them to remodel their armies on Prussian

---

[3]Reunited in 1938, they parted company once more in 1945.

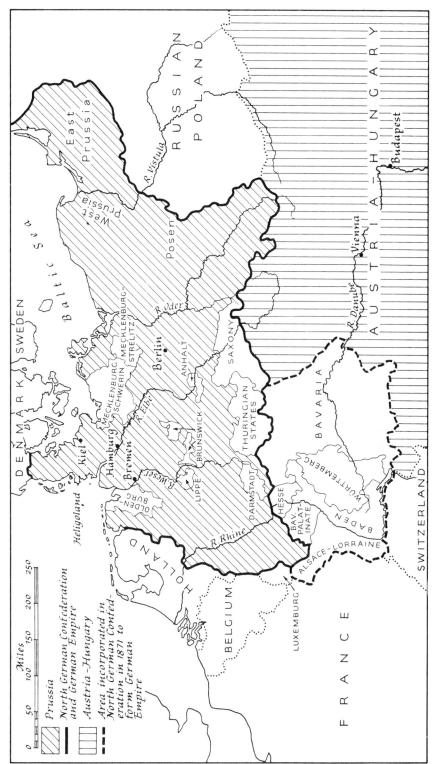

Map 2: The Unification of Germany 1867–71

lines and put their troops under Prussian command in wartime. This meant that the idea of a truly independent southern confederation had received a mortal blow before the Treaty of Prague was signed. Faced with determined Prussian resistance, Napoleon withdrew the demands and dismissed his foreign minister Drouyn de Lhys. Rouher, his successor, dropped the demands for German territory and tried instead to tempt Prussia with an offer of alliance on condition that Prussia allowed France to annex Luxemburg and Belgium. A French alliance did not interest Bismarck; though he hinted that he would not oppose France if she could acquire Luxemburg by negotiation with the interested parties. He carefully preserved a copy of the draft plan for the acquisition of Belgium written in the French ambassador's own hand; in 1870 this was put to good use to discredit France.

Sadowa made a deep impression on the political scene in North Germany. The Prussian opposition had already been weakened and divided by the Danish war. The victory at Düppel aroused memories of past military glories, and some liberals began to feel that Prussia had really acted for Germany in Schleswig-Holstein, however contemptuous Bismarck was of Duke Frederick; one-third of the *Nationalverein* resigned in the autumn and some prominent liberals, including Twesten, Mommsen and Miquel, came out openly in support of the annexation of the duchies by Prussia. But most liberals remained impaled on the horns of a cruel dilemma; to support annexation would be a repudiation of liberal principle and an act of abject surrender to Bismarck, the arch-enemy of liberalism; on the other hand, to oppose annexation was to oppose the expansion of the one power likely to promote unification. So the constitutional struggle continued throughout 1865 and was in fact reaching a new intensity on the eve of the war as a result of the government's prosecution of two deputies for critical speeches made in the lower house. Bismarck's reform proposals in April 1865 aroused little interest in Prussia, where liberals were generally apprehensive at the prospect of a long war and fearful of the social revolution which would assuredly follow Bismarck's defeat. Sadowa resolved their doubts. The voices of the critics were suddenly stilled and lost in a great wave of acclamation which arose from many parts of Germany. The atmosphere in the north was described vividly by a contemporary journalist: 'I never breathed in my life a more invigorating air than the one which blew in the autumn of 1866 through North Germany. It cast an incomparable spell over us. One felt as if one were standing at the threshold of a new period, a period which promised miracles. One lived under the impression of a surprise which had come so suddenly and with such overwhelming fullness that the patriots who a short while before had been full of fears and sombre premonitions suddenly felt like dreamers.'

The effects of the war were at once apparent in the elections to the lower house of the Landtag which by chance were held on the same day as

Sadowa, though the news of the battle was not known until later. Even so, the opposition suffered a sharp reverse being reduced to 148 seats whilst the conservatives who previously held only thirty-eight seats returned with 142. A few conservatives led by the high-principled Gerlachs were shocked by Bismarck's ruthless repudiation of the legitimacy principle where it suited his purpose in North Germany. But most of them were jubilant over the military victory and confidently expected a *coup d'état*, a domestic Düppel, and a return to the old absolutism. Bismarck did not oblige them. On the contrary, he introduced a bill to indemnify the government for illegal collection of taxes since 1862. Bismarck had not repented of his quarrel with the lower house; he was simply astute enough to see that a parliament of sorts was essential for the smooth running of the new Confederation and that he must win the support of moderate liberals if he was to keep control of it. As King William grew older, these new political allies would be a reinsurance policy against the day when Bismarck's enemy, the crown prince, ascended the throne. The stratagem succeeded; the indemnity bill was carried by a large majority on 3 September 1866, opposed only by a few Progressives and Catholics. German liberalism had suffered a serious defeat; the lower house had legalised the government's actions since 1862 in return for an admission that the government had violated the constitution; but there was no assurance that the constitution would not be violated again; indeed King William, replying to the address from the lower house, embarrassed the government by stating bluntly that he would do the same again if he had to.

The liberals, as Bismarck anticipated, were split asunder over the bill. The left-wing Progressives, led by Virchow and Waldeck, opposed it. The principles of constitutional government mattered as much as, if not more than, unification to this small group of high-minded and intransigent idealists; as the veteran radical Jacoby remarked, 'Unity without freedom is a unity of slaves'; to accept the bill without any guarantee of real progress towards constitutional government or any cessation of the relentless persecution of the opposition would be a craven act of surrender; no foreign political success, however great, could justify this betrayal of the ethical principles of liberalism.

Right-wing Progressives joined with moderate liberals of the centre in support of the bill. These right-wing liberals led by Twesten and Lasker coalesced with non-Prussian liberals – there were many of these in the new Reichstag of 1867 – to found the National Liberal party. Many members of this upper-middle-class party had an economic stake in a united Germany, and all of them were dazzled by Prussia's military achievements. They looked to Bismarck to complete the unification of Germany by bringing the southern states into the Confederation, and pledged unconditional support to Prussia in the field of foreign affairs. The *Nationalverein* had now served its purpose and dissolved itself in October

1867, its propaganda activities being continued by the new party.

At home the National Liberals, who had long wearied of the constitutional struggle, grasped gratefully at the straw of the indemnity bill. They were determined to avoid the 'sterile and doctrinaire' liberalism of the left. It seemed sheer futility to continue in opposition after the national triumph of 1866 – if they did so they were likely to lose votes to the conservatives. They were also much more aware than the followers of Virchow and Waldeck of the structural weakness of Prussian liberalism. In the new situation political realism seemed the only sensible policy. Miquel, co-founder of the *Nationalverein* and now a National Liberal leader, expressed their basic philosophy in a memorable passage: 'The time for idealism is over. German unification has descended from the realm of speculation to the prosaic world of reality. Today politicians should be much less concerned than ever before with what is desirable in politics as opposed to what is attainable.' National Liberals were not fervent believers in parliamentary government; their ideal was a 'constitutional system' in which parliament and the executive had equal rights. They sincerely hoped that the new Reichstag would, in the fullness of time, attain a position of equality with the government. And they were encouraged to believe that they could have the best of both worlds on the basis of their modest success over the 1867 constitution.

The draft constitution placed before the constituent assembly of the North German Confederation in 1867 bore the imprint of Bismarck. It was designed with the express purpose of preserving Prussian predominance in Germany. Bismarck achieved this only after strenuous efforts, and by exploiting the conflicts of interest in German society in masterly fashion to produce a fine balance of forces which left effective power in Prussian hands. Prussian ascendancy was openly recognised in that the king of Prussia became president of the Confederation; he was solely responsible for foreign policy; he alone could declare war and make peace, and as commander-in-chief he controlled the confederate army. But in order to appease conservative-particularist elements in the smaller states, where Prussia was feared and disliked, Bismarck allowed the princes to remain on their thrones (apart from the annexed territories), vested sovereignty in them and let them manage their own internal affairs. They were also given control of the most important organ established by the constitution, the Bundesrat or federal council. The council consisted of representatives from the twenty-four states in the Confederation; through a series of committees they supervised the administration and voted in accordance with instructions from their governments much as in Metternich's Federal Diet. Appearances were deceptive; the federal chancellor – the chief executive officer, chosen by Prussia – was to preside over Bundesrat meetings and, as Prussia had seventeen of the forty-three votes, she would have effective control over that body. To hold conservatism in check and to appease liberalism – a much stronger force in the non-Prussian territories than in Prussia itself – Bismarck created a Reichstag elected by universal suffrage. Again appearances were deceptive; the powers of this body were severely limited; it had no control over the Bundesrat; legislation passed by the Reichstag required the consent of the Bundesrat; the army establishment and the army grant were permanently fixed in the so-called 'iron budget', which was outside Reichstag control; all the Reichstag was permitted to discuss was the distribution of the non-military expenditure – less than one per cent of the total – and this only triennially. Clearly Bismarck did not intend this emasculated Reichstag to be much more than an organ of public opinion, a political safety valve playing an insignificant part in public life. Speaking in confidence to a Saxon minister, Bismarck admitted that he was trying 'to destroy parliamentarianism by parliamentarianism', in the hope that the antics of an impotent Reichstag would finally discredit parliamentary institutions in German eyes.

The National Liberals were dissatisfied and urged Bismarck to give the Reichstag a share of real power. With seventy-nine seats the National Liberals were the largest party in the constituent Reichstag, occupying a decisive position between the Free Conservatives and the older liberals who supported Bismarck unconditionally, and the handful of Progressives still fighting the battles of 1861. In the end Bismarck, being anxious to preserve a united front at home and abroad, conceded some ground to the critics. He refused to accept a National Liberal proposal that the heads of administrative offices countersign ordinances, fearing that this would open the door to responsible government. But he agreed to make the chancellor 'responsible' for all ordinances, whilst carefully leaving the nature of this responsibility undefined. This change enhanced the importance of the chancellorship and probably decided him finally to assume this office in addition to that of Prussian foreign minister. Faced with demands for increased budgetary powers, he allowed the Reichstag to debate all expenditure annually. In return the National Liberals accepted the 'iron budget' for a transitional four years, after which new arrangements would be made and submitted to the Reichstag for approval. Bismarck conceded the secret ballot in elections – a concession which National Liberals hoped would prevent the exploitation of universal suffrage (which they secretly disliked) by conservatives; he also allowed officials to seek election but refused to pay deputies a salary, fearing the growth of a class of professional politicians. There was no declaration of fundamental rights in this constitution, a Progressive motion to this effect being only narrowly defeated. These changes certainly increased the effective power of the Reichstag but they did not alter the authoritarian character of the new Confederation or weaken the overall power of Prussia. In its amended form the constitution was approved by 230 votes to 53.

The final votes were taken at the height of the Luxemburg crisis. Luxemburg was a small German-speaking grand duchy situated between France, Belgium and Germany. Originally part of the Holy Roman Empire, Luxemburg had changed hands frequently since the fifteenth century and in 1815 became a member of the German Confederation with the Dutch king as grand duke. In 1852 she became a member of the German Customs Union, although the population would probably have preferred union with Belgium. Luxemburg was neutral in the 1866 war. She did not join the North German Confederation, but the Prussian garrison which had been stationed in the federal fortress of Luxemburg was not withdrawn.

For some years France had wished to acquire Luxemburg as a stepping-stone to Belgium. In 1866 Bismarck assured the French that he would not oppose their designs on Luxemburg. In March 1867 the French practically persuaded King William III of Holland, a ruler with expensive tastes and limited means, to sell his sovereign rights in Luxemburg. By this time news of the private negotiations leaked out, causing a popular outcry in Germany. National Liberals, eager to cross the river Main, seized on this fresh evidence of French designs on German soil, and demanded that Prussia defend Germany's national honour even to the point of war. Bismarck cared little about the fate of the German-speaking people in a grand duchy of no strategic importance to Prussia. But the violence of the popular reaction possibly surprised Bismarck and compelled him to modify his accommodating attitude to France. At any rate he now had to struggle to retain control of the situation and to reduce the temperature on both sides of the Rhine. To impress the French with the danger of war and to warn them off Luxemburg, he revealed the existence of the alliances with the southern states. As the excitement mounted with rumours of the Dutch king's signature of a treaty of cession, Bismarck told the Reichstag on 1 April 1867 that the Luxemburg affair was a European question which would be settled by negotiation, although as a gesture of appeasement he assured his audience that German rights in Luxemburg would be defended. Bismarck certainly did not want war with France in 1867, when Prussia had not yet recovered from the effects of the 1866 war and when the international situation was unfavourable. Most important of all, as he remarked to an acquaintance, 'The chance of success is not a just cause for beginning a great war'; it would suffice if he could extricate himself from an unexpected crisis; as for the larger issue of Franco-German relations, Bismarck fully intended, as always, to examine every possibility of a peaceful settlement before resorting to violence.

The French were stranded again. They could not secure Russian or Austrian support for their scheme. and the king of Holland refused to sign the cession treaty without prior Prussian consent. Bismarck had no wish to humiliate France. On the contrary, he helped her save face by proposing that the Great Powers, who had regulated the affairs of Belgium and Luxemburg in 1839, be called together to solve the problem. Eventually the tension abated; France agreed to Bismarck's proposal, and a conference met in London in May 1867. The king of Holland was obliged to keep his grand duchy, its perpetual neutrality was guaranteed by the Great Powers, the Prussian garrison was withdrawn and the fortress of Luxemburg was demolished.

The crisis had passed without war, although a sense of crisis persisted in Europe, and war between France and Germany remained a distinct possibility in the near future. This was a decisive moment in Franco-German relations. Before 1867 Napoleon was virtually in control of French foreign policy. He had accepted great changes in Germany with a fairly easy conscience, since they accorded with his own views on nationality and because he hankered after an understanding with Prussia in order to weaken Austria, his uncle's old enemy. After the crisis Napoleon was bitterly disillusioned in Bismarck, hopes of a Prussian alliance were buried, and anti-Prussian advisers gained the upper hand over the ailing emperor. These men reverted to the old policy of keeping Germany weak and divided as far as this was possible by 1867; acutely conscious of growing discontent at home, they determined not to retreat any further east of the Rhine; if the second Empire was to survive, France must resist the union of North and South Germany at all costs.

This was possibly a decisive moment in German history as well. Bismarck had followed in the footsteps of his predecessors and had succeeded by skilful diplomacy in establishing Prussian ascendancy in North and Central Germany. But the defeat of Austria and the emergence of the North German Confederation decisively altered the balance of power in Central Europe and opened up the prospect of further conquests. Nationalist pressure for the completion of Little Germany coincided with the power-political interest of Prussia in absorbing South Germany. After the Luxemburg Crisis it was likely that this could be achieved only by war.

That does not mean that he expected to complete the unification of Germany in the near future. Certainly the tide in South Germany was running in favour of union in the summer of 1866. South-German liberal leaders meeting in Stuttgart expressed their desire for immediate union; in Württemberg a German party was formed to work for this goal; the Baden chamber passed a resolution favouring union, and a strong minority in the Bavarian chamber supported a similar motion. This was a temporary phenomenon. After the peace was signed the old particularism quickly reasserted itself. Particularist parties flourished in Württemberg and Baden, where the mass of the people – as opposed to the upper-middle-class minority – were deeply suspicious of Prussia and sympathetic to Austria. This widespread animosity was partly religious in origin, for Catholicism was a powerful and deeply entrenched force, especially in

Bavaria. It was also an instinctive reaction against any diminution of local privilege; the large-scale annexations in North and Central Germany as well as the constitution of the new Confederation confirmed the old fears of Prussian domination; the liberal-minded foreign minister of Baden bluntly described the Confederation as a 'union of a dog with its fleas'. Southern governments encountered difficulty in persuading their legislatures to accept the military treaties with Prussia. The Luxemburg crisis aroused great apprehension south of the river Main where there was little desire to be dragged into war. Only in Baden was the desire for union widespread and sustained, perhaps because proximity to France gave cause for alarm.

Reform of the Customs Union did relatively little to promote unification. In the old customs union, which was essentially a loose association of states, the veto rights enjoyed by members made the negotiation of commercial treaties a laborious undertaking. In 1867, under heavy pressure from Berlin, the machinery was overhauled and new institutions set up to determine common policies; this was done in effect by extending the machinery of the North German Confederation; nominated members from the south were added to the Bundesrat to form a *Zollbundesrat*, and elected members from the south took part in the deliberations of the Reichstag on commercial matters forming a *Zollparlament*. These contacts between north and south could not but erode barriers of prejudice, but when elections were held in the south in 1868 the result was a political reverse; Bismarck was bitterly disappointed when forty-nine opponents of union and only thirty-five supporters were returned.

Although Bismarck now believed final unification inevitable, he kept a completely open mind about the means and timing of unification. He was fully aware that popular resistance to union in the south was so strong that final unification in the near future would be possible only after a victorious war against France. War apart, unification would be the end-product of an evolutionary process spread out over the next twenty or thirty years. Early in 1869 he summarised his current attitude in a letter to the Prussian minister in Munich: 'That German unity would be furthered by violent events I also hold probable. But it is quite another question to assume the mission of bringing about a violent catastrophe and the responsibility for the choice of timing. Arbitrary interference in the course of history, motivated on purely subjective grounds, has never had any other result than the shaking down of unripe fruit. That German unity is not at this moment a ripe fruit is in my opinion obvious . . . We can put the clocks forward, but time does not on that account move any faster, and the ability to wait, while the situation develops, is a prerequisite of practical politics.'

While Bismarck waited on events, France took the diplomatic initiative, seeking allies to help her contain Prussia and prevent final unification. Russia was not to be bought, and Britain was in an isolationist mood. This left Austria-Hungary, and in the summer of 1867 Napoleon III met Francis Joseph at Salzburg. Beust, the new Austrian chancellor and a Saxon by birth, was eager enough for revenge; the difficulty was that Austria was rapidly losing interest in Germany and turning increasingly to South-Eastern Europe. She wanted a firm promise of French aid against Russia before she would commit herself against Prussia. No progress was made. Nor was the deadlock broken when the Italians joined the negotiations in 1868. Italy would only fight Prussia if the French garrison was withdrawn from Rome, a price Napoleon, being dependent on Catholic support, dare not pay. An approach to Russia in 1869 did not rescue France from her isolation; Russia had nothing to gain from war with Prussia and much to lose. Then in January 1870 French policy changed direction with the birth of the liberal empire. The new cabinet headed by Émile Ollivier, former leader of the opposition, recognised that unification was inevitable and decided not to intervene in Germany provided that the union of north and south was effected by peaceful means – a view which commended itself to the rapidly failing emperor. This seemed likely to bring about an improvement in Franco-German relations. Yet six months later the two powers were locked in mortal combat over the Spanish throne candidature.

In 1868 revolution occurred in Spain. Queen Isabella was driven out, and the Spaniards looked around Europe for a new ruler. After Portuguese and Italian candidates had declined the throne, the Spanish provisional government approached the Hohenzollern-Sigmaringens, a Catholic branch of the Hohenzollern house which had already supplied Rumania with a king in 1866. Early in 1870 General Prim, the Spanish envoy, asked Karl Anton, head of the Hohenzollern-Sigmaringen house, to allow his son Leopold, whose wife was a Portuguese princess, to accept the crown. At first Leopold was most reluctant. Apparently Bismarck had not known of the general's first visit to Germany in the autumn of 1869; informed of the second approach in February 1870, Bismarck urged the Sigmaringens to accept.

What were Bismarck's motives? As usual, complex. By the beginning of 1870 Bismarck seems to have been seeking ways and means of refloating the stranded ship of unification in the interests of domestic politics; local elections in Bavaria in November 1869 had revealed the strength of particularism and weakened the pro-Prussian ministry. In February 1870 Bismarck was accused of indifference to the national cause by the National Liberals when he opposed a motion in the Reichstag for immediate union with Baden on the grounds that it was ill-timed. Elections to the Reichstag were due in 1870, and it was clearly essential that the government control the newly elected assembly, as it would have the right of reviewing the 'iron budget'. Bismarck was working on a scheme to make William emperor of the Confederation, or perhaps emperor of Germany, in the hope that a prestige victory for the Hohenzollerns would impress the liberals and restore their faith in the chancellor. As he was making little headway with his scheme, the offer to the Sigmaringens came at an opportune moment. No doubt Bismarck feared that if the Sigmaringens refused, the reigning houses in Bavaria or Baden might supply candidates, an unwelcome development likely to strengthen particularism still further. Furthermore, he wanted to put a spoke in the wheel of the French, who were still hoping for an Austrian alliance; in the spring of 1870 Archduke Albrecht arrived in Paris to discuss the military terms of an understanding.

At first the Ollivier government seemed to hold out prospects of a permanent change in French policy. Then early in May, after a successful plebiscite, the Duc de Gramont was appointed foreign minister. Bismarck grew suddenly apprehensive, convinced that this dedicated opponent of Prussia would pursue a bellicose policy likely to end in war. The appointment was an added incentive for Bismarck to reanimate the faltering negotiations between the Sigmaringens and the Spaniards. What his real intentions were towards the French continues to be debated by historians. One view is that he hoped to deflate France by a sophisticated exercise in brinkmanship. Acceptance of the Spanish crown by a Hohenzollern could hardly fail to wound French pride; hopefully, the French would vent their fury on Napoleon, so weakening France that unification could be completed without fear of French interference. On the other hand, some historians nowadays incline to the much older view that Bismarck was working from the start for a war which could accomplish his ends at a stroke. Whichever view is favoured, one thing is certain: Bismarck kept war in mind throughout the crisis.

On 19 June Leopold was prevailed upon to accept the Spanish throne. Reluctantly King William endorsed the candidature. The Spanish envoy, Salazar, telegraphed his government that he would return in a few days; the Cortes would then formally elect Leopold, and Europe would be presented with a *fait accompli*. A Madrid cipher clerk decoded a crucial phrase in the telegram incorrectly, an error which led the government to order prorogation of the Cortes until the autumn instead of keeping it in session until Salazar's return. When he arrived in Madrid on 28 June the 'secret' was common gossip and by 3 July it was known in Paris.

The French government, assailed by opponents on the right and left for its feeble foreign policy, dare not suffer a fresh humiliation at the hands of Bismarck. With full cabinet support Gramont made a flamboyant statement in the chamber of deputies on 6 July in which he declared that a Hohenzollern on the throne of Charles V represented a threat to the balance of power, jeopardised the interests and honour of France and would not be tolerated. The Great Powers disapproved of the inflammatory language, but the chamber, packed with ardent imperialists, applauded the sentiments vigorously. The French press denounced the German strategem to put a Hohenzollern in a Spanish sentry-box to keep France in order, and demanded full satisfaction from Prussia. Not that the government wanted war; what it feared was another diplomatic defeat certain to destroy the empire; to prevent this and to retrieve French fortunes the government was ready to go to the brink of war, confident that if it stood firm and rattled the sabre Prussia would give way and the imperial throne would be saved. The declaration of 6 July had already served one of its purposes by stilling the clamour of Napoleon's opponents and uniting them behind the government.

Things went badly for Bismarck. Under French pressure Spain agreed that the Sigmaringens could withdraw the candidature. The Great Powers, who regarded the whole affair as an intrigue against France and wanted a peaceful settlement, urged the Sigmaringens to do so. Finally Karl Anton decided on withdrawal and telegraphed the decision to Madrid. King William was immensely relieved. Bismarck put on a brave front, pretending that he had expected this development. In fact he was badly put out by the turn of events; he felt betrayed by his king and was depressed by the diplomatic implications of withdrawal for Prussia. He did not resign, because he hoped somehow to minimise the French victory.

For victory it certainly was, a triumph sufficient to restore the fortunes of France. Napoleon and Ollivier felt that honour was satisfied. Gramont did not. He was intent on extracting the maximum out of the victory. Supported by influential newspapers and deputies and by a growing number of Frenchmen who felt that withdrawal was not enough, Gramont got his way. Benedetti, French ambassador to Prussia, was instructed to ask King William for confirmation of the withdrawal of the candidature – a perfectly proper request – and for a promise that it would never be renewed – a demand calculated to humiliate Prussia and reveal the degree of her dependence on Paris.

Benedetti visited the king at Bad Ems, where William was taking the waters, on 13 July. The king expressed his pleasure at the withdrawal and promised to inform Benedetti when the Sigmaringens officially confirmed the report. Repeatedly pressed by Benedetti for a formal assurance against renewal, William politely but firmly declined. Later in the day Karl Anton's letter arrived confirming the withdrawal, news which William conveyed at once to Benedetti. When the ambassador tried to renew the interview in order to discuss the question of a formal assurance, the king, through his adjutant, flatly refused and referred Benedetti to Bismarck.

In his memoirs Bismarck has drawn a vivid picture of the scene on 13 July 1870 when he was dining with Roon and Moltke, all of them deeply depressed by the news of the withdrawal. A telegram arrived from

Bad Ems containing an account of the interview with Benedetti and authorising Bismarck to inform the press of Benedetti's second demand if he thought it advisable. Bismarck read the telegram through a second time, asked Moltke whether Germany was ready for war, and receiving a favour-able reply, dictated a shortened version for publication. This version altered the spirit of the original; it omitted all reference to the polite behaviour of the king, laid emphasis on the humiliating character of the French demand and insinuated that the king had, as a matter of national honour, abruptly terminated diplomatic relations with France. According to Bismarck, Roon and Moltke were restored to high spirits and spoke elatedly of war. 'It has a different ring,' observed Moltke of the telegram; 'it sounded like a parley, now it is like a flourish in answer to a challenge.'

The account of the editing is true, but Bismarck undoubtedly over-dramatised the incident. There was no depression in Berlin. Bismarck, aware that the French had overreached themselves, was straining every nerve to retrieve the situation. With the agreement of Roon and Moltke, Bismarck had already telegraphed the king, advising him to send an ulti-matum to France to force her to declare her intentions. The Ems telegram gave Bismarck his chance. Strictly speaking, the edited version was not a forgery; but it was certainly designed to humiliate France and shift the advantage in the game of brinkmanship back to Berlin. Bismarck was determined to save his reputation at all costs, fully recognising that war was virtually inevitable. In that sense Bismarck certainly bears respon-sibility for the outbreak of the war.

The final decision still rested with France. Despite reports of Prussian military measures, the government was most reluctant to declare war and talked of calling a European congress – a proposal welcomed by Napoleon who had premonitions of defeat. In a perceptive moment the emperor admitted the truth; there was no legitimate *casus belli*; it was the chauvinist-minded editors and deputies clamouring for a victorious war to keep radicalism at bay who propelled a reluctant government over the brink. The empress was eager for war, and the generals confident of victory. On 15 July the government decided on war; on 19 July a formal declaration was delivered in Berlin and the Franco-German war had begun.

France had grossly over-estimated her chances. With a population of thirty-six millions she put 270,000 men in the field to face 284,000 Prussians. The diplomatic situation failed to develop as anticipated. No Great Power approved of the French demands on Prussia or of the declara-tion of war. Britain mistrusted Napoleon, and these suspicions were con-firmed when Bismarck arranged for *The Times* to publish Benedetti's draft treaty of 1866 (taking care to suppress the date). Russia remained neutral, feeling no vital interest was at stake, although she made her neutrality conditional on Austrian neutrality. There was no need to worry about Austria-Hungary; Gramont confidently counted on her support but failed to consult her; Beust, in fact, had no intention of being involved in war. Finally, Italy insisted to the last that she could not move as long as the French garrison stayed in Rome.

On 4 August the first serious passage of arms occurred. Within a month the French armies were defeated and the emperor taken prisoner; the battle of Sedan on 2 September 1870 was the decisive battle, a triumph for the superb staff-work and leadership of the Prussian armies and an unmistakable sign that the balance of power had moved to Berlin. Much to the surprise of Moltke and Bismarck, the war continued into January 1871. When the French provisional government discovered that Prussia wanted Alsace-Lorraine, they decided to fight on rather than cede an inch of their native soil. The German liberal press had launched a vociferous campaign for the return of Alsace-Lorraine with the encouragement of Bismarck. However, strategic not national considerations were probably uppermost in his mind; as long as Strasbourg remained French, South Germany would be at the mercy of French invaders. He realised that France would resent bitterly the loss of the provinces, but believed that lasting antagonism between the two peoples was the likely outcome of a war which was becoming increasingly bitter and bloody; irregular *francs-tireurs* attacked German units, and the Germans retaliated by taking hostages and burning villages. This was no 'cabinet war' but a national struggle, a step on the road to the total war of the twentieth century. It left its mark on Bismarck, who revealed a vicious and blood-thirsty streak in his nature by advocating the most ruthless measures against the enemy. Great tension existed between Bismarck and the generals, who resented civilian interference in military matters. While the Prussians besieged Paris, seeking to starve the city out, Bismarck fumed at the delay, aware that the longer the war lasted the greater the possibility of foreign intervention. In the end he got his way and the city was bombarded, an act of savagery which brought only discredit on the Prussians. On 28 January 1871 the French capitulated and signed an armistice followed by a preliminary peace in February and a definite treaty, The Peace of Frankfurt, in May.

How had the war affected Germany? Public opinion was aroused by the Ems telegram and the declaration of war; a great wave of white-hot patriotic fervour swept through the whole country including the south. After the battle of Sedan final unification seemed certain. Baden and Hesse both declared their wish for union with the north. However, Bismarck was involved in much arduous negotiation before the empire was created. Particularism was still a powerful force which needed careful handling. Bavaria, spokesman of the particularists, would only enter the Confederation in return for special privileges giving to her in effect an equal voice with Prussia. Skilfully playing off one state against another and encouraging the National Liberal press to attack particularism, Bismarck succeeded in isolating Bavaria and compelling her to modify her demands.

To conciliate the particularists, Bismarck agreed to extend the power of the Bundesrat. In addition, he conceded some special privileges to Bavaria, including the right to a permanent seat on the military committee of the Bundesrat, separate representation at peace negotiations and chairmanship of a committee on foreign affairs. These concessions amounted to little in practice, although they aroused National Liberal displeasure. Of greater significance were the reserve rights which allowed Bavaria and Württemberg to keep control of their postal and telegraphic services and armed forces. Much to Bismarck's relief, the new constitution was accepted by the Reichstag and by the southern parliaments. 'People don't know,' he grumbled, 'what the situation is like. We are balanced on the end of a lightning conductor – if we lose the equilibrium which I have created with such difficulty then we are finished.'

One question remained undecided: the title which the king of Prussia would assume as head of the new state. Bismarck felt that it would be easier to reconcile the princes to Prussian overlordship if the king was designated emperor with their voluntary agreement. William had welcomed the extension of Prussian territory in recent years but felt that the creation of an empire would be the end of Prussia. Bismarck brought pressure to bear on the Bavarian monarch, second in rank among the princes of Germany, to take a 'free' initiative; he actually drafted the *Kaiserbrief* in which Ludwig II, the romantic castle-building ruler of Bavaria, asked King William to become German emperor; in return Ludwig received an annual subsidy of 300,000 gulden, a transaction which only became public knowledge many years later. Reluctantly William gave way. All was now ready. On 18 December 1870 a Reichstag deputation arrived at Versailles led by Simson, who had offered Frederick William the crown of a united Little Germany in 1849. When he had received the consent of the princes, King William accepted and on 1 January 1871 the German Empire came into being.

Before the Empire was proclaimed in solemn ceremony on 18 January, the anniversary of the day in 1701 when Prussia became a kingdom, a further quarrel disturbed the harmonious relationship between king and chancellor, this time over the precise phrasing of the title. William preferred 'by the grace of God king of Prussia chosen Emperor of Germany'. Bismarck insisted on 'by the grace of God German emperor and king of Prussia'. Grudgingly William accepted Bismarck's arguments that the imperial title must come first, though to the end he insisted on being called 'emperor of Germany'. That was denied him. For at the end of the ceremony the grand duke of Baden (the king's son-in-law), at Bismarck's instigation, called for three cheers with the words: 'Long live his imperial and royal majesty Emperor William.' The old man shook hands with the chief dignitaries but walked past Bismarck without a sign of recognition. Before the day was out the quarrel was made up, and when the Peace of

Frankfurt was signed Bismarck became a prince. The king's annoyance was symptomatic; many old-fashioned conservatives feared that the creation of an empire would seriously diminish the power of Prussia, and were quick to blame Bismarck for the curious fate which had overtaken the Great Elector's principality.

Most liberals had no reservations. For them the war of 1870 was the culmination of the national revolution begun in 1866. The onward march of events since 1866 had been little short of miraculous in their eyes, and led easily to the growth of an exaggerated national pride. Liberals saw in the brilliant military victories of Moltke a sign of the moral as well as the material superiority of Prussia over Austria and France. They were not alone in this; Queen Victoria was pleased at this triumph 'of civilisation, of liberty, of order and of unity . . . over despotism, corruption, immorality and aggression'. In the brilliant afterglow of Sedan, war ceased to be a scourge of mankind; it was elevated into a healthy confrontation between opposing moral concepts and an infallible guide to the worth of a people and its culture. The German historian Gerhard Ritter has rightly pointed out that writers in other lands were saying much the same things; tired of peace and prosperity they, too, praised the high drama of war. Undoubtedly the contemporary adoration of material power had disastrous effects upon German liberalism, weakening still further the idealistic strands in its philosophy. Many liberals frankly lost faith in the ability of ordinary mortals to understand affairs of state; Baumgarten, an old South-German liberal and opponent of Bismarck, remarked as early as the end of 1866 that 'the citizen is born to work but not to be a statesman'.

Some critical voices were raised in 1870. The old liberal historian Gervinus, one of the Göttingen seven in 1837 and always an opponent of Bismarck, was bitterly critical of the militaristic spirit of Prussia, which he accused of transforming two-thirds of Germany into 'a warrior state ever ready for aggression', a permanent threat to the peace of Europe and the security of her neighbours. Gervinus felt that the lights were going out and that Europe was retreating to the outmoded and tyrannous militarism of bygone ages, leading inexorably to further wars. The only hope for Germany was that Prussia might undo her handiwork, liberate the lands wrongfully annexed and turn Germany into a true federation with Hamburg as its capital. Equally critical was Herwegh, the fiery liberal of the 1840s; he stubbornly maintained that unity without freedom was worthless; he never ceased to condemn Bismarck's methods: 'The watch on the Rhine will not suffice,' he wrote in 1871; 'the worst enemy stands on the Spree' – and insisted on being buried in the free soil of Switzerland rather than in his native Württemberg. Another opponent was Heinrich von Gagern, once president of the Frankfurt Parliament, who died in 1880 a forgotten man largely because he refused to come to terms with the new Germany.

Their opposition was undoubtedly somewhat naïve and unbalanced and their solutions impracticable; once the Habsburgs resisted the creation of Greater Germany, the union of north and south was almost inevitable with or without war given the prevailing nationalist ethos. But these men represented a precious heritage of radical dissent, a tradition with which no great country can dispense. They remained isolated figures partly because the tide of popular opinion was flowing strongly against dissent in the golden years of the new Empire, and partly because opponents of the new order were deeply divided amongst themselves. Catholics remained deeply suspicious of the new Empire but were far too traditional in outlook and too hostile to the ethical tenets of liberalism for any political *rapprochement* to be possible. Liberal suspicion of Catholicism was equally profound, although in fact Catholics and liberals – especially those on the left wing – might have found much common ground in their respective philosophies. As it was, half a century elapsed before this was realised. Nor did the working-class movement help to unite the opposition; Marxist-oriented, it was suspicious of Catholic and liberal alike; even a man like the veteran radical Jacoby found himself assailed not only by enemies on the right but by Socialists who saw in his valiant struggle for responsible government nothing more than 'petty-bourgeois ethics'.

5

The Development of the German Empire 1871–1890

To the very end of its existence in 1918 the German Empire bore the deep imprint of its origins in military victory. The French chose the Fall of the Bastille as their national day; the Germans commemorated a military battle, the battle of Sedan, emphasing by their choice the causal relationship between unification and the defeat of the 'arch-enemy' France. Inevitably the structure of the *Reich* was permeated with the autocratic spirit of victorious Prussia. The Empire did not emanate from the will of the people. Sovereignty resided in twenty-two rulers – four kings, six grand dukes, four dukes and eight princes – who, in company with the senates of three free cities, created the Empire by a voluntary act of association. In theory these princes were all equal; in practice no-one denied that the Prussian ruler was more equal than the remainder; as German emperor he was head of the imperial executive and civil service and supreme war-lord of all the armed forces of the Empire.

The *Reich* was, however, rather more than a simple extension of Prussian power over the southern states. Constitutionally it did not fit easily into any category known to the political scientists. Essentially the *Reich* was an uneasy compromise between the forces of conservative federalism, the liberal unitary principle and the military might of Prussia.

The federal basis of the Empire was enshrined in the Bundesrat or Federal council. This was an assembly of ambassadors from the various states. Constitutionally it was the executive body of the Empire and was endowed with considerable power and prestige. Its consent was necessary for all legislation, it could veto constitutional changes, and foreign policy was, in theory, supervised by a special Bundesrat committee. States were represented in accordance with size and power. Prussia had seventeen of the fifty-eight seats, Bavaria six and the smaller states one each. Theoretically Prussia could be outvoted on constitutional and military questions, as fourteen votes constituted a veto. In practice the smaller states never opposed Prussia on important issues. Bundesrat meetings were held in private and were always presided over by the emperor or the chancellor.

The Reichstag, elected by universal suffrage, represented a concession to the spirit of mass democracy and symbolised the unity of the Empire. It shared legislative power with the Bundesrat as well as the right to review annually all non-military expenditure. In 1874 Bismarck grudgingly allowed the Reichstag to review the army grants every seven years; in practice the effectiveness of the concession was reduced, for as Reichstags were triennial, only alternate Reichstags could exercise control over military expenditure, And, significantly, imperial ministers were not accountable to the Reichstag. Normally they were members of the Bundesrat and specifically excluded from sitting in the former body. Undoubtedly Karl Liebknecht's celebrated description of the Reichstag as a 'fig leaf covering the nakedness of absolutism' contains a good deal of truth. But as the structure of politics changed with the transition to a more mature economic society, the Reichstag after 1890 became the focal point of German politics. And, limited though its powers were, it was able to exert more influence – even if only of a negative nature – on the government's policies than either the Russian Duma or the Austrian Reichsrat ever exerted on their respective governments. On the eve of the First World War there were some faint signs that Germany might be moving towards a more flexible form of government. That the outside world did not notice these tentative beginnings was due in no small measure to William II's frequent hysterical outbursts and exaggerated claims for the imperial dignity, as well as to the growing power of the military after 1912.

The administration of the new Empire was supervised by the chief imperial officer, the chancellor, who exercised the enormous executive power vested in the emperor and the Bundesrat. The constitution referred to the chancellor as a 'responsible' officer; this was of little significance, for the Reichstag never defined the term. Chancellors were not obliged to act upon resolutions passed by the Reichstag; votes of no-confidence could not remove them from office; they were appointed by the emperor and remained in office as long as he reposed confidence in them. The other basis of a chancellor's power lay in Prussia; the office of chancellor was usually combined with the minister-presidency of Prussia. Bismarck relinquished control of this office for a few months in 1873 but soon changed his mind once he realised that his effective power was derived from the minister-presidency rather than the chancellorship. Throughout his twenty years in office Bismarck maintained the closest possible association between Prussia and the Empire. Ideally, he would have liked Prussian ministers to hold all the corresponding offices in the imperial administration. But close personal union of this kind was opposed by other states resentful of the growing power of the chancellery. However, Bismarck went some way towards achieving this in 1878 when the growing volume of work necessitated the appointment of a vice-chancellor and secretaries of state to supervise the new imperial departments in the chancellery; the new vice-chancellor was allowed to deputise for Bismarck at meetings of the Prussian council of ministers, and the secretary of state for foreign affairs was given a seat and vote in the council. Bismarck firmly resisted attempts to make the secretaries responsible ministers. They remained senior clerks working under the old man's orders. He alone had the right to appear in the Reichstag and explain and defend imperial policy. The close ties established between Prussia and the institutions of the Empire were continued and strengthened in some respects by his successors so that imperial policy was in effect Prussian policy writ large.

Although chancellors were under no constitutional obligation to adopt policies approved by the Reichstag, they were, of course, obliged to secure Reichstag support for their own legislative proposals. Bismarck accepted these limitations on his power. He appreciated that the Reichstag was a useful device for maintaining in good order the delicate balance between a unitary empire and the forces of federalism; and it was generally realised in ruling circles that the active co-operation of a popularly elected body was almost essential for the smooth running of a modern state. But it was characteristic of Bismarck that he was only ready to work with the Reichstag on condition that it accepted his legislative proposals or at any rate arrived at some compromise acceptable to him. If, however, Reichstag and government could not reach agreement, constitutional obligations ceased to count for Bismarck; the government was always right, and parliamentary opposition was merely factionalism, harmful to the best interests of the nation. On these occasions the chancellor often toyed with the idea of a *coup d'état* to reduce the powers of the Reichstag or modify the franchise to produce amenable majorities. In short, co-operation with the Reichstag was a matter of sheer expediency to Bismarck. As Crown Princess Victoria, eldest daughter of Queen Victoria and wife of the heir to the throne, aptly commented, '. . . he is medieval altogether and the true theories of liberty and of government are Hebrew to him though he adopts and admits a democratic idea or measure now and then when he thinks it will serve his purpose.'

It is a significant comment on the structure of German politics that despite Bismarck's cynical attitude to the Reichstag, he could usually count on its support. Most members were content to criticise government bills and showed little desire to have their hands on the levers of power. As a class German politicians undoubtedly failed to exploit to the full the potentialities of the Reichstag as an instrument for political and social change.[1] On the other hand, in the 1870s and 1880s the Reichstag undoubtedly played on important and constructive role in the implementation of liberal policies within the framework of an authoritarian system. In all the circumstances, at a time when the balance of power was tilted sharply in favour of monarchy, when the working class was hostile to

[1] It must be remembered that the Reichstag became an increasingly unrepresentative body, as no provision was made for a redistribution of seats to reflect changing population patterns.

the Empire and the middle class was deeply respectful of authority, these modest beginnings were perhaps all that could be expected at this stage in German constitutional development.

The Empire was not a homogeneous national state. There was a French-speaking population in Alsace-Lorraine, a Danish minority in North Schleswig, as well as the Poles in the eastern territories. Nor, as has been indicated already, was it a unitary state. Sovereignty was divided between the imperial authorities and the member states. The imperial government was responsible for defence, customs, coinage, banking, communications and the civil and criminal codes. States had considerable residual powers over education, justice, agriculture, relations with the churches and local government. Only states could levy direct taxation whilst the Empire was dependent for its revenue on indirect taxation. The power of the states was far from negligible. Occasionally states opposed Berlin with success. A notable example was the railway question; Bismarck wanted to bring railways under central control to enhance the power and prestige of Berlin. Bavarian opposition obliged Prussia to refrain from this course of action and resort instead to the infinitely more laborious task of negotiating with individual railway companies. The result was that it took Prussia thirty years to acquire control of two-thirds of the railways in Germany.

But although the very real power of the states remained as a check on the triumph of unitary tendencies, nevertheless this could not prevent a disproportionate increase in Prussian influence. Decision-making in all advanced countries was increasingly monopolised by the capital city. As the twentieth century dawned, Germany's public image was being created less and less in traditional cultural centres such as Munich and Dresden and more and more in the huge industrial metropolis Berlin. It was, therefore, of crucial importance for German development that the forces of conservatism were particularly deeply entrenched in the premier state in the *Reich*.

Conservative ascendancy in Prussia hinged on the military might of her armies. For two centuries the sons of Junkers and high officials had officered the army which had carried Prussia from Fehrbellin to Sedan. Bismarck agreed with Schweinitz, a diplomat of the old school, who remarked in 1870 that the limits of the Prussian system would be reached 'where we no longer have Junkers to fill our commissions in the army'. In return for their military services the Prussian aristocracy enjoyed a dominant position in the social, political and administrative structure of the kingdom. In the Reichstag Conservatives were never more than a minority party. In Prussia Conservatives controlled the Landtag from 1879 onwards, and as the archaic constitution of 1850 remained in force unamended, their monopoly of political power remained intact down to 1918. The Empire made a heavy price for the maintenance of Prussian conservatism. The new social and economic forces stirring in Germany at the turn of the century came into conflict with the entrenched force of agrarian conservatism. Conservatism survived the onslaught, but the clash of battle reverberated throughout Imperial Germany, generating new political tensions and rendering increasingly precarious the fragile balance of forces on which the *Reich* rested.

The Empire was essentially a by-product of military victory. Before Germany could claim to be a modern state a gigantic task of internal unification and consolidation had to be accomplished; the abolition of all legal and economic anomalies between the states, and the creation of a modern administrative structure, were two urgent necessities. Modernisation did not commend itself to conservative backwoodsmen, who eyed the Empire with cold suspicion. Fortunately Bismarck was not dependent on them politically. Throughout the 1870s he could rely on the enthusiastic support of the National Liberals, the largest party in the Reichstag, with 125 seats in 1871 rising to 155 in 1873. Indeed the tide was flowing so strongly in favour of National Liberalism in the early 1870s that even in Prussia itself the Conservatives suffered heavy defeats. The National Liberals were ideal allies for the chancellor. These solid middle-class Germans were bewitched by Bismarck's phenomenal success, filled with admiration for the great man and eager to help him put flesh on the adminstrative skeleton of the *Reich*. With the support of the National Liberals and of the Free Conservatives – a small group of Rhineland and Silesian landowners and industrialists who broke away from the main body of Conservatives in 1867 – a spate of progressive legislation poured through the Reichstag in the next decade. A uniform coinage and currency was created; in 1873 Germany adopted the gold standard; in 1875 a *Reichsbank* was created; the legal system was standardised and modernised; in 1879 an imperial court of appeal was established; and the remaining restrictions on trade and industry were swept away. However, in their attempts at modernising the political structure of Prussia the National Liberals were much less successful. The judicial powers of landowners were only partially curtailed; the aristocracy still held half the seats in *Kreis* diets; and nothing was done to extend self-government in the towns. Even the modest changes that did occur were bitterly opposed by Junkers east of the Elbe (where the centre of gravity of German conservatism lay) who, with a total lack of political insight, persisted in regarding Bismarck as a 'renegade Junker' hell-bent on the destruction of his own class. But in general the task of modernisation would have been a good deal more painful had it not been for the staunch support of the National Liberals who helped draft the new legislation and saw to its implementation in the various states.

The new *Reich* was hardly in existence before it was shaken to its foundations by a great conflict between Church and State, the so-called

Kulturkampf. In the last quarter of the nineteenth century Church and State came into conflict in several countries. As European liberalism reached its apogee, friction was inevitable with a conservative institution slow to adapt itself to the changing moods of secular society. In 1870 the First Vatican Council enunciated the doctrine of papal infallibility. The Council resisted the pressure of those who wanted to declare every papal pronouncement infallible and merely restated the ancient belief that the Pope, when speaking on matters of faith and morals as Vicar of Christ, could not teach erroneous doctrine. Even this more moderate declaration aroused great alarm in liberal and Protestant circles. At a time when the Church was suffering reverses in Germany and Italy, the declaration was seen as a last gesture of defiance from a Pope who had openly declared in 1864 that the Roman pontiff could not be reconciled with 'progress, liberalism and recent civilisation'. The implications were disturbing; might not this new doctrine inaugurate a new phase of militant Catholicism, with the Pope using his spiritual powers in medieval fashion to support worn-out political causes and to interfere in the domestic affairs of sovereign states? These fears were increased by the Catholic attitude to the temporal power of the papacy. In 1870 Italian troops entered Rome, ending the last vestiges of the Pope's temporal power. The intransigent old man on the chair of St. Peter refused to accept the *fait accompli*, arguing that without temporal power his spiritual independence would be endangered. Catholics rallied around him and urged their governments to help restore the Pope to his temporal possessions, a demand which no power was prepared to entertain.

Liberal and Protestant fear of the Church of Rome did not, however, cause the Kulturkampf. True, Bismarck had little affection for Catholicism and no great knowledge of Catholic doctrine either. But as a statesman and diplomat his instinct was to remain strictly impartial in all his dealings with a church which had been on good terms with the Prussian state since the days of King Frederick William IV. Bismarck regarded the Syllabus of 1864 and the Vatican Council as internal church matters of no concern to the state. When approached by the Curia in 1870, he refused to intervene in Italy on the Pope's behalf but offered him asylum in Germany, being quick to appreciate possible political advantages for the new Empire.

Events soon forced Bismarck to abandon neutrality in his dealings with the Church. Some Catholics led by Döllinger, a prominent German theologian and Church historian and a friend of Gladstone and Lord Acton, refused to accept the decree on papal infallibility and broke with the Church. In 1871 the bishops of Breslau and Ermland and the archbishop of Cologne asked Prussia to dismiss the Old Catholics, as the dissenters were called, from teaching posts in schools and in Catholic theological faculties at universities. The government refused, maintaining that as the state was committed to the principle of religious toleration, it could not interfere in disputes between warring sects. When the bishops persisted in their demands, the government retaliated by suspending state subsidies to the offending prelates.

This dispute on its own would hardly have led to a full-scale Kulturkampf. Political not theological considerations were, as usual, uppermost in Bismarck's mind. He was particularly worried by the activites of the Centre, a new political party formed in 1870. There had been Catholic groups in local parliaments in South and West Germany for many years, formed primarily to defend Catholic interests in disputes arising out of the secularisation of Church property. The war of 1866 gave the first impetus to the creation of a national Catholic party; in the old Confederation fifty-two per cent of the population was Catholic and forty-eight per cent Protestant; once Austria was excluded from Germany, the Catholics became a minority of thirty-seven per cent in a Protestant state under a Protestant emperor. As Catholics had mostly sided with Austria in 1866, they were objects of suspicion in the new state. After 1870 they were driven further onto the defensive. Fearful of the growing power of Protestant Prussia and aware of mounting liberal hostility to their church, Catholic members of the Prussian lower house formed their own national party, the Centre.[2]

The Centre was unique among German parties in drawing its support from all social strata: aristocracy, middle class and working class. In 1871 it was the second-largest party in the Reichstag with fifty-eight seats, and had a leader of outstanding ability in the former Hanoverian minister Ludwig Windthorst. The party was pledged to defend the Church, support confessional schools and oppose civil marriage. It resisted extensions of imperial power and favoured decentralisation and greater autonomy for the states; in short, it emphasised those tenets of Catholicism inimical to the power of Caesar largely because Caesar happened to be Protestant Prussia.

The Centre was also unique among non-socialist parties in its advocacy of social reform. Catholic interest in social problems reached back to the 1830s, when the Romantic writer and philosopher Baader attacked *laissez-faire* capitalism and proclaimed his belief in the superior virtue of the hierarchically organised *Ständestaat*. The work of Father Kolping and Bishop Ketteler made Social Catholicism an integral part of the German scene. Kolping founded associations for vocational training, the *Kolpingfamilien*, which soon spread over all Germany. Ketteler, the theorist of Social Catholicism, one-time member of the Frankfurt Parliament, bishop of Mainz and later Archbishop of Cologne, wrote a book in 1864 strongly critical of a system which allowed such extremes of wealth and poverty

[2]The name was first used in 1859 by the Catholics in the Prussian lower house.

that workers were alienated from the Church.[3] Ketteler advocated Christian trade unions, worker-producer co-operatives and assistance for those unable to work. Later he accepted the need for state intervention and aid to ameliorate working conditions. As the party grew in size and influence in the 1870s – largely on account of the Kulturkampf[4] – it adopted a positive social programme calling for factory legislation, the regulation of child and female labour, the establishment of arbitration courts and the encouragement of co-operative associations. For a half century the Centre exerted considerable influence on the social legislation of the *Reich* and of the republic which superseded it.

At first Bismarck was not hostile to the Centre party. He changed his mind when the Centre clamoured for intervention in Italy and tried to have included in the imperial constitution the religious guarantees contained in the Prussian constitution of 1850, despite the fact that it had been agreed in 1867 to leave religious matters completely in the hands of the states. The latter manoeuvre was unsuccessful, but this more than anything else convinced Bismarck that the Centre was a sectarian party, bent on putting religion in the forefront of politics at all costs. His suspicions of the party deepened still further when he observed how rapidly it was becoming a natural rallying-point for opponents of the Empire. The seven members of the Guelf party, sworn enemies of Prussia on account of the annexation of Hanover, the fifteen Alsace-Lorrainers seeking autonomy for their homeland, Danish members longing for union with Denmark, and the thirteen Polish nationalists, were all clustered together under the shadow of the Centre. Contrary to popular belief, Bismarck was an excitable and highly strung individual who easily took fright. His sense of realism deserted him completely on this occasion; he easily persuaded himself that an ephemeral anti-Prussian political alignment in the Reichstag was in reality a Vatican-inspired conspiracy of malcontents bent on destroying the Empire he had so painfully created. He tried repeatedly to persuade the Vatican and the German bishops to withdraw support from the Centre. Only when these attempts failed did he intensify the campaign against the Church, thoroughly enraged by her refusal to do his bidding.

There was one final consideration: the situation in Poland, which no Prussian minister could ignore. Bismarck had observed with mounting anxiety how the Catholic clergy and school inspectorate still encouraged the use of Polish, despite his attempts to promote the use of German. The preservation of the Polish tongue kept the flame of nationalism alight, and at a time when the indigenous population was increasing rapidly this constituted a serious threat to the stability of the *Reich* on its eastern

[3] *Diet Arbeiterfrage und das Christentum*, Mainz, 1890.
[4] In 1871 only half the Catholic vote went to the Centre.

frontier. By curbing the Church in Poland Bismarck hoped to loosen the ties between nationalism and Catholicism.

Up to 1872 the measures against the Church were only intended to delimit more clearly the spheres of influence of Church and State; the Catholic section of the Prussian ministry of public worship and education was dissolved on the grounds that it represented the interests of the Church rather than the State; and Prussian schools were removed from clerical control and placed nominally under state supervision;[5] this law, which affected Protestant as much as Catholic priests, led to an open breach between the old conservatives and the chancellor. By the spring of 1872 Bismarck finally abandoned hope of persuading the Vatican to discipline the Centre party and intensified the struggle, now with the intention of subordinating Church to State.

In this, the second phase of the Kulturkampf, legislation against the Church was passed by both the Prussian Landtag and the Reichstag. In 1872 the Reichstag forbade the Jesuit order to set up establishments in Germany and empowered governments to expel individual Jesuits from the country. In 1873 the Prussian Landtag passed the famous May Laws; all candidates for the priesthood had to attend university for three years before entering a seminary; and all church appointments were subject to a veto by the state authorities. In 1874 Prussia introduced civil marriage and required all births, deaths and marriages to be notified to the registrar, not to the church authorities; this law was extended to other states in 1875. In 1874 all states were given powers to restrict the freedom of movement of the clergy and to expel offending priests from Germany. In 1875 the Kulturkampf reached a climax with laws empowering Prussia to suspend subsidies to the Church in dioceses or parishes where the clergy resisted the new legislation; and all religious orders in Prussia, with the exception of nursing orders, were dissolved. The legislation was enforced vigorously in Prussia by Falk, an able jurist and a bitter anti-clerical, who was appointed minister of public worship by Bismarck. There was undoubtedly much popular support in North Germany for the Kulturkampf – the phrase was coined, significantly enough, by Virchow, a prominent Prussian Progressive. The Conservatives were ranged against Bismarck on this issue. Consequently the chancellor became heavily dependent on the National Liberals and Progressives; this helped to exacerbate the passions aroused by the new laws, for many of Bismarck's liberal supporters were hostile to all revealed religion and were seeking, not to restrict the activity of the Church, but to destroy her. Only a minority of liberals, led by Lasker and Bamberger, protested against the basic illiberality of the Kulturkampf.

The Catholic Church, with a long record of resistance to secular

[5]The clergy still acted as school inspectors but in the name of the State not of the Church.

interference behind her, refused to submit. Bishops instructed their flocks to resist. In 1875 Pope Pius solemnly condemned the legislation to the fury of liberals who denied the Church all right to sit in judgement on secular laws. The measures were rigidly enforced; by 1876 all but two of the twelve Prussian bishops were in exile or under arrest, and a quarter of all parishes were vacant. The Church thrived on persecution; the laity rallied round the clergy; the clergy rallied round the Pope; and the Centre party, the political arm of German Catholicism, had greatness thrust upon it. Not all Catholics had approved of a confessional party; some had feared the retrograde effects this might have on political life. The Kulturkampf allayed all doubts, confirming most Catholics in the belief that a separate party was essential for the defence of the Church. The Centre grew rapidly. Its vote doubled in 1874, and by 1881 it held 100 seats in the Reichstag. For the next fifty years it came to occupy an arbitral position in German politics and remained a constant but unpredictable political factor manoeuvring skilfully in its own interests, sometimes for and sometimes against the government of the day.

By 1876 it was beginning to dawn on the weary nerve-racked chancellor that physical force was unlikely to bring the Church to heel. The whole campaign was going badly; Catholics were ranged solidly against him, and there was growing opposition from other quarters; the emperor had serious reservations about the Kulturkampf; the empress sympathised with the Church, whilst the crown prince and princess openly disapproved of Bismarck's brutal enforcement of the May laws. The time had come for the chancellor to cut his losses before the Empire was seriously weakened by a campaign which so far had only succeeded in deepening the confessional divisions in Germany.

There were other considerations too. In the late 1870s the *Reich* was beset by serious financial and economic problems. Imperial revenue raised from customs duties and indirect taxation was proving woefully inadequate to cover the growing cost of armaments and administration. The states had to cover the deficits with matricular contributions raised from their own citizens by direct taxation. As the deficits mounted, the states dug deeper into their pockets, making the Empire, in Bismarck's words, 'a troublesome sponger who had to go begging at the door of the separate states'. Financial reform was clearly an urgent necessity both to ensure a plentiful source of revenue for the *Reich* and to pacify the states, who resented matricular contributions.

The expansion of the German economy was also creating problems quite outside Bismarck's ken. He had little knowledge of, or interest in, economic matters and left them in the hands of the president of the chancellery, Delbrück, a capable administrator who continued the free-trading policies which had made the Customs Union so powerful. Then towards the close of the 1870s German agriculture began to suffer from the effects of a series of bad harvests, coupled with the emergence of Russia and the U.S.A. as major wheat exporters. Slowly but surely Germany was becoming dependent on foreign grain; even in 1874 she imported two million tons of Russian wheat; East German wheat exports declined and prices fell. Industry, too, was experiencing a difficult period. Basic industries had been advancing steadily since the middle of the century. In the early 1870s the rate of expansion accelerated for several reasons; the acquisition of Alsace-Lorraine supplied Germany with new iron-ore deposits conveniently close to the Ruhr and Saar basins and with a flourishing cotton industry; and measures such as the unification of the coinage, together with improvements in banking, promoted the growth of trade. Unfortunately, the French indemnity of £200 millions sparked off an unhealthy speculative boom; in the twenty years before 1870 a total of 295 limited companies were formed; between 1870 and 1873 857 new companies sprang up. The inevitable crash came in 1873; over 160 companies failed, industry suffered a sharp set-back and the rate of expansion slowed down for several years. The result was that at the close of the 1870s landowners, great and small, and industrialists – who founded the Central Association of German Industrialists (*Zentral Verband deutscher Industriellen*) in 1876 – were clamouring for protective tariffs. This was part of a much wider picture. All industrial countries were experiencing difficulties in the last quarter of the century and all except Great Britain adopted tariff protection as their answer.

Being a landowner himself, Bismarck was close enough to the soil to appreciate instinctively the dangers of a prolonged agrarian depression; falling prices threatened the economic basis of Junkerdom, pointing the way to the ultimate decline of the Junkers as a class and the collapse of their political ascendancy in Prussia. And once the doctrine of self-sufficiency was breached by increasing dependence on imported wheat, then the military foundations of the Empire would be quickly undermined. Both in the interests of imperial defence and to protect the class interests of Prussian landowners agrarian protection was essential. This key unlocked several doors; protective tariffs and increased indirect taxation would between them make the *Reich* solvent and do away with the need for matricular contributions. Indirect taxation had other advantages; the necessary legislation would be voted once and for all by the Reichstag and remain unaltered until a new law was passed; the alternative of allowing the Reichstag to raise money by direct taxation would make it far too powerful for Bismarck's liking; and he also happened to be strongly opposed to direct taxation on economic grounds, believing it to be a disincentive to farmers and manufacturers; indeed one of his main ambitions – which he failed to achieve – was the complete abolition of direct taxation.

Bismarck had failed to win support for the new policy, which required an alteration to the existing law. This was far from easy. Free trade ideas were in the ascendancy in the early 1870s; a bill to retain the last tariffs on pig-iron was decisively defeated as late as 1876, despite the fact that half Germany's blast furnaces were idle that year. All the Progressives, many National Liberals and some Conservatives were still firmly committed to the doctrine of free trade. Support for protective tariffs came from a small but growing body of agrarians and industrialists in the Conservative parties and to a lesser extent in the Centre party. Already the chancellor was toying with the possibility of a new political alignment. The old conservatives had abandoned their bitter opposition to Bismarck and the *Reich*; in 1876, when the German Conservative party was founded, its programme was submitted to the chancellor beforehand for his approval. In the case of the Centre, support might well be forthcoming once the Kulturkampf was over; Bismarck had certainly no wish to prolong it; the difficulty was that as long as Pope Pius IX lived Bismarck could not disengage himself without surrendering unconditionally, which he would not do. And as the Conservatives and Centre together did not command a majority, Bismarck was still dependent on National Liberal support. He tried in the course of 1877 to persuade the right wing of the National Liberals to abandon their opposition to tariff protection. The bait dangled before them was the offer of a post in the Prussian cabinet. This was not enough for their leader Bennigsen; convinced that he had Bismarck at his mercy, he insisted on two additional posts for left-wing colleagues. Bismarck refused, and the negotiations deadlocked. In February 1878 Bismarck broke openly with the National Liberals during the debate on a government bill to increase the tax on tobacco. The National Liberals insisted on constitutional guarantees of the budgetary rights of Reichstag and Prussian Landtag in return for support of the bill.[6] Bismarck refused to accommodate them and went out of his way to declare bluntly that he was aiming at a government monopoly over the entire tobacco industry, an extension of state control totally unacceptable to liberals.

Bismarck made no attempt to appease his old allies, because at last the ice floes were breaking up. On 7 February 1878 Pope Pius IX died. His successor, the conciliatory diplomat Leo XIII, wished to end the Kulturkampf and wrote to Emperor William on 20 February expressing his earnest wish for improved relations. Bismarck accepted the offer with alacrity and in the summer of 1878 conferred with the papal envoy, Monsigneur Masella, at Bad Kissingen in an attempt to wind up the struggle between Church and State.

The chancellor was not yet out of the wood. Negotiations with the

---

[6]Bennigsen feared that the new revenues, by doing away with the need for contributions by the states, would make the *Reich* less dependent on the Reichstag, whose consent was required for matriculars. Furthermore, by relieving Prussia of the obligation to pay matriculars, the changes were likely to strengthen the government at the expense of the Landtag. Basically what Bennigsen was seeking was an assurance that the fiscal powers of Reichstag and Landtag would remain unaltered.

Church were slow and arduous; meanwhile the Reichstag remained adamantly opposed to tariff reform. Suddenly events played into his hands. In May a half-crazed apprentice plumber with anarchist leanings fired two shots at the emperor. The man had in fact no proven association with the Socialist party, but Bismarck, in common with many of his contemporaries, drew no clear distinction between anarchism and socialism; and many socialists were themselves lamentably vague on this point. All his life Bismarck had been haunted by the spectre of revolution. Socialism evoked memories of 1848 and aroused irrational fears and prejudices in him. Its internationalism was disturbing; Socialism, like Catholicism, had allegiances beyond the national state, and that was something which he could neither understand nor tolerate. Most of all he was frightened by the revolutionary language of socialism, with its strident talk of class warfare and the destruction of the bourgeois state; after all, Bebel, speaking in the Reichstag in 1871, had openly praised the French Commune as a foretaste of what was to come. And it must be remembered that contemporaries saw the attempt on the emperor's life as part of a wider subterranean movement; Russian anarchists made several attempts on the tsar's life in the late 1870s before finally murdering him in 1881. So it is not difficult to see why Bismarck believed that German socialism represented a most serious threat to the conservative-monarchist order of society in which he was rooted.

Bismarck had tried unsuccessfully in the past to persuade the Reichstag to place restrictions on freedom of the press and to make incitement to class warfare a punishable offence. After the attempt on the emperor's life he tried again, with no greater success. His hastily drafted bill against socialism was decisively defeated by the National Liberals and the Centre, not out of sympathy towards socialism, but because they felt that the discriminatory character of the proposals violated the basic tenets on which the *Rechtsstaat* rested. A week later there was a second attempt on the emperor's life. This time the old man was seriously wounded. Bismarck decided at once to dissolve the Reichstag. Bennigsen, under pressure from frightened industrialists, agreed to anti-socialist legislation in principle. Bismarck brushed the offer aside, scenting political advantage in the new situation; Germany was deeply shocked by the latest attempt on Emperor William's life; it would not be difficult to stampede the middle classes into voting against 'unpatriotic' liberals who had refused to protect the emperor against 'red assassins'; the outcome would be a Reichstag ready to do Bismarck's bidding. The manoeuvre succeeded; the two Conservative parties gained 600,000 votes and thirty-seven seats between them, the Centre stood firm and the National Liberals lost 130,000 votes and twenty-nine seats – only by supporting anti-socialist legislation during the election did they save themselves from a heavy defeat. Bismarck got his way in the new Reichstag. A new anti-socialist bill was passed by 221 votes to 149. It was supported by the National Liberals and Conservatives and opposed by Socialists, Progressives and Poles, and by the Centre, for whom the Kulturkampf was still a harsh reality. Under the new law socialist and communist meetings, societies and publications were forbidden; the police were empowered to expel socialist agitators; and states could declare a state of siege in disaffected areas for periods of up to one year. Socialist electoral activity was not however forbidden; to its everlasting credit the Reichstag refused to interfere with the freedom of elections. The result was that Socialists could still stand for election and speak freely in both Reichstag and state legislatures, an anomaly unthinkable in the totalitarian state of the twentieth century.

This is an appropriate point to leave the general narrative and describe briefly the development of German socialism since the death of Lassalle. At the close of the 1860s the small but growing Socialist movement was rent asunder by internal strife. In 1867 the General Workers' Association came under the influence of Schweitzer, an energetic and controversial figure. As an ardent supporter of Prussia and a staunch admirer of Bismarck, he soon incurred the wrath of Marx and Engels. By this time the works of the great prophets of socialism were becoming known in Germany, and a new Marxist-inspired movement was growing up with roots outside Prussia. The leading figures were August Bebel and Wilhelm Liebknecht, two of the greatest names in the history of German socialism. Bebel, a Silesian wood-turner, was first attracted to socialism by Lassalle and only became a Marxist under Liebknecht's influence. The latter, after being active in the 1848 revolution, fled to London, where he came under the influence of Marx and Engels before returning to Germany in 1862. Bebel and Liebknecht differed profoundly from Schweitzer on fundamentals. Schweitzer was a Little-German nationalist and a gradualist, believing like Lassalle in the power of universal suffrage to ameliorate working conditions. Bebel and Liebknecht were internationalists, bitter opponents of Prussia and dedicated revolutionaries who denied the possibility of achieving socialism by parliamentary means. The parting of the ways came in 1869, when Bebel and Liebknecht founded the Social Democratic Worker's Party (*Sozialdemokratische Arbeiterpartei*) at the Eisenach conference. This was a Marxist party, affiliated to the Second International and committed to the abolition of class domination and to the attainment of the complete economic and political emancipation of the working class. However, Lassalle's pervasive influence could not be easily eradicated from the movement; the party remained Lassallian in its belief that co-operative labour must replace the wage system, that political freedom was indispensable for the economic emancipation of the workers and that social questions could be solved only in a democratic state.

At first there was bitter rivalry between the Lassallians and the Eisenachers. Then for a number of reasons they drew closer together; the completion of unification ended the argument between the Little-German leaders of the Workers' Association and the Greater-German leaders of the Workers' Party; Schweitzer, whom the Marxists detested, resigned in 1871; and Bismarck's mounting hostility to socialism after the episode of the French Commune underlined the need for unity. In 1875 at the Gotha conference Lassallians and Eisenachers united to form the German Social Democratic Party (*Sozialdemokratische Arbeiterpartei Deutschlands*). The Gotha programme was inevitably an uneasy mixture of Marx and Lassalle. The party accepted the Marxist analysis of society and now declared openly that its aim was the overthrow of the existing order. But – an important point which Bismarck failed to appreciate – the party also declared that it would use only legal means in the struggle for economic and political freedom, and it still clung to Lassalle's state-aided producers' co-operatives as an economic panacea. Marx was strongly critical of the concessions to the Lassallians, while Engels did not expect the two factions to remain united for long.

Perhaps they would not have done so had it not been for Bismarck's anti-socialist law. This law had the same traumatic effect on Socialists that the May laws were having on German Catholics. It rallied the faithful and fortified them in their beliefs. Marxism, like Catholicism, supplied its followers with an eschatological view of life; in an age when orthodox religion was under heavy fire socialism became a secular religion for thousands of workers outside the influence of the churches. The Centre and Socialist parties both developed social and cultural activities to bind together members conscious of their sense of isolation in an alien world. Twelve years of persecution deepened the fortress mentality of the German working class. The party became more radical and class-conscious; at the Wyden Congress, held in Switzerland in 1880, the party committed itself to use 'all means' to attain its objectives. The anti-socialist law was enforced rigorously. Several Socialist leaders were arrested or exiled, and many periodicals were suppressed. At first the Socialist vote fell from 493,000 in 1877 to 312,000. But by 1884 it had risen to 550,000 – giving the party twenty-four seats in the Reichstag – and continued to rise until it was well over one million in 1890. The party simply went underground; it held congresses and published its journals as before but operated from outside Germany. By the beginning of the twentieth century, it had become a well-disciplined and highly organised mass-party, a model for all Socialist parties. In short, Bismarck had completely failed to bring the Socialists to heel; worst of all, his blundering ill-conceived policy had seriously retarded the integration of the growing working class in the new *Reich*.

By the autumn of 1878 the campaign for tariff reform launched by the industrialists two years previously was reaching a high intensity. An all-party association for tariff reform soon had the support of 204 deputies, mostly Conservatives and Centrists, with some National Liberals. Bismarck, now certain of a parliamentary majority, introduced a general tariff bill in 1879. The Conservatives were solidly behind the bill, and the support of the Centre was easily secured. Bismarck accepted their proposal for a division of the new revenues between *Reich* and states; this left the *Reich* formally dependent, as before, on matricular contributions, although as the states would dispose of plentiful funds to meet these demands, the new arrangement would cause less friction. Falk, symbol of the Kulturkampf in Prussia, had to be thrown to the wolves but by this time the struggle against the Church no longer mattered. It was not, in fact, finally wound up until 1887, and in the end Bismarck came out of it without losing too much face. He certainly lost the Kulturkampf inasmuch as he had failed to destroy the Centre party. But the Church did not win a complete victory either. During the negotiations Bismarck with his usual skill played off Centre party against Curia and benefited from the Pope's willingness to make substantial concessions. Bismarck had to dismantle the May laws, allow the exiled clergy to return and resume payments to the Church. On the other hand, civil marriage remained compulsory, Jesuits were still forbidden to enter Germany, the 'pulpit paragraph' forbidding 'political' sermons was not repealed and the Church agreed to submit the names of all permanent appointments to the state authorities. These were not inconsiderable achievements. Bismarck even persuaded Rome to exert pressure on the Centre in 1866 to support his army bill. However, to his credit Windthorst refused to tolerate Curia interference in party matters and the Centre voted against the bill.

The passage of the tariff bill in July 1879 profoundly affected the political and social structure of Germany. Bismarck's liberal honeymoon was over. Henceforth he relied for political support on the forces of conservatism. The great landowners in the Conservative party – and to a lesser extent in the Centre – were saved by protection from economic ruin and became devoted supporters of the chancellor. Heavy industry, too, had reason to be grateful, even if the duties on iron were much lower than those on cattle and grain. In the past, industrialists had been free-traders and liberals. Once free trade ceased to benefit them, they lost interest in liberalism. Instead they turned to conservatism and were accepted as junior partners by the landed aristocracy. A common interest in protection brought Ruhr industrialists and East Elbian Junkers together in a new 'alliance of steel and rye' which established the pattern of high society in Germany for the next forty years. The new alignment was not peculiar to Germany. In several countries at the close of the century the middle classes were becoming reconciled to the *status quo* after a long association with liberalism. This political realignment made possible periods of conservative rule in Britain, France, Italy (where governments were liberal only in name) and Russia, as well as in Germany.

The rise of conservatism was preceded by the decline of liberalism. Liberals were slow to adapt themselves to the pattern of industrial society; accordingly they fell from power in Austria-Hungary (1879), Sweden (1880), Belgium (1884) and Britain (1885). 1879 witnessed the destruction of German liberalism as an effective political force. Prussian peasants who voted liberal in the 1870s changed sides in 1879; consequently the Conservatives regained control of the lower house and retained it until 1918. Conservatism tightened its grip over the apparatus of government. By 1879 the last of the liberal-minded ministers had been forced out of the Prussian cabinet. Bismarck launched a ruthless campaign in the civil service to stamp out the last vestiges of the liberal tradition, which reached back to the days of Stein. Puttkamer, the reactionary Prussian minister of the interior, succeeded in the 1880s in turning the civil service into an ultra-conservative body, the preserve of the sons of the aristocracy and the politically reliable upper classes. As a result of these measures the *Obrigkeitsstaat*[7] took on a new lease of life as Prussia moved into the twentieth century.

The great National Liberal party of the 1870s was shipwrecked during the tariff-protection debate. The left-wingers, who still believed in free trade and parliamentary government, broke away and eventually united with the Progressives to form a new radical party called the *Deutschfreisinnige Partei* in 1884. The new party attracted support among small merchants, minor officials and intellectuals and became a formidable opposition group in the 1880s under the able leadership of Eugen Richter, but declined rapidly after 1893.[8] What remained of the old National Liberal Party was a group of bankers and industrialists, staunch supporters of the chancellor. They reformed themselves as a party in 1884 but never gained more than forty or fifty seats in the Reichstag and were a rapidly declining political force by the beginning of the twentieth century.

The fragile unity of 1871 was endangered by the Kulturkampf, which alienated many Protestants as well as Catholics from the *Reich*. Protective tariffs healed the wounds. A new impetus was given to national pride, and overnight the forces of conservatism rallied in defence of the Empire. This was partly Bismarck's doing. He openly intervened in the debate between protectionists and free-traders, praising high tariffs as a truly patriotic policy while denouncing low tariffs and neglect of agriculture, which free trade would lead to, as pure subversion, certain to weaken the fatherland seriously in time of war. Bismarck's readiness to equate patriotism with whatever policy he was currently pursuing affected political life adversely. Yet it would be foolish to deny that the appeal to national pride was a

[7]Authoritarian State.
[8]Only in terms of Reichstag seats. The radical popular vote was rising in 1907 and in 1912 totalled 1,497,041.

persuasive argument. Protective tariffs gave a new lease of life to the Empire. They consolidated the work of unification by drawing north and south closer together and accelerated the creation of a large internal market.

It was not all gain. In the long run protection encouraged the growth of a top-heavy economy with a built-in tendency to over-production. Germany could not dispose of her industrial surplus internally. She became increasingly dependent on the production of armaments and on the acquisition of new export markets to solve her problems. Not that this was a specifically German issue. The Russian economy exhibited similar symptoms on the eve of the war. Furthermore, protection meant lower living-standards for the German people. Armaments which German workers did not want had to be paid for by dearer bread which they could not do without. German wheat was thirty to fifty per cent dearer than foreign wheat; canned food and refrigerated meat were kept out of Germany to give assured markets to less efficient German producers. There would have been much more industrial discontent in Imperial Germany had it not been for the thrift of the housewife and rising wage levels which partially obscured these economic realities.

When Bismarck introduced his anti-socialist law in 1878, he did not suppose that coercion was the complete answer to socialism; from the beginning he had state socialism in mind. No doubt as a Christian Bismarck was conscious of a moral obligation to aid the needy members of society. But state socialism was not inspired primarily by religious conviction; in essence it was an attempt to wean the working classes from revolutionary socialism by offering them a modest stake in the Empire. Bismarck assumed naïvely that workers, like the peasants on his Pomeranian estate at Varzin, were simple folk, loyal to the crown at heart but woefully misled by red agitators; let the police deal with the trouble-makers, and welfare measures would quickly reconcile the workers to the Empire. In the background loomed military considerations; conservative circles were gravely alarmed by reports that recruits from industrial areas were unfit for military service; welfare socialism, like tariff protection, was essential if the fatherland was to survive in a hostile world.

Bismarck rightly enjoys the distinction of being the pioneer of state socialism. But he did not act in isolation. As so often before, he merely put his stamp on a well-established trend. The paternalist tradition had always been very strong in Germany. There was much less resistance to state intervention in the life of the community than in Britain and France, with their libertarian political traditions. Social Catholicism with its wide ramifications was part of the German scene, and its political arm, the Centre party, advocated limited state intervention in the industrial field. Protestants and Conservatives, though to a lesser extent, were also active in this field; on the extreme right wing the Protestant court chaplain, Stöcker, founded his short-lived Christian-Social party in 1878. Especially important in this context was the work of the so-called *Kathedersozialisten,*[9] a small group of influential economists and university professors, who founded the *Verein für Sozialpolitik* in 1872. Through its conferences and publications this association exerted a profound influence on social policy for the next sixty years. It did much to popularise the Hegelian belief that the state had moral objectives to encompass, one of the most important being the promotion of the material well-being of its citizens.

In 1881 Bismarck informed the Reichstag through the medium of an imperial proclamation that the repression of socialist excesses was not enough; the well-being of the worker must be actively promoted. Following this a comprehensive welfare system, the first in Europe, was created in the next decade. An act of 1883 provided medical treatment for three million workers and their families, the cost being borne jointly by workers and employers. In 1884 benefits and a burial grant were given to incapacitated workers under an accident-insurance act financed wholly by the employers. In 1886 accident and sickness insurance was extended to seven million agricultural workers. In 1889 workers were given a graduated pension at seventy, or earlier if disabled; this measure was financed by the workers, employers and the state. In 1891, after Bismarck's resignation, a code of factory legislation rounded off the system.

State socialism was supported in the Reichstag by the Centre and the Conservatives, the former out of genuine social conviction, the latter out of concern for the national interest. Opposition came from Socialists and Liberals, curious as this may seem at first sight. Socialists of the Eisenach school rejected welfarism as crumbs from the rich man's table; they realised only too clearly that state socialism would strengthen the power of the autocratic state and divert the working class from real socialism with its democratic connotations. Liberals were divided on the issue. Some fifty National Liberals supported Bismarck because a contented and docile working class was in the national interest as well as in their own economic interest as employers. The Radicals, on the other hand, clinging to the doctrinaire liberalism of 1848, firmly opposed state socialism on principle; to them insurance and state aid were violations of personal freedom and steps on the road to the omnipotent state. This outmoded attitude epitomised the strength and weakness of radicalism; a strength inasmuch as it made the Radicals champions of the individual against the state – a welcome corrective in the authoritarian climate of Imperial Germany. But electorally the attitude was a serious handicap, robbing the Radicals of any hope of building up a mass following in support of their advanced political views.

[9]Academic Socialists – a term of abuse coined by a liberal.

State socialism, continued and extended as it was in the reign of William II, became an integral part of the German scene. It undoubtedly helped the working class to acquire a modest stake in the Empire. This, in its turn, led to a gradual transformation in the attitude of the Socialist party to the state. By 1914 it could hardly be denied that German workers – largely by their own efforts – had more to lose by revolution than their chains; when Germany went to war, the Socialist party recognised this fact by rallying solidly round the imperial banner. But this was twenty years later in a vastly changed Germany. In Bismarck's day the success of state socialism was very much in doubt. The moody chancellor lost interest in it once it became clear that the working class still voted for 'the party of subversion' despite all his efforts. Workers were not likely to be won over as long as the police harried their representatives. That Bismarck thought this at all possible is an eloquent testimony to his complete failure to take the correct measure of social problems. There was other evidence of Bismarck's hostility to working people; he strongly opposed Socialist demands for state intervention to improve working conditions; he would not hear of legislation to regulate working hours, place restrictions on female and child labour and allow a Sunday rest, because he believed that employers must be masters in their own factories and that workers would not welcome restrictions of this kind. The psychological gulf between the patriarchal landowner and the Marxist-orientated factory worker was quite unbridgeable. Only when the Bismarck era was over could workers think differently about state socialism.

The 1880s were a difficult period for Bismarck at home and abroad. The emperor's advancing years suddenly cast a shadow over the chancellor's plans. Emperor William was in his eighties, and in the normal course of events Crown Prince Frederick must soon ascend the throne. Frederick, a man of liberal views married to the eldest daughter of Queen Victoria, had been an opponent of Bismarck over the years and had kept in touch with Radical leaders, including Richter and Bamberger. It seemed possible that Frederick would dismiss Bismarck and appoint a liberal chancellor. Such a change would be welcome to the Reichstag, where the majority was no longer in Bismarck's pocket. In 1881 the combined Radical parties won over 100 seats;[10] this was due in part to Bismarck's plans for a tobacco monopoly and for higher indirect taxation, which had aroused much popular criticism, whilst on the other side many upper-class liberals abstained from voting out of dislike for Bismarck's state socialism. In 1884 when the new party was formed, Crown Prince Frederick congratulated the Radicals on their good sense, an action which convinced Bismarck that Emperor Frederick would appoint a 'Gladstone cabinet' from this party. Bismarck could still rely on Conservative and National Liberal support in the 1880s,

[10]The secessionists who parted from the National Liberals in 1880 won fifty-five seats and the Progressives won sixty seats.

but only with support from the Centre could he scrape by in the Reichstag. And the Centre was unfortunately an unreliable ally, quite capable of voting with the Radicals when it suited Windthorst's book to do so. Many of Bismarck's measures were in fact mauled by the Reichstag; the tobacco monopoly and a proposed increase in indirect taxation were defeated in 1881; this ruined Bismarck's plans for financial reform; the *Reich* was once again in debt and had to resort to loans to pay for increased armaments and social welfare. State socialism was approved, but only in a modified form; originally Bismarck wanted only the state and the employers to finance his insurance schemes, fearing that workers would resent contributions. But Radical opposition to state subsidies forced him to modify his plans. Plagued by ill-health in the 1880s, and infuriated beyond measure by the uncertainties and complexities of a parliamentary situation where chance majorities could ruin his schemes, Bismarck lashed the parties, especially the Radicals – 'the crown prince's party', as he called them – with his vitriolic tongue. He complained to a friend that the Germans were ruining the toy that he had given them to play with. The thought of a *coup d'état* to abolish the Reichstag or reduce its powers undoubtedly crossed his mind from time to time. The corporate state with its authoritarian over-tones increasingly appealed to him; he wanted, for example, to turn the corporate bodies administering the insurance schemes into economic parliaments rivalling the Reichstag, but had finally to abandon the scheme for lack of funds.

The friction between chancellor and Reichstag came to a head in 1887 over the renewal of the army grant or Septennates. The current Septennates were not due to expire until 1888, but the darkening international scene alarmed the generals, who pressed for an early renewal. Accordingly, in November 1886, Bismarck asked the Reichstag to agree to substantial military increases. The Reichstag agreed, but the Radicals and the Centre insisted that Reichstags be allowed in future to review military expenditure every three years; thus every Reichstag, instead of only alter-nate Reichstags, would exercise some control over the army. Bismarck was furious. Twenty-five years before he had fought the Prussian Landtag on this very issue. 'The German army is an institution which cannot be dependent on transient Reichstag majorities,' he declared bluntly; 'This attempt to turn the imperial army into a parliamentary army maintained, not by the emperor and the associated governments, but by Windthorst and Richter will not succeed.' Brushing aside an offer from the parties to pass the estimates on certain conditions, he dissolved the Reichstag on January 1887. In the election campaign which followed, Bismarck exploited the international scene shamelessly in order to bring the Reichstag to heel. He quickly conjured up a picture of a revanchist France under General Boulanger ready for war at any moment; the fatherland would remain in grave danger until the Septennates were passed; only the

Kartell, the electoral alliance of Conservatives and National Liberals, could be relied upon to save the peace, and patriotic Germans should support it. Cynical and irresponsible exploitation of national feeling on this scale could not but retard the political education of the German people, and for that Bismarck bears a heavy responsiblity. In terms of the Reichstag the strategem succeeded; the Conservatives gained fifteen seats, the National Liberals forty-eight and his great enemies the Radicals were drastically cut back to thirty-two. Bismarck's dependence on the Centre was over at last; the *Kartell* had an absolute majority and the Septennates were passed. It was a sign of changing times that the Centre merely abstained during this vote. However, it is important to realise that Bismarck's success was much less complete in terms of the total poll. Government parties polled three-and-a-half million votes, opposition parties four million votes on an increased poll. Only the electoral device of the *Kartell*, plus the fact that the distribution of seats did not reflect the changing pattern of the population, gave Bismarck his victory.[11] Bismarck had not destroyed the grassroots of the German opposition; all he had done was obscure the tensions in German society temporarily by reshuffling seats in the Reichstag.

In March 1888 Emperor William died in his ninety-first year, and Crown Prince Frederick, the toast of the liberals, ascended the throne. The new era of liberal reform which might have swept Bismarck from office did not take place. Emperor Frederick was mortally ill and quite unable to resist Bismarck's determined efforts to isolate him from his Radical friends. The only change was the dismissal of Puttkamer whose name was a byword for reaction in progressive circles. Only on one occasion did the palace pursue an independent line, and that was in connexion with the Battenberg marriage. The empress set her heart on marrying her daughter Victoria to Alexander of Battenberg, the ex-prince of Bulgaria. Bismarck opposed the marriage on the grounds that it would prejudice relations with Russia, Alexander being *persona non grata* at St. Petersburg. Possibly Bismarck feared that the empress was grooming Alexander to fill his place one day. At any rate he had his National-Liberal allies launch a bitter press campaign against the empress, and he worked assiduously to turn Crown Prince William against his mother, with some success. In the end the project was abandoned, and Alexander settled for a German opera-singer from Darmstadt. The episode revealed only too clearly the vindictive streak in Bismarck's character, as well as the limits to his professions of loyalty to the Hohenzollerns. Frederick reigned only ninety-nine days and

[11]The Radicals lost only 30,000 votes but this cost them forty-two seats. The Centre gained 200,000 votes and lost one seat. Most striking anomaly of all, the Socialists gained 200,000 votes and actually lost thirteen seats.

died in June 1888. Historians have often felt that his death was a tragedy which robbed German liberalism of its one real chance to influence events decisively. No one can say what would have happened had Frederick lived, but it should be remembered that, although kindly and humane in outlook, the emperor was a somewhat indecisive individual, less committed to liberalism than friends thought, and most certainly a firm believer in the dignity and power of the monarchy.

When Crown Prince William ascended the throne, superficially Bismarck's position seemed secure again. He had cultivated the young prince's friendship, and William returned the compliment by expressing his admiration for the old man. Yet within two years it was all over; chancellor and emperor parted company for ever.

It was not possible to create the intimate friendship which bound William's grandfather to the chancellor for over a quarter of a century. A great psychological gulf separated the cantankerous old autocrat from the young prince of twenty-nine. As an impressionable boy of eleven, William trotted on his pony through the Brandenburg Gate when his grandfather returned as emperor from France. He had grown up in a noisy, ebullient and expanding Germany and was anxious to obtain for his country her rightful place in the sun. A man of great charm and with a quick mind and wide-ranging interests, a brilliant conversationalist and amiable companion, William was also a highly impatient and unstable personality. A restless individual with an insatiable appetite for activity, he played many parts with consummate skill; sometimes the soldier and lover of military pageantry, passionately devoted to his army; at times the modern ruler, interested in social problems; at times the intellectual, proud founder of the Emperor William Society for the Encouragement of Scientific Research. Unlike his grandfather, William would not stay in the background; he interfered in affairs of state, expressing his opinions in frequent after-dinner speeches much to the alarm of officials, whom he rarely consulted. Firmly convinced of his own infallibility, William threw caution to the winds on these occasions, declaring his intention of leading his people to a glorious future. Finally, he was a born autocrat with an exalted notion of his vocation and a contempt for the constitution, which he boasted he had never read – in short, a ruler unlikely to tolerate Bismarck's monopoly of political power for long. He had, in fact, resolved to dispense with the senile elder statesman as soon as decently possible.

The emperor was encouraged in his design by close friends like General Waldersee, whom he appointed chief of the German general staff on the retirement of Moltke in 1888. Waldersee was a prominent member of an influential group of extreme Conservatives which included Stöcker, the court chaplain. These men were seeking to capture the mind of the young ruler and overthrow Bismarck. Bismarck had not scrupled in the past to use intermediaries to turn William against his parents; the intermediaries now turned the emperor against his chancellor, and as he spent most of his time on his estate at Friedrichsruh near Hamburg, he could do little to fight back.

The open breach between emperor and chancellor began over social policy. In 1889 William intervened dramatically in the Ruhr miners' strike and settled the dispute by lecturing the employers on their responsibilities. With romantic visions of himself as a latter-day *'roi des gueux'*, William confidently believed that he could win over the working class by a modest extension of the social welfare system. Bismarck disagreed; he was deeply pessimistic about the future, had little faith in state socialism and believed that the forces of social anarchy could be kept at bay only by further repression. With this end in view, he proposed in 1889 to make the anti-socialist law permanent, including the clause which empowered municipal authorities to expel agitators from the towns. William was not against renewal for he, too, feared socialism. But he asked Bismarck to delete the expulsion clause, feeling that this was an unnecessarily harsh measure. Bismarck refused. In the end the Reichstag let him down. The *Kartell* was divided over the clause; some Conservatives supported it, while National Liberals and Free Conservatives favoured deletion. As Bismarck stubbornly refused to make any concessions to the parliamentary majority, the entire bill was rejected by the Reichstag in January 1890, an ominous sign that the chancellor's political power was crumbling away.

Early in February 1890, when the Reichstag elections were under way, William issued a proclamation promising new social legislation and announcing the calling of an international conference to discuss social questions. The absence of Bismarck's counter-signature from the proclamation caused a sensation. When his delaying tactics failed, Bismarck had bluntly refused to sign, and actually intrigued with foreign diplomats to frustrate the conference. Contemporaries sensed that the chancellor's days were numbered. The election results confirmed them in this belief. The *Kartell* of 1887 went down to an ignominious defeat; the Conservatives and National Liberals lost eighty-five seats between them; the Radicals gained forty-six seats and, most dramatic change of all, the Socialists won twenty-four seats; although still only the fifth party in terms of Reichstag seats, the Socialists polled more votes than any other party.[12] The electorate had in effect passed a massive vote of no-confidence in the chancellor and the opposition was once again in control of the Reichstag.

At long last Bismarck was trapped between an emperor bent on having his own way and a hostile Reichstag. He could not accept defeat gracefully but clung desperately to office. At first he thought of a *coup d'état*; he planned to put an anti-socialist bill and new military estimates before the Reichstag, certain that one or both measures would be rejected; the

[12] 1,427,298.

Reichstag would be repeatedly dissolved to bring it to heel; as a last resort he would summon a congress of princes to remake the constitution, drastically reducing the powers of the Reichstag. William, alarmed by the increased Socialist vote, readily agreed. Then, characteristically, he quickly changed his mind and ordered Bismarck not to renew the anti-socialist legislation.

In a last desperate attempt to stay in office, Bismarck revived an obsolete Prussian cabinet order of 1852 which required all Prussian ministers to consult their minister-president before communicating with the king. William demanded the repeal of an order which clearly restricted the exercise of his authority. Simultaneously Bismarck was busy in the Reichstag trying to create a fantastic new *Kartell* of Conservatives, Centrists, Poles, Guelfs and Danes. Windthorst, after discussions with Bismarck, commented sadly that he had just left the death-bed of a great man. The Conservatives bluntly refused even to discuss the matter. When Bismarck met William II on 15 March, they quarrelled violently. William disputed Bismarck's right to receive Windthorst and accused his chancellor of consorting with Jews and Jesuits.[13] The emperor insisted on repeal of the 1852 order; he reaffirmed his decision not to allow any dissolution of the Reichstag and ordered Bismarck to reduce the military estimates. Bismarck knew the sands had run out. Next day William demanded the instant repeal of the 1852 order, failing that, the chancellor's resignation. Bismarck was reluctant to resign over a triviality. Fate spared him this final humiliation. The emperor chanced to read a routine report referring to 'ominous' Russian troop movements in the Balkans. At once William accused Bismarck of gross dereliction of duty in failing to warn him in time to alert the Austrians. Bismarck now had his excuse for resigning over foreign policy, where he was undisputed master, rather than over domestic matters, where he was behaving like a petty tyrant. Bismarck's resignation letter of 17 March 1890 ignored the serious differences over domestic policy, merely remarking that the 1852 order was indispensable for good government; the real issue, he maintained, was the emperor's pursuit of an anti-Russian policy of which he could not approve. The resignation was accepted and his long reign was over. Only his son Herbert resigned with him. All the other ministers, his creatures, stayed on, feeling no gratitude to the old man, merely relief that the ogre had departed.

Bismarck retired to Friedrichsruh until his death in 1898. He could not break the habits of a lifetime and leave affairs of state alone. He resented his dismissal and was especially embittered by the emperor's refusal to install Herbert as chancellor. He remained a persistent and querulous critic of the regime, giving interviews to journalists, writing innumerable articles and dictating the notoriously unreliable *Reminiscences*.[14] Oddly enough,

[13]A reference to Bleichröder, Bismarck's Jewish banker friend.
[14]*Gedanken und Erinnerungen,* 6 vols., Stuttgart, 1898–1907.

he was more popular with the general public than in the past. But he failed completely to exert any influence on high policy, so that his last years were a bitter disappointment and a pathetic epitaph to a great career.

In Anglo-Saxon lands the propaganda of two world wars has made Bismarck a sinister figure; a direct line of descent is often traced from Bismarck through William II to Hitler. What can a historian writing in the last quarter of the twentieth century say of Bismarck? That he was a great man is undeniable. He towered above contemporaries, a veritable giant amongst pigmies. No other German exerted so profound an influence on German history in the nineteenth century. When he came to power in 1862, Germany was a confederation of independent states fossilised in the mould of 1815; when he left office, Germany was a united nation, a state of great stature, feared and respected by the Great Powers. Of course, once Germany became an industrial nation unification was probably inevitable. But this in no way detracts from his historical significance as the executant of a historical process. In his own lifetime and long after his death, Bismarck was idolised by millions of his fellow-countrymen who saw in him the embodiment of Germany's will to be a nation. Nor did his services to Germany end in 1871. As chancellor he helped shape the destinies of the new Empire for two decades, in fact nearly half its lifetime. He undoubtedly committed monumental blunders in his handling of the Church and the working class; and he was tenacious in defence of the class interests of the Junkers to whom he belonged. Yet, on the other hand, he helped to promote the modernisation of Germany and was responsible for a social welfare system which, though it disappointed its creator and did no more than file some of the rough edges off the system, did in the long run give working people some limited stake in the survival of the Empire.

Like all great men he had serious defects and limitations. He was petty, vindictive and ruthless in his treatment of those who stood in his way. His tyrannical methods, intolerance of independence of mind in others and his lust for power left their mark on the whole apparatus of government, infecting subordinates with the corruption of manners inevitable under a personal dictatorship. His most serious limitation was that he was cast in the mould of the eighteenth century. To him government was essentially a function of rulers and officials, not of peoples. Most certainly he had some understanding of the dynamic political and social implications of an industrial society. But his 'Bonapartist' methods – seeking to satisfy the material interests of aristocracy, middle class and (to some extent) working class whilst barring the way to more responsible government – seriously retarded Germany's political growth. The idea that the Reichstag might one day become an instrument for articulating the will of the people and effecting political and social change was quite outside his understanding. At best he treated the Reichstag with condescension. When it refused to do his will, he turned on it with primitive fury, fighting hostile parties as if they were hostile foreign powers. It was no accident that the best minds stayed out of politics, leaving the Reichstag, with some honourable exceptions, in the hands of mediocre bureaucrats incapable of broad vision. Nor does the Empire seem to have had any cosmic significance for Bismarck. Power was an end in itself. He could not envisage Germany after his day and made no attempt to train up any political class capable of steering Germany through the rapids of the twentieth century.

The sociologist Max Weber, writing in 1917, summarised these negative aspects of Bismarck's heritage succinctly and accurately:

'Bismarck left behind him as his political heritage a nation without any political education, far below the level which, in this respect, it had reached twenty years earlier. Above all, he left behind a nation without any political will, accustomed to allow the great statesman at its head to look after its policy for it. Moreover, as a consequence of his misuse of the monarchy as a cover for his own interests in the struggle of political parties, he left a nation accustomed to submit, under the label of constitutional monarchy, to anything which was decided for it, without criticising the political qualifications of those who now occupied Bismarck's empty place and who with incredible ingenuousness now took the reins of power into their hands.'

6

Bismarck's Foreign Policy 1871–1890

The proclamation of the German Empire at Versailles in 1871 turned a new page in the history of Europe. During the first half of the century, when Germany lay weak and disunited, Austria, France and Russia had been the dominant powers on the Continent. After the Franco-Prussian war, 'the German revolution', as Disraeli called it, the balance of power was deeply disturbed. In the 1870s France and Austria-Hungary were recovering from defeat; Russia was as interested in Central Asia as in Europe; and Britain was still in her isolationist interlude. These circumstances conspired together to assure for Germany, temporarily, a position of relative hegemony in Europe. For the time being she was, as one historian has remarked, more than a traditional Great Power but less than a World Power in the class of Britain and Russia.

Bismarck, who monopolised the conduct of German foreign policy for nearly twenty years, appreciated the essential precariousness of Germany's position. The multi-national empires of the Romanovs and Habsburgs were fixed points in Bismarck's diplomatic compass, not only because of his innate conservatism but because any attempt to disrupt the existing order of things by extending Germany's frontiers in any direction would bring the other Great Powers down on Germany. The 'nationalist' poacher had to become an imperial gamekeeper preserving the *status quo* of 1871 if Germany was to survive.

The chief danger to the new order of things came potentially from France. After her long period of hegemony reaching back to the days of Richelieu and Mazarin, France would have resented defeat under any circumstances. The annexation of Alsace-Lorraine (for which Bismarck bore heavy responsibility) merely put a sharper edge on her natural resentment. In the early 1870s she made determined efforts to throw off the effects of defeat. Her rapid military reorganisation on German lines and the prompt repayment of the indemnity of 1873 surprised and alarmed many Germans.

How could Bismarck contain the French and avoid a fresh conflagration? A means lay close at hand. Bismarck had helped to disrupt the old understanding between Austria, Prussia and Russia in order to make Prussia dominant in Germany. Once his purpose was accomplished, the chancellor's instinct as a conservative was to restore the *'entente à trois'*. The revival of France confirmed his instinct; a three emperors' league would keep France quiet and preserve the *status quo* in the east, where all three had Polish subjects to keep in order. Friendship with Russia was essential for geographical reasons as well; Germany faced the real danger of war on two fronts if she was on bad terms with France and Russia simultaneously. As relations with France were bad, the line to St. Petersburg had to remain open. At the same time Bismarck did not want to be completely dependent on the Russian colossus and be dragged willy-nilly into her disputes with Britain in Asia. The friendship of Austria was important to Germany not only because it deprived France of a potential ally, but because it gave Bismarck a welcome degree of independence in his dealings with Russia.

Austria and Russia were both anxious to have the friendship of Germany; Austria because of the growing antagonism with Russia in the Balkans; Russia because she did not want to face a hostile coalition of European powers if war broke out in Asia. Still, it did not prove easy for the three emperors to come to terms when they exchanged visits in 1872 and 1873. The deepening conflict between Austria and Russia cast a dark shadow over the proceedings. Francis Joseph bluntly refused to sign the military convention agreed to by William I and Tsar Alexander II. In the end the three emperors could agree only to consult on matters of common interest or if a third power disturbed the peace of Europe. So from the start the new 'Holy Alliance' lacked credibility; there was much talk of defending monarchy against republicanism and socialism – a Bismarckian device for holding the *entente* together – but precious little positive content.

Not surprisingly the Three Emperors' League quickly foundered. It was severely shaken as early as 1875 during the 'War-in-sight' crisis. Bismarck was irritated and alarmed by the growing confidence of France. At home the Kulturkampf was arousing great opposition, and French and Belgian clergy were openly encouraging German Catholics to resist the pretensions of the state. It did not take Bismarck long to conjure up a fanciful picture of a great clerical-royalist conspiracy against Germany directed by the war-mongering French royalists. Moltke's advocacy of preventive war did not impress Bismarck. He remained adamantly opposed on principle to the pre-emptive strike as interference with the workings of Divine Providence, quite apart from the damage it would do to Germany's reputation. But he saw no harm in scaring France into abandoning her rearmament. The export of horses to France was forbid-den – usually a prelude to mobilisation – and in April 1875 an article appeared in the influential *Berliner Post* entitled 'Is war in sight?', which concluded that it was, as France had just passed legislation increasing the size of her army. Radowitz, who was the German *chargé d'affaires* in St. Petersburg and a close colleague of Bismarck, hinted to the French ambassador over the port that some influential Germans favoured preventive war; the same day Moltke made similar comments to the Belgian ambassador. The remarks were reported to Paris, and the French foreign minister, Decazes, immediately asked Britain and Russia for protection. Decazes had tried frequently, and without success in the past, to rouse Britain to the dangers threatening France from Germany. Now he succeeded, for the conservatives, who came to power in Britain in 1874, hankered after an active foreign policy. Disraeli was suspicious of the Three Emperors' League and disliked Bismarck: 'another old Bonaparte again and he must be bridled', he remarked to the queen. Disraeli proposed a joint protest in Berlin by the Great Powers. Italy and Austria-Hungary refused but Russia saw no harm in putting Bismarck in his place. In May the British and Russian ambassadors made their joint *démarche* in Berlin, warning Germany of the dangers of war. The tsar and his chancellor, Prince Gortschakov, paid a visit to Berlin to reinforce the warning. Bismarck soon convinced his visitors that the rumours of preventive war were false and they departed satisfied.

So the 'War-in-sight' crisis ended in a defeat for Germany and a diplomatic victory for France. True, Britain and Russia would not have moved a finger to aid France had she attacked Germany, as the new order in Europe suited them perfectly well. More to the point, the crisis made it plain that these powers would not allow Germany to destroy France and become absolute master of Europe. Bismarck was angered by the turn of events. He could not bear to be outmanoeuvred and never forgave Gortschakov for his part in the *démarche*; in fact his enmity towards the Russian chancellor probably had permanent effects on his attitude to Russia. The whole crisis brought home forcibly the real danger of a war on two fronts and undoubtedly impressed him with the need for the utmost caution in the future.

The crisis revealed structural weaknesses in the Three Emperors' League; the Near Eastern crisis of 1877–78 destroyed it completely. In the closing decades of the nineteenth century the Christian peoples of the Ottoman Empire were stirred by the hope of independence. Austria-Hungary and Russia were deeply involved in the Balkans; Austria because she was worried about the impact of nationalism in her own empire; and Russia because of the Straits, which had immense economic and strategic importance for her. At first they contained their rivalry within the Three Emperors' League. Thus when the people of Bosnia-Herzegovina revolted in 1875, Austria-Hungary and Russia readily co-operated in an attempt to impose reforms on the sultan. The mediation attempts – of which Bismarck approved – failed; the Turks would not reform, the Bosnians wanted more than reform, and the Serbs complicated the situation by declaring war on Turkey. Then in November 1876 the tsar was converted to Panslavism and decided to pursue a forward policy in defence of the Slav peoples regardless of Austrian wishes. Russian and Austrian policy was suddenly out of step, and both turned to Germany for support.

What happened in the Balkans was of relatively little interest to Bismarck, who once remarked that the area was not worth 'the healthy bones of a single Pomeranian musketeer'. Russia could do as she pleased with the Turk as long as she acted in accord with Austria-Hungary. But the effect on Germany's international position of any serious disagreement between Russia and Austria-Hungary mattered a great deal. For if Germany was compelled to choose between them, the rejected suitor would find a willing ally in France, and an obscure Balkan dispute would quickly develop into a general conflagration. This *'cauchemar des coalitions'*, as Bismarck once called it, was a perpetual danger because of the resentment France bore Germany. Thus when the tsar asked Germany in December 1876 whether she would remain neutral in a war between Austria and Russia, Bismarck replied with masterly evasion that it was not in Germany's interests to see either power so seriously defeated in war that its independence was threatened. Similarly when Andrassy, the Austrian foreign minister, talked of an Austro-German alliance against Russia, Bismarck flatly rejected the proposal; balance between the two, not the victory of either, was his objective.

In January 1877 Russia came to terms with Austria-Hungary; in return for a Russian promise that no large Slav state would be created in the Balkans, Austria-Hungary promised benevolent neutrality if Russia attacked Turkey. When Turkey rejected another attempt by the powers to impose reform on her, Russia declared war. The war lasted longer than Russia expected. Not until the spring of 1878 did Russia impose the San Stefano peace on defeated Turkey. The most sensational feature of the treaty was the proposal to create a large Bulgaria with a foothold on the Aegean Sea. Britain took fright, fearing that Bulgaria would be a Russian satellite. Disraeli sent the fleet to the Straits, and war seemed imminent. Russia, however, was too weakened by her exertions to fight Britain and Austria-Hungary too – for the Austrians were infuriated by Russia's breach of agreement over Bulgaria. In the end a congress of the Great Powers met in Berlin in June 1878 to settle the questions at issue. This was a great diplomatic occasion, the first full-dress meeting of the Concert of Europe since 1856. Bismarck presided over the congress as the self-styled 'honest broker', seeking no territorial gain for Germany but intent only on arranging a settlement which would leave the balance of power unaltered. At critical moments, especially over Bulgaria, his energetic intervention saved the day, and in general he established a new reputation for himself as a peace maker. He was not, in fact, particularly well pleased by the turn of events; originally he wanted the congress to be held in Paris, and when Russia proposed Berlin he suggested a French president, no doubt hoping to avoid personal involvement in a settlement unlikely to please Germany's allies.

His instinct proved correct. The Near Eastern crisis dealt a mortal blow to the Three Emperors' League. Russia left Berlin a dissatisfied power. Influential circles in St. Petersburg, led by Gortschakov, felt that she had been cheated of her just reward. Frustrated by their failure but reluctant to admit that their own policy had been at fault, the Russians looked for a scapegoat and found one in Germany. The Panslav press accused Bismarck of leading an anti-Russian conspiracy at the congress and declared that the Three Emperors' League was no more. In vain did Bismarck protest that, far from being an honest broker, he had been a 'fourth Russian plenipotentiary'. Yet, when Russo-German relations deteriorated rapidly in the first half of 1879, this was very largely of Bismarck's own making. The situation was complex. In defence of the class interests of Prussian landowners he was committed to protective tariffs against Russian wheat, a measure certain to deepen anti-German feeling in a backward country so dependent on exports for its modernisation. But, in the interests of German hegemony in Europe and despite personal dislike of Gortschakov, Bismarck had also to persuade Russia that she could not do without Germany. That could be best achieved, he decided, by bullying tactics. In January 1879 he went out of his way in the Reichstag to emphasise those features of the tariff bill which did most harm to Russia. Soon afterwards he banned the import of Russian cattle, when an outbreak of cattle disease gave a pretext; in February he announced cancellation of clause five of the Treaty of Prague, which had committed Austria and Prussia to hold a plebiscite in North Schleswig, an action deeply offensive to the tsar on account of marriage ties between the Danish royal family and the Romanovs. In retaliation the Russians strengthened their frontier garrisons and made soundings in Italy for an alliance; finally, in August the tsar, who thought Bismarck a 'frightful scoundrel', warned William I of the dangers of a policy which Alexander attributed to Bismarck's dislike of Gortschakov.

Perhaps Bismarck felt that the situation was at last getting out of hand. At all events, even before the tsar's minatory epistle arrived, Bismarck was on his way to Bad Gastein, where he met Andrassy and discussed a formal alliance with Austria-Hungary. At first Bismarck proposed an ambitious all-embracing alliance against aggression, to be sanctioned by both parliaments. Andrassy rejected this because he saw no reason why Austria-Hungary should become involved in disputes between Germany and France. Bismarck, anxious that Austria should not succumb to Russian pressure, or, worse still, look to France for support, gave way. In October 1879 the formal alliance was signed. It was a straightforward defensive alliance committing Germany and Austria-Hungary to resist Russian aggression; but if Germany or Austria-Hungary was at war with a third power, the other partner would remain neutral unless Russia intervened. In effect Germany was bound to aid Austria-Hungary in the event of a Russian attack but Austria-Hungary was not bound to support Germany against France.

In his reminiscences Bismarck describes the Austrian alliance as the fruition of a grand design cherished since 1866. There is, in fact, no evidence that he had it in mind before 1879. The truth is that he acted once again on the spur of the moment to deal with an emergency situation largely of his own making. The alliance was a temporary expedient to preserve the precarious balance of power in the Balkans by warning Russia off Austria. In no sense was Bismarck making a final choice between them. He never wavered in his belief that the *'entente à trois'* was Germany's salvation. During the negotiations he actually suggested to Andrassy that Russia be brought in, a proposal which the Austrians flatly rejected. The alliance was signed only after a fierce struggle with the emperor. The upright old conservative for whom good relations with Russia were of paramount importance thought an alliance specifically directed against Germany's best friend an undue provocation. In the end Bismarck, with the support of the crown prince, of Moltke and of the Prussian ministers, forced the emperor's hand by threatening resignation. Reluctantly William gave way, but commented bitterly: 'Those men who have compelled me to this step will be held responsible for it above.'

The secret alliance of five years' duration was renewed regularly down to 1918 and became the very corner-stone of German foreign policy. It grew steadily in importance over the years until its preservation became the mainspring of German policy in the early twentieth century. Bismarck's concern was, however, not with the distant future but with the immediate situation and from that point of view the alliance of 1879 served its purpose; it strengthened Austria against Russia and ensured that she would not seek allies elsewhere. It had some value, too, inside Germany, where it helped to reconcile Catholics to the Empire; and it did something to bring the two German-speaking peoples together for the first time since 1866 by creating an identity of interest in the field of foreign policy. Only later were some of these advantages clear to Bismarck. For the present he had allayed Austria's fears of Russia, and he proceeded briskly to bring back Russia into the fold. This was not difficult. By the end of 1879 Russia was thoroughly alarmed by her diplomatic isolation and anxious for an understanding with Germany. Gortschakov retired in 1880, to be replaced by the conciliatory Giers, while Bismarck got on well with Saburov, the new Russian ambassador in Berlin. All the difficulties came from Vienna, where the new foreign minister Haymerle, a bitter Russophobe, was seeking an alliance with Britain, the natural enemy of Russia. Unfortunately for him the anti-Russian and pro-Austrian conservatives were defeated in 1880, and Gladstone, the great enemy of Austria, came to power. Reluctantly Haymerle knuckled under and in June 1881 the Three Emperors' Alliance was signed.

The alliance was a secret treaty of three years' duration. It stated that if one of the three powers was at war with a fourth, the others would remain neutral. The three signatories pledged themselves to keep the Straits closed to foreign warships and declared that they would permit no changes in the Balkan *status quo* except by mutual agreement. If one of them went to war with Turkey, the other two promised to remain neutral on condition that prior agreement had been reached about territorial changes after the war. Bismarck hoped to reduce tension between Austria and Russia by commending peaceful co-existence to the rivals; the eastern half of the Balkans was to be a Russian sphere of influence, the western half an Austrian sphere. Russia recognised the right of Austria-Hungary to annex Bosnia-Herzegovina. In return Austria acknowledged that Bulgaria was in the Russian sphere of influence and promised to raise no objection to the union of Eastern Roumelia and Bulgaria.

The alliance pleased Russia. Her partners had written off half the Balkans and promised not to side with Britain should she attack Russia; they were even committed to opposing Britain actively should she try to force the sultan to open the Straits. These gains did something to reinsure Russia against the effects of the Austro-German alliance, although she continued to resent the existence of an alignment directed against her.[1]

For Bismarck this was the conservative alliance restored. His confident assertion to William I that Russia would come back despite the 1879 alliance had proved correct. 'This is the best receipt for my Viennese policy,' he remarked to Radowitz; 'I knew that the Russians would come to us once we had pinned the Austrians down.' The liberal honeymoon was over, inside and outside Germany. It was not ideology but plain utility which kept the new combinations afloat; protective tariffs bound Conservatives and Centrists to Bismarck. Similarly with Austria-Hungary and Russia; Bismarck had accommodated the Austrians in 1879 and the Russians in 1881. What he could not do, however – and of this he was well aware – was to satisfy both powers indefinitely; the deep-seated antagonism between them could not be conjured away; peaceful co-existence was precarious in the short run and almost impossible in the long run. His private doubts were soon confirmed; once the rivalry between Austria and Russia was reactivated at the close of the 1880s, the Three Emperors' Alliance followed the Three Emperors' League into oblivion.

In 1882 Bismarck acquired a new and unexpected ally in Italy. Unexpected, as Bismarck had a poor opinion of Italy, remarking *à propos* of her

[1] William I, with Bismarck's permission, informed the tsar of the contents of the 'secret' alliance in November 1879.

colonial ambitions that she had a great appetite but poor teeth. Italy was attempting to ally with Austria-Hungary at this time. In 1881 France occupied Tunis and put an abrupt end to Italian aspirations in this part of North Africa. Italian public opinion was outraged and forced the government to seek allies; hence the approach to Vienna. The negotiations deadlocked, since Italy had nothing to offer her northern neighbour. There the matter might have rested had not Bismarck suddenly found a use for despised Italy. He became alarmed by signs that Panslav influences were gaining ground in St. Petersburg. When General Skobelev, a leading Panslav, visisted Paris, Bismarck feared a Franco-Russian understanding was in the making. An alliance with Italy might have some use, if only of a negative nature; it would deprive France of a potential ally and would relieve Austria-Hungary in the event of war in the Balkans. It might stabilise the crown in Italy; this was a factor of some importance, for Bismarck feared that if the Italian radicals succeeded in overthrowing the monarchy, this would encourage opponents of monarchy in all lands; these were troubled times for crowned heads and Bismarck saw Italian radicals, Russian anarchists and German Socialists as part and parcel of a vast subterranean plot to subvert the existing order of society. The negotiations between Rome and Vienna were reactivated and led to the Triple Alliance of 1882.

The Alliance was of five years' duration and committed the signatories to uphold the monarchical principle and the existing social and political order. More specifically the three partners agreed to aid each other if one or more was attacked, without provocation on their part, by two or more powers. In an Austro-Russian war Italy would remain neutral; in a Franco-German war Italy would aid Germany but Austria would stay neutral; and if France attacked Italy without direct provocation, Austria-Hungary and Germany would aid their ally. In a separate protocol the Italians, acutely conscious of their vulnerability to attack by sea, expressed the hope that the alliance would not disturb the traditional friendship with Britain.

The Italians were pleased with the alliance. It conferred prestige on the new kingdom and encouraged Italy to embark on colonial adventures in the Red Sea area. Certainly her allies were not committed to supporting Italy in North Africa, but the Italians hoped that this would come later. Austria-Hungary gained something, for the assurance of Italian neutrality enabled her to switch four army corps from the southern frontier in an emergency. Germany gained precious little. The German promise to defend Italy against unprovoked French aggression admittedly meant little, so remote was the eventuality. Yet even this was of more use to Italy than her promise to aid Germany against France. Bismarck carefully restrained Italy in Africa, as he restrained Austria in the Balkans. All the same, he could not escape the consequences of an alliance which, like that of 1879, was engineered to extricate him from temporary difficulties.

Certainly the alliance succeeded in its immediate objective but its long-term significance was to ally Germany with a restless and ambitious power whose basic hostility to Austria-Hungary was masked only by her desire for an African empire. Early in the twentieth century the alliance lost its *raison d'être* for Italy. In a sense the unintended outcome of Bismarck's diplomacy was to ally Germany with two unstable powers. Despite their solemn pledge to defend the existing order, one ended up fighting Germany, while ostensibly to defend the other Germany plunged recklessly into a world war.

The Bismarckian 'system' reached high noon in 1884. The solid structure of the Triple Alliance was supplemented by a secret agreement with Serbia (1881) which turned the country virtually into an Austrian satellite, and by an agreement with Rumania (1883) providing for joint military action against Russian aggression. The Three Emperors' Alliance was renewed in 1884, and Bismarck even managed to be on tolerably good terms with France.

There was a new and surprising departure in 1884 when Germany acquired the beginnings of a colonial empire in Africa. Previously Bismarck had opposed colonialism, remarking once that for Germany to acquire colonies would be like a poor Polish nobleman buying silks and sables when he needed shirts. Things changed in the 1880s. Colonialism became fashionable once the European powers partitioned Africa in earnest. In all lands enthusiastic pressure-groups sprang up agitating for colonies on economic grounds and as a sign of national greatness; in Germany the *Kolonialverein*, founded in 1882 with support from industry, did much to interest public opinion in overseas expansion. Already the state was intervening more extensively in overseas trade as the unavoidable consequence of the transition from free trade to protection. These factors all played their part in Bismarck's change of front. There were probably some political considerations as well; colonialism was a convenient stick with which to beat Radicals and Socialists at the 1884 elections; and by exploiting anti-British feeling in Germany he may have hoped to discredit Crown Prince Frederick's pro-English advisers and make reorientation of foreign policy difficult should the old emperor die. Official support was given to German merchants seeking concessions from native chieftains. Between 1884 and 1885 Germany acquired South-West Africa, Togoland, the Cameroons, German East Africa and some Pacific islands. Bismarck did not set much store by the new colonies. They were intended only to encourage German traders and never became military bases in his lifetime. He also insisted that all administrative costs be borne by the chartered companies, not by the *Reich*. For at bottom he knew that Germany could never cut a great figure overseas: 'my map of Africa lies in Europe,' he once remarked to an eager explorer. 'Here is Russia and here is France and we are in the middle; that is my map of Africa.'

Had colonialism not happened to fit in with the general objectives of his foreign policy, Bismarck would certainly not have embarked upon it. However, at this time he was watching with some satisfaction the growing rivalry in Africa between Britain and France. As long as it lasted it made the two powers more dependent on Germany and diverted French attention from Alsace-Lorraine. The rivalry might be turned to Germany's advantage in another way. As Bismarck grew increasingly dubious about the viability of the Russian connexion, he seriously considered the possibility of a lasting reconciliation with France as the only way of avoiding war on two fronts. Active co-operation with France in the colonial field was the first step; by picking quarrels with Britain over German colonial claims he aligned Germany on the side of France. Together they opposed British financial reform in Egypt and supported each other's colonial claims. Later Bismarck talked of a general *entente* and a maritime league to isolate Britain and force her to abandon her colonial monopoly. In fact Britain was quite prepared to do so and was more than a little puzzled by Bismarck's anti-British policy. The Franco-German *entente* reached its high-water mark at the Berlin Conference of 1884–85 called to regulate the affairs of Central Africa. All the European powers, except Switzerland and Luxemburg, were represented and the United States. The conference recognised the Congo Free State, upheld free-trade principles in Central Africa, prohibited the slave trade and laid down general rules for the occupation of the unpartitioned parts of Africa.[2]

Further proof that Bismarck's 'system' was operating effectively came in the spring of 1885 when a Russian army defeated the Afghans at Pendjeh. It is not certain that Bismarck actively encouraged the Russian operations in Central Asia as a further anti-British gesture, but he certainly knew of the Russian plans and approved them. The alarm-bells were set ringing in London, where it was firmly believed that if Afghanistan fell India would soon follow. Gladstone prepared to send a force through the Straits. The continental powers closed their ranks. France joined with the Triple Alliance powers in warning the sultan not to accede to the British request. The sultan agreed, and as Russia submitted the Afghan dispute to arbitration in May 1885, the crisis died away. But it was, as a historian of this period remarks, the most effective display of continental solidarity between Napoleon's continental system and the Russo-German pact of 1939.[3]

The solidarity of the European Great Powers was short-lived. By the autumn of 1885 the 'system' was showing serious signs of wear and tear. For one thing the Franco-German *entente* collapsed. Jules Ferry, the prime minister who had worked with Bismarck, fell from power in March 1885; nationalist elements, led by Déroulède's League of Patriots, gained

---

[2] They also banned the use of coloured troops in a European theatre of war.
[3] A.J.P. Taylor, *The struggle for mastery in Europe*, 1848–1918, Oxford, 1954, p. 300.

ground in France in the summer and autumn; in January 1886, when their hero, the revanchist General Boulanger, became minister of war, Franco-German relations began to deteriorate. The failure of Bismarck's brief essay in reconciliation was inevitable; France was willing enough to co-operate with Germany over colonies, but she carefully avoided talk of a general *entente* having no desire to become completely dependent on Germany and lose all hope of recovering Alsace-Lorraine.

Secondly, the Near Eastern question erupted once more, smashing the Three Emperors' Alliance beyond repair. Since 1881 Austria and Russia had been busily consolidating their respective spheres of influence in the Balkans. Austria met with great success in Serbia. Russia, however, ran into serious difficulties in Bulgaria, where there was much resentment of autocratic Russian officials and officers. Prince Alexander of Bulgaria struck out on an independent line, fully supported by the nationalist-minded Bulgarian assembly; in September 1885, without consulting his cousin the Russian tsar, Alexander engineered the union of Eastern Roumelia with Bulgaria. Russia deeply resented this unilateral action and demanded a return to the *status quo*. Meanwhile in November, Serbia, fearing that Prince Alexander's ambitions were growing, attacked Bulgaria. The Bulgars made short work of the Serbs at Slivnitza and prepared to invade Serbia. So enmeshed were the powers by this time in the web of commitments spun by Bismarck that an obscure local war might easily have developed into a major conflagration. Austria warned Bulgaria peremptorily that she would find Austrian troops waiting for her if she dared to cross the frontier. The warning stopped the Bulgarian offensive but it strained Austro-Russian relations to breaking-point. Bismarck, desperately anxious to remain friends with both powers, had to inform Austria bluntly that Germany could not fight Russia over this issue. In the end the Serbs extricated themselves from a highly embarrassing situation without territorial loss, and Austria and Russia finally agreed to the union of Eastern Roumelia and Bulgaria under the fiction of personal union.

This was not the end of the Bulgarian crisis. In August 1886 Prince Alexander was kidnapped by pro-Russian officers and was later ordered to abdicate by the Russian tsar. Alexander did so and retired into obscurity, pursued to the end of his life by the vindictive Bismarck who never forgave him for stirring up the Balkans; this was one reason why the chancellor was so bitterly opposed to the proposed marriage between Alexander and Princess Victoria, the daughter of Emperor Frederick. Having disposed of Alexander, the Russians sent a general to take over as governor of Bulgaria. But Bulgaria had come of age at last, and led by her peasant premier Stambulov resisted Russian dictation. In November the tsar broke off diplomatic relations, and it seemed probable that Russia would invade Bulgaria, if only to save face. This in its turn would arouse Austria, for her foreign minister, Kàlnoky, was opposed to the partition of the Balkans on which the Three Emperors' Alliance rested, and saw no reason why Austria should not control the whole of the Balkans if she could. In Germany there was some clamour for preventive war against Russia. Once again Bismarck warned Austria that Germany could not help her. Russia did not, in fact, intervene in Bulgaria but the situation remained tense for months to come.

As Austro-Russian relations reached their nadir, Bismarck's fears of France suddenly revived. General Boulanger was by this time an extremely popular figure; his army reorganisation was applauded by enthusiastic nationalists, who now talked openly of a war of revenge in alliance with Russia. To make matters worse, Panslav advisers sympathetic to France and hostile to Germany, were exerting great influence in official circles in St. Petersburg; in November 1886 the tsar remarked to the French ambassador that Russia and France must be able to rely on each other in the troubled times that lay ahead. Bismarck was suddenly alarmed by the prospect of a Franco-Russian alliance in the near future. It is true that, for domestic reasons, he deliberately exaggerated the danger of war; in April 1887, with the Reichstag safely in his pocket, he even made light of the whole episode: 'I couldn't invent Boulanger but he happened very conveniently for me,' he quipped. This was said with hindsight when it was clear that the general had much less popular support than was supposed. But it does not alter the fact that Bismarck was alarmed by the situation at the beginning of 1887 and felt that military and diplomatic precautions were needed to safeguard Germany.

Part of the price he had to pay for peace of mind was the renewal of the Triple Alliance in February 1887 on terms more favourable to Italy than she obtained in 1882. As the tensions grew in Europe, Italy seized her opportunity to extort better terms from her partners. Her threat of approaching France unless her wishes were respected forced Bismarck's hand. He persuaded the reluctant Austrians to promise to consult Italy on all matters affecting the Balkans, the Adriatic and the Aegean, and to compensate her for alterations in the *status quo* in that area. Germany went further; she promised military support for any retaliatory action taken by Italy in the event of a French occupation of Tripoli or Morocco. If it came to war, Germany agreed to support Italian demands for substantial territorial gains from France.

The new commitments were, in fact, less onerous than they appeared at first sight. Although the details of the new agreements remained a closely guarded secret, the knowledge of their signature would be enough, so Bismarck calculated, to deter France from further expansion in North Africa. He was also greatly heartened by the knowledge that Britain had in effect under-written these German commitments. This arose out of the anxiety of the British foreign secretary, the Marquess of Salisbury, to end

British isolation and to stop French interference in Egypt. In February 1887 Salisbury negotiated an agreement with Italy committing the parties to the maintenance of the *status quo* in the Adriatic, Aegean and Mediterranean seas *'autant que possible'*. When Salisbury asked Austria-Hungary to join in, Bismarck encouraged her, and in March the First Mediterranean Agreement came into being to defend the *status quo*. France was effectively isolated and unable to move, so that Germany was even less likely to be called upon to fulfil her obligations to Italy. And in the last resort, as Bismarck admitted in private, he would have found a loophole in the loosely worded protocol to evade all responsibility to the Italians. For the time being he was satisfied that Italy had been kept away from France and that Britain had been associated, even if only indirectly, with the Triple Alliance powers.

The Triple Alliance had been safely renewed but there was no hope of renewing the Three Emperors' Alliance which expired in the summer of 1887. Russia made it clear that she would sign no agreement with Austria, only one with Germany. Even that hung in the balance for several months; Panslavs at the imperial court pressed hard for an agreement with France, and the tsar was greatly attracted by the prospect of playing Germany off against France. But France, grown suddenly cautious since the exclusion of Boulanger from the government, avoided Russian feelers, and the conservative diplomats who believed firmly in the utility of a Russo-German pact got the upper hand at St. Petersburg. Reluctantly Alexander III accepted their argument that an agreement with Germany was better than nothing, and in June 1887 the Reinsurance treaty was signed.

Much controversy has surrounded this treaty. Between the world wars ardent defenders of the old chancellor hailed it as his masterpiece, 'the corner-stone' of the 'system'. This is a gross exaggeration. Bismarck certainly did not attach much importance to it. Herbert Bismarck, close confidant of his father, remarked that 'the only value of it was that in an emergency it might keep the Russians off our necks for six or eight weeks longer than otherwise might have been the case'. The agreement was very limited in scope. During the negotiations Russia wanted each power to remain neutral if the other was at war with a third power; in effect Russia wanted a free hand against Austria, in return for which she offered Germany a free hand against France. But Bismarck refused and told Russia that under the 1879 treaty Germany could remain neutral only if Austria-Hungary attacked Russia; if Russia was the aggressor, Germany was bound to aid Austria-Hungary. On learning this, Russia would only promise neutrality if France attacked Germany; if Germany was the aggressor, Russia would not promise to remain neutral. Thus the element of 'reinsurance' was slight; a Franco-Russian agreement to resist Austrian or German aggression was not excluded; indeed the 1894 alliance was perfectly compatible with the text of the Reinsurance treaty.

There was little improvement in Russo-German relations following the Reinsurance treaty. Russian troop movements continued on the western frontiers. There were renewed signs of *rapprochement* between France and Russia; French and Russian staff officers made contact with each other; Déroulède was greeted warmly during his Russian tour in August 1887; in October Grand Duke Nicholas, toasting officers on board a French steamer, welcomed the prospect of war against Germany with France as an ally. In March a ukase forbade foreigners to buy land in the western provinces or to accept posts as factors in Poland, measures which affected the many Germans employed in that country. In retaliation the German press, with Bismarck's tacit approval, launched a campaign against Russian state loans which were mostly raised in Germany; in November Bismarck ordered the *Reichsbank* not to deal in Russian securities, in order, as he said, 'to remove the possibility that [the Russians] wage war against us at our cost'; this only drove the Russians into the arms of the French, for when the former found the Berlin money market closed to them they simply turned to Paris, where French financiers were eager to accommodate them.

The Bulgarian question was still causing trouble. In a highly secret protocol to the Reinsurance treaty Bismarck had promised moral and diplomatic support for Russia if she took measures to protect her interests at the Straits; he also promised to support her in Bulgaria and to oppose the return of Alexander of Battenberg. When Ferdinand of Coburg was elected prince in July 1887, Russia took umbrage; she wanted to regain control of Bulgaria by appointing a Russian general as provisional regent, and it looked as if the long-awaited intervention was imminent. Bismarck broke off diplomatic relations with Bulgaria to please Russia. Russia was not grateful; she expected Germany to persuade the Great Powers to depose Ferdinand, a step Bismarck refused to contemplate. Nor could he please Austria, being obliged to warn her that Germany could not aid her over Bulgaria. So Austria and Italy, both alarmed by the likelihood of Russian intervention, looked elsewhere for support. They found that Salisbury shared their fears, and in December 1887 the Second Mediterranean Agreement was signed; in this secret pact the three powers pledged themselves to uphold the *status quo* in the Near East, at the Straits, in Asia Minor and in Bulgaria, and to come to Turkey's aid if Russia attacked her; should the sultan be reluctant to resist aggression, they agreed to occupy Turkish territory to remind him of his obligation to fight Russia. Bismarck gave his blessing to the agreement and helped it along actively behind the scenes, for in this way his promise to aid Russia at the Straits – a promise which was, strictly speaking, incompatible with the spirit of the Austro-German treaty and with the text of the Triple Alliance – was neutralised by the readiness of the Mediterranean powers to resist Russia.

This piece of Machiavellian diplomacy extricated Bismarck successfully from a difficult situation but brought no lasting relief. In the winter of 1887–88 Bismarck came under heavy pressure from Waldersee and Moltke to strike quickly at Russia before she was ready for war. As always, he resisted preventive war and warned Austria not to be provoked into attacking Russia. He was deeply pessimistic about the chances of peace but twisted and turned desperately to avoid war. In February 1888 he published the Austro-German treaty, partly to warn the Russian public that Germany would stand by Austria if it came to war, and partly to restrain the Austrians – and especially the belligerently anti-Russian Hungarians – by making it clear that Germany's obligations were limited to a defensive war. To the end he fought hard to keep Russia in play; in his last great Reichstag speech in February 1888 he defended Russian policy in Bulgaria. This problem was, incidentally, solved at last in March 1888. The publication of the Austro-German alliance and rumours of a Mediterranean agreement made Russia hold her hand; also her interest was turning away from the Balkans to Central Asia and the Far East. She contented herself with asking the sultan to declare Ferdinand's election illegal, which he did, and Russian honour was satisfied. As Ferdinand remained prince of Bulgaria the Bulgarians were equally pleased with the outcome.

When William II ascended the throne in July 1888 the sands began to run out quickly for Bismarck. France and Russia were moving closer to each other; in October 1888 Russia obtained her first big loan from France; in January 1889 Russia ordered French rifles, promising that they would never be used against France; and when Tsar Alexander visited Berlin in November he toasted William II in French, much to the latter's annoyance, and told the French ambassador that France must build up her army. The pattern of international politics was changing rapidly, and there was nothing Bismarck could do about it. In a last desperate attempt to stave off a Franco-Russian alliance he threw out the suggestion of an Anglo-German alliance directed against France. But Salisbury no longer trusted him and left the proposal lying on the table. Nor could Bismarck control the new emperor. Influenced by his anti-Russian friends, William was not even prepared to go through the motions of keeping Russia in play; when Francis Joseph visited Berlin in August 1889, William assured him that Germany would mobilise the day after Austria, regardless of the cause of the latter's dispute with Russia. When he decided to visit Constantinople in November, a journey which aroused apprehension in St. Petersburg, Bismarck could not restrain him and indeed made little attempt to. His policy was virtually in ruins; he was tired and old, and with the tide moving against him at home and abroad, he resigned in March 1890.

Bismarck has long enjoyed a formidable reputation in the field of foreign affairs. His apologists claim that he was largely responsible for preserving peace in Europe for twenty years; he did not want war himself, so it is argued, and he prevented others from going to war by enmeshing the Great Powers in such an intricate diplomatic web that war became too perilous an undertaking. This is to exaggerate his influence. A factor of equal importance was the desire of the powers to avoid a major war in Europe. The 1880s were a period of colonial expansion which acted as Nature's lightning conductor, diverting attention from Europe; Russia was moving slowly eastwards, while France and Britain were struggling for the mastery of Africa, developments which helped to take the pressure off the situation in Europe.

No one would deny that Bismarck was a past master in the diplomatic arts, equalled only by Salisbury; by cleverly exploiting and fostering the rivalries among the powers he prevented the formation of any hostile coalition against Germany and obtained for his country an assured place at the top table. These are solid achievements. But, equally, it cannot be denied that his policies ended in failure. His bullying tactics, however successful in the short term, were bitterly resented, especially by the Russians, and poisoned international relations in this period. And in any case, the cabinet diplomacy at which he excelled in the 1860s was no longer possible in the 1880s; public opinion was beginning to influence policy, making it impossible to turn friendships on and off at will. Bismarck could not reconcile France to the loss of Alsace-Lorraine, and his attempts to divert her attention overseas failed; public opinion would not allow the politicians to forget 1870. Nor could he keep both Austria-Hungary and Russia as his friends; public opinion in both countries as well as diverging economic interests widened and deepened their rivalry, and by 1890 German public opinion was firmly aligned on the side of Austria against Russia. In fact all Bismarck succeeded in doing was to involve Germany more deeply in the consequences of this rivalry. He did at least restrain the Austrians. His successors did not even try to in the end but deliberately encouraged them to attack Serbia in 1914. It is significant that in his last year or two in office Bismarck was himself acutely conscious of the failure of his policy; he stood by helplessly as France and Russia moved towards each other and Germany and Russia moved further apart.

It is an indictment of Bismarck – and of foreign ministers in other lands, too, it is only fair to add – that he conceived of international relations as nothing more than an exercise in power politics. He put his trust in secret alliances and large armies; German arms expenditure rose from nine-and-a-half million pounds in 1870 to twenty-four millions in 1890, a greater increase than for any other power; only France ran a close second with a thirteen-million-pound increase. Alliances and armaments are important ingredients in international affairs but not the only ones. Bismarck overworked power politics, partly because he was completely lacking in any wider vision of a community of nations subject to the same moral law with common aspirations for its peoples. It is well known that he had the greatest contempt for 'Professor' Gladstone's elevated view of the

Concert of Europe. 'I have always found the word Europe used by politicians when they are demanding from other powers something which they dare not ask for in their own name', he observed with cynicism. Maybe so. Yet already at the close of the century a new community of nations was emerging, as economic and technological advance drew all parts of the world into an increasingly intimate association. Bismarck was peculiarly blind to the forward march of events and too obsessed with the minutiae of the daily diplomatic round to ponder on the pattern of the future. On the other hand he was acutely aware of the precarious nature of Germany's semi-hegemonial position in Europe. Speaking in the Reichstag in 1887 he put it in these words: 'Any Great Power which goes beyond its sphere of interest and tries to exert pressure or influence on the policy of other countries, seeking to take charge of things is operating outside the sphere allotted to it by God. It is pursuing *Machtpolitik*, not a policy based on national interest; it is seeking only prestige. We will not do that.' True, he had bullied and intimidated other powers (with limited success). Yet in the last resort he had recognised certain limits beyond which it was dangerous to go. His successors were markedly deficient in this respect. Once they were in control of Germany and once the forward thrust of German imperialism propelled them into a bid for absolute hegemony in Europe, then the egocentric methods implicit in Bismarck's power politics proved a disastrous heritage for Europe.

7

The Germany of William II 1890–1914

When Bismarck departed from Lehrter railway station on 29 March 1890, a squadron of hussars and a military band lined the platform. Ministers, ambassadors, generals and a crowd of admiring citizens cheered the old man and sang *Die Wacht am Rhein* as the train steamed out of the station. But few Germans regretted his passing. There was much more concern in the foreign press than in Germany, where it was generally accepted that he had outlived his political usefulness. After 'a first-class funeral', as Bismarck called it, Germany turned to the future with confidence under the dynamic young emperor and his chancellor General Leo von Caprivi.

Caprivi was a middle-aged soldier with a good administrative record and few illusions about the difficulties facing him in his new post. A general was chosen to succeed Bismarck because it was hoped that a uniform would give its wearer more authority. Caprivi was singled out from among other generals simply because William II thought him an amenable character likely to do what he was told – in fact he quickly displayed a will of his own – and, like a good soldier, Caprivi had obeyed the summons with resignation. His task, as he saw it, was to recall the people 'from the mighty deeds and figures of the past to the prose of everyday life'. He repeated the emperor's dictum that the course remained the same and he confirmed the ministers in office. But Caprivi knew that this would not do; Germany expected him to break with the past. And in his first speech to the Prussian Landtag he made it plain that he was ready to steer 'a new course'; he announced that ministers would have more freedom in their own departments and declared his readiness to consider new ideas and proposals regardless of their origins.

Bismarck, oddly enough, recommended Caprivi for the post of minister-president in the belief that the general was a 'strong man' who would deal ruthlessly with the Socialists when the long-awaited revolutionary storm swept through Germany. Much to his surprise, Bismarck found that Caprivi preferred to conciliate potential opponents of the government in the new Reichstag. He went out of his way in his first weeks as chancellor to make concessions to Radicals, Socialists, Poles and Centrists. It is true that William II did not care much for this 'leftish' policy and only tolerated it as long as it succeeded. Yet conciliation proved a great success; for four years Caprivi was able to rely on a very wide measure of Reichstag support for government measures. The tension which had developed between government and Reichstag in the 1880s died away after 1890. The opposition parties took care not to inflict parliamentary defeats on Caprivi, because they had no wish to see Bismarck come back. This was an important development. Whatever William II said to the contrary in after-dinner speeches, the rough-and-ready partnership between Caprivi and the Reichstag represented a first tentative step away from the authoritarian practices of the Bismarckian era and towards a more flexible and less authoritarian form of government.

The new era got off to an excellent start when Caprivi introduced five bills into the Prussian Landtag; these included an important finance bill featuring a progressive income tax for the first time, and a bill to reform rural administration. Steps were taken to extend the social welfare system. In 1891 the Reichstag passed an act regulating working conditions; Sunday work and the employment of children under thirteen were completely forbidden; women were forbidden to work more than eleven hours, and youths under sixteen more than ten hours; and the Bundesrat was given power (which it used) to fix maximum working hours in factories where working conditions were exceptionally difficult. Another act set up courts, with representatives from both sides of industry, to arbitrate in industrial disputes; by 1902 the courts had become obligatory in most towns. The success of this limited experiment in industrial co-operation was only possible because the government prepared the way psychologically by lapsing the anti-socialist laws.

The German Socialist party could now organise openly and soon became the largest working-class party in Europe. Persecution had a curious double effect on the Socialists. It strengthened their Marxist faith, so that at the Erfurt Congress of 1891 the party committed itself to a thoroughgoing Marxist programme from which the last remnants of Lassallianism were expunged. The Erfurt programme faithfully summarised the main tenets of Marxism as laid down in the Communist Manifesto of 1848, and emphasised more forcibly than before the international character of the working-class movement; Lassalle's state-aided producers' co-operatives were abandoned in favour of the social-isation of the means of production. At the same time the party had grown in numbers during the period of persecution, and now polled more votes than any other party. This strengthened the Lassallian argument that gradualism, not violent revolution, was the only correct path for Socialists to follow. On this all-important point the Erfurt programme remained ambiguous. In the years that followed many Socialists did, in fact, act on the assumption that political power could only be won via the ballot box.

In practice more importance was attached to the party's so-called minimum programme, which outlined practical measures to be attained by parliamentary action within the framework of the capitalist system; new industrial legislation, tax reform, an extension of the social welfare system and full political and educational rights in all states; in short, a radical programme capable of winning mass support for the party whilst leaving full-blooded socialism to a distant utopian future. Here were the beginnings of Revisionism which will be referred to later in the chapter.

The most important single measure Caprivi laid before the Reichstag was a bill to reform the tariff act of 1879. The bread tax was causing widespread discontent; on top of this bad harvests and a world wheat shortage sent prices even higher. Caprivi did not reduce tariffs out of any humanitarian impulse to give the people cheaper bread or because he believed in the therapeutic value of free trade. On the contrary, the general believed firmly in agrarian protection and self-sufficiency for military reasons. It was the drying-up of markets for industrial exports which forced his hand. Other countries were raising tariff barriers – France increased her tariffs in 1892 – and in a competitive world it was obvious that new markets could be secured only on a *quid-pro-quo* basis. 'We must export,' declared Caprivi; 'either we export goods or we export men.' In the interests of imperial security Germany could not afford to lose manpower. The only alternative was the negotiation of a series of commercial treaties which assured Germany of markets for industrial exports for the next twelve years in return for a reduction of the tariffs on cattle, timber, rye and wheat. Between 1891 and 1894 treaties were signed with Italy, Austria-Hungary, Russia, Belgium, Switzerland, Rumania and several other countries.

When the first treaty with Austria was debated in the Reichstag it was approved by a massive majority. A policy which reduced the cost of living appealed naturally to the left wing, and for the first time the Socialists voted for a government measure. Even National Liberals and Free Conservatives supported Caprivi, despite Bismarck's fierce press campaign against acceptance. Only the German Conservatives voted against the Austrian treaty, although there was more opposition to the treaties with Rumania and Russia because wheat producers had more reason to fear competition from these lands.[1] But the treaties on the whole probably did less damage to Prussian landowners than the *Kreuzzeitung* alleged. Certainly the price of rye was halved in 1894, but largely because of record harvests in America which ended the world shortage; German tariffs were still high, and in addition the government offered farmers substantial freight reductions to promote wheat exports. In the long run German agriculture did not suffer too much; many landowners improved their

[1]The Russian treaty was passed by 200 votes to 146, with some National Liberals, Centrists and Free Conservatives supporting the German Conservatives on this occasion.

methods or switched from wheat-growing to cattle-breeding, and as the population continued to grow rapidly, wheat producers were still assured of markets, even if prices were lower.

The commercial treaties were the last straw for the German Conservatives. They were thoroughly dissatisfied with Caprivi on several counts. They disliked his bill to reform rural administration and successfully emasculated it in the Landtag. They were disturbed by Caprivi's readiness to reduce the period of service to two years at the request of the Reichstag. They were particularly incensed by his behaviour over the Prussian school-reform bill, which restored church influence in education and allowed Polish to be used in the schools in Posen and West Prussia. The bill was carried with Conservative and Centre support. There was great indignation in liberal Protestant circles, where the bill was condemned as a dangerous concession to particularism. In the end, the emperor, alarmed by mounting criticism, intervened personally in the dispute and the bill was dropped. The Conservatives were bitterly disappointed by what the *Kreuzzeitung* described as a second Olmütz. Weighed down under successive disappointments, the Conservatives broke with their past; in 1892 the party congress adopted the Christian-Social and anti-Semitic ideas of Stöcker. This was a calculated attempt to come to terms with the mass electorate. Realising that they could win little working class-support, the Conservatives hoped that defence of the old guild system, plus anti-Semitism, would capture the lower-middle-class vote. This flirtation with the politics of the lunatic fringe was no more successful in 1893 than it was to be forty years later. In 1933 the Nazis were the winners; in 1893 the Anti-Semites increased their Reichstag representation from five to sixteen seats. A much more effective recruiting sergeant for conservatism was the powerful and well-organised Agrarian League (*Bund der Landwirte*) founded in 1893. The league, which had enrolled 250,000 members by 1900, was an unashamed pressure-group; it eschewed all ideology, denounced Caprivi as a 'socialist' bent on ruining wheat producers, and it agitated in season and out of season for subsidies, import controls and minimum prices to protect farmers – measures which the Reichstag rejected as too 'socialistic'. Under the persuasive influence of the league, the Conservative party soon became little more than an agrarian pressure group itself, concerned only to promote the material interests of members, a far cry from the days of the highminded Gerlachs.

Caprivi's commercial treaties had a much wider significance. They helped to make Germany the leading industrial nation in Europe by 1900. This was by far the most important development in the history of these years, and one fraught with the most far-reaching social, political and international consequences for Germany. What Professor Rostow has described as the 'take-off' period of industrial growth was completed in the early 1870s. Germany now entered into the stage of economic maturity.

The emphasis in industry moved away from coal, iron and heavy engineering to steel, chemicals, electrical engineering and shipping. Statistics reveal something of the impressive story. The output of coal, the basic raw material of the early industrial revolution, continued to rise; in 1871 Germany mined 38 million tons to Britain's 118 million tons; by 1890 German output was 89 million tons, compared with Britain's 184 million tons; by 1914 Germany, with 279 million tons, had almost caught up with Britain at 292 million tons. Iron and steel output was even more impressive. In 1876 half Germany's blast furnaces were idle. The introduction of the Gilchrist process, which depended on the use of the phosphoric ores of Lorraine, caused a revival. Pig-iron output increased from 2,729,000 tons in 1880 to 4,658,000 tons in 1890. Steel output rose from 1,548,000 tons to 3,164,000 tons in the same period; by 1900 output rose to 7,372,000 tons, and by 1910 it reached 13,149,000 tons surpassing that of Britain.

Most impressive of all was the growth of the electrical and chemical industries. The electrical industry was founded by Werner Siemens, who had invented the dynamo in 1866. German manufacturers were quick to exploit this new form of energy and light. Two giant firms dominated the new industry; the *Siemens-Schuckert Werke* and the *Allgemeine Elektrizitäts Gesellschaft*, or A.E.G., directed by Walther Rathenau. By 1913 nearly half the world's trade in electrical products was in German hands. Equally impressive was the rapid expansion of the heavy chemical industries producing potash, potassium salts and ammonia. Perhaps the most spectacular advances were made in the light chemical industry on the basis of intensive research into the utilisation of coal by-products; for example, Hofmann's discovery of the first synthetic dye made possible the growth of a synthetic-dye industry in the 1860s. German industry was exceptionally enlightened in its encouragement of research; many trained scientists were employed by the large corporations; many important discoveries resulted from this policy, as, for example, Haber's discovery of synthetic ammonia, which enabled Germany to produce nitrates for explosives when Chilean supplies were cut off in 1914.

Foreign trade figures reflected the enormous expansion of the German economy. The value of exports increased from £173,250,000 in 1872 to £538,515,000 in 1914. An important change occurred in the nature of this trade; in 1873 only thirty-eight per cent of German exports consisted of finished industrial products; by 1913 this had risen to sixty-three per cent. Into the 1880s Germany was a net importer of capital. By 1914 Germany was an exporter of capital, with investments in the Americas, the Near East and Far East totalling nearly £1,250 millions. It is a significant comment on the changing balance of economic power in Europe that in 1913 the German share of world trade almost equalled that of Britain and was already twice the size of the French share. Germany had become Britain's most serious competitor, and the mark rivalled the pound sterling.

There were several reasons why Germany forged ahead so dramatically in the industrial field. Her population rapidly increased from 56.7 millions in 1901 to 67.7 millions in 1914, and its structure favoured expansion; only four per cent of the population was over sixty-five years and thirty-two per cent of young people were under fourteen years. It was also a mobile population, as more intensive methods of cultivation accelerated the drift to urban centres; in 1871 63.7 per cent lived in the countryside; by 1890 this had fallen to 57.5 per cent and by 1910 to 40 per cent. Industrial cities grew very rapidly as a consequence of this; the population of Berlin rose from 774,498 in 1870 to over two millions in 1910. Expansion was encouraged by an abundance of raw materials. The rich iron-ore deposits of Alsace-Lorraine, and the Ruhr coal fields, formed the most powerful industrial complex on earth. Credit facilities for expansion were readily available in Germany. German banks, which had always been important in the promotion of trade and industry, expanded their activities enormously at the close of the century and financed practically the whole of industry. Through their representatives on boards of directors banks were able to influence industrial policy profoundly. Banks played an active role in financing exports and in overseas industry; the *Deutsche Bank*, for example was active in Asia Minor. The readiness of the state to aid industrial expansion was another factor of importance. Tariffs, subsidies and preferential freight rates were a further extension of the long-established tradition of state intervention. Finally, Germany possessed a skilled working class and an extremely competent managerial class quick to adopt the latest techniques and inventions from other lands, so that industrial expansion was not impeded by out-of-date equipment or outmoded practices.

The expansion of the economy was accompanied by a marked trend towards industrial concentration. This took the form of cartelisation; firms were organised in cartels which controlled the price and quantity of goods produced and supervised marketing methods. Cartels were either horizontal or vertical; horizontal cartels were federations of firms producing the same raw material or product; vertical cartels were associations of firms engaged in different stages of production from raw material to finished product. In 1875 there were only some eight cartels in Germany, in 1885 about ninety; in 1905 a government investigation revealed 366, and the number rose to about 3,000 in the 1920s. Cartelisation was encouraged by several factors; collective action made it easier for firms to exploit fully the home market; in some cases a natural monopoly, as in potash, favoured combinations; in the more modern industries, especially chemicals and electrical engineering, only large units could raise sufficient capital; lastly, there was the infectious example of American trusts. In the extractive industries, and in trades dependent on mineral production, a few great cartels soon dominated the field; an example was the Rhenish-Westphalian Coal Syndicate controlling fifty per cent of total coal production and ninety-five per cent of Ruhr production; this syndicate had a virtual monopoly in the Ruhr and through its pricing policy it exerted a decisive influence on industries dependent on coal. The emergence of these industrial giants profoundly affected the capitalist system. Cartels fixed their own prices, and therefore their own profit levels, so that in effect, the self-regulating mechanism of the market economy was destroyed whatever the economic textbooks said; only later were the full political implications of cartelisation clear.

In Britain agreements restraining trade were not enforceable at law, the U.S.A. had its anti-trust laws, but in Germany cartels were respected and admired. They enjoyed legal protection and were actively encouraged by the state; in 1910, for example, the government insisted that the potash industry form a cartel. Public opinion took its cue from the government, and Germans learnt to look upon cartels with favour as rational devices for eliminating wasteful competition and for promoting German trade, prosperity and national prestige. Significantly enough, some Socialists were deeply impressed by the phenomenon of cartelisation, seeing in it a prototype of Socialist economic planning in the future.

Only once did Caprivi encounter serious difficulties in the Reichstag. That was in 1892 over his army bill. Caprivi was firmly convinced that war on two fronts was unavoidable sooner or later. His opinion was shared by Count Schlieffen, who succeeded Waldersee as chief of the general staff in 1891. Schlieffen believed that war under modern conditions could only be waged for a few weeks. It followed from this that a belligerent must win decisive victories in the opening stages of a war. Germany had hitherto planned to stand on the defensive in the west and concentrate her main effort in the east to defeat the Russians. Schlieffen decided that Russia was too large to be defeated quickly; the only alternative was an all-out offensive against France, to drive her out of the war in a week or so. To make this strategy feasible, massive military increases were essential. Caprivi accepted these arguments and in November 1892 introduced an army bill which increased the peace-time strength by 84,000. To appease the left, Caprivi reduced the period of service from three to two years and allowed the Reichstag to debate the army grant every five instead of every seven years. It was not enough. Public opinion was strongly opposed to increases of this order; only the National Liberals and Conservatives stood by the government. The bill was defeated, whereupon Caprivi dissolved the Reichstag.

Elections fought on military issues tend to favour right-wing parties. That was the lesson of 1887. And once again the National Liberals and Conservatives improved their position. The left liberals suffered a very serious reverse, losing over a third of their seats.[2] The Radical party was split asunder. Two liberal parties fought each other during the election; the *Freisinnige Vereinigung*, which supported military increases, and the rump of the old party, renamed the *Freisinnige Volkspartei*, which steadfastly opposed increases. True, the Radicals recovered the lost votes, and more, by 1907 but they never regained their old influence in the Reichstag. However, apart from the spectacular defeat of radicalism, the balance of forces had not been greatly altered, because Caprivi firmly resisted the temptation to make real political capital out of the situation. The new Reichstag passed the bill but only by a narrow majority. Caprivi would have been defeated again had not the nineteen Polish members voted for the bill out of gratitude to the government for its reversal of Bismarck's anti-Polish policies in Posen and West Prussia.

Extreme left as well as extreme right increased slightly in strength in 1893; the Socialists in fact gained more votes than any other party and secured another nine seats, bringing them up to a total of forty-four. This was no isolated phenomenon. Socialism was on the march in Europe in the 1890s. Trade-unionism was growing in strength and militancy in all industrial countries as the unskilled workers were brought into the ranks of organised labour. Several Socialist parties were founded in these years; the Polish and Italian parties in 1892, the Independent Labour Party in 1893. Socialists were at last securing substantial representation in many national parliaments; in 1893 forty Socialists were elected to the French chamber of deputies and thirty to the Belgian chamber.

Fear of socialism played a significant part in bringing the New Course to an end. William II was worried by the steady advance of German socialism. When President Carnot was assassinated by an Italian anarchist in 1894, his fears knew no bounds. He was easily persuaded by court advisers that the lives of his wife and children were in danger. In September 1894, in a speech at Königsberg, he appealed to the Conservatives to rally round the throne: 'forward into battle for religion, for morality and for order against the parties of revolution,' he cried in hysterical vein. He asked Caprivi to draft a law against 'subversive elements'. Caprivi kept his head and refused, knowing full well that the Reichstag would not tolerate a new anti-socialist law. Conservative extremists, supported by the Prussian minister-president, Count Botho Eulenburg,[3] won the emperor over to the idea of a *coup d'état à la* Bismarck which would reduce the Reichstag's powers. Again Caprivi stood firm and dissuaded William from this anachronistic and highly dangerous course of action. Then later in 1894, despairing of ever controlling the young ruler, Caprivi resigned. The New Course was over. The Agrarian League had its revenge at last for 'tariff socialism'. The general retired into obscurity, wrote no memoirs and

[2]They held seventy-six seats in 1890 and forty-eight in 1893.
[3]Caprivi had resigned from this post in 1892 when his school reform bill was opposed by the emperor.

burnt material likely to aid future historians, remaining a loyal servant of his ungrateful master to the end of his days. It was characteristic of the fickle-minded emperor that nothing came of his blustering talk of a *coup d'état*, although as late as May 1895 he talked eagerly of supplying his soldiers with 'cartridges for the last stand', when the sedition bill was defeated.

Fear of socialism and anarchism had another important effect upon domestic politics; it brought landowners and industrialists together again. The alliance of 'steel and rye' had broken down in 1892 when Caprivi reduced agrarian tariffs; by the end of the 1890s it was fully restored. Industrialists still believed in cheap food and disliked Conservative talk of state subsidies. It was the rising tide of social unrest which drew them back to their natural allies, the Prussian landowners. Miquel, the National Liberal leader, welcomed the Agrarian League, shrewdly perceiving that an understanding would be easier once Conservatives behaved like National Liberals and pursued material interests wholeheartedly without the encumbrance of old-fashioned principles.

The Conservatives were equally alarmed by the growth of socialism and readily supported National Liberal demands in 1895 for an anti-socialist law. The heat had gone out of the landowners' quarrel with the government, since the new chancellor, Prince Hohenlohe, promised to increase the wheat tariff when the treaties were renewed in 1904. Conservatives found a new champion against socialism at the close of the century in the person of Baron von Stumm-Halberg. This powerful Saar industrialist was a violent opponent of socialism and trade-unionism and a leading practitioner of industrial paternalism. He offered his workers high wages and social amenities but denied them the right to think for themselves; workers needed his permission to marry and could be dismissed for reading Socialist papers. Not for nothing was his Saar ironworks dubbed *'Saarabien'*. He likened the running of industry to a military operation and often boasted that in 'the kingdom of Stumm' only one will reigned supreme – that of 'His Majesty the King of Prussia'. Naturally he quickly became William's favourite philosopher-industrialist and exerted great influence on conservative thinking in the so-called 'Stumm era'.

The new chancellor, Prince Hohenlohe, was a Bavarian nobleman of mildly liberal views. But he was too old and too evasive a character to become a decisive voice in the formulation of policy. It was the emperor's advisers, notably Miquel, who had been Prussian finance minister since 1890, and Köller, the new Prussian minister of the interior, who devised the new 'policy of concentration' to rally the middle classes round the monarchy. Caprivi's social-reform policy had failed to win over the working class; all it had done was drive the middle classes, the natural supporters of monarchy, into opposition. To redress the balance Miquel and Köller advocated the defence of middle-class interests plus strong measures against socialism.[4] They tried to put the clock back twenty years in their fight against socialism; progressive elements were winkled out of important posts in Prussia; by 1897 the last representative of the New Course, Bötticher, *Reich* minister of the interior and deputy minister-president of Prussia, was forced to resign on account of his alleged 'softness' towards Socialists. As part of the new policy the Reichstag was asked in 1894 to pass a subversion bill which made it a punishable offence to incite citizens to class hatred, to make public attacks on the family, marriage and property, or to denigrate the state. In 1899, at the emperor's express wish, the Reichstag was asked to pass a further law threatening stiff penalties for workers who compelled fellow-workers to form unions or come out on strike. The struggle against socialism was carried on in the states as well; Saxony introduced a three-class system in 1896 which effectively eliminated Socialists from the Landtag; and in 1897 the Prussian Landtag was asked to give the police power to dissolve all societies threatening law and order or the security of the state. It added up to a highly dangerous and anachronistic policy calculated to polarise German society into two antagonistic camps; the forces of law, order and respectability on the one hand, and the forces of radical dissent and non-conformity on the other. Stresses and strains were inevitable in a society where the working class was growing in strength but where agrarian-feudal forces clung tenaciously to their power and privilege. In these circumstances the adoption of policies deliberately directed against the working class made the situation explosive in the extreme.

Fortunately the danger passed; the policy of concentration was abandoned before it caused irreparable harm to the social fabric of the *Reich*. For one thing, the middle classes failed to rally to the crown as Miquel and Köller expected. In the Reichstag only the Conservatives supported the subversion bill without reservation, and it was in fact soundly defeated in 1895.[5] Similarly in 1899 the middle-class parties were solidly opposed to the bill which would have penalised trade-union activity. In the Prussian Landtag the Liberals and the Centre opposed the 1897 bill, fearing that they might suffer as much as the Socialists if the powers of the police were vastly increased. In effect, the politically active spearhead of the middle classes appreciated that draconian methods against the working class were inappropriate in a sophisticated industrial society; so deep was their respect for the rule of law that they could not bring themselves to pervert the law even to repress a movement they loathed and feared. Furthermore, Hohenlohe had never favoured the policy of concentration and had the

---

[4]An example of the positive side of their policy was the 1897 law which stifled free competition in the interests of the guild system; local authorities were given power to make guilds compulsory in any trade where a majority of masters demanded it.

[5]The Centre eventually succumbed to the temptation to support it on condition that 'subversion' was extended to cover attacks on the Christian religion.

good sense to realise that talk in extreme conservative circles of over-throwing the constitution was wild and irresponsible. Even the emperor saw this in the end, and by 1897 had ceased to take it seriously. Last, but not least, the Socialists, though subjected to great provocation, acted with caution and restraint. As the party and the trade-union movement grew in strength, many Socialists felt that the working class had too much to lose to risk a direct confrontation with the power of the state. There was a case for turning the other cheek and waiting for better days to come. Because the middle classes had failed to support the policy of concentration, a state of deadlock now existed between government and Reichstag, much as in the last years of Bismarck's reign as chancellor; the government would not introduce legislation acceptable to the majority, and the majority refused to accept bills presented by the government. In the past, governments had usually won. This time the government gave way; in 1899 the penal bills were dropped and the policy of overt repression was abandoned. Although there was still talk in court circles after this of a *coup d'état* to discipline the Reichstag, responsible politicians knew that the days were long past when a lieutenant and ten men could close that body down at the emperor's bidding.

The close of the nineteenth century was a real turning-point in German history. The *Reich* broke with Bismarck's foreign policy and embarked on *Weltpolitik*, with all that this implied for the future. Germany suddenly evinced a new interest in colonial expansion and acquired some posses-sions in the Pacific; she initiated the scramble for China; she laid the basis of a powerful navy and she became more deeply involved in the affairs of Asia Minor than ever before. Like any broad trend in foreign policy, Germany's transition to *Weltpolitik* was a response to internal pressure, part economic, part psychological and part political.

Industrialisation impelled all advanced countries to look beyond their frontiers for raw materials to feed the new factories, for markets for manu-factured goods and for outlets for accumulated capital, all of which could only be found outside Europe. Inevitably the search for new markets and investment possibilities overseas had political implications. Turkey is an excellent illustration of this point. Behind the growth of German political influence in Asia Minor lay a story of commercial success reaching back to the 1880s. In 1887 Turkey imported six per cent of her goods from Germany; by 1910 this rose to twenty-one per cent. In 1881 Germany controlled five per cent of the Turkish national debt; by 1914 this rose to twenty per cent. And German trade with Turkey rose from £5,500,000 in 1908 to £8,500,000 in 1913.

Secondly, psychological pressures operated in the same direction. When France was defeated in 1870, the victory was hailed in Germany as a vindication of the superior moral and cultural power of the German way of life. By the turn of the century a profound change had come over nationalism in all lands. The biological ideas of Lamarck and Darwin robbed nationalism of its idealism; nationality was now equated with a community of blood rather than a community of ideas; Natural Selection applied to relations between states as much as to the animal kingdom; the struggle for markets and raw materials and the urge to expand overseas were interpreted as outward signs of a deep unceasing struggle between nations in a world 'red in tooth and claw' where the right of the strongest was law. In this age of 'national missions' Germany was well to the fore, determined to play a role overseas commensurate with her economic and military might. As Bernhard von Bülow observed in a speech in 1897, 'we do not wish to put anyone in the shade but we do demand our place in the sun'.

Thirdly, there were political pressures. By the end of the century demographic change and accelerated economic development were altering the structure of German politics. The National Liberals, the middle-class party *par excellence* in the days of Bismarck but one which never quite overcame its gentlemanly distaste for mass politics, was a declining force outflanked by the emergence of a virile and popular middle-class movement. The peasantry, the old middle class of small producers and shopkeepers, and the new – and rapidly growing – middle class of white-collar workers in state and private industry began to mobilise themselves in the 1890s in a variety of organisational forms. Left as well as Right derived benefit from this radicalisation process. Thus many white-collar workers suffering economic hardship voted socialist. Those who moved rightwards were also highly critical of aristocracy and government alike. Bodies such as the German Middle Class Association (*Reichsdeutscher Mittelstandsverband*) were ultra-nationalist, anti-semitic, anti-socialist and critical of parliamentary government, attitudes which have led some historians to see the seeds of fascism already present in Wilhelmine Germany. Not until 1913 when the Cartel of Productive Estates (*Kartell der schaffenden Stände*) was formed by a number of right-wing organisations did official conservatism – frightened by the socialist advance in 1912 – attempt to build bridges to this new political force.

These right-wing radicals were active supporters of *Weltpolitik*. They supplied the membership for numerous pressure groups originating mainly in the 1890s including the Pan-German League (*Alldeutscher Verband*), the Navy League (*Flottenverein*), the German Defence League (*Deutscher Wehrverein*) and the Eastern Marches Association (*Ostmarkverein*). Unlike earlier pressure groups they sought mass support and exerted more influence on the government than did the Reichstag. The best-known was the Pan-German League which nurtured a particularly repulsive type of nationalism, a mixture of anti-semitism and Darwinian racialism, crossed with crude expansionism. It preached hatred of France, Britain and Russia and supported the creation of a great mid-European union including Austria, Holland, Belgium, Luxemburg and Switzerland. Many of Hitler's ideas were probably derived from Pan-German League pamphlets. It attracted much support from professional men, business men and teachers, and was financed by the industrialists Emil Kirdorf, Hugo Stinnes and Karl Röchling. It is true that the League had only 20,000 members in its heyday, and few government contacts – only thirty-eight Reichstag members joined it – and it certainly did not exert direct influence on government policy. Its influence was more intangible but no less insidious. It probably did more than any other body to create and sustain a climate of opinion favourable to *Weltpolitik*. Not least of its disservices was the bad name it earned for Germany abroad.

A school of German historians led by Hans-Ulrich Wehler has argued that, as Germany entered the twentieth century, the ruling *élite* succeeded in holding in check the pressures for democratisation in German society by using Bonapartist methods – the defensive strategies of 'concentration', 'negative integration' and 'social imperialism'. The building of the German navy, for example, was designed to rally the middle classes around the emperor – an integrating figure in a deeply divided society – and so divert attention away from the socialist threat at home. The manipulation theory has, however, been criticised by other historians on the grounds that the ruling *élite* was too disunited to pursue a consistent policy and, far from manipulating the middle classes, was struggling to come to terms with the radical movement referred to above.

The two schools of thought are not necessarily incompatible. Indeed, pressures from above and below were involved in the building of the fleet. The emperor's role was of crucial importance. The *Reisekaiser*[6] was a dedicated *Weltpolitiker* who made it his mission in life to transform Germany into a global power of the first rank. Believing passionately that Germany's future lay on the high seas, he was dissatisfied with a fleet only seventh in the world when Germany's foreign trade was almost equal to Britain's. After an abortive attempt to obtain funds from the Reichstag he denounced his opponents as 'rogues without a fatherland' and talked wildly of dissolving that body and restricting the franchise. Quickly recovering his composure, he tried more subtle methods appointing Admiral Alfred von Tirpitz secretary of state for the navy in 1897. Tirpitz's bill to create seventeen ships of the line in seven years was accompanied by a noisy manipulative campaign to popularise the navy carried out by the Navy League (which Tirpitz helped to found in 1898 with financial assistance from Krupp and Stumm). Through its press organs the League drummed up middle-class support by depicting naval expansion as a truly 'national' policy strengthening the Reich and not the states. Friedrich

[6]'The travelling emperor'.

Naumann, the greatest radical of the day, even coined the slogan 'the fleet against reaction' to express his conviction that naval expansion was a 'progressive' development simply because Conservatives opposed it. While the National Liberals supported the bill, seeing in a navy a sign of imperial greatness as well as a guaranteed market for steel masters and shipping magnates, Conservatives felt that a fleet detracted from the prestige of the army. However, they voted for the bill having no desire to rub shoulders with Radicals and Socialists in opposing defence expenditure. But the decisive factor – and evidence of the influence of grass-roots politics on national policy-making – was the changing attitude of the Centre Party. This was being transformed into a lower-middle-class urban party increasingly anxious to escape from the oppositional stance of the Kulturkampf period and demonstrate the complete loyalty of Catholics towards the Wilhelmine state. Only when two-thirds of the parliamentary party decided to vote for the bill did Tirpitz win the day. The bill was carried by 212 votes to 139 in March 1898.

The emperor soon wanted more. In October 1899, immediately after the outbreak of the Boer War, William demanded further naval increases. A second bill was presented to the Reichstag in 1900 to the accompaniment of a noisy popular campaign in which most of the ultra-nationalist groups took part. A chance incident helped to swing public opinion behind the bill; a German ship, the *Bundesrat*, was detained by Britain in South African waters on suspicion of carrying contraband of war; the nationalist press inferred from this that only when Germany had a really strong fleet would her ships be safe on the high seas. In the end the second bill, which increased the ships of the line to thirty-six, was passed by a larger majority than the first.

By 1900 the dangerous policy of concentration, which had failed to win middle-class support or to retard the growth of socialism, had been abandoned. Symptomatic of the change was the readiness of the Socialists, who had opposed naval expenditure, to support the legislative programme put forward in the 1900s by Count Arthur von Posadowsky-Wehner, secretary of state for the interior since 1897. The defeat of the 1899 bill convinced this civil servant that there was no future in barren anti-socialism. As the new chancellor Bülow was absorbed by foreign policy and intervened only spasmodically in home affairs, Posadowsky was virtually his own master. He resumed, in effect, the policy of the New Course, believing, like Caprivi, that only by extending social welfare benefits could the growing working class be reconciled with the state and the tension taken out of German society. The new measures included an extension of accident insurance (1900), a law making industrial courts compulsory in all towns with a population exceeding 20,000 (1901), an increase in the length of sickness insurance (1903) and an extension of the prohibition on child labour (1903). These measures had the support of the Centre and of the

Socialists, who now recognised the importance of social welfare for working people. It was symptomatic of the new spirit that in several instances Posadowsky discussed his draft laws with the party leaders before introducing them and then presented the Bundesrat with a *fait accompli* which it reluctantly accepted.

Government and Reichstag were also broadly in agreement over the renewal of Caprivi's commercial treaties, one of the most important issues facing Germany in the early years of the century and one which aroused great controversy. Socialists and many Radicals called for lower tariffs to reduce the price of bread. On the other side the Agrarian League swung into action demanding even higher tariffs. This was one of the few domestic issues which interested Bülow. A man of landowning stock, he wanted to go down in history as an 'agrarian chancellor'. But he did not on that account capitulate to the demands of the Agrarian League; on the contrary he tried, as he expressed it, to pick a path between the twin lighthouses of protection for farmers and trade treaties for manufacturers. The Reichstag agreed with him. By a huge majority it restored tariffs to the pre-1892 level, which still fell far short of what the league wanted. When the treaties were renegotiated, Germany's partners accepted the tariff increases, and her exports to these countries were not greatly affected. Even though the middle-class electorate on the whole endorsed the action of the Reichstag at the 1903 election, popular opposition to higher tariffs helped the Socialists to win nearly a million extra votes and an additional twenty-six seats.

As the Conservatives had lost seats, the immediate result of the election was to give the Centre party a dominant position in the government coalition. Under the influence of a radically-minded younger element led by Matthias Erzberger, an ambitious Württemberg politician, the Centre began to pursue an independent line which quickly embarrassed the government. When Bülow, faced with mounting budget deficits, attempted to increase indirect taxation and introduce an inheritance tax, the Centre joined the left-wing parties in reducing the proposed tax increases while Conservative opposition emasculated the second bill. Similarly, over military increases Centre support of the Socialists ensured the defeat of government measures.

The inevitable breach with the Centre came finally over colonial affairs. In 1904 a serious native revolt broke out in German South-West Africa. German troops soon restored order in 1905, but unrest in the colony continued for several years. In the Reichstag there was much criticism of defects in the colonial administration. For once the Centre sided with the critics; it opposed government attempts to compensate white settlers; it ensured the defeat of a bill to elevate the colonial department into a *Reich* ministry; and finally, when the government asked for a twenty-nine million mark appropriation to put down guerrilla activity in South-West Africa, the Centre allied with Socialists, Poles and Guelfs to defeat the bill by a narrow majority. Bülow decided to bring the unreliable Centre party to heel and in 1907 abruptly dissolved the Reichstag.

To accomplish his ends he reverted to Bismarck's tactic of inventing 'national' crises to subdue political opponents. In attacking the Centre and Socialist parties Bülow switched attention away from domestic issues and beat the nationalist drum vigorously with the aid of the *Kolonialverein*. 'The government,' he declared, 'ought not to submit to the wishes and interests of individual parties when its most supreme task, the defence of the nation, is in question . . . what is at stake is our whole national political position and more than that, our position in the world.'

The 'Hottentot' election aroused great popular interest, and the results were acclaimed as a victory by emperor and chancellor. So they were, though, as usual, only in terms of Reichstag seats. The Centre managed to return with five more seats. But the Socialists, whom Bülow had attacked during the campaign, suffered their first major reverse, falling from eighty-one to forty-three seats.[7] And, as always when national issues were in the forefront, Conservatives and National Liberals – and Radicals too – gained votes and seats.

There was an important sequel to the 1907 election. As the Radicals had sided with Conservatives and National Liberals against the Centre, a new political possibility opened up for Bülow. These parties had between them 187 seats; with the support of smaller groups who normally voted for the government they commanded a substantial majority in the Reichstag. If the government pursued a policy acceptable to the *'bloc'*, the support of the Centre could be dispensed with. This is precisely what Bülow did. He removed ministers objectionable to the majority and gave the *bloc* some say in new appointments; for example, Posadowsky, 'the red count', as liberals and conservatives called him on account of his active social policy, was dismissed and replaced by Bethmann Hollweg, a sober-minded bureaucrat of moderate conservative views. To keep the *bloc* together Bülow introduced some mildly liberal measures. These included a bill on the stock exchange and a law regularising the right of association. It is interesting to note in passing that one clause of this 'liberal' bill made it obligatory to use German at public meetings; only where more than sixty per cent of the population was non-German could other languages be used, and that only during the next twenty years. Of course the 'Bülow *bloc*' was a highly artificial creation; it lacked a real community of interest and collapsed in the summer of 1909. But the fact remains that this was the first firm association between a government and the majority parties and, as such, might have been a step on the road to parliamentary rule. When the *bloc* threatened to fall apart in December 1907 Bülow actually summoned the

---

[7]The Socialists actually polled 240,000 more votes in 1907. But on second ballots, held in constituencies when there was no clear majority, the anti-socialist parties combined to squeeze the Socialists out.

party leaders and threatened resignation unless they continued to support him. In other words, a chancellor was suggesting that his continuation in office depended not only on the emperor's pleasure but on the willingness of majority parties to co-operate with the chancellor.

Before the 'Bülow *bloc*' fell to pieces, Germany was swept by a serious political storm, the *Daily Telegraph* Affair of 1908. During a visit to England in 1907 William II stayed with a pro-German soldier Colonel Stuart-Wortley. On the basis of conversations with the emperor then and later, Stuart-Wortley, who was desperately anxious to improve Anglo-German relations, wrote an article for the *Daily Telegraph*. It was full of the emperor's usual inept comments and was certain to offend the maximum number of people in the shortest possible time. In it William declared that although large sections of his people were anti-British, he and the best elements in Germany wanted friendship with Britain; during the Boer War he had remained neutral despite pro-Boer feeling in Germany; he had personally prevented the formation of an anti-British coalition of powers and had actually shown Queen Victoria how to win the war; finally, he defended the German navy and expressed the hope that Britain and Germany would stand together against Asiatic powers in the Pacific.

The article was published in the *Daily Telegraph* on 28 October 1908. It aroused much criticism abroad, but this was completely dwarfed by the tremendous uproar in Germany. On 31 October, in a desperate attempt to allay criticism, Bülow issued an official statement in which he accepted responsibility for what had happened but cleverly shifted the blame on to the shoulders of the foreign office; according to the statement, he had offered his resignation to the emperor, who had refused to accept it. This clumsy manoeuvre only added fuel to the fire. All the major parties, including the Conservatives, vehemently attacked the chancellor and his officials for their ineptitude in allowing the article to be published; nor did they spare the emperor, who was severely censured for meddling once more in matters which were the proper concern of the government.

In fact William acted with constitutional propriety on this occasion. When Stuart-Wortley sent him the article, the emperor passed it to Bülow for approval. The latter was too preoccupied with the Bosnian crisis to bother about trifles of this sort. Most likely he only glanced at it casually before passing it on to the foreign office. Minor corrections were made by a junior official at the Wilhelmstrasse, where it was assumed that the chancellor understood the implications of the article and approved of its general tenor. When it was returned by the foreign office, Bülow passed it unread to the emperor, who forwarded it to the *Daily Telegraph*. It can hardly be denied that Bülow's negligence was largely to blame for what happened. However, once the storm broke in the Reichstag, after some initial and characteristic hesitation, 'the eel' – as his enemies called Bülow – followed the line of least resistance and joined in the attacks on

Williams's 'personal government'. Under heavy pressure from all parties, Bülow declared that unless the emperor exercised more restraint in the future, chancellors would have no alternative but to resign. Shortly afterwards William promised in writing to respect the constitution and declared his complete confidence in the chancellor.

The emperor's declaration mollified the opposition and the crisis blew over without leading to structural alterations in the constitution. There was some pressure for change from the Radicals, who wanted to define the chancellor's responsibilities more precisely. The majority parties did not support these demands. It ill became Conservatives and National Liberals, the parties of strong monarchy, to initiate constitutional reform; as for the Centre, they were only awaiting an opportunity to dish Bülow, and on that account did not wish to offend the emperor. Many deputies also felt that, at a time of international crisis when Germany seemed to face encirclement, national unity must be preserved at all costs.

The emperor's boundless self-confidence was severely shaken by the knowledge that he was extremely unpopular with many Germans. After his capitulation to Bülow William suffered a breakdown and talked wildly of abdication. But he quickly recovered his nerve and never forgave the chancellor who had 'betrayed' him in the Reichstag. From that day forth he sought an excuse to be rid of him.

He did not have long to wait. As naval and colonial expenditure continued to mount, Imperial Germany's deficit steadily increased. To cover a 500-million-mark deficit Bülow introduced a finance bill increasing indirect taxation and extending the scope of the death-duties tax first introduced in 1906. The latter was a modest enough measure, affecting only 130,000 landowners. But the propaganda machine of the Agrarian League swung into action against it. There was no majority for the bill in the Reichstag. Socialists opposed it because indirect taxes were increased; Conservatives and Centrists opposed death duties as a matter of principle. This was not the real reason for their opposition. The 'bloc' had really outlived its usefulness in Conservative eyes. They were greatly alarmed by agitation for reform of the Prussian franchise and feared that Bülow, the supreme opportunist of the day, might be tempted to exploit the situation in his own interests. The Centre was simply determined to have its revenge on Bülow for 1906, and the Poles their revenge for his anti-Polish policy. The finance bill was defeated, and four days later Bülow tendered his resignation, as he had hinted he might do in the event of an adverse vote. Admittedly this was only a tactical manoeuvre; Bülow wished to avoid ignominious dismissal at the emperor's hands and was confident that William would have to recall him before long. The plan misfired for Bülow never returned to office. Nothing had changed. The new chancellor, Theobald von Bethmann Hollweg, was appointed by the emperor as Bülow had been. True, Conservative and Centre proposals for alternative taxes to replace the ill-fated death duties bill were accepted by the new chancellor. And once again the Bundesrat had to acquiesce in a *fait accompli*. But although this development, taken in conjunction with Bülow's attempt to establish a causal relationship between resignation and the defeat of his legislation, seems to represent a faltering step forward politically, appearances were largely deceptive. The power of autocracy remained in fact very largely unbroken – especially in the Prussian core of the German empire – on the eve of the First World War.

At the beginning of the twentieth century the burning political issue in Germany was not the future of the Reichstag but the need for reform of the archaic Prussian constitution. In the Reichstag Conservatives were only a small party, politically isolated after 1909 and unable to prevent the passage of progressive legislation. Yet in Prussia the conservative position was virtually unassailable. They had a stranglehold over the civil service, they controlled the upper chamber and had close on a majority in the lower house, which was still elected by the outmoded three-class system. Their entrenched position in the army and at court enabled Prussian landowners to exert a good deal of influence on imperial policy as well. The offensive against Prussian conservatism was started by a Radical, Theodore Barth, with a motion in 1900 calling for reform of the Prussian constitution. It was promptly defeated but Barth reintroduced it annually in the Landtag and focused public attention on the problem. It was becoming more acute in the early years of the century for other reasons. In the first place the democratisation of the South-German states was proceeding apace; in 1905–6 the principle of direct election was adopted by Baden and Bavaria, and in 1906 Württemberg decided to elect all members of its lower house on the basis of universal suffrage. Secondly, in 1900 the Socialists decided to take part in Prussian elections for the first time; the fact that they could obtain only seven seats with twenty-three per cent of the poll at the local election of 1908, whereas the Conservatives with sixteen per cent had 212 seats, illustrated the glaring injustice of the prevailing system. There were working-class demonstrations in Prussian cities, ending in clashes with the police, and the emperor hastily agreed to constitutional changes. Nothing came of it; Bülow had no wish to fall foul of the Prussian Conservatives. Early in 1910 further demonstrations occurred. This time the new chancellor, Bethmann Hollweg, decided to do something. A bill was introduced in the Landtag to strengthen the middle-class voters at the expense of landowners and workers. Even this modest measure was bitterly opposed by Conservatives, with support from the Centre, and was withdrawn. The dichotomy between Prussian Landtag and Imperial Reichstag was intensified the following year, 1911, when Alsace-Lorraine received a democratic constitution with two-chamber government and universal suffrage. Bethmann Hollweg took the initiative over Alsace-Lorraine in the hope that timely concessions would keep the population loyal to the

Reich. With one eye on Prussia, his original intention was to restrict the franchise. The Reichstag overruled him and he gave way. The curious outcome was that a conquered province enjoyed democratic institutions, with powers comparable to those of the Reichstag, whilst the Prussian nucleus of the *Reich* was still denied them.

The Reichstag election of 1912 registered the growing dissatisfaction of the German people with obstructionism from the right. The Conservatives and Centre went down to defeat, as expected. The sensational feature was a massive increase in the Socialist vote; with 110 seats and over four million votes the Socialists became the largest party in the Reichstag. One in every three Germans had voted Socialist, an impressive testimony to the power of the new working class. This would not have been possible without the support of the Radicals. The warring radical groups amalgamated in 1910 to form the *Fortschrittliche Vereinigung*. The new party entered into electoral pacts with the Socialists, supporting them on the second ballot. For it had at last dawned on the radical left that this was the high road to political advancement. As Barth observed in 1903, 'Liberal politics in Germany, as in all countries with a highly developed industry, can only be carried on with the aid of the class of wage workers. This is the alpha and omega of all political knowledge.' The Reichstag took a sharp turn to the left. Socialists and Radicals were within sight of an over-all majority. All they needed was support from the forty-five National Liberals. This was not a completely forlorn hope; when Spahn of the Centre was elected president of the Reichstag by a narrow majority, some twenty National Liberals voted for the runner-up, the Socialist leader Bebel. They also voted for the Socialist Scheidemann, who was elected vice-president, again by a narrow majority. Too much should not be read into isolated votes, but the willingness of these National Liberals to support Socialist candidates contains the first hint that even in the upper middle class, one of the bulwarks of Imperial Germany, there was some awareness of the need for political change on the eve of the war.

Nearly forty years had elapsed since the foundation of the Socialist party and over twenty since the end of Bismarck's anti-socialist legislation. It has already been pointed out that the growing electoral strength of the party gave substance to the view that a peaceful transition to socialism was perfectly feasible and ought to be the objective of the party. The old hostility between working class and state was at last beginning to wear thin; it could hardly be denied that working people derived substantial benefits from social legislation or that their living-standards were rising slowly as a result of the continuous activity of trade unions. In the light of these developments some Socialists decided that it was time to modify the Marxist base of the party. This led to a bitter ideological struggle at the turn of the century between the orthodox Marxists and the so-called Revisionists. The ideas of the Revisionists were expressed most clearly by

Eduard Bernstein, a Berlin Jew and London correspondent of the Socialist paper *Vorwärts* from 1882 to 1901. According to Bernstein, Marx was wrong in his belief that the contradictions in capitalism would deepen and lead to its early collapse. There was much evidence to the contrary; there had been no serious economic crisis for a decade; the workers had not grown poorer as Marx prophesied; the middle classes were more powerful than ever before; and the sharp edges of the class struggle were being blurred by the growth of a great army of white-collar workers. In short, capitalism had stabilised itself and the Revisionists demanded that the party accommodate itself to this fact, which was precisely what the Fabians were saying about British socialism. Instead of talking about the Day of Revolution, Socialists should concentrate wholeheartedly on the task of transforming Germany into a democratic state by parliamentary means. Socialism would not follow hard on the heels of a cataclysmic upheaval; it would come like a thief in the night, the end-product of an evolutionary process. The party's role, like that of the trade unions, was to fight for the improvement of conditions within the framework of capitalism. Socialists must abandon their isolationist attitude and seek the widest possible political support for peaceful change on the basis of the minimum programme. Finally, as the workers had a stake in Imperial Germany, they must be patriotic enough to defend her against aggressors; support for *Weltpolitik* and colonial expansion followed easily from the denial of Marx's thesis that the worker had no fatherland. Revisionism had an appeal for trade-union leaders concerned with bread-and-butter issues, and for many intellectuals. The strongest support came from South Germany, where electoral co-operation with liberals was a well-established practice, which had led Socialists to assume some responsibility for the government of Baden and Bavaria.

Revisionism was firmly opposed by the party executive, by leading Socialists such as Bebel and Liebknecht and probably by a majority of rank-and-file members. These were the orthodox Marxists, who heatedly maintained that the conflict between capital and labour, far from dying away, was deepening. On the eve of war real wages were falling, prices rising, unemployment growing and the state authorities were dealing more ruthlessly with strikers than ever before, as political tensions mounted in Imperial Germany. Capitalism was plainly on the eve of crisis; at such a moment it would surely be the height of folly to rely exclusively on parliamentary methods and neglect the truly revolutionary weapon of the general strike. And quite apart from the economic case against Revisionism, many rank-and-file Socialists felt instinctively that belief in revolution at some point in the future was the essential *élan* holding the party together. So Revisionism was condemned at one party conference after the other. In 1904 at the Amsterdam Congress of the Second International the Germans even persuaded the meeting to endorse the principle of strict non-co-operation with all bourgeois parties, a principle which all Socialist parties observed down to 1914. Many Socialists applauded Bebel when he declared passionately in 1903: 'I want to remain the deadly enemy of this bourgeois society and this political order in order to undermine it in its conditions of existence and, if I can, to eliminate it entirely.' Socialists continued to live as a race apart, almost a state within a state, developing their own cultural, educational and sports associations in their anxiety to avoid the corruption of capitalism. They treasured their sense of isolation, rejected the values of capitalist society, derided organised religion and denounced militarism and xenophobic nationalism.

The attitude of the parliamentary Socialist party calls for special comment, as it occupied a position of growing importance in the party as a whole. There were a few revisionists and some extreme left-wingers in the Reichstag, but the great majority of Socialist deputies were men of the centre seeking the best of both worlds. In practice they were deeply committed to democratic socialism. They did their best to damp down the revolutionary feeling of the masses, being firmly of the opinion that workers had too much to lose to risk that confrontation with the power of the state which advocates of the general strike dreamt of. At the same time, in the interests of party unity the men of the centre had to maintain a *façade* of revolutionary respectability. Seeking the best of both worlds, they ended up by getting the worst of both. They were easily vulnerable to the accusation of left-wingers, such as Rosa Luxemburg, that they were not revolutionaries in any recognisable sense of the word. Yet they went on uttering the old revolutionary incantations and refused to co-operate whole-heartedly with bourgeois parties; the result was that they alienated progressive elements in the middle classes without whose support Socialists could never, in fact, hope to secure a majority in the country.

On the very eve of war Germany was shaken by one last political storm, the Zabern incident. Relations between Alsace-Lorraine and the rest of Germany were bad, despite the constitution of 1911; the memory of the French connexion died hard; and as national animosities deepened in Europe there was much friction between the local populace and garrison troops who regarded the locals as unreliable. Zabern was a small town in Alsace where an infantry regiment was stationed. A young lieutenant made contemptuous remarks about Alsatian recruits which aroused indignation and led to several demonstrations in Zabern. During one of these disturbances, in November 1913, the commanding officer, a Colonel von Reuter, ordered his men to clear the streets. In the ensuing *mêlée* twenty-eight citizens, including a judge and a lawyer, were detained overnight in the barracks. The Zabern incident unleashed a great roar of disapproval in Germany; for one of the fundamentals of a *Rechtsstaat* was that only civilian courts or the police could interfere with the liberty of citizens. An animated debate took place in the Reichstag. The minister of war brusquely rejected criticism of the army, on the grounds that commanding officers were responsible only to the emperor and certainly not to the Reichstag. The Reichstag passed a vote of censure on the chancellor by a large majority; only the Conservatives stood by the government. In January 1914 Reuter was court-martialled but acquitted on the grounds that, as the police had failed to keep order, military intervention had been justified. Reuter was actually decorated, and the Prussian upper chamber passed, by a large majority, a resolution upholding the prestige of the army. In a sense, the Zabern affair was a lightning-flash which suddenly illuminated the horizon. The imperial constitution was devised by Bismarck so that Germany could be ruled by chancellors responsible only to the emperor; in practice the emperor intervened only spasmodically in affairs of state while the Reichstag became a more significant body under chancellors such as Caprivi and Bülow. The emperor's sharp defence of the military in 1914 revealed the strict limits within which the new system operated. It is equally significant that there was little support in the Reichstag for Scheidemann's proposal that appropriation bills be rejected until satisfaction was obtained. Wickham Steed, the English liberal journalist, commented on the court martial in these words: 'In Prussia the army is supreme and through Prussia the army rules Germany. This is the first lesson of the trial for those who lightly imagine the German empire to be even as other states.' A somewhat exaggerated judgement, but typical of much comment abroad where the Zabern incident encouraged the belief that arrogant militarists were in complete control of Imperial Germany.

Like most countries, Germany was a land of sharp contrasts. No one would deny that an exaggerated and unhealthy respect for military virtues was a disturbing feature. At the same time, Germany was an urbane and civilised country, the home of Theodore Fontane and Thomas Mann as well as Treitschke and Nietzsche. And, compared with lands east of the Elbe, the ordinary German citizen enjoyed much greater personal freedom. On the other hand, Socialist propagandists were frequently in trouble with the authorities; their meetings were supervised (and often dissolved) by the police; troops were often employed to uphold the rights of private property in strike-ridden areas; trade unionists were frequently dismissed for their activities; and even solid middle-class citizens could pay a heavy price for dissentient opinions, as witness the case of the distinguished historian Ludwig Quidde ruined professionally after a satirical piece in 1896 poking fun at the histrionic posturings of the emperor and his Byzantine court. Nationally, a state of political deadlock existed with a left-inclined Reichstag at loggerheads with a conservative chancellor. In some southern states local legislatures were already playing an increasingly significant role in political life. By way of contrast in the Mecklenburgs, in

Saxony and especially in Prussia a tightly knit complex of landowners and industrialists, with support from court and military circles, clung desperately to their entrenched positions determined to resist change to the very last. Opposed to this power complex was 'the other Germany', a growing army of Socialists, and lower-middle-class Radicals, with some support from rank-and-file Centrists, all demanding immediate political change in these states. Obviously the political temperature in Germany had been rising since the *Daily Telegraph* affair. It is, therefore, tempting to suppose that a confrontation between the forces of reaction and the army of progress was inevitable once boom conditions faded, and that within a very few years the institutions of the Empire would have been thoroughly democratised. This is to oversimplify a complex political situation containing possibilities for peaceful change as well as stagnation likely to end in revolution. It also underestimates the power of the forces of law and order in Germany. The middle classes, backbone of this industrialised and urbanised empire, were still pretty solidly on the side of the Establishment. They were alarmed by the darkening international scene and concerned above all else to defend the fatherland in the crisis which loomed ahead. This is one reason why the genuine anger over Zabern evaporated so quickly in the winter of 1913–14. It is significant that Bethmann Hollweg handled the 'left' Reichstag of 1912 with ease only when it was asked to approve military increases. Socialists and Poles always opposed military appropriations. It is not without interest that in 1913 Socialists relented sufficiently to support the capital levy which Bethmann Hollweg introduced to cover the increased defence expenditure; this, at least, was a progressive measure even if Socialists could not bring themselves to approve of the army measures which it financed. It is true that a majority of the Reichstag favoured constitutional changes of some sort. But at the same time most members including many Socialist leaders had the greatest respect for the monarchy and on that account made no attempt to force the pace of what seemed an inevitable movement towards parliamentary government. In short, there was much political tension and frustration in Imperial Germany – as in other countries in 1914 – but revolution was less likely here than elsewhere. It took four hard years of war to shake the Germans' deeply ingrained respect for authority and make revolution possible in the land of Hegel and Kant.

8

The Foreign Policy of Imperial Germany 1890–1914

The resignation of Bismarck in 1890 was an event of major importance in German history. It is true that the old man's foreign policy lay in ruins by this time; the understanding between Austria, Russia and Germany was shattered beyond repair and the inexorable pressure of events was drawing France and Russia together. Nevertheless the disappearance from the international scene of a familiar figure, who at any rate in his later years had worked for peace, aroused anxious speculation in the foreign press. And despite the young emperor's confident assertion that the course remained the same, the dropping of the pilot was followed by an important reorientation of policy, the so-called New Course, which lasted for the next four years.

The first sign that German policy was changing was Caprivi's refusal to renew the Reinsurance treaty. Bismarck accused his successors of criminal stupidity for allowing the treaty to lapse and so making a Franco-Russian understanding certain. That was a pardonable exaggeration of a frustrated old man. He had, in fact, helped to alienate Russia from Germany. More fundamentally the ruling *élites* in both empires were politically dependent on agrarian and industrial circles whose demands for protective tariffs had driven Russia and Germany apart. Even so, conservative diplomats were still influential enough in 1890 to insist on preserving a connexion which kept Austria quiet and left Russia free to face Britain in Asia. When approached by Russia Bismarck was naturally agreeable to renewal. Even after his resignation William II assured Russia that Germany would renew it.

Why, then, was the Reinsurance treaty allowed to lapse? Basically because William II was quite incapable of giving a firm lead in policy matters; his anti-Russian prejudice and Anglophile sympathies did not amount to a coherent policy. Nor was there any outstanding personality among his advisers strong enough to assume complete control of foreign policy; Herbert Bismarck, who knew most about his father's complex diplomacy, refused to serve as secretary of state for foreign affairs; and Chancellor Caprivi and Secretary of State Marschall were complete novices in the field. Lack of direction at the top played inevitably into the hands of other advisers, both civilian and military, who were able to exert some influence on policy from time to time. One of the most influential of these advisers was Baron Holstein, permanent head of the political department in the foreign office. Holstein was an able and dedicated civil servant, an ex-*protégé* of Bismarck with an unrivalled knowledge of foreign affairs. But 'the Grey Eminence', as he was called by contemporaries, was also a pessimistic, lonely and neurotically suspicious character, whose attempts at copying the tortuous and secretive diplomacy of the Bismarckian era did a great deal of harm to Germany during the next fifteen years. However, on this occasion he did not stand alone. His colleagues in the foreign office were unanimous in the view that the Reinsurance treaty was basically incompatible with Germany's other obligations; they feared that if the terms leaked out, then Austria, Italy and Britain would be estranged from Germany. Professional diplomats agreed with this assessment. Caprivi, too, doubted the viability of a renewed treaty in view of the strength of anti-German sentiment in Russia. So he finally advised William against renewal, unaware that his sovereign had already encouraged the Russians to expect a favourable outcome to the negotiations. William agreed at once, remarking with light-hearted abandon: 'Then it isn't possible, much as I regret it'; and the treaty was lapsed.

Germany assured Russia that she still desired friendly relations, but Caprivi's brusque refusal to entertain further written agreements with Russia aroused misgivings in St. Petersburg. Germany did not think the course had altered, but Russia did. She was annoyed by the growing intimacy between Austria and Germany; and she was positively alarmed by the attempts William II was making to ingratiate himself with Britain, Russia's greatest enemy. William paid frequent visits to his grandmother Queen Victoria; the British government welcomed the friendship of Germany and made the young emperor an honorary admiral of the fleet; in 1890 Britain and Germany signed a colonial agreement, the Anglo-German Convention, which restored Heligoland to Germany in return for a limitation of German claims in East Africa and a recognition of the British protectorate over Zanzibar. This was followed in 1891 by rumours that Britain had joined the Triple Alliance. That was the last straw for Russia. Fear of isolation drove her into the arms of France. In August 1891 France and Russia negotiated an *entente*, which was followed by a military convention in 1892 and blossomed into a full-blown alliance in 1893–4.

The significance of this momentous change in the balance of power was not immediately apparent. For by 1894 the New Course was over. Relations with Britain were clouded by colonial disputes, whilst at home the emperor was worried by the growth of socialism and quickly repented of his anti-Russian attitude. His new chancellor, Prince Hohenlohe, was related to the Russian aristocracy by marriage and believed firmly in the need for friendship with Russia. In March 1894 the Reichstag approved the commercial treaty with Russia, which assured German industrialists of markets in the east and turned them into ardent Russophiles; this was one occasion when William listened to his industrialist friends, not to the landowners who were bitterly critical of tariff reductions. The treaty did something to restore Russian confidence in Germany; after this the Panslav press was more restrained in its references to France. After 1894 Germany no longer stood four-square behind Austria-Hungary; William II warned her bluntly that Germany would not fight to keep Russia out of Constantinople. In effect the emperor was returning to Bismarck's policy – or as near as he could get to it by 1894.

On the face of things Germany's position in Europe seemed secure enough in the 1890s. Austria and Italy were allies; Russia was her friend again; relations with France were better than they had been under Bismarck; and by the close of the century Britain was on such bad terms with France and Russia that she was thinking of an alliance with Germany. It seemed to the Germans that if they manoeuvred the ship of state with care, remaining on good terms with all the powers but profiting wherever possible by dissensions among them, then Germany would soon become the arbiter of Europe. That was indeed the aim of Holstein's so-called 'free hand' policy. With hindsight it is easy to see that an over-confident Germany mistook the transient animosities between Britain, France and Russia for permanent features of the international landscape. By 1907, when the three powers had overcome many of their differences, Germany had to face the disagreeable fact that her arbitral position was a thing of the past.

Germany never possessed as much freedom of manoeuvre as the Wilhelmstrasse supposed.[1] Once Germany had pledged herself to Austria-Hungary in 1879, Russian friendship was a precarious bloom at the best of times. William II was on excellent terms with his cousin Nicholas II, a sovereign who did not share the Panslav sympathies of his predecessor. But the personal friendship enshrined in the 'Willy-Nicky' letters and the existence of important economic ties did not alter the fact that the French alliance remained the sheet-anchor of Russian policy. And as long as the Franco-Russian alliance remained in being, Germany's freedom of manoeuvre in Europe was seriously restricted, and the threat of war on two fronts at some future date was a very real one, as Caprivi appreciated. This was not immediately apparent simply because Russia was absorbed in Asia, and France in Africa. Moreover Italy was an unreliable ally; the Italians were thoroughly dissatisfied with the *Triplice* and by 1902 they had patched up their quarrel with France, though they remained nominal members of the alliance. Only Austria-Hungary remained loyal to

---

[1] The German foreign office was situated in Berlin's Wilhelmstrasse.

Germany. The fact that Germany would not commit herself whole-heartedly to supporting Austria at this time merely obscured the reality of the situation; it could not alter it.

A momentous change occurred in German policy in the closing years of the nineteenth century. She began to pursue *Weltpolitik*, looking beyond the narrow confines of Europe to a wider world overseas in Africa and in the Far East. In Africa, where Germany already possessed the nucleus of a colonial empire, she watched with jealous eyes the rapid expansion of British rule, and in the mid-1890s was co-operating with France to obstruct Britain, much as Bismarck had done a decade earlier. In the Far East German expectations of territorial expansion grew as the Chinese Empire tottered on the brink of collapse. In 1895 Germany joined with Russia and France to compel Japan to moderate her territorial gains after the defeat of China. In 1897 Germany used the murder of two missionaries as an excuse to occupy the harbour of Kiao-Chow, which she had long desired as a coaling station. This, incidentally, was the signal for other Great Powers to acquire strong-points along the Chinese coastline. In 1898, during the Spanish-American War, Germany compelled the Span-iards to sell the Carolines, the Pelews and the Marianne islands to her. In 1899, by agreement with Britain, Germany acquired part of the Samoan group of islands. In the Near East, too, German influence grew apace after the emperor's tour of the Ottoman Empire in 1898; at Damascus he made a famous speech in which he rashly assured the 300 million Mohammedans, many of whom were under British and Russian rule, that the German emperor was their true friend. Finally, between 1898 and 1900 Germany embarked on the building of a powerful navy.

Germany's desire to be a World Power as well as the dominant power in Europe had decisive effects on her policy. Her restless search for colonial possessions and more especially her naval policy led to serious disagreements with Britain. At the same time German penetration of the Near East caused some anxiety in St. Petersburg. It is true that no disagreement occurred between Russia and Germany on this account, and on the eve of the First World War even the colonial rivalry between Britain and Germany was dying away. But when the Triple Entente between Britain, France and Russia came into being in 1907, these side effects of *Weltpolitik* gave the members some grounds for their suspicion of Germany; France because she had never reconciled herself to German domination of Europe; Russia because she did not wish to see Turkey passing under German control when her own dependence on the Straits as a vital economic artery was increasing; and Britain because she regarded the German navy as a challenge to her maritime supremacy, and also because she deeply resented Germany's diplomatic methods.

Economic and social forces far beyond the control of the Wilhelmstrasse impelled Germany forward on a course which other Great Powers were already pursuing with vigour. What might perhaps have been avoided were maladroit diplomatic methods which gave offence to other powers. German intervention in South Africa is an excellent illustration of this. Britain's quarrel with the Boer republics was reaching a climax at the close of the century. For Britain vital strategic interests were at stake; as long as the Boer republics remained independent, Britain could not unite Cape Colony with the Rhodesias and so consolidate her position in South Africa. Germany had intervened in South Africa for the first time in 1894, when Cecil Rhodes tried to gain control of the railway the Boers had built from Pretoria to Lourenço Marques. German protests obliged Rhodes to abandon his attempt. In December 1895 Jameson, an agent of Rhodes, invaded the Transvaal with 800 men in an attempt to seize Johannesburg and overthrow the republic with the aid of the Uitlanders, as the non-Boer settlers were called. The raid was a miserable failure, quickly repudiated by the British government. The German emperor was highly incensed by the Jameson Raid and insisted on immediate action. He talked wildly of declaring a protectorate over the Transvaal and sending troops to the Republic. His advisers persuaded him to settle for what they thought was a less harmful gesture of protest in the shape of a congratulatory telegram to Krüger, president of the Transvaal Republic. Anxiety about German investment in the Transvaal and concern for the 15,000 Germans working in the gold fields were subordinate considerations in the emperor's mind. He was resentful of British success and determined to teach her a sharp lesson which would make her see that Germany had as much right as Britain to be in Africa. In a muddled fashion he and his advisers hoped that by bringing pressure to bear on Britain at a weak and vulnerable point they could force her to come to terms with the *Triplice*.

The Krüger Telegram was warmly applauded in Germany; Radical nationalists shared William's resentment of Britain and welcomed the ostentatious gesture of protest as a sign that Germany was now playing her rightful role in world politics. As a diplomatic manoeuvre the telegram was inept and unsuccessful. It did nothing to hinder British plans in South Africa, nor did it draw Britain closer to the Berlin-Vienna-Rome axis. On the contrary, a serious shadow was cast over Anglo-German relations for the first time. Much to the surprise of the emperor and his advisers, the telegram aroused great indignation in Britain where it was condemned as a piece of unwarranted meddling in a purely British concern by a hitherto friendly monarch. The incident helped to crystallise subconscious resentment of Germany's commercial rivalry and gave encouragement to the very small minority of Englishmen who positively hated Germany; their views found expression in the famous article in the *Saturday Review* in September 1897 which concluded with the ominous phrase: 'Ceterum censeo, Germaniam esse delendam.'[2] Nor did anything come of the

[2]'For the rest, I think Germany ought to be annihilated.'

attempts of the emperor and Holstein to create a continental league as an alternative means of isolating Britain and compelling her to come to terms with Germany. This proved an empty threat which merely laid bare fundamental weaknesses in German policy; neither France nor Russia had any wish to tangle with Britain in South Africa in order to strengthen Germany in Europe.

Yet it was not Germany but Britain who had most cause for alarm at the turn of the century. The international complications arising out of Britain's extended imperial commitments were casting doubts on the efficacy of 'Splendid Isolation', at least in the minds of some Englishmen. Britain no longer possessed a colonial monopoly; in Africa she clashed frequently with France and brushed with Germany; more serious still was the rivalry with Russia in Asia, where the fate of China was hanging in the balance. In March 1898 Russia acquired a lease on the key naval base of Port Arthur, a forward move likely to lead to Russian domination of China. The British government was alarmed, and Joseph Chamberlain, the forceful and thrusting colonial secretary, approached Germany in the first of three attempts between 1898 and 1901 to secure an alliance with her. During the unofficial negotiations Chamberlain, who believed that Germany was Britain's 'natural ally',[3] proposed a defensive alliance between the two countries, to be ratified by the British Parliament.

Germany's reaction was negative. This was hardly surprising in view of the prevailing hostility to Britain. Bülow, who became secretary of state in 1897, and Holstein both had more weighty objections. As they saw it, Britain was seeking cheap insurance in the shape of a continental ally to save her from the effects of her rivalry with Russia. If war broke out in the Far East, as seemed likely, Britain would fight a naval war against Russia. But Germany as the ally of Britain would find herself bearing the brunt of a two-front war in Europe. This was *Perfide Albion* with a vengeance. Geography dictated German policy as much as any other power's. German interests were best served by remaining on good terms with Russia. This was not difficult, because Russia, being deeply involved in the Far East, had signed an agreement with Austria-Hungary in 1897 preserving the Balkan *status quo*. Indeed a kind of continental league had at last come into being, for France was an anxious as Russia and Austria to keep the peace in the Balkans. The Balkan truce confirmed Germany in the belief that it was perfectly possible to remain on good terms with all the continental powers. Why endanger this for the sake of British investments in China? There were other reasons why Germany wished to avoid positive commitments towards Britain. If she waited, war between Britain and Russia or between Britain and France seemed highly probable; Britain would then become dependent on Germany and would join the *Triplice* on Germany's terms.

[3]Chamberlain used this expression in a public speech at Leicester on 30 November 1899.

For the present, Britain needed careful handling until Germany passed through 'the danger zone', i.e. the period when her new fleet was weak enough to tempt Britain into a surprise attack *à la Copenhagen* before it posed a serious threat to her naval supremacy. All things considered, Holstein's policy of the 'free hand' seemed correct. Germany must avoid new commitments and remain friends with both Russia and Britain as long as possible. Skilful diplomacy would reap a rich harvest. Germany would slip past envious rivals and dominate Europe absolutely within a few years by virtue of her unrivalled industrial power, without a shot being fired – by German guns at any rate. As the German ambassador in London remarked in 1901, 'If people in Germany would only sit still, the time would soon come when we can all have oysters and champagne for dinner.'

This was largely wishful thinking on his part. For it was quite clear that much scepticism existed in London about the possibility of a German alliance; significantly enough the initiative came not from the government but from individual ministers and diplomats; indeed no official alliance offer as such was made to Germany; nor can it be denied that British opinion was anti-German, a fact which would have made parliamentary approval of a formal treaty difficult, whatever the optimistic Chamberlain pretended. This does not exonerate the Germans from all blame for the failure of the negotiations. The makers of policy in Germany were excessively suspicious of other powers; whatever chance there might have been of securing a British alliance was lightly thrown away by the Germans. For basically they grossly overestimated Germany's freedom of manoeuvre, arrogantly assuming that understandings between Britain, France and Russia were out of the question. Supremely confident that Britain would come to them in the end, they insisted throughout the negotiations that Britain join the *Triplice* as a full member, a condition no British government was prepared to accept; 'the whole or none' summed up the German attitude in 1901, as Lord Landsdowne remarked to a British diplomat. In this intransigent frame of mind they rejected British offers of limited local agreements to cover the Mediterranean and the Persian Gulf, agreements which might conceivably have made a gradual *rapprochement* between the two countries possible at a later date.

Britain looked elsewhere for an ally. The Far East erupted in June 1900 with the Boxer Rebellion. The foreign legations in Peking were besieged by the Chinese, and the German *chargé d'affaires* was murdered. The White powers intervened at once to protect their investments and their nationals. For years the German emperor had tried to alert Europe to the danger of the 'Yellow Peril'. He now took the initiative in organising an international expedition under General Waldersee to restore law and order. This was the occasion for one of William II's most tactless speeches, in which he urged his soldiers to be ruthless towards the Chinese rebels and made the name 'German' as feared in China as the Huns had been centuries before in Europe. The Great Powers did not stay united for long. Russia had invaded Manchuria under cover of the Boxer Rebellion. Germany feared that this would make Britain seize the Yangtze basin. To safeguard German economic interests in the basin, Germany persuaded Britain to sign the Yangtze Agreement in October 1900. Under this agreement Britain and Germany renounced further territorial ambitions in China, promised to maintain the Open Door policy and agreed to consult together if other powers upset the *status quo*. Britain hoped to use the agreement against Russia, although Germany insisted from the beginning that she was not committed in this direction. In 1901 a new crisis occurred when Russia insisted on retaining political control in Manchuria before withdrawing her forces. Britain turned hopefully to Germany. It was the old story; Germany dare not risk a European war for the sake of British investments in China. In March 1901 Bülow, now chancellor, declared officially that Russian action in Manchuria did not concern Germany. This was the parting of the ways for Britain. She terminated the alliance negotiations and in January 1902 allied with Japan, a power eager to challenge the Russian colossus.

Bülow and Holstein welcomed the Anglo-Japanese alliance, confident that it would greatly increase the likelihood of war between Britain and Russia on which they pinned their hopes for Germany. When Britain came to terms with France in April 1904 there were faint misgivings, but Bülow brushed them aside, declaring in the Reichstag that the Anglo-French entente was a purely colonial agreement not directed against Germany. He could afford to be complacent, for in February the Russo-Japanese war had broken out. German hopes rose. It was confidently assumed that the Anglo-French entente would founder once Britain was dragged into the war by her Japanese ally. In October, when Russian warships passing through the North Sea on their way to the Far East fired in error on British fishing-smacks, Germany thought war certain. She attempted to exploit the situation by offering Russia a defensive alliance against Britain. Her calculation was that this would either compel France to come to terms with Germany, loosening the entente with Britain and bringing a continental league into being at last; or, if France refused, then at least the Franco-Russian alliance would be disrupted.

The high hopes were quickly dashed. The Dogger Bank incident passed off without war; Britain and Russia had no wish to fight each other and allowed the Hague Court to settle the dispute; the continental league was stillborn; and the Anglo-French entente was stronger than ever. Bülow had to admit ruefully that German policy had failed. But the clouds had a silver lining; the war in the Far East had not led to an Anglo-Russian conflict but it had at least weakened Russia seriously; in January 1905 revolution broke out in St. Petersburg, and for the rest of the year Russia had no time to bother about Europe. Overnight the threat of a two-front war disappeared, and France was suddenly weakened. This was a decisive moment for Germany. German policy had been essentially negative and pacific in the past; since 1890 she had relied on the forward march of events to make her supreme in Europe. In 1905 she adopted a more positive and aggressive policy designed to exploit the temporary disequilibrium in the balance of power and score a great diplomatic triumph at the expense of France.

Pressure was applied to France at her most vulnerable point, Morocco. In the past Germany had raised no objection to French penetration of Morocco. Now German agents began to intrigue in the country and advised the sultan to resist French encroachments. Bülow took care to warn the sultan that Germany could not fight over Morocco, for war never entered into his calculations in 1905. He realised that French predominance in Morocco was inevitable in the long run. German pressure was only intended to warn France that Germany was not to be ignored and to show her that British support would be of little avail; in despair the French would abandon the entente and gravitate to Berlin – or so the Germans hoped. In February 1905 France attempted to squeeze more concessions out of the sultan. Whereupon Bülow and Holstein decided on an ostentatious gesture of protest; they asked the emperor to visit Tangier during his spring cruise in the Mediterranean. William was annoyed; he had no wish to quarrel with France in North Africa, feeling that involvement in Morocco kept her mind off Alsace-Lorraine. Eventually he knuckled under and in March 1905 landed at Tangier; during his three-hour visit he was received by the sultan's uncle and assured the latter, in tones reminiscent of the Krüger telegram, that Germany considered Morocco an independent state and expected her to resist French pressure.

Europe was startled by the Tangier incident. The French were taken aback at the sudden German interest in North Africa and even more surprised to discover that Germany could not be bought off with offers of compensation elsewhere in Africa. Bülow insisted that an international conference be called to discuss Morocco. He felt supremely confident that a majority of the Great Powers in conference would uphold the independence of Morocco; France would suffer a humiliating defeat in public, and Germany would win a diplomatic victory at no cost to herself. Delcassé, the French foreign minister, urged his colleagues to resist German pressure for a conference. Unfortunately the cabinet was deeply divided, a fact known to the Germans. Bülow played on this weakness; hints were dropped that Germany would attack in the west if French troops invaded Morocco. This was bluff, as Delcassé knew, but a majority of his colleagues were not prepared to call it. Defeated in cabinet, Delcassé resigned in June 1905. Germany had won a great victory. Bülow had his hour of triumph and was made a prince by his jubilant master.

The French expected that Germany would now negotiate privately over

Morocco. To their dismay they found Germany more truculent than ever and absolutely insistent on a conference. Reluctantly France accepted the German demand. This was another victory for Germany, as the Great Powers were unlikely to agree to French annexation of Morocco. Yet the victory was dearly won, for it cost Germany the goodwill of the French left wing, which up to then had been a staunch advocate of reconciliation with Germany.

When the Algeciras Conference met in January 1906 the Germans had a rude awakening; their confident assumption that France would be isolated at the conference table was soon exploded. As expected, the conference upheld Moroccan independence and guaranteed commercial equality to the interested powers. But when the organisation of the Moroccan police and the creation of a state bank were discussed, German complacency was shaken at last; only Austria-Hungary and Morocco supported the German proposals; Britain, France and Russia were ranged solidly against Germany. Holstein, who had toyed with preventive war from the beginning of the crisis, would have gladly wrecked the conference at this juncture. Wiser counsels prevailed in Berlin. Holstein resigned and Germany withdrew her proposals. In the end France obtained a major influence in the financial and policing arrangements of Morocco with the agreement of the powers.

The Moroccan adventure had ended disastrously for Germany. A lasting diplomatic victory eluded Bülow's grasp after initial successes. Whatever the Act of Algeciras, signed in April 1905, said about Moroccan independence, the door in Morocco was now open to further French advances. The Anglo-French entente, which Bülow and Holstein had fondly believed they could shatter, was stronger than ever after its baptism of fire. Germany, not France, had been publicly humiliated by the revelation of her diplomatic isolation at the conference table; and whilst Russia stood by France at Algeciras, Italy's failure to support Germany spotlighted the weakness of the once mighty Triple Alliance. Few people in 1906 seriously believed that Germany was bent on the domination of Europe by force of arms; but there was much resentment of German brinkmanship, and of her veiled hints of war and brash attempts to tip the balance of power in her favour. Not only had Bülow suffered a personal defeat. The most serious aspect of the First Moroccan Crisis, as far as Germany was concerned, was that it brought home to her rulers the discrepancy between her massive economic and military power and her diplomatic achievements. This revelation engendered a dangerous feeling of resentment, irritation and frustration in Berlin.

The growing sense of malaise deepened when Britain and Russia came to terms in August 1907. The agreement was not directed at Germany. No doubt alarm at the growth of the German navy and resentment of Germany's blustering and arrogant diplomatic methods played some part on the British side; but first and foremost this remained a colonial agreement designed to reduce British commitments overseas. Nor was there much dislike of Germany on the Russian side; Iswolski, the new foreign minister, was anxious only to turn his back on Asia and raise Russia's prestige by diplomatic victories in the Balkans. Yet the very fact of the agreement emphasised Germany's isolation; the confident assumption that Britain and Russia could never come to terms had been finally exploded. It is significant that German newspapers complained in 1907 of the ring closing round Germany. There was little substance in the accusation of 'encirclement'. The Triple Entente powers were not banded together to destroy Germany. All the same, Germany's eagerness to find scapegoats was a sure sign that those who controlled her foreign policy were conscious of its bankruptcy.

Germany's suspicions of the Triple Entente were increased by her experiences over the Berlin-to-Baghdad railway. German banks had been active promoters of railways in the Near East since the 1880s. In 1889 the *Deutsche Bank* played a prominent part in the formation of the Anatolian railway company. After the emperor's visit to Constantinople in 1898 the company secured the right to survey the ground in Mesopotamia and in 1903 received a concession to build a line down to the Persian Gulf. The dream of a German railway link stretching from the North Sea to the Gulf had an irresistible appeal in an era of *Weltpolitik* which made every German heart swell with pride. Russian opposition to the project did not surprise or daunt Germany; despite repeated German assurances that the line had a purely commercial significance, Russia not unnaturally feared the consequences of German intervention in Turkey. Bülow confidently expected Britain and France to assist in building a line which would strengthen Turkey against Russia. To his surprise both governments declined to put up money. The emperor's attempts to talk Britain round during a visit to Windsor were unavailing: he offered Britain control of the line from Baghdad to the Gulf to ally her fears about India; when the government made acceptance of the offer dependent on French and Russian agreement, William felt convinced that the Triple Entente powers were maliciously obstructing Germany.

German suspicions of the Triple Entente were growing in 1907 and 1908. So were Entente suspicions of German intentions. When the First Hague Conference met in 1899, it was Germany who incurred public odium by refusing to discuss arms reductions. Again in 1907, when a second conference was called by the Americans, Bülow declared curtly in the Reichstag that Germany would not take part in any discussions on disarmament, as she considered this to be impracticable. Germany joined fully in other aspects of the work of the conference. But it was German opposition which wrecked a proposal for compulsory and universal arbitration of disputes. True, Germany was only saying what other powers were thinking about disarmament and compulsory arbitration. Neverthe-less, public opinion in many countries was deeply offended by the negative attitude of the Germans. Germany's behaviour during the Bosnian Crisis of 1908–9 seemed to confirm growing doubts about her ultimate inten-tions and convinced many contemporaries that she was seeking to domi-nate Europe by force.

The Balkans were in a highly disturbed state in the first decade of the twentieth century. As the Turkish Empire declined, the independent Balkan states were becoming increasingly restive. The 1897 truce had lapsed by this time. Russia had turned back to the Balkans with renewed interest after her defeat in Asia, while Austria-Hungary was drawn deeper into Balkan politics through her feud with Serbia. Aehrenthal, the new foreign minister, was intent on making the Dual Monarchy count for more in the Dual Alliance. Germany, too, was more deeply involved in the Balkans than ever before; growing economic interests in Asia Minor gave her a vital stake in the future of the Ottoman Empire. And, most important of all, the steady deterioration in her international standing made her increasingly dependent on her one loyal ally, Austria. Horse and rider were changing places at last. In Bismarck's day Germany had restrained Austria from adventurous policies against Russia; under Bülow Germany began to underwrite the efforts of the restless and ambitious Aehrenthal to preserve the unstable empire of nationalities by some brilliant stroke of policy.

Thus when Aehrenthal decided to annex Bosnia-Herzegovina in Octo-ber 1908 he could count on German support. William II was displeased when he heard the news, for he feared the effect on German investment in Asia Minor. But he agreed with Bülow that Germany must keep in step with her ally. 'Our position would indeed be dangerous', remarked the chancellor, 'if Austria lost confidence in us and turned away . . . on eastern questions above all we cannot place ourselves in opposition to Austria, who has nearer and greater interests in the Balkan peninsula than our-selves. A refusal or a grudging attitude in the question of the annexation . . . would not be forgiven . . . in the present world constellation we must be careful to retain in Austria a true partner.' Shortly afterwards Bülow told Aehrenthal that Germany would approve whatever action Austria considered appropriate against Serbia. This momentous decision com-pletely reversed Bismarck's policy towards Austria and carried Germany to the threshold of war.

The annexation caused a great international crisis. There were protests from the Turks, and from the Serbs, who hoped one day to incorporate Bosnia in their own state. Britain and France denounced the annexation as a breach of treaty. Russia was furious. Iswolski had in fact agreed to the annexation beforehand but only on the understanding that the Straits Convention was revised in Russia's favour; Aehrenthal's precipitate action seemed a betrayal, for Iswolski had not yet secured the agreement of the powers to his side of the bargain. In vain Russia tried to save face by getting Austria to the conference table. She refused point-blank to attend unless the powers accepted the *fait accompli*, and Germany supported her faithfully in her defiant stand. In the final stages of the crisis Germany even forced the pace; in March 1909 she suggested that Russia formally recognise the annexation. As Russia hovered on the brink of decision, the Germans reiterated their proposal and declared bluntly that if Russia failed to do so she must take full responsibility for the subsequent course of events. This amounted to an ultimatum, and such was indeed the intention of its author, Kiderlen-Wächter, a rising star in the Wilhelmstrasse. A close friend of Holstein, Kiderlen was recalled from the Bucharest embassy and appointed acting secretary of state by Bülow. It was Kiderlen who won Bülow for a policy deliberately intended to drive Russia into a corner and humiliate her as much as possible to win a cheap diplomatic victory. This was brinkmanship without the usual risks, for Russia could not fight over Bosnia as Germany was well aware. Russia gave way, the annexation was recognised by the Great Powers and the crisis ended.

Germany had little cause for self-congratulation. The diplomatic triumph was dearly bought. Germany remained encircled. Russia was deeply resentful of her humiliation and drew closer to Britain and France for protection in the future. And the sharp tones of the note to Russia aroused much suspicion of Germany. Significantly enough, the lion's share of the blame for the crisis was laid not at Austria's door but Germany's. 'My German colleague', noted the Austrian ambassador in St. Petersburg, 'has become overnight a terrifying and sinister . . . figure.' This was not an untypical reaction in the Entente countries where the general public was beginning to assume that deep-laid aggressive designs lay behind Germany's irresponsible brinkmanship.

In his eagerness to secure some kind of victory for Germany and break the chain of encirclement, Bülow tagged along tamely behind Austria in military matters. Bismarck always resisted Austrian proposals for a co-ordinated military strategy, having no wish to be dragged into a Balkan war through inadvertence. In January 1909 Count Helmuth von Moltke, nephew of the victor of 1870 and chief of the general staff since 1906, was authorised by William II and Bülow to inform his Austrian counterpart, Conrad von Hötzendorff, that if Austria invaded Serbia and Russia went to war with her, then Germany would go to war with France and Russia; in accordance with the Schlieffen Plan Germany would leave a holding force on the eastern front and launch her major offensive against France. Eleven years after the death of Bismarck the military implications of the Dual Alliance were at last accepted in full by Germany. The German commitment was of more than academic interest, for when the tension between Austria and Serbia was at its height in the winter of 1908–9, Aehrenthal seriously considered preventive war to solve the Serbian problem once and for all. Had it not been for second thoughts in Vienna, Germany would have been involved in a major war over Bosnia.

Unhappily for Germany, the Bosnian Crisis coincided with a sharp deterioration in Anglo-German relations. This was a direct result of naval rivalry between the two countries. The navy was the brain-child of William II and Tirpitz both of whom were convinced that Germany's future lay on the oceans. To become a world power she needed a navy. Recent research suggests that the fleet was more than a symbol of imperial greatness; Tirpitz secretly hoped to wrest mastery of the seas from Britain either by blackmail or by force. In the 1890s much was made of the 'risk theory' – the notion that the navy need only be strong enough to make the risk of attack too great: i.e. if Britain attacked the German fleet she would be so badly mauled as to be incapable of facing the combined Franco-Russian fleets. What Tirpitz did not emphasise was his hope of defeating Britain in such a conflict. A strong navy also supplemented the 'free hand' policy, for the Germans naïvely supposed Britain would be better disposed towards them if they represented a potential naval threat.

It all worked out very differently. The creation of the Triple Entente completely changed the strategic picture and exploded the 'risk theory'. Britain was stronger at sea than ever before; Japan was her ally, France her friend, and the Russian Baltic fleet now lay at the bottom of the Tsushima Straits. By 1905 Britain had only one political rival on the high seas – Germany, whom she could easily outbuild if she chose to and with whom she was on bad terms as a result of the Moroccan crisis.

It was not easy for Germany to admit that her calculations had gone badly astray. Once public interest had been aroused, and Krupp committed to the necessary steel production, the navy became a prestige symbol which could not be lightly abandoned. Moreover it was not immediately obvious that Germany was on the brink of a disastrous naval race. In 1906 Britain launched the first *Dreadnought*, a craft which rendered all existing vessels obsolete. John Fisher, first sea lord since 1904, thought that the cost of building the new battleships and adapting her docks to take them would be beyond Germany. But Tirpitz and the emperor grasped eagerly at this possibility of building on what seemed to be equal terms with Britain. The other encouraging factor for Germany was the obvious desire of the new liberal government at Westminster to save money on defence. Fortified by this, Germany deepened her ports and commenced to build *Dreadnoughts*. At the turn of the century Britain was not seriously worried by the German navy. By 1908 her naval experts had changed their minds. Britain had only a slight lead in the building of *Dreadnoughts*; Germany had fourteen battleships projected to seven British, and with the resources of a first-class industrial power behind her, she would quickly close the gap, or so it was feared. The British public, shocked by the thought that the navy was not invincible, demanded immediate government action to remedy the deficiencies. British suspicion of Germany increased in the summer of 1908 when the emperor wrote a tactless letter to Lord Tweedmouth, first lord of the admiralty, in which he ridiculed British fears of a German invasion and tried to persuade the government to cut the navy estimates. Finally, in the spring of 1909 it was rumoured that Tirpitz was secretly accelerating the rate of building as stipulated in the schedule passed by the Reichstag.[4] Popular anti-German feeling burst into the open. 'We want eight and we won't wait,' roared the Unionist opposition. The Asquith government gave in to the popular clamour, and an additional eight ships were promised.

The subsequent course of the naval rivalry simply deepened the suspicion on both sides. Bethmann Hollweg realised that the only way of detaching Britain from the Triple Entente was by coming to terms with her over the naval question. His attempts to do so ended in failure. There was precious little room for manoeuvre by this time; German public opinion would not tolerate significant concessions to Britain; Tirpitz still believed with incredible naïveté that the stronger the fleet became, the more likely Britain was to come to terms; and Tirpitz and his fellow-admirals exerted much more influence on the emperor than Bethmann Hollweg. Nor was Britain prepared to make sacrifices to secure an agreement with Germany. At all costs Britain was determined to preserve her naval supremacy, the key to her standing as a world power. The fleet, in Churchill's words, was a 'kind of luxury' for Germany, but a sheer necessity for Britain; if Germany continued to build it must be that she intended to destroy Britain. All that Bethmann Hollweg could offer Britain between 1909 and 1911 was retardation of German building, in return for which he demanded a promise of British neutrality in a European war. Britain was interested only in an absolute reduction in the size of the German fleet, a demand totally unacceptable to the emperor, to Tirpitz and to German public opinion generally. Nor would Britain entertain a neutrality agreement; German attempts to persuade her merely aroused suspicion that Germany was trying to separate her from her friends.

The abortive attempts to terminate the naval race were interrupted in 1911 by another North African crisis which added greatly to the general fear and suspicion of Germany in Entente countries. The Entente was showing signs of wear and tear. There was friction between Britain and Russia in Persia and in the Far East. And much to Britain's alarm Russia was actually negotiating the Potsdam Agreement with Germany, in which the latter recognised Russia's railway monopoly in Northern Persia in

[4] It is still not clear whether Tirpitz was trying to steal a march on Britain when he gave out two contracts ahead of time in the autumn of 1908.

return for a Russian promise not to oppose the Berlin-to-Baghdad railway. The negotiations deadlocked only because Germany insisted on a promise that Russia would not support Britain's anti-German policies, an undertaking Russia would not give. The mistrust between Britain and Russia weakened the Entente and tempted Kiderlen, now secretary of state for foreign affairs, to try and redress the balance of power in Germany's favour by some bold stroke of policy. Following in Bülow's footsteps, he decided to put pressure on France in Morocco where disorders had broken out, necessitating the dispatch of troops to Rabat and Fez in April 1911 to protect French interests. Kiderlen was confident that this was the prelude to a French protectorate over Morocco; as this would be a clear violation of the Algeciras Act, Germany could claim substantial compensation, in return for which she would readily agree to the extinction of Morocco's purely nominal independence. France, conscious of the weakness of her position, started negotiations with Germany. Unfortunately Kiderlen could not leave well alone; he wanted spectacular results and believed that Germany would only secure substantial compensation by rattling the sabre vigorously. With the reluctant agreement of the emperor and the chancellor, Kiderlen sent the gunboat *Panther* to the Moroccan port of Agadir, ostensibly to protect German nationals and their interests, but in reality to remind France that Germany must not be ignored in the Moroccan question. When the *Panther* appeared off Agadir on 1 July, an international crisis occurred. France bitterly resented this provocative action, coming as it did without warning in the middle of successful negotiations with Germany. Kiderlen made matters even worse on 15 July by suddenly demanding the whole of the French Congo as compensation. Though able enough in his own way, and certainly no war-monger, Kiderlen, 'the man of Agadir', was a natural bully, sadly lacking in finesse and restraint, who supposed that he could force the French to do his bidding by 'thumping on the table', as he put it.

The stratagem misfired. The French immediately broke off the negotiations and Britain rallied to their side. Lloyd George, speaking at the Mansion House dinner on 21 July, solemnly warned Germany that Britain would not tolerate dictation where her vital interests were at stake. The speech caused widespread anger in Germany, where it was regarded as unwarranted interference by Britain in a matter which did not concern her. The crisis deepened as Britain, fearing a German attack, prepared the fleet for action. War did not break out, for France knew that she could not go to war for the sake of Morocco and reopened the negotiations with Germany. Germany readily agreed, for however much Kiderlen blustered and threatened, he was sobered by the prospect of war. Any lingering doubts in his mind were dispelled by the emperor who insisted on a peaceful settlement before things got worse. After weeks of negotiation the Moroccan question was settled in November 1911; Germany recognised the right of France to establish a protectorate in Morocco, in return for which she received 275,000 square miles of jungle in the French Congo.

Germany had little cause for jubilation; at a time when the diplomatic situation called for great skill and delicacy Germany was ill-served by pseudo-Bismarckians such as the brash and arrogant Kiderlen who believed that more could be accomplished by bluster and sabre-rattling than by friendly negotiation. Far from weakening the Entente and bringing France to heel, Kiderlen's barrack-square diplomacy confirmed Entente suspicions of Germany and exposed her to the danger of war. But Kiderlen was not an isolated figure in Germany; he enjoyed wide support in middle-class circles, where the '*Panther* Spring' was applauded as a welcome sign of political virility. When Bethmann Hollweg informed the Reichstag of the terms of the final agreement, he was shouted down by indignant right-wing deputies, who accused him of surrending abjectly to Entente pressure. For the first time Britain superseded France as the great enemy of the fatherland; there was a roar of approval on the right wing when the Conservative leader declared that 'these events have shown the German people, like a flash of lightning in the night, where their real enemy is'.

Curiously enough, although Anglo-German relations reached their nadir in 1911, another attempt was made shortly afterwards to end the naval race. Bethmann Hollweg, acutely conscious of Germany's isolation, was keen to prevent further naval expenditure which Tirpitz was currently advocating. Through the good offices of Albert Ballin, a German shipping magnate and friend of the emperor, negotiations were started. Haldane, the British minister of war, visited Berlin in February 1912. This time Britain, seriously worried by Russian intrigue in Persia, was ready for an agreement; she was prepared to accept the existing level of German building (provided there were no increases) and even to enter into a political agreement (provided it preserved her freedom of action). However, Tirpitz insisted on the inclusion of a new navy bill in Germany's existing naval strength, a demand which Britain flatly rejected. In any case Britain would never agree to remain neutral if Germany went to war. Each side felt the other asked too much and offered too little. Momentarily the emperor wavered, but when Britain moved her fleet from the Mediterranean to the North Sea, he sided with Tirpitz. The new naval programme was published in March 1912, and the last attempt to end the naval race ended in failure.

Oddly enough, by 1914 Anglo-German relations were in a better state of repair than ever before. For as Britain rapidly outstripped Germany at sea after 1912, her fears diminished. In the summer of 1914 Britain reached agreement with Germany over the Berlin-to-Baghdad railway and a naval squadron visisted Kiel for the annual regatta.

By the end of 1911 the Germans were already drawing their own conclusions from the mounting cost of a naval race Germany could not afford and could never win. The 1912 naval bill was, in fact, more modest than Tirpitz's original proposals and was presented to the Reichstag in conjunction with large increases in the army. For as the situation in Europe deteriorated, the pressure of the army for substantial increases became irresistible. The defence of continental Germany against France and Russia became the overriding priority. One unfortunate by-product of this shift in the balance of armaments was an increase in the influence of the military leaders, the advocates of preventive war, in the corridors of power.

Since the outbreak of war between Italy and Turkey in September 1911, tension had been mounting in the Balkans. By October 1912 the restless Balkan states could contain their ambitions no longer. They attacked Turkey and within a few weeks tore the Ottoman Empire to pieces. This was a severe blow to Austria-Hungary, for it was commonly believed in Vienna that the Habsburg monarchy would hardly survive the fall of the Ottomans. The dramatic expansion of Serbia aroused the gravest alarm in the Ballplatz, for Belgrade looked forward with confidence to the liberation of Bosnia in the not-too-distant future. Berchtold, a vain and effeminate diplomat who had succeeded Aehrenthal as foreign minister in February 1912, was an indecisive character. He could not pluck up courage to attack Serbia, as Conrad, the Austrian chief of staff, advocated from time to time. Subsequent attempts to blame this indecision on lack of German support were unconvincing. Kiderlen, like Bülow before him, pledged unconditional support for any Austrian action, despite his own serious misgiving; speaking to the Bundesrat committee, Kiderlen declared that 'if Austria has to fight to defend her position as a Great Power, whatever the reasons, we must be at her side so that we do not have to fight alone later on next to a weakened Austria'. Nor could Berchtold bring himself to pursue the alternative policy of conciliating Serbia. In the end he chose a disastrous middle road, sponsoring the creation of an independent Albania in the hope of containing Serbia, a policy which did not win him friends in Belgrade. By this time Kiderlen was dead. His successor Gottlieb von Jagow, a former ambassador to Italy, was completely overshadowed by Bethmann Hollweg. As the chancellor had just failed in his efforts to restrain Tirpitz from further naval expenditure, he was all the more determined to urge moderation on Berchthold, hoping that he might in this way detach Britain from her friends. Moltke, too, wrote to Conrad advising him to await the break-up of the Balkan League before attacking Serbia. When the Second Balkan War broke out in 1913, Bethmann Hollweg repeated his advice; once again Berchtold was racked with indecision, talking of war but fearing the consequences of decision.

People who pursue weak and inconsistent policies have occasional moments of decision. Such was the case of Berchtold in the autumn of 1913. Deeply offended by Germany's lack of support in recent months, he decided to strike out on an independent line in a despairing attempt to arrest the steady erosion of Austria's position. The pretext was the presence of Serbian troops on what was technically Albanian soil. Berchtold thought war was too risky; instead he sent a brusquely worded ultimatum to Belgrade in October 1913 ordering the troops out of Albania. William II endorsed Austria's action enthusiastically; he deplored the possibility of Serbian acceptance: 'now or never – some time or other peace and order will have to be established down there,' he exclaimed. Serbia knuckled under. Berchtold was elated by his cheap victory. This was the curtain-raiser for 1914. Berchtold did not forget the eager promise of support given so lightly by William II. When he sent another ultimatum to Serbia in 1914, Berchtold was confident of German support for his last desperate gamble to keep Austria-Hungary afloat.

In the eighteen months before the Sarajevo Crisis tension in Europe rose perceptibly. Impressed by the swift victory of the small Balkan states, the powers overhauled their military machines. Significantly Germany took the lead in this. In January 1913 a new army bill creating three army corps was put before the Reichstag; Germany's peace-time strength was raised from 663,000 to 761,000 men rising to 800,000 in 1914, by which time Germany would possess a striking-force capable of dealing the knock-out blow at France on which German strategy pivoted. In August France extended the period of service with the colours. Finally, in December Russia decided to add 500,000 men to her peace-time strength. Each power supposed that increases in armed might would augment its power of diplomatic coercion and enable it to survive the next crisis without loss of face. But inevitably the rapid accumulation of armaments of an increasingly destructive character only aggravated the situation and made the Great Powers less inclined to make sacrifices for peace.

Rearmament was accompanied in all countries by propaganda campaigns to persuade the ordinary citizen that the growing risk of war justified additional military expenditure. The anxiety-neurosis which had afflicted diplomats for some years now gripped the peoples of Europe. The articulate section of public opinion now believed war to be inevitable, a belief which encouraged the growth of bellicose nationalism in all lands. In Germany, where a leftish Reichstag passed the new army bill, there was much talk of the. impending war between Slav and Teuton; the Pan-Germans and the newly formed *Deutscher Wehrverein* vied with each other in bellicosity; one of the great literary successes of 1913 was General Bernhardi's book, *Vom heutigen Kriege*, which expounded the thesis that war was a biological necessity and a convenient means of ridding the world of the unfit. These views were not confined to a lunatic fringe but won wide acceptance, especially among journalists, academics and politicians.

By the beginning of 1913 William II believed in the inevitability of war and had ceased to care whether Austria was held in check or not. When Colonel House, an American politician and friend of President Wilson, visited Berlin in 1913, he was appalled by the bellicosity he encountered in military circles and depressed by the prevailing mood of chauvinism and fatalism in high places. 'The whole of Europe is charged with electricity,' he wrote. 'Everyone's nerves are tense. It needs only a spark to set the whole thing off.' An apt comment indeed, for the war mentality, though more pronounced in Germany than elsewhere, was not peculiar to that country; the politically active classes in France and Russia were equally chauvinistic and believed just as firmly that war was inevitable.

Nevertheless, one cannot overlook the fact that Germany's leaders were more inclined towards warlike solutions than the leaders of other countries. Some historians, notably Fritz Fischer and John Röhl, argue that the war of 1914 was, in fact, a premeditated act of aggression; that at a Crown Council meeting on 8 December 1912 called to discuss ominous international developments[5] the emperor and his military advisers decided not to launch a major war there and then – as William II and Moltke wanted to – but to postpone it until 1914 when work on the widening of the Kiel Canal would be completed. While it seems doubtful whether any ruling *élite* could be so united in its objectives that it could work relentlessly to bring about a great war in eighteen months' time, it cannot be denied that Germany's leaders were deeply pessimistic about the worsening diplomatic situation of the *Reich* even before the Crown Council meeting. War may not have been deliberately 'planned' for 1914 but it was clearly thought to be a likely eventuality and war preparations were accordingly accelerated by the military and civilian authorities.

Nor can the domestic situation be ignored in explaining the decision for war. Germany was deadlocked politically by 1914. Chancellor Bethmann Hollweg would neither appease the Reichstag by introducing leftish legislation nor align himself with Conservatives who favoured repressive anti-socialist policies. His so-called 'policy of the diagonal' meant in effect that he by-passed the Reichstag and ruled by decree thereby becoming more dependent on court advisers than any chancellor since 1890. And these circles were filled with gloom by the leftward trend in German politics. A *coup d'état* to dissolve the Reichstag was an impossibility as they knew full well; working-class recruits indoctrinated by 'socialist agitators' had made the greatly expanded army a less reliable instrument of coercion. There remained one last desperate remedy: a victorious war to rally the forces of conservatism and keep socialism at bay. What part, if any, such considerations played in 1914 it is quite impossible to determine. But because

[5]William II was particularly incensed to learn that Grey and Haldane had warned the German ambassador in London that if a European war resulted from an Austrian attack on Serbia it was unlikely that Britain would stand aside and certain that she would not tolerate the defeat of France.

chancellor and Reichstag were at loggerheads it made it that much easier for military advisers to exert decisive influence on German policy.

These last months before the Sarajevo crisis saw a sudden deterioration in Russo-German relations. In May 1913 Turkey requested German assistance in reforming her armies, mauled in the Balkan wars. Germany agreed as a routine matter, having previously assisted Turkey with her military reorganisation. A certain General Liman von Sanders was sent to Turkey in charge of a five-year military mission. To guarantee him effective power over the Turkish army, he was given command of the first Turkish army corps, stationed at Constantinople. Much to Germany's surprise Russia protested vigorously, maintaining that Turkey was passing under German military control, a development which threatened Russia's vital interests at the Straits. However Britain was not greatly alarmed by the mission and Germany, who had never intended to provoke Russia, found a way out in January 1914 by relieving Sanders of his command. But Russia was not satisfied. She launched a vast rearmament programme and determined to transform the Entente into an alliance so powerful that Russia would never again be threatened by Germany. This was a real turning-point in Russo-German relations. In February 1914 William II commented aptly: 'Russo-Prussian relations are dead once and for all. We have become enemies.' Their relations deteriorated rapidly into the summer of 1914; the German press openly discussed the coming conflict with the Slavs, whilst the Russian press talked of Russia's historic mission at Constantinople and called on France to hold herself in readiness for war.

Against this darkening sky another Balkan crisis in the summer of 1914 came as no surprise. In June Russia scored a diplomatic triumph when she detached Rumania from the *Triplice*, offering her Transylvania in return for a promise of neutrality when war came. Austria stood by helplessly as the balance of power in the Balkans moved steadily in favour of Russia. Another heavy blow followed on 28 June when the heir to the throne of the Dual Monarchy, Archduke Franz Ferdinand, and his wife Sophie were murdered by Bosnian terrorists during a visit to Sarajevo, the capital of Bosnia.

The news of the assassination engendered a mood of desperation in Vienna. Ballplatz officials called for stern measures, for it was clear from the outset that the murders had been planned by a powerful Serbian secret society. Conrad urged preventive war against Serbia; Tisza, the Hungarian minister-president, opposed war, while Berchtold hesitated as usual. The factor which tipped the scales in favour of war was the unofficial advice from Berlin to the effect that Germany expected her ally to stand up to Serbia. When Austria approached Germany formally for her assistance, she was left in no doubt that Berlin favoured stern measures. It was high time to make a clean sweep of the Serbs, declared the emperor; and without waiting for the chancellor William II pledged full support, whatever the consequences, to the Austrian ambassador over lunch on 5 July. Bethmann Hollweg readily agreed with the emperor and on 6 July told the ambassador that 'Austria must judge what is to be done to clear up her relations with Serbia. But whatever Austria's decision, she could count with certainty upon it that Germany would stand behind her as an ally.' In fact, Bethmann Hollweg and Jagow did not leave Austria free to decide on a course of action. They urged her most strongly to go to war with Serbia, convinced that this was the only way to show the world that Austria still counted in the Balkans. They believed that war between Austria and Serbia could be localised and was not likely to develop into a major conflagration; Russia and France were too weak to intervene; Germany's relations with Britain were better than they had been for many years; and it was thought highly unlikely that Britain would go to war over an obscure Balkan issue; if Austria and Germany stood firm, they might well bring Serbia sharply to heel and win a great diplomatic victory.

At the same time it is abundantly clear from the evidence that the rulers of Germany were prepared to face a major war if this should prove the only way to bolster up Austria-Hungary and preserve the Triple Alliance. The diaries kept by Bethmann Hollweg's secretary and confidant, Kurt Riezler, show that from the beginning of July the chancellor recognised the very real danger of a general war breaking out over Serbia. What depressed Bethmann Hollweg most of all was the growing power of Russia. He shared the widespread belief in middle-class circles that a conflict between Slav and Teuton was inevitable; the longer Germany waited, the greater the chances of Russia winning this war. As he remarked to the Austrian ambassador, 'If war must break out, better now than in one or two years' time, when the Entente will be stronger.' Such was the view of the general staff; Moltke declared in May 1914 that Germany was now ready for war but by 1917, when Russian rearmament was complete, Germany's strategic position would be practically hopeless. Everything pointed to 1914 as the year of decision for Germany; she could either seize this last chance of breaking the ring of encirclement and asserting her 'right' to absolute hegemony in Europe, or, if a diplomatic victory was no longer possible, she would at least fight for hegemony in the most favourable circumstances. When a Great Power is prepared to run such appalling risks, it must bear a major share of responsibility for the outbreak of war should the gamble fail. This by no means exhausts the question of war guilt. Other powers contributed to the general deterioration in the international situation and committed tactical errors in July 1914. Can one be sure in a period of feverish rearmament and bellicose nationalism that other powers might not have reacted in the same way had what they supposed were their 'vital interests' been at stake and had they been convinced that the balance of military power was moving inexorably against them? That certainly is not intended to excuse German brinkmanship nor minimise German responsibility for the outbreak of war. It is merely a reminder, where questions of war guilt are concerned, that the conduct of Great Powers should not be judged in isolation but must always be seen in the contemporary context of international politics.

By 14 July Austria made up her mind; if she wanted to arrest the steady decline in her power and keep Germany as an ally, she must use force against Serbia. She sent an ultimatum to Serbia drafted in terms so severe that it was certain to be rejected, as Berlin and Vienna calculated, and would then serve as a pretext for military action. At first Serbia decided to bow to the inevitable, expecting little aid from Russia. Then at the last minute, emboldened by signs that Russia would stand by her, Serbia inserted reservations in her reply, refusing, for example, to allow Austrian officials to work on Serbian soil to unravel the murder plot. When Austria received the Serbian reply on 25 July, she at once broke off diplomatic relations with that country.

Meanwhile Germany attempted to keep the ring clear for Austria. On 21 July in a note to the powers she denounced Serbia's intrigues, expressed her sympathy with Austria and declared that the matter concerned only Serbia and the Dual Monarchy. Once the terms of the ultimatum were known on 24 July, there was a flurry of diplomatic activity. Britain took the initiative in an earnest endeavour to prevent the dispute ending in war. However, at this stage, Germany was not prepared to restrain Austria. When Grey proposed that the ambassadors of Britain, France, Italy and Germany discuss the Serbian reply on condition that Serbia, Austria and Russia promised not to commence military operations, Germany refused, declaring that she could not allow Austria to be humiliated at the conference table. It is true that Germany passed on other British proposals to Vienna, but without comment, and in private she made it clear that she did not expect Austria to act upon them. On 28 July William II suddenly intervened in the crisis; back from his Norwegian cruise, he decided that the Serbian reply was highly satisfactory, and ought to be accepted by Austria who must abandon her plans for war and only occupy part of Serbia temporarily as a guarantee of good behaviour. The foreign office was thoroughly alarmed by the emperor's characteristic change of heart. Bethmann Hollweg and Jagow took evasive action, so that William's proposal for a 'Halt in Belgrade' arrived too late to influence the situation; they also deleted from his instructions the comment that war with Serbia was unnecessary. On the contrary, fearing that Austria might be diplomatically out-manoeuvred before she had the satisfaction of declaring war, the Germans redoubled their efforts to force Berchtold's hand. His lingering doubts were finally overcome by German pressure; on 28 July Austria declared war on Serbia and on the following day she bombarded Belgrade.

On 29 July Bethmann Hollweg had second thoughts. Probably he believed the gamble had succeeded, the balance of power had been redressed in favour of the Triple Alliance, and that the moment had come to step away from the brink to facilitate a peaceful settlement. If so, the news that Russia had ordered partial mobilisation upset his calculations by increasing enormously the danger of a general war. Seeking now to moderate Austrian policy, he urged Vienna to accept a British version of the 'Halt in Belgrade' and advised her not to refuse to discuss the Serbian question with Russia. But it was too late; so accustomed were the Austrians to German support, that they ignored the warnings. Certainly they resumed negotiations with the Russians, but this was more than neutralised by their decision on 31 July to order general mobilisation at the prompting of the chief of the German general staff.[6]

The intervention of the military was a new and highly dangerous development. Once Russia started to mobilise, military planning took precedence over diplomatic considerations in Berlin. Falkenhayn, the war minister, wanted to order a pre-mobilisation alert; every hour's delay added to the gravity of the situation, reducing Germany's chance of dealing a knock-out blow in the west without interference from Russia. Bethmann Hollweg resisted the pleas of the generals. Instead he informed Russia that unless she cancelled partial mobilisation Germany would have to order mobilisation. Tactical considerations entered into the chancellor's calculations at this point; if war could not be avoided, then at least Russia might be manoeuvred into ordering general mobilisation first, thereby incurring the grave responsibility before History of transforming a Balkan dispute into a major war – for no one doubted that mobilisation made a general war quite certain. But even at this late hour he probably still hoped that Russia would back down. Moltke agreed to wait until midday on 31 July for a decision, but in fact, as indicated above, he went behind the chancellor's back and on 30 July urged Austria to order mobilisation and pledged full German support if she did so. Russia's nerve cracked first. Partial mobilisation against Austria had been ordered only as a means of bringing pressure to bear on that power. It had not been intended as a prelude to war. But in view of Germany's warning Russia had either to suffer a fresh humiliation by cancelling that order or order general mobilisation to defend herself against a possible German attack. Russia opted for the latter. News of her decision reached Berlin just before midday. Bethmann Hollweg's manoeuvre had partially succeeded. Russia could at least be blamed for taking the first certain step to war and German mobilisation could be represented as a defensive measure, an important consideration which helped to rally the German working class round the emperor on 4 August.

The German war-machine swung into action. General mobilisation was ordered and an ultimatum dispatched to Russia demanding cessation of all

---

[6]Although already at war with Serbia, Austria had not yet ordered general mobilisation against Russia.

measures within twelve hours. Russia refused to comply and on 1 August Germany declared war. German diplomacy was now completely subordinate to the needs of the Schlieffen Plan. War had to be declared on France as quickly as possible, but it proved difficult to find a pretext. On 31 July Germany asked France what course of action she would pursue in the event of war between Germany and Russia. France replied that she would act in accordance with her interests. Then a dramatic telegram arrived from London suggesting that Britain might stay out of the war, provided Germany did not attack France. The emperor was jubilant. He ordered champagne and asked Moltke to change the plan of campaign. Moltke was appalled by such frivolity and threatened resignation. 'It is utterly impossible to advance except according to plan: strong in the west, weak in the east.' The deadlock was resolved a few hours later when a further telegram made it clear that Grey's remarks were purely speculative, whereupon William withdrew his instructions and mobilisation against France continued. To the very end Germany tried to put the blame for war on France, staging several clumsy border incidents before declaring war on 3 August.

Britain's failure to make her position crystal-clear hardly altered the course of events in the summer of 1914. Once Germany was committed by the Schlieffen Plan to attacking France and violating Belgian neutrality, British participation in the war was inevitable sooner or later, as Bethmann Hollweg seems to have realised only too well. Of course he wanted to keep Britain neutral as long as possible, in order to dishearten France and Russia. On the evening of 29 July he spoke with the British ambassador. He realised, he said, that Britain could not stay neutral if France were crushed. Such was not the German intention. If Britain promised to stay neutral, Germany would promise not to annex French territory and would restore Belgian neutrality after the war. Immediately after the interview he received his answer in the shape of a telegram from the ambassador in London reporting Grey's clear warning that Britain would not remain neutral if France went to war.

Grey was convinced that it was not in British interests to let Germany dominate Europe, and this she would surely do if Britain stood aside and allowed France and Russia to be defeated. The invasion of Belgium simply made it easier for Grey to carry the country with him. Power considerations do not move people to fight; but an attack on a small friendly people who fought bravely against the invader raised a moral issue for which the British people were ready to fight. The invasion came as no surprise. The outlines of the Schlieffen Plan were known in military circles. On 31 July Britain asked France and Germany whether they would respect Belgian neutrality. France gave the undertaking, Germany was evasive. On 2 August Germany delivered her ultimatum to Belgium demanding free passage for her troops. Belgium refused. On 4 August German troops crossed the frontier. At once Grey sent an ultimatum to Germany ordering her to withdraw from Belgium within twelve hours. Germany declared this to be an impossibility, and when midnight struck in Berlin on 4 August Britain and Germany were at war. The world war which Bethmann Hollweg had probably hoped to avoid was now a dreadful reality.

9

Germany at War 1914–1918

The outbreak of war was greeted with enthusiasm in all belligerent countries. On 4 August the Reichstag met to hear the emperor's speech from the throne. William insisted that Germany had done all she could to avoid war and now drew her sword with a clear conscience. 'I know no parties any more, only Germans,' he declared to the assembled deputies, and invited their leaders to pledge full support to him in the coming struggle. The party leaders responded with alacrity and agreed to a political truce, the *Burgfriede*, for the duration of hostilities. There was thunderous applause from all sides when Bethmann Hollweg described Germany as the victim of unprovoked aggression and declared that Germany drew her sword in a righteous cause: 'Our army is in the field, our navy is ready for action and behind them stands the German people – the whole people united to the last man.' That Belgium and Luxemburg had been invaded in defiance of international law, he admitted with regret, adding that this wrong would be put right later, when Germany's military objectives had been attained. The war credits were passed unanimously, and the Bundesrat was empowered to put the economy on a war footing. The Reichstag then adjourned, perfectly content to leave the conduct of the war to the government, and did not reassemble until 2 December, when it approved a second request for war credits. Political differences were submerged in the great wave of patriotic fervour, 'the spirit of 4 August', which united the people as they had not been united since 1870. Most Germans confidently expected victory within a matter of weeks.

If the war had been over by Christmas, Germany would have been deeply grateful to the Hohenzollerns, and political change might have been retarded for a generation. At first all went well. In accordance with the Schlieffen Plan three armies swept through Belgium and into France. The French armies fell back, and the government decided to leave Paris. But then inherent weaknesses in the German plan were revealed. Schlieffen had always known that this plan was a gambler's throw dictated by Germany's need to win the war before the numerical strength of her opponents led inescapably to her defeat. Even when fully mobilised in

1914 Germany was short of eight army corps essential for the plan's success. Moreover, the chief of the general staff, Moltke, was a neurotic character whose nerves were scarcely equal to the task. Already he had severely weakened the plan by leaving an inordinately large force behind in Alsace-Lorraine to repel a French offensive towards the Rhine. He weakened the right flank of the invading German armies still further by detaching two army corps during the campaign and dispatching them to the east to repel the Russians. The result was that Kluck's First Army was too weak to encircle Paris. Instead, Kluck by-passed the city and moved eastwards in pursuit of the retreating French armies. By so doing he exposed his flank to an attack from Paris where the French commander Joffre had assembled a new army. On 5 September 1914 Joffre ordered a general offensive and the great battle of the Marne began. Kluck repelled the French, and forward reconnaissance units of the First Army were within sight of the Eiffel Tower. But in the heat of battle a thirty-mile-wide gap had opened up between Kluck's army and Bülow's Second Army. Into the gap moved the British Expeditionary Force, more by luck than good management. Back at General Headquarters in Luxemburg there was complete panic. Moltke, who had never believed in the Schlieffen Plan, was completely broken by the news of the British advance. The emperor had arrived at Headquarters by this time, but the supreme war lord was no more capable than Moltke of dealing with the situation; had the First Army been ordered to dig in, it might have quickly turned the tables on the advancing British. Instead, Moltke sent a young intelligence officer Colonel Hentsch to the front, armed with plenary powers to order a retreat if circumstances warranted it. Hentsch, having ascertained that the British were across the Marne, ordered a general retreat to the line of the river Aisne. By 14 September the Germans had taken up new positions, from which the French and British failed to dislodge them. The first battle of the Marne was over.

This battle was a real turning-point in the war. It cost Moltke his command; he suffered a complete breakdown and was replaced by Falkenhayn, the minister of war. More important, the Marne ended Germany's hope of quick victory. Her initial advances had given her control of the whole of the Belgian industrial complex, eighty per cent of France's coal resources and all her iron-ore. On the other hand, she faced a prolonged two-front war which it had been the constant endeavour of her statesmen and generals to avoid. By November Falkenhayn's endeavours to retrieve the situation by driving towards the Channel ports had failed, and the opposing sides had dug themselves in. The spade and the machine gun came into their own along a four-hundred-mile front from the North Sea to Switzerland. The Entente powers could not win final victory at this stage of the war, but in the three years of trench warfare that followed they had an opportunity to exploit their superiority in manpower resources which eventually ensured the defeat of Germany.

The Russians were quicker off the mark than had been expected. While the Germans were advancing through Belgium, the Russians launched two offensives. The first was directed at Austria-Hungary and resulted in the capture of most of Galicia by December; as the Austrians retreated in disorder, the Germans had their first taste of war on two fronts with a mortally sick power as their junior partner. The second Russian offensive was launched against East Prussia. In military terms this was not a serious development; temporary losses would be made good once Germany had annihilated the enemy in the west, where the bulk of her forces were committed. In practice the effect on German morale of losing the bastion of Junkerdom, even temporarily, proved too much. The emperor was deeply disturbed by the Russian invasion and persuaded a reluctant Moltke to send two divisions to the east at once. Not only did this weaken the armies in the west at a crucial moment, but it proved a worthless gesture; the troops arrived too late to have any influence on the outcome. For Moltke had just appointed Paul von Hindenburg, a retired general with an unrivalled knowledge of the terrain, to be commander of the Eighth Army in East Prussia with General Ludendorff as his chief of staff. The tide quickly turned at the battle of Tannenberg, where between 25 and 30 August 1914 one of the two invading armies was annihilated by a numerically inferior German force. In September the second invading army was beaten at the battle of the Masurian Lakes. These victories made Hindenburg and to a lesser extent Ludendorff popular heroes in Germany. In February 1915 they won another great victory, the winter battle of the Masurian Lakes, and finally flung the Russians out of East Prussia. The myth of Russian invincibility was destroyed for ever in these battles, which cost Russia over 200,000 men, nearly a quarter of her mobilised strength. By the end of 1914 the eastern front was stabilised along the line of Russia's western frontier running from the Baltic southwards to Rumania. Yet Russia was not mortally wounded as France would have been; Russia had manpower enough to replace her losses and continue the war; meanwhile her Galician offensive was so successful that by the spring of 1915 it seemed possible that she might launch a fresh offensive over the Carpathians, capture Vienna and Budapest and force Austria-Hungary to her knees.

The German public knew nothing of the dangers which faced the fatherland when the Schlieffen Plan failed. Even the Reichstag did not discover the truth about the battle of the Marne. All the High Command allowed the people to know was that a battle had occurred and was going well, and that adverse reports could be discounted as enemy propaganda. Because the public was lulled into complacency by the High Command, it was confidently assumed – long after the facts had ceased to justify the assumption – that a German victory was certain. The question which exercised the mind of the public in 1915 was not whether Germany would win the war, but what use her victory should be put to.

The controversy about Germany's war aims started in the spring of 1915. In its early stages war always strengthens the hand of conservative forces. Emboldened by victories over the Russians, landowners dreamt of a ring of satellite kingdoms and principalities in Poland and the Baltic lands; heavy industrialists wanted control of the coal and iron resources of Belgium; generals a string of fortresses from Verdun to Belfort; naval officers control of the strategically important Flanders coastline; colonialists a mid-African empire. Bethmann Hollweg's so-called September programme of 1914 already incorporated most of the essentials of what became known as the *Siegfriede*, or peace of victory, propagated with passionate energy by the Pan-Germans. Conservatives did not support the *Siegfriede* simply out of a chauvinistic desire for expansion. The more perceptive aristocrats and industrialists sensed that, whatever the outcome of the war, the social and political ascendancy of the ruling class would be gravely endangered. If Germany lost the war, their own destruction was certain, so they believed – subsequent events in postwar Germany showed how grossly they underestimated the resilience of vested interests. The situation would be little better if Germany won the war and demanded only the restoration of the *status quo*. Then the people would have borne the burden of war for nothing. The abandonment of their monopoly of political power was unthinkable to Conservatives under any circumstances, likewise reform of the Prussian constitution; this left them with only one way of reconciling the people to the continued ascendancy of conservatism, namely by taking territory from the enemies of Germany or by imposing a huge war indemnity on them or by some combination of both.

It would be quite wrong to suppose that belief in the *Siegfriede* was confined to the upper classes. On the contrary, it was supported by practically the whole of the middle class. Before the war the exaggerated nationalism of the Pan-Germans appealed to a small minority of the people. Once the fighting started, Pan-German propaganda made rapid headway. The middle class was soon persuaded that military victory would enable Germany to achieve the break-through to world power which had eluded her diplomats for so long. Intellectuals were solidly behind the *Siegfriede*, as was a majority of the Reichstag until 1917. In December 1915 Spahn of the Centre presented a declaration on behalf of all the non-Socialist parties in which he demanded territorial acquisitions to safeguard Germany's military, economic and political interests. Even Erzberger, the prime mover behind the Peace Resolution of 1917, started out in 1914 believing in German domination of Belgium and the French Channel coast as well as the separation of Poland, the Baltic provinces and the Ukraine from Russia, although admittedly he gradually modified his views as the war dragged on. The *Siegfriede* found some support among Socialists; a small group of Socialist Imperialists led by Lensch, Haenisch and Kolb equated a German victory with the triumph of socialism and world revolution; Germany, being an advanced industrial economy, was ripe for socialism, and mobilisation, by transforming her aristocratic army into a people's militia, made social change inevitable after the war.

The idea of a *Siegfriede* was repugnant to most Socialists. For them the war was purely defensive. Their leaders had hoped to avoid war up to the very last moment. They only voted for the war credits because Tsarist Russia, the great enemy of democracy and socialism, was about to attack the fatherland. 'The freedom and future of our people is at stake if Russian despotism wins,' declared Haase, leader of the parliamentary party, on 4 August; '. . . it is up to us to defeat this peril on our frontiers and to safeguard the culture and independence of our country.' No doubt many Socialists genuinely believed, like the radicals of 1848–49, in the superiority of German cultural values and in Germany's mission to defeat barbaric Russia. They were confirmed in their beliefs by the great wave of patriotic anti-Russian feeling which swept through Germany from north to south on the outbreak of war. A party whose star is in the ascendant finds it difficult to resist popular pressures and the Socialists were no exception. The fact that their own supporters were second to none in their patriotic desire to defend the fatherland against aggression could not be ignored by the party leaders. In any case defensive war was perfectly compatible with the principles of the International, as Haase pointed out in his speech. What Socialists would not do was prolong the war in the interests of the upper classes. Haase condemned 'wars of conquest' and declared that once Germany was safe from attack she must seek a peace of reconciliation with her neighbours, remarks which Conservative members listened to in stony silence. In the months that followed the controversy between the advocates of a *Siegfriede* or 'Hindenburg' peace and the supporters of the 'Scheidemann' peace[1] generated great bitterness and helped to reactivate the old political disputes temporarily obscured by 'the spirit of 4 August'.

Despite some initial disappointment that the war was not over by Christmas, ordinary Germans continued to believe confidently in final victory throughout 1915. On the western front Germany held her own, repelling several enemy offensives and inflicting severe losses on the French and British. On the eastern front Russia suffered a major defeat. In May 1915 Germany and Austria launched a combined offensive which rolled the Russians out of Galicia and resulted in the capture of all Poland as well as Lithuania and Courland. The pressure on the weak link, Austria-Hungary, was at last relieved. The Russians lost a total of 250,000 men

[1] The Socialist Philipp Scheidemann put the case for a peace of reconciliation.

killed, wounded or taken prisoner. If Hindenburg and Ludendorff had had their way, the Russian armies might have been encircled and annihilated, but Hindenberg was overruled by Falkenhayn who, as chief of the general staff, had to take account of the needs of other fronts. In the Balkans Turkey, the ally of the Central Powers, survived the Dardanelles campaign and in October 1915 a joint Austro-German army, with Bulgarian support, launched a successful offensive against Serbia. She was defeated and passed under the control of Austria and Bulgaria. The campaign had also strengthened the lines of communication with Turkey and weakened Russia's position still further. Thus the balance of material gain seemed to favour the Central Powers, who by the end of 1915 controlled a compact mass of territory stretching from Antwerp to Baghdad and from Bremen to Basra. Significantly enough, there was a revival of interest in the concept of *Mitteleuropa*; Friedrich Naumann's book, published in October, quickly became a best-seller with its proposals for a supranational state in Central Europe. On the other hand, Germany had won no decisive victory in 1915; the Russians, despite a severe mauling, were able to launch a new offensive in 1916, while in the west, France and Britain were undefeated. The truth of the matter was that Germany had little idea of how to end the war; she had pinned her hopes on quick victory in 1914 and still lacked a long-term war strategy at the end of 1915.

On the high seas the Entente had the upper hand. Germany's colonies were quickly overrun by the enemy. Graf von Spee's cruiser squadron, as well as isolated cruisers such as *Emden, Möwe* and *Seeadler*, which caused considerable damage to Entente shipping by their daring exploits, were soon put out of action. Meanwhile the German high-seas fleet remained in port. Her admirals were sharply divided on its war-time role; Tirpitz wanted to do battle with the British fleet, while his opponents wanted to keep the fleet in reserve until a more decisive point in the war. The emperor had lost faith in Tirpitz and sided with his opponents. So the German fleet stayed on the defensive, guarding the German coastline and the Baltic. It could do nothing to break the blockade which Britain had imposed on Germany and which was already making it difficult for her to obtain supplies through neutral countries. This would have affected her even more seriously, had she not taken measures to mobilise her own economic resources early in the war.

Economic mobilisation was a universal feature during the First World War. It was soon apparent to all belligerent powers that modern war was not entirely a matter of land armies. Numbers counted, but wars were no longer won because one side could draw up a more imposing list of allies with superior manpower. Victory in the field under modern conditions called for total mobilisation of a country's economic potential. Consequently the war accelerated the pace of government intervention in the economic sphere, a trend noticeable in all advanced industrial countries before 1914. All the belligerents were affected to a greater or lesser degree by this development, but Germany was affected much more than the others simply because her resources were totally inadequate for prolonged campaigns. Stocks of coal, iron-ore, lead and zinc were adequate only because Belgium and Northern France were in German hands. She experienced chronic shortages of hardening agents (required to produce the finest quality steel) and of special metals including copper, nickel, tin and mercury. She was completely dependent on imported supplies of cotton, rubber, nitrates and petroleum, all essential ingredients of the modern war machine, and on imported fertilisers, fats and oils. Germany's allies were of little help in this respect; indeed they were a positive encumbrance, for the Austrians were averse to controls, Bulgaria was dependent on her allies for most supplies, and Turkey, normally an importer of Russian wheat, was in great difficulty from the day she entered the war. In short, Germany was thrown upon her own resources; self-sufficiency was forced upon her if she was to feed sixty-seven million Germans, maintain armies in the field and support ailing allies.

The first tentative steps towards planning a war economy were taken by Walther Rathenau, the director of *A.E.G.*, one of the great men of the war, an unusual combination of practical administrator and philosopher. As early as 8 August 1914 he believed Germany was likely to face a long war. He persuaded Falkenhayn, then war minister, to establish a War Raw Materials Department (*Kriegsrohstoffabteilung*) affiliated to the war ministry. This department, under Rathenau as director, was given the task of ensuring that Germany had adequate supplies of raw materials to wage the war. Rathenau delegated the task to several war-industries companies (*Kriegswirtschaftsgesellschaften*) modelled on the great industrial combines and staffed with business men. These companies were non-profit making concerns whose task it was to sequestrate available raw materials and reallocate them to manufacturers working on government contracts. By April 1915 Rathenau had completed his task. Essential supplies had been secured and the vast complex of companies was handed over to the Prussian war ministry.

It was not sufficient to conserve available resources. The wastage of war was so tremendous that imported materials had to be replaced as far as possible. Scientists and technicians applied themselves diligently to the task of discovering substitutes. The era of *Ersatz* started in Germany; aluminium formerly imported from Switzerland was extracted from German clays and replaced copper in munitions and electrical fittings; wood-pulp products kept textile mills going; nitrate of cellulose replaced cotton in the manufacture of explosives; oils were produced from animal tissues and seed; by the end of the war Germany was even producing small quantities of synthetic rubber. The outstanding achievement was the manufacture of nitrates from air. Nitrates were, of course, the basis of high explosives and artificial fertilisers. Before the war Germany imported half her nitrates from Chile and produced the remainder at home as a by-product of coal-carbonisation. The outbreak of war cut off supplies from Chile, and the dislocation of industry in the autumn of 1914 seriously reduced domestic supplies. The nitrogen-fixation process perfected by Haber and Bosch saved Germany. It led incidentally to a further stage in the extension of state control over industry; in addition to placing contracts with civilian firms, the government built two plants to produce the nitrates urgently needed by agriculture. In fact the army's appetite for nitrates proved insatiable, and the *Reichswerke* were soon producing nitrates for explosives.

The government was obliged to assume control of Germany's foreign trade at an early stage in the war. All belligerents faced a similar problem; trading patterns collapsed with the outbreak of war, and exports declined suddenly, as markets dwindled and resources were switched to war production. The demand for imports was greater than before. The result was fierce competition for the exports of neutral countries and a sharp decline in the exchange rates of belligerent currencies in favour of neutral ones. Germany was anxious to preserve some of her export trade to avoid paying for imports with gold. To this end, as well as to facilitate the purchase of imports in neutral countries, Germany established a Central Purchasing Company (*Zentral-Einkaufs-Gesellschaft*) at the end of 1916. This company became the greatest trading organisation in the world, with a turnover of several million marks. It managed to retain some of the old export markets and maintained a steady flow of imports throughout the war.

With imports scarce and dear, it was essential not only to control and allocate raw materials, but to try to protect civilians against the worst effects of scarcity, which, if unchecked, leads naturally to high prices and unfair shares. Early in the war maximum retail prices for food and clothing were decreed. In January 1915 bread-rationing started, to be followed by the rationing of all foodstuffs. Another invasion of private enterprise occurred when the government took over the grain and milling business, vesting control in the Imperial Grain Office (*Reichsgetreidestelle*) which controlled supplies and issued ration cards. One by one every type of foodstuff was placed under similar offices in the course of 1915 and 1916.

These measures undoubtedly helped Germany weather the crisis of war up to the summer of 1916. But 'war-time collectivism' – as David Thomsen aptly calls it – was the undoing of the German government in the long run. Precisely because the state was intervening so actively in the regulation of the economy ordinary Germans began to blame it for its manifest failure to protect their living standards in the second half of the war. No longer did discontented people in town and countryside vent their anger on an imaginary socialist 'enemy' but openly criticised state officials for their inability to cope with the situation, a crucially important psychological development which prepared the way for the revolutionary situation of 1918–20.

Falkenhayn was well aware that time was on the side of Germany's enemies. The growing power of the Entente countries – of which there were some ominous signs in 1915 – would tip the scales against Germany unless she was victorious in 1916. He decided to seek final victory in the west and in the early spring launched a great offensive against Verdun, pivotal point in the defence system of Lorraine and a fortress of immense sentimental significance for France. Falkenhayn's aim was to lure France into a costly war of attrition, bleed her white and break her will to resist. France rose to the bait; within five months 315,000 Frenchmen died stemming the German advance. But it did not lead to final victory. It proved almost as costly to attack as to defend; between February and June 1916, when Falkenhayn broke off the battle, Germany lost 281,000 men in and around Verdun.

The plain fact was that Germany had lost the initiative in the west. The failure at Verdun was followed by the British offensive on the Somme, which lasted from July to October 1916. There were no victors in this battle either; it cost Britain 420,000 men to gain a few square miles of territory and Germany 450,000 men in desperate and misguided attempts to recover their lost trenches. Meanwhile Russia had launched a new offensive, much to Falkenhayn's surprise. Initially it was a success. Brusilov swept into Galicia and conquered Bukovina before the offensive ground to a halt. Before long the Germans had rolled the Russians back. What they could not do was escape from the remorseless logic of a two-front war; at a critical stage of the fighting round Verdun Falkenhayn was forced to send seven divisions to the eastern front. His reputation suffered a further blow in August 1916 when Rumania joined the Entente. As Austria reeled back before the Brusilov offensive, little Rumania thought her hour had come to seize Transylvania. She was wrong; by the end of 1916 the Central Powers had driven her out of the war. But this came too late to save Falkenhayn, who was dismissed by the emperor on 29 August.

In the summer of 1916 the German public began at long last to despair of victory. The rumours that Verdun had been a costly failure were confirmed when the casualty lists went up in every town. Since August 1914 Germany had lost two-and-a-half million men killed, wounded and missing. There were some signs of material hardship. Although the mass of the people did not suffer seriously until the terrible 'turnip winter' of 1916–17, nevertheless the monotony of war-time shortages and the decline in living-standards was wearing down the patience of the people. The 'spirit of 4 August' was dead, buried at Verdun and on the Somme. The ineffectiveness of price controls, the growth of the black market and the ostentatious display of wealth by the new class of war profiteers aroused widespread discontent. Class differences deepened; while economic interest drew many small producers closer to the great industrial concerns, white collar workers – whose living standards were falling to proletarian levels – and farmers, disgruntled by low prices for their produce, began to move leftwards; and in the factories the unequal distribution of burdens sharpened the antagonism between employer and worker.

The critical military situation in August 1916 aroused great alarm in Conservative circles and led to dramatic changes in the direction of the war effort. For some time the Conservatives had been critical of Bethmann Hollweg. The chancellor realised that some reorientation of domestic policy was essential to ensure the continued loyalty of the people, especially when all hope of early victory had disappeared. From the very beginning of the war he had courted the Socialists and obtained their active co-operation in the war effort. In January 1916 he even succeeded in persuading William II to promise reform of the Prussian constitution. Conciliatory gestures to the left were deeply resented in Conservative circles. So was the chancellor's opposition to unrestricted submarine warfare. There was growing pressure from naval and military authorities in 1915 for the employment of this weapon; once Tirpitz discovered that the emperor refused absolutely to let the fleet engage the British in battle, he championed unrestricted submarine warfare and boasted that this 'secret weapon' – which he had rightly neglected before 1914 – would win the war. This was a classic example of the wish being father to the thought, for in sober fact it was unlikely that Britain could be brought to her knees by submarines. The chancellor advised against unrestricted warfare, dimly aware that such a violation of international law would seriously endanger Germany's relations with neutral powers. On the other hand, Britain was already violating the rules governing sea blockade; she was blockading, not the entrances to German ports, but the whole North Sea; nor had she restricted herself to the seizure of contraband of war on neutral ships but was trying to stop all neutral trade with Germany, including the shipment of food supplies. The British hunger-blockade aroused widespread indignation in Germany. Bethmann Hollweg gave in to military pressure and popular clamour and agreed to retaliate in kind. In February 1915 Germany declared the waters round the British Isles a war zone and announced that enemy merchantmen would be sunk without warning. In May the liner *Lusitania* was sunk off the Irish coast, and 1,200 passengers, among them over one hundred American citizens, were drowned. The United States sent a stern warning to Germany. Bethmann Hollweg took fright and persuaded the emperor to override the unrepentant admiralty. By September unrestricted submarine warfare had ceased in British waters. There was an uncanny repeat performance in 1916, when Falkenhayn pressed for a resumption of unrestricted submarine warfare to break the deadlock in the west. Reluctantly Bethmann Hollweg bowed once more to 'expert' opinion, and in February 1916 German submarines were ordered to sink all enemy merchantmen in the war zone without warning. Again disaster threatened when the passenger ship *Sussex* was sunk in April; this time the United States threatened to break off diplomatic relations, and Bethmann Hollweg again intervened, to the annoyance of the Conservatives, and had restrictions placed on submarine warfare.

In the summer of 1916 the Conservatives, shaken by the sudden reversal in Germany's fortunes, demanded the replacement of Falkenhayn by General von Hindenburg, the victor of Tannenberg, a 'strong man' whom the right wing respected. Surprisingly, Bethmann Hollweg joined in the intrigue to unseat Falkenhayn. Originally an ardent annexationist, the chancellor had become deeply pessimistic about final victory; but, conscious of his own indecisiveness and unpopularity, he believed that only a popular hero like Hindenburg could bring the nation to its senses and make a negotiated peace palatable to the right wing, a monumental miscalculation if ever there was one. On 29 August Falkenhayn was dismissed, and General von Hindenburg became chief of the general staff. He brought with him from the eastern front General Ludendorff, who was appointed chief-quarter-master-general and given joint responsibility with Hindenburg for the conduct of operations.

This was a turning-point in the history of war-time Germany. Under the constitution the emperor, as supreme war-lord, was responsible for military operations. During the war his obvious incapacity to master strategy led to his being virtually ignored by the generals. The significance of 29 August was that William in effect surrendered the supreme command to Hindenburg. After this the emperor's authority for operations was a mere formality. It was a defeat for the chancellor as well as the emperor. All his life Bismarck stoutly resisted the view that the chief of the general staff had equal status with the chancellor. Ludendorff succeeded in establishing his equality by the simple expedient of threatening resignation if chancellors advocated policies of which he disapproved. Hindenburg relied heavily on the brusque, dynamic and efficient Ludendorff and automatically sided with him in disputes with successive chancellors. The emperor dare not allow these popular heroes to resign, and consequently Ludendorff got his way in the end. As a German historian has aptly commented, the Bismarckian constitution ended on 29 August 1916. For the next two years supreme military and political power resided very largely in the hands of Erich Ludendorff.

Hindenburg and Ludendorff made an immediate and determined effort to mobilise Germany's resources more thoroughly than before. The Somme bombardment brought home to the Germans the growing power of the Entente in terms of men and material. Ludendorff, a dedicated and ruthless militarist, believed that total war called for the total commitment of all Germans. He demanded the immediate mobilisation of the entire civilian population for war service, compulsory labour for women, restriction of the worker's freedom to change his job and the closure of universities, measures which he hoped would establish an equality of sacrifice between soldiers and civilians and rekindle the patriotic fervour of 4 August. In fact, by the time the Auxiliary Service Act was passed by the Reichstag, it was a more modest measure, much to the disgust of Hindenburg and Ludendorff. Direction of labour was introduced for all males between seventeen and sixty, but the right of the working population to change jobs was safeguarded; women and children were excluded from the act, but intensive campaigns were launched to recruit female labour, and children were encouraged to form salvage teams, collecting rags and bones to aid the fatherland. The administration of the law was vested in a Supreme War Office (*Kriegsamt*), which was set up in the Prussian ministry of war and given wide powers over industry and labour. Trade unions co-operated loyally with General Groener, head of the *Kriegsamt*, and set up works committees to raise the production of munitions of which there was now an acute shortage. The new measures were rough-and-ready in their effects and did not prevent serious shortages of coal and transport in the winter of 1916–1917. Nevertheless General Groener was able in May 1917 to report a substantial recovery in iron and steel output and a threefold increase in munitions production.

In other directions Germany paid dearly for the Ludendorff dictatorship. Political change was seriously retarded precisely when the demand for it was growing as the *Burgfriede* crumbled away. The working class was becoming restive in the summer of 1916. Already a split had occurred in the parliamentary Socialist party. In June both the Majority Socialists and the Labour Fellowship (as the secessionists were called) voted against the budget.[2] Then came the terrible 'turnip winter' of 1916–17, when early frosts destroyed the potatoes and the turnip became the staple diet of the people. After the appalling hardship of that winter Bethmann Hollweg knew that serious disturbances were inevitable unless some attempt was made to reform the Prussian franchise and modify the Bismarckian constitution. On 17 March 1917 he hinted cautiously at the need for change in a speech to the Prussian Landtag. A few hours later the news of the Russian Revolution transformed the situation. The German working class was profoundly stirred by the overthrow of tsardom, an encouraging sign that the age of revolution had not passed. The Reichstag woke up from its long war-time slumber. The Radicals demanded universal suffrage in all states, the newly formed Independent Socialists called

[2]Ebert made it clear, however, that this was only intended to be a formal protest against the government's failure to produce plans for political reform. The Majority Socialists were still loyal to the war effort, and once the budget had been passed, they voted for supplementary credits.

for parliamentary government and peace without annexations, and the Majority Socialists, with National Liberal support, succeeded in establishing a Reichstag committee to consider constitutional reform. Bethmann Hollweg persuaded the emperor to issue an Easter message in April promising reform of the Prussian upper chamber after the war and the introduction of the secret ballot and direct election (but not universal suffrage) for the lower house. This modest promise did not arouse public enthusiasm. But it caused consternation in conservative circles; Ludendorff indignantly denounced it as a 'kowtow to the Russian revolution'. After this the chancellor's days were numbered. He was too weak and irresolute a character to survive the political pressure of this period. He knew that reform, or at least a substantial promise of reform, was essential to sustain the loyalty of the sorely tried civilian population. Yet he could never summon up enough courage to challenge the forces of conservatism, whose resistance to change had been reinforced by the events of 29 August 1916. Ludendorff was an outstanding strategist but a most reactionary political figure. Though totally lacking in political instincts and experience, unlike his predecessor Falkenhayn he meddled extensively in matters of domestic policy. He resisted fiercely all proposals for political reform, on the grounds that change would undermine the morale of fighting men. Whatever the problem, he insisted on giving priority to narrow military considerations. Bethmann Hollweg was constitutionally quite incapable of standing up to this resolute and brutal soldier, whose position was rendered well-nigh impregnable by the curious paradox that the mass of the people, though progressively disillusioned with the civilian authorities, had complete confidence in him almost to the very end of the war.

Ludendorff sabotaged what slender hope there was of a separate peace with Russia. He shared with Hindenburg all the illusions of the annexationists and rejected utterly the thought of a compromise peace, stoutly maintaining that officers would not go into battle without the sure knowledge that Germany would gain masses of territory when the war was over. Bethmann Hollweg had put out feelers to Russia and was prepared to settle for something like the *status quo* in the east, when Ludendorff suddenly destroyed all hope of negotiations; in his anxiety to raise men for the western front he persuaded the German and Austrian emperors to promise Poland her independence. The Poles were not tempted to join the German armies by this fraudulent offer. All the proclamation of 5 November 1916 succeeded in doing was ending what slender hope there was of peace with Russia, who was not likely to abandon Poland.

At the end of 1916 Bethmann Hollweg faced a new danger: renewed pressure for unrestricted submarine warfare. Hindenburg and Ludendorff could see no way of winning a decisive victory in the west and fully appreciated that the longer they waited the worse their chances would become. It was the sheer hopelessness of Germany's position which made them swallow the exaggerated claims of the navy and press for the resumption of unrestricted submarine warfare. The chancellor suspected that this would be the ruin of Germany. In a desperate attempt to postpone the moment of decision he tried to start peace negotiations and found a willing ally in William II. On 12 December 1916 Germany announced her willingness to negotiate with the Entente, much to the disgust of Ludendorff. However, in his anxiety not to offend the Conservatives, Bethmann Hollweg represented the offer as a magnanimous gesture by victorious Germany who wished to spare her enemies further losses. The note contained no concrete proposals, although it is clear that the chancellor wanted some control over Belgium and gains in the east. Not that it mattered greatly, for the Entente was not ready to negotiate. Believing final victory possible, Britain and France quickly rejected the note.

There was now no holding the admirals and generals. Against his instincts Bethmann Hollweg bowed to the opinions of so-called experts, such as Holtzendorff, head of the admiralty staff, who confidently predicted Britain's defeat within five months of a new submarine offensive. He accepted the inevitability of war with the United States but declared that the risk of American troops landing in Europe was practically nil. Although there were no plans for a break-through in the west in 1917, the experts blithely assumed that the war would soon be over once Britain had been beaten to her knees. Public opinion was firmly on the side of the experts. In the Reichstag the Conservatives, National Liberals and Centre declared that if the Supreme Command favoured unrestricted submarine warfare, it was the chancellor's bounden duty to accept this advice. Finally the emperor succumbed to the feverish optimism gripping ruling circles. On 9 January 1917 he came down on the side of the experts, and on 1 February unrestricted submarine warfare commenced. It was a desperate gamble with only a slender chance of success. As Bethmann Hollweg had predicted, technical advances enabled Britain, after some anxious months, to win the battle against the submarine. And once the enormous economic potential of the United States was thrown into the battle, following her declaration of war in April 1917, the fate of Germany was sealed. The financial and economic problems of the Entente were solved overnight, the blockade of Germany increased in efficiency and a vast reserve of manpower made victory quite certain.

In the summer of 1917 signs of war-weariness appeared in all the belligerent countries. Three years of food-shortages and enormous casualties undermined the loyalty of civilian populations everywhere. The spectacle of Russia contracting out of the war added to the growing unrest. In Britain there were munitions strikes, in France serious army mutinies and in Germany a dramatic parliamentary revolt occurred in July. Popular disillusionment with the duration and conduct of the war was at last strong enough to affect the behaviour of the Reichstag. Rumours that submarine warfare had failed were already circulating when the government foolishly called a special session of the Reichstag to grant new war-credits. No one was surprised to hear Ebert calling for peace before the winter. The sensation was Matthias Erzberger's speech. Erzberger, a rising figure on the left of the Centre party, was at one time an ardent annexationist and supporter of unrestricted submarine warfare. By July 1917 he had lost faith in the Supreme Command. Visiting the eastern front he learnt of Germany's military plight from the commanding general Hoffmann. In Vienna Erzberger obtained a copy of a report to Emperor Karl from Czernin, the new foreign minister, which made it abundantly clear that Austria could not survive another winter of war. On 6 July Erzberger put into words what many Germans were thinking. The web of fantasy spun by the annexationists was broken when he bluntly declared submarine warfare a failure and urged Germany to face realities by repudiating annexationism and committing herself publicly to a peace of reconciliation. Erzberger swung his party into line with Socialists and Radicals, and on 19 July 1917 the peace resolution was carried by 212 votes to 126. The new Reichstag alignment reflected the changing class alignment in Germany; middle-class and peasant supporters of the Centre moving leftward under the pressure of economic hardship dragged the right-wing leadership after them.

The peace resolution was a fine moral gesture which unfortunately had no influence on German policy. The one positive result was to bring about the downfall of Bethmann Hollweg. Hindenburg and Ludendorff refused to work any longer with a man who doubted final victory and could not keep the Reichstag in order. The chancellor, as usual, had the worst of both worlds. He opposed the resolution on the grounds that it was a tactical error to admit publicly that Germany wanted peace. He now had all parties against him for one reason or another.[3] He tried in vain to weather the storm by persuading the emperor to promise a new franchise for Prussia. It was too late. The party leaders refused to work with him any longer. The decisive blow came from the Supreme Command. Hindenburg and Ludendorff threatened resignation unless the peace resolution was withdrawn. Bethmann Hollweg happened to be at the palace when the peremptory telegram arrived. William preferred Bethmann Hollweg to all known alternatives but he knew full well that power resided at Headquarters in Kreuznach. To spare the emperor further embarrassment, Bethmann Hollweg quietly resigned. This was a decisive moment. By bowing to the will of the Supreme Command against his better judgement, William II destroyed one of the foundation stones of the Bismarckian constitution, which had enabled successive chancellors to remain in office as long as they had the emperor's confidence.

[3] Only the Radicals remained loyal to him.

Bethmann Hollweg's resignation was not a victory for the Reichstag. The only candidate they could agree upon was Bülow, a nominee quite unacceptable to the emperor, who never forgave the prince for 1909. The crisis in fact gave the Supreme Command a chance to assert its superiority over chancellors. It was Ludendorff who gave Bethmann Hollweg the *coup de grâce*; it was Ludendorff who played the decisive role in naming his successor. Out of discussions between the head of the cabinet secretariat, the head of the military cabinet and the emperor's adjutant emerged a name which Hindenburg and Ludendorff would accept – that of George Michaelis, a Prussian administrator who had impressed Ludendorff during a brief interview. Michaelis was a completely insignificant figure, quite bewildered by the turn of events which brought him back off holiday to the chancellor's desk. Michaelis clearly did not possess the confidence of the Reichstag. The general feeling of members towards the puppet chancellor was expressed by a Socialist who likened Michaelis to 'the fairy angel tied to the Christmas tree at Christmas for the children's benefit'.

What emerges most clearly during the crisis of confidence in July 1917 is the extreme reluctance of the Reichstag to launch a frontal assault on the system of government. At the height of the crisis the members confined themselves to the peace resolution and never pressed for those political reforms in which a majority of them believed. Successive chancellors sidetracked the constitutional committee's proposals with ease. The Reichstag even allowed the new chancellor to make a complete mockery of the peace resolution; he accepted it with the saving clause 'as I interpret it' and on condition that the Reichstag voted new war-credits.[4] At no time did the Reichstag use its power of refusing war-credits to prise major concessions out of the government. It was content with minor victories. As a sop to the parties Michaelis gave office to several prominent party members, including the Socialist Müller, who became under-secretary at the foreign office and Spahn of the Centre, who was given the Prussian ministry of justice. And the day after his appointment Michaelis arranged for Socialist deputies to be presented at court, an astute move which did not fail to impress the representatives of the working class. Further than this Michaelis would not go, being a declared opponent of parliamentary government. It is a fact of equal significance that the Reichstag agreed to stop at this point. Those who had power in Germany had no insight, those who had insight had no power and made only half-hearted attempts to obtain it. True, there was no great parliamentary figure to weld the hesitant parties into an irresistible pressure-group, and some deputies undoubtedly feared that too much pressure would force Ludendorff to set up an open military dictatorship. But the real reason for the continued forbearance of the Reichstag was that most members of this conservative-minded assembly

[4] Writing to the crown prince, Michaelis boasted that he 'had removed the greatest danger from the notorious resolution. One can after all now make any peace one likes under its terms.'

felt that it was unpatriotic to embarrass the government and the Supreme Command and divide the nation over constitutional issues at a time of national crisis.

Outside the Reichstag as a counter-blast to the peace resolution radical nationalists founded the Fatherland Party or *Vaterlandspartei*. Led by Wolfgang Kapp and Admiral Tirpitz, heavily subsidised by industry and aided by the army's propaganda service, this party soon had over one million members, overwhelmingly middle-class in complexion. The party was bitterly opposed to all political change, demanded annexations in west and east and supported wholeheartedly the dictatorship of the 'strongman' Ludendorff. Some historians have seen in these beginnings a proleptic hint of the Nazi party; Drexler, the founder of the German Workers' Party (which Hitler joined) was a prominent member of the new party.

Only on the occasion of Michaelis's downfall did it look as if real progress was being made towards parliamentary government, and that only by accident. Michaelis came to grief when he attempted to lay the blame for a naval mutiny at Kiel in June 1917 on the subversive activities of certain Independent Socialist deputies. Irritated by his mismanagement of the affair, the Reichstag demanded his resignation. On 1 November Michaelis was dismissed, to everyone's satisfaction. The Reichstag hoped to have a decisive say in the appointment of his successor and was not disappointed at the outcome. The emperor chose Count von Hertling, an elderly half-blind Bavarian aristocrat, who disliked parliamentary government. But he had enough political understanding to appreciate the need for consulting the parties. He promised to base his foreign policy on the peace resolution and to reform the Prussian franchise, and as an earnest of good faith he appointed Payer, the Radical leader, vice-chancellor. To this extent the appointment of Hertling represented a step on the road to parliamentary government. On closer investigation it becomes clear that the decisive factor was not the agreement with the Reichstag parties, but the attitude of the Supreme Command. Ludendorff, busy with preparations for the 1918 offensive, favoured a conciliatory gesture; Hertling was a reliable man who could keep the home front quiet long enough for Germany to win in the west. For once Reichstag and Supreme Command were in agreement. The *Burgfriede* was restored, a great calm descended on Germany and all eyes turned eastwards where great events were in the making.

In November 1917 the Bolsheviks came to power. The Supreme Command played some part in this revolution inasmuch as it had arranged for Lenin and his associates to travel back to Russia in the spring of 1917. They lived up to expectations, overthrowing the Kerensky government, and immediately took Russia out of the war. Early in December an armistice was signed and peace negotiations started at Brest-Litovsk. Strictly speaking only the chancellor was entitled to make peace. This did not deter

Ludendorff from sending General Hoffmann to represent the interests of the Supreme Command during the negotiations. Germany and Russia agreed that this would be a peace without annexations. They paid lip-service to the principle of self-determination, which each power thought it could manipulate in its own interests. On the German side Kühlmann, a career diplomat who became foreign minister in July 1917, believed that the implementation of self-determination was not incompatible with the maintenance of German hegemony in the east. However, the Supreme Command with its usual lack of subtlety favoured outright annexation and flatly refused to evacuate German troops from Poland, Courland and Lithuania, all vital sources of food supply for the army. Negotiations deadlocked as the Russians played for time, hoping that world revolution would relieve them of the need for negotiation with imperialists. In the end the Supreme Command, anxious to transfer troops to the western front without delay, lost patience. Hoffmann brushed aside Trotsky's celebrated 'No war, no peace' formula and ordered the resumption of hostilities in February 1918. The Germans advanced rapidly and would have entered Petrograd had Lenin not agreed to an immediate peace.

The Treaty of Brest-Litovsk in March 1918 was disastrous for Russia. She renounced all rights to Poland, Courland and Lithuania, and agreed that Germany and Austria-Hungary decide the future of these territories in accordance with the wishes of the population. She also promised to evacuate Finland, Estonia and Livonia and even recognised the independence of the Ukraine. It was a Carthaginian peace, which signified the destruction of Russia as a great imperialist power and shifted the balance of power in the east decisively in favour of Germany. The Entente powers denounced the treaty as a piece of unashamed annexationism and a fair warning of the fate awaiting them if Germany won. In August 1918 Germany blackened her reputation further in the eyes of the Entente when she used her military superiority in the east to impose reparations on Russia and secured complete control of Livonia and Estonia.

The Reichstag approved the Treaty of Brest-Litovsk by a large majority. Many members, intoxicated by the hope of final victory, easily persuaded themselves that the detachment of this huge mass of territory from Russia was only the first step on the road to genuine self-determination; this in its turn would lead eventually to the establish-ment of German hegemony in the east by agreement with the liberated peoples who feared and mistrusted Russia. Only the Independent Social-ists voted against it. Even the Majority Socialists abstained. Scheidemann admitted that the treaty was probably incompatible with true self-determination but declared bluntly that the party could not vote against a treaty bringing peace. In reality abstention was a tactical manoeuvre to disguise the fact that the party was divided and that some members were ready to vote for the treaty.[5]

Outside the rarefied atmosphere of the Reichstag, reactions to the treaty were much less favourable. Rumours that the generals were planning a harsh peace in the east roused widespread misgivings, implying as they did that the war was being prolonged in the interests of the upper classes. The fantastic arrogance and elation which gripped conservative circles in the early months of 1918 seemed to confirm these fears. The German princes, oblivious of the mounting frustration of the people, spent their time discussing the division of the spoils of war. For example, the kings of Bavaria and Saxony planned the partition of Alsace, whilst the emperor was busily designing a personal coat of arms for the day when he became duke of Courland. In January 1918 the real world broke in on these fantastic day-dreams when 400,000 Berlin workers went on strike. The strike spread to other cities, and soon one million men were idle. The strikers followed the lead of the Berlin committee in demanding democratisation of the government and a peace without annexations. The strike was not a random outburst motivated by economic hardship but a carefully organised attempt by the Revolutionary Shop Stewards to influence the course of the negotiations at Brest-Litovsk.

This is a convenient point to explain briefly the development of left-wing politics since 1914, when the Social Democrats voted unanimously for the war-credits. As the war dragged on, critical voices were heard in the parliamentary party. As early as December 1914 Karl Liebknecht, son of the Socialist pioneer, cast a lone vote against the war-credits. In March 1915, during the budget debate, and again in August, during a debate on war-credits, thirty members abstained. In December twenty members voted against war-credits and another twenty-two abstained; shortly afterwards Haase, the party leader who had suppressed his doubts about the war in 1914, resigned, to be replaced by Friedrich Ebert. Finally in March 1916 eighteen members led by Haase, Dittmann and Ledebour broke away and formed the Labour Fellowship. The schism in the parliamentary party was repeated in constituencies all over Germany. Even *Vorwärts*, the party organ, was gripped by internecine warfare and emerged a much less radical paper controlled by the right wing.

Opponents of the war inside and outside the party accused the Socialist leaders of wilfully closing their eyes to the fact that the war had ceased to be defensive in nature (if it ever had been) and had become a blatantly imperialist struggle waged in the interests of the upper classes. A few members of the parliamentary party, such as Lensch, Haenisch and Kolb,

[5]A group of Socialist deputies visited the Supreme Command in the spring of 1918 and were so impressed by initial victories during the last offensive that they felt they could no longer take the peace resolution seriously.

were undoubtedly out-and-out imperialists. Some others had gradually drifted rightwards in the shadow of the *Burgfriede* and were anxious not to jeopardise their newly won respectability and influence by challenging the government. But a great many Socialists found themselves impaled on the horns of a very real dilemma. They were as unhappy as their critics about the influence of the Supreme Command and strongly opposed unrestricted submarine warfare from the beginning. However, they could not bring themselves to resist the government on that account; this would be an act of treason prejudicial to the war effort and likely to bring discredit upon the ideals of parliamentary democracy in which they firmly believed. The path of duty, as they saw it, obliged them to continue co-operation with non-socialist parties and suspend class-warfare in the national interest for the duration of hostilities.

While the parliamentary Socialists wrestled with their consciences, many disillusioned Socialist voters were transferring their allegiance to the Independent Socialist party founded in April 1917 when the Labour Fellowship finally broke with the Majority Socialists. Forty-two members of the parliamentary party joined the new party; the remaining sixty-eight reconstituted themselves as the Majority Socialist party with Ebert as chairman. In the first instance the Independents differed from the Majority Socialists only on the issue of the war. They made no attempt to sabotage the war effort but acted as a ginger-group in the Reichstag, pressing for a speedy conclusion to hostilities. As material conditions worsened, the area of differences between the parties widened. The Majority Socialists continued to lose support, despite their belated efforts to prod the government into political reform. In the winter of 1917–18 the Independents were becoming a mass party representing left-wing socialism. Loosely associated with them were two other groups, the Spartacus League and the Revolutionary Shop Stewards. The league was founded by a small group of socialist intellectuals and admirers of Lenin led by Karl Liebknecht and Rosa Luxemburg. It had no mass following and exerted little influence on the course of events but is of some historical interest as being the nucleus of the future Communist Party. The Revolutionary Shop Stewards, on the other hand, exerted considerable influence in 1917–18. They were working-class activists, versed in conspiratorial techniques, who tried to organise mass action in the factories and workshops of Berlin in an attempt to end the war. Many Independents were firmly wedded to constitutional action, whereas the Spartacus League and the Shop Stewards believed that working people must use the imperialist war to destroy capitalism and inaugurate world-revolution.

The Shop Stewards were largely responsible for the great strike of January 1918, which the Majority Socialists and the trade unions denounced as an unpatriotic act at a particularly critical moment in the war. The Shop Stewards and Independents decided to call it off, largely because the authorities acted firmly. They placed the largest plants under military control, declared Berlin to be in a state of siege and prohibited public meetings. Right-wing extremists denounced the January strike as a 'stab in the back'. In fact it had little bearing on the military situation; munitions factories were already on short-time working and had actually dismissed workers owing to a coal shortage. The strike was a warning shot across the bows; if the new offensive failed, the government could expect serious internal disorder.

The collapse of Russia freed Germany from the nightmare of war on two fronts and in so doing gave her one last chance to avoid certain defeat. Ludendorff decided to strike a decisive blow in the west before the arrival of the Americans in great numbers tipped the scales in favour of the Entente. That winter fifty-two divisions were switched westwards, and by the spring of 1918 three-and-a-half million men were poised for attack in the west. On 21 March 1918 the long-awaited 'victory' offensive began. Germany threw half-a-million men into battle along a forty-five mile front at the junction of the British and French armies with the object of driving the British towards the sea. In the first forward lunge the Germans broke through, advanced thirty miles and captured many guns and prisoners before Foch succeeded in closing the gap and halting the attack. In April Ludendorff lunged towards Armentières but failed to break through. In May he attacked the French holding the Chemin des Dames. Again the Germans advanced many miles and for the second time in the war reached the Marne before the offensive ground to a halt. In Germany hopes of final victory remained high, and when Kühlmann ventured a contrary opinion in the Reichstag, he was attacked by all parties, save the Independents, and dismissed by the emperor at the request of Hindenburg and Ludendorff.

Kühlmann was right. The gamble in the west had failed. Germany did not possess the necessary superiority in manpower to exploit the initial breakthrough. The Supreme Command had chosen to keep one-and-a-half million men in the east controlling, directly or indirectly, vast territories from the Baltic to the Crimea which were ruthlessly exploited to supply the needs of the German war machine. Meanwhile American reinforcements arrived more quickly than Ludendorff bargained for; in March there were some 300,000 Americans in France; by July the figure had risen to over one million. In the high summer the initiative passed to the Entente. The Germans fell back when Foch launched his counter-offensive in July. On 8 August, 'the black day of the German army', as Ludendorff called it, thirteen British divisions supported by 450 tanks overran the German positions between the Somme and the Luce, taking 16,000 prisoners. The Germans never recovered from the psychological effects of 8 August; their will to fight was fatally weakened by the realisation that the tide had turned against them. They had lost all the gains made in the spring offensive and continued to retreat slowly but in good order. When the armistice was signed in November 1918, they were holding a line running from Antwerp to the Meuse.

Hindenburg and Ludendorff were stunned and bewildered by the turn of events and could not bring themselves to face the awful truth. Throughout August they talked of wearing the enemy down by going onto the defensive in France. Whilst they hesitated, the ground was crumbling away under their feet. Austria-Hungary tried in vain to make peace as her dominion over the Slav peoples waned; the Turkish front in Syria collapsed completely in September; finally a combined Entente offensive compelled Bulgaria to sue for an armistice on 29 September. Ludendorff's nerve broke. At the Spa Conference he admitted to the emperor and the chancellor that Germany could not win the war; if she did not end the fighting at once the enemy would break through in the west, drive the Germans over the Rhine and bring revolution to Germany. The chancellor must approach Wilson without delay and ask for an immediate armistice and a peace based on his Fourteen Points. In view of Wilson's belief that a lasting peace could only be concluded between democratic states, Ludendorff calmly proposed to transform Germany into a parliamentary democracy. This cynical ruse might secure better terms for Germany; if not, negotiations would at least give the generals time to regroup their forces and rally the people for a last stand. The emperor was appalled by the realisation that all was lost and he meekly accepted the general's advice to form a government enjoying the confidence of the people. Hertling could not stomach this 'revolution from above' and resigned on 30 September. He was replaced on 2 October by Prince Max of Baden, a moderate conservative, who quickly formed a government from the majority parties in the Reichstag. Thus the first parliamentary cabinet in German history came into being, not as the result of a struggle between Reichstag and government, but by order of the Supreme Command and in the very hour of defeat, ominous portents for the future of democratic government.

At first Prince Max, to the surprise of the Supreme Command, wanted to wait a month before suing for an armistice out of a genuine fear that over-eagerness would encourage the enemy to demand total capitulation. 'I am opposed to the offer,' he began in the crown council on 2 October, to be cut short by the emperor, who remarked curtly: 'You have not been brought here to make things difficult for the Supreme Command.' Exposed to tremendous pressure from a panic-stricken Ludendorff, who declared that Germany could not hold out another twenty-four hours, Prince Max gave way reluctantly. On 3 October he wrote formally to President Wilson asking for an armistice and a peace based on the Fourteen Points.

Any hopes Prince Max cherished of limiting Germany's losses by negotiations with the enemy were speedily dispelled in the correspondence which followed. Wilson insisted on immediate evacuation of all occupied territory, the cessation of submarine warfare and firm guarantees that the new German government was truly democratic and free from military influences. On 23 October Wilson declared bluntly that in his opinion the power structure of Germany was unchanged, and he warned Prince Max that 'if it [the American government] must deal with the military masters and the monarchical autocrats of Germany now, or if it is likely to have to deal with them later in regard to the international obligations of the German Empire, it must demand not peace negotiations but surrender'. Ludendorff had recovered his nerve by this time. He vigorously opposed acceptance of the armistice terms and issued an order to army commanders calling on all ranks to resist a humiliating surrender. Further resistance was sheer lunacy, as Prince Max realised. Ludendorff had also embarrassed the government by issuing his notorious order without consultation. This inopportune action seemed to confirm the doubts Wilson expressed about the government's control over the military. Prince Max grasped the nettle firmly, informing the emperor that he must choose between Ludendorff and the cabinet. On 26 October, after a heated exchange with the emperor, Ludendorff resigned and slipped across the frontier on his way to Sweden wearing blue spectacles and false whiskers.[6] The government had won its first battle. On 27 October Prince Max replied to Wilson's last note, reiterating Germany's wish for an armistice and emphasising that the military authorities were at last subject to the government.

On 28 October the constitutional changes set in motion by Ludendorff in a fit of panic were completed. Germany had become a parliamentary monarchy by agreement with the Bundesrat and the emperor. The chancellor and the secretaries of state were at last responsible to the Reichstag as well as to the Bundesrat. The emperor's powers over the army, the most cherished prerogative of the Hohenzollerns, were severely curtailed; all military appointments in future required the counter-signature of the minister of war. In addition the three-class system was abolished in Prussia, and parliamentary reforms were introduced in a number of South-German states.

These were important changes. Power had been transferred peaceably from the emperor to the Reichstag in the short space of three weeks. Unfortunately it all happened too late. In the last days of October 1918 the people were overwhelmed by the realisation that Germany had lost the war. The dismantlement of the Bismarckian constitution passed almost unnoticed. The significance of this event escaped the ordinary citizen. After all, the emperor was still on the throne, a prince was still chancellor, the power of the officer corps was unbroken, a state of siege (under which strikes were illegal) was still in force in the cities, and the war continued.

[6]Hindenburg remained at his post, much to the relief of the members of the government, who considered the victor of Tannenberg indispensable to Germany in her hour of crisis.

Nor did the Reichstag behave as if the revolution from above was a turning-point in German history; it adjourned on 5 October and did not meet again until 22 October when it immediately adjourned until 9 November.

By the end of October a revolutionary situation existed in Germany. Four years of war-time privation and hardship had gradually eroded the old relationship between ruler and subject. The shock of military defeat was the last straw. The stunned and disorientated people were only too ready to blame the Hohenzollerns for the misfortunes which had befallen Germany. Wilson helped to focus attention on this issue by making it plain that the emperor was an obstacle to peace. Once Wilson's notes were made public, popular pressure for the emperor's abdication grew rapidly. By 25 October an influential section of the press, representing the Socialist, Centre and Radical parties, considered abdication an essential preliminary to a just peace. The emperor was not willing to be a scapegoat for the politicians. He left Berlin and returned to Spa on 29 October, ostensibly because he believed his place was with the troops, in reality because he sensed that the pressure for abdication would overwhelm him if he stayed in the capital city. At Spa he persuaded his sons not to succeed him in the event of his deposition and, encouraged by Hindenburg's remark that the army would fall to pieces without the emperor, dreamt of riding home at the head of the army to restore order and crush revolution as he had dreamt of doing in 1894. It was twenty-five years and a whole war too late for that. At Kiel on 29 October sailors on board the cruisers *Thüringen* and *Helgoland* refused to obey orders. The German Revolution had begun.

10

The German Revolution
1918–1920

On 28 October 1918 the German naval authorities ordered the fleet assembled at Wilhelmshaven, to put to sea and make a cruiser raid in the English Channel. As unrestricted submarine warfare had been stopped out of deference to Wilson, it was hoped that a modest naval diversion would ease the pressure on the German armies. The morale of the sailors was perilously low. They resented the arrogance of their officers, the strictness of naval discipline and the disparity in rations between officers and men. The latest order seemed a lunatic gesture designed to appease fanatical officers and likely to endanger the armistice negotiations – many sailors thought this was the real aim of the officers who were notorious for their extreme right-wing views. The crews of two cruisers, *Thüringen* and *Helgoland*, mutinied and damped down their fires. Whereupon the naval authorities ordered the arrest of 600 sailors on these ships. Other sailors, fearing a repetition of the harsh sentences meted out after the mutiny of 1917, demonstrated in Kiel on 3 November. Shots were fired and eight sailors killed. This was the signal for a general mutiny. Sailors' councils were set up on nearly all ships. On 4 November dock-workers and the local garrison in Kiel joined the mutinous sailors and set up their own workers' and soldiers' councils. Independent Socialists were certainly in close touch with some mutineers, but on the whole this was not a politically motivated mutiny but a genuine protest against intolerable conditions. The sailors' councils were not disloyal to the government. On the contrary, they asked for representatives to come and listen to their grievances. The government sent Noske, the Majority Socialist expert on defence. He quickly reassured the sailors that there would be no 'suicide offensive', and promised better conditions for naval ratings, the ending of the state of siege and the liberation of all political prisoners. The grateful sailors promptly made him governor of Kiel.

Noske could not confine the disturbances to Kiel. Sailors quickly carried the torch of revolution from Kiel to other North-German ports. By 6 November workers' and soldiers' councils had been set up in all major cities and ports. The German Revolution, like the March Revolution in

Russia, was spontaneous in its origins. As the old order crumbled away under the strain of war and defeat, a political vacuum appeared which the politically active sections of the people filled. It was also a bloodless revolution. The old order offered no resistance, perhaps because the most fanatical monarchists were still at the front. Garrisons all over Germany and on the western front went over to the revolution. Overnight officials found their authority superseded by soldiers' councils. The new workers' and soldiers' councils varied in composition; in the small towns they were mostly controlled by Majority Socialists, in the cities by Independent Socialists. All the councils claimed executive power over their own area and co-existed rather uneasily with pre-revolutionary bodies. In practice the councils allowed the old imperial officers to remain at their desks and life went on much as before. They were not revolutionary bodies at all. The name was an accidental by-product of a revolutionary situation; it certainly did not imply that the councils were seeking to overthrow the existing order of things. Only occasionally did a socialist note creep in, as in Dresden and Leipzig, where the councils promised to socialise the economic system and arm the people to defend the revolution. Most councils were local *ad hoc* bodies, manned by patriotic Germans anxious to maintain law and order and ensure the smooth functioning of local services at a time of national crisis. All they had in common was a wish to be rid of the emperor and see a fully democratic form of government established in Germany.

The decisive moment in the German Revolution occurred on 8 November, when a republic was proclaimed in Bavaria. The Bavarian peasants were frightened by the prospect of invasion following the collapse of Austria-Hungary and were desperately anxious for peace. There was already much resentment of the Berlin government, which the Bavarians blamed for the economic hardship they had endured. The suspicion that Berlin was in no hurry to make peace deepened their resentment. Encouraged by the near-separatist mood of the people, the Independent Socialists, a minority group led by the romantic and theatrical Kurt Eisner, seized the initiative and forced the pace of the revolution. On 8 November the Independents set up a council of workers, soldiers and peasants which deposed the Wittelsbachs and proclaimed the Bavarian Democratic and Socialist Republic. The disgruntled Bavarians acquiesced in the *fait accompli*, and the Majority Socialists, who had been content to organise demonstrations calling for peace, hurriedly joined with the Independents to form a government. The new government was in fact democratic, not socialist, in character, because Eisner believed that a radical middle-class revolution was all that could be achieved at this stage in German development. Accordingly the government confirmed the old officials in power and promised to maintain law and order, protect property and convene a constituent assembly. It affirmed its belief in socialism, but declared bluntly that the means of production could not be socialised at a time of economic dislocation.

The proclamation of the Bavarian Republic was undeniably a revolutionary act. This transformed what had been a rather haphazard movement led by unknown workers and soldiers into a serious political revolution. And it brought home forcibly to Prince Max's cabinet the gravity of the situation. Berlin was a restless and turbulent city in the early days of November 1918, with the tide of revolution sweeping across the surrounding countryside. The most active group of revolutionaries, the Shop Stewards led by Barth and Müller, had been planning an armed uprising for several months. On 2 November they conferred with the Independent Socialist leaders to determine the exact date of their bid for power, only to discover that their colleagues were completely divided on the question. Haase, now leader of the Independent Socialists, counselled caution; a representative of the right wing of the party, he was a firm believer in parliamentary methods and opposed insurrectionary tactics. Not so Ledebour on the party's left and Liebknecht of the Spartacists, both of whom spurned parliamentary institutions and called for the immediate seizure of power and the establishment of the dictatorship of the proletariat. In the end the perplexed Shop Stewards decided by twenty-one votes to nineteen to postpone the uprising.

Whilst Shop Stewards and Independents debated the advisability of armed insurrection, the Majority Socialists were able to play a major role in determining the course of the revolution. The Majority Socialists, under their leaders Ebert and Scheidemann, were thorough-going and convinced constitutionalists, who believed that the working class would come to power via the ballot-box as Lassalle and Engels had predicted. When the Socialists won a popular mandate for change, then, and then only, would the time be ripe for the socialisation of the means of production. The steady increase in the Socialist vote before 1914, together with the constitutional changes in October 1918, encouraged the Majority Socialists to believe that they would be forming a Social Democratic government in the not-too-distant future. The prospect of bloody revolution appalled and offended them. Insurrection had no place in their tidy scheme of things. It would only add to the difficulties facing defeated Germany and might even endanger the unity of the *Reich* for which their sons had fought and died. A deep sense of patriotism and a firm belief in the efficacy of parliamentary institutions guided them to the conclusion that law and order must be restored as quickly as possible, so that the constitutional system of government could be established firmly in the minds and hearts of the people.

Nor did Majority Socialists object to monarchy as such. They only joined in the growing clamour for William's abdication because their own supporters were deserting the party *en masse* and joining the Independent

Socialists. If they were to regain the support of active party workers and prevent civil war – this seemed distinctly possible in view of the determination of the extreme left to come to power – then they must place themselves at the head of the popular movement and divert it into constitutional channels. On 2 November Scheidemann wrote to Prince Max requesting the emperor's abdication. Nothing happened. Five days later on 7 November the party executive adopted a firmer line, threatening to withdraw support from the government unless the emperor abdicated within twenty-four hours and the Socialists were given greater representation in the cabinet. Prince Max concluded, reluctantly, that abdication was the only way of avoiding civil war and preserving the monarchy in some form. Unfortunately, he could not convince the emperor of this unpleasant truth. On 8 November the Socialist ministers Scheidemann and Bauer resigned, and the party agreed to call a general strike for 9 November unless the emperor had abdicated by then. Only with reluctance did the Majority Socialist leaders, many of whom had come up through the trade-union movement, agree to use the strike weapon for political purposes. Their hand was really forced by the Shop Stewards, who had already called a strike for 9 November in protest against the arrest of some of their leaders in connection with the plans for an armed uprising of which the government had got wind.

So, on 9 November most workers left their factories for one reason or another and demonstrated on the streets. A deputation of Socialists headed by Ebert and Scheidemann called on Prince Max. They informed him that the local garrison was on their side,[1] and that a new democratic government must be formed at once. This was not a revolutionary act. Ebert made it clear that he was not assuming power on behalf of the Berlin workers' and soldiers' councils but on a strictly constitutional basis. Prince Max hesitated no longer. At noon he announced the abdication of the emperor and the crown prince. By this time Hindenburg and Groener, Ludendorff's successor, realised that the emperor must go. Groener told him the terrible truth; the soldiers would not march behind the emperor, nor would they march against bolshevism; all they wanted was an armistice. Even now the emperor wriggled and twisted, hoping to remain king of Prussia. Prince Max's announcement finally shattered the illusion. Abandoned by his generals and his ministers, the angry emperor left for exile in Holland, never to return to Germany.

Prince Max handed over the seals of office to Ebert in the early afternoon of 9 November. Strictly speaking this was an unconstitutional act. What counted most with Prince Max at this critical moment was his conviction that Ebert was 'a man determined to fight the revolution tooth and nail'. Later he was engagingly frank about his motives: 'I said to myself:

[1] The work of Otto Wels, who became chairman of the parliamentary party in 1931 and is remembered for his defiant Reichstag speech in March 1933.

the revolution is on the eve of success; we can't smash it, but perhaps we can throttle it . . . if Ebert is introduced to me as the tribune of the people, then we shall have a republic; if it's Liebknecht, bolshevism; but if the abdicating emperor appoints Ebert chancellor, there is a faint hope still for the monarchy.'

It was certainly not Ebert's fault that the republic was proclaimed on 9 November. The Majority Socialists stumbled into this decisive event quite by accident. Scheidemann was having lunch when a crowd of excited workmen broke in to tell him that Liebknecht was about to proclaim a soviet republic from the balcony of the castle. The report was erroneous; all Liebknecht wanted was a 'free Socialist republic'. Subtle distinctions of this kind escaped Scheidemann and his colleagues. They were morbidly suspicious of all who stood further to the left than themselves. Later, like Social Democrats in other lands, they were shocked by Lenin's dissolution of the Russian constituent assembly in January 1918; 'soviet rule' they regarded as synonymous with 'the bolshevik reign of terror'. With such thoughts in the forefront of his mind Scheidemann rushed onto the balcony of the Reichstag, determined to prevent Liebknecht turning Germany into a 'Russian province'. He harangued the crowd and ended his peroration with the fateful words 'Long live the great German republic!' He was taken severely to task by Ebert for his enthusiasm. 'You have not the right to proclaim the republic,' shouted Ebert, livid with rage; 'whether Germany becomes a republic or something else is a matter for a constituent assembly to decide.' Ebert had clearly hoped even at this late hour to save the monarchy by avoiding any mention of the word 'republic' until the constituent assembly met. After Scheidemann's speech this hope was buried for good.

Ebert issued his first proclamation to the people on 9 November, signing himself 'imperial chancellor', a title deliberately chosen to emphasise continuity between his government and that of Prince Max. This device conferred some semblance of legitimacy on the new government and helped to rally the officer corps and the civil service behind it. Ebert declared that the goal of the government was to bring peace to Germany as quickly as possible and 'to establish firmly the freedom which it has achieved', a significant phrase clearly implying that, as far as the Majority Socialists were concerned, the revolution had ended. Citizens were exhorted to maintain food supplies, to keep off the streets and to preserve law and order.

Ebert was under no illusions about the position of the new government. Its authority did not extend with certainty beyond Berlin, and it was not even accepted in all parts of the capital city. If only for tactical reasons, Ebert needed to broaden the basis of the government. That was not the only consideration. The revolution had generated a spirit of fraternity; Majority Socialists and Independents were collaborating amicably enough in workers' and soldiers' councils up and down Germany; it seemed only reasonable to give them representation at government level, thus preserving the solidarity of the Socialist movement. After leaving Prince Max on 9 November, Ebert at once asked the Independents to accept office with the Majority Socialists, offering them parity of seats in the government.

The Independents had arrived at a political cross-roads. The party was deeply divided on this issue. The right wing favoured acceptance. The left wing bitterly opposed collaboration with opportunists like Ebert, who had 'smuggled himself into the revolution' in Ledebour's graphic phrase, and demanded instead the assumption of plenary powers by the workers' and soldiers' councils. By a slender majority of twenty-one votes to nineteen the Independents finally decided to accept Ebert's offer. As a sop to their left wing they insisted on a number of concessions from the Majority Socialists. Only Socialists must be included in the government – not liberals as Ebert had hoped – the government must declare that all powers resided in the workers' and soldiers' councils, and, finally, the calling of the constituent assembly must be delayed until the revolution was consolidated. Reluctantly Ebert accepted the conditions, and on 10 November a new government, the Council of Peoples' Representatives (*Rat der Volksbeauftragten*), was formed. It consisted of three Majority Socialists: Ebert, Scheidemann and Landsberg; and three Independents: Haase, Dittmann and Barth; with Ebert and Haase acting as co-chairmen.

Ebert's government was not the only authority in Berlin. On 10 November elections to form workers' and soldiers' councils were held in all the factories and garrisons in Berlin. At a mass meeting of the councils, called in the evening by the Independents, the delegates approved the composition of the government by a huge majority. An executive committee of twenty-eight members was elected to manage the affairs of the Berlin workers' and soldiers' councils. The executive committee, which consisted of seven Majority Socialists, seven Independents and fourteen soldiers – many of whom were not socialists at all – at once started negotiations with the government to define the precise relationship between the two bodies. On 22 November agreement was reached on a new constitutional form for the transitional period before the constituent assembly met. All executive and legislative power was formally vested in the workers' and soldiers' councils of 'the German Socialist Republic'. Executive power was to be exercised by the government but in the name of the workers' and soldiers' councils. The executive reserved the right to appoint and dismiss members of the government. The task of the republic was defined as being the protection and development of the achievements of the revolution and the suppression of counter-revolution. Finally it was agreed that an assembly of delegates from workers' and soldiers' councils in all parts of Germany be convened as quickly as possible.

Ebert accepted the agreement with reluctance. Like most Majority Socialists he viewed the workers' councils with grave suspicion as a possible rival to parliamentary government. Friction soon developed between the Majority Socialist members of the government and the executive committee, which was swayed by an active minority of Independents. The calling of the constituent assembly was not in dispute. Only left-wing Independents and Spartacists opposed this; most Independents believed as firmly as the Majority Socialists in parliamentary democracy. But whereas Majority Socialists maintained that the revolution was over, the Independents believed that the gains of the revolution must be consolidated before the assembly met. They argued that authoritarian habits were so deeply ingrained in the minds of the citizens that democracy would shrivel up and die unless it was preceded by a period of socialism. In order to dissolve those great concentrations of political and economic power which they believed inimical to the development of a healthy democracy, the Independents called for the socialisation of key industries, the breaking-up of the great estates and the democratisation of the civil service, the judiciary and the army. Workers' and soldiers' councils had an important role to play in their scheme of things. They supposed, rather naïvely, that these popularly elected bodies were the embodiment of the revolutionary will of the people for change, and therefore eminently suited to supervise the implementation of a crash programme of socialism. Most Independents did not think the councils should supersede the constituent assembly, but rather supplement the activities of the parliamentary body by extending grass-roots democracy into the political and industrial field and giving the people a real sense of participation in decision-making.

Throughout November and December a silent struggle was going on between Majority Socialists and Independents on this vital issue inside and outside the workers' and soldiers' councils. The government extended the social-welfare system in these months; the eight-hour day was recognised, agricultural workers and officials were given the right to form trade unions, there was legislation to provide work for demobilised soldiers and improvements in sickness insurance and unemployment benefits. Beyond this the Majority Socialists did not want to go, feeling that the transition to full-blooded socialism was a matter for the constituent assembly to decide. As the weeks slipped past, Ebert's position was growing steadily stronger. Permanent officials co-operated willingly enough with Ebert, seeing in him the legitimate successor of Prince Max; but they would not work with the executive committee of the councils. Important, too, in this context was the fact that the officer corps had pledged full support to Ebert.

On 10 November Ebert had the first of several telephone conversations with General Groener on the secret line linking the chancellery with the Supreme Command at Spa. Groener, the ablest technician in the army and Ludendorff's successor as quarter-master-general, was desperately afraid that the revolution would destroy the authority of the officer corps and lead to a disastrous civil war which would weaken Germany and deliver her into the hands of her enemies. There was in fact little foundation for these exaggerated fears; the general staff underestimated the mood of the German working class in the autumn of 1918 as much as Liebknecht and the Spartacists underestimated it from a diametrically opposed view-point. Ebert was tailor-made to calm the generals' fears. Groener recognised in the new chancellor a deeply patriotic German who had lost two sons for the fatherland and would do his utmost to preserve law and order. With the full agreement of Hindenburg, Groener telephoned Ebert and assured him that the general staff would support the government and would do its best to see that the three million soldiers in occupied territory, who had to be withdrawn by 12 December in accordance with the armistice terms, retired in good order across the Rhine. As Groener was well aware, this manoeuvre could only be carried out successfully with the full co-opera-tion of the government; that was why he asked Ebert to help the generals uphold the power of the officers against the soldiers' councils. Entering boldly into the political arena, Groener went on to say that the officer corps naturally expected Ebert to defend Germany against bolshevism and was placing itself at the government's disposal for this purpose. Ebert quickly assured Groener that the government fully intended to resist bolshevism and to call a constituent assembly as quickly as possible. In return for the offer of military support, Ebert agreed to curtail the power of soldiers' councils, and on 12 November the cabinet sent a telegram to Hindenburg upholding the officer's power of command.

This was the celebrated Ebert-Groener pact, which left-wing critics denounced bitterly over the years as proof positive that Ebert had betrayed the revolution. Its importance has probably been exaggerated. From Ebert's point of view it was not betrayal; Majority Socialists never made any secret of their distaste of revolution; as the government had no reliable forces at its disposal, the understanding with the general staff was an elementary precaution to protect it against violence from the extreme left. When put to the test Groener was not, in fact, able to protect the govern-ment properly. On the other hand, the pact sealed the fate of attempts to democratise the army. In December the All-German Congress of Workers' and Soldiers' Councils endorsed the so-called Hamburg points, which were designed to subordinate the military authorities to the government and to the executive committee of the workers' and soldiers' councils. All ranks would be abolished, officers would be elected and the standing army would be replaced by a peoples' militia. Hindenburg and Groener were highly indignant and threatened to resign unless Ebert repudiated the action of the congress. Ebert, still in no position to defy the executive committee, had to pay lip-service to the points whilst privately assuring Groener that they would not be applied to the field army in the east.

Implementation of the points in the home forces was delayed. In January, when Ebert finally issued an order regulating the position of soldiers' councils, the latter were given far fewer powers than the Hamburg points envisaged. What slender chance there had been of breaking the power of the officer corps had gone for good by this time.

As relations between the government and the executive committee deteriorated, Ebert did his utmost to accelerate the calling of the constituent assembly. Late in November he convened a conference of state governments to discuss this question. The states, having no wish to be ordered about by the Berlin executive committee, readily agreed to call the constituent assembly as quickly as possible. The question was also submitted to the All-German Congress of Workers' and Soldiers' Councils which met in Berlin from 16 to 21 December. 'The revolutionary parliament of 1918', as it is sometimes called, was in fact controlled by the Majority Socialists. Over 300 of the 500 delegates supported the Majority Socialists and only ninety the Independents, a not altogether surprising result, for the Majority Socialists had a well-organised party machine at their disposal and help from the trade unions.

In some respects the Congress was more radically inclined than the government. Despite warnings from the right wing against precipitate action, the delegates passed a resolution demanding the immediate socialisation of key industries. Similarly in connection with the democratisation of the army; as indicated above, the Congress endorsed the Hamburg points. But it was just as clear that the delegates wanted Germany to be a parliamentary democracy. On 19 December Congress approved by an overwhelming majority the government decision to hold elections to the constituent assembly on 19 January[2] and decided that all executive and legislative power be vested in the government until this assembly met. At the same time the Berlin executive committee was to be replaced by a central council with powers of supervision over the German and Prussian cabinets. However, Ebert successfully persuaded the Congress to forbid the central council from interfering in the day-to-day business of government. The Independents were annoyed by this and, feeling that they would be unable to use the new council to bully the government into a socialist path, committed the tactical error of boycotting elections to the council. The result was a council packed with Majority Socialists whom Ebert could control with ease.

Shortly after the dispersal of the Congress, Ebert scored another victory over the Independents when Haase, Dittmann and Barth resigned from the government over the sailors' revolt. Tension was rising again in Berlin early in December. On 6 December soldiers fired on Spartacist demonstrators, killing sixteen of them. On 23 December the sailors' division, which

[2]It is indicative of the widespread support for this decision that it was approved at the Independent Socialist party congress in mid-December by 485 votes to 195.

had come from Kiel in November to defend the government and generally sympathised with the Independents, was ordered to evacuate its quarters in the palace. The disgruntled sailors decided to march on the chancellery and arrest the government. They seized Otto Wels, commandant of the republican civic guard, and barricaded themselves in the palace. Ebert telephoned Groener for assistance. Next day a detachment of 800 soldiers attacked the palace and released Wels. Then, having practically forced the sailors to surrender, the soldiers lost heart and allowed a crowd of civilians to disperse them. This was, incidentally, a serious rebuff for the army and might have had serious repercussions had the men of the left not been too divided by their internal feuds to exploit the new situation. The Independents were highly incensed by Ebert's action, undertaken without their knowledge, and referred the incident to the central council. Their three ministers were already frustrated by the slow progress towards socialism and highly suspicious of the ties between Ebert and the general staff. They were also under constant pressure from their own left-wingers, who opposed collaboration with the Majority Socialists and applauded the provocative utterances and demonstrations of the Spartacists, with whom they had much more in common than with their own leaders. When the central council sided with the government over the sailors' revolt, the three ministers resigned on 29 December.

The resignations were a blunder of the first magnitude. For by contracting out of practical politics at this moment of crisis the Independents destroyed what hope there had been of bridging the yawning gulf between the government and the Spartacists. The left was now polarised in two hostile camps: on one side the Majority Socialists driven more and more to the right by the insurrectionary language of their opponents, on the other side the Spartacists embittered by what they regarded as Ebert's betrayal of the revolution. On the last day of December 1918 the Spartacists, meeting in congress in Berlin, broke finally with the Independents and founded the German Communist Party. They carried with them some left-wing Independents, although most of the party remained loyal to Haase. The leading figures in the new party were Karl Liebknecht, a gifted orator and son of the Social Democratic leader Wilhelm Liebknecht, and Rosa Luxemburg, a Polish Jewess of immense personal charm and formidable intellectual qualities.

The Communists contemptuously dismissed Ebert's government as the 'enemy of the working class'. In December they declared that the new national assembly would be an organ of counter-revolution and called instead for government by workers' and soldiers' councils. They refused even to participate in the forthcoming general election despite the pleas of Liebknecht and Luxemburg that a national assembly might be used as a forum for revolutionary propaganda. But despite the promptings of Russian revolutionaries such as Radek, that their German comrades should try and seize power at once, most Communists were sincere democrats, deeply critical of the growing power of bureaucracy in pre-war German society and painfully aware that Germany was not ripe for a socialist revolution. Their forward strategy of strikes and demonstrations was designed to educate the masses to political awareness, not to mobilise them for an immediate seizure of power.

The Communist uprising in the early days of January 1919 – 'the battle of the Marne of the German Revolution' – was the act of misguided idealists who wanted to give History a push forward. When the Independent Socialist members of the Prussian cabinet resigned on 3 January, Eichhorn, chief of the Berlin police, refused to leave his post declaring that he had a duty to protect the revolution. On 4 January the Prussian government summarily dismissed him. On 5 January the Revolutionary Shop Stewards and the Berlin Independents joined with the Communists in a call for mass demonstrations against Eichhorn's dismissal. At first the Communists did not think the moment had arrived for the overthrow of the government. Then, encouraged by promises of armed support from shop stewards, they changed their minds and decided on an uprising. Rosa Luxemburg bowed to the will of the majority only with reluctance, for she sensed that the Communists had not yet won over the mass of the working people without whose support the dictatorship of the proletariat would be a hollow mockery. On 6 January a revolutionary committee of fifty-three Communists and Shop Stewards was set up. It issued a proclamation deposing the Ebert government and announcing the establishment of a new revolutionary government, led by Liebknecht, Ledebour and Scholze. At the same time armed Communists occupied newspaper offices and various public buildings in the city.

Faced with this clear challenge to its authority, the government acted promptly. Ebert made Noske, the new defence minister, responsible for restoring order. The self-styled 'bloodhound of the revolution' quickly discovered that the Majority Socialists in Berlin were reluctant to fight for the republic, largely because anti-militarism was an extremely powerful tradition on the left. Noske turned to the generals. Groener had taken to heart the lesson of the sailors' revolt, when front-line soldiers had succumbed easily to revolutionary propaganda on being put to the test. Far more reliance could be placed on irregular bands of volunteers, like those being formed in the Baltic lands and in Poland to fight the Russians and defend the frontiers of the *Reich*. Noske approved the idea and with the help of several generals succeeded in recruiting and training some hundreds of officers and men, who were organised in the so-called Free Corps, a German version of the notorious Black and Tans. On 10 January 1919 Free Corps men, led by General von Lüttwitz, attacked the Communist positions in Berlin. By 13 January the revolt was crushed after savage street-fighting in which prisoners were mishandled and summarily shot.

The Communist leaders Liebknecht and Luxemburg were captured and cruelly murdered on the way to the Moabit prison. The Majority Socialist leaders were shocked by the brutality of their new allies during Spartacus week and sharply condemned the murders, but were virtually powerless to restrain the fanatics and adventurers who flocked to join the various Free Corps.

The defeat of the Communists made it possible to hold elections to the constituent assembly later in January. But the German Revolution was not yet over. On the contrary, the election results helped to revive revolutionary sentiment in the spring of 1919 inasmuch as they destroyed widespread hopes on the left of a solid socialist majority. The Weimar assembly, dominated by the middle classes, was opposed to socialist experiments. The authorities were already attempting to suppress the councils in the factories, much to the alarm of the workers. Noske's use of the Free Corps also aroused great bitterness among the workers, who felt that the forces of reaction were in control once more. The Independent Socialists, still a considerable political force, were moving steadily leftwards; in March 1919 at their annual congress they rejected parliamentary democracy entirely and came out in favour of government by workers' councils. In February widespread strikes were organised by the Communists in defence of workers' councils. In some cities this led to sporadic street-fighting and to attempts to proclaim soviet republics. In Berlin, early in March, the Communists called for a general strike as a first step to a second revolution. The Independents and the Berlin workers' and soldiers' council endorsed the strike appeal. At first even the Majority Socialist union leaders joined the strike committee in their anxiety to retain the loyalty of their members, but later, when the committee attempted to deprive the people of light, water and power, they quickly resigned. Again Berlin became the scene of disorder and street-fighting, largely spontaneous in origin. Again Noske ordered the Free Corps to assist the police and break the back of the resistance in East Berlin. By the middle of March order had been restored at the cost of over one thousand dead, many of them summarily shot by the Free Corps for possessing arms.

Dramatic events occurred in Bavaria in April 1919. The elections to the Bavarian parliament in mid-January resulted in an overwhelming defeat for Eisner's Independents.[3] Eisner, a convinced adherent of parliamentary democracy, summoned the new parliament but on his way to the opening session on 21 February was murdered by a right-wing fanatic. Disorders broke out in Munich, and the new coalition government, led by Majority Socialists, eventually retired from Munich on advice from Berlin, leaving the city in the hands of Independents and Communists neither of whom had any support in the Bavarian countryside. On 7 April a group of

[3]They won only three seats.

starry-eyed Independents set up a soviet republic in the firm belief that world revolution was on its way. The local Communists contemptuously brushed them aside and proclaimed their own soviet republic on 9 April. Meanwhile the coalition government, following the example of Berlin, called upon a local Free Corps led by *Ritter* von Epp for assistance. Supported by Prussian and Württemberg soldiers, Epp marched into Munich at the end of April and restored order after some days of savage fighting. In the 'white terror' which followed, hundreds of workers were summarily shot, including all the local Communist leaders, Bavarian politics took a sharp turn to the right and during the next few years this part of Germany acquired a reputation as a hotbed of right-wing radicalism and separatism. In 1920 following the Kapp Putsch a fresh outbreak of revolutionary activity occurred with the formation of the Red Army in the Ruhr. This was eventually suppressed by *Reichswehr* and Free Corps units. Finally, in March 1921 when armed miners at Mansfeld clashed with the police the Communists called a general strike in their support. Few responded and the uprising was quickly put down. With this the 'second revolution' came to an end.

The German Revolution has often been dismissed as a purely negative event largely because the Weimar Republic is seen, unhistorically, as a mere prelude to the Third Reich. It is true that, unlike the 1848 Revolution, this revolution was not preceded by a period of intellectual ferment discrediting the values of the old order. But those values were just as effectively discredited by the strain of war. A revolutionary situation did exist in 1918 in as much as the people was no longer prepared to obey the old rulers. The power and popularity of the workers' and soldiers' councils indicate quite clearly that ordinary people did feel some sense of liberation in these months and were dimly aware that the balance of power had shifted momentarily in their direction.

All the same, the achievements of the Revolution were undoubtedly limited. The empire had gone and the dynasties too – but they were harmless anachronisms by this time. Universal suffrage and the secret ballot were introduced in all states and the reign of parliamentary democracy began – but all this had been achieved before the November Revolution which merely confirmed a new political order brought into being by the fiat of the Supreme Command. By 1920 very few Germans took pride in the part they had played in the Revolution. The Republic was accepted by many Germans not as a superior form of government but as a convenient means of filling a void left by the collapse of monarchy. It was widely – but quite erroneously – believed that the alternative to a conservative parliamentary regime was a Red dictatorship which only a tiny minority wanted. The structure of German society was hardly affected by the revolution. The spirit of Imperial Germany lived on in the unreformed civil service, the judiciary and the officer corps. Nor did the powerful industrial barons have much to fear from the revolution. If one believes, as many socialists did in 1918, that democracy is fatally weakened unless the citadels of power and privilege are stormed and subjected to the general will, then the German Revolution was certainly a failure for which the three Socialist parties bear much of the responsibility.

Firstly, the Majority Socialists. The sincerity of their belief in the principles and practice of parliamentary democracy cannot be doubted. What can be called in question is their imperfect understanding of the socio-political complex of post-imperial Germany. Their obsession with correct constitutional procedures blinded them to other equally important considerations. They stubbornly resisted demands by the workers' councils – of which they were inordinately suspicious – for the immediate democratisation of the administrative apparatus and the socialisation of key industries, on the grounds that these were matters which could only be decided by a constituent assembly; the difficulty was that this body would, of necessity, represent the anti-socialist middle class as well as the socialist working class. The Majority Socialist leaders were harassed men, deeply concerned about the German fatherland but morbidly suspicious of left-wing critics and far too immersed in the day-to-day problems of government to perceive the general direction in which they were drifting. The Communist uprising made matters worse in this respect. For, as they had conspicuously failed to arm their own supporters, the Socialists were forced to turn to the Supreme Command for support; almost without noticing it, they became deeply dependent on the sworn enemies of democracy and socialism. They received little thanks for their strenuous efforts to preserve democracy. The Communists never forgave them for 'betraying the revolution'; while the right wing soon forgot what it owed to Ebert and his associates and denounced all socialists indiscriminately as 'November traitors' who had 'stabbed the fatherland in the back', a legacy which weighed heavily on the party throughout the Weimar period. Half a century later, when the fire has gone out of these quarrels, one can see that the Majority Socialist leaders were a good deal more honourable and well-meaning, according to their lights, than their critics allowed. But it is equally clear that the Majority Socialists were woefully misguided in their glib assumptions about the future of parliamentary democracy, and that they grossly underestimated the strength and tenacity of the forces in Germany opposed to all that Weimar stood for.

The Independent Socialists, on the other hand, were much more perceptive in their social analysis. From the start they insisted that a considerable degree of political and economic change was essential if democracy was to flourish in the uncongenial climate of post-imperial Germany. For a time they seemed well on the way to becoming a mass party combining democratic beliefs with socialist principles. The high hopes were not realised. Throughout the whole of its short life this party was gravely weakened by internecine strife between the parliamentary right and the revolutionary left. When the Independents were in the government, the left wing continually sniped at them and reduced still further what limited influence the ministers had on their Majority Socialist colleagues. By the time they decided to withdraw from the government the Independents had lost many supporters to the Communists, who now became the focal point of resistance to Ebert in Berlin. Indeed the very act of withdrawal was a blunder which dangerously accentuated the tension between right and left and made conflict unavoidable. During Spartacus week the Independents were hopelessly divided. In March 1919 they abandoned their belief in parliamentary methods and declared in favour of government by workers' councils, although they were careful to point out that the dictatorship of the proletariat could only be established with the full support of the working class. The fortunes of the party revived in 1920.[4] But when the Independents decided to seek affiliation with the Third International, the party was finally split asunder; a third of the members joined the Communists, and the remainder eventually found their way back to the Majority Socialists by 1922. This was the end of a party which showed more awareness of the problems facing parliamentary democracy than either Majority Socialists or Communists. It is tempting to suppose that the Independents represented a viable alternative to Ebert and Liebknecht. The sad truth is that the party lacked basic cohesion and simply could not rely on the support of all members at times of crisis. Had the Independents remained inside the Social Democratic party, they might conceivably have arrested its progress to the right and compelled Ebert to modify his views on socialism. Alternatively, had they joined the Communists *en bloc* they might well have diverted the new revolutionary party from a disastrous course of action. As it was, the Independents fell tragically between two stools and so exerted little positive influence on the course of events.

Finally, the Communists must bear some share of responsibility for the failure to give the Revolution a positive social content. Radical utopians who got the upper hand in the party in December 1918 were hypnotised by the spectacle of the Russian Revolution and easily persuaded themselves that Germany, too, was ripe for proletarian revolution. This was a monumental miscalculation. Rightly or wrongly the German working class was solidly committed to parliamentary democracy. The ill-advised *coup d'état* merely drove Ebert further to the right into the arms of the forces of reaction. It finally extinguished what admittedly slim chance still remained of achieving a measure of socialism before the constituent assembly met. The long-term consequences were even more serious. Communist

[4] They polled 5,046,800 votes to the Majority Socialists' 6,104,400 at the general election of 1920.

support of insurrectionary tactics cut the party off from the main stream of the working-class movement, and kept it divided at a time when proletarian solidarity was essential for the future of democracy in Germany. When the left Independents joined them in 1920 it looked as if the Communists might at last become a mass party and adopt more realistic tactics. Once again they missed the chance when they sided with the Mansfeld miners in March 1921. Party membership fell sharply (though it recovered substantially in 1922) and the division in the working-class movement deepened still further, fatally weakening German democracy in the long run.

11

The Weimar Republic: The Critical Years 1919–1924

On 19 January 1919 the German people went to the polls to elect a constituent assembly. All the non-socialist parties reconstituted themselves in time for the elections. They appeared under new names but with much the same personnel and general objectives as before. The Centre temporarily changed its name to the Christian Peoples' Party but soon reverted to the old name and remained the party of political Catholicism. Under the leadership of Erzberger and Wirth, middle-class democrats who had wrested control of the parliamentary party from South-German aristocrats during the war, the Centre adjusted fairly easily to a new order of things. Unfortunately, attempts to create a united liberal party failed, and the old schism persisted into the Weimar period. Left-wing liberals, greatly strengthened by the accession of many intellectuals disillusioned with monarchy, formed the German Democratic Party. Of all the non-socialist parties this was the one most sincerely committed to democratic ideals, which it combined with a deep sense of patriotism. On the right wing the National Liberals continued as the German Peoples' Party, or Populists, a somewhat misleading nomenclature for the party of the wealthy industrial middle class, nationalist-minded, devoted to private enterprise and luke-warm towards the republic. Conservatives naturally found adjustment most painful in a world which had pulled up all the dynastic signposts. To meet the challenge, Free Conservatives and German Conservatives ended their forty-year-old division and formed the German National People's Party. The party was controlled, as always, by a hard core of landowners with some help from heavy industry. But it was much more broadly based than the pre-war Conservatives, having a considerable following in the middle class until 1930. As a party the German Nationalists paid lip-service to the republic, but many members made little secret of their deep monarchist sympathies.

Contrary to widespread expectations, the Socialists failed to secure an absolute majority; there had been some reaction against socialism on account of Spartacus Week, and women, voting for the first time, showed an inclination to support the parties of the *status quo*. Even so, the Socialists secured 187 seats, of which 165 were won by Majority Socialists and only twenty-two by Independents, a testimony to the power and efficiency of the Majority Socialist electoral machine, which unfairly depicted the Independents as fellow-travelling Communists. The Centre won ninety-one seats, the Democrats seventy-five, the German Nationalists forty-four and the Populists nineteen.[1] The central council of workers' and soldiers' councils handed over its powers to the assembly without demur. On 10 February 1919 Ebert was elected first president of the republic by 277 votes to fifty-one. He immediately asked the Majority Socialists, as the largest party in the assembly, to form a government. Having no over-all majority, the Socialists needed allies and found them in the Centre and Democratic parties. The new government was headed by Chancellor Scheidemann and consisted of six Socialists, three Centrists and three Democrats. This was the famous Weimar Coalition, so called because the assembly met in the new theatre at Weimar, conditions in Berlin being too unsettled to risk meeting in that city.

The assembly turned at once to the task of drafting a new constitution. In November 1918 Hugo Preuss, a left-wing liberal and well-known professor of law, had been appointed secretary of state by Ebert and asked to prepare a draft constitution. Preuss set out to combine democracy and parliamentary government with a high degree of centralisation, for left-wing liberals had always held the unitary state in high esteem. He was also convinced that without a strong central authority the unity of the *Reich* would be endangered in the troubled days that lay ahead. He proposed the dismemberment of Prussia – a state which left-wing liberals had always suspected as a bastion of particularism – and the complete reorganisation of Germany into twelve roughly equal administrative units (fourteen with German Austria and Bohemia-Moravia). These drastic proposals aroused fierce opposition, especially in Bavaria, Württemberg and Baden. In the end a revised version of the Preuss draft was adopted in the assembly by 262 votes to seventy-five.

What emerged from the debates was a compromise between the full-blooded unitary state favoured by Preuss, and the old Bismarckian structure, which recognised the existence of individual states. The unitary principle was implicit in the first clause of the new constitution: 'The German *Reich* is a republic. Political authority is derived from the people.' Sovereignty was no longer dispersed among twenty-five states as in 1871, but concentrated in one body, the constituent assembly, elected by the whole people. Incidentally, the retention of the word *Reich* was deliberate; Preuss, a deeply patriotic German, as most Democrats were, declared in the assembly that 'the tradition of centuries, the entire yearning of a divided German people for national unity are bound up with the name

[1]The Majority Socialists polled 11,509,100 votes; the Independents 2,317,300; the Centre, 5,980,200; the Democrats 5,641,800; and the Populists, 1,345,600.

Reich and we would wound the feeling of wide circles without reason and to no purpose if we gave up this designation of an older Germany'. The special relationship between Prussia and the *Reich* embedded in the 1871 constitution came to an end. In theory Prussia was only one of several *Länder*.[2] So too were Bavaria and Württemberg, both of which lost the special privileges accorded them in 1871. The supremacy of the *Reich* over the *Länder* was clearly established; the *Länder* had to have republican governments whether they liked it or not; the *Reich* reserved the right to enunciate fundamental principles for the guidance of *Länder* over a wide range of subjects; and the *Reich* assumed the power of direct taxation over all citizens, leaving only some items of indirect taxation to the *Länder*. Growth in the power of the central government was not peculiar to Germany; in this respect the Weimar constitution merely reflected an inevitable trend in the modern world and one which had been greatly accelerated by war-time experiences. Socialists welcomed increased state control as a signpost on the road to the socialist millennium. With their support the unitary concept prevailed in the assembly over the federalist concept supported by the Centre and the German Nationalists.

Germany did not become a completely unitary state in 1919. The reorganisation into administrative units advocated by Preuss did not take place. The states were renamed *Länder* but were more than administrative units inasmuch as they retained their old powers over education, police and the churches. The boundaries between the *Länder* remained virtually unchanged.[3] Prussia was not dismembered as Preuss had suggested. True, she suffered considerable territorial losses under the Versailles treaty; in the north North Schleswig returned to Denmark; in the west Eupen-Malmédy was ceded to Belgium; and in the east most of Posen and West Prussia went to form the new Polish state. But Prussia was still by far the largest *Land* in the republic, and she continued to play a major role in German affairs. In one respect Preuss's fears proved unfounded; Prussia became a model of republican propriety under a coalition government of Socialists and Centrists which remained in power from 1920 to 1932 under the able leadership of the Socialist Otto Braun; it was Bavarian not Prussian particularism which threatened the republic in its infancy.

At national level Germany was to be governed by a president, a Reichstag and a Reichsrat. The president was elected every seven years. He represented the *Reich* in foreign affairs; he appointed all officers, civil and military, including the chancellor; he was supreme commander of the armed forces; he alone convened and dissolved the Reichstag; and he could only be removed from office by a referendum supported by two-thirds of the Reichstag. Far-reaching powers were conferred upon the president

[2]Roughly equivalent to the English county.
[3]There were a few minor changes. The seven small Thuringian territories fused into a larger unit in 1920; later Coburg joined Bavaria, and Pyrmont and Waldeck were merged with Prussia.

under the notorious clause forty-eight; in an emergency he could suspend civil liberties and take whatever steps he deemed necessary to restore law and order. Emergency powers were deemed essential in 1919 to strengthen the executive in troubled times and were intended to be used only with the approval of the Reichstag. All decrees issued by the president, whether emergency or not, required the counter-signature of the chancellor or appropriate minister. Unfortunately the use of these special powers was never properly defined by the Reichstag, so that during the continuing emergency which existed in Germany after 1930 governments were able to derive their effective power from the president rather than the Reichstag, a contingency quite unforeseen by the authors of the constitution. In fact it was felt in 1919 that the president was a rather weak figure in danger of being completely overshadowed by the Reichstag. To adjust the balance and give the president a measure of independence, the assembly decided that he should be elected, not indirectly by the legislature as in France, but directly by the whole people as in the United States. This, it was hoped, would popularise the office of president and place him far above all party strife. Only later did it become apparent that a popularly elected president could overshadow the Reichstag and make the presidency the real centre of authority in a disturbed and disorientated Germany.

Legislative power was vested in the Reichstag, elected every four years by all men and women over the age of twenty. The electoral system was based on the principle of proportional representation, which ensured that political divisions in the country were faithfully reflected in the Reichstag – too faithfully, in fact, for proportional representation encouraged a multiplicity of parties and made the task of government more difficult than it need have been. In accordance with normal democratic procedures the chancellor and his ministers had to possess the confidence of the Reichstag and were obliged to resign when they forfeited it.

The Reichsrat was a much less important body, a kind of second chamber designed to give the *Länder* a voice in the making of national policy. It consisted of nominees from the various *Länder* governments, each *Land* being represented in accordance with population. No *Land* was allowed to have more than two-fifths of the seats, a device designed to prevent Prussian preponderance as in the old Bundesrat. In practice the powers of the Reichsrat were very limited; it possessed a modified power of veto over legislation, which could be removed by a two-thirds majority in the Reichstag. Alternatively the president could resolve a dispute between Reichstag and Reichsrat by holding a national referendum (*Volksentscheid*). This device, borrowed from Switzerland, proved a failure. Four referendums in all were held in the lifetime of the republic; they proved expensive and indecisive, and unnecessarily exacerbated political passions.

The Bismarckian constitution contained no declaration of basic rights, an omission which was repaired in 1919. In his opening address to the constituent assembly Ebert remarked that the Revolution of 9 November would continue where the Revolution of 18 March 1848 had left off. In a special section of the constitution the German people were guaranteed personal liberty, equality before the law, freedom of movement, expression and conscience and the right of association. But where the Paulskirche had been content to enunciate the rights of the individual against the community, the Weimar assembly restored a proper balance by emphasising the duty of the individual to the community and by declaring that citizens must use their intellectual and physical powers in the interests of the community.

Trade-unionists were well represented in the assembly,[4] which was one reason why the constitution made special reference to economic affairs. Labour was placed under the protection of the *Reich*, all Germans were guaranteed the right to work, employees were promised equal rights with employers in determining working conditions and provision was made for taking private property, where appropriate, into public ownership.

Little use was made of the latter provision. A socialisation committee was set up in November 1918 under the chairmanship of Kautsky, the Socialist theoretician and historian. The commission recommended the nationalisation of coal, land and power but was obstructed by the civil service and given scant encouragement by the Scheidemann government. True, the coal industry was reorganised in March 1919 into cartels under a *Reichskohlenverband* which supervised the organisation, sale and consumption of coal. Above it was a *Reichskohlenrat* representing mine-owning *Länder*, miners, consumers and coal-merchants under the supreme control of the ministry of economic affairs. This body guided the industry, fixed prices and regulated exports in the national interest. A similar reorganisation took place in the potash industry. This was not socialism but compulsory cartelisation, part of a continuous process of rationalisation which strengthened capitalism by making it more efficient. Not that most Socialists were unduly perturbed by their failure to grasp the levers of economic power. On the contrary, they believed that socialisation could only be effective when industry was healthy and flourishing; at a time of economic dislocation and chronic raw-material shortages it seemed madness to embark upon risky experiments which might retard Germany's recovery. Socialisation would solve no economic problems and might well displease the victorious powers, who would either veto it or earmark socialised enterprises for reparations. In July 1919 the Scheidemann government opted in effect for the private enterprise system, when the cabinet rejected unanimously the proposals of the minister of economic affairs, Rudolf Wissel, for the extension into peace-time of the planned economy of the war years.

---

[4]Ninety-four of the 423 deputies belonged to trade unions.

The trade unions were ranged solidly behind the government in its oppo-sition to radical changes, for early in the Revolution trade unionists had made substantial gains which they did not intend to jeopardise by dubious 'socialist' experiments. Vested interests displayed a remarkable facility for adaptation in the Germany of 1918; Groener saved the army from socialism by coming to terms with Ebert; likewise the industrialists safeguarded their economic power by making concessions to the unions. In an important agreement, signed on 15 November 1918, both sides of industry declared that co-operation between capital and labour should form the basis of indus-trial relations in the future; the employers accepted collective bargaining without reservation, agreed to the eight-hour day and promised to allow the workers' councils to help regulate wages and working conditions at shop-floor level; the workers for their part promised to submit disputes to mixed tribunals for discussion before resorting to strike action. This agreement, which the government quickly endorsed, went a good way towards satisfy-ing genuine grievances on the shop floor while diverting attention from the more fundamental issue of the ownership of the means of production. In fact it did not prevent industrial strife in the early years of the republic; the con-flict between capital and labour deepened between 1919 and 1923; in 1923 the agreement of 1918 broke down completely when the employers repu-diated the eight-hour day; in December 1923 the government used its emer-gency powers to increase working hours. If industrial relations did improve after 1924, it was due much more to a general economic revival than to any sense of community between capital and labour.

Out of respect for the revolutionary mood of the working class in the spring of 1919, the Weimar assembly decided to give institutional form to the workers' councils which flourished in most factories. Under a law of 1920 works councils (*Betriebsräte*) were made mandatory in all factories employing over twenty workers and were intended to represent their 'social and economic interests'. At district level, economic councils of workers and employers were to be formed, and at the apex of the pyramid a national economic council (*Reichswirtschaftsrat*), composed of workers, employers and other interested groups, was to be established under the aegis of the ministry of economic affairs. The national council, a curious blend of Marx and Bismarck, was to advise the government on economic legislation and could submit its own draft bills to the Reichstag. Little came of the fine words. District economic councils were never formed; a provisional national council was set up but never became an economic parliament; and the works councils, though rather more successful, found their powers carefully circumscribed from the beginning, simply because trade union leaders had no wish to share effective power with them. Thirty years elapsed before the German Federal Republic revived these ideas in its Co-determination legislation.

In the summer of 1919 the Weimar assembly faced a moment of supreme crisis when the terms of the peace treaty were made known. The assembly had assumed that Germany would be treated leniently; whatever sins she had committed had surely been expiated by the destruction of Hohenzollern rule and the establishment of a fully democratic form of government. The moment of truth arrived on 7 May when the peace terms were handed to the German delegation. Germany was given only fourteen days (later extended to twenty-one) in which to make written representations to the victorious powers. A wave of indignation swept through the assembly. Speaker after speaker from right to left of the political spectrum denounced the peace terms. Chancellor Scheidemann accused the Entente of betraying its ideals: 'What hand would not wither which placed this chain upon itself and upon us?' he observed bitterly. At the end of the special session in the hall of Berlin University the members, regardless of party, stood and sang the *Deutschlandlied* together, a vivid testimony to the potency of national sentiment even in the hour of defeat. On 16 June a final text was handed to the German delegation with a peremptory order to sign within five days (later extended to seven). On 19 June the cabinet rejected the treaty by eight votes to six and resigned. Only entreaties from his colleagues kept Ebert at his desk. Rejection logically implied the resumption of hostilities. But when Hindenburg's opinion was asked, the old man declared that though he personally preferred honourable defeat to a shameful peace, nevertheless he had to admit that the outcome of further military operations was extremely doubtful; Germany could hold out in the east but not against the Entente in the west simultaneously. Groener fully agreed; if military operations were resumed he feared internal disorders – on 1 May a Rhineland republic was proclaimed in Mainz and Wiesbaden – and he foresaw the complete destruction of the *Reich* and the officer corps. Peace was the only way out, and as long as civilians bore the responsibility for it Groener did not mind too much.

The coalition parties were now deeply divided over the peace terms. The Democrats strongly opposed acceptance. The Majority Socialists and the Centre eventually agreed to sign on being assured that the army would remain loyal, and on condition that signature did not imply recognition of war-guilt or any obligation on Germany's part to surrender the ex-emperor and others for trial as war-criminals. A new government of Socialists and Centrists was formed under Chancellor Gustav Bauer, the former Socialist minister of labour. On 22 June, by 237 votes to 138, the assembly authorised the government to sign the treaty with the above-mentioned reservations. Unfortunately for the government, news had just arrived in Paris that the Germans had scuttled the fleet at Scapa Flow instead of surrendering it as required by the armistice, and that certain captured battle honours due to be returned to France had been deliberately burnt by Free Corps men in Berlin. The victorious powers were deeply incensed by this evidence of bad faith and insisted on unconditional acceptance of the treaty. Bauer faced a new crisis with many army officers threatening resignation if the government knuckled under. Once again Groener, speaking for the Supreme Command, made it clear to Ebert that there was no alternative to surrender. The assembly swallowed its pride, and one-and-a-half hours before the time limit expired Bauer informed the Entente that Germany would sign unconditionally. The foreign minister, the Socialist Hermann Müller, accompanied by the minister of justice, Johannes Bell of the Centre, travelled to Versailles and signed the treaty on 28 June in the historic Hall of Mirrors, where William I had been pro-claimed German emperor forty-seven years earlier.

The territorial provisions of the Treaty of Versailles bore heavily on Germany. In the west Alsace-Lorraine was restored to France. To allay French fears of Germany, the left bank of the Rhine and a fifty kilometre strip on the right bank were permanently demilitarised, and an allied army of occupation stationed in the Rhineland; this army was to be progressively reduced every five years, provided Germany fulfilled her treaty obliga-tions, and finally withdrawn in 1935. As compensation for the mines deliberately destroyed by the retreating Germans, France was allowed to exploit the coal mines and plant of the Saar basin. The Saarland was separated from Germany and placed under a League of Nations commis-sion for fifteen years, when the national future of the area would be determined by plebiscite. There were some frontier adjustments in favour of Belgium, and in Schleswig a plebiscite resulted in the return of the northern districts to Denmark. In the east Germany suffered heavy losses. Most of Posen and West Prussia and parts of Pomerania were incorporated in the new Polish state. As a result of these changes one-and-a-half million Germans came under Polish rule and East Prussia was separated from the rest of Germany by the Polish Corridor. Danzig, an indisputably German city, became a Free State under a League-of-Nations High Commissioner. The town and environs of Memel, another indisputably German territory, were placed under a French High Commissioner and then seized by the Lithuanians in 1923. Originally the whole of the rich industrial area of Upper Silesia was assigned to Poland. Then, in response to German representations, the Entente relented and ordered a plebiscite which resulted in sixty per cent of the inhabitants choosing to stay in Germany. The Poles were reluctant to see Silesia returned to Germany and staged an uprising. Finally, in 1922, the League of Nations decided on partition, which left Poland with much of Silesia's industrial potential. Austria was forbidden to unite with Germany despite the express wish of the Austrian constituent assembly for an *Anschluss*. Germany lost all her colonial pos-sessions, which became mandated territories under the League of Nations and were in practice allocated to the victorious powers. Altogether Ger-many lost some 25,000 square miles of territory, approximately six-and-a-

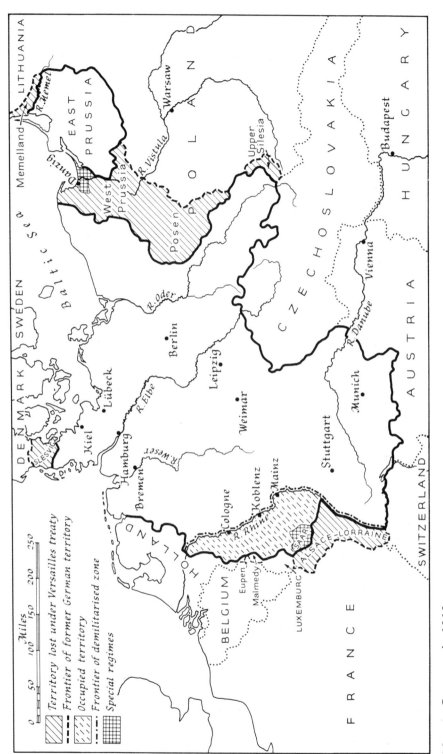

Map 3: Germany in 1919

Miles
0 50 100 150 200 250

Territory lost under Versailles treaty
Frontier of former German territory
Occupied territory
Frontier of demilitarised zone
Special regimes

LITHUANIA
Memelland
R.Memel
EAST PRUSSIA
Danzig
West Prussia
Posen
Warsaw
R.Vistula
Upper Silesia
P O L A N D
Baltic Sea
SWEDEN
DENMARK
SLESVIG
Kiel
Lübeck
Hamburg
Bremen
R.Elbe
R.Oder
Berlin
Leipzig
Weimar
R.Weser
HOLLAND
BELGIUM
Eupen
Malmedy
LUXEMBURG
Cologne
Koblenz
R.Rhine
Mainz
SAAR
ALSACE-LORRAINE
FRANCE
SWITZERLAND
Stuttgart
Munich
AUSTRIA
R.Danube
Vienna
C Z E C H O S L O V A K I A
H U N G A R Y
Budapest

half million subjects, of whom half were German-speaking, and considerable proportions of her most valuable raw materials.[5]

The disarmament clauses were understandably severe. Germany was required to surrender or destroy all heavy weapons and to dismantle all fortifications in the Rhineland and on Heligoland. The general staff was dissolved and conscription forbidden. Germany was allowed only a small professional army of 100,000 men to preserve order at home, and was forbidden to manufacture tanks, gas, aircraft for military purposes and submarines. The navy was drastically reduced to 15,000 men, six battleships and a few smaller craft.

Finally, Germany was required to pay an unspecified sum in reparations to the victorious powers. Under the armistice agreement Germany promised to pay compensation for damage caused to allied civilians and their property. Feeling against Germany was running high in Britain and France in the winter of 1918–19, and there was a move afoot to make the Germans pay the total costs of the war. President Wilson objected strongly and finally a compromise was arrived at. Britain and France waived all claims to total war costs, and in return the United States agreed to the so-called 'War-Guilt clause', clause 231, which required Germany to admit responsibility for all loss and damage sustained by the allies 'as a consequence of the war imposed on them by the aggression of Germany and her allies'. But clause 232 went on to admit that Germany was not capable of paying the total costs of the war and would only be expected to pay compensation for war damage. Moral indignation overflowed in other clauses which accused the ex-emperor William of violating international morality, and called on Germany to hand over several hundred individuals for trial as war criminals.

Severe as the treaty of Versailles seemed to many Germans, it should be remembered that Germany might easily have fared much worse. If Clemenceau had had his way, instead of being restrained by Britain and America, the Rhineland would have become an independent state, the Saarland would have been annexed to France and Danzig would have become an integral part of Poland. The Peace Conference is often accused of inconsistency in applying the principle of self-determination to the ex-enemy states; what is often overlooked is the difficulty which faced the peace-makers in trying to combine the facts of history and geography and the traditional demands of power politics with the claims of nationality; the result, for the most part, was a rather uneasy compromise. In this respect Germany fared quite well compared with Austria-Hungary. Alsace-Lorraine would not have opted for Germany even if a plebiscite had been held. In Schleswig the loss of the Danish-speaking area north of Flensburg was a foregone conclusion in view of past history; Germany did at least

[5]She lost seventy-five per cent of her iron-ore, sixty-eight per cent of her zinc ore and twenty-six per cent of her coal.

retain Zone II, the area between Flensburg and the Schlei estuary. Even in the east, where most of the changes occurred without plebiscite, exceptions were made in disputed areas. Thus plebiscites were held in Silesia, around Allenstein in East Prussia and around Marienburg and Marienwerder in West Prussia; and when the inhabitants of Allenstein and Marienwerder voted overwhelmingly for Germany, their wishes were respected. True, the Memelland was lost to Germany, but only because the allies had insufficient forces in the area to compel the Lithuanians to restore it and allow it to become a free city as originally planned.

However, the Germans as a nation were not inclined to count their blessings in 1919. Though they accepted as inevitable the loss of Alsace-Lorraine, they were angered by the changes in the east. To them the resurrection of Poland was no long overdue act of justice to an oppressed people, but a deliberate attempt to weaken Germany by separating historic East Prussia from the rest of the *Reich*. The loss of the colonies also rankled because of the lofty pretence that this was a punishment for Germany's bad record as a colonial administrator instead of – what it really was – a penalty for losing the war. Most of all they resented the moral stigma of sole war-guilt which they did not feel, and which historical research soon showed to be an untenable imputation. Reparations were a further source of resentment. Finally, the fact that the treaty was not negotiated but dictated to Germany and signed in humiliating circumstances made it certain that the German people would accept no moral responsibility for its fulfilment. To the discerning it was clear from the beginning that the Versailles settlement would last only as long as the victorious powers were in a position to enforce it on a bitterly resentful people.

The signature of the peace treaty cast a long shadow over the political life of the 1920s. Before the government signed the treaty it took the precaution of asking its chief opponents, the German Nationalists, the Populists and the Democrats, to declare that those who had voted for signature were not lacking in patriotism. The Democrats and Populists readily agreed. The German Nationalists were more guarded and only agreed reluctantly because they could see no alternative to unconditional surrender. What the German Nationalists could not do in the months that followed was bring themselves to accept the fact of Germany's military defeat. Deep down they felt the need for a different explanation of Germany's plight which would preserve the army from the stigma of defeat. They found what they were looking for in the *Dolchstosslegende*. The Weimar assembly set up a commission to investigate the causes of Germany's defeat. In November 1919 Hindenburg was called as a witness. His visit to Berlin was the occasion for nationalist demonstrations, and at the end of his statement to the commission he added the fateful words: 'An English general has said with justice: the German army was stabbed in the back. No blame is to be attached to the sound core of the army. Its performances call like that of the officer corps for an equal admiration. It is perfectly plain on whom the blame rests.' The stab-in-the-back myth had been born and was accepted without question on the right wing; the army could be exonerated from all blame for Germany's defeat; those responsible were the 'November traitors', the coalition parties – primarily the Socialists – who had sabotaged the war effort by their agitation for a peace of reconciliation, had engineered the revolution and had signed the shameful Versailles 'dictate'. From then onwards the right wing, led by the German Nationalists, lost no opportunity of denigrating prominent republican politicians – both Erzberger and Ebert were the object of vicious personal attacks – and of pouring abuse on democratic institutions. The coalition parties made only feeble attempts to defend themselves against this pernicious propaganda. The tragic outcome was that precisely when the young republic needed maximum support to establish itself in the minds and hearts of the people, influential sections of the community, anti-democratic by instinct and tradition, were confirmed in their opinions by the open hostility on the right wing towards the republic as an institution.

Right-wing resentment of the republic was the cause of an abortive *coup d'état*, the Kapp *Putsch*, in the spring of 1920. This was the work of disgruntled army officers and Free Corps men, angered by the progressive reduction of the armed forces to 100,000 men in accordance with the Versailles treaty. A group of officers led by Freiherr von Lüttwitz, commanding general in Berlin, and Wolfgang Kapp, one of the founders of the extreme right-wing *Vaterlandspartei* in 1917, plotted to overthrow the government and hold new elections. Their plot came to a head when the Inter-Allied Military Control Commission insisted on the disbandment of two marine brigades of Free Corps men recently returned from the Baltic. One of the brigades, stationed at Döberitz outside Berlin, was led by the famous adventurer Captain Ehrhardt. When Lüttwitz refused to disband the Ehrhardt Brigade and tried to dictate terms to the government, his arrest was ordered. Whereupon Lüttwitz's men and the Ehrhardt Brigade marched into Berlin on 13 March 1920, greeted at the Brandenburg Gate by a crowd of admirers including General Ludendorff.

The Kapp *Putsch*, amateurish in design and execution, had little hope of ultimate success. What was memorable about it was the ambiguous attitude taken by the army chiefs. The generals, who had never failed to help Ebert against Communism, would not move against Lüttwitz. To his credit General Reinhardt, commander of the *Reichswehr*, was ready to use force immediately. But General von Seeckt, head of the *Truppenamt*, spoke for most generals when he bluntly informed Ebert that 'troops do not fire on troops . . .; when *Reichswehr* fires on *Reichswehr* all comradeship within the officer corps has vanished.' Seeckt sympathised with the putschists; only natural caution restrained him from an open declaration of support. Ebert was bitterly disappointed by this disloyalty. Instead of challenging Seeckt and insisting on military action, as they had every right to do, Ebert and his colleagues decided that discretion was the better part of valour and withdrew from Berlin to Dresden. Meanwhile a new government headed by Kapp and Lüttwitz was installed in Berlin. From the start it had little support in the city and even less in the rest of Germany. Some army units in East Prussia, a notorious bastion of reactionary militarism, supported Kapp, but elsewhere officers remained loyal to the Bauer government. Before the government left Berlin the Socialist members called for a general strike. The trade-unionists, unlike many generals, did not let the government down. The strike was completely effective; the life of the great city was paralysed and all industrial activity ceased. Nor would the civil servants in Prussia accept orders from Kapp; the *Reichsbank* refused to recognise his signature, thus depriving the rebels of financial support. After four days Kapp and Lüttwitz fled from Berlin and the *Putsch* collapsed completely.

Supporters of the republic were greatly alarmed by these unwelcome signs of right-wing extremism barely eighteen months after the November Revolution. Trade-unionists who had played a key role in overthrowing Kapp called for strong measures against counter-revolution. Noske, a favourite target of left-wing critics, was forced to resign in the aftermath of the *Putsch*, and some politically unreliable civil servants were dismissed. However, nothing came of the proposal made by the trade-union leader Karl Legien for an all-Socialist government for the defence of the republic. In the end another coalition government emerged, this one headed by Hermann Müller. Despite widespread criticism on the left of the generals' behaviour during the *Putsch*, little was done to discipline recalcitrant officers, because the government needed the support of the army to suppress fresh disorders. In the Ruhr the Communists led an uprising in mid-March 1920 in protest against the Kapp *Putsch*, and a Red Army, 50,000 strong, soon controlled the whole region. When the Communists refused to disband the army, Müller ordered the *Reichswehr* in, supported by Free Corps elements, to restore order. This the army did with alacrity and not a little brutality. Further disturbances in Saxony and Thuringia in April were also ruthlessly suppressed. A grateful government repaid its debt by drawing a veil over the Kapp affair. Even the conspirators themselves got off fairly lightly. Kapp died in prison while awaiting trial, Traugott von Jagow, Kapp's minister of the interior, was sentenced to five years' imprisonment, of which he served three, Lüttwitz was retired from the army and Seeckt successfully prevented the arrest of Ehrhardt.

The leniency which the authorities habitually showed towards declared enemies of the republic seems to confirm the pessimistic diagnosis of left-wing Socialists such as Crispien, the Independent Socialist leader, who roundly declared at his party conference that 'a year after November 1918, when the powers of the past were overthrown, the old forces are again the power of the present'. Foreign observers were generally agreed that German society had come through the dislocation of war and revolution virtually unchanged. The power of the landowners and industrialists was unbroken. The old apparatus of the state survived the revolution intact; high officials and judges, who looked back nostalgically to the golden days of the Empire, continued in office. The educational system was controlled from top to bottom by officials lukewarm in their commitment to democracy – it is significant that no attempt was ever made to infuse into school curricula a spirit more in keeping with the demands of a new age. The universities, far from generating enthusiasm for democratic ideals, remained ultra-conservative strongholds in the Weimar period. Certainly it would be an over-simplification of a complex historical situation to say that the republic was automatically doomed to destruction because of the entrenched power of vested interests in 1920. After all, one of the encouraging things about the Kapp *Putsch* was the loyalty of most officers and civil servants to the Bauer government. At the same time it would be unrealistic to ignore the plain fact that the mental attitudes of the Wilhelmian period lingered on under a thin democratic veneer, and that unless a real effort could be made to inculcate a democratic spirit in the institutions of the republic, the Weimar system seemed doomed to founder in the first serious storm.

One institution which successfully resisted attempts at democratisation was the German army. The way in which the new *Reichswehr* became 'a state within a state', in Scheidemann's phrase, is one of the most fascinating themes in the history of these years and one of great political significance in view of events in the early 1930s.

The *Reichswehr* owed its privileged position in part to the efforts of Hans von Seeckt, a gifted Prussian officer who was appointed commander of the *Reichswehr* in March 1920 despite his lukewarm feelings for the republic. Seeckt was one of the few really outstanding personalities in the Weimar period. He had one object in life; the restoration of German military power, and this end he pursued for the next six years with great tenacity, shrewdness and sophistication. As a British ambassador noted with some surprise, he 'had a broader mind than is expected in so tight a uniform, a wider outlook than seems appropriate to so precise, so correct, so neat an exterior.' Within the limits imposed by the treaty, he set out to create a superb fighting machine which would one day restore Germany to her former greatness. It was not so much this ambition as Seeckt's elevated view of the army's place in society which constituted the real threat to democracy. He believed that the *Reichswehr* owed loyalty not to the transitory republic, of which he had a low opinion, but to the imperishable *Reich*. The army was the very foundation stone of the *Reich* without which it could not exist, and it was in no way subordinate to the state machine. It represented the 'national interest' in its purest form, and for this reason, whilst forbidding his officers to meddle in politics in an individual capacity, Seeckt reserved the right of the *Reichswehr* as a corporate body to intervene in affairs of state whenever the commander thought it necessary. Despite these anti-democratic views and his own thinly veiled contempt for republican politicians, Seeckt had little difficulty in handling successive governments. Under the constitution he was strictly accountable to the *Reichswehr* minister, in practice Seeckt concentrated direction of policy and training as well as the power of command in his own hands, and was in fact left free to circumvent the treaty of Versailles as he saw fit.

Seeckt succeeded in transforming the *Reichswehr* into a formidable fighting force, the nucleus of the armies which swept through France and the Low Countries in the summer of 1940. The brain of a modern army, the general staff, had survived under the guise of a *Truppenamt*, from which all civilians were rigidly excluded. Seeckt continued to train new staff officers despite the vigilance of the Control Commission. The limitation on size was overcome partly by placing the emphasis in training on speed and mobility, and partly through a system of short-term enlistments which trained cadres for the large army of the future. Recruits were most carefully chosen; only thoroughly reliable 'national elements' were selected, but not political adventurers such as Ehrhardt, who were unlikely to make perfectly disciplined soldiers. Sports clubs and paramilitary formations such as *Stahlhelm* helped to provide a plentiful supply of reliable recruits by inculcating a military spirit in German youth with Seeckt's full approval.

Soldiers are of little use without guns, and to ensure a plentiful supply of the latest weapons when the time came to expand the *Reichswehr*, Seeckt made arrangements with German industry. Krupp of Essen and other industrialists co-operated enthusiastically in this exercise. Although one should not exaggerate the extent of secret re-armament, certainly prototypes of heavy armaments were manufactured abroad by anonymous limited companies with foreign subsidiaries, aeroplane and chemical factories were set up in Russia, submarines were produced in Spain, tanks and field guns in Sweden, and other weapons in Holland, Denmark and Switzerland. So successfully were the disarmament clauses of the treaty evaded in these and in other ways, that Brigadier-General Morgan, writing in 1924, declared that it would take Germany only twelve months to attain her maximum production of 1918 in guns and munitions, once controls were removed.

One of the most intriguing aspects of Germany's secret rearmament was the co-operation between the *Reichswehr* and the Red Army. This was part of a much broader canvas. It soon occurred to influential groups in Germany and Russia that their two countries had something in common as outcasts in a hostile world. The Communists, fearful of a great anti-socialist crusade against Russia, perceived the advantage of weakening their capitalist enemies by playing off Germany against Britain and France.

On the German side pressure for agreement came from various quarters; some industrialists wanted commercial agreements to secure new markets in the east; some foreign-office officials hoped to strengthen Germany's diplomatic position by restoring 'the old line to St. Petersburg'; and Seeckt and his colleagues were primarily interested in a military agreement to facilitate secret rearmament, although from time to time Seeckt urged the government to enter into close economic and political agreements as well. In 1920 Seeckt formed a special department, *Sondergruppe R* (Special Group Russia) to pave the way for co-operation with Russia. From 1921 the *Reichswehr* arranged technological assistance to help Russia build an arms industry, and in return Russia trained German pilots and tank crews and provided sites for Krupp's factories near Moscow. Leading members of the government knew of these contacts and approved of them, though their knowledge was scanty because Seeckt successfully resisted civilian interference in this field.

Clearly the *Reichswehr* could not have attained such a high degree of autonomy without the tacit approval of the Reichstag. From time to time left-wing politicians and organisations questioned the large budgetary requirements of the army, or raised a corner of the veil of secrecy drawn over secret rearmament. On these occasions there were howls of protest from the right wing, and the revelations were effectively buried in the appropriate Reichstag committee. The truth was that most deputies on the right and centre of the Reichstag regarded evasion of the disarmament clauses as a perfectly legitimate exercise; as long as the victorious powers remained armed, it was sheer hypocrisy to refuse Germany adequate armaments on the pretext that this was a step towards general disarmament – or so it seemed to most Germans anxious to see their country strong again. There was some sympathy for these views outside Germany. Major-General Temperley, British military expert at Geneva in 1932, readily excused secret rearmament: 'one wondered', he remarked, 'to what extent other high-spirited nations in similar circumstances would have refrained from doing their utmost to circumvent a treaty which had been forced on them at the point of the bayonet.' Successive governments, as indicated earlier, adopted the same attitude. Otto Gessler, the Democrat who succeeded Noske as minister of war in 1920, although not in agreement with Seeckt on every issue, loyally shielded him from civilian critics. So powerful did Seeckt become, that he could even deny President Ebert, supreme commander of the *Reichswehr* under the constitution, the right to review his own soldiers. When Hindenburg became president the relationship between the army and the head of state naturally improved. In 1926 Seeckt, for whom the president had no great liking, was forced to resign over a trivial incident which aroused much indignation in republican circles.[6] This was in a sense a victory for the forces of democracy over a

---

[6] He permitted a grandson of the ex-emperor to take part in army manoeuvres in South Germany.

masterful army commander. But this did not lead to any fundamental change in the relationship between army and Reichstag, so that when democratic institutions faltered in the early 1930s, the army emerged as an influential centre of power in a fluid political situation.

A particularly disquieting feature of the post-war scene was the continuance in being of para-military formations, despite a law in 1920 requiring all citizens to surrender fire-arms. A few of these formations were left-wing in character, such as the *Roter Frontkämpferbund*, founded in 1925, and the republican *Reichsbanner Schwarz-Rot-Gold*, founded in 1924. But the real danger came from right-wing organisations, which at one time in 1920 had a total of 300,000 men under arms. When the government dispensed with the services of the Free Corps, many of the disorientated ex-soldiers, quite incapable of adjusting to civilian life, joined illegal organisations in various parts of Germany but especially in Bavaria, the home of extremist parties and a hotbed of neo-separatism in the early 1920s. These para-military formations, whether indigenous or imported, had certain characteristics in common; they were hostile to the republic, ultra-nationalist and anti-semitic in outlook, tinged with an incoherent radicalism and addicted to violence.

The views of the war-veterans and students in these illegal bands were confirmed – and to some extent shaped – by contemporary political writers. The Weimar Republic produced a diversity and wealth of cultural experience and intellectual speculation, much of it broadly democratic in inspiration. Many writers such as Lehmann, Forster and Unruh readily condemned the atavistic nationalism and militarism of the old days and upheld the traditional liberal values of the Greco-Roman-Christian heritage. But anti-democratic and authoritarian trends were also present, lurking in the intellectual undergrowth. Many young people were attracted by a brand of 'revolutionary conservatism', a many-sided ideology which owed something to Oswald Spengler's *Der Untergang des Abendlandes* (a book which won its author international fame), and found its fullest expression in the writings of the circle led by Ernst Jünger and Möller van den Bruck. These writers rejected what they called 'the technocratic materialistic civilisation of the west', much as the Romantics a century before had rejected the rational Enlightenment. Contemptuous of democratic values, they exalted the power of the irrational and subconscious in place of the rationality of the republican philosophy. Early nineteenth-century Romantics were restrained by religious belief from pursuing their ideas to a logical conclusion. Not so the young conservative revolutionaries of the 1920s. Life had no meaning for them outside a biological struggle for existence; conflict and war was the very essence of life, and history showed that in this struggle young nations survived and old ones went down to destruction. Once the youth of Germany grasped this truth they would sweep the politicians aside in a great 'national revolution' and lead

Germany to the pinnacle of greatness. The new Germany, as described in van den Bruck's book, *Das dritte Reich*, would save the people from Marxism and from plutocratic capitalism. It would be a 'socialist' Germany where the common good superseded the private profit motive. It would be a national Germany based on the authoritarian concept of the corporate state where all citizens believed in the old Prussian virtues of discipline, obedience and service to the state; the Roman legionary, who died at his post while volcanic ash rained down at Pompeii, was held up as a model of martial virtue to be emulated by all young men. Curiously enough, some of these young writers were attracted by Communism, partly because it rejected liberal-capitalist values, and partly because its use of violence commended it to men who at times took a perverse pride in German barbarism. The attempts made by right-wing extremists and Communists in the 1920s to find a basis for co-operation in their common hostility to western capitalism – National Bolshevism as it was called – did not succeed, but the story is a fascinating one in the light of later Russo-German co-operation.

Authoritarian ideologies were not peculiar to post-war Germany, even if they took root here more easily than elsewhere for historical, political and social reasons. They must be seen as part of a much wider wave of disillusionment among young people in all lands, a revulsion against the old order which had died in 1914. One should not overstress the importance of 'revolutionary conservatism' in the genesis of National Socialism; the young people attracted by these ideas played only an intermittent part in politics, and in fact neither Jünger nor van den Bruck approved of Hitler's movement. On the other hand, an ideology which was in essence a protest against state and society could not fail to pave the way for more extreme movements, inasmuch as it eroded respect for law and order and condoned the use of violence. The brutalisation of political life after the war was a reflection of this. Between 1919 and 1922 there were 376 political murders in Germany, 356 of them attributed to right-wing extremists, often members of para-military formations. Prominent politicians fell beneath the bullets of assassins, Erzberger in August 1921 and Rathenau in June 1922, both victims of *Organisation Consul*, led by Ehrhardt of Kapp *Putsch* fame. The slaying of the gifted patriot Rathenau aroused great anger in republican circles. The Reichstag passed a law for the protection of the republic which only the German Nationalists opposed; a special court was set up at Leipzig to handle anti-republican crimes, and several para-military bands, including *Stahlhelm*, were dissolved. As so often happened when the political crime was committed by men of the right, those accused of complicity in the Rathenau murder were dealt with leniently by the courts. One of them, Ernst von Salomon, later wrote a best-selling novel, *Die Geächteten* (the outlaws), a document of great social interest exposing the mental processes of these self-styled 'executioners'.

The republic was burdened with intractable economic problems arising out of the war. By 1919 Germany's internal finances were in a parlous state, largely because she had financed her war effort through short-term loans and by inflating the currency in the firm expectation that her enemies would pay the war costs. Defeat left her saddled with a huge internal debt of 144,000 million marks and with a currency which had lost over one-third of its pre-war value. The task of recovery was complicated by other factors. Germany was running a trade deficit; she had little hope of attracting foreign investment when capital was in short supply; her industrial potential was severely crippled by the loss of the Saarland and Upper Silesia, and her pre-war trading pattern was shattered. Faced with the problem of monetary inflation and a falling mark successive governments shied away from the drastic remedies of currency stabilisation and balanced budgets for several reasons. At a time of political instability governments hesitated to increase direct taxation or restrict credit too much and risk alienating support for the young republic. And as the mark fell in value, Germany's export trade increased and unemployment fell sharply, benefiting the working class. Right–centre governments between 1920 and 1923 were also sensitive to the advice of industrialists who derived benefit from continued inflation.[7] The state benefited, too, for inflation reduced the volume of internal debt. Finally, it seemed inadvisable to try to put Germany's economic house in order as long as the dark cloud of reparations hung over her; the stronger she became the more she was likely to have to pay; conversely, the weaker she was the more leniently she might be treated.

The allied powers failed to agree on a total reparations figure at the Paris Peace Conference. Instead they asked Germany to submit proposals for a settlement within four months of the end of the Conference, failing which a Reparations Commission would decide the amount of Germany's liability by May 1921. As the allied powers were anxious to reach agreement as quickly as possible, they held several summit conferences on reparations and invited Germany to attend some of them. Germany naturally tried to drive as hard a bargain as she could. The climax came at the London Conference in March 1921, when Germany proposed a drastic scaling-down of allied proposals, making the offer dependent upon the evacuation of the Rhineland and the retention of Upper Silesia. It was too early for blackmail. The allies were thoroughly annoyed and showed their teeth. They sent an ultimatum to Germany threatening to occupy three Ruhr towns unless she accepted the allied figures proposed in January 1921 or made acceptable counter-proposals. When Germany refused, the towns were occupied, an act of doubtful legality for which the allies tried to find *ex-post-facto* justification in the announcement by the Reparations

[7]The Socialists did not join the Fehrenbach government (June 1920–May 1921) or the Cuno government (November 1922–August 1923).

Commission that Germany had not completed the interim payment of £1,000 million required of her pending agreement on her total liability. In April 1921 the Reparations Commission presented the long-awaited report, which recommended a total liability of £6,600 million (132 billion marks) payable in annual instalments of £100 million (two billion marks) together with annual payments equivalent in value to one-quarter of all German exports. The allies approved the figures and sent another ultimatum to Germany giving her six days in which to accept. The Fehrenbach government resigned in protest, causing a political crisis in Berlin. There was no alternative to acceptance, any more than in 1919. Joseph Wirth, a left-wing Centrist and former finance minister, formed a Weimar coalition government (Centre, Democrats, Socialists) and, with authorisation from the Reichstag, signified Germany's acceptance of the ultimatum twenty hours before its expiration. Thus began the policy of fulfilment usually associated with Stresemann. The new policy did not imply acceptance of any moral obligation to make restitution. On the contrary, Wirth and his minister of reconstruction, Walther Rathenau, calculated that only by attempting to fulfil the terms could their impossibility be demonstrated and a more reasonable figure obtained later.

The added burden of reparations increased the difficulties facing Germany. The efforts of the Wirth government to secure the necessary foreign exchange depressed the mark still further. In November 1921 a particularly sharp fall occurred when Germany tried to repay a £50-million loan with which she had financed the first instalment of reparations. By the end of 1921 it was clear that Germany would soon be in default. In January 1922 the Reparations Commission granted her a moratorium on the January and February payments, while Germany's creditors met at Cannes to discuss the situation. Britain and France had not seen eye to eye over reparations for some time. Britain, suffering from a post-war depression, was anxious to restore Germany, her best pre-war customer, to health as quickly as possible and consequently favoured lenient treatment. The differences with France became acute when Poincaré, the embodiment of French fears and suspicion of Germany, came to power in January 1922. He pressed French claims to the utmost, insisting rigidly on the letter of the law; Germany had promised to pay, Germany could pay but did not want to and must, therefore, be made to pay. Clumsy German diplomacy played into his hands. In the midst of the European Economic Conference at Genoa in April 1922 the allies were startled by the news that Russia and Germany, who were both participating in the conference, had signed the treaty of Rapallo on Easter Sunday. Diplomatic relations between the two countries were re-established, Russia waived all claim to reparations from Germany, and in return Germany waived all claims to compensation for expropriated German property. On the Russian side this was a diplomatic manoeuvre to keep the capitalist powers divided; for Germany it was intended to be the beginning of an independent foreign policy. In practice it was little more than a futile act of defiance which confirmed French suspicion of Germany without obtaining for the latter the advantages of alliance with a strong power. When Germany requested further moratoria in July and August 1922, France refused point-blank unless she was given in return 'productive guarantees', including the right to exploit the Ruhr coal fields. Meanwhile conditions in Germany continued to deteriorate. In December 1922 the Reparations Commission, against the protest of the British member, announced that Germany was technically in default in her deliveries of timber.[8] This supplied Poincaré with a pretext for intervention in Germany. A last-minute attempt to reconcile Britain and France at the Paris Conference in January 1923 ended in complete failure. On 9 January the Reparations Commission announced that Germany had deliberately defaulted over coal deliveries. Two days later French and Belgian troops entered the Ruhr, ostensibly to protect a Franco-Belgian control commission sent in to supervise reparations payments. Britain and America protested, the latter withdrawing her occupation forces from the Rhineland.

Poincaré calculated that the occupation of the industrial heart of Germany would bring the Germans to their senses and make them face their obligations; if it did not do this, then France would stay indefinitely in the Ruhr exploiting its economic resources, and by her presence there she would prevent an early resurgence of German military power; either way France would win. Germany was outraged by Poincaré's action, a clear violation of the treaty of Versailles, which required all allied decisions to be unanimous. A wave of anti-French feeling swept through Germany, and she was united as she had not been since August 1914. All parties denounced the French; the Communists, though reluctant to support the Cuno government, called for a general strike in protest; only Hitler's diminutive National Socialist German Workers' Party stood alone, calling for action against the 'November traitors' before dealing with France. The people of the Ruhr resorted to passive resistance, refusing to co-operate with the French and Belgian forces. In retaliation France brought in her own workers to operate mines and public utilities, declared a state of siege in the whole area, incorporating it in effect in the Franco-Belgian customs union, and imprisoned or expelled resistance leaders from the Ruhr. Germany retaliated by breaking off diplomatic relations, suspending all reparations payments to France and giving official sanction to passive resistance. Right-wing extremists of all shades (except the National Socialists) converged on the Ruhr where, despite government warnings, they committed numerous acts of sabotage, blocking canals and blowing up railway lines to prevent the removal of coal from the area. One of the

[8]She has failed to deliver 100,000 telephone poles to France.

saboteurs, an ex-Free Corps officer named Schlageter, was captured by the French, court-martialled and executed. Overnight he became a national hero; even Radek, in his speech to the executive committee of the Comintern, praised Schlageter as a 'brave soldier of the counter-revolution'.

The Ruhr occupation was the last straw for the German economy, which was gripped by catastrophic inflation never seen before or since. The new burden of paying wages and salaries to workers and officials on strike in the Ruhr proved too great. The mark fell to a quite meaningless level; early in 1923 the dollar was worth 18,000 marks; by August it was worth 4,600,000 marks and by November it reached the astronomical figure of four billion marks. Two thousand printing presses worked night and day to supply the *Reichsbank* with useless currency. Prices soared ahead of wages. Strikes and disorders occurred in the Ruhr, where workers were unable to make ends meet. The crowning irony was the printers' strike in August 1923, which threw the economy into even greater chaos and made currency stabilisation absolutely imperative in the interests of economic survival.

Many sections of the community undoubtedly thrived on inflation. Landowners and middle-class householders paid off their mortgages in inflated currency. Industrialists enjoying cheap credit facilities from the *Reichsbank* easily repaid loans and turned inflated profits into permanent assets by expanding their plant. Vast industrial enterprises sprang up in these troubled months. One of the greatest presided over by Hugo Stinnes controlled twenty per cent of German industrial potential, its interests ranging from iron and steel to timber, shipping and newspapers. These gigantic concentrations of power were, in fact, only a temporary phenomenon. Once inflation was over the trusts, deprived of liquid assets, soon collapsed. Moreover as long as boom conditions lasted workers, too, benefited from inflationary conditions. It is more difficult to assess the impact of hyper-inflation on the middle class as a whole. While Stresemann was probably exaggerating when he declared in 1927 that inflation wiped out the savings of the middle class, nevertheless, some sections of that class – those on fixed incomes or living on inherited wealth – were impoverished and consequently alienated from the republic and more inclined to listen to political radicals at the close of the 1920s.

Ominous cracks were appearing in the structure of the *Reich* in the summer of 1923. In the Rhineland the French authorities were giving active support to local separatists in the hope of detaching the area from Germany and bringing it under French control. The separatists had a negligible local following but were plentifully supplied with arms by the French, and were encouraged to proclaim a Rhineland republic which they eventually did in October. In the south there were threatening signs of disaffection in Bavaria, a constant thorn in the side of the *Reich* authorities. And in Saxony and Thuringia Socialist governments had joined forces with Communists in forming working-class defence organisations and seemed likely to admit Communists to the cabinet, a development which caused alarm on the right wing.

On 12 August 1923 the Cuno government, faced by mounting Reichstag opposition, fell and Gustav Stresemann was appointed chancellor. Within twenty-four hours he formed a government of Populists, Centrists, Democrats and Socialists, the so-called 'great coalition', which received an overwhelming vote of confidence in the Reichstag, only the German Nationalists and Communists opposing it. Stresemann's 'hundred days' as chancellor marked a real turning-point in the republic's history. He took office when the republic was at its lowest ebb politically and economically; by the time the great coalition collapsed in November 1923, the republic was well on the road to recovery. Stresemann was one of the few really outstanding political figures in the Weimar period. A statesmanlike figure of immense ability and industry, he was a gifted orator and a dynamic and vigorous personality with some of the mental qualities and attitudes of Winston Churchill, whom he resembled both in temperament and physique. The son of a Berlin innkeeper, Stresemann made a name for himself in business circles before 1914 and became a National Liberal deputy in 1907. During the war he was an out-and-out annexationist and an ardent admirer of Ludendorff. In 1919 he seemed to have repented of his previous political beliefs but was kept out of the Democratic party on account of his annexationist record. With help from industrialist friends, he founded the small Populist party and became its first chairman.

Chancellor Stresemann acted upon the simple truth that a government which lacks power cannot play power-politics. The economic resources of Germany were strained to breaking-point, the wheels of industry were grinding to a halt and the powers of resistance of ordinary Germans were reaching an end. Stresemann tried in vain to obtain some concession from the French. On 24 September leading industrialists warned him that Germany was at the end of her tether. He was left with no alternative but to call off passive resistance unconditionally on 26 September, with the agreement of most minister-presidents, and to announce Germany's willingness to resume reparations payments. Poincaré had won the nine-months-long struggle.

Precisely because it was an act of unconditional surrender, Stresemann's bold action multiplied his difficulties at first. The nationalist cauldron in Bavaria bubbled over. In protest against the abandonment of passive resistance, the right-wing Knilling government declared a state of emergency and appointed *Ritter* von Kahr, a former minister-president, as state commissioner. Kahr was in close touch with the nationalist organisations in Bavaria, a number of which had banded together under the leadership of Hitler's National Socialist German Workers' Party for the purpose of overthrowing the *Reich* government and inaugurating the 'national revolution'. Throughout October preparations went ahead for a 'march on Berlin' along the lines of Mussolini's march on Rome. Radical nationalists hoped in this way to rid Germany of her 'Marxist' government and set up a national dictatorship over the whole country, whilst the more conservative Bavarian nationalists, such as Kahr and Lossow, were primarily concerned to regain for Bavaria the privileged status she once enjoyed under the Wittelsbachs, a difference of objective which proved decisive in November when Hitler attempted to seize power. Late in October General von Lossow, commander of the seventh (Bavarian) division, was ordered by Gessler, the *Reichswehr* minister, to close down the *Völkischer Beobachter*, a newspaper recently acquired by the National Socialists, on account of insulting remarks made in an article about Seeckt. Lossow refused and was dismissed by Gessler. Whereupon Kahr promptly reinstated Lossow as Bavarian commander and ordered all soldiers to obey the Bavarian government, a clear and open act of rebellion against the *Reich*.

When Bavaria declared her state of emergency in September, Stresemann at once obtained Ebert's consent to a declaration of national emergency. Emergency powers were at once given to the *Reichswehr* through Gessler. Seeckt was not particularly well-disposed towards Stresemann. There was much talk in right-wing circles at this time of making Seeckt dictator, an idea to which he was by no means averse – in fact he drafted a programme for an authoritarian-style government with greatly increased executive powers. Certainly he did not plan to seize power with the aid of the *Reichswehr*. At the same time he was as reluctant as ever to use the *Reichswehr* against right-wing putschists; when asked by Karl Severing, the Prussian minister of the interior, what the *Reichswehr* would do if Lossow marched on Berlin, Seeckt repeated the remark he made to Ebert in 1920: *Reichswehr* did not fire on *Reichswehr*. On the other hand, he could not tolerate signs of indiscipline; when Major Buchrucker, a political adventurer who commanded four battalions of the Black *Reichswehr* – a secret organisation trained by the *Reichswehr* to defend Germany against a possible Polish attack – tried to seize power at Küstrin on 1 October, Seeckt at once ordered his arrest. The *Putsch* failed and Buchrucker was sentenced to ten years' imprisonment, of which he served only a fraction, being pardoned by President von Hindenburg.

Stresemann was anxious to avoid a major conflict with Bavaria at all costs, fearing that this would be the signal for further 'national' uprisings, the downfall of his government and the establishment of a military dictatorship. Worst of all, under cover of civil war, the French would tighten their grip on Rhineland and Ruhr. To avert these dangers he had to reassure the right wing that he had the 'national' interest very much at heart. The obvious way to do this was by striking a blow at the extreme left wing at its most vulnerable point in Central Germany. Socialists in Saxony and Thuringia were greatly alarmed by events in Bavaria and by mounting evidence of close links between the *Reichswehr* and the extremist organisations in Bavaria and elsewhere. To defend the *Reich* against fascism these left-wing Socialists were prepared to cooperate with the (still) putschist-minded Communist party and gave Communists seats in the newly formed *Land* governments. In both *Länder* Red militias were set up. Saxony defied an order from the local *Reichswehr* commander, General Müller, disbanding the militias. The Saxon parliament ordered Müller to obey it and not Berlin; Stresemann, already under pressure from Saxon industrialist friends to intervene and 'restore order', told the new minister-president, Zeigner, to dismiss his Communist ministers. Zeigner refused, whereupon Stresemann ordered the *Reichswehr* into Saxony and Thuringia at the end of October and deposed both governments. This was an act of doubtful legality; these governments had the full support of their parliaments and, unlike the Bavarian government, had committed no treasonable act.[9] Needless to say, it established a highly dangerous precedent; when the Prussian government was deposed in 1932, Hindenburg was able to justify the action in terms of 1923. The Socialists in Stresemann's government had supported him reluctantly against Saxony, but were angered by his subsequent refusal to end the military state of emergency there and proceed with equal vigour against Bavaria. They resigned in protest on 2 November 1923 and later in the month were instrumental in causing the collapse of the 'great coalition', thus bringing Stresemann's hundred days to an end.

Stresemann's stratagem served its political purpose. The more moderate nationalist elements in Bavaria were impressed by the chancellor's firm stand against Communism. Kahr and Lossow were wavering in their opposition to Berlin when Hitler suddenly staged his own *Putsch* in a desperate attempt to begin the 'national revolution' before time ran out. At the head of a band of Brown Shirts, the small private army of the Nazi movement, Hitler burst in on a public meeting being addressed by Kahr in the Munich Bürgerbräukeller on the evening of 8 November, and forced him at pistol point to agree to a march on Berlin. Hitler declared the Bavarian and *Reich* governments dissolved and assumed leadership of a provisional national government, naming ex-General Ludendorff, one of his admirers and supporters in Munich, as the new army chief. Once out of sight of Hitler, Kahr and Lossow quickly changed their minds and banned the Nazi party. Undeterred, Hitler led a procession of his followers several thousand strong through the city next morning. When the procession reached the Feldherrnhalle the police fired on it, sixteen demonstrators were killed –

---

[9]Leading Russian Communists, it is true, encouraged their German comrades to seize power at this time. But the Saxon and Thuringian Socialists refused to resist the *Reichswehr* when it moved in. Only in Hamburg did the Communists attempt a completely abortive uprising in October. After that fiasco the party buried putschism for good.

the first martyrs of the National Socialist movement – and the *Putsch* collapsed ignominiously. Hitler was a convenient scapegoat for Kahr and Lossow, who were able to come to terms with Berlin without difficulty; Kahr resigned, Lossow retired and Berlin overlooked their treasonable conduct. As for Hitler, he, together with Ludendorff and eight others, was put on trial in Munich in 1924. Ludendorff was acquitted, much to his disgust, whilst Hitler and three others received five years' imprisonment with possible probation after six months, an extremely lenient sentence for self-confessed traitors. It was indicative of the nationalist mood in Bavaria that Hitler was allowed to turn his trial into a great political attack on the republic, and that the court actually declared its belief that all the accused had been inspired by 'the pure spirit of patriotism'.

The activities of the separatists in the west reached a climax in October and November 1923. Earlier attempts by separatists to set up a Rhineland republic in the summer of 1919 failed miserably in the face of united opposition from the local inhabitants. Under cover of the confusion caused by the Ruhr occupation, and with the connivance of the French and Belgian authorities, the separatists tried again. Small bands of separatists – many came from outside the region and several had police records – seized power in October 1923 in Aachen, Bonn, Trier, Wiesbaden and Mainz and proclaimed the Rhineland republic. A provisional government headed by the separatist leaders was set up at Koblenz. Britain protested vigorously and refused to recognise autonomous governments set up in defiance of the Versailles treaty. In fact separatism attracted negligible support in the Rhineland and had collapsed in most places by the end of the year. Separatism took a more serious turn in the Palatinate. The commanding French general, encouraged by Bavaria's defiance of Berlin, recognised the Palatinate as an autonomous state in October. With this encouragement separatists seized power in November and proclaimed a republic. In January 1924 the Rhineland High Commission recognised the Palatinate Republic against the protests of the British representative. When the French eventually withdrew their support, as a result of a changing international situation, Palatinate separatism collapsed dramatically in February 1924 with the burning of Pirmasens town hall by local inhabitants and the murder of seventeen separatists hiding in the building. By the end of the month Berlin had the situation well in hand. The emergency powers given to Seeckt on 9 November 1923 were withdrawn and the state of emergency was officially ended.

When Stresemann called off passive resistance in September 1923, one of the most urgent tasks facing him was the restoration of Germany's finances. The problem of runaway inflation could no longer be ignored. Armed with plenary powers from the Reichstag, Stresemann acted boldly. Within three days he established a *Rentenbank* with power to issue a new currency, the *Rentenmark*. This was a temporary expedient only, for the new notes lacked solid backing; in lieu of gold, which Germany did not possess in sufficient quantities, the *Rentenmark* was covered by a mortgage put on all industrial and agricultural land. Two thousand, four hundred million Rentenmarks were issued, half to the government, half to the *Reichsbank* to supply credit to industry. To supervise the delicate operation of launching a currency with so little backing, Stresemann appointed a currency commissioner (*Reichswährungskommissar*) in the person of Hjalmar Schacht, a director of the *Darmstädter und Nationalbank*. Much of the credit for the effectiveness of the *Rentenmark* belongs to this financial genius. He ensured that the new notes superseded the paper marks and all other emergency currencies, and when the first issue was quickly swallowed up, firmly refused to authorise further issues. The government curtailed expenditure, cut salaries, reduced the number of officials and government employees by 300,000 and increased taxation. The drastic treatment together with the fact that no reparations were being paid then, did the trick. To the surprise of the outside world, who called it 'the miracle of the *Rentenmark*', confidence was restored and the danger of inflation vanished from the German scene.

A contributory factor in the restoration of confidence was the settlement of reparations in 1924 known as the Dawes Plan. When Stresemann called off passive resistance, Poincaré had won a victory. It proved a hollow triumph, as he soon discovered that reparations could not be collected indefinitely at the point of the bayonet. True, he struck a highly favourable bargain with Ruhr industrialists for coal and other deliveries in kind in November 1923, which had a ruinous effect on the German economy but could not have been maintained for very long. A more ominous sign was that the franc lost a quarter of its face value as a result of the Ruhr occupation. Poincaré was brought up at last against the real dilemma facing France. If she hung on in the Ruhr, taking what she could by way of reparations in kind, she could so weaken and depress Germany as to make a revival of militarism impossible. But if she wanted substantial reparations, then Germany must be allowed to recover economically and earn the necessary foreign exchange. The catch was that once Germany recovered economically her military potential would revive and she would be in a position before long to repudiate all payments. While Poincaré hesitated, impaled on the horns of this dilemma, Britain seized the initiative and appealed to the United States to take part in an international investigation into Germany's capacity to pay reparations. The proposal was warmly welcomed by the Americans, who were anxious to stabilise conditions in Central Europe in the interests of their investors. In the face of strong Anglo-American pressure France gave way reluctantly. In November the Reparations Commission, in response to a German request, agreed to set up two committees of financial experts, one to deal with the problems posed by the flight of capital from Germany, the other, chaired by the American general, Dawes, to consider ways and means of stabilising the German currency and balancing her budget. The latter committee met in Paris in January 1924 and published its report, the Dawes Plan, in April.

Several factors worked in favour of Germany at this juncture. American Secretary of State Hughes paid visits to the leading European capitals in the summer of 1924, bringing pressure to bear on governments to accept the new reparations plan. Britain welcomed it, for Ramsay MacDonald was now in office and Labour had always believed the impoverishment of Germany to be bad ethics (as well as bad business). Then in May the chief obstacle to agreement was removed when Poincaré's *Bloc National* was defeated at the polls. The radicals under Herriot came to power, a change of some importance, for the radicals were internationalists in the tradition of the French left. It was a matter of practical politics as well as sentiment; Germany was a land of great industrial potential with a population of sixty millions compared with thirty-eight million Frenchmen; within a decade or so Germany would inevitably become a Great Power again; to ensure that she remained a peaceful power, conciliation was the only practical alternative where coercion had failed.

So the Dawes Plan was accepted with some modifications by the creditor nations and by Germany at the London Conference in July and August 1924. Germany's total liability remained unchanged not because the financial experts thought it a credible figure but simply because Herriot dare not offend nationalist opinion at home by agreeing to a reduction. But the important thing was that Germany's payments were at last geared to her economic capacity. Over the first five years Germany was to make payments rising from an initial £50 million (1,000 million marks) to £125 million (2,500 million marks). After this the sums paid would vary according to the index of German prosperity. The reparations were secured by a form of 'productive guarantee' in the shape of a mortgage on the German railway system, which was turned into a special corporation run by a mixed board of directors. Further securities were provided by certain customs and excise duties and by a mortgage on German industry. Special steps were taken to safeguard Germany's balance of payments, reparations being paid into the *Reichsbank* account of the agent-general, Parker Gilbert, an American banker, who had to arrange the transfer of payments to the creditors without endangering the balance of payments. Germany also received a loan of £40 million (800 million marks) to help her stabilise the new currency. Penalties were not to be imposed on her except for deliberate large-scale default. Even then sanctions would require the unanimous support of all creditors in conjunction with the Americans, a device to safeguard investors against a repetition of the economically

disastrous Ruhr occupation. During the conference the German delegation pressed the French to announce a date for the evacuation of their
troops from the Ruhr, although this item had been excluded from the
agenda at the insistence of the French government. With active support
from MacDonald, Stresemann finally persuaded Herriot to agree to an
immediate withdrawal from certain towns and in private conversation
Herriot promised to complete the evacuation within a year.

Under Stresemann's guidance the republic had survived its darkest hour;
threats to the unity of the *Reich* were overcome, confidence in the economy
restored and reparations put on a realistic footing. These were considerable achievements, for which much, though by no means all, of the credit
must go to Stresemann. Yet his policies were not universally popular at
home; mostly he had to fight for them in the teeth of bitter opposition and
savage personal attacks from the extreme right and extreme left as well as
from the right wing of his own party. The situation was especially difficult
in the summer of 1924. At the general election in May the political
extremes were strengthened at the expense of the middle-of-the-road
republican parties; the National Socialists polled nearly two million votes
and obtained thirty-two seats;[10] the Communists gained over three million
votes, capturing most of the Independent Socialist vote and increasing
their representation from four seats to sixty-two; while the German Nationalists gained over one million votes and became the largest party in the
Reichstag.[11] In all, over eleven million of the twenty-nine million electors
voted for enemies of the republic of one kind or another, a disheartening
portent for the future. The Nationalists failed to form a government,
largely because they could not bring themselves to accept responsibility
for the Dawes Plan, having attacked it so bitterly during the elections. So
the Marx cabinet, with Stresemann as foreign minister, stayed in office
while the Nationalists continued their irresponsible attacks. During critical stages of the London Conference Stresemann was gravely embarrassed
by continual fire from left and right. Indeed only with the greatest difficulty did he secure the two-thirds majority necessary for the passage of a
law giving the creditor nations certain rights of control over German
railways, as required by the Dawes Plan. There were dramatic scenes in
the Reichstag when forty-eight Nationalists voted for the bill at the third
reading, ensuring its passage by the necessary majority. There was really
no alternative, as many Nationalists were well aware; big business was
prepared to accept the Plan, and Ebert threatened new elections if the Plan

[10]The National Socialists amalgamated with extremist groups to form the *Nationalsozialistische
Freiheitspartei*, polling 1,918,300 votes.
[11]They polled 5,696,500 votes and won ninety-five seats. They were joined in the Reichstag by the ten
members of the *Landbund* and by some right-wing Populists who had left their own party.

foundered. So in return for a government declaration repudiating sole war-guilt, half the German Nationalists supported Stresemann and the crisis was over. In the second half of 1924, as economic conditions improved, political extremism started to decline in popularity. When elections were held again in December 1924 to resolve the political deadlock in the Reichstag, Communists and National Socialists suffered a sharp setback whilst Democrats, Populists and Socialists slowly recovered their strength.[12]

[12]The Communists lost nearly one million votes and seventeen seats, the National Socialists over one million votes and eighteen seats.

12

The Rise and Fall of the Weimar Republic 1924–1933

Gustav Stresemann's contribution to the stabilization of the Weimar Republic was not over with the collapse of the great coalition in November 1923. Between 1924 and 1929 when Germany was regaining much of her old status as a Great Power, he was in continuous control of the foreign office.

Controversy has raged around his work as foreign minister. In 1918 Stresemann apparently turned his back on the rabid annexationism of the war years and became a staunch democrat and dedicated European working for a lasting reconciliation between Germany and France. The first doubts about the genuineness of his liberalism were raised by the publication in 1933 of his letters and diaries, which revealed the depth, subtlety and deviousness of his policies. With the National Socialists in power in Germany, there was a reaction against Stresemann, especially in France where he was denounced as a hypocritical Pan-German who had deliberately thrown Europe off the scent while Germany rearmed secretly. The pendulum swung in the opposite direction after the Second World War when, in the aftermath of defeat, a few German historians attempted to rehabilitate him and show that his conversion to liberalism in 1918 was genuine and that with a few minor lapses he remained true to his beliefs all his life. Since then historians have had access to material from the German foreign-office archives which throws fresh light upon his policies.

A final judgement on Stresemann may not yet be possible but a clear enough picture emerges from the available evidence. His aim was quite simply to make Germany a Great Power once more, freeing her as quickly as possible from the shackles of the Versailles treaty. He was working for the speedy withdrawal of all foreign troops from German soil, for the recovery of the territory lost to Poland, for the removal of the moral stigma of the war-guilt clause and for Germany's entry into the League of Nations. And, although it occupied a secondary place in his thoughts, he did what he could to keep the idea of the *Anschluss* with Austria alive, having played a prominent part with Friedrich Naumann in the *Mitteleuropa* movement during the war. That he pursued a foreign policy corresponding to Germany's national interests should evoke no surprise. In sharp contrast to the right-wing extremists who ranted ceaselessly (and impotently) against the victorious powers, he did appreciate the need for care and finesse if Germany was to recover her old position. A Bismarckian in his understanding of power realities, he possessed the mental agility and adroitness of the old chancellor, seizing opportunities as and when they presented themselves. With his eyes fixed firmly on the ultimate goal of complete independence, he cheerfully made use of whatever argument seemed appropriate to the matter in hand: 'We need not always be too careful about the method if only it gets us forward,' he noted in his diary, 'for in the end the results decide which method is the right one. But we shall not always follow a straight path as might please the more theoretically minded.' He approved of secret rearmament but not because he was planning aggressive war, much less was he paving the way for Hitler. Brought up in the high noon of Imperial Germany, he assumed as a matter of course that only when Germany had a powerful army would other powers respect her and pay attention to her wishes. Writing to a friend in 1927, he complained that at League of Nations meetings all he had behind him was the spiritual power of German culture and the economic power of the republic: 'But I lack the material power of an army and this, in the nature of things, despite all the pacific assurances of the peoples of the world, still remains the really decisive factor as far as the influence of Great Powers is concerned.' Like the men of the Wilhelmstrasse in the days of William II, with whom he had so much in common, Stresemann wanted to make Germany dominant in Europe. He was probably sincere enough in his desire to achieve this by peaceful means and in his profound belief that it was in the interests of Europe as a whole to see the Versailles Treaty revised as quickly as possible.

It started with the Dawes Plan in 1924 when Stresemann seized a favourable moment to drive as hard a bargain as circumstances permitted. He did not obtain all he had hoped for in 1924, but at least some foreign troops were withdrawn from Germany and the day brought nearer when the industrial heart of Germany would be free from foreign control. Stresemann turned a defeat into a victory, thanks to the desire of Britain and America to see economic stability return to Central Europe. France had argued that Germany could pay but would not do so; the financial experts, as Stresemann noted with satisfaction in his diary, had come to her rescue, saying that she could not pay and must not be forced to. Most important of all, Germany was accepted as an equal at the conference table. The pretence of sole war-guilt was already wearing thin; Stresemann was careful to point out that Germany accepted the Dawes Plan only 'because the war has been lost and not because she felt morally guilty of the origin of the war.' The day after the Reichstag ratified the agreement, Chancellor Marx publicly repudiated the war-guilt clause and promised to inform the creditor nations that as long as Germany was regarded as a 'criminal against humanity' there could be no hope of reconciliation between victors and vanquished.

Stresemann did not even believe in the Dawes Plan; in private he referred to if as 'no more than an economic armistice' in the rivalry between France and Germany. The Plan was accepted simply in order to secure the foreign loans without which economic recovery was impossible. In September 1925 he told Crown Prince William, son of the ex-emperor, that by 1927 the demands of the plan would strain Germany beyond endurance, and that a new conference would then have to be called to relieve her of the burden. Like Wirth before him, Stresemann was pursuing a policy of fulfilment simply in order to prove the impossibility of reparations.

In 1925 Stresemann scored a great diplomatic triumph on the occasion of the Locarno Pacts. At the close of 1924 the international situation clouded for Germany. MacDonald, the friend of Germany, went down to defeat and the Conservatives came to power. The new foreign secretary, Austen Chamberlain, was much less cordial towards Germany. Shortly afterwards Britain and France declared that they would only evacuate Zone I of the Rhineland and the bridgeheads on the right bank of the river in January 1925 on condition that the report of the Inter-Allied Control Commission on German disarmament was satisfactory. However, the report accused Germany of failing to disband the general staff, of training reserves in excess of the 100,000 men allowed her, and of failing to dismantle certain industrial installations. Accordingly the ambassador's conference announced that the evacuation of Zone I and the final evacuation of the Ruhr would not now take place. Overnight Stresemann's fulfilment policy was exposed to heavy attack from the right wing. A further worry was the gnawing fear that the new friendship between Britain and France would lead to an alliance directed against Germany.

How could Stresemann avoid a disastrous set-back to his policies? An unexpected opportunity presented itself in connexion with the related problems of security and general disarmament. The victorious powers pledged themselves to disarm in 1919 but made no progress, owing to French fears of Germany. France insisted on fool-proof guarantees against German aggression before she would disarm. In an attempt to allay French fears, MacDonald sponsored the Geneva Protocol which strengthened the Covenant of the League of Nations against aggression. At the last minute the new Conservative government upset everything by rejecting the Protocol out of respect for the isolationist mood of the Dominions. Acting on a hint from his friend the British ambassador, Stresemann sprang into the breach with a proposal that the powers directly interested in the Rhineland, that is, France, Germany and Belgium, with Britain and Italy acting as guarantors, should solemnly declare their intention never to go to war again over their western frontiers. A similar proposal had been made by Cuno in 1922 but had foundered on the rock of French intransigence. This time, with Briand at the Quai D'orsay once more, France welcomed the proposal. Britain was equally pleased by the German initiative. The negotiations at Locarno in October 1925 were crowned with success.

The central feature of the Locarno agreements was the Rhineland Pact, a treaty of mutual guarantee binding the signatories to respect the frontier between France, Germany and Belgium, including the demilitarised Rhineland. France and Germany shook hands over their western frontier and solemnly renounced war as a means of resolving future differences. What Stresemann had done in effect was make a virtue out of necessity. Germany was in no position in 1925 to re-militarise the Rhineland or alter the western frontier by force; in any case she was quite resigned to the loss of Alsace-Lorraine. When stated in the form of a solemn guarantee, these simple facts earned rich dividends for Germany. At a stroke of the pen France was neutralised and the fear of an anti-German coalition removed. The complaints about German rearmament were quietly dropped. The Ruhr was finally evacuated in August 1925 and Zone I of the Rhineland by January 1926. Negotiations started for the reduction of the remaining occupation forces, and in December 1926 the allies relaxed their control of disarmament still further by abolishing the Inter-Allied Control Commission. Renunciation cut both ways; as a *quid pro quo* for the German guarantee of the *status quo* in the west, France was obliged to respect Germany's frontiers and refrain from unilateral action against her. In short, by tying his own hands in the west Stresemann tied those of France as well.

The French suspected, quite rightly, that Germany was deliberately cutting her losses in the west in order to gain freedom of manoeuvre in the east. Writing to a German diplomat in April 1925, Stresemann observed that 'our policy regarding the security offer was undoubtedly correct; it secured the Rhineland against a French policy of aggression, split the Entente and opened new prospects for the east.' There was little France could do about it. Stresemann flatly refused to guarantee the eastern frontiers, and Britain declined to act as guarantor where her interests were not directly involved. Nor could France persuade Germany to accept her full obligations under the Covenant in the likely event of her being admitted to the League of Nations. Stresemann was determined not to allow Germany to become a battleground in the event of war between Poland and Russia. If she applied sanctions against Russia, Germany might be exposed to Russian attack and would have to allow French troops to march through the fatherland to help Poland, an equally unpalatable prospect. In the end it was agreed that, as Germany was (theoretically) disarmed, she need only apply sanctions in so far as this was compatible with her military security and geographical position, which meant in effect that Germany could veto punitive measures against Russia. All that Germany would agree to at Locarno were arbitration conventions applying to the Polish and Czech frontiers. As a further safeguard Briand reaffirmed the existing treaties between France, Poland and Czechoslovakia, providing for mutual assistance against unprovoked German aggression.

Contemporaries hailed the Locarno agreements as a turning-point in the post-war period; the past was finally buried now that Germany was again a respectable member of the West European community of nations. The ghost of Rapallo had been laid at last – or so it seemed. In fact the Locarno Pacts did not keep Germany away from Russia. In April 1926 they signed the Treaty of Berlin, which reaffirmed and strengthened the Rapallo agreement. Geography, economic necessity and common prudence obliged Germany to be on good terms with Russia, as Stresemann was well aware. Soldiers such as Seeckt wanted to rely entirely on Russia and win her as an ally for a war of revenge against Poland and France. This was a course of action which Stresemann would not consider for a moment, for he was deeply convinced that Germany needed to be on good terms with east and west simultaneously. He also hoped to regain Germany's old markets in the east believing on the basis of Lenin's New Economic Programme that Russia would in time revert to a free-market economy. And while always suspicious of Comintern policy and fully aware that Russia was too weak to be of much assistance, nevertheless he tried to keep her in play to facilitate treaty revision in the east and exclude the possibility of an understanding between France and Russia at Germany's expense. This he succeeded in doing in 1926. In the Berlin treaty Germany promised to remain neutral in the event of Russia's being involved in war with other powers, provided Russia was not the aggressor – a proviso making the commitment compatible with German membership of the League of Nations; all the same, Russian fears that Germany might side against her in a moment of crisis were allayed. Germany and Russia also promised not to form coalitions for the purpose of imposing economic or financial boycotts on each other. The treaty was widely acclaimed in Germany and ratified with enthusiasm by the Reichstag. Only three votes were cast against the Berlin treaty whereas when the Locarno pacts were ratified in November by 292 to 174 votes, it was only after a bitter parliamentary battle, in the course of which the German Nationalists (who had accepted office for the first time in 1925) withdrew from the cabinet and voted against the treaty.

The success at Locarno opened another door for Germany: entry into the League of Nations. Actually this was delayed until late in 1926 because Spain, Portugal and Brazil were offended by the Great Powers' decision to give Germany a permanent seat on the council. A Brazilian veto kept Germany out when she applied for membership in March 1926. Not until September was the difficulty resolved and Germany admitted to full membership. Stresemann attached great importance to being in the League. But whilst France hoped that membership would turn Germany into a loyal defender of the *status quo*, Stresemann hoped that it would have precisely the opposite effect and enable the *status quo* to be altered in Germany's favour. Regular attendance at Geneva had other advantages, as Stresemann remarked to Crown Prince William: 'all the questions that lie so close to German hearts as, for instance, war-guilt, general disarmament, Danzig, the Saar, etc., are matters for the League of Nations, and a skillful speaker at a plenary session of the League may make them very disagreeable for the Entente.'

To keep the question of frontier revision in the east well to the fore, Stresemann raised the question of the treatment of German minorities under foreign rule whenever possible. The defence of the rights of the ten to twelve million Germans under Polish, Czech, Yugoslav and Rumanian rule was a major preoccupation with successive governments. Organisations were formed to help preserve the German language and culture abroad, so that long before Hitler came to power Germany had built up an elaborate network of contacts with her minorities abroad. In the hope of shaming Britain and France into a speedy withdrawal from the Rhineland, Stresemann seized every opportunity of contrasting the Locarno spirit and the new idealism generated by the Franco-German *rapprochement* with the continued presence of foreign soldiers on German soil. Disarmament was another favourite theme at Geneva, where he constantly drew attention to the incompatibility between the fact of German disarmament and the failure of other powers to follow suit. Not that he expected to bully them into disarmament; his objective was simply to embarrass France and to mobilise world opinion for the removal of all limitations on Germany.

Stresemann scored his last success in 1929, when the allied powers withdrew their remaining forces from the Rhineland in return for a final settlement of the reparations question. The Dawes plan was never intended to be more than an interim measure until such time as Germany had recovered economically. In 1927 the agent-general Gilbert Parker suggested that the time had come to redefine Germany's total liability and end foreign supervision of payments. At first Stresemann was reluctant to agree, fearing that the creditors would propose too high a figure in view of the superficial signs of prosperity in Germany. He only gave way when it became clear that otherwise France would not evacuate the Rhineland. All his efforts to persuade France that the presence of her troops on German soil was out of keeping both with the Locarno agreements and the Kellogg Pact – recently signed by Germany – failed to move her. France refused to treat reparations and the Rhineland evacuation as separate issues; having recently funded her own war debt to the U.S.A., France wanted to see Germany's total liability finalised and was not prepared to throw her best bargaining-counter away beforehand. Stresemann was left with no alternative but to agree to a re-examination of the reparations burden by a committee of financial experts. The committee, chaired by Owen Young and with Schacht as one of Germany's representatives, met in Paris early in 1929 and worked out a new reparations plan which was accepted with some minor alterations by the creditor nations at the Hague Conference in August.

Under the Young Plan Germany agreed to pay reparations until 1988. For the first thirty-seven years annual payments would rise from 1700 million marks to 2400 millions, and then continue at a reduced rate for the remaining twenty-two years; in all Germany would pay 37,000 million marks (£1,850 million), a considerable reduction on the 132,000 million marks (£6,500 million) demanded in 1921. Furthermore, all foreign control of reparations ended. The Reparations Commission was dissolved, all mortgage commitments on German railways and industry terminated and the burden of payment became the sole responsibility of the German government. A Bank of International Settlement was set up in Basle to handle the payments. In the event of default the creditors' only redress would be an appeal to the International Court. In return Britain and France agreed to withdraw their troops from the Rhineland. Zone II was evacuated by November 1929 and Zone III by June 1930, five years ahead of the Versailles schedule.

Before the negotiations were completed, Stresemann, in failing health for some time, saddened by vitriolic right-wing attacks on his policies, worn out by his endeavours, died suddenly of a heart attack on 3 October 1929. Without a doubt Stresemann's contribution towards the steady improvement in Germany's international fortunes was a significant one. On the other hand, a favourable international situation, American financial support and Germany's growing economic power probably contributed just as much to the final outcome. And although Stresemann succeeded in removing all foreign troops and control-officers from German soil, the demilitarised Rhineland remained as a reminder that Germany had not yet regained complete sovereignty over her own territory.

It is sometimes said that Weimar Germany experienced boom conditions between 1924 and 1929 comparable to those in the Federal Republic in the 1950s. Certainly iron and steel, coal, chemicals and electrical products recovered quickly after the war – though even in 1929 they only attained the output and export levels of 1913. This recovery was due to a burst of rationalisation; the introduction of up-to-date management techniques and more efficient methods of production brought about a tremendous increase in productivity; blast furnaces, for example, trebled their output. Rationalisation was actively encouraged by the government and much of the 25,000 million marks of foreign capital which poured into Germany in the late 1920s was applied to this end.

Rationalisation was accompanied by the related phenomenon of industrial concentration: the amalgamation into great industrial empires of enterprises engaged in similar or allied productive processes. The best-known examples of 'trustification' are *I.G. Farbenindustrie* (1925) and *Vereinigte Stahlwerke* (1926). The former quickly became the largest concern in Europe with a capital of 900 million marks and interests ranging from rayon to dynamite. A perfect example of the vertical trust, *I.G. Farben* possessed a virtual monopoly of synthetic dye-stuffs and nitrogen production and had extensive interests in the new industries developed by chemical science. *Vereinigte Stahlwerke* with a capital of 800 million marks linked together the coal, iron and steel interests of Thyssen, Stinnes, Phoenix and the Otto Wolff groups which, between them, controlled between forty and fifty per cent of total iron and steel production and thirty-six per cent of coal production. Similar trends were observable in the chemical industry, where Siemens had a virtual monopoly, and in shipping and cement where the *Wiking Konzern* was dominant. Economic power was being concentrated into an ever-diminishing number of hands, a development of some social and political significance.

Recent research, however, suggests that the extent of the 'boom' has been greatly exaggerated. Germany experienced high growth rates and low unemployment between 1919 and 1924. In the late 1920s growth rates were unsteady, rising in 1924–5 and 1927 but falling in between to a minus rate by 1928–9, while compared with the American economy which grew by seventy per cent between 1913 and 1929, the German grew by only four per cent. Capital investment was already falling by 1929; unemployment consequent upon rationalisation was never less than 1.3 million and reached 3 millions by February 1929. Contrasting sharply with the spectacular growth of heavy industry was the poor performance of agriculture and small industry, both starved of capital and still largely geared to pre-war markets. The true position was disguised by two factors. First, the massive inflow of foreign capital. Second, the extensive welfare system. The genuine concern of the republic for the living standards of its citizens was reflected in improved sickness benefits, the introduction of unemployment benefit (1927) and the practice of state intervention to resolve industrial disputes (usually in favour of the workers). Railways and postal services were thoroughly modernised in these years; roads were improved to accommodate the growing volume of traffic; and public authorities embarked upon a lavish building programme of schools, hospitals, sports grounds and housing financed by government subsidies and easy credit facilities. Consequently social expenditure, which in 1913 had been fifteen per cent of the GNP, had risen to twenty-six per cent by the end of the 1920s and budget deficits were mounting.

The relative affluence of these years was reflected politically in a sharp decline of support for parties on the extreme right and left. The National Socialists won thirty-two seats in May 1924 but held only fourteen of them in December and lost two more in 1928, when they polled only 810,000 votes. The Communists had sixty-two seats in May 1924 but only forty-five in December, though they had admittedly regained much of the lost ground in 1928. Middle-of-the-road parties were making steady progress. The Centre and the Democrats roughly held their own. The Majority Socialists made substantial gains; in 1928 they reached their high-water mark (excluding 1919) with a total of 153 seats and over nine million votes. When the republic celebrated its tenth anniversary in 1929, there seemed reasonable grounds for optimism. The Kapp *Putsch* was a thing of the past; all hope of a monarchist restoration had been abandoned long ago; the Weimar coalition ruling Prussia felt safe enough in 1928 to raise the ban on public speaking by Hitler; much to the alarm of ex-Emperor William, the German Nationalists actually voted in 1928 for the renewal of the 1922 law for the protection of the republic which banned him from returning to Germany; and the fact that a 'great coalition' of Populists, Centrists, Democrats and Socialists could be formed in 1928 under Hermann Müller might suggest to the unwary that a good deal of common ground existed in German politics.

A closer look at political life in the late 1920s quickly destroys those illusions. Superficial prosperity and the growing international stature of the republic served to mask a state of chronic political weakness. From the start the existence of a multi-party system, inherited from Wilhelmine Germany, made the task of creating a viable democracy difficult. Proportional representation accentuated the difficulty. No party secured an absolute majority at a German national election until 1957.[1] Consequently the republic had to make do with coalition government, a delicate operation at the best of times. It proved immensely difficult to form coalitions with majority support in the Reichstag; only eight of the twenty-one governments from Scheidemann to Schleicher were in that happy position. The basic problem was the presence of extremists at each end of the political spectrum. As they refused to participate in any cabinet, regular alternation between right and left was impossible. On their own the Weimar parties, Socialists, Democrats and Centre, could not secure a majority, nor could the right-wing parties (German Nationalists and Populists). The political deadlock was obscured by two factors: the flexibility of the Centre which was prepared to move left or right as circumstances dictated,[2] and Socialist 'tolerance' of right-centre governments which they adamantly refused to join. These conditions maximised party intrigue in the Reichstag. Governments emerged only after long and arduous horse-trading behind the

[1] See p. 381.
[2] In Prussia the Centre ruled for many years in coalition with Socialists and Democrats; but at national level Catholics frequently formed coalitions with the right-wing parties.

scenes by party bosses who forced their shaky compromises on successive chancellors, who, in theory at least, were supposed to be forming the government. Even when the negotiations succeeded, the all-powerful party committees kept a vigilant eye on the government and were always ready to sacrifice a cabinet to party advantage. Interference by party committees led to some quite absurd and alarming situations. For example, in 1928 the Müller government agreed to the construction of a pocket battleship, Cruiser A, at the behest of the military authorities. During the election campaign the Socialists vehemently denounced this expenditure. In the new Reichstag the party committee criticised their ministers for voting for the bill but, because it wanted to keep the government afloat, instructed them to remain in the cabinet. To confuse matters still further the committee finally insisted that all members, including ministers, vote for a motion (subsequently defeated) calling for a halt to construction work on the battleship, a Gilbertian situation which brought nothing but discredit on the parliamentary party.

Incidents of this kind, trivial in themselves, do not enhance the credit of party politics at any time, least of all in a country where democracy has insecure foundations. From the beginning the Reichstag tended to be a debating-chamber remote from the people; the single-member constituency of pre-war days was superseded by thirty-five vast electoral areas where the electors voted for party lists. There were no by-elections; deputies were simply replaced from the list. When the deputy arrived in the Reichstag he became little more than a puppet controlled by party committees which ruthlessly stamped out individualism. Curiously enough, when party politics were rapidly losing their meaning and permanent officials were carrying out many of the essential functions of government, party divisions were deeper than ever. They thrived on questions like the disposal of the property of the old ruling houses, around which a fierce debate raged in 1925 and 1926; on the issue of support for church schools, which wrecked a cabinet in 1927; and on the issue of the flag in 1926, when President von Hindenburg ordered the merchant ensign with the old black, white and red colours to be flown alongside the republican colours at all consulates, a dispute which actually led to the downfall of a government. All matters of secondary importance in the grand scheme of things, which nevertheless aroused deep passions and kept old feuds alive. It was significant that interest in party politics was declining in these years.[3] Party politics – '*das System*', as many started to call it – were clearly falling into disrepute. There were ominous signs of *malaise* after the 1928 elections. That sensitive barometer, the Centre party, was aware of it. 'Never has the German soul asked more vehemently and impatiently for leadership in the grand style than in these days . . .' observed Mgr.

[3]The percentage of non-voters increased from sixteen per cent in 1919 to twenty-six per cent in 1928.

Kaas, newly elected chairman of the Centre. And the liberal *Deutscher Volkswirt*, urging democracy to rise to the challenge of the times, spoke of 'a deep longing for the strong will of a leader and saving ideas sweeping across Germany'. Small wonder that many people, who were losing what little faith they had in democratic institutions, looked elsewhere for a saviour when the great crisis broke on Germany.

The Weimar parties did far too little to combat this dangerous drift from democracy. The Socialists, despite their numerical strength, were ill at ease in the republic. Their spokesmen were still mouthing the slogans of revolutionary Marxism, yet in practice Socialists were reformists, defenders of the republic and staunch anti-Communists. But they never became a truly national party; hostility to the middle classes – although 40 per cent of their members were white-collar workers – and a blend of pacifism and old-fashioned anti-clericalism were insurmountable obstacles in that direction. Their leaders were solid, unimaginative trade unionists, deeply committed to democratic procedures but inept tacticians sadly lacking in *élan* and incapable of arousing enthusiasm for the republic as an institution. They retained the allegiance of the older working class but failed lamentably to win youth to the party. Only at the very end of the republic did the Socialist intellectual, Carlo Mierendorff, gather some able young men around him, modernise the party organisation and try to change the mental attitude of the party. It all came too late to save a well-meaning but ageing party.

The Centre party played a much more active role in the political life of the republic. Having no ideological objection to bourgeois parties, it was represented in nineteen of twenty-one cabinets, and in fact without the Centre's support government-making would have been impossible. But the party had advanced little beyond the days of Bismarck. Defence of Church interests was still the *raison d'être* of the Centre, perhaps because it could agree on little else, being deeply divided on social and economic policy. In the early days the left wing, led by Erzberger and Wirth, was in control, pursuing policies broadly akin to the Socialists. By the end of the 1920s the right wing under Kaas and Brüning had reasserted its old dominance, a development which did not greatly assist the cause of democracy. The Democrats were a great disappointment. A strong party in 1919, full of enthusiasm for parliamentary democracy, the Democrats failed to generate a liberal dynamic to sustain the republic. They lost their most able leaders, Friedrich Naumann and Max Weber, very early on; and the small bankers and industrialists, the party's backbone, were a declining economic force in the late 1920s, swamped by the great industrial combines.

Reference was made earlier to the active opposition which faced the republic from extreme left and extreme right. On the left the German Communist party in the early 1930s was the most numerous and powerful outside Russia. After a confused period in the mid-1920s the party came under Russian influence via the Comintern. Faced with the rise of National Socialism, German Communists adhered slavishly to the Moscow line. With a cavalier disregard for reality, they persisted in describing fascism as the twin sister of social democracy. Both were denounced as the lackeys of monopoly capitalism operating within the framework of a bourgeois republic daily becoming more fascist as the economic crisis deepened. Furthermore, as fascism was held to be the final and unavoidable stage of capitalism, the establishment of a fascist regime would soon be followed by the collapse of capitalism and the victory of socialism. Such an interpretation grossly minimised the significance of a Nazi victory and weakened the will of the working class to resist fascism. And even when on the eve of Hitler's appointment as chancellor some Communists at last showed willingness to work with Social Democrats, the intransigence of the former and the deep-rooted suspicions on both sides prevented the emergence of a united working-class movement which was the one hope of preventing a fascist victory.

It was not only the Communists who had abandoned all intention of seizing power. Most right-wing opponents of the republic had done the same. The Kapp *Putsch* was an isolated episode. As putschist politics went out of fashion, the German Nationalists started to reassess their position. It was a slow and arduous process, but by 1927 the more perspicacious Nationalists had realised that irresponsible opposition would lead them into a *cul-de-sac*. By accepting the republic as a fact and acknowledging the success of Stresemann's policy, they could hope to exert a positive influence on policy, especially on tariffs and taxation. The decision to join the Marx cabinet in 1927 was a turning-point in their evolution.[4] One of the factors which encouraged this new mood was the election of President von Hindenburg in 1925. Whatever hopes some right-wing supporters may have cherished, the election of the victor of Tannenberg set the seal of respectability on the republic. Of course the seventy-eight-year-old field marshal was never more than lukewarm towards the republic; before accepting nomination he insisted on obtaining privately the consent of the ex-emperor. That half of the electorate which preferred him to his opponent, Marx of the Centre party, undoubtedly saw in the venerable warrior an *Ersatzkaiser*, a reincarnation of the spirit of Wilhelmine Germany. As Stresemann perceptively remarked, the Germans were not really happy as long as the head of state was a civilian in a top hat; they longed for a respectable figure in uniform with a chestful of medals. This they obtained in 1925. But as long as the political machinery of the republic functioned, Hindenburg played the game according to the constitutional rules. Only when the great crisis came in the 1930s did the presence of this authoritarian-

---

[4] They joined the Luther cabinet in January 1925 but withdrew in October.

minded old gentleman in the presidential palace prove a serious liability for the republic.

It was little short of tragic that precisely when the more moderate German Nationalists were starting to play a constructive political role, the forces of reaction should have triumphed in the party. Their instrument was Alfred Hugenberg, an ambitious and ruthless business man, who became party chairman in 1928. Known as the 'silver fox' on account of his acumen and organising ability, Hugenberg owned a vast newspaper- and cinema-network through which he disseminated virulent nationalist propaganda. A fervent Pan-German, he was deeply hostile to the republic and all it stood for and a bitter opponent of the fulfilment policy. His hour came at the close of the 1920s when the leaders of heavy industry, with whom he was on excellent terms, transferred their allegiance from the Democrats and Populists to the German Nationalists, partly in protest against growing state intervention in the economy and partly because they feared that a new reparations settlement would penalise industry. It so happened that the Nationalists suffered a heavy electoral defeat in 1928, losing nearly two million votes, largely because they had joined the Marx cabinet. In the aftermath of defeat Hugenberg was elected chairman by a narrow majority, and Count Westarp, the parliamentary leader, finding his position impossible, resigned. This was the end of constructive opposition. Under Hugenberg moderates were squeezed out of the party and it lapsed once more into blind opposition to the republic.

The first fruits of this disastrous change were seen in 1929 when Hugenberg launched a major political campaign against the Young Plan. In July a national committee representing the German Nationalists, the Pan-German League, *Stahlhelm* and the National Socialists, was formed to promote a law 'against the enslavement of the German people', which would oblige the government to repudiate war-guilt and secure the immediate evacuation of occupied territory (how this could be done was not explained); finally, ministers who signed agreements such as the Young Plan were to be prosecuted for treason. The extremists succeeded in obtaining the bare ten per cent of the electorate's support required for the submission of their absurd 'freedom bill' to the Reichstag. Here it was ignominiously defeated, and in the subsequent referendum only 13.8 per cent of the electorate supported the bill. Hugenberg's irresponsible campaign had failed miserably. Some of the more able Nationalists, led by Gottfried Treviranus, broke with the party, thoroughly disgusted by the vulgarity and blatant dishonesty of the campaign. The real victor was Adolf Hitler. The campaign came at a most opportune moment for this small-time Bavarian politician, whose party had only secured twelve seats in the 1928 elections. Overnight Hitler became a national figure, and for the first time his propaganda reached hitherto inaccessible middle-class circles, thanks to Hugenberg's vast press network. Having extracted the

maximum publicity out of the campaign, Hitler simply severed his connection with elements he regarded as 'reactionary' and went his own way
again.

The collapse of the Wall Street Stock Exchange in October 1929 was the
beginning of the end of the tinsel prosperity of Western Europe. A super-
abundance of capital led to a wave of speculative investment in the United
States. Share values increased out of all proportion to the earning power of
assets, and when statistics revealed that production was actually declining,
the bubble burst. Within a month American investors lost 40,000 million
dollars. Europe was so heavily dependent on American investment by this
time that she could not escape the consequences of the Wall Street Crash.
Foreign investment had started to decline as early as 1928. The decline
rapidly gathered momentum in the winter of 1929–30, when many short-
term loans were called in. Withdrawals from Germany were greatly accelerated by the National Socialist electoral victory in September 1930,
although it was still not apparent how dependent Europe had become on
American prosperity. The awful truth dawned in the summer of 1931.
The Austrian *Kreditanstalt* collapsed in May; in the first two weeks of June
foreign funds totalling 1,000 million marks left Germany; the *Norddeutsche
Wollkämmerei* of Bremen collapsed, and the *Darmstädter und Nationalbank*, one of the four great German deposit banks, suspended payments.
Other banks were in no position to help their associate. On 14 July the
government intervened, proclaimed a two days' bank holiday and closed
the stock exchange to avert the complete collapse of the banking system.

The crisis was industrial as well as financial. The price of food and raw
materials was already falling in the late 1920s. The Wall Street Crash was
the last straw. Advanced industrial nations drastically reduced overseas
purchases, causing prices to fall catastrophically. This quickly boomer-
anged on the advanced countries when primary producers, deprived of
their income, were obliged to reduce drastically manufactured imports,
causing serious unemployment in Europe and America. As world markets
contracted, Germany's export trade declined sharply, being heavily
dependent on capital goods, which are the first to suffer cuts in times of
economic uncertainty. Unemployment grew by leaps and bounds; in the
summer of 1929 approximately 900,000 were out of work in Germany; the
figure rose to over three millions in December 1930, five-and-a-half millions by July 1931, reaching a peak of over six millions at the beginning of
1932.

German agriculture was seriously affected by the crisis. Prices fell
disastrously and rye exports virtually ceased, causing widespread distress
among the heavily mortgaged farmers, especially in East Prussia. As early
as March 1929 the landowners' organisations banded together in the

Green Front to fight for greater tariff protection. In the summer there were sporadic disturbances in Schleswig-Holstein when bankrupt farmers were obliged to auction their homes. The state did in fact give considerable assistance to agriculture in 1930 – the so-called *Osthilfe* – but no amount of aid could turn embittered land-owners into friends of the republic.

The political crisis which ended in Hitler's accession to power in January 1933 started in March 1930 when Heinrich Brüning was appointed chancellor. By the end of 1929 there were many alarming signs of impending crisis; mounting unemployment, falling tax-receipts and a budget deficit of 1,700 million marks which called for drastic action. On the issue of unemployment benefits the great coalition was fatally divided. The middle-class parties, Populists, Democrats and Centre, though favouring retrenchment, had actually agreed on a compromise formula but the Socialists, fearing that even this would lead to a reduction of benefits, rejected it. With the cabinet hopelessly divided, Müller had no alternative but to resign. Parliamentary government, properly so-called, ended with the fall of Müller. For on 28 March 1930, when Hindenburg appointed Heinrich Brüning, it was made clear that the new chancellor could rely on the president's emergency powers for the conduct of business if Reichstag support was not forthcoming. This was the thin end of the wedge for parliamentary government, for under the new arrangement – presidential government as it was called – the balance of power began to move from the legislature back to the executive, where it had been in 1914.

A growing body of contemporary opinion welcomed this retrograde development. Strong government appealed to business men eager to break the power of the unions and to reduce the social contributions they paid to support the welfare state, and to agrarian circles full of nostalgia for the old *Obrigkeitsstaat*. It came frankly as a relief to many politicians on the right and centre, all too conscious of their inability to make parliamentary government work. Hindenburg had always taken an exalted view of his own powers and lent a ready ear to the suggestions of military and civilian friends who believed the time ripe for non-party government. The leading figure among the unofficial advisers clustered round the president, and a man who came to exert great influence over the eighty-three-year-old warrior over the next three years, was General von Schleicher, chief of the *Ministeramt*, a wily political soldier who acted as permanent liaison officer between the *Reichswehr* and the government. Schleicher feared that extremists on right and left would be encouraged by the weakness of the Reichstag to make a bid for power certain to plunge Germany into civil war and invite a Polish attack in the east. What Germany needed, in Schleicher's opinion, was a period of strong non-party government, drawing on presidential powers and relying on the *Reichswehr* to keep order and preserve the unity of the *Reich*. Brüning seemed ideally suited to be 'the army's chancellor'; a highly intelligent, rather aloof man of authoritarian views who favoured the restoration of the monarchy and the emasculation of the parliamentary system, he was well-disposed towards the army; during the war he served as a machine-gun officer and won the Iron Cross, important recommendations in the president's eyes. Hindenburg, unable at first to win Hugenberg's support for a 'national' government, had been inclined to give Müller emergency powers to get an agreed budget through. To this Schleicher was adamantly opposed. And as Hindenburg's request for yet more aid for East Prussian landowners was being currently delayed by Müller, the president finally decided to let him go.

Brüning's 'non-party' government – basically Müller's without the Socialists – was tolerated at first by the Reichstag. Brüning survived a no-confidence motion after warning the deputies that his government represented a 'last attempt' to solve Germany's economic problems in co-operation with the Reichstag. Then in July 1930 he presented a retrenchment budget featuring sharp tax-increases and cuts in expenditure. When it was clear that a majority would not be forthcoming, Brüning promulgated the budget by decree, a controversial use of clause 48 not envisaged in 1919. A few days later, when a Socialist motion demanding the withdrawal of the decrees was carried by a narrow majority, Brüning promptly dissolved the Reichstag and ordered fresh elections.

The election of September 1930 intensified Germany's political crisis. Naïvely Brüning hoped to rally moderate opinion in support of presidential government. The omens were not encouraging; the chancellor was far too shy and aloof to arouse great passion on the part of the electorate at the best of times; nor was there much hope of a united middle-class front emerging to save Brüning. Therefore some increase in right-wing extremism was certain. Already in 1929 the Nazis increased their support significantly at the Land elections. However, no one expected such a phenomenal increase in the National Socialist vote; even Hitler counted on a maximum of fifty seats in the new Reichstag. In September 1928 the Nazis polled 810,000 votes, in 1930 they polled nearly six-and-a-half million votes and with 107 seats became the second largest party in the Reichstag. The Communist vote also increased sharply; they gained well over one million votes, mostly from the Socialists, and now had seventy-seven seats instead of fifty-four. Taken over all, the great increase in the extremist vote was ominous; two out of every five Germans voted for parties bitterly opposed to the principles on which the republic rested.

The international repercussions were also serious. Foreign investors accelerated the withdrawal of funds from Germany; in September and October she lost 633 million marks in gold and foreign exchange. The good relations with France, so carefully cultivated by Stresemann, were suddenly clouded. Briand had arrived in Geneva to negotiate with

Brüning about the French plan for a united Europe (about which admittedly Brüning had serious reservations, fearing that acceptance would end all hopes of revision of the eastern frontier). When news of the Nazi successes came through Briand terminated the negotiations.

The Nazi landslide merits closer examination. During the lean years the hard core of Nazi support came from the 'white-collar proletariat' – clerks, small shopkeepers, teachers and people on the lower fringes of the professions. It is no coincidence that many of the Nazi leaders stemmed from this *milieu*. But the Nazis only became a mass party when the broad middle class and the farming community abandoned their traditional political allegiances, deserting the German Nationalists – who lost half their total support – the Democrats and the Populists. Lacking an agrarian programme until 1930 the Nazis simply latched on to agrarian discontent and won massive support in the countryside with promises of higher prices and protection. In the cities the working-class vote was, however, relatively unaffected – the unemployed did not in the main vote Nazi but Communist in the early 1930s. It was in the small towns especially in the Protestant north and centre that the Nazis won over the broad middle class. Some young voters turned to the Communists, many more to the Nazis, attracted in part by the physical violence of the Brown Shirts whose attacks on opponents were tolerated by respectable middle-class citizens as long as 'Marxists' were the target. The young end of the army was greatly attracted by Hitler. Schleicher and Groener in an attempt to preserve the army from contamination placed three young officers on trial for spreading Nazi progaganda. Hitler, star witness for the defence, publicly announced his intention of creating a large army, a promise calculated to weaken opposition to him in *Reichswehr* circles.

What had National Socialism to offer the discontented in town and country? A clever combination of promises of concrete measures designed to appease interest groups (farmers, civil servants, small manufacturers etc.) coupled with bombastic rhetoric directed against the 'Marxist republic'. Instead of rational analysis Nazi speakers blamed Germany's ills on a series of scapegoats: 'Marxists', 'November traitors' and 'Jews' – although for tactical reasons anti-semitic propaganda, once so prominent a feature of the party in the early 1920s, was toned down. Like other right-wing parties they promised strong government, inspired leadership and the restoration of national pride. The difference was that they beat the nationalist drum more vigorously than their rivals; *Deutschland erwache*[5] was the theme at every rally and on every street corner; and with reckless abandon they called for the immediate repudiation of the Versailles Treaty. And of their followers they demanded whole-hearted commitment to the party and

[5]Germany awake!

faith in the leader's ability to carry out the 'National Revolution' to restore Germany to greatness.

There can be little doubt that the Nazis owed at least some of their spectacular success to the extraordinary political ability of their leader, Adolf Hitler. The details of his early life are well known. The son of an Austrian customs official, Hitler was born at Braunau-am-Inn just inside the Austrian frontier in 1889. His youth was unhappy; attempts to become an artist ended in failure, and after the death of his parents he migrated to Vienna. Shy, morose and awkward as a young man, Hitler lived in Vienna for several years supported largely by a state pension. His bitter hatred of Jews, Marxists and democrats and his passionate belief in Pan-Germanism and racism date from this period. In 1913 he moved to Munich, apparently to avoid conscription in the Austrian army. On the outbreak of war, swept along on a tidal wave of patriotic emotion, he enlisted in a Bavarian regiment. For the next four years he experienced true peace of mind in front-line service, became a corporal and was decorated for bravery. The end of the war came as a bitter blow while he was recovering in a Pomeranian hospital from a gas attack. Returning to Bavaria with no clear plans for the future, he was appointed 'education officer' to maintain contact between the army and small extremist groups springing up in and around Munich. Asked to investigate one of these parties, the German Workers' Party, he quickly accepted an invitation to join its executive committee. Soon he discovered his remarkable gift for public speaking, and by 1921 was party leader. Imprisoned for his part in the abortive 1923 *Putsch*, Hitler spent a year in comparatively comfortable surroundings in Landsberg prison, where he dictated *Mein Kampf*, a long rambling and repetitive political text which became the bible of the movement and eventually netted a fortune for the author. Upon his release at the end of 1924, Hitler returned to Munich and set to work to rebuild the Nazi party, which he had allowed to fall to pieces in his absence. With great skill and perseverance he welded the scattered fragments into a small but compact and well-organised party under his personal control. By 1926 the party had a following in North Germany, thanks to the efforts of the Strasser brothers and their *protégé*, a certain Josef Goebbels, whom Hitler put in charge of propaganda in 1928.

Hitler's personality was unattractive in the extreme. He was a changeable and moody individual, excessively vain, full of overweening pride and ambition, not without intellectual ability but shallow and superficial in his judgements and firmly convinced of his own infallibility over the whole range of human experience. At bottom Hitler was a profoundly lonely and isolated human being, deeply contemptuous of mankind in general, inordinately suspicious of his fellow men, unscrupulous, brutal and utterly ruthless in his methods and totally lacking in human compassion and consumed by paranoid hatred of Jewry. But his political gifts were of the very highest order. He possessed tremendous energy and remarkable will-power and in his quest for high office displayed the singlemindedness of a fanatic. A supreme opportunist, he had an uncanny sense of timing and an unerring instinct for the course of action most likely to advance his interests. As a political propagandist he was quite unsurpassed, a supreme master of the psychology of mass politics, with an unrivalled gift for exploiting contemporary discontent. Without doubt Hitler was one of the greatest demagogues of modern times. His violent tirades, often lasting for hours on end, were full of repetition, half-truths and down-right lies, but his rasping voice rarely failed to exert an uncanny hypnotic effect on the audience – objectors were speedily ejected by the brown-shirted *SA*. He never reasoned with audiences but simply put into words what they were longing to hear, feeding on their hidden resentment, playing on their anxieties, unleashing elemental passions and forcing his listeners to sur-render their will to that of the leader; literally a man possessed, a mass psychologist of diabolical genius, as Schacht once remarked. While it would be quite wrong to attribute the phenomenal success of the party to Hitler's efforts alone, it is equally apparent that his personal qualities – his charisma for many (though not all) Germans and his ora-torical skills – are factors of major importance in explaining the rise of the Nazis.

Brüning, backed by Hindenburg, remained in the chancellery despite electoral defeat. The parliamentary deadlock was now complete. The Nationalists, the Nazis and the Communists were ranged against Brüning. For support he could rely only on the Centre and, less certainly, on the small right-wing splinter groups. Everything depended on the Socialists. Once again the party was impaled on the horns of a cruel dilemma. Support of Brüning, quite apart from the natural repugnance of demo-cratic Socialists for presidential government, meant acquiescence in deflationary policies bearing most heavily on the working class; their only alternative was to oppose Brüning and precipitate new elections certain to strengthen the Nazis still further and likely to end in a fascist dictatorship. After an agonising appraisal the Socialists concluded that Brüning was the lesser of two evils, and with their help he survived a no-confidence motion. Some quarters praised the Socialists for a patriotic and statesmanlike act, others condemned them for betraying the working-class movement and, significantly enough, their vote declined appreciably at subsequent elections. One thing is certain. By tolerating Brüning and his use of clause 48, the Socialists enabled presidential government to function with a semblance of Reichstag support for the next two years; in effect Germany reverted to the pre-1914 situation where chancellors consulted the major-ity parties from time to time but always retained in their own hands ultimate responsibility for policy.

Economic strategy, foreign political objectives and a desire to steal the thunder of nationalist extremists were closely intertwined in Brüning's policies. Clearly he hoped to exploit the economic crisis to rid Germany of her huge foreign indebtedness and secure the abolition of reparations. He cut wages, salaries and public expenditure, increased consumer-goods taxes and ordered price cuts, a deflationary package designed to stimulate demand at home and exports abroad. Retrenchment and the conquest of export markets at the expense of the creditors would surely convince them of the absurdity of reparations. In pursuit of this objective 3,000 million marks were handed out in subsidies to industry (and to agriculture out of deference to agrarian interests) but only 500 million marks to combat unemployment directly.

Brüning succeeded in building up a considerable export surplus which enabled Germany to pay reparations without recourse to foreign loans. But before the implications dawned on the creditors Germany was overwhelmed by a great financial crisis. In June 1931 Brüning announced that she could no longer fulfil her obligations under the Young Plan. At last the creditors changed their mind. A month later the Hoover memorandum suspended all reparation and war debts payments for one year. And when Brüning insisted that Germany could not possibly recommence payments in 1932 the Bank of International Settlement agreed with him and recommended a meeting of creditors to revise the Plan. Because of well-founded French fears that Germany was seeking complete abolition the conference scheduled for January 1932 was postponed until June. When the Lausanne Conference met reparations were wound up in return for a final payment of 3,000 million marks (which Hitler never paid). But it was Brüning's successor Papen who enjoyed the political fruits of his labours.

Similarly over disarmament. In an attempt to head off the Nazis whose vote continued to rise at Land elections, Brüning pressed hard at the Disarmament Conference (which opened in February 1932) for recognition of Germany's right to absolute equality in armaments. Whether other powers disarmed down to her level or allowed her to arm up to theirs mattered little to Brüning as it had to Stresemann. Predictably the French, being determined to preserve their military superiority as long as humanly possible, fiercely resisted Brüning. Eventually the issue was resolved in Germany's favour but, once again, too late to save Brüning.

Nor did Brüning's ambitious Austrian plans succeed. Hoping to prove to the nationalist right that he was just as anxious for *Anschluss* with Austria, Brüning announced in March 1931 that Germany and Austria intended to form a customs union to consolidate economic ties between the two countries. He was also attempting to break into the markets of South-Eastern Europe and establish Germany as the dominant economic power there – as Schacht was to attempt after him. The news aroused alarm in France and the Little Entente countries where it was regarded as proof positive that the old expansionist spirit was still alive. Reluctantly Brüning agreed to refer the matter to the League of Nations Council and to the Hague Court. Meanwhile the economic crisis deepened; Austria in a state of collapse was forced to ask the League for a loan which gave France and her allies a golden opportunity to make it conditional on the abandonment of the proposed customs union. On 5 September 1931 the Hague Court decided – though only by eight votes to seven – that the union would have been incompatible with the Treaty of Versailles. Brüning suffered a sharp reverse and Foreign Minister Julius Curtius resigned.

By the end of 1931 the centre of gravity of German political life was rapidly moving away from the Reichstag and chancellery to the streets, where the Nazis and their opponents came into frequent collision. Quasi-military formations and uniforms were back in fashion in the early 1930s; the Nazis had enrolled over 400,000 men in the *SA*, a huge private army which protected party meetings and intimidated political opponents; the *Stahlhelm*, representing the more conservative nationalists, had also become a considerable political force; whilst on the left *Reichsbanner Schwarz-Rot-Gold*, trade unions and workers' athletic clubs formed the *Eiserne republikanische Front zur Abwehr des Faschismus* in December 1931. Against this back-cloth of mounting tension and violence, which the Reichstag was powerless to stop, the presidency emerged as the stable point in a fluid political situation. Effective power resided partly in the presidential palace, partly on the streets, but less and less in the Reichstag or in the chancellery.

The crucial importance of the presidency was emphasised in the spring of 1932, when Hindenburg's term of office expired. The old man, now in a state of mental and physical decline, wanted to retire to Neudeck, his country estate, to end his days in peace. Brüning insisted that he remain at the head of affairs, firmly convinced that Hindenburg was the only alternative to Hitler. Naturally Brüning wished to avoid the excitement of a presidential election at a time of nationalist ferment when the Nazi vote was increasing at every *Land* election, so he tried to obtain the agreement of the parties to a constitutional amendment extending Hindenburg's term of office to 1934. Neither Hitler nor Hugenberg would agree to this expedient, and reluctantly Hindenburg agreed to stand for re-election. That the Socialists and Centre supported him, while the German Nationalists ran a candidate against him, greatly upset the old man, whose sympathies lay completely on the right. After some initial hesitation Hitler agreed to stand; on the eve of the election he hastily assumed German citizenship by accepting the post of *Regierungsrat* (government adviser) in the little Nazi-controlled *Land* of Brunswick. A bitter and frenzied campaign ensued, marked by further street violence. In effect it was a plebiscite for or against National Socialism, a contest between the power of the streets and the magic of an old warrior's name backed by the power of the *Reichswehr*. On the second ballot in April 1932 Hindenburg received

19,359,000 votes, Hitler 13,418,000, and the Communist Thälmann, 3,706,000. Though defeated, the Nazis had won a great moral victory; since 1930 their vote had nearly doubled, and between the first and second ballots Hitler succeeded in capturing an extra two million votes. Nor had those republicans who reluctantly supported Hindenburg, as the only alternative to a reign of lawlessness under Hitler, much cause for congratulation. They had no guarantee that the weary octogenarian would respect the spirit of the constitution or display sound judgement in affairs of state; within a matter of weeks there was proof of his lack of political insight when he dispensed with the services of his faithful and devoted chancellor who had worked zealously to secure his re-election.

The resignation of Brüning in May was very largely the work of Schleicher. In the course of 1931 Schleicher changed his mind about Brüning, once it was clear that the latter had failed to rally moderate opinion in defence of the presidential system. As radical nationalism grew in strength, Schleicher concluded that the only certain way of avoiding a Nazi uprising, likely to strain the loyalties of the *Reichswehr*, was to come to terms with Hitler and include him in a presidential cabinet under a more right-wing chancellor. Immediately after the election Brüning had yielded to pressure from several *Länder*, notably Prussia, and banned the *SA* and *SS* as a serious danger to state security. Schleicher was alarmed, not out of any respect for these ill-disciplined rowdies, but simply because he feared the reaction of the right wing to a ban on a nationalist organisation. The time had come, he decided, to end 'the drift to the left' and appoint a new chancellor who would show no favour to Socialists but would do his best to prepare the ground for a *rapprochement* with Hitler. Looking back over the years, it is only too apparent that Schleicher was a vain and self-confident intriguer, who grossly underestimated the nature of the Nazi party, lightly assuming that it was a healthy nationalist movement which he could tame and exploit by adroit political manipulation. The general was digging his own grave as he intrigued first against Groener, whom he forced to resign, and then against Brüning. The president was already out of sympathy with Brüning's policies and lent a ready ear to the advice of Schleicher, eagerly reinforced by his son Oskar von Hindenburg. Early in May 1932 Schleicher overcame the president's lingering doubts by informing him that Hitler had now agreed not to oppose a new chancellor, on condition that the ban on *SA* and *SS* was lifted and new elections were ordered.

The scene was set for Brüning's dismissal. Ironically enough, the chancellor was confident that the tide was turning at last, both at home and abroad. Well aware that his deflationary policies had failed to cure unemployment, now topping the six million mark, he was preparing cautiously to reflate the economy and had drafted a programme of public works, including proposals for the break-up of some inefficient East Prussian estates and the resettlement of 600,000 unemployed on them.

Landowning circles got wind of this and their spokesman, Oldenburg-Januschau, visited Hindenburg at Neudeck and easily persuaded the disgruntled president that Brüning was an 'agrarian bolshevik' bent on socialising agriculture. When Brüning appeared with new emergency decrees the old man refused to sign, and insisted on the formation of a more right-wing cabinet. Brüning was deeply offended by Hindenburg's ingratitude when the government was allegedly 'only a hundred metres from the goal', with reparations and disarmament likely to be resolved in Germany's favour. Characteristically, he made only a half-hearted attempt to justify himself, meekly tendering his resignation and that of his cabinet, which was at once accepted.

The fall of Brüning was a turning-point in these critical years. His dependence on Hindenburg hardly compensated for his lack of tactical ability and mass appeal. And though his deflationary policies contributed materially to the abolition of reparations, they did so only by deepening the domestic crisis. Still, Brüning was a man of integrity and a deeply patriotic German who won the respect of foreign statesmen. And once he had departed the prospects for the survival of even a mildly authoritarian regime suddenly looked much bleaker.

The eight months which came between the resignation of Brüning and the appointment of Hitler as chancellor were full of feverish political activity and complex political manoeuvring. There could be no clearer sign of the bankruptcy of the political system than the appointment of Franz von Papen as chancellor. A charming and accomplished socialite and close friend of Schleicher, Papen was a Westphalian aristocrat with industrial connexions, a former general-staff officer in the old Prussian army, a Catholic with authoritarian views, a crafty intriguer certainly, but a man of little political insight or stature. A storm of disapproval greeted his government of 'national concentration', which represented the interests of business men and landowners so blatantly that contemporaries dubbed it 'the cabinet of barons'. The left was automatically against Papen; the centre bitterly hostile to the man who had ousted Brüning; even the Nationalists were annoyed because Papen had been preferred to Hugenberg. And much to his surprise Schleicher discovered that Hitler was not a man of his word; despite Hitler's promise, the Nazis attacked Papen as they had attacked Brüning before him. Clearly there was no hope of the Reichstag's 'tolerating' Papen as it 'tolerated' Brüning. So fresh elections were ordered at once and, in accordance with Schleicher's promise to Hitler, the ban on the *SA* was lifted, a step which resulted in a new wave of street violence sweeping through Germany in the high summer of 1932.

To curry favour with the right wing before going to the polls, and also to strengthen the government's hand *vis-à-vis* Hitler by securing control of the police in the largest German state, Schleicher and Papen decided on a *coup d'état* to unseat the Prussian government. For years the extreme right had resented the Socialist-Centre government which had made Prussia a bulwark of the Weimar system. In April 1932 local elections destroyed the 'red-black' majority, but as Nazis, Communists and Nationalists were not likely to reach agreement, the Braun-Severing government remained in office on a caretaker basis. On 20 July 1932 Papen declared a state of emergency in Prussia, appointed himself *Reichskommissar*, and dismissed the Prussian ministers on the grounds that they had favoured the Communists and had failed to prevent fresh street violence (for which Papen's raising of the ban on the *SA* was to blame). Neither Centrists nor Socialists were prepared to resist Papen. The Socialists acquiesced in the situation, as their predecessors had done when Stresemann struck at Saxony in 1923. One police captain and five men sufficed to remove Socialist ministers from office in the most industrialised and powerful *Land* in Germany. Of course they made out a compelling case for inaction; resistance would have led to useless bloodshed because the *Reichswehr*, the *Stahlhelm* and the Nazis would have been thrown into battle against them, and the *SA* might well have seized power in the general confusion; there were legal doubts whether a mere caretaker government would be justified in offering resistance at all; nor did it make sense to call a general strike with six million men unemployed. Instead the Socialists turned to the Supreme Court and sought an injunction against Papen. 'I have been a democrat for forty years and I am not going to become a condottiere now' remarked Minister-President Braun, as he rejected suggestions that he lead the resistance to Papen; an understandable attitude perhaps, in the light of the party's traditions of non-violence, rational discussion and peaceful evolution. But whatever may be said for or against the decision of Braun and Severing and their trade-union colleagues, one thing is quite certain; the cause of democracy suffered a mortal blow when the Prussian government capitulated without a struggle. Papen followed up the *coup d'état* with a thorough purge of the Prussian civil service; many loyal republican officials were retired and the *Land* completely integrated with the Reich.

The Prussian *coup d'état* pleased the right wing, but it did not enable Papen to woo nationalist support away from Hitler at the elections on 31 July 1932. The Populists lost over one million votes, the German Nationalists nearly 300,000, whereas the Nazi vote actually showed a slight increase on that of the presidential election; with 13,745,000 votes the Nazis held 230 seats in the Reichstag. As leader of what was by far the largest party, Hitler had a constitutional right to try and form a government. Schleicher and Papen agreed that he must come into their cabinet. The difficulty was Hitler, who was in a thoroughly intransigent mood, confident (as he had every reason to be) of ultimate victory in the near future. Called to the palace for consultations, he bluntly demanded full powers for his party. The president was unimpressed by 'the Bohemian corporal', refused to offer him more than inclusion in a presidential cabinet and warned him to exercise more control over lawless elements in the Nazi party – shortly after the election Papen had been obliged to impose the death penalty for political murders and to set up special courts to deal with political offences. Hitler rejected Hindenburg's offer out of hand, but as he had no intention of seizing power, despite much wild talk, the political deadlock was complete.

When the Reichstag met in September 1932 Papen, well aware that he had no hope of success, promptly dissolved it, but not before Goering, newly elected Reichstag president, had humiliated him by allowing the deputies to carry a motion of no confidence in the Papen government by 512 votes to 42, a sufficient comment on Papen's unpopularity in the Reichstag and in the country as a whole.

The election on 6 November did not resolve the deadlock. But it revealed a significant fall in the Nazi vote; this time they polled only 11,730,000 votes – a loss of two millions – and returned with 196 seats. The decline, which was confirmed at subsequent *Land* elections, was due at least in part to the fact that Papen's withdrawal from the Disarmament Conference, until Germany was conceded equality in armaments, had impressed nationalist opinion – for the first time since 1924 the German Nationalists increased their vote by almost 800,000 and returned with fifty-two instead of thirty-seven seats. This time Hitler was desperately short of funds and fighting hard for every vote; some of the more restless supporters were undoubtedly disillusioned by the leader's failure to seize power in August and drifted over to the extreme left – this was partly the reason why the Communist vote increased by 700,000 to a total of nearly six millions, giving them 100 seats in the Reichstag. Some middle-class supporters were probably scared away by Hitler's vain attempts to capture the working-class vote; the Nazis reviled the Papen cabinet as 'a class government of reactionaries' and actually collaborated with the Communists during the Berlin transport strike which paralysed the great city in early November.

What Papen might have made of this changing political situation will never be known, for in November he fell victim to another Schleicher intrigue. As Papen had no support in the Reichstag, apart from Nationalists and Populists, he tendered his resignation, a purely tactical manoeuvre, for he assumed that Hitler would not be able to form a government and that Hindenburg would then reinstate his old friend in office. As expected, Hitler still insisted on plenary powers which the president refused to give him. So Papen re-emerged from the wings, this time with a new plan. He proposed to declare martial law, dissolve the Reichstag, postpone elections and rule by decree until the constitution had been amended along authoritarian lines and a reflationary programme given time to work. Hindenburg was willing enough to support Papen in this but

Schleicher was not. He believed that he could divide the Nazi party and hive off a section of some sixty deputies led by the left-wing National Socialist Gregor Strasser. With their support and the backing of sympathetic trade-union elements in the Socialist and Centre parties, where he had been taking soundings, Schleicher hoped to build a Reichstag majority for a progressive social programme within the framework of the constitution. While Hindenburg hesitated, Schleicher played an ace. He informed the cabinet that Papen's policy would lead to civil war, a general strike and probably a Polish invasion; to defend Germany against several perils simultaneously was simply beyond the *Reichswehr*'s capacity. When Papen now tried to have Schleicher dismissed, Hindenburg refused and with tears rolling down his cheeks allowed 'little Franz' to depart.

On 2 December 1932 Schleicher became German chancellor, rather reluctantly, as he would have much preferred to continue his intrigues behind cover. Nothing went right for him in office. It was soon apparent that he had grossly over-estimated his ability to divide the Nazis. Strasser was easily outmanoeuvred by Hitler, who reasserted his control over the party and nipped signs of rebellion in the bud. Then Schleicher approached the left with a programme of public works, price-fixing, restoration of wage- and relief-cuts, and land resettlement in East Prussia, measures which naturally turned the right wing against him. But he could not overcome the mistrust of Socialists and Centrists and had finally to return to the presidential palace to take up where Papen left off. Admitting that he could not obtain a majority in the Reichstag, Schleicher proposed to dissolve it, declare a state of emergency, ban the Nazis and Communists and postpone elections indefinitely.

The role of industry in the winter of 1932-3 in ousting Schleicher and helping Hitler to power has been the subject of much controversy. In the boom years German industry had been uninterested in the Nazis. What support Hitler received before 1932 came from mavericks such as Fritz Thyssen and Emil Kirdorf. Industry was deeply suspicious of the anti-capitalist veneer of Nazism. In October 1930 just after their spectacular electoral victory the newly arrived Nazi deputies introduced a bill to nationalise banks and control interest rates which Hitler obliged them to withdraw. Over the next two years as the crisis deepened Hitler – who had no interest whatsoever in socialism – redoubled his efforts to win industrial support but without success. Industrialists preferred Brüning and Papen to Hitler. Consequently, far from being in the 'pocket of big business', the Nazis were desperately short of funds from June 1932 to January 1933, as Goebbels lamented in his diary.

Certainly some (but not all) leading figures in the cartelised coal and steel industries, which were in dire trouble, sympathised with the Nazis. For the latter promised to destroy parliamentary government, smash the trade unions (ensuring that wage-levels remained low) and dismantle the welfare system (lowering the employers' social contributions). Possibly Schleicher's willingness to co-operate with the trade unions, introduce labour legislation and a public works programme putting money in the hands of municipalities not big business worried industrialists. But this turned them not to Hitler but back to Papen. Recent research suggests that although much of industry was ready enough to tolerate a Hitler cabinet and had little love for Weimar, nevertheless, heavy industry exerted only marginal influence on Hitler's appointment.

More important in this deadlocked political situation caused by the Reichstag's unwillingness to assume responsibility and by the unwillingness of both Nazis and Communists to seize power was the influence exerted by the president's political advisers. 'Little Franz' was working assiduously to encompass Schleicher's downfall. Hugenberg's decision to support a Hitler cabinet was equally crucial. When Hitler, worried by signs of disaffection in his own ranks, decided to accept office in a Nationalist–Nazi cabinet provided he became chancellor the intrigue moved forward. Papen, a frequent and welcome visitor to Hindenburg's house, persuaded the old man that a viable alternative to Schleicher now existed. The Nazis and Nationalists would have a reasonable chance of obtaining a majority in the Reichstag; and the fact that Hitler seemed prepared to share power and had broken with the 'left wing' Nazi Otto Strasser reassured Hindenburg. On top of Papen's promptings came pressure from landowners alarmed by the plans of the 'socialist general'; the *Landbund* went into action accusing Schleicher, like Brüning, of 'agrarian bolshevism', a serious charge in Hindenburg's mind. Disturbing rumours were circulating that the budget committee of the Reichstag had uncovered evidence of misuse of public money given to inefficient landowners under the *Osthilfe*; it was even alleged that relatives of the president were implicated, although whether this influenced Oskar von Hindenburg's decision to press Hitler's candidature on his father is uncertain. The *Reichswehr* inclined to Hitler's side; General von Hammerstein, the commander-in-chief, thought Hitler preferable to another Papen government whilst General von Blomberg, commander in East Prussia and the soldier earmarked for minister of defence in the new cabinet, reflected the views of younger officers in his enthusiastic advocacy of the Nazi cause. Whatever the decisive factor may have been, the old man determined to be rid of Schleicher. So when the general requested emergency powers at the end of January, Hindenburg turned him down; had not the chancellor argued seven weeks before that a military dictatorship meant civil war? There was nothing left for Schleicher but resignation on 28 January.

On 30 January 1933 Hindenburg received Hitler in audience and appointed him chancellor. That night and into the early morning Hitler stood on the chancellery balcony in salute as a huge torchlight procession of 100,000 excited supporters marched past in triumph, singing the *Horst*

Wessel song. This was a great hour for the rank and file; all the efforts of a handful of reactionary advisers in the presidential palace had failed to keep the leader from power; at last the long-awaited 'National Revolution' would begin.

In fact Hitler did not stand alone. A hundred metres away a slightly bewildered Hindenburg stood at an open window of the presidential palace as the procession passed. It was a timely reminder that Hitler had not seized power; he had come to office by a sordid backstairs intrigue and with the president's consent. He was chancellor, but in a government of 'national concentration', surrounded by such orthodox reactionaries as Hugenberg and Seldte of the *Stahlhelm*. There were in fact only two Nazis in the cabinet, Frick, minister of the interior, and Goering, minister without portfolio and Prussian minister of the interior. Papen, vice-chancellor in the new cabinet, was elated by the success of his intrigue, believing that he had taken Hitler prisoner and succeeded where Brüning and Schleicher failed; 'in two months we'll have pushed Hitler into a corner so hard that he'll be squeaking,' Papen boasted to a friend.

Hitler encouraged his new friends to think that the Nazis had made their peace with the forces of reaction. In the early part of 1933 he posed as a reasonable-minded nationalist, deploring *SA* excesses and claiming that sound Christian-Conservative principles guided the Nazi movement. As late as 21 March, at the impressive ceremony to mark the opening of the new Reichstag, Hitler still played this role with skill and sophistication. Outside the garrison church at Potsdam, where Frederick the Great and Frederick William I lay buried, *Reichswehr* detachments and *SA* stood on guard. Inside were assembled the generals and admirals in full-dress uniform and the Reichstag deputies (excluding the Socialists and Communists), with the Nazis in uniform as usual. The crown prince was in attendance, sitting behind the empty chair reserved for his father, the ex-emperor. Before the great array the venerable old warrior-president and the frock-coated chancellor shook hands to symbolise the marriage of the old Prussia with the new 'national awakening'.

Behind the scenes it was a very different story. Hitler was bent on absolute power from the start. The key lay in new elections, which Hitler had insisted upon as a condition of appointment, arguing that the electorate should pass judgement upon this new political combination. He made scant effort to establish whether the Centre would support him in the Reichstag and with Papen's support quickly persuaded Hindenburg to dissolve the Reichstag. Now Hitler had the apparatus of the state at his disposal, an advantage which he exploited ruthlessly. Through Goering he controlled the Prussian police. The jovial ex-air-ace did his work thoroughly; he purged the police, replacing senior officers with reliable men, and recruited 50,000 auxiliary policemen, mostly *SA*, *SS* and *Stahlhelm*, who were encouraged to use violence against left-wing political opponents.

By February a reign of terror had begun in Prussia, and the election campaign of the opposition was effectively sabotaged. Similar campaigns were launched in all *Länder* controlled by the Nazis. They were plentifully supplied with funds from industry after the meeting between Hitler and representatives of the world of industry and finance on 20 February in Berlin. At this gathering Goering openly boasted that 'the elections will certainly be the last for the next ten years, probably even for the next hundred years'. And before the March elections at least three million marks flowed into party finds. With this aid and with the radio network working for him, Hitler looked forward with confidence to the outcome of the election.

On 27 February, a few days before polling day, the Reichstag was burnt down. Whether van der Lubbe, a half-crazed Dutch Communist, was solely responsible, or more likely, was used by the Nazis to divert attention from their own involvement remains unproven. But it is undeniable that the incident occurred at precisely the right moment for the Nazis. At once they claimed that the fire was the signal for a Communist uprising which they knew full well was a remote possibility. On the strength of this, Hitler obtained the president's agreement to a decree suspending most civil and political liberties – a purely 'temporary' measure which remained in force for twelve years. The Nazi dictatorship had begun. In the early days of March the left-wing press was muzzled, hundreds of Communists and Socialists were arrested, meetings broken up and hundreds wounded and many killed in street clashes, while *Reichswehr* and police stood by helplessly. When the country voted on 6 March the Nazi vote increased significantly; they polled 17,277,200 votes and secured 288 seats. This was less than they had hoped for; Centre and Socialists had stood firm under unprecedented intimidation and even the Communists lost only one million votes. Still, Hitler had secured 43.9 per cent of the poll and with the help of the German Nationalists' fifty-two seats he now had an absolute majority in the Reichstag. The Nazi success at the polls was due in large measure to an eight per cent increase in the poll which brought out apolitical voters anxious to clamber on the current band-waggon. Broadly speaking, the middle classes, who were drifting away from Hitler in the autumn of 1932, were stampeded back again by fear of the 'Red peril'. Whatever doubts contemporaries had about the origins of the fire, it had rid Germany of 'Marxism', and as the Nazis grew irresistibly in power, with their leader in the chancellery, many felt it expedient to make peace with the new order of things. Nor could it be denied that Hitler had more claim on power than the Papens and Schleichers with their petty intrigues.

The last scene in the death of the republic was enacted on 23 March 1933. Hitler demanded that the Reichstag approve an enabling bill conferring general powers on the government for the next four years to take whatever action was deemed necessary, including the proclamation of new laws to consolidate the 'National Revolution'. For constitutional amendments to be valid, two-thirds of the deputies had to be present and two-thirds of those present had to support the bill. At first the Nazis feared the Socialists might obstruct the bill's passage by absenting themselves; eighty-one Communists were already excluded (mostly under arrest); if 120 Socialists stayed away and persuaded another fifteen deputies to do likewise the necessary majority could not be obtained. To defeat this stratagem Hitler insisted on a procedural change whereby all deputies were counted present unless excused, and the (Nazi) president of the Reichstag would decide whether they were excused or not. In fact it was not necessary to invoke this procedure. The German Nationalists, the small right-wing splinter groups and the Centre all supported Hitler, a pathetic comment on the bankruptcy of the middle-class parties. Fear of the personal consequences if they refused, vain hopes that they might avert outright tyranny by preserving some semblance of constitutionalism, trust in the ability of the aged president to restrain the Nazis and a naïve belief that Hitler would keep his promise to restore civil and political liberties and respect the power of the Reichstag, the Reichsrat and the presidency, all these factors played their part in the melancholy decision. Only the Socialists refused to bend. When the bill was passed by 444 votes to 94, the Nazi deputies sang the *Horst Wessel* song and crowds of supporters outside the Kroll opera house joined in.

The Nazi dictatorship had commenced already with the decree suspending civil liberties on 28 February. Nevertheless, the Enabling Act was of great psychological importance. Many sober-minded officials and soldiers brought up in the strict law-abiding Wilhelmian atmosphere were repelled by the rowdy street hooligans in uniform and their vulgar ranting leader. The act, which seemingly placed the legality of the régime beyond all doubt, enabled these Germans to suppress their anxieties and fears and serve their new masters as faithfully as the old. The continued presence of Hindenburg at the head of affairs and the fact that non-Nazis remained in the cabinet was a reassuring sign that all was well. After all, Hitler was indisputably the strongest man in Germany and should be given his chance to put Germany's house in order and end the state of near civil war which had threatened Germany for two years. It was significant that when the Socialist party was dissolved on 22 June 1933, the middle-class parties hastened to dissolve themselves, the German Nationalists on 27 June and the Centre on 5 July. On 14 July, an unfortunate choice of date, the National Socialist German Workers' Party was proclaimed the only legal party in Germany. The Reichstag still remained in being but ceased to be a forum for democratic discussion. The one-party state had arrived and the 'National Revolution' began.

The collapse of the Weimar republic was a complex historical phenomenon into which many separate strands were interwoven; the shock of the great depression, the tenuous roots of parliamentary democracy, the failure of the parties to grapple effectively with Germany's problems or even to coalesce against the Nazis, the power and drive of Hitler's movement, the antipathy of the middle class for democratic institutions, the vulnerability of the old president and the intrigues of his advisers and of pressure groups; all these factors, indigenous to the German situation, played a part in this tragedy. This does not exhaust the problem by any means. No country lives in a vacuum. Liberalism, nationalism and industrialism, the forces which moulded Germany's history in the nineteenth century and brought the German *Reich* into being, were part of a broad historical movement affecting the whole of Western Europe. Similarly in the 1930s, the crisis of German democracy was not peculiar to that country, but a reflection of a more general crisis of democracy throughout the western world.

Already in the second half of the 1920s, during a period of relative prosperity, there were ominous signs of impending crisis when parliamentary democracy was superseded by dictatorship in Italy, Spain, Portugal and Yugoslavia. The drift from democracy was greatly accentuated by the depression. Because parliamentary institutions seemed incapable of dealing boldly with mass unemployment, critics on right and left called into question the basic liberal concepts of freedom and the rule of law even in the well-established democratic countries. Authoritarianism in the 1930s was generally accompanied by a resurgence of nationalism. Without doubt nationalism assumed a more virulent and destructive form in Germany than elsewhere. However, looked at in a broader perspective, resurgent nationalism was no isolated phenomenon but a disease affecting the whole of Europe, where the economic crisis obliged all nations to take unilateral action in defence of their interests. Economic nationalism was the order of the day and this, in its turn, stimulated the growth of political nationalism, intensifying the rivalries between nations. In short, the tragic death of German democracy can be properly understood only as part of a wider canvas.

13

National Socialist Germany 1933–1945

In the spring and summer of 1933 Hitler established the apparatus of party dictatorship in Germany. Fortified by the Enabling Act, he concentrated all power in the hands of the government without difficulty, dissolved the trade unions and abolished all political parties except the Nazis. However, Germany had not yet become the brutal tyranny which was to appal the conscience of mankind within a very few years. Admittedly much violence had already occurred; hundreds of political opponents died between 1930 and 1933 in street battles or at the hands of Nazi assassins; thousands more languished in hastily constructed concentration camps; discrimination against Jews had begun; and police and courts were virtually powerless to deal with innumerable acts of lawlessness committed by gangs of *SA* men. But this was largely the work of over-zealous or unscrupulous supporters at local level; at this stage terror and brutality had not been rationalised and systematised into an instrument of government. Indeed throughout 1933 and into 1934 the Nazis were carried forward on the crest of a wave of disillusionment with the republic and hope for a better order of things in the future. There were few protests against the dissolution of political parties or the wholesale destruction of democratic institutions; in fact, the almost total collapse of organised opposition took Hitler completely by surprise. In November 1933 the first plebiscite under Nazi auspices showed that eighty-eight per cent of the electorate supported the Führer. Naturally the Nazis stage-managed this and subsequent plebiscites. But it was not all trickery by any means; an overwhelming majority might well have voted for Hitler without the techniques of coercion and intimidation employed on these occasions. Already he had done much to restore the faith of ordinary Germans in themselves and in the future of their country. Catholics were deeply impressed by Hitler's readiness to sign a concordat with the Vatican in July; and when he withdrew Germany simultaneously from the Disarmament Conference and the League of Nations in October 1933, on the eve of the plebiscite, the news was received with satisfaction by most Germans. Those who had doubts were inclined to suppress them and hope for the best under the new régime.

Hitler certainly did his utmost to dispel lurking fears and anxieties about Nazi intentions by a studied display of statesmanlike moderation. He quickly made it plain to his followers that conditions must now return to normal after the feverish excitement of the previous nine months. On 6 July he solemnly warned his *Reichsstatthalter*, assembled together in the chancellery, that revolution was not a permanent state but that 'the stream of revolution released must be guided into the safe channel of evolution.' At Leipzig later in July he informed his audience that the second phase of the struggle for Germany was over; the next phase was the educational task of winning over the masses to National Socialism. Hitler's efforts to make the *Machtergreifung*[1] respectable reassured the middle class that life would go on much as before. It had precisely the opposite effect on many party activists, who watched the conciliation of the Establishment with deep misgivings. So much so that by the spring of 1934 there was talk of a 'second revolution' among rank-and-file members, especially those enrolled in the Brown Shirts.

The *SA*, commanded by Ernst Röhm, a tough, able and earthy ex-*Reichswehr* captain, had played a vital role in Hitler's accession to power; without command of the streets, won by the Brown Shirts in innumerable and bloody battles with political opponents, the Nazi party would never have become a formidable mass movement and Hitler might never have arrived in the chancellery, as he was well aware. Having put the Führer in power, the *SA* men expected a privileged status with well-paid posts to compensate them for long years in the wilderness.

They were quickly disillusioned. Hitler had no intention of disrupting the economic and commercial life of Germany; on the contrary, he forbade the party to interfere with the work of economic experts whose services were indispensable if Germany was to solve the problem of unemployment. The Nazi victory was followed inevitably by a great influx of members into the party – the *Märzgefallene*,[2] as contemporaries dubbed them – who were allowed to retain their jobs, much to the disgust of unemployed *SA* men. In August Goering dismissed the auxiliary policemen recruited from the *SA* earlier in the year and took steps to prevent local commanders turning the Prussian police into an *SA* stronghold. Röhm concluded – not without great reluctance, for he was an old friend of Hitler's – that the Führer no longer shared the objectives of the *SA*. Röhm, like many *SA* leaders, was a man of the left, filled with what Gregor Strasser once described as 'the great anti-capitalist longing' of the lower middle classes. He had expected to come to power not by the back door but on the barricades in classic revolutionary fashion. A 'National Revolution' of the kind symbolised by Hitler's meeting with Hindenburg in the Potsdam garrison church was totally inadequate; what Germany needed

[1] The seizure of power.
[2] Those who fell in March.

was a 'National Socialist Revolution' to destroy the power of the reactionary upper classes and to alleviate unemployment by adopting those socialist measures to which the party was at least nominally committed. Hitler seemed to have been taken prisoner by capitalists and Junkers out to sabotage the revolution. That being so, the *SA* must look to its defences and stand ready to carry out a 'second revolution', if necessary, to purge Germany of the enemies of National Socialism. Of central importance in the quarrel between Röhm and Hitler was the question of army reform. There was no love lost between Röhm's private army and the professional soldiers who ran the *Reichswehr*. Röhm was bitterly critical of Hitler's failure to deal with this 'stronghold of reaction' and pressed upon Hitler his plan for the amalgamation of *Reichswehr* and *SA* to create a people's militia, a truly revolutionary army under Röhm as minister of war.

Hitler was in fact every bit as resentful and contemptuous as Röhm of the upper classes and certainly had no love of generals. Where he differed from Röhm, a revolutionary of the old style, was in his political realism and tactical cunning. For the time being he needed the generals; that did not mean that he would let them lord it over him indefinitely, as events were to prove. But the highly disciplined *Reichswehr* was indispensable for a dynamic foreign policy; a loosely disciplined people's militia would be useless in this regard. And without the full co-operation of his generals how could the *Reichswehr* be expanded rapidly and still remain an efficient fighting force? As early as 28 February Hitler informed *Reichswehr* and *SA* leaders that only the army could carry arms. There was another urgent reason for caution. Hindenburg's life was drawing to a close; to consolidate his power Hitler had to take over the presidency which, of course, carried with it supreme command of the army, a delicate operation which could scarcely succeed if the generals were hostile to him. Fortunately Blomberg, the new *Reichswehr* minister,[3] and Reichenau, chief of the ministerial office, were both enthusiastic Nazis, only too ready to co-operate fully with Hitler. There is no positive evidence of any formal agreement between Hitler and leading generals in the spring of 1934. It sufficed that a community of interest already existed; Hitler had no intention of taking Röhm's side against the army or of being overshadowed by a man who had never fallen under the spell of the Führer; the generals were equally alarmed by Röhm and made it plain that they would only support Hitler's claim to the presidency on condition that he put Röhm in his place and let them keep their privileged position in German society.

The situation was further complicated in the summer of 1934 by stirrings on the right wing. The approaching demise of the old president revived monarchist hopes of a restoration, a solution personally favoured by Hindenburg. Several conservatives were employed in the vice-

[3]The title was changed to minister of war in 1935.

chancellery and some of them had a hand in drafting the sensational speech delivered by Papen at Marburg university on 17 June 1934. No one was surprised when the vice-chancellor condemned the talk of a second revolution likely to end in a Marxist bloodbath. More significant was his sharp criticism of the Nazis; he condemned their hostility to the churches and the suppression of opposing viewpoints; and he declared that a one-party state was acceptable only as a transitional stage on the way to an authoritarian state based on Christian corporate principles, a passage clearly intended to rally moderate conservative opinion, not least in the *Reichswehr*, in favour of a restoration. Hitler was suddenly alarmed by the possibility of an intrigue between the *Reichswehr* and the extreme right to keep him from the presidency. On 21 June when Hitler visited Hindenburg at Neudeck, Blomberg was waiting to warn him that if the government could not reduce the tension in Germany the *Reichswehr* would not hesitate to proclaim martial law and restore order. For months Hitler had postponed the moment of decision, partly because he still felt sentimental attachment for old comrades like Röhm, partly because it suited his book to play off *SA* against *Reichswehr*. Forced into a corner at last, he finally decided to put the *SA* in its place and to deal with right-wing opposition at the same time.

As the tension mounted in June 1934, influential party leaders, especially Goering and Hess, were already hard at work intriguing against Röhm. Hitler let himself be persuaded on the flimsiest evidence that Röhm was plotting against him. Himmler, head of the Prussian *Gestapo*, played a highly significant role behind the scenes, manufacturing evidence against Röhm and spreading false rumours in order to screw up the tension to breaking-point. On 25 June General von Fritsch, commander-in-chief of the *Reichswehr*, alerted his troops and confined them to barracks, so convinced was he that *SA* units might attempt to seize power.

On 30 June, 'the night of the long knives', Hitler struck at the *SA*. Directing operations in person from Munich, he ordered the arrest and execution of Röhm and his immediate associates. The ease with which the order was carried out disproves the allegation that an *SA Putsch* was imminent. Simultaneously Goering and Himmler, ably seconded by Heydrich, the up-and-coming chief of the Berlin office of the *Gestapo*, conducted a more extensive purge in North Germany. It was carried out by the *SS* and *Gestapo* with arms and transport supplied by the *Reichswehr* in accordance with an agreement between Himmler and Reichenau. Summary execution was the fate of all who appeared on the secret *SS* lists; in Berlin the victims were shot in the Lichterfelde cadet school, placed at the disposal of the *SS* by the *Reichswehr*. The purge continued for three days and met with no resistance. On 3 July a new law announced that the executions were legitimate acts of self-defence carried out by the state authorities against traitors. On 13 July Hitler, speaking in the Reichstag, dismissed out of hand the suggestion that the guilty men should have been tried according to the due processes of law, and remarked ominously that he had assumed personal responsibility as supreme judge of the German people at a moment of crisis. He admitted to seventy-seven victims. In fact several hundred people were slain, including prominent right-wing personalities; Schleicher and his wife were brutally shot down in their own home; General von Bredow, Schleicher's assistant at the *Reichswehr* ministry, *Ritter* von Kahr the former state commissioner for Bavaria during the 1923 *Putsch*, and the Catholic Action leader Klausener were among the victims. Had Brüning remained in Germany he would have shared their fate. Two of Papen's closest associates in the vice-chancellery were murdered and he was under house arrest for four days; he owed his life to the protecting hand of the president.

The brutal purge of 30 June was a decisive event in the history of Nazi Germany, setting the pattern for much that followed. The victory of the party over the *SA* was absolute. Overnight the Brown Shirts became a harmless mass organisation devoid of all political significance. The law which had conferred ministerial status on Röhm at the height of his power was repealed, and Viktor Lutze, a reliable ex-*Reichswehr* officer, became the new *SA* chief of staff. From now on until the end of the Third Reich there was no serious opposition to Hitler inside the Nazi movement. The primitive brutality of the purge, with its clear implication that the liberal *Rechtsstaat* had been superseded by a personal tyranny, undoubtedly shocked and frightened many Germans. But as the true facts were carefully concealed from the people, it was easy to believe that Hitler really had saved Germany from the horrors of civil war. Ironically enough, the purge was construed as a victory for the moderate men over the notoriously lawless *SA* ruffians who had disturbed Germany for so long. The fact that all talk of a 'second revolution' came to an abrupt halt after the purge was a further reassuring sign that things were returning to normal.

The elimination of their *SA* rivals seemed to put the generals in a very strong position. Hitler took care to reassure them on 13 July 1934 that the *Reichswehr* was the only armed force in the state and would remain a 'non-political' instrument. In reality the *Reichswehr* was fatally compromised once Blomberg issued his order of the day on 1 July congratulating Hitler on his action and assuring him of the continued loyalty of the army. Two senior generals, Schleicher and Bredow, had been brutally murdered – a crime which appalled many of the older officers – yet Blomberg publicly endorsed Hitler's gangster methods without a murmur of protest from the officer corps.[4] No thought of resistance to Hitler entered the minds of the generals when Hindenburg died on 1 August. Within the

[4] General von Hammerstein started a campaign in the army to have the names of the murdered generals restored to the roll of honour, from which they were removed in June 1934. In 1935 Hitler, for tactical reasons, privately admitted that the generals had been killed in error and allowed their names to be restored.

hour Hitler amalgamated the offices of chancellor and president and assumed the new title of *Führer* and *Reichskanzler*. On 2 August Hitler won a further victory over the army when Blomberg and Fritsch agreed to swear an oath of personal allegiance to him. Shortly afterwards all officers and men were required to take this oath, which ran as follows: 'I swear by God this holy oath, that I will render unconditional obedience to the Leader of the German *Reich*, Adolf Hitler, supreme commander of the armed forces and that, as a brave soldier, I will be ready at any time to stake my life for this oath.' This far-reaching oath bound all soldiers (and civil servants as well) so completely to the régime that resistance later on was, from a moral standpoint, a dubious and hazardous undertaking – a factor of the utmost importance during the Bomb Plot of 1944.

The generals were too full of their victory over the *SA* to notice that Hitler was well on the way to being senior partner in the alliance between *Reichswehr* and state. For the next few years rearmament and army expansion absorbed their interest. But their political influence was waning. Hitler paid scant attention to their opinions and as the army grew in size after 1935 National Socialist influence began to erode the position of the officer corps.

At the beginning of 1938 a new stage was reached in the subordination of the army to the state. When Hitler revealed plans for a more expansionist foreign policy to a select meeting in the chancellery in November 1937 Blomberg and Fritsch expressed grave reservations. Hitler, therefore, determined to purge the high command as soon as possible. His chance came in January 1938 when Blomberg re-married, with Hitler and Goering as the principal witnesses. A few days later Goering produced evidence that the general's wife, the former Luise Gruhn had a police record for theft and indecency, a revelation which shocked fellow-officers who called for Blomberg's resignation. Somewhat reluctantly Hitler, who valued Blomberg's services highly, dismissed him. But the suggestion that Fritsch should succeed Blomberg as war minister was not acceptable to the Führer. Very conveniently Himmler, who like Goering wanted to discredit the officer corps, produced evidence that Fritsch was a homosexual, a completely false accusation which the general indignantly denied. He, too, was dismissed. At the same time Hitler abolished the post of war minister and assumed personal command of all the armed forces. Out of the armed forces office in the old ministry Hitler created a separate high command, the *Oberkommando der Wehrmacht*, to act as his personal staff under the command of General Wilhelm Keitel, an admirer of the Führer. Keitel received a seat in the cabinet but was to take orders directly from Hitler. To succeed Fritsch as commander-in-chief of the army, Hitler chose another enthusiastic supporter, General von Brauchitsch. Some sixteen generals were relieved of their posts and another forty-four transferred in this major upheaval which firmly established Hitler's ascendancy over the armed forces.

Finally, the purge of 30 June saw the beginning of the meteoric rise to power of the *SS*, an organisation which soon symbolised for millions of people all over the world everything that was evil and bestial in Nazi Germany. The *Schutz Staffel* or *SS* was founded in 1925 as a personal body-guard for Hitler with duties indistinguishable from those of the *SA*. The *SS* became a significant organisation when Henrich Himmler was put in charge of it in 1929 with specific orders to transform it into an *élite* force. Within a few years Himmler built up the *SS* from 200 men into a carefully selected formation 50,000 strong, with a distinctive black uniform and it own *esprit de corps*. At this stage the *SS* was still subject to the over-all control of the *SA*. However, Himmler had another string to his bow; he was also head of the political police. He started off as head of the Bavarian political police and within months secured control of the political police in all *Länder* except Prussia. Finally in April 1934 he was appointed head of the Prussian secret police, the *Geheime Staatspolizei* or *Gestapo*, formed by Goering in 1933 as an instrument of personal power. As *Reichsfuhrer* of the *SS*, and with all the secret police of Germany under his control, Himmler was already a powerful figure, who played a key role in the great purge. On 20 July, as a reward for their 'great services', Hitler made the *SS* an independent organisation inside the party and subject only to his immediate authority.

The next important step came in June 1936 when Hitler amalgamated the separate police forces into one body and placed it under Himmler's control. This decision formalised the intimate connexion between *SS* and police and created a formidable power complex, the very core of the totalitarian system. Himmler had at his disposal a vast security network stretching out over the whole of Germany and penetrating into the very corridors of power; soon no one was immune from the surveillance of some branch of the ubiquitous secret police. Those arrested for the slightest sign of opposition to the régime usually passed quickly from *Gestapo* cells to one of the eighteen concentration camps, originally intended for the temporary detention of political prisoners but now permanent institutions manned by *SS Totenkopfverbände* (Death's Head detachments). In these camps the more sadistic guards – and there were many of them in them *SS* – were more or less free to inflict indescribable cruelties on the inmates without fear of diciplinary action. Other *SS* activities included the handling of racial problems, which Himmler regarded as his special province. A fanatical adherent of Nazi racial theories, Himmler planned to breed a new race of pure Aryans, an *SS* version of the medieval knights, to rule Europe from the Atlantic to the Urals; there were special 'Lebensborn' homes for unmarried mothers with impeccable racial antecedents, and special schools – the *SS Junkerschulen* – for training the *SS élite* of the future. And despite Hitler's promise to the *Reichswehr* Himmler was allowed to establish armed *SS* formations, known as *SS Verfügungstruppen* (emergency troops), from which the divisions of the *Waffen SS* emerged in the war years. By 1939 Himmler's *SS* exerted enormous influence over the whole apparatus of government and overshadowed the party; many high-ranking party officials took care to hold *SS* ranks, while Himmler had become a dreaded figure, one of the Führer's most trusted advisers.

Germany was well on the way to becoming a totalitarian state before the purge of 30 June. All political parties except the Nazis had been dissolved, and a law in December 1933 declared the National Socialist Party to be the pillar of the state and bound indissolubly to it. Early in 1934 the cabinet was empowered to enact new laws; in effect these plenary powers were in Hitler's hands, for he quickly relegated the cabinet to the background and rarely summoned it; when war broke out in 1939 the members of the cabinet first heard the news on the radio like most other Germans. Similarly with the Reichstag; one-party elections in November 1933 produced a Nazi-packed assembly which was called together only occasionally to hear the Führer's special pronouncements. The rights of the *Länder* were systematically destroyed as part of the general process of co-ordination, or *Gleichschaltung*, which concentrated effective power in the hands of the Berlin government to a degree previously unknown. Eighteen *Reichsstatt-halter* (special commissioners), all Nazis, were put in charge of the *Länder*, with full power over *Land* governments and all local officials. In 1934 the Reichsrat and all Landtage were abolished, the residual powers of the *Länder* transferred to Berlin and the *Reichsstatthalter* put under the ministry of the interior. The only exception was Prussia, where Hitler agreed to act as *Reichsstatthalter* but delegated his powers to Goering, who was also allowed to keep the title of minister-president. The elective principle was snuffed out in local government in accordance with the new *Führerprinzip* which recognised only the right of the *élite* to rule on behalf of the masses; in practice elected bodies were replaced by party nominees. The civil service was thoroughly purged of Jews and other 'undesirables' and transformed into a completely subservient body with party members in the senior posts.

Curiously enough, *Gleichschaltung* did not lead to a clear and more orderly system of government as one might expect. On the contrary, Nazi Germany was a confused jungle of overlapping authorities all ultimately dependent on the Führer but usually in conflict with each other. The Nazi hierarchy was riddled from top to bottom with bitter rivalries and feuds between individuals and institutions; *Wehrmacht* and *Waffen SS* clashed over military matters; in wartime the *OKW* and the general staff were locked in endless rivalry; Gauleiters eager to turn their areas into private empires feuded with Frick, the minister of the interior; Goebbels at the propaganda ministry had to defend his empire against the pretensions of

Rust at the new ministry of science and education, and of Rosenberg the leading party ideologue; Schacht, Frick, Ley and Goering continually clashed over the conduct of the economy; while in the field of external affairs Ribbentrop's office, Rosenberg's rival party office, and an *SS* organisation were all in competition with the foreign office. A truly chaotic picture, but one that was undoubtedly to Hitler's liking; he deliberately blurred the frontiers of authority, allowed new organisations to proliferate and stood aside while rivals struggled with each other so that his own authority was the one stable and constant factor in an uneasy balance of forces.

Gleichschaltung applied to every aspect of life in Nazi Germany. Few could escape involvement in one or more of the innumerable organisations run by the party. Special attention was paid to education, which was removed completely from the control of the *Länder*. Politically unreliable teachers were removed from the classroom and the remainder regimented in the *NS Lehrerbund*, which saw to it that Nazi texts were used in all schools, especially in the teaching of biology and history. Boys from the age of ten were bullied into joining the *Hitlerjugend*, the only youth organisation allowed by the Nazis, which spent much of its time imparting rudimentary military skills to its members. For girls there was the parallel organisation, *Bund deutscher Mädel*. Young men between eighteen and twenty-five were obliged to spend six months in the *Arbeitsdienst* engaged on public works and receiving further military training. This was followed by two years' compulsory military service. Industrial workers were organised in the *Deutsche Arbeitsfront* run by Robert Ley, and women in the *NS Frauenschaft*. Separate organisations were created for doctors, civil servants, lawyers, university teachers, students and technicians. For farmers, a group specially favoured by the Nazis on account of their affinity with the soil, there was the *Reichsnährstand*, directed by Walter Darré, a comprehensive organisation dealing with every aspect of agriculture from the marketing of produce to the collection of folk tales.

Like any totalitarian state Nazi Germany relied heavily on control of the mass media of communication. With press, radio and cinema firmly under their control, the Nazis were able to subject the German people to a ceaseless flood of propaganda devised with great skill and ability by the minister of propaganda, Josef Goebbels, a malevolent but highly intelligent Rhinelander. In itself Nazism was a pathetically thin and unsophisticated creed, little more than a transient amalgam of social resentment and national frustration. But Goebbels was helped enormously in his task by the psychology of the German situation. The crude and over-simplified *Weltanschauung* projected by Nazi propaganda agencies had a soporific effect on millions of Germans, who were completely overwhelmed by the great crisis of the early 1930s and only too ready to suspend their rational faculties and surrender to the mystique and anti-rationalism of Nazism.

There were positive as well as negative aspects to this propaganda. When the Nazis appealed to the spirit of idealism and self-sacrifice in German youth or harped on the need for a truly integrated society – the *Volksgemeinschaft* – they touched on psychological needs which the republic with its deep social divisions had failed to satisfy. A sense of national solidarity against Germany's foes was the new social cement which would overcome class differences and bind the people together under the party. No effort was spared by party propagandists to maintain national feeling at fever pitch; impressive parades, enthusiastic rallies, an abundance of flags and uniforms and constant reiteration of racialist themes were all part of the grand design to give the Germans a sense of purpose and a fanatical pride in the fatherland and in the race. Nor can it be denied that the cult of the infallible leader had an irresistible appeal for millions of Germans, young and old alike. The republic had failed to arouse the intensity of devotion formerly given to dynastic rulers; Hitler was a father-figure in whom disillusioned and weary people could repose confidence and trust at a time of unusual stress and strain. As long as he was successful, people supported him. Those who disliked the régime simply immersed themselves in their work and in their private lives and tried to shut out the incessant clamour of propagandists.

The xenophobic nationalism of the Nazi movement was sustained by a fanatical belief in the alleged superiority of the Aryan race. Marx had taught that all history was the history of class struggle; the Nazis revived the arguments of the nineteenth-century racialists such as Gobineau and Houston Chamberlain and maintained that history was nothing more than a biological struggle for existence between inferior and superior races. According to them, the one civilising influence throughout world history had been the Aryan race, of which the Germans represented the purest strain; in the present century it was the German racial mission to strengthen the position of the Teutonic people of Europe and to rule over inferior races in the east – a dynamic concept which had radical implications for German foreign policy as will be seen later. Intimately bound up with these racial fantasies was the phenomenon of anti-Semitism. Hitler's hatred of the Jew was pathological. Jews were not simply members of an inferior race to be despised by pure Aryans; in his eyes they were a 'counter-race' whose aim it was to enslave and ultimately destroy the Aryan race. Jews symbolised all that was evil in Hitler's world. They stabbed Germany in the back in 1918: they were the moving spirit behind Marxism and monopoly capitalism; they were disseminating the pernicious doctrines of pacifism, internationalism and democracy in order to undermine the will of the people to fight for living-space. Sooner or later Hitler intended to cut this 'cancerous growth' out of the body politic without mercy.

Although a violent anti-Semitic propaganda campaign commenced as soon as the Nazis were in power and many Jews suffered physical assault at the hands of Nazi hooligans, in general Hitler moved cautiously in the early years. Many (but not all) Jewish officials were dismissed; a boycott of Jewish shops in April 1933 was ended after the first day because of the adverse effects on the German economy; and pressure from rank-and-file Nazis for the expulsion of all Jews from the economy was successfully resisted because of their importance to economic recovery. One incident which attracted widespread attention abroad was the burning of books by Jewish writers carried out in May 1933 by members of the *NS Studentenbund* on Berlin's Odeonplatz with the enthusiastic approval of Goebbels.

Persecution of the Jews reached a new stage with the passage of the so-called 'Nuremberg laws' promulgated at the Nazi party congress of 1935. Jews were deprived of full citizenship and forbidden to marry Aryans, while extra-marital relations between Jews and Gentiles became a punishable offence. The pace quickened still further in 1938 after a seventeen-year-old Jewish boy murdered a German embassy official in Paris. This was the pretext for a large-scale pogrom organised by the *SA*. During the *Reichskristallnacht*[5] of 9–10 November Jewish shops were looted; houses, schools and synagogues burnt down; several Jews were murdered; and thousands manhandled by *SA* hooligans enjoying their first taste of violence for five years.

The pogrom, which aroused widespread horror abroad, was followed by a spate of laws which at last drove the Jews out of commercial life, confiscated their industrial assets and turned them into a race of 'untouchables' in their own country. They were practically deprived of the means of livelihood; they could not enter cinemas, theatres or swimming pools; they could not own cars; their children were expelled from school and university; and they were obliged by law to wear the yellow star of David in public as a mark of degradation. That a still worse fate might be their lot was hinted at by Hitler in January 1939 when he declared in a Reichstag speech that if war broke out it would lead to the annihilation of the Jewish race in Europe.

Friction between Church and State is inevitable under a totalitarian régime. Tyrants cannot tolerate for long institutions which have any claim to an independent existence outside the state. True, the Nazis were not officially hostile to religion; in the party programme they spoke of commitment to 'positive Christianity' and promised to respect freedom of religion – provided that it did not endanger the security of the state or offend the moral sense of the Germanic race. Hitler was himself a Catholic (although lapsed like other Nazi leaders) and in the early days he paid lip-service to Christian beliefs and promised to respect the position of the various churches.

---

[5]'Crystal night;' so-called because of the innumerable panes of glass broken by the *SA*.

Christians were reassured by Hitler's behaviour, as he hoped they would be. In fact Nazism was a deeply anti-Christian creed. It spurned the Christian virtues of charity, mercy and humility, exalted the use of violence and gloried in war for its own sake. Nazis showed a complete disregard and contempt for those fundamental human rights and liberties on which all civilised communities are founded. The state for them was not a means for assisting individuals to realise their full potential but an end in itself, the embodiment of the racial will to survive. Leading Nazis were well aware of the incompatibility between Nazism and Christianity. Hitler was himself a religious nihilist full of contempt for Christianity. To his intimates he declared that it was of crucial importance for Germany's future to decide whether she wanted 'the Jewish Christ creed with its effeminate pity-ethics or a strong heroic belief in God in nature, in God in our own people, in God in our destiny, in our blood. . . .' Although in private he ridiculed Alfred Rosenberg's turgid *Mythos des zwanzigsten Jahrhunderts*, he made no secret of his belief that the churches would wither away and that after the war he would withdraw their state subsidies.

That lay in the future. For the present he had to move warily. And indeed he could not repress a certain grudging admiration for the Catholic Church, because of its power and superb organisation. Like Napoleon and Mussolini before him, Hitler recognised the tactical advantages of coming to terms with Catholicism and promptly offered to negotiate a concordat with the Vatican. His aims were simply to gain international prestige for the new régime and to keep the Catholic clergy out of German politics. Many Catholic bishops had been critical of the Nazis before 1933 and even those such as Mgr. Pacelli, one-time Papal Nuncio in Berlin and a future Pope himself, who advocated a conciliatory policy towards Hitler, were deeply concerned about the future of the church under the Nazis. On the other hand, precisely because the Nazis were unfriendly towards religion, a written agreement seemed a desirable safeguard. Hitler's offer was accepted and a concordat negotiated by Mgr. Pacelli and Papen was signed in July 1933. The Church was assured of full religious freedom, her bishops were promised freedom of communication with Rome and the right to publish pastoral letters, religious orders were allowed to continue with work of a pastoral character, and assurances were given about church schools. In return the Church ordered bishops to take the oath of loyalty to the state, agreed to the dismantling of the Christian trade-union movement and the dissolution of the Centre party and prohibited clergy from taking part in political activities. The concordat did much to allay Catholic fears at a popular level; what the Church could not obtain from the republic had been achieved overnight under Hitler. However, it is a sufficient comment on the Nazis' respect for the spirit of the concordat that only five days after its signature a sterilisation law utterly contrary to Catholic teaching was announced.

It was soon apparent that Hitler had no intention of abiding by the concordat. There was interference with the rights of bishops to communicate with Rome and publish pastoral letters, restrictions were placed on charitable institutions, including the famous *Karitasverband*, church schools were turned into undenominational schools, and Catholic lay organisations were suppressed. When the bishops protested at the teaching of racialism in schools, the Nazis did not hesitate to employ the shabbiest methods of defaming the character of priests and religious; in 1935 a number of priests were charged with violation of currency regulations, and in 1936 several members of religious orders were accused of immorality. By the end of 1936 the hierarchy was completely disillusioned with the Nazis and several bishops denounced them from the pulpit. An open breach occurred in March 1937 with the publication of an encyclical letter '*Mit brennender Sorge*' in which Pope Pius XI made a trenchant and outspoken attack on the Nazi creed. The campaign against priests and religious was intensified, and by 1939 hundreds of clergy were in concentration camps. Only with the outbreak of war did open persecution cease for tactical reasons.

Relations with the Protestant churches were no better. At first the Nazis were confident of an easy victory over the twenty-eight separate territorial churches (*Landeskirchen*). Their aim was to capture the machinery of church government and create a united national church under a national bishop acceptable to the party. A new church constitution was promulgated, and when church elections were held in the summer of 1933 the German Christians, an evangelical group which wanted to synthesise National Socialism and Christianity, secured large majorities with Nazi assistance. *Gleichschaltung* went ahead rapidly; non-Aryan pastors were dismissed and the new national synod, meeting at Wittenberg, elected Müller, the Nazi favourite, to be the first *Reichsbischof*. He promptly put his nominees in charge of the various churches and the Nazi victory seemed complete.

In fact this was the beginning of a long struggle inside the Protestant Evangelical Church. A group of pastors led by an ex-submarine commander, Martin Niemöller, refused to accept the 'Aryan paragraph' and protested against secular interference with the church. By Christmas 1933 6,000 pastors supported the Niemöller group, and only 2,000 stayed with the German Christians. Out of this opposition grew the Confessional Church (*Bekennende Kirche*), which took its stand on the Bible and refused to be dictated to by the state in matters of conscience. The protest movement grew, and a rival church organisation was set up in some *Länder*. In an attempt to reconcile the opposing viewpoints Hitler appointed Kerrl minister for church affairs with wide powers. After a brief and unsuccessful attempt at conciliation Kerrl resorted to persecution. The Confessional Church was in effect made illegal, and in 1937 800 pastors and laymen were arrested, many of them being sent to concentration camps. By 1938 confessional pastors had been deprived of financial support and the German Christians were in complete control of church organisation. But the opposition did not abate and Kerrl's last attempt to reconcile all evangelicals on the eve of the war ended in failure. Out of the struggle against totalitarianism came much suffering, as well as a deepening of Christian experience and witness in all churches and a new awareness amongst Catholics and Protestants of the fundamentals of the Christian heritage which they held in common.

When the Nazis came to power they had no detailed economic plans. Hitler was careful to avoid specific commitments contenting himself with the announcement in February of a Four Year Plan to cure unemployment and rescue the farming communities. Once he felt secure in power he ordered the party to stop interfering in economic matters and turned to the great industrial magnates without whose active co-operation he could neither solve unemployment nor in due course obtain armaments for an ambitious foreign policy. In May industry was offered tax cuts, reductions in social contributions and wage-pegging at 1932 levels. This package coupled with the suppression of the free trade unions the same month encouraged industry to overcome to some extent its suspicions of the regime and mastermind the German economic recovery.

Although re-armament was built into the recovery programme from the very beginning, it did not assume significance until 1935. Overall control of the economy was at first vested in Hjalmar Schacht, the financial wizard of 1924 and a highly respected figure in industrial and banking circles. Hitler appointed him president of the *Reichsbank* because, unlike his predecessors, Schacht was prepared to give the government unlimited credit to stage an economic revival. Already in 1932 the Nazis had begun to show interest in the highly unorthodox theory of deficit financing later to be associated with John Maynard Keynes (whose seminal work did not, in fact, appear until 1936). According to this theory, governments should increase, not cut, expenditure to lift the economy out of a deflationary crisis. On this basis the public works programmes drawn up by Brüning and introduced by Papen were continued but greatly extended; up to the end of 1935 5000 million marks were pumped into work-creation schemes.

The spectacle of thousands of young men working on afforestation and water conservation schemes impressed the outside world. It is now thought that work creation was not as important as investment in the construction and automobile industries in getting the economy moving. But the overall effect of Nazi measures was impressive. By 1934 unemployment fell to 2.7 millions, to 1.7 millions in mid 1935 and on the eve of war a shortage of skilled labour existed in some industries. Because the Nazis feared that if the public realized how the recovery was being financed its confidence in the regime might be undermined, Schacht hit on the ingenious device of *Mefo-bills*; government contracts were paid not in cash but in *Mefo-bills* guaranteed by the *Reichsbank* and repayable in four years. A total of 12,000 million marks was spent in this way. This, together with a failure to publish statistics, disguised the reality from the German people. Not that it would have mattered had the bills been redeemed in 1937, i.e. had the pump-priming money been taken out of the economy by higher taxation.

Though the Nazis borrowed the technique of deficit financing from the German Keynesians, they were not true Keynesians. The latter expected private business to take over from the state-financed recovery and return to the multilateral trading pattern of pre-war days. Not so the Nazis. After 1936 consumer-goods production slowed down and expenditure on armaments increased sharply from 5400 million marks in 1935 to 17,200 million marks by 1938, accounting for 44 per cent of total state expenditure. As Germany was heavily dependent on imports for crucial raw materials such as high-grade iron ore and oil, the Nazis aimed from the very start at autarky, or economic self-sufficiency. This was the order of the day almost everywhere in the 1930s. The only difference was that Germany was more thorough-going and ruthless in her pursuit of autarky than other countries. In addition, Schacht made strenuous efforts to reduce inessential imports and employed a whole range of devices such as dumping (selling goods below cost) to increase exports. The central controls set up by Brüning over foreign exchange were extended and under Schacht's New Plan (1934) raw materials were allocated to industry in accordance with Nazi priorities. A significant shift in the pattern of German trade occurred in the 1930s. To save precious foreign exchange, Schacht negotiated bilateral trade agreements with several countries in South-Eastern Europe and Latin America. Germany offered guaranteed markets for raw materials but paid for them in blocked marks which could only be spent in Germany. This development brought into being a *Grossraumwirtschaft* or common market in South-Eastern and Central Europe which prepared the way for political domination.

The drive for autarky intensified in 1936 with the introduction of the Second Four Year Plan under Goering's direction. The first aimed at eliminating unemployment. The second launched in a great blaze of publicity was really designed to place Germany on a war footing. In August in a top secret directive Hitler ordered the army and the economy to be ready for war in four years. Great efforts were made to increase domestic production of synthetic rubber (buna), petrol and oils regardless of cost. Nazi control over industry tightened considerably after 1936. Thus when the iron and steel combines refused to exploit low-grade indigenous iron ore reserves – thereby reducing dependence on costly Swedish imports – the

Nazis rode roughshod over them and established the Hermann Goering *Konzern* at Salzgitter to exploit German ore. In the next few years this state-owned enterprise became a gigantic corporation with ramifications in many branches of industry and quite overshadowed privately-owned combines.

Schacht's influence had declined sharply by 1937, partly because he feared that autarky was being taken to extremes and partly because he was stoutly opposed to Hitler's insistence on increasing armaments expenditure regardless of the economic consequences. At the end of 1937 Schacht resigned and was replaced by Walther Funk, a party man and a nonentity completely under Goering's thumb. That the economics ministry had been demoted was apparent from the way in which Hitler buttonholed Funk during the interval at an opera, appointed him and told him to await orders from Goering. After 1937 the state financed re-armament by increasing the public debt, forcing financial institutions to loan money to the government in return for treasury bills which were not redeemable. Inflation – the natural consequence of expanding the non-productive goods sector – was kept in check through tight control of the money market and by slowing down consumer spending and by taxation increases.

The Plan was on the whole successful. Certainly it did not produce arms as quickly as Hitler and the army wanted, and in 1938 absolute priority was given to the production of certain vital war materials. Nevertheless autarky succeeded in that although Germany was still dependent on imports in 1939, her degree of dependence had not increased despite her economic expansion. And though Germany went down to defeat in 1945 the greatly expanded production goods industries were the cornerstone of the economic recovery of the Federal Republic in the 1950s, an interesting example of economic continuity.

In 1939 the German economy was neither a wholly war nor wholly peacetime economy. It was on a war-footing in the sense that much more was spent on armaments than in Britain and France and Germany had a formidable striking force at her disposal. But she was certainly not totally mobilized in 1939. Many historians think this was due to a deliberate decision to wage only short wars requiring much less than total mobilisation and enabling the Germans to have both guns and butter at least until the winter of 1941–2. More recently it has been argued that, on the contrary, Hitler was aiming at a long war from the very beginning, that total mobilisation was the aim and that consumer-goods production had been sharply curtailed by 1939 but that preparations for this type of war had not been completed when Hitler attacked Poland.

Summing up on the German scene in 1939 is not easy. The Nazis undoubtedly enjoyed much support in all classes because of the economic revival of their country and its foreign political successes. Many intellectuals left Germany in 1933 but many more became ardent supporters of the Führer. Thus Werner Sombart, an economist and historian of international repute, speaking at one of the last meetings of the *Verein für Sozialpolitik* in 1935 warmly welcomed the substitution of the *Führerprinzip* for free discussion. Sociologists and literary figures joined in a chorus of praise for the regime. Gerhard Hauptmann, the most renowned literary figure in Germany, treasured his meeting with Hitler much as Goethe treasured his conversation with Napoleon over a century before.

Most industrialists and business men had been pretty lukewarm towards the republic. They did not mourn its passing. After the destruction of the free trade unions they were masters in their own factories. But while all shared in the general recovery of the economy, some benefited more than others. The general trend towards industrial concentration was greatly accelerated by re-armament at the expense of small businesses. The coal and steel industries flourished and *I.G. Farben* became a key concern in the Four Year Plan while less important industries were starved of raw materials. Yet though profits soared in armaments-linked industries, even these industrialists found that they were no longer free agents; the state, not the private entrepreneur, controlled investment, regulated profits and determined priorities. Had the Nazis won the war, industry would have been relegated to a subordinate role in the Nazi scheme of things.

In the countryside the Nazis had their most loyal supporters. Rural folk occupied a special position because of the drive for agricultural self-sufficiency and because of the role they were expected to play in the mythology of blood and soil. The elaborate structure of the *Reichsnährstand* controlling prices and distribution certainly ensured that Germany's dependence on imported food did not increase in line with the expansion of the economy. At first all farmers benefited from increased prices. But after 1936 large farmers did much better than the small dairy farmers because the Nazis refused to raise their prices. Nor were the *Erbhöfe* or hereditary farms very popular. Significantly, the Nazis could do nothing throughout the 1930s to stem the drift to the towns where wages were higher.

How did the industrial working class react to the regime? There were substantial gains in the shape of full employment, stable rents, more paid holidays, and (for some) the cultural and recreational facilities of *Kraft durch Freude* with its cheap theatre tickets and subsidised holidays in Norway and Italy. But, on the other hand, workers had lost the right to strike; the power of employers was vastly increased; working hours were longer; and wage rates rose only very slowly.

It is true that in industries associated with re-armament such as metals, building and building materials workers were able to exploit the mounting economic difficulties in 1938–9 by squeezing more money and fringe benefits out of employers busily engaged in poaching scarce labour from each other. That was not typical of working people as a whole. Nevertheless, the failure of the regime to combat these practices effectively or more broadly to combat inflationary pressures (of which there were some signs by 1938) has led historians to wonder whether the Nazis were afraid of straining working-class loyalties. For example, measures in 1938 to impose wage maxima in key industries and to conscript labour were not rigidly enforced. And a package of measures introduced in September 1939 limiting bonuses and wages was quickly withdrawn because of shop-floor discontent. Possibly the Nazi leadership did fear a repetition of the 1918–20 Revolution if they imposed too heavy a burden on the people. On the other hand, in a dictatorship where no free press exists the regime cannot gauge opinion accurately and the Nazis probably erred on the cautious side in assessing working-class discontent. What is certain is that the Nazis themselves exacerbated the economic difficulties by demanding ever-increasing quantities of armaments which it was beyond the capacity of the economy to produce.

The outbreak of war accentuated the totalitarian character of the Nazi régime. Nazi leaders no longer felt any need to respect foreign opinion, and in a world conditioned to accept large-scale violence and destruction the adoption of the most brutal measures against each and every critic of the régime passed relatively unnoticed; though it is significant that the Nazis displayed more restraint in Germany than elsewhere, fearing that the revelation of the extent to which terror was now a normal instrument of government would undermine the morale of a people at war.

One of the most important consequences of the war was the rapid growth in power of the *SS*. With a large part of Europe under German control, *SS* organisations expanded to cope with the increasing burden of security work. Thus by 1945 the *Gestapo* alone numbered over 40,000. The *Waffen SS* grew from three divisions in 1939 to thirty-five in 1945. Originally Hitler planned to dilute the officer corps by training up a new Nazi-oriented officer class. As the war dragged on he changed his mind and came down in favour of a large *Waffen SS* which would replace the *Wehrmacht* as the standing army of the future. Himmler's personal power grew by leaps and bounds during the war, reaching its apogee in July 1944 when he was appointed commander-in-chief of the new reserve army and succeeded at last in placing the *Wehrmacht* under *SS* surveillance.

The number of prisoners in the hands of the *SS* increased rapidly during the war. In 1939 21,000 political prisoners were incarcerated in six concentration camps; in 1945 there were 800,000 prisoners in twenty-two camps. The *SS* also had charge of millions of foreign slave-labourers working in the munitions industry, on the land and on projects organised by the *SS*. Keeping prisoners in 'protective custody' was no longer a major *SS* activity. By the middle of the war an acute labour shortage existed in Germany; in 1942 Hitler gave top priority to the mobilisation of labour and appointed the ruthless and inhuman Fritz Sauckel, Gauleiter of Thuringia, as plenipotentiary-general for manpower. Sauckel solved the immediate problem by setting political prisoners to work. But the need for labour intensified. Voluntary recruitment of foreign labour produced fewer than 200,000 men. And, oddly enough, the conscription of German women was resisted by the régime partly for ideological reasons and partly because it feared unfavourable reactions from the population. Instead, the *SS* was ordered to scour occupied Europe for manpower. Thousands of men and women were deported to Germany in the most brutal and arbitrary fashion. Treatment of occupied territories varied according to the Nazi estimate of the 'racial worth' of the inhabitants. Scandinavians, Dutch and Flemings came off best, being classed as fellow Aryans.[6] The worst treatment was meted out to Russians, Poles and Greeks as 'racial inferiors' fit only for slave labour; of the 4,795,000 foreign workers in Germany at the end of the war nearly two millions were Russians living in frightful conditions, brutally treated and systematically worked to death in the interests of the German war-economy.

Exploitation of slave labour fitted in with Nazi plans for the depopulation of Eastern Europe and the resettlement of Aryan colonists in the area in a new and more terrible version of the medieval *Drang nach Osten*. Himmler, who was charged with responsibility for racial questions in October 1939, busied himself with the details of this fantastic scheme to create a new German *Reich*, 120 millions strong, dominating Europe from the Atlantic to the Urals; Poles, Czechs, White Russians and Ukrainians would be deprived of any possibility of advancement, material or spiritual, and ground down under the iron heel of the 'master race'; within twenty years – so Himmler told senior *SS* officers in 1943 – Germany might have moved her racial frontier five hundred kilometres eastwards and would breed a new race of supermen to control this vast empire and lead Europe against Asiatic barbarism. Deportation to Germany was an easy method of depopulating Eastern Europe, although at first, as Himmler admitted with regret in 1943, the *SS* allowed thousands of Russian prisoners of war to die of hunger and exhaustion instead of working them to death in Germany. Hitler took a lively interest in these nightmare schemes and was second to none in his brutality and ruthlessness towards the Slavs; it was on his express orders that mass executions of members of the Polish ruling class took place in 1939 in a cold-blooded attempt to deprive the Poles of their natural leaders.

[6]Had Great Britain been conquered, Himmler planned to deport all males between seventeen and forty-five to slave settlements in the Baltic countries.

The Nazis adopted the most severe measures to deal with growing opposition to German rule in many parts of occupied Europe. Hitler's *Nacht und Nebel* order in 1941 prescribed the death penalty for offences endangering occupation forces; those offenders who were not shot at once were transported to Germany as slave labour. More drastic still was the Terror-and-Sabotage decree of July 1944 which ordered that all acts of violence by non-Germans in occupied territory be construed as treason and sabotage. Keitel extended the decree to cover all persons endangering the war effort in any way. Senior *SS* officers were empowered to extend the decree so widely that any offence committed by a non-German in occupied territory was punishable under it. The utmost severity was meted out to those involved in partisan activity. By agreement with the military authorities, *SS Einsatzgruppen* (combat groups), were attached to each army group to combat partisans and were encouraged to terrorise and intimidate the affected areas. Partisans were shot out of hand, and those harbouring them were taken off to labour camps. Hostages were taken and executed as reprisals for attacks on German soldiers; in October 1941, a month after Keitel ordered the execution of fifty to a hundred 'Communists' to avenge the death of one German soldier, a station commander in Yugoslavia reported that 2,300 people had been shot after the killing of ten soldiers and the wounding of another twenty-six.

The most frightful chapter in the history of war-time Germany remains the extermination of the Jews. Words are quite inadequate to convey the enormity of a crime without parallel in the whole of modern history. With cold-blooded deliberation several million Jews, men, women and children, from all parts of occupied Europe were murdered in the short space of three years by specially formed execution squads.[7] However, although in one sense the murder of the Jews was a logical consequence of the savage anti-semitic propaganda over the years, it would be wrong to assume that the Nazis had planned the holocaust in detail long ago. An element of improvisation characterised Nazi policy here as elsewhere.

During the Polish campaign *SS* units had already murdered Jewish members of the Polish ruling class. When some *Wehrmacht* commanders tried to restrain the *SS*, Hitler deprived the army of any share in the administration of Poland and conferred full police powers on Himmler's *SS*. Meanwhile Heydrich herded other Polish Jews into ghettos in the larger towns preparatory to deportation to a huge reserve near Lublin. Then, after the fall of France, Nazi leaders toyed with the possibility of settling four million Jews in Madagascar under a governor of Himmler's choosing. But continued British resistance made this impossible. Meanwhile in Germany and all over occupied Europe Jews were bowed down by fresh restrictions and completely deprived of civil rights.

[7]Possibly between four and four-and-a-half millions perished, though some estimates are higher.

The attack on Russia sealed the fate of the Jews. Almost certainly Hitler ordered the extermination of European Jewry in the summer of 1941 when the Russian campaign was going well. Four *Einsatzgruppen* were already rounding up and massacring 'bolshevik' functionaries in Russia – including thousands of Jews – an operation planned by the *RSHA*[8] in collaboration with army high command. The *SS* units were given every assistance by most field commanders who were greatly relieved that the Führer had not assigned the grisly task of extermination to front-line soldiers. In the autumn of 1941 all German Jews were transported to the east, where special *SS* units were in readiness to carry out their dreadful task. Some of these people were practised murderers already, for in October 1939 Hitler ordered euthanasia of the incurably ill. By 1941 over 70,000 had been gassed in special institutions. When the camouflage around this operation began to wear thin, there were protests from church leaders, and Hitler ordered the suspension of the euthanasia programme in August 1941, although mentally defective and Jewish children were still murdered after that. In any event the 'mercy killers' soon found new employment in the east; the *SS* decided that shooting was too wasteful and harrowing a method of extermination and ordered gassing instead. Special camps were constructed at Chelmno, Belzec, Sobidor, Treblinka, Maidanek and at Auschwitz-Birkenau, where gas chambers were built on Himmler's orders as early as June 1941. The camp commandant at Auschwitz calculated in 1945 that two-and-a-half million Jews had been gassed there and a further half-million had died of hunger and illness, a total of three million Jews murdered coldly and scientifically by 'Zyklon B', a gas supplied by a subsidiary of *I.G. Farben*. Perhaps the most horrible feature of all was the meticulous care and thoroughness with which the camp staff disposed of personal effects; clothes and shoes were carefully counted, gold fillings from teeth (torn from the jaws of the victims immediately after death) were sent to the *Reichsbank*; hair was cut off and used for stuffing chairs; their bones were used for fertiliser and the fat of their bodies boiled down and used in soap-making. Most Germans had little direct knowledge of what went on in these remote death camps; there were whispers of fearful deeds, but the Nazis went to some pains to disguise the whole operation, and exposed as he was to the immense pressures of a totalitarian state in war-time, the average citizen quickly suppressed his doubts and restrained his curiosity.

The outbreak of war was not greeted with any enthusiasm by the mass of

---

[8]The *Reichssicherheitshauptamt* was the *SS* agency responsible for the work of the *Gestapo*, the *Sicherheitsdienst* and the *Sicherheitspolizei*.

the people. The tumultuous excitement of August 1914 belonged to a distant age; a grey, sober realism gripped the peoples of Europe in the early autumn days of 1939. However, after the victorious summer campaign of 1940 confidence in Hitler and in the outcome of the war was fully restored. Most historians have believed that the standard of living of the people was little affected by the war; that even in 1942 consumer expenditure was still roughly equal to the 1937 level; and that few restrictions were placed on the economy that were not already operative in 1939. Raw materials, the Achilles' heel of the German war effort, were scarce but Germany deliberately ran down her stocks to dangerously low levels confident that her armies would be in Moscow by Christmas 1941. According to this view it only became apparent in the traumatic winter of 1941–2 that the *Blitzkrieg* era was over and that Germany must mobilise for a total war of some duration.

More recently some doubt has been cast on this interpretation. It is argued that, *Blitzkrieg* victories in Poland and France notwithstanding, Germany was already mobilising the economy in 1939–40 for what Hitler was certain would be a major war. Arms expenditure mounted steeply and an acute shortage of consumer goods already existed in 1940. That industry failed to produce the vast quantities of arms Hitler expected was due to general inefficiency and to the conflicts between competing authorities characteristic of the Nazi administrative machine; three separate military agencies bore responsibility for the equipment of the armed forces; arms production was controlled by the ministry of munitions but industry and commerce came under the ministry of economics; in fact, the only effective form of overall control was the Führer-command, top-priority directives which regulated the level of arms production on Hitler's instructions. It is even argued that Hitler was already trying to shake industry out of its complacency before he appointed Albert Speer as minister of munitions and armament in February 1942.

However, there can be little doubt that Speer, the ex-architect friend of Hitler, was an organising genius cast in the mould of Walther Rathenau. Speer quickly established centralised machinery of control – the Central Planning Board – which proved so effective that by 1943 he had complete control of the whole economy. From 1942 onwards production rose steadily despite allied bombing, a phenomenon which baffled allied experts who had not appreciated how inefficient German industry had been. Thus, Germany attained her highest level of munitions production in August 1944, of aircraft in September and of weapons in December. Centralised planning was only part of the explanation. The other half of the picture was the ruthless exploitation of occupied Europe; without food supplies from the east German living standards would have fallen dramatically; and without Sauckel's brutal use of foreign labour and Goering's indiscriminate plundering of raw materials from all corners of Europe, the war-machine would have ground to a halt long before 1945.[9]

After the winter crisis of 1941–2 the Nazi grip on Germany tightened. In April 1942 Hitler assumed absolute powers to conduct the war as he saw fit. Judges were now ordered to dispense only 'National Socialist' justice in the 'national interest' regardless of legal niceties, Hitler expressly approved the use of torture by the *Gestapo* to extract confessions. And when he appointed Roland Freisler president of the Peoples' Court (*Volksgerichthof*) in August 1942 a bloody reign of terror commenced.

As totalitarian pressures weighed more heavily on Germany in 1943 and allied bombing brought the war to the people, opposition to the régime showed at all levels in German society. Of course, under the watchful eye of *Gestapo* and *SS* organised resistance by the people as a whole was virtually impossible, and in any case most of those who criticised the Nazis were not prepared to take active steps against them. More determined critics were already meeting in secret to discuss their grievances. These groups were small, scattered, loosely organised, had little contact with each other and varied greatly in their objectives. Many prominent and influential figures were involved in this clandestine activity; in the foreign office Adam von Trott zu Solz, Ulrich von Hassell, a former ambassador to Italy, and Count von Schulenburg, a former ambassador to Russia; in the civil service the Kordt brothers and Johannes Popitz, Prussian finance minister; in the *Wehrmacht* Field Marshal von Witzleben, Generals Beck and Olbricht and a few young officers, notably Count von Stauffenberg; in counter-intelligence the departmental head, Admiral Canaris and his chief aide Major-General Oster; the most prominent civilian was Karl Goerdeler, ex-mayor of Leipzig and leader of a group which planned to overthrow the Nazis by *coup d'état*; Goerdeler was in touch with Socialist and Catholic trade unionists such as Leuschner, Mierendorff, Leber and Kaiser; the churches were represented by priests such as Protestant pastor Bonhoeffer and the Jesuit father Delp; representatives of various social groups met together in the aristocratic Kreisau circle presided over by Count Helmuth James von Moltke, a descendant of the general who led Prussia to victory in 1870, and planned the political and social structure of a free Germany. Communist groups were actively engaged in industrial sabotage at this time but had few contacts with the middle-class and aristocratic groups.

Considerable differences of opinion existed about the future of Germany and about the desirability of active steps against Hitler – the Kreisau circle opposed a *coup d'état* almost to the end. Some wanted a planned economy after the war, others – such as Goerdeler – favoured

---

[9]Speer might have had even greater success had he not been opposed by jealous rivals such as Goering, by Gauleiters hostile to any central control and by the *SS*, which had its own economic empire largely outside his control. See chapter VI in A. Milward, *The German Economy at War* (London, 1965).

free enterprise; many were monarchists at heart and longed for the return of the social and political order of 1914; some were staunch democrats, while others hoped to salvage something out of the wreckage of National Socialism; and while some pinned their faith on lasting friendship with the west, others looked, in the Bismarckian tradition, towards Russia. What these heterogeneous elements had in common was a strong feeling of moral revulsion against the barbarity and inhumanity of Hitlerism and a desire to return to a civilised *Rechtsstaat*; in this sense the German resistance movement can be regarded as part of a much wider European reaction against fascism. Secondly, those who were resolved on direct action to remove Hitler were convinced that unless they acted quickly the Führer would drag Germany down to utter destruction and catastrophe.

It was to the army, the only institution with any remaining vestige of independence, that the activists looked for a lead; for without military co-operation no plot had any chance of success. As far back as 1938 Beck sounded out the generals about a possible *coup d'état* but met with a negative response. Halder, his successor, continued in the same vein, plotting with Witzleben and Weizsäcker of the foreign office with a view of removing Hitler and his associates in the event of war. Goerdeler was sent to London with details of the plot, hoping to encourage resistance to German demands for the Sudetenland. But Chamberlain was (rightly) sceptical about their chances of success. And after Munich opposition was damped down for the time being.

The outbreak of war made resistance much more difficult; 'mutiny' and 'revolution' were not words in a soldier's dictionary, as Beck commented in 1938. This was even more true in war-time; senior officers suppressed what doubts they had and immersed themselves in their professional duties. And Hitler's brilliant victories from 1939 to 1941 clearly reassured many of the critics, earned promotion for some of them and generally cut the ground from under the feet of Halder and Witzleben.

By 1943 the situation had changed substantially; many of those close to the corridors of power doubted whether Germany could win the war. In fact Hitler himself doubted in absolute victory as early as the winter of 1941–2 although he was still prepared to go on fighting to the bitter end whatever the cost to Germany. Consequently the group led by Beck and Goerdeler decided that only one course of action remained open: assassination of the Führer, which would free the *Wehrmacht* from its oath of allegiance and make a successful *coup d'état* possible. Even if this would not secure better terms from the allies – who now insisted on unconditional surrender – the conspirators felt deep down that they would at least save the nation's soul. After several abortive attempts Colonel von Stauffenberg placed a bomb in the conference room at 'Fort Wolf' in East Prussia on 20 July 1944, the anniversary of Papen's *coup d'état*. After Hitler's death it was planned to set up a provisional government under

Beck and Goerdeler and sue for peace. The bomb exploded but, unknown to Stauffenberg who returned at once to Berlin, Hitler survived. Himmler and Keitel acted promptly and announced the news of Hitler's escape on the radio, a move which threw the conspirators, waiting in Berlin, into confusion. Troops on which they relied to seize the radio station failed to arrive. In the end a group of loyal soldiers led by a certain Major Remer arrested the conspirators.[10] Beck was allowed to commit suicide, Stauffenberg and Olbricht were shot out of hand. A four-hundred strong *Gestapo* commission moved into action, uncovered the far-reaching ramifications of the plot, which greatly surprised the Nazi leaders, and made thousands of arrests. After a farcical trial by the People's Court the chief conspirators, including Witzleben, were executed. In all some 5,000 opponents of the régime, whether implicated in the plot or not, were executed in the next few months.

The Bomb Plot came too late in the day to succeed. Perhaps it could never have succeeded at any time, given the totalitarian conditions of war-time Germany. The oath of personal loyalty to Hitler made outright opposition extraordinarily difficult even for soldiers who hated Hitler's methods; once it was clear that he was unharmed, those who had been ready to support a new government quickly changed their minds. A deeper difficulty was that the conspiracy had to succeed on its own before it could expect the support of the people; a mass uprising was impossible as long as the *Gestapo* and the *SS* were in command. The very fact that the attempt was made with little hope of success gives it its real significance as a moral gesture of atonement for the horrible crimes of the Nazis.

In the aftermath of the Bomb Plot the Nazi party reached the height of its power. Hitler had always mistrusted the old officer corps and had done his best over the years to weaken its position. Now his fury knew no bounds. The last lingering vestiges of army independence were ruthlessly stamped out. With Himmler as commander-in-chief of the home forces, the army passed under *SS* control; the *Waffen SS*, long despised by many regular officers, came into its own at last; the Nazi salute was made compulsory throughout the *Wehrmacht*; all general-staff officers were ordered by General Guderian, the new army chief of staff, to co-operate fully in the political indoctrination of the armed forces; and to make certain his orders were obeyed Hitler attached political officers, a Nazi version of the Red Army's old political commissars, to all military headquarters.

With allied armies fighting in France in the summer of 1944 and Russian armies moving steadily westwards, Hitler tried to brace the people for a last effort to win the war. Goebbels, who had always been on the radical left of the party, was back in favour with the Führer. In August 1944 he was appointed plenipotentiary for total war and at once ordered

[10]Remer was promoted major-general by the grateful Führer. After the war Remer was for a time the leader of an extreme nationalist organisation in West Germany, the *Deutsche Reichspartei*.

total mobilisation; all theatres, cinemas and restaurants were closed, the civil service was ordered to work at least a sixty-hour week, and all leave was cancelled. Desperate efforts were made to strengthen Germany's dwindling labour force. Taking advantage of the pause in military operations in the west in the late autumn of 1944, Hitler busied himself with fantastic plans for the creation of a new mass army to roll back the invaders; all it meant in practice was that instead of bringing depleted units back to strength, he created new divisions adding to the list of active units without increasing his total manpower. As a final resort he ordered a *levée-en-masse*; all men between sixteen and sixty were liable for service in the *Volkssturm*, a home-defence force organised, not by the army, but by the party and operating under Himmler's command. Meanwhile Goebbels tried to boost flagging morale with desperate talk of vast reserves and new weapons – the V rockets – which when operational would win the war for Germany; in an attempt to whip up a spirit of fanatical resistance he painted a grim picture of the terrible fate awaiting them if they lost the war – rumours of the Morgenthau Plan to pastoralise Germany lent credibility to his frenzied propaganda. The judicial terror rose to a climax; slighting references to the Führer or unguarded words about the outcome of the war were sufficient to cost unwary citizens their lives.

It was all in vain. There was no escape for the Third Reich from the plight to which Hitler and his associates had brought her. The German people struggled grimly on but with little hope. The economic base for further resistance no longer existed; the war-economy was breaking down rapidly at the beginning of 1945. Germany was using up raw materials which could not be replaced as the allies liberated the occupied territories from which they were obtained; an acute fuel shortage developed, largely because of allied bombing of synthetic-oil plant; and in February 1945 Jodl, chief of operations at the *OKW*, had to forbid the use of the *Luftwaffe* in all but the most grave military situations. Intensive bombing by the allies resulted in a serious breakdown of communications. This in its turn created supply problems and shortages (sometimes artificial, as in the case of coal). Labour shortages assumed dangerous proportions as all available men were drafted into the *Volkssturm*. Speer, who had done so much to mobilise Germany for total war, had ceased to believe in a German victory, and warned Hitler in January 1945 that the war was virtually over. This the Führer knew in his heart even though he clung pathetically to the forlorn hope that when Russia and her allies fell out – as he was certain they would – the latter would make peace with Germany and turn against Russia. The end came in the spring of 1945. When the allied armies swept across the Rhine in March, they met with little resistance on the other side. In the east the Russians were closing in on Berlin. In the last days of April the Third Reich fell to pieces in a welter of confusion and disorder, and the victorious allied powers assumed responsibility for the administration of Germany.

14

Foreign Policy and War
1933–1945

Looking back in retrospect over the twenty years separating the armistice from the collapse of Czechoslovakia, it is not altogether surprising that Germany recovered her old power and prestige so quickly. Several factors were in her favour from the beginning. The strategic situation in Europe was potentially more promising in 1918 than ever before. For one thing the old balance of power in the east was completely destroyed by the war. From the days of Bismarck Germany had never been free from the danger of war on two fronts. This nightmare ceased to trouble her for several years after 1918 when Communist Russia was a weak and isolated power, ostracised by victor and vanquished alike. The Habsburg and Romanov empires had crumbled away, throwing the political geography of Central and Eastern Europe into the melting-pot. In the place of these venerable empires there arose small weak states likely sooner or later to turn to Germany for economic support and protection against Communism. Even the victors, Britain and France, were seriously weakened by the strain of four years of war; only with American help had the scales been tipped decisively against the Central Powers. Germany, on the other hand, though temporarily exhausted, had survived without the work of unification being seriously disrupted as it was to be in 1945. It was really only a matter of time before a country of Germany's size and potential tried to shake off the shackles of a treaty which her people detested and which had its critics from the start, especially in Britain. Under republican auspices Germany had by 1932 regained much of her former status as a great power. Inasmuch as Hitler was seeking to repudiate the remnants of Versailles, he was travelling along a road signposted by preceding chancellors.

  Was Nazi foreign policy, then, simply a continuation of the revisionist policy of preceding régimes? In *Mein Kampf* Hitler made it perfectly plain that the restoration of the frontiers of Bismarck's *Reich* had no special significance for the Nazis. Reunion with 'German Austria' – a step towards the creation of *Grossdeutschland*, the dream of 1848 – was Hitler's declared ambition on the first page of the book. Furthermore, Germany's task was to gather together all German-speaking people in one great *Reich*, wherever they lived in Europe. That was only the beginning. Memories of the huge territories the Germans held under the Brest Litovsk treaty convinced Hitler that the true destiny of the Germans lay in the east where they could find living space at the expense of 'Jewish-bolshevik' Russia. A new and mighty *Reich* would arise dominating Europe from the Atlantic to the Urals. And the Slav peoples would be largely expelled to make room for German settlers. Although the living-space theme was played down in the 1930s when the Nazis became a mass party, it is significant that within three days of becoming chancellor Hitler informed his army commanders privately that rearmament was the first priority; this might, he admitted, help Germany find new export markets but the most desirable outcome would be the conquest of *Lebensraum* in the east and its 'ruthless Germanisation'. Several historians now think that Hitler had world ambitions: once Germany had conquered Europe from the Atlantic to the Urals she would make a bid for world power which would almost certainly mean war with the United States. That, however, lay in the distant future.

Many people inside and outside Germany assumed that once in office Hitler would quickly outgrow the racialist imperialism of *Mein Kampf*. Hitler encouraged this view by his cautious behaviour both at home and abroad. There was no sudden change of course in 1933. The Disarmament Conference was still meeting, and when the second session commenced in February 1933 the German delegation was in its usual place. When MacDonald produced his draft convention proposing *inter alia* a reduction of French land forces from 500,000 to 200,000 men and an increase in Germany's forces up to 200,000, Hitler gave it a guarded welcome, reiterating his longing for peace and Germany's readiness to remain disarmed on condition the other powers disarmed. In fact he was playing for time, hoping that the French would sabotage the scheme and supply Germany with a pretext for leaving the conference. The gamble succeeded. France, already seriously alarmed by evidence of secret rearmament in Germany, could not believe that Hitler would be satisfied indefinitely with equality of armaments and insisted on a pause of four years before disarmament commenced. When the conference reassembled in October, Hitler denounced the failure to concede immediate equality of armaments to Germany and withdrew the German delegation. For good measure, he withdrew from the League of Nations at the same time, an action which represented the first clear breach with Stresemann's conciliatory policy. Throughout he acted with the support of foreign office, diplomatic corps and army command, all just as anxious as Hitler to make Germany the dominant power in Europe. And though Germany's lapse into isolation was deplored and regretted by the other powers, there were no repercussions; Britain and Italy sympathised with the German argument for immediate equality of armaments while France on her own was not prepared to move against Germany.

Sometimes Hitler pursued policies which surprised his conservative partners as in January 1934 when he signed a Non-Aggression Pact with Poland, a state Weimar governments had felt only hostility towards. In view of German territorial ambitions in the east the Poles were greatly alarmed by the resurgence of German militarism. Threatening military movements in the Danzig area were intended by the Poles as a warning to the Nazis. Whereupon Hitler offered to negotiate with Poland. Ostensibly a sign that Germany was settling down to normal diplomatic life, in reality the pact was a serious blow to the French defensive system in Eastern Europe which rested on the Polish alliance. It is possible that Hitler toyed with the idea of turning this authoritarian state into an obedient German vassal and using her against Soviet Russia at a later date. In any event German territorial claims on Poland were not abandoned, but merely put in cold storage until a more convenient moment.

Hitler was not always so successful. After the *Machtergreifung* the Austrian Nazis intensified their disruptive activities with Hitler's support – for surprisingly he supposed that the powers would regard the absorption of 'German' Austria as a purely internal affair. In July 1934 the Austrian Nazis attempted to seize power in Vienna. Dollfuss, the Austrian chancellor was murdered, but the *Putsch* quickly collapsed. Dollfuss, with his authoritarian ideas, had been a favourite with Mussolini, who regarded independent Austria as a useful buffer to keep Germany at arm's length as well as a handy counter to French influence in the Danubian basin. Alarmed by these signs of German interest in Austria, the Italian dictator immediately sent troops to the Brenner pass and assured Schuschnigg, Dollfuss's successor, that Italy was ready to defend the independence of Austria. A timely warning had been served on Hitler that he could not yet do as he pleased in Central Europe. Whether he was party to the *Putsch* or not, he quickly retreated at the first sign of real opposition and for the next two years acted with great restraint towards Austria. The German minister in Vienna, who had been deeply implicated in the *Putsch*, was recalled, and Papen sent in his place as extraordinary ambassador in a calculated attempt to win the favour of Schuschnigg.

Hitler was still moving with great caution in the early months of 1935. In January, when the Saarland returned to Germany after a plebiscite which showed that ninety per cent of the inhabitants wanted reunion, Hitler assured France that the last obstacle to friendly relations was now removed. Shortly after this Britain and France tried to interest Germany in a general agreement fixing arms levels, in a mutual assistance pact covering Eastern Europe and in a five-power air pact, proposals which Hitler was careful not to reject out of hand. Then on 4 March 1935 a British White Paper appeared defending some modest air-force increases on the grounds that Germany was rearming in defiance of treaty obligations. There was much indignation in Germany, which increased still further when a week later the French increased the period of conscription from twelve to eighteen months. Hitler was glad of this pretext for ending tiresome negotiations in which he had never been interested. At last he saw his chance of scoring a cheap prestige victory by a bold stroke of policy.

On 9 March 1935 Goering announced the existence of a German air force, no great surprise, as it was generally known that Germany possessed one despite the treaty. The real sensation was the reintroduction of conscription on 16 March and the announcement that, in view of British, French and Russian rearmament, Germany felt obliged to build up a peace-time army of 550,000 men, a figure considerably higher than the 300,000-strong army Hitler had proposed to settle for in 1933. World reaction was much as Hitler expected. Britain, France and Italy, meeting at Stresa, solemnly condemned Germany's unilateral action and reaffirmed their resolve to maintain Austrian independence. Beyond that they did not go; the fact of the matter was that many people in Britain and Italy felt that Germany had simply removed an intolerable disability which any self-respecting power would resent after the failure of the Disarmament Conference. Similarly at Geneva the Council of the League of Nations condemned Germany's action and set up a committee to consider what steps to take – but only in the event of future breaches of international obligations. Britain was still prepared to negotiate with Hitler and in June 1935 actually signed a naval convention with Germany which formally annulled the naval provisions of the Versailles treaty and allowed Germany to have a navy thirty-five per cent of the strength of the British Fleet.

This was not because the British government did not realise that the general thrust of German policy posed a threat to British interests. But Japanese aggression in China and Mussolini's ambitions in the Mediterranean raised the dreadful spectre of a three-power alliance directed against the British Empire. As Britain was too weak militarily to face such a conflict and had no wish to be trapped into another arms race, it made sense to try to ease the tension in Europe by negotiating limited agreements with Germany and Italy – here were the roots of the appeasement policy associated with Neville Chamberlain. But for Hitler the convention was the first step towards the British alliance he spoke of in *Mein Kampf* as a *sine qua non* for German expansion in Europe. Although Hitler possessed considerable political skill in handling opponents (e.g. Schuschnigg and Hacha) his understanding of British policy was fatally flawed. His assumption that Britain would accept German hegemony in Europe in return for a guarantee of her maritime supremacy and imperial power completely ignored the well-documented fact that Britain had traditionally opposed attempts by any Great Power to dominate Europe. An equal partnership was never on offer; at best Britain would have been a junior partner. And if those historians are right who argue that after conquering Europe Hitler (or his successors) intended to make a bid for world power then war with Britain and the United States to wrest control of the seas from them would have been a likely outcome.

The failure of Britain to consult France and Italy before signing the convention greatly weakened the Stresa Front. During the winter of 1935-6 it foundered completely over Abyssinia, much to Hitler's satisfaction. He watched with close attention the half-hearted attempts of Britain and France to coerce a fellow-dictator, realising that if they succeeded it might well be more difficult for Germany to complete the dismantling of the treaty. As long as the issue remained in doubt Hitler, with characteristic caution, avoided giving offence to them. Once it was obvious, in the spring of 1936, that Mussolini had won the war, Hitler lost what lingering respect he may have had for the League of Nations and struck another blow at the crumbling edifice of Versailles; on 7 March 1936 German troops marched into the demilitarised Rhineland.

The reoccupation of the Rhineland was an event of major importance. This was a violation of the freely negotiated Locarno Pacts as well as the Versailles treaty and on the face of it a dangerous gamble. As always, Hitler had a ready excuse; the Franco-Soviet Alliance, ratified by the French Chamber in February 1936, was, so he maintained, incompatible with the Locarno Pacts, and by drawing 'Bolshevik' Russia into European affairs it threatened the integrity of all countries and not only Germany – an argument calculated to appeal to the widespread fear of communism in ruling circles. To allay the anxiety of the Locarno powers, Hitler offered to create a new demilitarised zone on each side of the Franco-German frontier, to sign an air pact and negotiate a new non-aggression pact with the western powers and even to return to the League of Nations. Opinion in the foreign office, diplomatic corps and army command was divided. The pessimists were convinced that the Rhineland was so essential to the French defensive system that she could not possibly allow German soldiers to remain there and as Germany could offer no more than token resistance, the enterprise would end disastrously. Hitler sided with the optimists, among them Neurath. In the event France did not intervene; foreign complications were highly unwelcome on the eve of a general election in a deeply divided country; and the general staff, having grossly overestimated German strength, feared that a major war would be required to force the Germans out of the Rhineland. Britain was frankly relieved that an anomalous situation had been clarified and wanted to negotiate with Hitler on his latest proposals, a course of action unacceptable to France. So the Locarno powers confined themselves to verbal protests, a lead followed by the Council of the League of Nations.

Germany had won a great diplomatic victory without a shot being fired. In so far as the demilitarised Rhineland gave France security against

German aggression, that advantage was lost overnight. True, France never seriously intended to aid her East European allies, and once she commenced to build the Maginot Line in 1929 her strategy was purely defensive. All the same, once Germany had refortified the Rhineland – which she was remarkably slow in doing – France could not even envisage the possibility of a successful offensive strategy. More serious still was the psychological defeat France suffered in 1936. It was not that she lacked military strength to deal with Germany. Her weakness was more fundamental; her people lacked the will to fight, partly because they were preoccupied with political conflict at home and partly because of a deep-seated sense of their own inability to keep Germany down; it was easier to hope that inaction might win German favour in the long run.

After this Hitler's faith in his own star was unbounded. Changes in the pattern of international affairs after the reoccupation of the Rhineland encouraged him to believe that the time had come to advance more rapidly towards his ultimate goal. One of the most important developments was the *rapprochement* with Italy. Mussolini's fears of German ambitions in the Danubian basin were set at rest by an Austro-German agreement in July 1936 in which Germany promised to respect Austrian independence and refrain from interference in her internal affairs – an agreement which Hitler entered into because he felt he could afford to await the day when Austria moved into the German orbit of her own volition. Austria for her part, aware that she could no longer rely on the protection of the Stresa Front, readily agreed to improve relations with Germany; political prisoners were to be released and some members of the 'national opposition' were promised a share in political responsibility. But the decisive consideration, as far as Mussolini was concerned, was the fact that Italy was deeply involved in the Spanish Civil War which made her vulnerable to attack and more dependent on German support. This suited Hitler, who appreciated that as long as the war continued Italy could not interfere with German plans in Central Europe. Discussion in October led to the signature of an agreement for political, economic and ideological co-operation. Speaking in Milan on 1 November 1936, Mussolini revealed the existence of a pact and declared that Europe would soon revolve round the new 'axis'. In November Ribbentrop negotiated the Anti-Comintern Pact with Japan for both the foreign minister and his master saw in her a useful counter to British and Russian influence in the Far East. A year later, when Italy finally left the League of Nations and adhered to the Anti-Comintern Pact, the 'Rome-Berlin-Tokyo Axis' was born. Whatever reservations existed on all sides about ultimate objectives, the Axis represented a new power alignment, a fascist 'Holy Alliance' utterly opposed to the values of western democracy. To some extent, too, it meant that Hitler had lost faith in the possibility of a general agreement with Britain to underwrite German expansion in Europe and had aligned himself with powers hostile to Britain.

By this time the League of Nations was a completely broken reed. Power politics had returned to the forefront of international relations, and states great and small alike were adjusting themselves to the reality of a balance of power moving rapidly back to Berlin. Britain and France were driven onto the defensive. The Locarno system to which they pinned their faith lay in ruins; all attempts to resurrect it failed and when Belgium declared her neutrality in 1937, the strategic position of France *vis-à-vis* Germany was rendered even more serious. The Franco-Soviet alliance counted for little, with Russia racked by internal convulsions and weaker than ever, while in Central Europe the Little Entente was rapidly disintegrating. The semi-authoritarian states of the Danubian basin were already dependent on Germany economically; realising that they could no longer play off Italy against Germany, they tried to make their peace with fascism; Yugoslavia came to terms with Italy and Bulgaria in 1937 while Rumania disengaged herself from the French alliance as quickly as possible. This left Czechoslovakia high and dry, virtually isolated in a hostile world and a tempting prize for an aggressor.

At the famous Hossbach Conference in November 1937 Hitler outlined to Foreign Minister von Neurath, Minister of War Blomberg and the three commanders-in-chief his determination to exploit this favourable international situation as quickly as possible. In the course of a long and rambling discourse (of which Hossbach, Hitler's adjutant, took notes) – his political testament as Hitler called it – he reiterated his belief that Germany's future depended on the acquisition of *Lebensraum*. To obtain it Germany must be prepared to use force and run risks. At the very latest the problem of *Lebensraum* must be solved by 1943–5. Otherwise the rearmament of Britain and France would tip the balance of advantage against Germany – just as in 1914 Germany's leaders agreed that by 1917 Russian rearmament would prevent them realising their ambitions. Secondly, the diplomatic situation was deteriorating; Britain was now classed with France as a 'hate-inspired' opponent and the possibility of American support for Britain conjured up the spectre of a grand anti-German alliance against which Germany could not prevail. Thirdly, Germany's economic difficulties would become more acute; the scarcity of foreign exchange and the need to import food and raw materials meant that Germany could not maintain indefinitely both a large army and the living standards of the people; the stark alternatives were a decline in these standards or expansion. In his address Hitler discussed various scenarios: civil war in France under cover of which Czechoslovakia could be seized; or war between France and Italy, possibly in 1938, when Germany could seize both Austria and Czechoslovakia.

Blomberg and Fritsch doubted whether Germany would be ready for war in 1940 let alone in 1938. Moreover they doubted whether Britain and France would stand idly by – as Hitler asserted they would – should it come to war. A few days later Hitler had striking confirmation of his intuitive judgement when Lord Halifax, Lord President of the Council, visited Germany on a good-will mission. Speaking to Goering Halifax praised Germany as the 'bulwark of the west against bolshevism' and admitted that Germany had legitimate grievances in respect of Austria, Czechoslovakia and Danzig. Britain would not oppose alterations in the status quo provided these were effected by peaceful evolution and 'that methods likely to lead to far-reaching disturbances were avoided'. Britain had re-stated her traditional policy of disinterestedness in East European affairs at precisely the right moment for Hitler. Though he now considered Britain to be an opponent of German policy, nevertheless he concluded that she would stand aside and let him do much as he pleased in the immediate future.

Before embarking on a more aggressive policy, Hitler rid himself of tiresome critics in high places. Reference was made in the last chapter to the upheaval in the army early in 1938 which ended with Hitler assuming the functions of commander-in-chief of the armed forces. This purge was extended to the foreign office. Papen was recalled from Vienna, Hassell from Rome and Dirksen from Tokyo, and Neurath was replaced by Joachim von Ribbentrop, a fanatical Nazi and German ambassador in London since 1936. Under Ribbentrop's control the foreign office at last became a servile tool of the Führer's.

By the end of 1937 Hitler, anxious to end the stalemate in Austrian affairs in recent months, proposed a meeting with Schuschnigg. The latter, concerned about Austria's growing isolation, agreed. At the meeting on 12 February 1938 at the Berghof, Hitler's mountain eyrie on the Obersalzberg just inside the German frontier, Schuschnigg was to his surprise subjected to moral blackmail. The Führer stormed and raved about 'intolerable conditions' in Austria, declared that his patience was exhausted and threatened to use force unless Schuschnigg agreed at once to a series of demands which practically turned Austria into a German satellite. Seyss-Inquart, a Nazi fellow-traveller, was to become minister of the interior, all Nazi activity in Austria was to be legalised and all Nazi prisoners amnestied, and Austria had to promise to co-ordinate her foreign policy and economic system with Germany's. As Schuschnigg capitulated to this pressure, the Berchtesgaden Agreement represented a great victory for Hitler. Confident that the peaceful absorption of Austria was now only a matter of time, he ordered the Nazis to stop their subversive activities; a frontal assault was unnecessary once the citadel had collapsed from within.

However, the tension continued to mount inside Austria, where local Nazis prepared for the *coup de grâce*. Threatening demonstrations were held in several large towns, whereupon the government banned meetings and processions and forbade the wearing of Nazi emblems. In a last desperate attempt to stop further erosion of his authority Schuschnigg suddenly announced his intention to hold a plebiscite on 13 March to let the people decide whether they wanted Austria to remain free and independent. If a massive majority voted yes, as seemed probable, this would give Schuschnigg a moral base on which to resist further Nazi encroachments. Hitler's hand was forced. He dare not risk a public rebuff certain to retard the prospect of an early *Anschluss*, and at once ordered the army to prepare for the invasion of Austria. Plans were hastily improvised and army units took up positions on the frontier. On 11 March Seyss-Inquart was instructed by Goering to demand the postponement of the plebiscite. Schuschnigg turned in vain to the Great Powers. Mussolini refused even to answer the telephone, having written Austria off months before. Britain disapproved of Germany's bullying tactics but refused to help Schuschnigg; it was felt in London that *Anschluss* with Germany was inevitable and broadly in accordance with the wishes of the Austrian people. France was paralysed by a ministerial crisis, a convenient alibi for a power who had no intention of helping Austria. Schuschnigg had no option but to postpone the plebiscite. Hitler now insisted on his resignation and replacement by Seyss-Inquart. At first President Miklas refused, whereupon Goering warned him through Seyss-Inquart that Germany would invade at once unless Schuschnigg went. Finally Miklas gave way and let Schuschnigg resign. By this time the Nazis had taken over in many parts of Austria. Hitler at last made his mind up to invade. Goering actually dictated the telegram in which the newly appointed chancellor Seyss-Inquart asked Berlin to send troops in to restore order. On 12 March 1938 German troops marched into Austria and Hitler drove to Linz, his boyhood home, where he was greeted by jubilant crowds. Only at this late hour did he decide to annex Austria rather than allow it satellite status in the shadow of Germany. On 13 March Seyss-Inquart proclaimed the union of Austria and Germany; independent Austria ceased to exist and a *Reich* of seventy million Germans came into being.

This was Hitler's greatest triumph to date, a feat which captured the imagination of the German people and enormously enhanced his personal prestige. Again he had successfully defied Britain and France, who did no more than protest at the illegality of his methods. The strategic implications of the *Anschluss* were immensely important. Germany now had contiguous frontiers with Italy, Hungary and Yugoslavia. With Vienna in his hands Hitler had military and economic control of the mid-Danubian basin; South-Eastern Europe was more dependent on Germany economically than ever before, and the Little Entente was virtually buried; overnight the western defence perimeter of Czechoslovakia was outflanked and the Czechs were suddenly exposed to German pressure.

Barely a month after the *Anschluss* Hitler turned his attentions to Czechoslovakia. Since his early days in Vienna he had hated and despised the Czechs as a 'sub-people'. That they were the allies of France and Russia and the bastion of democracy in Central Europe made them even more obnoxious in his eyes. But military considerations were decisive for Hitler; until the Czechs were 'neutralised', German ambitions in the east could never be realised. All he needed was a pretext for intervention in her internal affairs and this was ready to hand in the existence of a three-and-a-half-million German minority in the Sudetenland.

Throughout the 1920s the Weimar Republic did its best to sustain the Sudeten Germans in their cultural and political aspirations. National Socialism spread quickly in the Sudetenland after 1933, feeding on economic discontent and on grievances about the predominance of Czech officials in German-speaking areas. After the *Anschluss* the local Nazi party, led by an ex-schoolmaster, Konrad Henlein, grew bolder and demanded complete autonomy for the Sudetenland in the Czech state and a reorientation of Czech foreign policy. By the end of 1937 Henlein had opted for *Anschluss* with Germany and was following the policy dictated to him by Berlin; on 28 March 1938 he met Hitler, Ribbentrop and Hess and was instructed to negotiate with the Czechs but to avoid binding agreements by continually raising his demands, in short to cause the maximum difficulty for the Czechs until Hitler was ready to exploit the situation in a decisive manner.

On 21 April Hitler discussed with Keitel various pretexts for a lightning attack on Czechoslovakia before the Great Powers had time to intervene. With Austria still to digest Hitler did not intend to launch this attack in the near future. By 30 May he had changed his mind and in the directive for Operation Green – the plan of attack – he stated that 'it is my unalterable decision to attack Czechoslovakia by military force in the near future'. The decisive factor was Hitler's visit to Italy in early May which confirmed Hitler in the belief that Italy would not interfere with German plans for expansion in Central Europe. The May Crisis at the end of the month when Czech President Eduard Beneš ordered partial mobilization on the basis of (false) rumours of German troop movements may well have enraged Hitler and confirmed him in his decision, already taken, to strike at the Czechs as soon as possible.

The behaviour of Britain and France encouraged him to believe that they would not intervene in his little war. From the beginning Britain refused to give any guarantee to Czechoslovakia or to France if she went to war over Czechoslovakia. It was equally obvious that France had no intention of aiding the Czechs. Significant, too, that no attempt was made by the western powers to co-ordinate policy with Soviet Russia, despite the Franco-Soviet and Franco-Czech alliances. Chamberlain's well-meaning attempts to mediate between Czechs and Germans merely confirmed

Hitler in his belief that Britain wanted peace at any price. Badgered by Chamberlain and Halifax, Beneš agreed reluctantly to negotiate with Henlein, but as the latter was still under orders to avoid agreement, no progress was made. Nor could Lord Runciman, sent out in the high summer as mediator, achieve anything. By early September the situation had deteriorated alarmingly; clashes between Czechs and Germans were of frequent occurrence in the Sudetenland; threatening German army manoeuvres were taking place on the Czech frontier and a vituperative anti-Czech campaign commenced in the German press. The climax came on 12 September with Hitler's violent speech at the Nuremberg party rally, when he demanded the right of self-determination for the Sudeten Germans. This was the signal for renewed disturbances in the Sudetenland; Henlein broke off negotiations with Beneš, staged an abortive uprising and fled to Germany.

At this critical juncture Chamberlain suddenly flew to Germany in a desperate attempt to settle the Czech-German dispute and avoid war. He met Hitler at the Berghof on 15 September and agreed at once to accept the principle of self-determination as a basis for settlement; provided Hitler did not attack Czechoslovakia in the meantime, he offered to return home and obtain cabinet approval of his offer. It cost Hitler nothing to agree as he had never intended to attack Czechoslovakia before 1 October. He was greatly surprised and none too pleased by Chamberlain's visit; he thought the British prime minister a ridiculous figure and supposed he had seen the last of him; for it seemed inconceivable that Britain and France could accept the self-determination principle and serve him Czechoslovakia on a plate, as he put it later.

He was wrong. Chamberlain secured the support of the British and French cabinets to the outright cession of the Sudetenland; all areas where over fifty per cent of the population was German were to be handed over to Germany without plebiscite. Subjected to tremendous pressure from London and Paris, Beneš agreed. On 22 September Chamberlain reappeared this time at Bad Godesberg confident that the crisis was over. To his dismay Hitler rejected the proposals on the grounds that they were too dilatory; instead he insisted on the immediate occupation of the Sudetenland within two days – he finally moved the date to 1 October, making great play with this 'concession'.

Why had he become so intransigent? Confident that Britain and France would not fight, he was simply raising his terms as a pretext for breaking off negotiations and going to war. On 26 September at the Berlin Sportpalast in a most belligerent speech he gave the Czechs twenty-four hours in which to agree to return the Sudetenland by 1 October, a ploy to place the onus for peace or war on Beneš's shoulders. Warned on 27 September by Sir Horace Wilson, Chamberlain's personal envoy, that if Germany attacked Czechoslovakia France would honour her obligations to Czechoslovakia and Britain would fight on her side, Hitler remained unmoved. It seemed that war was inevitable.

Why, then, did he suddenly change his mind and agree to the Munich Conference? He seems to have been assailed by last-minute doubts. The chances of destroying Czechoslovakia by a surprise attack and presenting Europe with a *fait accompli* diminished once the Czechs mobilised. Now France had mobilised some troops and the British fleet left Invergorden. It looked as if a local war might escalate into a major one. His generals took fright, fearing that France would intervene and quickly overwhelm the dozen divisions which was all that could be spared to guard the western frontier. Hitler personally experienced the lack of enthusiasm for war on the part of the German people as he stood at the chancellery window and watched the silent crowds as guns and tanks roared past. Party leaders were divided; Ribbentrop and Himmler were for war while Goering pleaded for negotiation. Finally Mussolini, alarmed by the prospect of war, sponsored a new British proposal for a further conference which would – as he pointed out to Hitler – enable the Germans to begin the occupation of the Sudetenland on 1 October, the deadline for military action. In the end Hitler agreed reluctantly to negotiate and Chamberlain, Daladier and Mussolini joined him at Munich on 29 September.

There was little negotiation at the Munich Conference. Britain and France quickly agreed that the Sudetenland be occupied by German troops between 1 and 10 October, the details to be worked out by an international commission. What remained of Czechoslovakia, after Polish and Hungarian claims had been satisfied, would be guaranteed by the four powers. After the conference Chamberlain sought out Hitler in an attempt to secure a more general understanding. The result was the Anglo-German declaration signed in Hitler's Munich flat on 30 September. Chamberlain attached great importance to this document which stated that Britain and Germany were resolved never to go to war again but always to settle disputes around the conference table. The British and French public accepted the Munich Agreement with uneasy approval as the only alternative to war. In Germany the Führer's prestige rose to new heights. Significantly enough, he was in a bad mood after Munich; far from regarding this as a great triumph he complained bitterly to his intimates that through Chamberlain his 'entry into Prague had been spoilt'.

He was determined to complete the destruction of Czechoslovakia as quickly as possible. As early as 21 October, three days after the formal signature of the Munich Agreement, in a secret memorandum counter-signed by Keitel, Hitler declared that he must be able to smash Czechoslovakia should her policy become hostile to Germany, and plans were drawn up for a surprise attack. However, in the end Czechoslovakia collapsed from within. After Munich the Slovaks were given a large measure of autonomy which only whetted their appetite for complete independence. Hitler gave every encouragement to the Slovakian separatists, receiving their leader, Tuka, in audience in February. Early in March the Czechs, in a desperate attempt to prevent the disintegration of the state, dismissed Tiso, the Slovakian premier, and most of his ministers and sent in troops to restore order. This was the opportunity for which Hitler had been waiting. Under pressure from Berlin Tiso declared Slovakia independent. Faced with the destruction of their state, the Czechs turned in despair to Hitler. President Hacha visited Berlin where he was mercilessly bullied into placing Bohemia and Moravia under German protection; the alternative, as Goering delighted in explaining to the old man, was the destruction of Prague by aerial bombardment. Early on 15 March 1939 German troops entered Prague. On 16 March Hitler incorporated Bohemia and Moravia in the *Reich*, declaring as his excuse that these provinces had been part of Germany for a thousand years – the historical argument had now superseded the national one. On the same day Tiso asked Hitler to take Slovakia under his wing – the proclamation was drafted during the Slovakian premier's visit to Berlin on 13 March – which the Führer agreed to at once. Simultaneously Hungarian troops seized Carpatho-Ukraine, the eastern tip of Czechoslovakia in which Hitler had no interest. Hitler's victory was complete. To round off the events of this momentous spring he compelled Lithuania on 22 March to hand back the Memelland, a territory taken from Germany in 1919.

Hitler was right in supposing that the western democracies would, as usual, only protest at the rape of Czechoslovakia. What he did not anticipate was the deep impression the events of March 1939 made upon public opinion in Britain. Overnight, appeasement was discredited; Hitler had not acted in a civilised fashion, as Chamberlain had hoped; on the contrary he had deliberately plotted to destroy Czechoslovakia. Nor could Hitler claim to be reuniting Germans any more; Czechs and Slovaks were not German by any stretch of the imagination. At last it dawned on public opinion that Hitler was seeking to dominate Europe by force. Although Chamberlain did not completely abandon the appeasement policy, he began to pay more attention to rearmament and at long last tried to create a diplomatic front in Europe capable of containing the Germans. In accordance with this new policy and on the basis of rumours of threatening German troop-movements Britain offered a guarantee to Poland on 31 March 1939, promising to come to her aid if her independence was threatened. Overnight Britain had reversed her traditional policy of non-involvement in the affairs of Eastern Europe. And the Danzig problem suddenly moved into the forefront of the diplomatic scene, for the Polish attitude to Germany hardened at once; she now saw no reason why she should make concessions to Hitler over Danzig and the Corridor.

For Hitler settlement of the German demands on Poland was a secondary objective. His hope that Britain would allow Germany to dominate

Europe had been destroyed by Chamberlain's intervention over Czecho-slovakia. Hitler concluded that he would have to fight Britain as well as France before he could realise his eastern ambitions. Significantly, in October 1938 he ordered a five-fold increase in the *Luftwaffe* to create a strategic (long-range bombers) as well as a tactical airforce. Already in the winter of 1938-9 the *Luftwaffe* started to plan for war with Britain. In January Hitler gave the highest priority to the so-called Z Plan for the building of a large battle fleet. The fact that these plans would not be completed until the mid 1940s indicates that Hitler was not thinking of war against the western powers in 1939 but in the mid 1940s as he told his associates in November 1937.

Meanwhile he intended to expand his continental empire and in the case of Poland eliminate what he regarded (perhaps wrongly) as a potential threat in Germany's rear. War was not at first in his mind. Strenuous efforts were made in the winter of 1938-9 to win the Poles over as junior partners by dangling before them the prospect of territorial gains in the Ukraine. Though attracted by the offer, Foreign Minister Beck dared not contemplate a pact with Germany for fear of Russian reactions. By the end of March Hitler was already moving round to the view that Poland must be crushed by force. The news of the British guarantee confirmed him in this belief.

Naturally he did not want to fight on two fronts even though he declared to senior generals on 22 May that if Britain and France intervened he would fight them too. His expectation was that he could scare the western powers off Poland and avoid war with them until total mobilisation had been completed. The war of nerves to isolate Poland had started already; on 28 April he denounced the Non-Aggression Pact with Poland and the Anglo-German Convention of 1935. In the months that followed Hitler carefully cultivated good relations with Hungary, Bulgaria and Yugoslavia to keep Poland isolated; non-aggression Pacts with Latvia, Estonia and Lithuania were part of the same strategy. Important, too, in this connexion was the signature in May of the Pact of Steel, the formal alliance with Italy which Hitler valued as much for its effect on Britain and France as for the military assistance which Mussolini promised in the event of war.

A greater prize still was to be his before the summer was out – an agreement with Soviet Russia which took the western world by surprise and made war certain. Since the spring of 1939 Britain and France had been trying to come to terms with Russia as part of their plan to contain Germany. By May it had dawned on the Russians that the western powers were not likely to give them the security they needed, much less a free hand in Eastern Europe. The only alternative was an understanding with Germany. To this possibility Hitler was not averse. He had realised for some time that if only he could neutralise Russia the isolation of Poland would be complete; for without Russian support the western powers could not possibly come to her aid. Expediency was the sole criterion; the long anti-bolshevik tirades over the years were conveniently forgotten – the German press was ordered to moderate its language towards Russia – and the ambitions for *Lebensraum* in the Ukraine were temporarily shelved. In July trade talks between Russia and Germany were reactivated and Ribbentrop broached the question of a political agreement, to find the Russians interested but still suspicious of the Nazis. In the middle of August, as the German press campaign against Poland reached a new intensity, Hitler became alarmed by the dilatoriness of the Russians and intervened personally in the negotiations. On 20 August he requested Stalin to receive his plenipotentiary Ribbentrop in audience at once. Stalin agreed, and on 23 August Ribbentrop and Molotov signed a ten-year non-aggression pact in Moscow. Russia and Germany declared their intention of remaining neutral if either partner went to war with a third power. In secret protocols they cynically defined their respective spheres of influence in Eastern Europe; Western Poland and Lithuania would be in the German sphere of influence, the Baltic states, Eastern Poland and Bessarabia in the Russian. Provision was made for economic co-operation – on the strength of this Germany received valuable iron-ore and petrol supplies until 1941 – and Germany promised to restrain Japan. Russia was more than satisfied. In return for a simple promise of neutrality she had regained her old frontiers and was relieved of the fear of a German attack for the time being at any rate; Stalin fully expected the capitalist powers to tear themselves to pieces in a long war leaving Russia at peace.

This was Hitler's greatest moment of triumph. 'Now I have the world in my pocket,' he exclaimed. At a stroke of the pen he had ended Germany's fear of a war on two fronts and in the event of an allied blockade had ensured supplies of essential raw materials from the east. Already in an exultant mood on 22 August, while the negotiations were still proceeding in Moscow, he told his senior army commanders assembled at the Berghof that the chances of British and French intervention were now slight and in any case they could not help Poland if they did intervene. Whatever happened, the moment had arrived for Germany to strike while her chances of success were greater than they would be in two or three years' time, a theme he referred to frequently in these months. Moreover, economically Germany could 'only hold out for a few more years. . . . We have no other choice; we must act' – though his use of economic arguments on this and on other occasions should not be interpreted as a sign that this was a primary cause of his aggressive policy; that is to be sought in his strategic and ideological thinking. The next day he fixed the date for attack on Poland for the early hours of 26 August. On 24 August he was back in Berlin waiting to greet Ribbentrop on his return from Moscow as a 'second Bismarck'.

Much to Hitler's surprise, Britain and France were not scared off by the

Russo-German agreement. Instead they declared their intention of standing by Poland. On 25 August the Anglo-Polish Alliance was signed, a step which made general war quite certain if Hitler attacked Poland. Then Mussolini informed Hitler that, the Pact of Steel notwithstanding, the state of Italian rearmament precluded her from immediate entry into a general war. Hitler's caution asserted itself over his martial inclinations; 'Stop everything at once,' he shouted to Keitel; 'fetch Brauchitsch immediately. I need time for negotiations'; that is, he needed time for one last attempt to detach the western powers from Poland. On 25 August Hitler offered to guarantee the British Empire on condition Germany was allowed in effect a free hand to settle the Danzig problem – a counterpart in fact to the pact he had achieved with Russia. Through a private emissary and friend of Goering's, a Swedish business man named Dahlerus, he repeated the offer. Britain replied on 28 August that she stood by the Polish alliance but all the same she recommended direct Polish-German negotiations over Danzig. The reply probably reassured Hitler that he need not fear western intervention, for both Britain and France were clearly half-hearted in their support of Poland. True, on 29 August Hitler offered to negotiate with a Polish plenipotentiary if one was sent to Berlin the next day. This was not a serious proposal; had negotiations started Hitler expected them to founder on the rock of Polish obstinacy and intended to allow the attack to go ahead as planned. In fact the Poles refused the offer and began to mobilise. In the early hours of 1 September 1939 the attack on Poland began. Possibly Hitler still hoped that Britain and France would stay out of the war; indeed only on 3 September did they formally declare war after vainly hoping that Hitler might withdraw from Poland.

A major war for which Germany was not prepared and which Hitler had not expected had broken out. Nevertheless, in the early stages Germany enjoyed a military advantage over her opponents. The Polish campaign was a victorious promenade, the first example of the *Blitzkrieg* or lightning war. Within eighteen days the Polish army was destroyed, pounded from the air by the *Luftwaffe* and out-manoeuvred by German armour on the ground. On 17 September Russian troops occupied Eastern Poland, meeting the Germans at the historic town of Brest-Litovsk. At the end of the month Germany and Russia partitioned Poland; Danzig, West Prussia and Posen were re-united with Germany, and the remainder of Western Poland was formed into the *Generalgouvernement* under Hans Frank, the Nazi party's legal expert. In spite of desperate appeals from Warsaw, Britain and France had not tried to help Poland by attacking in the west. Not only did this make it easier for Hitler to concentrate on the destruction of Poland – there were only eleven regular infantry divisions guarding

Germany's western frontier – but it encouraged him to think that the western powers were unlikely to offer any serious resistance. Certainly they would have welcomed an end to the war but could not bring themselves to make peace on the basis of the new *status quo* in the east as Hitler proposed in October. Not that Hitler believed in his own offer; it was really intended to prove to the German people, who had shown little enthusiasm for the war, that Germany must fight on and exploit the favourable situation while it lasted. Before Hitler's offer had been formally rejected, he had ordered an attack in the west to begin in November. His generals were greatly alarmed by his optimistic assessment of German strength and managed to dissuade him from this plan with the help of adverse weather reports. In January 1940 he reluctantly agreed to postpone the attack until the spring or summer. Thus Europe enjoyed the illusion of peace during the first winter of the war, the period of the so-called 'phoney war' or *Sitzkrieg*.

When the spring of 1940 arrived, Hitler's attentions were diverted temporarily to Scandinavia. Britain and France were trying to aid Finland in her struggle against Russia in the winter of 1939–40, and it seemed likely that they would occupy Norway to open up lines of communication with the Finns. This would bring the British into the Baltic and endanger the iron-ore supplies from Sweden on which Germany was heavily dependent. On 8 April the British navy mined Norwegian waters and British and French forces embarked to occupy selected Norwegian ports. Germany struck first. On 9 April she occupied Denmark and attacked Norway, defeating her and driving out the allied forces in a few weeks. After the flight of the Norwegian monarch and his government to Britain, Hitler installed a puppet administration headed by the collaborator Quisling. Germany had won a notable victory; her iron-ore supplies were safe, the key to the Baltic was in her pocket, and with new Atlantic bases the German navy and air force could extend the scale of their operations against Britain.

By the late spring all was ready for the *Blitzkrieg* in the west. Thanks to Russian neutrality, Hitler could afford to leave a mere ten divisions in the east and concentrated the other 141 in the west. On 10 May 1940 Germany invaded Holland, Belgium and France. It was an immediate success. Within five days the Dutch capitulated but not before Rotterdam was virtually destroyed in a fearful aerial bombardment while armistice negotiations were acutally under way. Within eighteen days King Leopold of the Belgians had capitulated. Meanwhile, German armoured columns, strongly supported from the air, swept through the Ardennes, took the French by surprise and quickly reached the Somme estuary, cutting off the first French Army and the British Expeditionary Force. At this critical moment Hitler made a slight tactical error which was to have enormous consequences. Halder and Brauchitsch wanted to continue the advance to the coast, but Rundstedt proposed to halt in front of Calais before the B.E.F. was completely encircled. Hitler agreed with him largely because he wanted to switch his armour southwards without delay to deal with the main French armies. The pause enabled the B.E.F. to establish a bridge-head at Dunkirk, which they held long enough to evacuate 338,000 men despite the efforts of Goering's *Luftwaffe* to prevent it. Two days later Hitler reversed the order but by then the damage had been done. The plight of the French was desperate. On 14 June Paris fell. The main French army was trapped in the south and Mussolini, eager for cheap victories, stabbed France in the back. On 22 June a new government led by the veteran defender of Verdun, Marshal Pétain, signed an armistice. Hitler, with an eye to the dramatic, insisted that it be signed in the same dining-car and in the same place where Erzberger and Bell had signed the armistice in 1918.

The free world was stunned by the completeness of the German victory. Within six weeks Hitler had defeated Holland, Belgium and France. He now had the industrial potential of these lands at his disposal and he controlled the entire Atlantic coastline from Spain to Norway. The balance of power swung decisively to Berlin. Even the generals, some of whom had doubted the wisdom of the whole campaign, were at last impressed by the Führer's military ability and political intuition.

At first Hitler seemed to think that Britain, too, would accept the logic of history and recognise German hegemony in Europe. For this reason he restrained Mussolini, who wanted to humiliate France and strip her of her colonial possessions. Hitler decided to occupy only the northern half of France and the west coast; the French fleet was allowed to remain disarmed in French ports; French colonies would not be seized; and a French government was tolerated at Vichy in unoccupied France. Speaking to the Reichstag in July 1940, Hitler declared that if only Britain would recognise the *fait accompli* in Europe and return Germany's colonies the war could end. As Britain showed no signs of wavering under her defiant new premier, Winston Churchill, Hitler ordered 'Operation Sea-Lion', the invasion of Britain.

From the start Hitler recognised that British naval superiority made invasion a particularly difficult operation. In the end he decided it would only be feasible if Germany had air superiority over the Channel ports. In August Goering attempted to establish this in readiness for an invasion early in September. The great air battles fought over Britain in the next few weeks were crucial for the whole course of the war. The *Luftwaffe* struck first at ports and RAF bases, and later at London and major industrial towns, but suffered such crippling losses that Hitler decided in October to postpone 'Sea-Lion' until at least the spring of 1941. In fact this was the end of the operation, which was quietly dropped in 1942.

There was another reason why Hitler lost interest in 'Sea-Lion'.

Eastward expansion was never far from his thoughts for several reasons; memories of the Brest-Litovsk conquests; hatred of 'Jewish' Russia; and, once the war had begun, the need for the oil and wheat of the Ukraine to keep the 'New Order' afloat. Furthermore, since 1939 Russia had neglected no opportunity of improving her position in Eastern Europe. In the autumn of 1939 she compelled the Baltic states to give her bases. In November she attacked Finland and by March 1940 had gained key strategic points from that little country. In June after the armistice with France Russia compelled Rumania to hand over Bessarabia and Northern Bukovina. Molotov had already forced the Baltic states to appoint governments friendly to Russia. In August these states became part of the Soviet Union. Alarmed by the growth in Russian power which cut across German ambitions in the east, Hitler and the general staff started to plan an attack on Russia for the autumn but finally decided that it would not be feasible before 1941. Once 'Sea-Lion' had been postponed Hitler advanced the new argument that the defeat of Russia would dishearten Britain as well as deterring the United States from intervention in Europe; for once Russia had collapsed, Japan would exert pressure on the Americans in the Pacific. However, military preparations, which continued throughout the autumn, did not preclude negotiation with Russia to redefine their respective spheres of influence and to allay Russian suspicions about the presence of German troops in Finland and of a German military mission in Rumania. In November Hitler attempted in a daring manoeuvre to divert Russia from the Balkans to the Indian Ocean and Persian Gulf, offering Molotov a partnership with the three Axis powers in a new division of the world along geopolitical lines. Molotov showed no interest in Hitler's fantastic global plans but made it clear that Russia was interested primarily in Europe, where she wanted complete control of the Baltic and Black Sea. Confirmed in his decision to attack Russia, Hitler approved the first directive for Operation Barbarossa, the attack to take place in the spring or early summer of 1941.

Before Hitler could strike at Russia he was forced to turn his attention to the Balkans. Mussolini, incensed by Hitler's complete failure to consult Italy and anxious to assert the importance of his end of the Axis, attacked Greece in October 1940. It proved a disastrous mistake; the Greeks drove the Italians out of their country and Britain came to their assistance; using Crete as a base British bombers savagely mauled the Italian fleet in Taranto harbour in November. A further blow followed in December 1940 when the Italians were driven out of Cyrenaica. Italy was the weak link of the Axis chain, much as Austria-Hungary had been the millstone round Imperial Germany's neck in the First World War. It was clear to Hitler that he must remove this threat to Germany's flank before the attack on Russia commenced. Hungary, Rumania and Bulgaria, all virtually German satellites, agreed to allow the transport of German troops through their countries. Under the pro-German Regent Paul, Yugoslavia, like Hungary and Rumania, had at first adhered to the new Three-Power Pact drawn up by the Axis powers in September 1940. Then in March 1941 a palace revolution ousted Paul, and young King Peter II took over. Hitler was furious at the possibility of resistance from little Yugoslavia and postponed the Russian campaign by four weeks in order to attack Yugoslavia as well as Greece. In April 1941 Germany launched her third *Blitzkrieg* which was as successful as the first two had been. Yugoslavia capitulated within eleven days and Greece within fifteen. In May German paratroopers captured Crete in ten days and drove the British out.

Heartened by his latest victory, which secured the Balkans against further British landings. Hitler turned to his life's ambition, the conquest of *Lebensraum* in the east. On 22 June 1941 187 divisions, supported by Finnish and Rumanian troops, attacked Russia on the flimsy pretext that she was about to attack Germany. Hitler's armies pressed deep into the heart of Russia, the Russians reeled back under the weight of the offensive, large parts of the Ukraine and the whole of Western Russia were soon occupied, and by the end of 1941 German armies besieged Leningrad and Moscow. Hitler's empire had reached its zenith, stretching from the Channel Islands in the west to the Caucasian mountains in the east, from Norway in the north to the Aegean islands in the south. Nazi propagandists supremely confident that the 'New Order' had come to stay, started to build up a new image of Hitler as the great European, another Charlemagne who was saving western civilisation from 'bolshevism' and 'Jewish plutocracy' and building a strong united Europe, independent of Britain and America. This was a travesty of the truth, a hollow sham which could not conceal the ruthless exploitation of occupied and conquered territories, satellite and enemy alike, in the interests of the German warmachine.

At the very pinnacle of Nazi power shadows were already falling. Despite heavy Russian losses and Hitler's confident boast that the enemy was already annihilated, never to rise again, the unpalatable fact was that Russian resistance was still unbroken. Hitler's plan had been to encircle and destroy the enemy; the Russians did not oblige him; because of a shortage of mechanized vehicles on the German side they were able to escape before the trap closed and adopted scorched earth tactics as they retreated. Not only did this deprive Germany of the food and raw materials on which she counted, but as the German armies pressed deeper into Russia in pursuit of the enemy their lines of communication became dangerously over-extended. Now Hitler and his advisers quarrelled about the appropriate tactics. Hitler ordered the central army to halt its advance on Moscow. Part of its armour was switched north to help in the capture of Leningrad and the rest transferred to the south to help conquer the Ukraine. Hitler may well have been right in thinking the wheat of the

Ukraine was of prime importance. But when Hitler allowed the attack on Moscow to re-commence in October it was already too late for success.

Of course, the Germans had grossly underestimated Russian strength in the first place, assuming that the campaign would be over in three months at most. Hitler was reluctant to admit that the Russians were in fact capable of putting huge armies in the field despite their reverses. Britain had come to Russia's assistance and tanks, planes and guns were soon pouring in from the U.S.A. An even more powerful ally came to Russia's assistance – one of the worst winters on record which set in early, catching the German army in summer uniforms. In December Hitler was taken completely by surprise (for which faulty intelligence was largely to blame) when Russia threw 100 divisions into a counter-offensive on the central front. Only with the greatest difficulty and at heavy cost did the Germans hold the line. The series of brillant victories was over at last. The *Blitzkrieg* had failed, and Germany was committed to a long war for which she was singularly ill prepared.

Another decisive event occurred in December 1941; the Japanese suddenly attacked and destroyed the American fleet anchored at Pearl Harbor. On 8 December the U.S.A. declared war on Japan, and the European war became a global one. Hitler had not been informed of the Japanese plan but he approved of the attack and, feeling that the U.S.A. would soon join in the war in any event, he seized what marginal advantage there was in declaring war on her at once.

Hitler had no appreciation of the enormous strategic implications of American intervention, which sealed Germany's fate in the long run as surely as Wilson's declaration of war in 1917 had done. The Führer was completely absorbed in the Russian campaign, which was now an obsession with him. In December he accepted Brauchitsch's resignation and assumed personal command of the army in the field. In failing health and at last feeling the strain of the war which was going wrong, he easily persuaded himself that his generals were to blame for the failure to defeat Russia in 1941. Confident that he could win the war in 1942, he ordered a great offensive in May along the southern front, the objectives being the capture of Stalingrad and the seizure of the Caucasian oilfields. Initial successes were encouraging; the Germans advanced 450 miles, reached Stalingrad and hoisted the German flag on the highest Caucasian peak. In June the combined Axis forces in North Africa commanded by General Rommel drove the British back into Egypt; by the end of the month Rommel was within fifty miles of Alexandria. This was a crucial point in the war; if Germany had conquered the Caucasian oilfields and swept southwards to join up with Rommel's forces in Egypt, British power in the Middle East would have been destroyed and the prospects of final victory for the Axis powers would have been considerably brighter.

It was not to be. Though Hitler certainly had some appreciation of

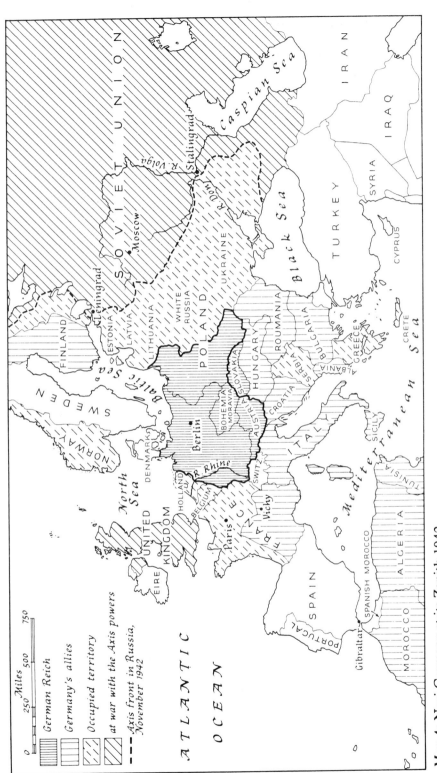

Map 4: Nazi Germany at its Zenith 1942

global strategy, he and his advisers failed to see how important the Mediterranean was to Britain. Africa for him was, like the Atlantic, a quite secondary theatre of operations, a diversion from the main task of crushing Russia. Rommel's supply lines across the Mediterranean were always tenuous because Hitler neglected to take Malta, and when petrol supplies ran out Rommel had to halt at El Alamein. Meanwhile in Russia it was clear that Hitler had taken on too much; stubborn Russian resistance in the ruins of Stalingrad deprived Hitler of complete victory here, while his troops on the Caucasian front were too weak and exhausted to seize the oilfields. In November the Russians launched a counter-offensive which relieved Stalingrad and cut the lines of communication of the German Sixth Army. A month before, British forces led by General Montgomery launched a surprise attack at El Alamein; Rommel's Africa Corps and their Italian allies were routed and retreated. A further blow followed; on 7–8 November 1942 Anglo-American forces landed at Algiers, Oran and Casablanca, sealing the fate of the Axis powers in North Africa. Hitler was taken completely aback by this landing, which he had insisted would come in Norway, whither he had dispatched powerful reinforcements. In a desperate attempt to retrieve the situation Hitler poured reinforcements into Tunisia instead of allowing Rommel to withdraw while there was still time. By January 1943 the British Eighth Army had reached the eastern borders of Tunisia, while a combined American, British and French force under General Alexander was massing on the western borders. The end was not long delayed. In the spring of 1943 a combined operation drove the Axis forces northwards into a great bottle-neck. On 3 May 250,000 German and Italian soldiers surrendered and the desert campaign was over. An even worse disaster occurred in January 1943. Paulus's Sixth Army at Stalingrad was completely encircled by three Russian army groups. Hitler adamantly refused to allow Paulus to try and break through this ring and escape before the inevitable happened. At the end of January, after his men had suffered fearful privations, Paulus surrendered, and what remained of the Sixth Army went into captivity; over 300,000 men had been wantonly sacrificed in a vain attempt to hold an untenable position. This was a real turning-point in the Russian campaign. Germany had made her maximum effort and failed. From July onwards Russian offensives grew in number and intensity and the Germans fell back slowly but surely through Poland towards their own frontiers.

At the beginning of 1943 the Nazis claimed that whatever happened elsewhere, they were at least invincible in *Festung Europa* (Fortress Europe); Scandinavia, France with the west wall, the line of the Pyrenees, Italy and the Balkans acted as a shield preserving the *Reich* from attack. This claim was quickly exploded. On 30 May the R.A.F. launched the first 1,000-bomber raid on Cologne, which was followed by others in the summer. By the autumn allied bombing grew more intensive. With the

Americans attacking by day and the British at night, the German people felt the horror and devastation of war at long last. The *Luftwaffe* was unable to protect Germany; Goering's proud boast that no enemy aircraft would ever penetrate Germany's defences was turned to bitter ashes. With Germany trapped in a total war the allied insistence on unconditional surrender could only strengthen Hitler's determination to continue a war which, objectively speaking, Germany could not win.

In July *Festung Europa* was breached when Anglo-American forces landed in Sicily. The Italians had no heart for a new struggle, and the Fascist Grand Council soon deposed Mussolini, though for the time being Italy continued the war. Hitler did not lose his nerve at this critical juncture. He had no intention of giving up the fight, and quickly switched *SS* divisions from the Russian front to Italy. When the Italians signed an armistice in September 1943, Hitler struck back; the Germans disarmed the Italian army, seized key points, freed Mussolini and virtually assumed control in most of Italy. By this time Allied forces had landed in Southern Italy but the Germans were able to hold out south of Rome until the end of 1943 and were only driven back slowly into Northern Italy, where they were still in control until the closing stages of the war. No doubt the stiff German resistance pinned down allied forces in Italy much longer than had been expected. But it gave Germany a third front to fight on when she was hard pressed in the east, suffering immense losses in the desperate struggle against the advancing Russians, and at a time when Hitler was obliged to build up his western defences in the expectation of an Anglo-American landing. Germany had sixty divisions, a quarter of her mobilised strength, stationed in the west during the crucial battles on the eastern front; she was paying the price of a two-front war with a vengeance.

Even so, when the assault in the west began on 6 June 1944 Germany was taken by surprise. Rundstedt and Rommel expected an attack in the Pas-de-Calais area, but in fact it came in Normandy, where Hitler expected it. Without command of the skies the Germans could not prevent the consolidation of allied bridgeheads. As usual Hitler blamed his generals for incompetence, but when Rundstedt and Rommel suggested an armistice he flatly refused and relieved Rommel of his command. At the end of July the First American Army broke through the German lines and spread out in all directions. A new war of movement started, with the Germans on the losing side. The German armour was encircled at Falais and annihilated. What remained of the German forces retreated to the Seine. On 25 August General de Gaulle entered Paris; early in September Brussels was liberated. Meanwhile in the east the Russians had launched a new offensive coinciding roughly with the Normandy landing. By August they reached the Vistula and crossed the Rumanian frontier. The Balkan front quickly collapsed; Rumania sued for an armistice, in September Bulgaria surrendered, and German forces began to evacuate Greece and Yugoslavia.

The allied forces in the west had planned originally to sweep into Germany before the winter. However, a combination of bad weather, supply problems, differences of opinion within the allied command and, not least, unexpected German resistance compelled them to bring their offensive to a halt in the early autumn. The Germans managed to stabilise their front along a line running from the Vosges through Southern Holland to the sea. The temporary lull in the fighting in October and November encouraged Hitler to think that his enemies were exhausted and that a new offensive might incline them to make peace with him and turn together against Russia. On 16 December he threw twenty-eight divisions, Germany's last reserves, into an offensive against the American positions in the Ardennes in a desperate attempt to capture Antwerp. After initial successes the Germans were quickly thrown onto the defensive; a second attempt at the end of December to break through the Ardennes and take Strasbourg was equally unsuccessful. On 8 January Hitler agreed to withdraw the German armour from the Ardennes front. The last offensive had failed. In all Germany lost a total of 120,000 men killed or captured, 1,600 planes and 600 tanks and guns.

The end came in the spring of 1945. On 12 January the Russians launched a general offensive with 180 divisions which swept through the German positions; by the end of the month East Prussia was cut off and the Russians were within 160 kilometres of Berlin. By now Hitler had returned to the capital. Ageing rapidly and exhausted by the strain of war and the effects of drugs, he stormed at all who ventured to hint at the possibility of defeat. The next blow came in the west when the Anglo-Americans launched a new offensive, crossed the Rhine on 7 March and soon occupied the Ruhr, Lower Saxony and South Germany. Many Nazi leaders, reading the signs correctly, hurriedly left Berlin and tried desperately to save themselves by coming to terms with Germany's enemies. Still the Führer remained in encircled Berlin with Martin Bormann, his deputy, and Goebbels at his side. The last scenes in this epic tragedy were enacted in the eerie atmosphere of the underground bunker in the chancellery grounds. Almost to the very last Hitler continued to believe in his ability to win the war. Completely isolated from reality, he remained convinced that, if only Germany could hold out long enough, the hostile coalition would melt away as it had done for Frederick the Great, whom he admired so much.

At last old friends turned on him. On 23 April Goering telegraphed from Bavaria with a request that he be allowed to assume full powers to act in the best interests of Germany. Hitler, who had clearly misled Goering by earlier remarks on this subject, retorted by accusing him of treason and stripped him of all his numerous offices. Hard on the heels of this 'betrayal' came news of a second defection; it was announced on the allied radio that Himmler had put out peace-feelers to the allied powers, an offer they had summarily rejected. At once Hitler ordered Himmler's arrest and had Fegelein, Himmler's personal representative at headquarters, summarily shot in the grounds of the chancellery. Overcome by rage and despair, Hitler decided on suicide. On 29 April he legalised his liaison with Eva Braun, his mistress, and dictated his will, a political testament in which he blamed the war on the Jews and Germany's failure to win on the generals, whom he despised to the very last. For the German people he showed not the slightest concern or compassion; they had failed him and deserved to be annihilated or ruled over by the 'sub-people' from the east. Indeed in the last few weeks of his life he revelled in a mood of nihilism; on 19 March he issued the famous 'sorched earth' order which commanded the Germans to destroy all installations and factories in the path of the advancing enemy armies; thanks largely to Speer this order was not obeyed. On 30 April, with the Russians only a street or two from the chancellery, Hitler shot himself and, like Eva Braun, probably swallowed a poison capsule as well. Their partially destroyed bodies were found later outside the bunker by the Russians. Goebbels and Bormann made despairing attempts to negotiate with the Russians to no effect. Goebbels then posioned his children and he and his wife shot themselves. Bormann vanished on 1 May. For many years it was thought that he alone of the leading Nazis had escaped certain retribution; however, in 1973 human remains accidentally unearthed during excavations in Berlin were positively identified as those of the wanted man.

Hitler had designated Grand Admiral Dönitz his successor. On 1 May Dönitz informed the German people that Hitler had died like a hero at the head of his soldiers and appealed for a continuation of the war, vainly hoping to divide the allies. There was no escape for Germany. On 2 May Berlin capitulated. On 7 May Admiral von Friedeburg and General Jodl signed an instrument of unconditional surrender of all German forces on Lüneburg heath. A few days later Dönitz was taken into custody by the allies to await trial as a war-criminal. On 23 May the provisional government set up at Flensburg by Schwerin-Krosigk, on orders from Dönitz, was dissolved. The four powers assumed supreme power in Germany and the Third Reich passed into history.

15

The Two Germanies

From 1900 to 1914 and from 1933 to 1945 Bismarck's Reich shaped the course of history to an unprecedented degree plunging the world into two major conflagrations within twenty-five years. One of the most striking changes in the forty years since the end of the Second World War has been the relative decline in German influence. Though of major importance within their respective alliance systems, neither the German Federal Republic nor the German Democratic Republic has exerted comparable influence on international affairs.

In the summer of 1945 Germany was utterly devastated. Great cities had been reduced to heaps of smoking rubble, communications were totally disrupted and the administrative apparatus shattered. The German people were dazed and bewildered by the ordeal of total war. Over three million German soldiers had been killed in action, one million were prisoners of war in Russia, many never to return, and half a million civilians had been killed in air raids. *Heim ins Reich*, the proud Nazi slogan of the 1930s, took on a new meaning as millions of panic-striken refugees streamed westwards before the advancing Red Army.

Before the fighting ended the 'Big Three' – Roosevelt, Stalin and Churchill, meeting at Yalta in September 1945 – set the seal of approval on arrangements for the occupation of Germany which were dictated in large measure by the nutcracker strategy they had pursued. Temporarily Germany would be divided into four occupation zones: the Russians in the east, the British in the north-west, the Americans in the south-west and the French in a small zone in the west carved out of the British and American zones. Authority would be vested in an Allied Control Council consisting of the four commanders-in-chief meeting in Berlin. That city, to be occupied by the four powers, would remain the German capital. Germany would be demilitarized, denazified and obliged to pay reparations, not in money – the error of the 1920s – but in kind. While no formal figure was agreed, 50 per cent of the reparations would be given Russia in recognition of the immense devastation caused by German aggression.

With their armies firmly in control of Germany the Big Three met at

Potsdam in July 1945. By this time the Americans had abandoned the Morgenthau Plan to pastoralize Germany and divide it into several small states. German unity was preserved although for the time being a central authority would not be re-established. But political recovery would be encouraged along democratic lines in all zones. A more immediate task was denazification which the occupying powers undertook enthusiastically – indeed this turned out to be the only subject on which complete agreement could be reached. The most spectacular example of four-power unity was the Nuremberg Trial of 1945–6, when a representative selection of leading Nazis and their advisers were tried and in nearly all cases found guilty of conspiracy to commit wars of aggression and crimes against humanity. The reparations arrangements were shrouded in some ambiguity. Each power was to dismantle industrial plant in its own zone and take goods from current production. At the same time the German economy was to be treated as a whole and the German people permitted a standard of living no higher than that of neighbouring peoples. To co-ordinate economic activity in the zones five central administrative offices staffed by Germans would be set up. Already deeply uneasy about Russian actions, President Harry S. Truman and Clement Attlee, the newly elected British Prime minister, promised Russia only 25 per cent of reparations deliveries from their zones. Finally – and with great reluctance – they acepted a major territorial change in Germany's eastern frontiers ahead of a peace treaty: *de facto* Polish administration of former German territory up to the line of the Oder and Neisse rivers and the partition of East Prussia between Russia and Poland.

The Potsdam Conference – significantly codenamed Terminal – represented the high-water mark of allied unity. Even before the guns fell silent, relations were seriously strained. As the Red Army rolled westwards entering Warsaw, Prague, Budapest and Bucharest fear of Soviet ambitions – never far below the surface – re-emerged. And as western resistance to Russian actions and demands stiffened, Stalin's suspicions that the 'imperialist powers' still posed a threat to the Soviet Union must have deepened. Several issues clustered together to form a vicious spiral of mistrust in the First Cold War between East and West which reached a height in the early 1950s. The allied Declaration on Liberated Peoples of 1945 envisaged free elections in all parts of Europe freed by the allies. Russia soon made it clear that these elections must return governments favourably disposed to her. Molotov's demand for a Soviet base on the Dardanelles and the refusal of Russia to withdraw troops from northern Persia aroused fears of Russian expansionism, while America's refusal to share atomic secrets, her possession of the atomic bomb and the construction of a ring of bases around Russia aroused fears of American ambitions.

German reparations contributed significantly to the Cold War.

Understandably the Russians stripped their zone of capital equipment and took goods from current production regardless of its effect on German living standards. Meanwhile, as refugees crowded into the western zones, pressure increased on limited food supplies. As British and American tax-payers were in effect feeding the Germans and had much less need of reparations, they argued that these should only be taken from current production after the German economy had fully recovered. The situation was further complicated by French and Russian opposition to the creation of centralized offices treating all zones as one economic unit. Secondly, the Level of Industry Agreement approved by the four powers in March 1946 – a measure to prevent the emergence of a powerful German econ-omy with warlike potential by prohibiting many industries of a military nature – set steel production at seven million tons, roughly half the 1938 figure. Though this suited the Russians who wanted a low figure to maximise surplus capacity for dismantling as reparations, the western powers realised that the figure was too low to stimulate rapid German recovery. Consequently each power ended up implementing those parts of the Potsdam Agreement suiting its interests and zonal frontiers assumed a significance not originally intended.

The turning-point came in May 1946 when Britain and America halted the dismantling of plant not already scheduled for Russia. By September their zones were merged into Bizonia. At Stuttgart Secretary of State James Byrne announced a change of policy declaring that it was 'not in the interests of the German people or . . . of world peace that Germany become a pawn or a partner in the military struggle for power between East and West'. He called for the immediate establishment of central German agencies to accelerate German economic recovery.

Once the Germans were given a leading role in their economic recovery a serious revival of political life could not be long delayed. In fact, this began in the summer of 1945 when Russia created four parties in her zones: the Communists (KPD); the Socialists (SPD); the Christian Democrats (CDU); and the Liberals (known as LDPD in that zone). In allowing 'bourgeois' parties to co-exist with the KPD Russia was acting in accor-dance with the Marxist belief that the whole of Eastern Europe had to undergo a 'bourgeois democratic' revolution before socialism was pos-sible. Nevertheless, from the start Russia intended to keep a tight rein on developments. On 30 April a group of German Communists led by Walter Ulbricht returned from Russian exile and were quickly installed in key positions. By the end of 1945 the Russians decided to fuse the KPD and SPD. Many Socialists and Communists, brought together in the common fight against Nazism, favoured close co-operation to effect radical social change on Marxist lines. However, Kurt Schuhmacher, the dynamic and bitterly anti-Communist Socialist leader in the British Zone, vigorously opposed the union and succeeded in persuading the Berlin SPD to hold a

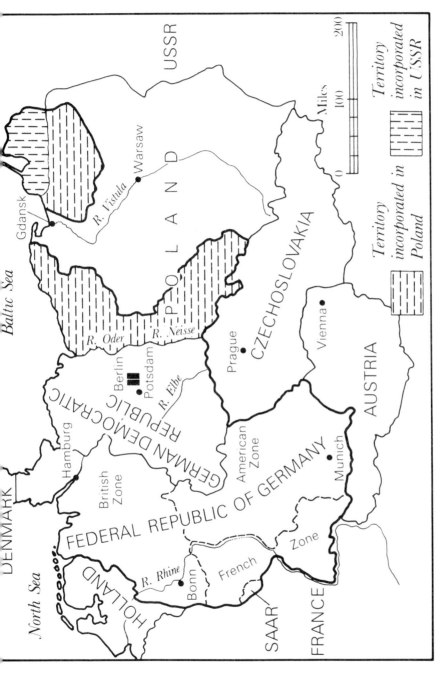

Map 5: Germany Divided post 1945

referendum on it. The referendum – prohibited in East Berlin by the Russians – showed that 80 per cent were against fusion although 60 per cent still favoured close co-operation with the Communists. In April the Socialist Unity Party (SED) was founded and the SPD banned in the Russian Zone. In October at the *Land* elections the SED obtained 47.5 per cent of the popular vote and, as it had a majority with the support of the SED-dominated farmers organization over the CDU (24 per cent) and the LDPD (24.5 per cent), took over effective control of the *Landtage* in the five *Länder* in the eastern zone. In Berlin, however, where the western powers insisted that the SPD be permitted, even in the Soviet sector only 29.8 per cent voted SED and 43.6 per cent SPD, a result greatly embarrassing to the Russians. In subsequent elections in the Russian Zone electors were presented with a single list of candidates in a 'united anti-fascist front' to approve or reject. Inside the SED Stalinists had the upper hand by the end of 1948. Taking Russia as their model, they imposed 'democratic centralism' on the party and purged many former SPD members. Meanwhile radical social change was well under way. By the end of 1945 land reform, i.e. the break-up of estates over 100 hectares – a popular measure with the rural population which benefited 500,000 peasants – was being carried out while most of heavy industry was already in Soviet hands.

In the anti-capitalist atmosphere of the immediate post-war world left-wing parties were expected to do well in the western zones. Popular reactions to Stalinism in the Russian Zone sealed the fate of the KPD. Even so in the federal elections of 1949 it obtained 5.7 per cent of the vote and 15 seats in the Bundestag. At the second elections in 1953 after the suppression of the uprising in East Germany it netted only 608,000 votes and disappeared from the Bundestag. Banned by the Federal Court in 1956 – largely for propaganda reasons – the Communists were allowed to re-form as the German Communist Party (DKP) in 1968 but secured only 0.3 per cent of the vote in the 1970s.

The SPD fared much better. Despite the loss of the Prussian heartland it became the second largest party in the Bundestag with 131 seats and 29.2 per cent of the popular vote – only 400,000 votes behind the CDU/CSU. Schuhmacher's robust nationalism and fierce anti-Communism did much to give the lie to Adenauer's charge that the SPD was unpatriotic but Socialist insistence on public ownership and a planned economy frightened away voters concerned to preserve their material gains since 1948 whilst its old-fashioned anti-clericalism alienated many Catholics, now a considerable force in the GFR. Although it participated in several *Länder* governments, not until 1966 did the SPD exercise power at federal level in coalition first with the CDU and then with the FDP.

The largest party in 1949 with 31 per cent of the vote and 139 seats in the Bundestag was the CDU and its associated Bavarian wing, the

Christian Social Union (CSU). This was an amalgamation of various political elements: ex-Centre party voters and former supporters of the German Nationalists and Populists expressing the new-found ecumenical spirit between Catholics and Protestants forged under the Hitler tyranny and embracing a wide spectrum of opinion from that of left-wing trade unionists such as Jacob Kaiser to that of right-wing industrialists. Initially surprisingly anti-capitalist in attitude, denouncing state capitalism as fervently as Marxism, by 1949 the CDU/CSU found its natural centre of gravity on the right, becoming the champion of the 'social market economy' practised by Ludwig Erhard, Economic Director of Bizonia. Under the leadership of the wily Konrad Adenauer the CDU/CSU remained in office in Bonn for twenty years leaving an indelible stamp on the GFR. In the early days it was assisted enormously by the patronage of the Catholic Church which favoured this and similar parties in France and Italy as bulwarks against Communism. The typical CDU voter was Catholic – now 45 per cent of the population in the GFR compared with 30 per cent in pre-war Germany – and lived in a small town or rural area.

The fourth party, the Free Democratic Party (FDP), heir of the old Democratic Party, espoused the cause of individualism being equally opposed to the Marxism of the left and the religious colouration of the CDU/CSU, especially its support of confessional schools. Supported by white collar workers and the professional classes – a growing social group in the GFR – the FDP has exerted disproportionate political influence for a party which at its peak in 1961 obtained only 12 per cent of the vote and 67 seats in the Bundestag. Nevertheless, as neither CDU/CSU nor SPD has been able to secure an absolute majority (1957 was an exception), the FDP has been an arbitral force in German politics. It has served in federal coalitions for twenty-nine of the last thirty-six years and supplied two of the GFR's five presidents. Subject to the fissiparous tendencies at work in all middle-of-the-road parties as they veer left or right as circumstances dictate, by 1983 the FDP secured only 6.8 per cent of the vote and is now threatened by the rise of the Green Party which appeals to the same social strata. The FDP might in the future conceivably fall victim to the 5 per cent clause (see p. 373).

By 1947 the western and eastern zones were going their own way, constructing different political and economic systems. Representatives of the four powers meeting in Moscow in March 1947 and in London in December made no progress on reparations or towards the treatment of Germany as an economic unit. The Cold War took a turn for the worse when, alarmed by the support Greek guerilla forces were obtaining from neighbouring Communist countries and by the prospect of British withdrawal from Greece because of economic difficulties, Truman enunciated his famous 'Doctrine' declaring that the United States would aid 'free peoples' struggling against 'totalitarianism' and immediately offered assistance to Greece and Turkey.

The Marshall Offer widened the gulf between East and West. By the summer of 1947 Europe was on the point of economic collapse. The continent was suffering acute food and raw material shortages and was quite incapable of restoring former production levels or re-capturing lost markets. The Americans, who had initially intensified the crisis by abruptly winding up the United Nations Relief and Rehabilitation Administration (UNRRA) and insisting on convertibility of sterling as the condition of a British loan, now relented. In June General George Marshall called on Europe to draw up a co-ordinated plan for recovery; America, desperately anxious to prevent Europe going Communist and to preserve valuable markets, was prepared to foot the bill. Sixteen nations accepted the offer of American aid. The western zones were included in the plan for without the industrial power of Germany recovery would be much slower. Whether Stalin, in desperate need of financial aid to help restore Russia, would have continued the wartime co-operation with the West on the basis of mutual recognition of each other's spheres of influence had America been willing to deal bilaterally with her clients – which she was not – we do not know. Fearing that joint planning would impair Russian sovereignty, Stalin ordered the satellite states to withdraw from the Paris Conference. Russia now attacked the European Recovery Programme as 'American imperialism' designed to tie Europe to the 'chariot wheels of the American war machine'. From the autumn of 1947 Russia tightened her grip appreciably over Eastern Europe.

The failure of the London Conference brought matters to a head in Bizonia. Elected German governments were already running the new *Länder* into which the western zones had been divided. In June 1947 an Economic Council drawn from members of the *Landtage* was given control of the five central offices established by Britain and America. When the London Conference broke down the way was opened for the establishment of a West German state. External events accelerated the pace of events. In February 1948 Communists assumed control in Czechoslovakia and the Foreign Minister, Jan Masaryk, committed suicide, dramatic events which convinced many in the west that the Russians were poised for a new thrust westwards and not simply consolidating what they regarded as their sphere of influence. In March 1948 Britain, France and the Benelux countries concluded the Treaty of Brussels, a mutual defence pact. In April these powers were joined by the United States and meeting in London declared that the time had come for the German people to establish political institutions. In July the minister-presidents of the *Länder* were asked to draw up a constitution on federal–democratic lines. A council meeting in Bonn chaired by Adenauer and composed of 27 CDU, 27 SPD and 5 FDP members with 6 others representing three smaller parties produced the Basic Law in May 1949. After approval by the military governors this was ratified by all *Länder*. In a separate statute of occupation the western powers reserved certain rights over the GFR in respect of foreign relations, demilitarisation and control of the Ruhr. The military governors were replaced by high commissioners exercising supreme allied authority in the GFR. In the first federal elections in August 1949 the CDU gained 139 seats, the SPD 131, the FDP 52 and eight smaller parties shared eighty seats. Theodor Heuss was elected president and Adenauer chancellor by one vote. On 21 September the GFR came into being.

The Basic Law drew heavily on liberal–democratic traditions dating back to the 1848 Revolution and also incorporated the lessons learnt from the demise of the Weimar Republic. The republic is based on four main principles. First, the rule of law. A Federal Constitutional Court safeguards basic rights – more or less identical with those enunciated in the 1849 constitution – and adjudicates in cases where federal or *Land* legislation is thought to conflict with Basic Law. Second, democratic participation in affairs of state is guaranteed to all citizens. The Bundestag or Federal Parliament is elected normally every four years by universal suffrage. Half the members are elected directly and half via party lists. Twenty-two members are delegated to the Bonn Parliament from the West Berlin Assembly. To discourage lunatic-fringe politics parties polling under 5 per cent of the vote are not represented in the Bundestag. Third, power is divided between the federal government and nine *Länder*. The *Länder* are not mere administrative units as under Weimar but exert very real political influence. They control administration, education and culture in their own territories through their own elected *Landtage*. At federal level the government has to submit all bills to the Bundesrat or Federal Council which is composed of members from the *Länder* governments. On some bills the Bundesrat can only make comments which the Bundestag can override by simple majority. Over other bills the Bundesrat has a veto. By the 1970s this category accounted for 60–70 per cent of all legislation so that the power of the Bundesrat is very real. Federal governments are constantly obliged to modify their proposals to secure Bundesrat approval.

The president is essentially a ceremonial figure. Elected indirectly by a federal assembly of members from the Bundestag and the *Länder* governments, he can stand only once for election; he is not supreme commander of the Bundeswehr or armed forces – that office is exercised by the Minister of Defence – he has no power to declare a state of emergency; nor can he appoint or dismiss chancellors or dissolve the Bundestag. The chancellor is now the key political figure. He can only be removed by a constructive no-confidence motion, i.e. one proposing a named successor. This occurred in 1982 when Chancellor Helmut Schmidt leading an SPD–FDP coalition was toppled by Helmut Kohl of the CDU/CSU with FDP support. Kohl then engineered his own defeat on a government confidence motion on which his supporters abstained, thus forcing a dissolution of the Bundestag two years ahead of time, and incidentally securing a majority for a renewed CDU/CSU–FDP coalition.

Fourth, the federal government is committed to the establishment of a social welfare state thus continuing the tradition of welfarism from Bismarck onwards. To achieve this aim state intervention is allowed and basic rights may be restricted. While private property rights are guaranteed, the Basic Law does not rule out the possibility of land, property and the means of production being taken over by the state.

Finally, it should be noted that the minister-presidents insisted in 1949 upon the term 'Basic Law' on the grounds that they were not creating a new state but entering into provisional arrangements pending German re-unification. Meanwhile the Reich of 1937 – with which, so it was said, the GFR was identical – continued in being. The Federal Court, asked to rule on the compatibility of the Basic Treaty of 1972 with the Basic Law, decided that the task of re-unification was still binding on the GFR, a sore point with the GDR.

The GFR and the GDR came into being in the middle of a serious international crisis over Berlin in 1948–9, a crisis which accelerated their emergence. The Russians were no doubt genuinely alarmed by the prospect of a separate West German state – a clear violation of the Potsdam Agreement and one which they rightly supposed would soon lead to German re-armament. Their protest took a characteristically insensitive form: the blockade of Berlin. As part of the recovery programme a new currency (the Deutschmark) was introduced into the western zones in June 1948 but not in Berlin. When the Russian commander-in-chief announced the introduction of a new currency into the Soviet zone and in Berlin, the western powers immediately introduced the DM into the western sectors of the city. The same day the Russians closed the road, rail and canal links with the west and abruptly cut off electricity from the western sectors.

What may have been a hamfisted attempt to prevent the establishment of a West German state and promote four-power discussions leading to the creation of a united but demilitarized Germany, was construed in the west as Russian aggression. If Russia succeeded in forcing the western powers out of Berlin would she not then force them out of West Germany and station Red Army units on the Rhine? So the west argued and responded vigorously with a spectacular airlift which commenced in July and continued throughout the winter of 1948–9 supplying the western sectors with food and raw materials. The courage of two million Berliners in standing up to Russian pressure became a by-word in the western world. The Russians finally admitted defeat and raised the blockade in May 1949. The crisis had a lasting effect on Berlin; by the end of 1949 separate local authorities were operating in the two halves of the city.

Once it became clear that the west was determined to establish a West

German state, the Russians accelerated parallel developments in their zone. From its inception the SED was committed to the creation of a 'united peace-loving anti-fascist democratic German republic'. In the autumn of 1949 a 400-strong People's Council started work on a draft constitution obligingly supplied by the SED. In May 1949 the draft was approved by an elected People's Congress. On 11 October the GDR came into being. Wilhelm Pieck was elected president and Otto Grotewohl, former leader of the SPD in Berlin, became minister-president in a cabinet which though it included CDU and LDPD ministers, was controlled by the SED. In November the Soviet military command transferred its administrative functions to the GDR and turned itself into the Soviet High Commission.

The 1949 constitution vested legislative power in an elected *Volkskammer* or Parliament to which the council of ministers was responsible, and in a *Länderkammer* representing the five *Länder* into which the Soviet zone was divided. Basic rights including freedom of speech, press, assembly, religion and the right to strike were guaranteed. A pluralist political system was permitted – the CDU and the LDPD still exist in the GDR although they have long since attuned themselves to the dominant ideology. But the SED, by 1949 a highly-centralised Leninist party, has remained the controlling party in the republic. At first the new government took its orders from the High Commission. Only after the Berlin uprising in 1953 did Russia begin to relax her control and allow the GDR some limited freedom of development within the socialist camp.

While the GDR remained under dominant Russian influence, the GFR, rapidly regaining self-confidence, carved out a niche for herself in the new Europe. Her new international status was underpinned by economic recovery masterminded by Ludwig Erhard. A passionate believer in the regenerative force of private enterprise, Erhard while Economics Director for Bizonia dismantled the control system inherited from the Nazis; rationing and price controls were abolished and taxation reduced. The so-called 'German miracle' which completely transformed West Germany from a devastated and demoralised country into a thriving industrial state by the end of the 1950s was made possible by a coincidence of favourable factors of which Erhard's measures were only one. The GDR was also a recipient of 4.4 million dollars of American aid. She was fortunate in not carrying an armaments burden much less fighting ruinously expensive and hopeless colonial wars as the victors were. No doubt it helped that the German people displayed Teutonic singlemindedness of purpose in concentrating wholeheartedly on *Wiederaufbau* and avoided debilitating conflicts between employers and trade unions over the distribution of the gross national product. But above all it was the demand for industrial equipment caused by the Korean War (1950–3) which gave a decisive boost to the West German economy; exports boomed thanks to an undervalued currency and American encouragement of free trade in

Europe. This enabled Erhard to reduce unemployment from 1.9 millions in 1950 to 200,000 by 1961 and to successfully integrate into the economy the influx of refugees from Eastern Europe totalling 7.9 millions in 1950. Important, too, was the creation in the 1950s of an elaborate welfare system (family allowances, pensions and unemployment and sickness insurance) in accordance with the GFR's commitment to a 'socially responsible' market economy. Of particular significance was the Equalisation of Burdens Law (1952) which in the course of twenty years transferred 90,000 million DM from those who suffered least in the war to those who lost everything. Without such measures social peace could hardly have been maintained when economic growth was uneven – as government policy was aimed at stimulating investment and restricting domestic consumption – and while wage rates were low by international standards.

From 1949 to 1963 the destinies of the GFR were presided over by Chancellor Adenauer. Already seventy-three when elected in 1949, Adenauer, a Rhinelander, a Catholic and a staunch anti-Communist, had been Lord Mayor of Cologne from 1917 to 1933. Dismissed by the Nazis, he was re-appointed by the Americans in March 1945 only to be curtly dismissed by the British in October for political intrigue. Devoting himself full-time to politics, he soon established his ascendancy over the CDU/CSU. He proved himself a strong authoritarian-minded chancellor who dominated his cabinet and won from opponents the kind of grudging respect Bismarck earned in the Reichstag. Adenauer's major achievement was not his domination of Bonn politics for over a decade – 'chancellor democracy' was not without its severe critics and ended on a sour note over the *Spiegel* affair in 1962 when he tolerated actions of dubious legality by the minister of defence, Franz Josef Strauss. Equally lamentable was Adenauer's outrageously dishonest denigration of his socialist opponents as a stalking horse for Communism, the 'enemy within' who could not be trusted with power.

His achievement was, as a foreign admirer commented, that 'he met the great imperative of his moment in German history – the restoration of national self-respect without the record of intransigence.' Adenauer contributed more than any other German political leader to the re-establishment of his half of Germany to a position of equality among the western nations by tenacious political tactics, relentless anti-Communism and wholehearted commitment to the west. Above all a realist cast in the mould of Bismarck and Stresemann, Adenauer realised that the temporary division of Germany was likely to be of long duration and that West Germany's only hope of recovery lay in full co-operation with the western powers. He was helped enormously by the American and British desire to see the GFR tied firmly to the·west – much as they had supported Stresemann in the 1920s for similar reasons – and by European initiatives such as the Coal and Steel Community and the European Economic Community. Adenauer welcomed with enthusiasm steps towards the integration of Western Europe. Whether this was because he hoped to contain the restless German spirit within the European movement or, more likely, because being a Rhinelander he was basically uninterested in the fate of Eastern Germany and wanted the GFR to play the dominant role in a united Europe is open to question. What cannot be denied is that if any chance of re-unifying Germany by four-power agreement ever existed, Adenauer's staunch pro-western orientation helped to destroy it.

In 1949 he persuaded the western powers to suspend further dismantling of industry in exchange for German agreement to international control of Ruhr industry, a device to prevent the re-emergence of giant combines which many people in 1945 held responsible for the rise of Nazism. Early in 1952 the western powers agreed to a federal foreign ministry. A month later they restored sovereignty to the GFR and the occupation ended.

Only over German re-armament did Adenauer experience difficulties. In 1945 the four powers, absolutely determined to stamp out militarism, had no thought of ever allowing the Germans to bear arms again. Some years later NATO was formed to defend the North Atlantic area and Europe against Soviet aggression. To strengthen the western allies against numerically superior Russian ground forces the Americans insisted on a German military contribution. That demand disturbed many Germans – the *'ohne mich'* ('count me out') movement flourished in the GFR in the early 1950s – as well as many westerners who feared that it would diminish still further all hopes of re-unification. Adenauer, however, never doubted that the GFR must play a military role commensurate with her new-found status. He welcomed a French proposal that the German forces be part of an integrated European army: the so-called European Defence Community (EDC). To justify this *volte-face* to the Germans, Adenauer beat the anti-Communist drum loudly, insisting that an unarmed Germany would only encourage Russian aggression; far from postponing re-unification, the armed might of the west, augmented by German divisions, would eventually force the Russians to negotiate, a dangerous illusion – if Adenauer ever believed it – which he shared with the American Secretary of States John Foster Dulles. However, despite western approval of the EDC, the European spirit was too weak to allay French fears of a re-armed Germany; in August 1954 the French Assembly defeated the project.

This was a bitter blow for Adenauer especially as difficulties had also arisen during negotiations over the future of the Saarland. This territory, under French control since 1945, had declared itself autonomous and was bound to France by a customs union. In addition the much-heralded Four Power Conference on Germany had failed to make progress despite Adenauer's sanguine predictions. Out of this dangerous impasse he was rescued by British and American determination to have the GFR share in the defence of Europe. In October 1954 at the London Conference Britain, France and the Benelux countries invited the GFR to join them in an enlarged alliance: the Western European Union. In return the GFR promised not to manufacture atomic weapons and to place her armed forces directly under the supreme allied commander. France and the Benelux countries then agreed to give the Saarland European status in the WEU. In February 1955 the Bundestag ratified the agreement. On 5 May the GFR became a fully sovereign state and on 9 May a member of NATO. Seldom in history has a defeated power recovered so quickly.

By now Russia's attitude to the GDR had begun to change as a result of the June 1953 uprising. While the GFR economy was beginning to recover in the early 1950s, the GDR's position steadily deteriorated. Russia was exacting reparations regardless of the effect on the GDR. Ulbricht's unrealistic plans for the 'building of socialism' announced in July 1952 which laid emphasis on rapid industrialisation and on the collectivisation of agriculture strained the economy to breaking-point. They were accompanied by punitive measures against farmers, the middle classes and the churches. Labour shortages were intensified by an accelerated flight of refugees to the west which the authorities, who fortified the frontier in 1952, failed to halt. Ironically enough the Soviet High Commission newly appointed after Stalin's death was reversing Ulbricht's breakneck dash for socialism. More consumer goods, price reductions and higher wages had already been promised when a building workers' demonstration in East Berlin demanding a lowering of work norms escalated into an uprising affecting several towns by 17 June. Russian soldiers and German policemen quickly restored order; dozens of demonstrators died and thousands were arrested. The Soviet authorities, deeply shaken by the experience, modified their German policy; reparations were ended and firms in Soviet hands were given back to the GDR. At first Ulbricht promised to persevere with the New Course announced before the uprising. Some economic improvement did occur. But by 1954 Ulbricht had reverted to the 'building of socialism' concentrating effort on the expansion of heavy industry at the expense of consumer goods. After Nikita Khruschchev's deStalinisation speech at the 1956 Party Congress pressures built up in the SED for greater economic freedom with less state control. Ulbricht, always a reluctant deStaliniser, purged the party of all opponents of the new Russian line which combined state supervision of the economy with decentralised control mechanisms. In 1958 to complete the march to socialism collectivisation was extended still further and a drive launched against the remaining small businesses and shops. These measures coupled with growing anxiety about the future of Berlin accelerated the exodus of skilled workers to the west. As the 8 per cent growth rate of the 1950s fell to 2.3 per cent between 1960 and 1962, the GDR faced a most serious economic crisis.

Stalin's death in March 1953 and the end of the Korean War in June brought the First Cold War to an end. Whilst neither East nor West ceased to accuse each other of aggressive designs, dialogue between them did at least re-commence. In January 1954 the four foreign ministers met in Berlin to discuss Germany. Molotov repeated re-unification proposals first advanced in 1952: the German governments would set up a provisional all-German government to supervise free elections, and a reunited Germany would not belong to any alliance system. The western powers, deeply suspicious of the GDR, insisted on United Nations' supervision of elections, and confident that the numerically superior West Germans would opt for the western alliance, insisted that reunited Germany have complete freedom of action. Behind the arguments lay strategic pre-occupations. Russia, hoping to prevent the ratification of the EDC and to remove American troops from Europe, proposed a European Collective Security Treaty to supersede NATO. As this was completely unacceptable to the western powers who wanted to keep their forces in the GFR, the talks ended in failure. Shortly afterwards Russia restored sovereignty to the GDR and withdrew the Soviet High Commission. When the Warsaw Pact, a defensive alliance of East European states, was set up in 1955 the GDR became a member. In January the GDR established a People's Army. But in fact the frontier police and transport police established in 1947 had been more like soliders from the beginning. In 1952 most of them were turned into a People's Police and stationed in barracks.

Nor was progress towards re-unification made when the heads of state met in Geneva during the high noon of *detente* in May 1955 or when the foreign ministers met later that year. By the close of the 1950s the four powers tacitly accepted that re-unification was now highly improbable. In 1958 the GFR entered the European Economic Community enmeshing her economy closely with Western Europe; the GDR was a member of the much more loosely structured Comecon organisation in Eastern Europe. Russia also accepted the inevitability of the continuing division of Germany. Already in 1958 she was arguing that re-unification would not be brought about by holding free elections but only by negotiation between the two Germanies. In November the ebullient and volatile Russian leader Khruschchev demanded that the western powers sign a peace treaty with the two Germanies. To compel them to do so, he applied pressure at their weakest point: Berlin. This started a second Berlin crisis which rumbled on until 1962.

When Russia announced triumphantly in August 1957 that she had tested an intercontinental ballistic missile and would by implication soon have the capacity to bombard America with nuclear warheads, the Americans redoubled their efforts to maintain their nuclear superiority. They persuaded NATO to arm with tactical nuclear weapons and to agree to station intermediate-range missiles in Europe targeted on the Soviet Union. Alarm at the prospect of missiles on German soil may have prompted Khruschchev to use Berlin as a lever to force the western powers to rethink their strategy. Other motives may have been conservative pressure at home for a tougher policy and a wish to obtain international recognition for the GDR to strengthen the socialist camp for the coming confrontation with Communist China. Over Berlin Khruschchev argued that a peace treaty with the GFR and the GDR was long overdue. If the western powers failed to respond, Russia threatened to sign one with the GDR within six months. Because the western powers had violated the Potsdam Agreement and were using West Berlin as an 'espionage centre' they had forfeited their occupation rights. West Berlin would become a demilitarised city and access would be controlled by the GDR.

The deadline was moved forward because Khruschchev did not want war over Berlin and carefully avoided a repetition of the 1948–9 blockade. A second Geneva Conference in the summer of 1959 failed to resolve the issue although, significantly, East and West German observers attended for the first time. Meeting President John F. Kennedy in Vienna in June 1961 Khruschchev renewed his threat setting December as his new deadline. Kennedy, newly elected to office, decided on a tough line. Calling Berlin 'the great testing place of western courage' which America would defend 'at all costs' he ordered a rapid build-up of conventional forces in Europe and called for extra military expenditure to guarantee a convincing non-nuclear response to Russian ambitions.

While the international crisis deepened the GDR faced a serious economic crisis as the drain of professional people and skilled workers to the west accelerated; within six months 100,000 had fled and in all about three million had opted for the west with their feet since 1945. On 13 August the GDR authorities started to build a wall physically dividing East from West Berlin, ostensibly to prevent 'spies and diversionists' from entering their capital city but in reality to prevent the collapse of the East German economy. The western powers protested at this dramatic action which revealed for all to see the bankruptcy of the Ulbricht regime. But as the East Germans avoided interference with western access routes to Berlin, the crisis did not escalate. A few weeks later Kennedy offered to negotiate on Berlin. Although the negotiations did not result in any weakening of the western position, Khruschchev seized the chance to cancel the deadline and the crisis ended. Khruschchev had gone some way towards achieving one of his objectives: the division of Germany had been finalised despite western objections and another nail driven into Adenauer's policy of 'maintaining tension' between the two Germanies and obstinately refusing to recognize the GDR.

During the Adenauer Era the GFR established itself as a major European power. As we have seen already, the 1950s was a period of unparalleled economic growth during which the GNP trebled, 'full' employment was achieved (by 1961) and the basis laid for what is today the third most powerful industrial nation in the world. Abroad, Adenauer continued to profit from the West's support. In 1957 France agreed to a plebiscite in the Saarland which resulted in the inhabitants rejecting a proposed European status for the territory and returning triumphantly to the GFR. Adenauer's last diplomatic achievement was the signature in January 1963 of the Franco-German Friendship Treaty which symbolised the vastly improved relations between the old enemies.

During these years the SPD, for long a bitter opponent of all Adenauer stood for, changed course. Under Schuhmacher, party leader up to 1953 and then under Erich Ollenhauer the SPD strenuously opposed German membership of the Coal and Steel Community, the European Economic Community and NATO on the grounds that such commitments diminished the chances of re-unification. Although the Socialist vote rose steadily from 29.2 per cent in 1949 to 31.8 per cent in 1957, the CDU/CSU stayed well ahead securing 50.2 per cent of the vote in 1957. At the Bad Godesberg Party Congress in 1959 the SPD took a decisive step away from its Marxist past. The new programme declared that democratic socialism was rooted in 'Christian ethics, humanism and classical philosophy'. In economics it was a pragmatic creed combining a belief in essential planning with a belief in the social market economy – 'as much competition as possible, as much planning as necessary' summed up the new position. The SPD no longer wanted to be a class party but aspired to be 'the party of the whole people'. Old-fashioned anti-clericalism went out of favour and the party accepted the principle of national defence. In 1960 Herbert Wehner, the SPD defence spokesman, came out in support of NATO and a bipartisan foreign policy became a reality at long last.

The Bad Godesberg *volte-face* was the end product of a reappraisal going on throughout the late 1950s. Electoral considerations were only one factor. Many Socialists now believed that excessive centralisation as exemplified by the GDR was inimical to human freedom. Willy Brandt, party leader since 1964 and a man who had spent his years in exile after 1933 in Scandinavia, brought a broader perspective and a new energy to an ageing party.

At the beginning of the 1960s Adenauer's long reign drew to a close. The CDU/CSU was becoming increasingly restive under the old man. In 1960 he was involved in an unseemly wrangle to become the new president while still retaining control of foreign policy. When the party refused to swallow this he abandoned the plan but not before he defiantly declared that he intended to stay on indefinitely as leader. When the Berlin Crisis erupted in 1961 it was Willy Brandt, then mayor of Berlin, who captured the popular mood of defiance in the city in striking contrast to Adenauer's lethargic response. At the 1961 elections the CDU/CSU share of the poll fell to 45.3 per cent (242 seats) while the SPD's rose to 36.2 per cent (190 seats). Only after protracted negotiations was the CDU/CSU–FDP coalition renewed and only on condition that Adenauer promised to resign by 1965. The *Spiegel* affair dealt the *coup d'grâce*. When the magazine published an article critical of the *Bundeswehr*'s performance during NATO manoeuvres the minister of defence, Franz Strauss, ordered the arrest of the author and several of the editors on charges of treason after a midnight occupation of the *Spiegel* offices. The subsequent explosion of protests against high-handed action reminiscent of the Third Reich forced Strauss out of office and disrupted the coalition. When it was patched up in December 1962 the FDP insisted that Adenauer must go in 1963. The CDU/CSU Party Congress elected as his successor the economic wizard Erhard whom Adenauer heartily detested. Even Adenauer's last diplomatic coup, the Franco-German Friendship Treaty, was seen not as an act of reconciliation with the old enemy but as a damaging blow to relations with the United States for the autocratic General de Gaulle was highly unpopular in Washington after his personal veto dashed Britain's hopes of entering the EEC, a step strongly favoured by the Americans. Finally, in October 1963 the 87-year-old chancellor resigned. A controversial figure over whose foreign policy historians will probably argue as hotly as they have done over Stresemann's, Adenauer left the imprint of his personality on the GFR. And, despite the negative features of 'chancellor democracy', it is greatly to his credit that he reconciled the older generation to a pluralist democracy which after nearly forty years is remarkably stable. It had been seen of him that he was the first German statesman who succeeded in overcoming 'the unconscious tendency of his fellow countrymen to believe that statesmen could only be taken seriously when they wore a uniform'. But, like Bismarck in his last weeks of office, Adenauer demonstrated by his actions that he could not conceive of Germany without him.

For the next three years Chancellor Erhard tried to maintain the CDU/CSU's dominant role in West German politics but without the force and authority of the old man. From the outset he was beset with problems at home and abroad. The old international signposts were disappearing. A mood of *détente* was in the air in Washington and Moscow, opening up the possibility of improved relations with the GDR but only if Erhard was prepared to abandon the unbending policy of the Adenauer era. The chancellor's hesitant steps in this direction will be discussed later. A firm believer in maintaining good relations with the United States on whom the defence of the GFR ultimately rested, Erhard found it increasingly difficult to approve of de Gaulle's stridently anti-American stance in the 1960s. Erhard was not helped by bitter feuds in the CDU/CSU parliamentary party where Adenauer – who remained party chairman until 1966 – and

Strauss advocated a pro-French and anti-American line, and bitterly opposed any conciliation of the GDR. That the CDU/CSU did so well at the 1965 election winning 47.6 per cent of the vote against 39.3 per cent for the SPD was a tribute to Erhard's continued popularity with the electorate as the jovial father of the 'economic miracle'.

The electoral victory did not save him. Abroad de Gaulle's withdrawal of French forces from NATO placed new strains on the triangular relationship with Paris and Washington. Meanwhile the much vaunted economic miracle started to fade. The growth rate fell from 6.2 per cent in 1964 to 4.5 per cent in 1965, unemployment rose from 100,000 to 200,000, prices increased by 4 per cent and higher wage demands raised the spectre of inflation. Rather than agree to tax increases to cover the budget deficit the four FDP ministers left Erhard's coalition in October 1966. A new shadow was cast over Bonn democracy when at *Land* elections in Hesse and Bavaria the National Democratic Party (NDP) secured 7.9 per cent and 7.4 per cent of the vote and obtained seats in the *Landtage*. This neo-Nazi party founded in 1964 was anti-American, anti-Russian, bitterly critical of Bonn politicians, hostile to foreign workers attracted in increasing numbers to the GFR by higher living standards and was insistent that Germany must never renounce her claims to the 'lost provinces', i.e. the land east of the Oder/Neisse rivers. As the political crisis deepened, Erhard was deserted by his party who chose Kurt Kiesinger, a Swabian Catholic, as their chancellor-nominee. As the differences with the FDP could not be patched up and as the SPD was anxious to widen its appeal and destroy the 'red' image for ever by participating in government, a Grand Coalition of the two main parties was formed, a marriage of convenience to deal with the pressing problems suddenly facing Bonn democracy. In December Kiesinger became chancellor and SPD members sat in a German cabinet for the first time since 1930.

Despite much initial scepticism the Black–Red coalition steered the GFR through its first major crisis. The economic situation continued at first to deteriorate with unemployment reaching 500,000 in 1967. The government got the economy moving again through a characteristic mixture of Keynesianism and monetarism. Under the stability and growth act of 1967 new machinery was set up to co-ordinate spending by federal, *Land* and local authorities; banks were given a major role in initiating economic acitivity; and the state encouraged trade unions and employers to agree moderate wage increases. Price rises were halted and unemployment fell to 200,000 by 1969.

The political situation remained a cause of grave anxiety. Throughout 1967 the NDP continued to poll 7–9 per cent of the vote at several *Landtag* elections and reached 10 per cent in Baden-Württemberg in April 1968. A more immediate threat was extra-parliamentary activity spearheaded by the student movement. Though part of a much broader movement of revolt in the west against the conformist monetary values of 'bourgeois democracy' and against American involvement in Vietnam there were also specifically German grievances: demands for reform of the archaic and autocratic university system and frustration at Bonn politics where the coalition's crushing majority emasculated effective opposition. The movement was radicalised by the death of a student during demonstrations in West Berlin against the shah of Iran's visit in June 1967 and spread to other cities. The protest movement reached a peak at Easter 1968 with extensive rioting in West Berlin reminding many observers of the street battles in Weimar Germany in the early 1930s. Fortunately for the GFR the student movement lacked a sense of purpose, failed to win much support from the populace at large and burnt itself out in the 1970s. It was fortunate, too, that the NDP – which clearly profited from the 'law-and-order' stance it adopted during the street disturbances – did not break through the 5 per cent barrier at the 1969 election and declined rapidly thereafter.

Cracks soon appeared in the Grand Coalition partly because of differences over foreign policy to be discussed later. It was also divided over responses to the student protest and over a proposal to abolish second votes and introduce single-member constituencies throughout the GFR in an attempt to consolidate the two-party system. This was strongly opposed by the FDP which owed all its seats to second votes. In March 1969 the coalition partners, having failed to agree upon a joint candidate for the forthcoming presidential election, made separate nominations. Significantly the FDP – which under Walter Scheel had swung to the left – voted for Gustav Heinemann, the SPD candidate, thus ensuring his election. At the Bundestag election in September the CDU/CSU vote fell to 46.1 per cent while the SPD rose to 42.7 per cent though the FDP fell dramatically from 9.5 per cent to 5.8 per cent, perilously close to elimination point. In October Willy Brandt was elected chancellor and with FDP support formed a government which remained in office for thirteen years.

The SPD–FDP coalition headed by Brandt until 1974 and by Helmut Schmidt from 1974 until 1982 had no easy passage. Foreign policy caused the first explosion. Ideological conflict between SPD and CDU/CSU so characteristic of the Adenauer era was dying away by the late 1960s in view of the convergence of their party programmes. The conflict flared up again in the passionate debate over *Ostpolitik* (to be discussed later) which reached a peak in 1972 when the CDU/CSU attempted to remove Brandt by a constructive no-confidence motion. After the Bundestag elections – forced by Brandt who asked for a vote of confidence in the government on which his supporters then deliberately abstained – confirmed coalition policy, a foreign policy consensus re-emerged for improved relations with the GDR.

Secondly, the urban unrest centred on universities persisted into the

1970s. A much more potent threat to the state was the outbreak of terrorism associated with the infamous Baader-Meinhof gang. Bank hold-ups, bomb outrages and murders of prominent citizens called for tough measures from which Brandt did not flinch. The anti-terrorist measures approved by the Bundestag in 1972, which greatly extended police power, curbed the violence but worried many who feared that the GFR was becoming an increasingly authoritarian state. Sharp criticism was also levelled at the *Berufsverbote* which *Länder* governments introduced in 1972 with Brandt's approval. Under these measures applicants for civil service posts – including the teaching profession and affecting roughly 50 per cent of all students – are required to submit to close political scrutiny. To date thousands have been excluded by virtue of their left-wing politics or association with known extremists.

Thirdly, an economic crisis infinitely more serious than the recession of 1966–7 struck the GFR in the 1970s. The first Middle Eastern oil crisis in 1973 trebled oil prices overnight and the second in 1979 doubled them. Unemployment shot up from 300,000 in 1973 to 600,000 in 1974 and reached 1.1 millions by 1975. Though government measures were initially successful in boosting growth rates through investment programmes based on cheap credit success was necessarily limited because of long-term trends still plaguing the western world in the 1980s. Like other advanced industrial lands, the GFR has had to accept that the days of spectacular growth are over and that the Germans are entering an age of computer technology and of intensified competition for markets. Unemployment was stabilised in the late 1970s but at a significantly higher level. After the second oil crisis it crept up from 1.8 millions in 1982 to 2.2 millions in 1985 under the CDU/CSU–FDP coalition.

Nevertheless, Brandt and Schmidt undertook an ambitious reform programme in part at least because the lasting effect of the student protest had been to create a new awareness of the need to revitalise – and to democratise – a society fossilised in the Adenauer era into a stifling conformism and authoritarianism. It was no coincidence that Brandt chose to work not in the Palais Schaumburg where CDU chancellors had worked but in a concrete-and-glass chancellery built in the palace grounds between 1969 and 1976.

Despite differences in the coalition, increasing financial constraints in the late 1970s with growing budget deficits, and despite CDU/CSU opposition exerted through the Bundesrat much was achieved. Marriage and family law was modernised though a bill to legalise abortion fell foul of the Federal Court. Social welfare was extended with a reform of family allowances and rents and improvements in sickness benefits. Major educational reforms re-structuring all institutions from schools to universities were started in this period. Finally, the co-determination system in industry was extended. The 1951 law gave workers in the coal, iron and steel industries parity with employers on boards of management and one-third representation on boards in other industries. After considerable internal strife the coalition agreed in 1976 (with CDU support) to give workers equal representation on boards of all large companies. Shareholders, however, still have the decisive voice in the event of conflict.

The coalition finally collapsed in 1982 when FDP and SPD failed to agree a budget. The FDP, now moving to the right, supported a CDU/CSU constructive no-confidence motion. Helmut Kohl of the CDU replaced Schmidt as chancellor in a CDU/CSU–FDP coalition. At the 1983 Bundestag election the CDU/CSU secured 49 per cent of the vote, the SPD 38.8 per cent and the FDP 6.7 per cent. A new feature was the emergence of the Green Party which secured seats in several *Landtage* in 1979. Campaigning on environmental issues, especially the development of nuclear power (favoured by the major parties as an alternative to costly oil), and opposing the stationing of missiles on German soil, the Greens obtained 5.4 per cent of the vote and have 27 seats in the Bundestag. It is too early to predict whether the Greens represent a serious threat to the major parties or whether they will share the fate of small parties in the past.

Summing up on the GFR in the mid 1980s, one may say with some confidence that 'Bonn is not Weimar' if only because historical phenomena never repeat themselves exactly. Bonn is, however, a viable democracy with a distinctly conservative colouration. Certainly revelations in 1984 of close financial ties between the giant Flick concern and Bundestag members of all parties, widespread evasion of tax on party funds and the charges of corruption against two former economics ministers suggest that the standard of political morality still leaves much to be desired. On the other hand, extremist parties have received short shrift at the hands of the electorate even at times of economic dislocation. Nor has the *Bundeswehr* formed in 1956 become a state within a state as the *Reichswehr* did. Now numbering 500,000 men – some 50 per cent of NATO's ground forces – it remains firmly under civilian control and takes its operational orders directly from the NATO supreme commander in Europe. Finally, although Bonn now faces intractable economic problems which raise serious questions about the funding of the elaborate welfare state, it shares them with other industrial lands in the west. As the foremost exporter, banker and industrial nation in the European Economic Community it is more likely than most to overcome them.

Both Germanies came into being with natural autocrats at the helm: Adenauer in the GFR and Walter Ulbricht in the GDR. A dedicated Communist who returned to Germany in 1945, Ulbricht became deputy minister-president in 1949, first secretary of the SED's Politburo (later Central Committee) in 1953 – holding the post until 1971 – and in 1960 chairman of the council of state formed after President Pieck's death. Ulbricht helped transform the SED into a highly selective cadre party subservient to the wishes of the Soviet Union. In economic matters he slavishly copied Russian-style five- and seven-year plans which emphasised state control and the expansion of heavy industry at the expense of consumer-goods production. Besides being an able administrator in Stalin's mould, Ulbricht possessed a well-defined instinct for political survival. In spite of strong criticism of his hardline policy just before the 1953 uprising he managed to stay in office afterwards. His loyalty to Moscow during the Hungarian uprising of 1956 enabled him to resist large-scale deStalinisation and silence critics inside and outside the SED. In 1961 with the economy virtually at breaking-point Moscow sanctioned the building of the Berlin Wall and once again Ulbricht survived.

Economically, the GDR suffered from major disadvantages compared with the GFR. She possessed only 30 per cent of former *Reich* industrial capacity, chiefly in the glass, ceramics and electrical goods sectors; she was chronically short of natural resources most of which had to be imported; and while the population of what became the GFR increased from 40 millions in 1948 to 54 millions in the 1950s, the GDR's population fell from 19 millions in 1945 to 17.8 millions as a result of an unprecedented outflow of skilled labour attracted by better conditions in the west. Industrial development was heavily dependent on Russia which after 1953 saw advantages for the eastern block in building up the GDR's heavy industrial base. Significant progress was made in the 1950s at the expense of the consumer. In the 1960s Ulbricht, following the current Russian wisdom, allowed economic experts more say than SED functionaries in drawing up and monitoring the plans. Decentralisation of decision-making, the use of pricing policy and the re-introduction of the profit motive improved efficiency and brought about a significant improvement in living standards. Though shortages of consumer goods and poor service standards remain characteristic of East European economies, nevertheless between 1965 and 1970 the percentage of GDR workers owning refrigerators rose from 25.9 to 36.4, washing machines from 27.7 to 53.5 and television sets from 48.5 to 69.1. Improved material conditions were underpinned by an extensive welfare system and by considerable efforts to improve educational facilities. To reflect these changes a new constitution was introduced in 1968 which described the GDR as a 'socialist state of the German nation'. Basically the constitution codified the increase in state power since 1949. The *Länder* had been superseded by *Bezirke* (administrative districts) in 1952; the *Länderkammer* was abolished in 1958; and in 1960 the presidency was abolished and replaced by a council of state. Though nominally elected by the *Volkskammer*, effective power resides in the council whose members are also key SED functionaries.

The 78-year-old Ulbricht was finally forced to resign in 1971. The

GDR was running into serious economic difficulties at home; Ulbricht was stubbornly resisting *détente*; and his didactic tone towards other Communist parties irritated Russia's Leonid Brezhnev. Under the aegis of his successor Erich Honecker, a protégé of Ulbricht who had master-minded the building of the Berlin Wall, and was, like him, a devoted friend of Russia, the GDR has become the most powerful industrial economy in the Eastern block after the Soviet Union. Production, flagging in 1969–70, recovered again in the first half of the 1970s when Honecker reverted to a more centralized control of the economy. All semi-private enterprises were nationalised and by 1972 the state was virtually the sole employer of labour. The dominance of industry in the economy and the rising level of skill in a labour force augmented by thousands of university graduates produced an increase in national income of over 4 per cent annually in the early 1970s.

Inside the socialist block the GDR became a major partner of the Soviet Union. Already under Ulbricht German soldiers had invaded Czechoslovakia in 1968 – the second time in twenty years – to put down the Czech Spring. As a result of the steadfast loyalty of the GDR to the Soviet Union during the Solidarity unrest in Poland in 1980–1 the GDR ranks even higher in the eyes of Moscow. And as a result of the normalisation of relations with the GFR the GDR has at last obtained international recognition. But in one respect the GDR has not changed since 1949: the SED's grip over all aspects of life in the republic is tighter than ever. The security organs are more powerful than in any other eastern state. And the signs of cultural liberalism which accompanied the early Honecker years ended abruptly in 1976 when Wolf Biermann while living in the GFR was summarily deprived of GDR citizenship for criticism of the state. Artists and writers who protested on his behalf were arrested and fined or expelled from the GDR.

Finally, we turn to relations between the two Germanies. Throughout the 1950s relations were extremely bad. Adenauer pursued a policy of 'maintained tensions' to discourage contact with the GDR. In 1955 Foreign Minister Heinrich von Brentano announced that diplomatic relations would be broken off with states recognizing the GDR. The Hallstein Doctrine – so called after Dr Walter Hallstein, a confidant of Adenauer – led to the severance of relations with Yugoslavia in 1957 and with Cuba in 1963. Nor did the leaders of the GDR wish to improve relations with the 'revanchist puppet state' west of the Elbe.

After the Second Berlin Crisis and the Cuban Missile Crisis of 1962 when Kennedy and Khruschchev brought their countries to the brink of war, the ice-floes began to melt. It seemed to a growing number of West Germans that the time had come to recognise that re-unification had receded into the distant future and to try to improve the lot of East Germans by negotiating with their leaders. Erhard's New Opening to the East in March 1966 proposing a reduction in the number of nuclear weapons in Europe, a ban on the transfer of nuclear warheads to non-nuclear nations and a pact between NATO members and the GDR renouncing the use of force in settling disputes was an expression of the new mood. But with Adenauer and Strauss fiercely hostile to any 'appeasement' of the GDR Erhard insisted that the GFR remained the only legitimate government, which condemned the initiative to failure from the outset.

Meanwhile the SPD committed itself to work for a policy of peaceful co-existence with the GDR. Nothing came of SPD attempts in 1966 to interest the SED in exchanges to improve relations. But when the Grand Coalition was formed the SPD insisted that Kiesinger adopt a more positive policy towards the GDR. Accordingly in 1967 he proposed that the two Germanies seek to improve relations in respect of travel, trade and cultural exchanges – small steps but clearly implying the abandonment of the Hallstein Doctrine. In 1968 Kiesinger offered to negotiate directly with the Chairman of the Council of Ministers, Willi Stoph. The movement towards normalisation was accelerated by Rumania's decision to break ranks and establish relations with the GFR, much to Ulbricht's chagrin. For he, Canute-like, did his best to turn the tide by rebuffing Bonn's approaches and maintaining the unrealistic demand that the GFR formally recognize the GDR.

However, his hardline stance fell foul of the Soviet Union for whom a general *détente* in Europe held attractions partly because of the alarming deterioration in her relations with China and partly because Russia was anxious for western aid to rescue her ailing economy. Coupled with this was the SPD's victory at the 1969 election which gave Brandt a clear mandate for full co-operation with the GDR at all levels, though stopping short of formal recognition. The SPD made *Ostpolitik* a major election issue whilst the CDU/CSU, fearful of being overtaken on the right by the NDP, upheld the old discredited line. Significantly at the end of 1969 opinion polls showed that 74 per cent of the GFR electorate favoured negotiation with the GDR while 50 per cent were even ready to recognise the GDR formally and renounce the 'lost provinces'.

In a series of agreements between 1970 and 1972 the GFR normalised relations with Eastern Europe. As long as the intransigent Ulbricht remained in control in East Berlin, negotiation had to commence with Moscow. In August 1970 the GFR and the USSR signed an agreement promising to respect the territorial integrity of all states in Europe within their existing frontiers including the Oder/Neisse line and the frontier between the GFR and the GDR. In December the GFR signed a treaty with Poland recognising the Oder–Neisse line. In September 1971 the

United States, Russia, Britain and France signed a four-power agreement on Berlin promising to settle all differences by negotiation not by force. Russia promised to allow unimpeded traffic between the GFR and West Berlin and to permit West Berliners to visit the GDR for humanitarian, cultural and commerical reasons. Finally, in December 1972 the two Germanies signed the Basic Treaty which governs their present relationship. In it they agreed to develop normal neighbourly relations, settle all differences without resorting to force and to respect each other's independence.

Despite bitter opposition in the Bundestag the CDU/CSU eventually abstained and the Basic Treaty was approved. Though much of the high optimism invested in the treaty has evaporated over the years and some have suggested that the GFR gave too much and gained too little, on balance some significant improvements have occurred especially in respect of traffic and communications. Visits to East Berlin by the two million West Berliners are now much easier. The three million who left the GDR illegally after 1949 are now able to visit relatives without fear of arrest. And between 1971 and 1983 visits to the GDR have risen from 1.3 millions to five millions. Postal services and telephonic communications have also improved.

The GDR achieved at last the international recognition she had been seeking since 1949. She was admitted with the GFR to the United Nations Organisation in 1973 and by 1984 132 states had established diplomatic relations with her. Trade between the two Germanies tripled in the 1970s and reached 11,000 million DM in volume in 1980. On the other hand, growth in the GDR has slowed down in the 1980s as a result of the sharp increases in world energy prices. The terms of trade have turned dramatically against the GDR increasing her foreign indebtedness and threatening a shortage of consumer goods. The hoped-for credits from the west have been slow in materialising because of the general difficulties in increasing trade between the western and eastern systems.

The people of the GDR have paid a price for international recognition. The SED leadership, acutely aware of the dangers to its own monopoly of political power through western contacts, has tightened its grip on its own citizens. The clamp-down on intellectuals in 1976 must be seen in the context of *Abgrenzung*, i.e. the limitation of the effects of the normalization of relations. To combat the danger of 'contamination' Honecker ridiculed all idea of re-unification from the start and emphasised the separate character of the GDR. For Brandt's optimistic slogan 'two German states in one nation' Honecker substituted his own slogan: 'two German states and two German nations' and insisted that the GDR was 'a socialist nation of workers and peasants', as the 1974 constitution expressed it, 'a historical epoch ahead' of the GFR. Positive efforts have been made to create a separate East German national consciousness. This has taken the form of a resurrection of the old Prussian virtues: order, discipline, diligence and devotion to duty. Old heroes: Scharnhorst, Gneisenau and (to some extent) Bismarck have been rehabilitated while, as if to symbolise the new spirit, the statue of Frederick the Great re-appeared again on Unter den Linden in 1980. Military training has been introduced into schools at all levels in recent years to inculcate into the young the desire to defend the socialist fatherland against its 'imperialist enemies', amongst whom is the GFR. Simultaneously, heavy emphasis is laid on friendly relations with the Soviet Union, to which according to the 1974 constitution the GDR is 'for ever and irrevocably allied'.

It would be unwise to make predictions about the future of the two Germanies. While completely separate nations have not come into being at this time, nevertheless two distinctive socio-economic systems each with its own *raison d'être* have now existed peacefully as long as Bismarck's *Reich*. Each has become the most important member (outside the Super-powers) of its respective alliance system both in terms of economic and military power. Their pre-eminence has been greatly enhanced by the normalisation of relations, which in turn depends upon maintaining a friendly relationship with the Soviet Union.

Since the onset of the Second Cold War which began in 1979 when the Soviet Union invaded Afghanistan – once again reviving fears of Russian ambitions – considerable strains have been placed upon the Bonn–Moscow and Pankow–Moscow axes. The escalation of the arms race, NATO's decision to station Cruise missiles in Europe and America's development of the Strategic Defence Initiative point up the latent conflict between the GFR's *Westpolitik* and *Ostpolitik*. When the Kohl coalition – anxious to maintain its relationship with the United States – agreed to station Pershing missiles in the GFR and indicated readiness to partici-pate in Star Wars research designed to put nuclear warheads in outer space, the Soviet Union warned of the effect these decisions could have upon the normalisation of relations with the GDR. Similarly, Honecker, despite his wish to pursue a fairly independent foreign policy, can do so only by grace and favour of Moscow. Thus he was obliged to cancel a projected visit to the GFR in the autumn of 1984 because it did not fit in with the Soviet Union's global strategy.

It seems likely that the division of Germany will continue into the foreseeable future because it is the cornerstone of a stable Europe. It remains very much in the interest of the two Germanies to continue to exert influence inside their rival alliances to encourage all signs of *détente*, such as the Reagan–Gorbachev connection, simply because increased international tension must carry with it the threat of the reduction of the area between Rhine and Oder to a pile of radioactive rubble. That is the new *Realpolitik* which ensures that the 'German Question' is not likely to disturb the peace of Europe again.

Bibliography

General Histories

Hajo Holborn, *A History of Modern Germany 1648-1945* (New York, 1964-8) 2 vols; Gordon Craig, *Germany 1866-1945* (Oxford, 1978); T. Nipperdey, *Deutsche Geschichte 1800-1866. Bürgerwelt und starker Staat* (München, 1983) good on economic and social development; for constitutional details H.W. Koch, *A Constitutional History of Germany* (London, 1984); on nineteenth century economic and social change M. Kitchen, *The Political Economy of Germany 1815-1914* (London, 1978).

1815-1848

T.S. Hamerow, *Restoration, Revolution and Reaction: Economics and Politics in Restoration Germany 1815-1871* (Princeton, 1958) is excellent. W.O. Henderson, *The Zollverein* (London, 1959) is still the standard.

The 1848 Revolution

V. Valentin, *Geschichte der deutschen Revolution von 1848-9* (Berlin, 1930) is the most detailed account, abridged in *1848: Chapters of German History* (London, 1940). The most detailed account of the Frankfurt Parliament is F. Eyck, *The Frankfurt Parliament 1848-9* (London, 1968). Still useful are R. Stadelmann, *Social and Political History of the German 1848 Revolution* (Ohio University Press, 1975) written in 1949; and W. Mommsen, *Grösse und Versagen des deutschen Bürgertums. Ein Beitrag zur Geschichte der Jahre 1848-9* (Stuttgart, 1949). Entertaining but unfair is L.B. Namier, *1848: The Revolution of the Intellectuals* (Oxford, 1944).

The Unification of Germany

Emphasis has been laid in recent years on the socio-economic background; a pioneering work was H. Böhme, *Deutschlands Weg zur Grossmatcht: Studien zum Verhältnis von Wirtschaft und Staat während der Reichsgründungszeit 1848-1881* (Cologne and Berlin, 1960). For detailed analysis of the ideological and socio-economic background see T. Hamerow, *The Social Foundations of German Unification 1858-1871* (Princeton, 1969-72) 2 vols.

Much has been written on Bismarck. An earlier and sharply critical work is E. Eyck, *Bismarck. Leben und Werk* (Zürich, 1941-4) 3 vols; a shortened version in *Bismarck and the German Empire* (London, 1950). Scholarly and balanced are W.N. Medlicott, *Bismarck and Modern Germany* (London, 1955); A.J.P. Taylor, *Bismarck. The Man and the Statesman*; and W. Mommsen, *Bismarck, ein politisches Lebensbild* (Munich, 1959). When completed down to 1898 the standard is likely to be O. Pflanze, *Bismarck and the Development of Germany* (Princeton, 1963). The latest biographies are L. Gall's penetrating *Bismarck. Der weisse Revolutionär* (Propyläen, 1980) and E. Engelberg's more conventional *Bismarck. Urpreusse und Reichsgründer* (Siedler Verlag, 1985).

The role of the Great Powers is investigated by W.E. Mosse, *The European Powers and the German Question 1848-71* (Cambridge, 1958).

The German Empire

A stimulating general analysis emphasising the economic and social determinants of policy is H-U. Wehler, *The German Empire 1871-1914* (Leamington Spa, 1984). See also the essays edited by J. Sheehan, *Imperial Germany* (New York, 1976).

The Wehler thesis – postulating manipulations of the people by a ruling elite determined to retain its privileged position – is challenged in R. Evans (ed.) *Society and Politics in Wilhelmine Germany* (London, 1978) and in D. Blackbourn and G. Eley, *The Pecularities of German History. Bourgeois Society and Politics in Nineteenth-Century Germany* (Oxford, 1984) a stimulating but not entirely convincing book. See also G. Eley, *Reshaping the German Right: radical nationalism and political change after Bismarck* (London, 1980).

On the emperor's political influence see J.C.G. Röhl (ed.) *Kaiser Wilhelm II. New Interpretations* (Oxford, 1982). A good general account of William II is M. Balfour, *The Kaiser and his Times* (London, 1964).

On post-Bismarck there is J.A. Nichols, *Germany after Bismarck: The Caprivi Era* (Cambridge, Mass. 1967) and J.C.G. Röhl, *Germany without Bismarck: The Crisis in Government in the Second Reich 1890-1900* (U. of California Press, 1967).

On the army and officer corps still outstanding is Gordon Craig, *The Politics of the Prussian Army 1640-1945* (Oxford, 1955). For a more sociological orientation see K. Demeter, *The German Officer Corps in Society and State 1650-1945* (London, 1965); and M. Kitchen, *The German Officer Corps 1890-1914* (Oxford, 1968). A conservative standpoint in G. Ritter, *The Sword and Sceptre: The Problem of Militarism in Germany* (Coral Gables, Fla., 1969) 4 vols.

The vast literature on the Social Democratic Party includes V.L. Lidtke, *The Outlawed Party 1878-1900* (Princeton, 1966); C.E. Schorske, *German Social Democracy 1905-1917* (Cambridge, Mass., 1955); and on

Socialism generally Dick Geary's incisive *European Labour Protest 1848–1939* (London, 1981). Important books on economic aspects are H. Rosenberg, *Grosse Depression und Bismarckzeit* (Berlin, 1972) and H-U. Wehler, *Bismarck und Imperialismus* (Cologne, 1972).

On Anglo-German relations see Paul M. Kennedy, *The Rise of Anglo-German Antagonism 1860–1914* (London, 1960).

The First World War and the Revolution

The origins of the war are still a highly controversial area. A pioneer work was F. Fischer, *Germany's Aims in the First World War* (London, 1967). His *War of Illusions* (London, 1973) argued that Germany planned a major war from 1912. A useful symposium is H.W. Koch (ed.), *The Origins of the First World War. Great Power Rivalry and German War Aims* (London, 1972). Balanced short accounts are L.C.F. Turner, *Origins of the First World War* (London, 1970) and J. Joll, *Origins of the First World War* (London, 1984).

An excellent GDR symposium is F. Klein, *Deutschland im I Weltkrieg* (Berlin, 1968) 3 vols.

On the Hindenburg-Ludendorff dictatorship see M. Kitchen, *The Silent Dictatorship: the Politics of the German High Command 1916–1918* (London, 1978). Still good on the war years and the approach of revolution is A. Rosenberg, *The Birth of the German Republic 1871–1918* (London, 1931).

On the 1918–19 Revolution A.J. Ryder, *The German Revolution of 1918: A Study of German Socialism in War and Revolt* (Cambridge, 1967). Wider in scope is F.L. Carsten, *Revolution in Central Europe 1918–1919* (London, 1972). Indispensable for the causes of revolution is J. Kocka, *Facing Total War: German Society 1914–1918* (Leamington Spa, 1984).

The Weimar Republic

General Histories

S. William Halperin, *Germany Tried Democracy: A Political History of the Reich from 1918 to 1933* (New York, 1946) is still probably the best. From a liberal standpoint E. Eyck, *The Weimar Republic* (Harvard, 1962–4) 2 vols. Informative but hostile G. Scheele, *The Weimar Republic: Overture to the Third Reich* (London, 1944). See also John Hiden, *The Weimar Republic* (London, 1974).

Monographs

On the army F.L. Carsten, *The Reichswehr and Politics 1918 to 1933* (Oxford, 1967) is outstanding. On Hindenburg J.M. Wheeler-Bennett, *Hindenburg The Wooden Titan* (London, 1967) and A. Dorpalen, *Hindenburg and the Weimar Republic* (Princeton, 1964). On the history of the left see R.N. Hunt, *German Social Democracy 1918–1933* (Chicago,

1970) and W.L. Guttmann, *The German Social Democratic Party 1875-1933* (London, 1981).

On the collapse of the Republic see the essays in Peter D. Stachura, *The Nazi Machtergreifung* (London, 1983). A most detailed account in K.D. Bracher, *Die Auflösung der Weimarer Republik. Eine Studie zum Problem des Machtverfalls in der Demokratie* (Villingen, 1971).

National Socialism
General Histories

A solid account in K.D. Bracher, *The German Dictatorship: The Origins, Structure and Consequences of National Socialism* (New York, 1970); K. Hildebrand, *The Third Reich* (London, 1984); domestic development is covered in M. Broszat, *The Hitler State. The Foundation and Development of the Internal Structure of the Third Reich* (London, 1981); an acute analysis of the main problem areas in I. Kershaw, *The Nazi Dictatorship. Problems and Perspectives of Interpretation* (London, 1985); see also John Hiden and John Farquharson, *Explaining Hitler's Germany. Historians and the Third Reich* (London, 1983).

Monographs

Of the many Hitler biographies A. Bullock, *Hitler: A Study in Tyranny* (London, 1952) is still a classic. Runners up are J. Fest, *Hitler* (London, 1974) and J. Toland, *Adolf Hitler* (New York, 1976). Different in approach is W. Carr, *Hitler. A Study in Personality and Politics* (London, 1978).

On relations between Nazis and soldiers see R.J. O'Neill, *The German Army and the Nazi Party 1933-1939* (London, 1966). A less favourable view in K-J. Müller's important book, *Armee Politik und Gesellschaft in Deutschland 1933-1945* (Paderborn, 1979) soon to appear in English.

On the economy a good survey is D. Petzina, *die deutsche Wirtschaft in der Zwischenkriegszeit* (Wiesbaden, 1977); also R.J. Overy, *The Nazi Economic Recovery 1932-1938* (London, 1982). Specialised works include A. Milward, *The German Economy at War* (London, 1965) which advances the view that limited resources compelled the Nazis to prepare for short wars; R.J. Overy, *Goering. The 'Iron' Man* (London, 1984) challenges this arguing that the Nazis were preparing for a long war; Bernice A. Carroll, *Design for Total War; Arms and Economics in the Third Reich* (The Hague, 1968); and for the GDR D. Eichholtz, *Geschichte der deutschen Kriegswirtschaft 1933-1945: vol. I 1933-41* (Berlin, 1971); vol. II 1941-43 (Berlin, 1985).

On the system of terror H. Krausnick, H. Buchheim, M. Broszat, H-A. Jacobsen, *Anatomy of the SS State* (London, 1968). On the persecution of the Jews there is R. Hilberg's massive *The Destruction of the European Jews* (Chicago, 1961). For a perceptive discussion of the dispute between 'intentionalists' and 'functionalists' about the extent to which the Nazis always intended to murder the Jews see I. Kershaw, *The Nazi Dictatorship*. Karl A. Schleunes emphasises the improvisation element in *The Twisted Road to Auschwitz. Nazi Policy towards German Jews 1933-1939* (London, 1970).

On public opinion quite excellent is I. Kershaw, *Public Opinion and Political Dissent in the Third Reich: Bavaria 1933-1945* (Oxford, 1983).

On foreign policy an authoritative if rather dogmatic account is G.W. Weinberg, *The Foreign Policy of Hitler's Germany. Diplomatic Revolution in Europe 1933-1936* (London, 1970) and *The Foreign Policy of Hitler's Germany. Starting World War II* (London, 1980). W. Carr, *Arms, Autarky and Aggression. German Foreign Policy 1933-1939* (London, 1972) attempts to relate foreign to economic policy. John Hiden, *Germany and Europe 1919-1939* and K. Hildebrand, *The Foreign Policy of the Third Reich* (London, 1973) are both useful. On the German side four volumes have appeared to date of the monumental 10 vol. history of the Second World War *Das deutsche Reich und der Zweite Weltkrieg* (Stuttgart, 1979) being written by a team at the Freiburg Militärgeschichtliches Forschungsamt.

On the war itself there is David Irving, *Hitler's War* (London, 1977); Andreas Hillgruber, *Der Zweiter Weltkrieg 1933-1945. Kriegsziele und Strategie der grossen Mächte* (Stuttgart, 1985); and on the early stages W. Carr, *Poland to Pearl Harbor. The Making of the Second World War* (London, 1985).

The Two Germanies
For the GDR see D. Childs, *The GDR. Moscow's German Ally* (London, 1983) and Martin McCauley, *The German Democratic Republic since 1945* (London, 1983). For the GFR D. Childs and J. Johnson, *West Germany. Politics and Society* (London, 1981) and essays in William E. Paterson and Gordon Smith, *The West German Model, Perspectives in a Stable State* (London, 1981). Detailed but dated is Alfred Grosser, *Germany in Our Time. A Political History of the Post-War Years* (London, 1971).

Index

For emperors, kings and popes dates are those of reigns.

Honecker, Erich (b. 1912), chairman of council of state in GDR, 388, 390
Hoover Moratorium, 302
Horst Wessel song, 309–10, 312
Hottentot election, 178
House, Edward (1858–1925), personal envoy of President Wilson, 206
Hugenberg, Alfred (1865–1951), German Nationalists' leader, 295, 298, 303, 309–10
Hughes, Charles Evans (1862–1948), American secretary of state, 280
Humboldt, Wilhelm, Freiherr von (1767–1835), writer and statesman, 8
Hungary, 7, 36, 47, 50, 61–2, 68, 348, 353, 359

IG Farbenindustrie, 290, 334
Imperial Grain Office, 220
Independent Socialist Party and Independent Socialists, 224–5, 229–31, 237–43, 245–8, 250–1, 254, 265–6
Industry: in Napoleonic period, 17–18; in 1830s, 21–2; expansion in 1840s, 28–9; crisis 1846–8, 33–4; unrest in 1848, 37; in 1850s, 66–7; in 1870s, 128–30; and protective tariffs, 129–30, 133–4; and commercial treaties, 165–7; in 1890s, 167–9; and *Weltpolitik*, 173; and wartime planning, 219–20; and socialism, 257–8; and loss of industrial potential, 260; and hyperinflation, 274; in 1920s, 289–90; and German Nationalists, 295; and 1929 Crisis, 296; and role in 1932–3, 308–9; in Third Reich, 327–30; in Second World War, 335–6, 339; in 1950s, 375
Inter-Allied Military Control Commission, 264, 285
Interim Agreement (1849), 62
Isabella II (1833–68), queen of Spain, 111
Iswolski, Alexander (1856–1919), Russian foreign minister, 197–9
Italy: balance of power in, 1; and unrest in, 18, 25, 32, 36; and Schwarzenberg's view of, 50; remains divided, 57; and Austria extended in, 61; in 1859–61, 74; Austria opposes nationalism in, 92, 95; allies with France, 98, 100; gains Venetia, 101; Austria defeated in, 102, 108; approached by France, 111; remains neutral in 1870, 115; and church in, 124; and Centre Party, 126; and conservatives in power in, 135; and Bismarck's foreign policy,

152–3, 157–9; and German Empire, 165, 188–9, 196, 204, 209; and Locarno, 285; and dictatorship in, 313; and German workers holiday in, 330; and Hitler, 342, 345–6, 348, 353, 358, 363

Jacoby, Johann (1805–77), radical politician, 51, 105, 118
Jagow, Gottlieb von (1863–1935), imperial foreign minister 1913–16, 204, 208–9
Jagow, Traugott von (1865–1941), Prussian official and Kapp conspirator, 265
Jahn, Friedrich (1778–1852), German patriot, 9, 15, 25, 41, 43–4
Jameson, L. Starr (1853–1917), colonial administrator and conspirator, 191
Japan, 190, 194, 200, 345, 354, 360
Jews, 299–300, 314, 323–4, 333–4
Jodl, Alfred (1901–46), chief of operations *OKW*, 339, 365
Joffre, Joseph (1852–1931), marshal of France, 214
John, Archduke (1782–1859), *Reichsverweser*, 41, 62
Jordan, Wilhelm (1819–1904), Berlin radical, 19
Jörg, Joseph (1819–1901), Bavarian historian, 73
Joseph II (1765–90), Holy Roman Emperor, 7
Jünger, Ernst (b. 1895), writer, 269
Junker Parliament *see* League for the Protection of Landed Property

Kaas, Ludwig, (1881–1952), Centre Party leader, 292–3
Kahr, Gustav, *Ritter* von (1862–1934), Bavarian minister-president, 275–8, 318
Kaiser, Jacob (1886–1961), Christian trade unionist, 336
Kaiserbrief, 116
Kalnoky, Gusztav Siegmund, Count von (1832–98), Austro-Hungarian foreign minister 1881–95, 157
Kapp, Wolfgang (1858–1922), instigator of Kapp *Putsch*, 229, 264–5
Karl I (1916–8), emperor of Austria and king of Hungary, 227
Karl II (1804–73), duke of Brunswick, 18
Karl XV (1859–72), king of Norway-Sweden, 90
Karl August (1757–1828), grand duke of Saxe-Weimar, 13, 15

KU-224-488

BRAND
IDENTITY
NOW!

Ed. Julius Wiedemann

BRAND IDENTITY NOW!

LEARNING
RESOURCES
CENTRE
HAVERING
COLLEGE

TASCHEN

HONG KONG KÖLN LONDON LOS ANGELES MADRID PARIS TOKYO

658.827 WIE

AG

203354
739900

Contents

Learning, thinking, branding at Pentagram

By John Rushworth

There's an idea out there that designers are either simply intuitive in the way they go about their business, or they fall on the other side of the coin and are purely rational in their approach. This may be true for some, but at Pentagram we aim to be both – at the same time. Although partners here have their own particular style and talent, with their own clients and design teams, we do all share a number of understandings. One of these is that using both sides of the brain when designing leads to the most appropriate and the most elegant result. No tricks or sleights of hand here, just a matter of keeping your wits about you.

How we go about a branding project is a case in point. Pentagram learned very early on that to get well ahead of the game, and the competition, you have to do the research, analysis, and thinking about every job very thoroughly and at the right time. This would then lead to a creative solution whose validity was not left to chance.

The legacy endures. We still do the learning and thinking as a deliberately distinct and thorough part of the design process. On branding projects, this may make us brand strategists or brand consultants, but not as ends in themselves. Our goal is the end result: brand creation, where a brand is the unique character and purpose of an organisation or service, not just its visual look or logo.

❝ Branding has grown to be more than visual identity. ❞

Until quite recently the word "brand" referred simply to the look of the trademark that identified a product or manufacturer – it is derived from the branding iron used to burn a designed mark into the hide of an animal to identify ownership. But branding has grown to be more than visual identity.

A corporate visual identity is generally a symbol or logotype and all the rules that govern its use. It can also encompass the visual management of the various promotional activities that a company engages in. However, now that is just the first part of brand creation, as branding includes all of these things but extends its experience further and deeper – into environments, sounds, smells, and attitudes. The point about these is that they can all be managed to a common end.

Every enterprise must have its brand. It is the essential character on which is based all aspects of identity and market communications. You cannot *not* have a brand identity; it may be bad or wrong, but never non-existent. It is a consequence of how well it is formed and managed that determines its success.

The first part of creating a brand is a rational process. Deliberate, controlled, and incremental, it allows us to become thoroughly familiarised with the organisation or service we are working for. It involves finding out and satisfying ourselves about identity and then organising the findings under three headings into simple definitions: 1.) Who you are. 2.) What you do. 3.) How you do it.

The next part of the learning and thinking process is synthesising these definitions into a "brand description". This involves pinpointing the client's particular values and qualities. Our conclusions are finally distilled into a positioning statement. This is the benchmark or reference that provides the "managing idea" for taking us on into the development of the brand's attitude or behaviour.

The final part of building a brand is the creative expression: how the behaviour or attitude is delivered to the market. So, from the learning and thinking findings the visual identity of the brand is first formed. The work then continues to create "stories" and deliver "hands-on experiences" that always support and express the brand authentically and precisely. By understanding and expressing the brand, this creative execution also adds to it.

Alan Fletcher, one of Pentagram's founding partners, tells the story in *The Art of Looking Sideways* of a lady who found herself sitting next to legendary designer Raymond Loewy at a dinner and struck up conversation by asking: "Why did you put two Xs in Exxon?" "Why do you ask?" he replied.

"Because", she said, "I couldn't help noticing."

"Well", he responded, "that's the answer."

There are two points here: the story itself says a great deal about the act of creativity in brand building, how the profound and apt does not have to be complicated – in fact it is better that it isn't. The other point is about the storyteller himself, Alan Fletcher, who was meticulous to a fault and spent more time getting under the skin of his clients and their businesses than he did on the creative execution. He saw it as the same thing: the rational and the intuitive as one. These points were understood early at Pentagram. They have not been forgotten.

John Rushworth has been a partner at Pentagram in London since 1983, and previously worked for Michael Peters and the Conran Design Group. He has also exhibited his work in countries including the USA (New York Art Directors Club), Italy (AOSTA), and Israel (Tel Aviv Museum of Art), and is currently an external assessor at Falmouth College of Art.

Lernen, Denken und Markenentwicklung bei Pentagram

Von John Rushworth

Die Vorstellung, dass Designer ihrem Geschäft entweder rein intuitiv nachgehen oder – ganz im Gegenteil – völlig rational arbeiten, ist weit verbreitet. Für jede dieser Arbeitsweisen gibt es gute Beispiele, doch uns bei Pentagram ist beides gleichermaßen wichtig. Obwohl die Partner bei Pentagram jeweils ihren eigenen Stil und ihr individuelles Talent haben und eigenverantwortlich mit Kunden und Designteams arbeiten, stimmen wir doch in vielem grundlegend überein. Dazu gehört, dass man die elegantesten Resultate erzielt, wenn man mit beiden Gehirnhälften arbeitet. Damit sind keine besonderen Kniffe oder Taschenspielertricks gemeint, sondern stets wach und aufmerksam zu sein und einen klaren Kopf zu behalten.

Ein typisches Beispiel hierfür ist unsere Vorgehensweise bei einem Branding-Projekt. Bei Pentagram lernt man schon früh, für jeden Auftrag gründlich und frühzeitig zu recherchieren, analysieren und reflektieren, will man sich von den Konkurrenten abheben. Das führt zu kreativen Lösungen, die nicht dem Zufall überlassen bleiben.

Dieses Erbe hat Bestand. Für uns gehören Nachforschen und -denken zu einem wohlüberlegten, gründlichen Designprozess. Bei Branding-Projekten macht uns das vielleicht zu Markenstrategen oder Markenberatern. Unser Ziel aber ist das Endergebnis: die Schaffung einer Marke, also der einzigartige Charakter und Zweck einer Organisation oder einer Dienstleistung, und nicht einfach nur deren visuelles Erscheinungsbild oder Logo.

,, Doch beim Branding geht es mittlerweile um viel mehr als nur die visuelle Identität. ''

Noch bis vor Kurzem bezog sich das Wort „Brand" (Marke) lediglich auf die Anmutung eines Markenzeichens, anhand dessen man ein Produkt oder einen Hersteller identifiziert. Dieser Begriff leitet sich von dem spezifisch geformten Brandeisen ab, mit dem man Tiere brandmarkt, um die Eigentümerschaft eindeutig zu kennzeichnen. Doch beim Branding geht es mittlerweile um viel mehr als nur die visuelle Identität.

Die visuelle Identität eines Unternehmens wird meist durch Symbole oder Logos verdeutlicht, wozu auch alle Anweisungen gehören, die deren Verwendung regeln. Sie kann auch die visuelle Verwaltung der verschiedenen werbewirksamen Aktivitäten beinhalten, mit denen sich eine Firma befasst. Allerdings ist das nur die erste Phase der Schaffung einer Marke: Umgebungen, Klänge, Düfte und auch Einstellungen und Haltungen werden mit einbezogen. All dies wird einem gemeinsamen Zweck unterworfen.

Jedes Unternehmen muss seine eigene Marke besitzen. Das ist der wesentliche Charakterzug, auf dem die gesamte Identität und Marktkommunikation mit all ihren Aspekten beruht. Man kann nicht *keine* Markenidentität haben – vielleicht ist sie schlecht oder verkehrt, aber niemals nicht-existent. Ihr Erfolg hingegen wird davon bestimmt, wie gut sie gestaltet und gemanagt wird.

Die erste Phase der Erstellung einer Marke ist ein rationaler Vorgang. Wohlüberlegt, kontrolliert und schrittweise machen wir uns dabei vollständig mit der Organisation oder Dienstleistung vertraut, für die wir arbeiten. Dazu gehört, dass wir wirklich herausfinden, worin die Identität besteht, und die Ergebnisse dann unter drei Überschriften in einfachen Definitionen strukturieren: 1.) Wer sind Sie? 2.) Was machen Sie? 3.) Wie machen Sie es?

Der nächste Teil des Kennenlern- und Reflektionsprozesses ist die Zusammenführung dieser Definitionen in der Synthese einer „Beschreibung der Marke". Dazu bringen wir die besonderen Werte und Qualitäten des Kunden auf den Punkt. Unsere Schlussfolgerungen fassen wir abschließend zusammen, und das ist dann der Referenzpunkt, aus dem wir die Einstellungen der Marke oder deren Verhalten entwickeln.

In der Abschlussphase geht es um den kreativen Ausdruck: Wie wird das Verhalten oder die Einstellung auf dem Markt vermittelt? So entsteht aus den Ergebnissen der Recherchen und Reflexionen zunächst die visuelle Identität der Marke. In der weiteren Arbeit geht es um die Schaffung von Stories und griffigen, gut vermittelbaren Erfahrungen, die die Marke authentisch und präzise ausdrücken. Das Verstehen, Umsetzen und Vermitteln der Marke baut die kreative Ausführung noch weiter aus.

Alan Fletcher, einer der Gründungspartner von Pentagram, berichtet in *The Art of Looking Sideways* von einer Dame, die bei einem Dinner neben dem legendären Designer Raymond Loewy saß. Sie kam mit ihm ins Gespräch und fragte: „Warum haben Sie für Exxon zwei Xe genommen?" „Warum fragen Sie?" antwortete er. „Na ja", meinte sie, „ist mir einfach aufgefallen." „Tja", entgegnete er, „das ist schon die Antwort."

Hier gibt es zwei Punkte anzumerken: Die Geschichte sagt sehr viel über den eigentlichen kreativen Akt bei der Schaffung einer Marke aus, nämlich dass das Tiefgründige und Treffende nicht notwendigerweise auch kompliziert sein muss – tatsächlich ist es sogar besser, wenn es genau das nicht ist. Zum anderen geht es um den Erzähler selbst: Alan Fletcher war absolut akribisch und verbrachte mehr Zeit damit, sich in seine Kunden einzufühlen und ihnen und ihrer Branche „unter die Haut" zu gelangen, als mit der kreativen Ausführung. Für ihn war es ein und dasselbe: Das Rationale und das Intuitive verschmelzen. Diese Punkte hat man bei Pentagram schon sehr früh begriffen und seitdem nie wieder vergessen.

John Rushworth ist seit 1983 Partner bei Pentagram in London und hat davor bei Michael Peters und der Conran Design Group gearbeitet. Seine Arbeiten hat er u.a. in den USA (New York Art Directors Club), Italien (AOSTA) und Israel (Tel Aviv Museum of Art) ausgestellt. Derzeit ist er als externer Assessor am Falmouth College of Art tätig.

Apprentissage, réflexion et branding chez Pentagram

Par John Rushworth

Une idée circule sur les designers : soit ils exercent leur activité de façon simplement intuitive, soit ils suivent au contraire une approche purement rationnelle. Ceci se vérifie peut-être pour certains, mais notre objectif chez Pentagram est d'être les deux à la fois. Même si les associés ont leur propre style et des talents particuliers, et travaillent avec leurs propres clients et équipes de design, nous partageons tous une série d'acquis. L'un d'eux est que le design le plus adéquat et élégant s'obtient en faisant travailler les deux hémisphères du cerveau. Ni ruse, ni tour de passe-passe : il s'agit juste de rester attentif.

Notre façon d'aborder un projet de branding est un bon exemple. Très tôt chez Pentagram, nous avons appris que pour avoir une longueur d'avance au jeu et sur la concurrence, il faut faire des recherches, des analyses et réfléchir à chaque projet en profondeur et au bon moment. Cette démarche conduit à une solution créative dont la validité n'est pas le fruit du hasard.

L'héritage demeure. Nous continuons à voir l'apprentissage et la réflexion comme une partie délibérément distincte et minutieuse dans le processus de design. Pour les projets de branding, nous devenons éventuellement des stratèges ou des consultants en marque, mais ce n'est pas une fin en soi. Notre objectif est le résultat final : la création d'une marque, laquelle est le personnage unique et le seul horizon d'une organisation ou d'un service, et pas uniquement son apparence visuelle ou son logo.

> **« Mais le branding a évolué et va bien au-delà de l'identité visuelle. »**

Récemment encore, le mot « marque » faisait simplement référence à l'aspect de la marque commerciale identifiant un produit ou un fabricant. L'idée découle du fer à marquer employé pour brûler la peau d'un animal afin d'en identifier le propriétaire. Mais le branding a évolué et va bien au-delà de l'identité visuelle.

En général, l'identité visuelle d'une entreprise correspond à un symbole ou logo et à toutes les règles qui en régissent l'usage. Elle peut aussi englober la gestion visuelle des diverses activités promotionnelles d'une entreprise. Il faut toutefois savoir qu'elle n'est que la première étape dans la création de marque, car le branding inclut tous ces éléments, mais étend aussi son influence au-delà et en profondeur, dans les environnements, les sons, les odeurs et les attitudes. L'idée est que tous ces aspects peuvent être gérés pour servir une cause commune.

Toute entreprise doit posséder une marque, l'essence sur laquelle se basent tous les aspects de l'identité et des communications sur le marché. Vous ne pouvez pas ne *pas* posséder d'identité de marque : qu'elle soit bonne ou mauvaise, elle doit exister. Sa qualité et sa bonne gestion conditionnent alors son succès.

La première phase de la création d'une marque est un processus rationnel. Réfléchi, contrôlé et progressif, il nous permet de nous familiariser dans le détail avec l'organisation ou le service en question. Il s'agit pour nous de trouver l'identité et d'en être satisfaits, avant d'organiser les résultats en trois blocs simples : 1) qui vous êtes, 2) ce que vous faites, 3) comment vous le faites.

La phase suivante du processus d'apprentissage et de réflexion consiste à synthétiser ces définitions dans une « description de la marque ». Pour ce faire, il faut bien cerner les valeurs et qualités propres au client. Nos conclusions se matérialisent finalement dans une déclaration de positionnement. Il s'agit du benchmark (référence) qui donne une « idée directrice » conduisant au développement de l'attitude ou du comportement de la marque.

La dernière phase de création d'une marque correspond à l'expression créative : la présentation du comportement ou de l'attitude sur le marché. L'identité visuelle de la marque se forme donc d'abord à partir des résultats de l'apprentissage et de la réflexion. Le travail consiste ensuite à créer des « histoires » et à présenter des « expériences pratiques » favorisant et montrant toujours la marque de façon authentique et précise. C'est en comprenant et en exprimant la marque que cette exécution créative vient l'enrichir.

Alan Fletcher, l'un des partenaires fondateurs de Pentagram, raconte dans *The Art of Looking Sideways* l'histoire d'une femme qui s'est un jour retrouvée assise à côté du designer légendaire Raymond Loewy lors d'un dîner. Elle a entamé la conversation en demandant : « Pourquoi avez-vous écrit Exxon avec deux X ? » « Pourquoi cette question ? », a-t-il répondu.

« Parce que je n'ai pas pu m'empêcher de le remarquer », lui a-t-elle dit.

« Et bien c'est ça, la réponse », a-t-il répondu.

L'anecdote souligne deux aspects : l'histoire en soi en dit long sur le processus de créativité dans la création d'une marque, et illustre que la profondeur et la pertinence ne sont pas forcément compliquées (mieux vaut d'ailleurs qu'elles ne le soient pas) ; l'autre aspect concerne Alan Fletcher lui-même, méticuleux à l'excès et qui passait plus de temps à se mettre dans la peau de ses clients et leur activité qu'à s'occuper de l'exécution créative. Pour lui, c'était un tout : le rationnel et l'intuitif ne faisaient qu'un. Ces aspects ont été assimilés très tôt chez Pentagram. Ils n'ont depuis jamais été oubliés.

Depuis 1983, **John Rushworth** est partenaire chez Pentagram, à Londres ; il a auparavant travaillé pour Michael Peters et Conran Design Group. Il a également exposé son travail dans plusieurs pays, dont les États-Unis (New York Art Directors Club), l'Italie (AOSTA) et Israël (Tel Aviv Museum of Art), et exerce actuellement comme expert au Falmouth College of Art.

Stand and Deliver

By Peter Knapp

There is a new era upon us. The profound changes in the world economy continue to leave in their wake a hefty slug of uncertainty and insecurity – everyone is affected in some way and it is all-pervasive. For the consumer, lack of goodwill is rubbing shoulders with distrust and jostling with diminishing confidence and the consequences are far-reaching and significant. There is more scrutiny of messages, more interrogation of promises, and generally more cynicism.

Challenging times indeed.

The downstream impact for design and branding is, not surprisingly, immense. No longer will companies feel able to make flimsy far-reaching claims that they may never have to substantiate, or proffer grandiose statements and eye-catching boasts with little requirement to back them up. The smart consumer is quick to shun hyperbole and demands much more transparency from brands these days. Put simply, we have been jolted into a new age of honesty and clarity.

If you are going to say it… then you have to *do* it.

There is now a real and definite requirement to assess carefully the capability of a brand to deliver its promise credibly, *before* making a claim in the market-place. Should brands and the individuals who drive and steer them decide not to "do what they say", they take the risk of being found wanting – of being found out. If the brand is "caring" then it must show, very clearly, how it delivers this. If it claims to be "dynamic" it must clearly communicate this characteristic. It cannot be "innovative" without regularly demonstrating its inventiveness.

If the claims fail to deliver then the consumer will de-select, move on, and invest in a brand that keeps its word, a brand that delivers against its promise. Apple customers remain loyal because the brand delivers. The objects are desirable and we feel "big love", but more importantly they are desirable objects that work. When the iPhone launched the communications strategy focused on the simple, user-friendly functionality – claims proffered, claims substantiated. Beauty and brains.

The industry sector possibly facing the most challenging brand building is, and will continue to be, finance and banking. At the epicentre of the financial crisis there is not only a lack of trust amongst consumers but real animosity. The typical "off the cuff" platitudes, robotic customer interfaces and selective hearing will no longer suffice and customer dissatisfaction will churn faster and faster. Banks that once upon a time liked to say (shout) "yes" are now adopting a lower profile with a softer sell. Northern Rock, which was the first to suffer the indignity of public scorn and scrutiny, has a website that simply says "welcome". Hyperbole exchanged for low-key, low-expectation messaging.

> **❝ The objects are desirable and we feel 'big love', but more importantly they are desirable objects that work. ❞**

Virgin Money's credit-card website pitches its offering as: "The card that gives you plenty of breathing space". It sounds great, reassuring, comforting even – but how much space and at what cost? The general public is wising up as to how the financial world operates and it is a knowledge database that financial brands would be wise to respect, react, and respond to. Take away respect, say goodbye to the custom.

However there *is* an upside to all this – a huddle of optimism emanating from the commercial anxiety. Branding can now truly be an essential cornerstone in the communications mix. The accuracy of the content and its subsequent delivery must be carefully crafted to ensure that real trust is built. Once trust has been earned, it is essential that it continues to deliver, so as to enable the brand in question to grow credibility with its difference and relevance clearly expressed.

This new era for brands – which has no choice but to react and respond to global shifts – is one based on clarity and honesty, promise and delivery.

Product "truths" will have to be built on really solid foundations, brand benefits will have to be tangible and real. Vapid brands will ultimately wither and perish whilst brands that are committed and doggedly determined to deliver against their claims could find that this is their time to go from strength to strength.

For the smart brands and the brains behind them it is crystal clear – clarity is all.

Peter Knapp has been a creative director at Landor Associates for more than 15 years, taking over for European and Middle Eastern markets in 1996, following a period in the Hong Kong office. He specialises in integrated branding and design programmes where graphic and three-dimensional designs are used together to form total branded experiences for consumers.

Für Versprechen einstehen und sie einlösen!

Von Peter Knapp

Wir befinden uns in einer neuen Ära: Die tiefgreifenden Umwälzungen der Weltökonomie bringen es mit sich, dass eine große Ungewissheit um sich greift. Jeder ist irgendwie davon betroffen. Mit der mangelhaften Umsetzung der ideellen Werte einer Firma geht ein Misstrauen gegenüber den Produzenten einher; dieses sinkende Vertrauen führt zu deutlich spürbaren Konsequenzen: Werbebotschaften werden genauer geprüft, die Versprechen der Werbung werden hinterfragt, und es herrscht mehr Zynismus.

Diese Zeit stellt uns also tatsächlich vor große Herausforderungen!

Es überrascht daher nicht, dass die Auswirkungen auf Design und Branding immens sind. Heutzutage können sich Unternehmen keine fadenscheinigen Behauptungen mehr leisten, weil sie sie möglicherweise untermauern müssen. Es geht nicht mehr, dass Kunden mit augenfälligen Protzereien gelockt werden, ohne dass diese dann auch wirklich eingelöst werden. Der informierte Konsument lässt sich von Übertreibungen nicht mehr beeindrucken, sondern verlangt von den Marken mehr Transparenz. Kurzum: Wir sind in einem neuen Zeitalter der Ehrlichkeit und Klarheit angekommen!

Wer Behauptungen aufstellt ..., muss auch entsprechend handeln!

Bevor Werbeclaims auf den Markt hinausgeschrieen werden, lautet die wahre Anforderung nun, die Fähigkeit einer Marke einzuschätzen, um das Werbeversprechen glaubwürdig umsetzen zu können. Sollten die Personen, die die Marken steuern, beschließen, nicht „das zu tun, was sie sagen", dann gehen sie das Risiko ein, dabei ertappt zu werden. Wenn die Marke in den Vordergrund stellt, dass sie sich um bestimmte Werte kümmern will, dann muss sie dies eindeutig umsetzen. Wenn sie behauptet, „dynamisch" zu sein, muss sie diesen Charakterzug klar kommunizieren. Eine Marke kann nicht „innovativ" sein, ohne ihren Ideenreichtum regelmäßig unter Beweis zu stellen.

Erfüllen die Werbeversprechen nicht die Erwartungen, wendet sich der Verbraucher von der Marke ab und investiert in eine Marke, die die in sie gesetzten Erwartungen erfüllt. Apple-Kunden bleiben ihrer Marke treu, weil sie genau das vermittelt. Die Produkte sind begehrenswert und reizvoll, und wir empfinden eine „große Zuneigung" für sie. Wichtiger ist jedoch, dass sie *funktionieren*. Als das iPhone auf den Markt kam, konzentrierte sich die Kommunikationsstrategie auf die benutzerfreundliche Funktionalität. Hier wird der angebotene Anspruch umgesetzt: Schönheit und Köpfchen.

Der Finanz- und Bankensektor bietet die größte Herausforderung bei der Schaffung einer Marke. Im Epizentrum der Finanzkrise mangelt es den Kunden nicht nur an Vertrauen – echte Feindseligkeit kennzeichnet das Verhältnis. Typische Allgemeinplätze und roboterhaft geführte Kundenkontakte werden nicht länger ausreichen, um die Kunden zu überzeugen. Banken, die ehemals ganz laut „Ja" gerufen haben, lassen nun leisere Töne anklingen und kümmern sich um unaufdringlichere Vermarktungsaktivitäten. Northern Rock gehörte zu den Ersten, die unter der Demütigung prüfender Blicke zu leiden hatten. Auf deren Website steht heute einfach nur „Welcome". Übertreibungen werden durch maßvolle Formulierungen und Botschaften ersetzt, die keine übergroßen Erwartungen auslösen.

Die Website für Kreditkarten von Virgin Money verspricht: „Diese Karte verschafft Ihnen jede Menge Luft". Das hört sich großartig und beruhigend an – aber wie groß ist diese Menge, und was kostet das alles? Die breite Öffentlichkeit versteht immer besser, wie die Finanzwelt operiert, und dies sollten die Finanzmarken respektieren – denn ist der Respekt erst verloren, kann man sich vom Umsatz verabschieden.

Allerdings gibt es auch noch Positives zu berichten: ein optimistisches Zusammenrücken, das aus dieser Sorge hervorgeht. Branding kann in diesem Kommunikations-Mix tatsächlich zu einem wesentlichen Pfeiler werden. Der korrekte Inhalt und dessen Vermittlung müssen sorgfältig ausgearbeitet werden, um echtes Vertrauen aufzubauen. Hat man dieses Vertrauen erst einmal gewonnen, muss es unbedingt weiterhin vermittelt und eingelöst werden, damit die jeweilige Marke an Glaubwürdigkeit zunimmt und deren Unterschied und Relevanz klar und eindeutig ausgedrückt werden.

Diese neue Ära für die Markenbildung – die keine andere Wahl hat, als auf die globalen Veränderungen und Verwerfungen zu reagieren – ist eine, die auf Klarheit und Aufrichtigkeit, auf Versprechen und deren Einlösen basiert.

Die „Wahrheit" von Produkten wird man auf fundierten Grundlagen aufbauen müssen, und die Vorteile einer Marke müssen greifbar und real sein. Marken, die schal und fade sind, werden letzten Endes verschwinden. Doch Marken, die ernsthaft und hartnäckig daran arbeiten, ihre Behauptungen einzulösen, stellen möglicherweise fest, dass nun ihre Zeit gekommen ist, um sich immer besser und stärker zu entwickeln.

Für clevere Marken und die Köpfe dahinter ist eines kristallklar: Klarheit ist alles!

Peter Knapp ist seit über 15 Jahren Executive Creative Director bei Landor Associates. 1996 übernahm er die Verantwortung für die Märkte in Europa und im Mittleren Osten und arbeitete anschließend zeitweilig in der Niederlassung in Hong Kong. Er hat sich auf die Arbeit mit Integrated Branding und Integrated Design spezialisiert. Dabei greifen grafische und dreidimensionale Designs ineinander und formen gemeinsam ein umfassendes Erlebnis für Anwender und Nutzer einer Marke.

Faire des promesses et les tenir

Par Peter Knapp

Une nouvelle ère se profile. Les profonds changements de l'économie mondiale laissent dans leur sillage une grande dose d'incertitude et d'insécurité. Personne n'y échappe et le phénomène se fait sentir partout. Pour le consommateur, le manque de bonne volonté coudoie la méfiance, et la bousculade va de pair avec une assurance à la baisse ; les conséquences sont de poids et d'une portée considérable. On assiste à une analyse plus rigoureuse des messages, à une interrogation accrue des promesses, et en général à plus de cynisme.

Une véritable gageure.

En toute logique, l'impact en aval est immense pour le design et le branding. Les entreprises ne se sentiront plus autorisées à faire de grandes déclarations creuses qu'elles n'auront peut-être jamais à justifier, ni à proférer des déclarations grandioses et des fanfaronnades accrocheuses qui ne reposent sur pas grand chose. Le consommateur intelligent fuit rapidement l'hyperbole et exige dernièrement une plus grande transparence de la part des marques. En d'autres termes, nous avons été projetés dans une époque d'honnêteté et de clarté.

Si vous le *dites*... vous devez le *faire*.

De façon manifeste, la capacité d'une marque à tenir sa promesse avec crédibilité doit maintenant être évaluée avec soin, et ce *avant* de l'annoncer sur le marché. Si les marques et les personnes qui les gèrent et les orientent décident de ne pas « faire ce qu'elles disent », elles prennent le risque d'être démasquées et jugées déficientes. Si la marque se veut « à visage humain », elle doit montrer très précisément comment elle s'y prend. Si elle s'annonce comme « dynamique », elle doit transmettre clairement cette notion. Elle ne peut pas être « innovante » sans prouver régulièrement son inventivité.

Si ce qui est annoncé ne se vérifie pas, le consommateur se retirera, ira voir ailleurs et investira dans une marque qui tient sa parole, une marque qui tient ses promesses. Les consommateurs d'Apple lui restent fidèles car la marque respecte ses engagements. Les objets sont attirants et nous en tombons « amoureux », mais ce qui compte c'est que ces objets attirants fonctionnent. Lorsque l'iPhone a lancé sa stratégie de communication centrée sur une fonctionnalité simple et conviviale, les annonces faites ont été vérifiées. Esthétique et matière grise.

Le secteur le plus problématique du point de vue de la création de marque est, et restera, celui de la finance et de la banque. À l'épicentre de la crise financière, on constate non seulement un manque de confiance chez les clients, mais aussi une véritable animosité. Les typiques lieux communs « au pied levé », les interfaces robotiques et l'écoute sélective ne suffiront plus et l'insatisfaction des consommateurs montera en flèche. Les banques qui, il fut un temps, aimaient dire (crier) « oui » adoptent désormais un profil bas et des techniques de vente moins agressives. Sur son site Internet, Northern Rock, qui a été la première à souffrir l'humiliation publique de la dissection et du mépris, dit simplement « bienvenue ». L'hyperbole a fait place à un message discret et créant peu d'attentes.

Le site Internet pour la carte de crédit de Virgin Money présente son offre par : « La carte qui vous laisse respirer ». Le message est intéressant, rassurant, voire réconfortant, mais qu'entend-on exactement par là, et combien cela coûte-t-il ? Le grand public s'informe sur le fonctionnement de la sphère financière ; les marques financières devraient vraiment respecter cette base de connaissances, y réagir et y répondre. Sans respect, vous pouvez dire adieu à la clientèle.

Une dose d'optimisme émanant de l'anxiété commerciale vient toutefois contrebalancer tout cela. Le branding peut à présent être une véritable pierre angulaire de la stratégie de communication. L'exactitude du contenu et sa diffusion doivent être pensées avec soin pour établir une vraie confiance. Une fois la confiance acquise, il est crucial de continuer à tenir ses engagements, afin que la marque puisse gagner en crédibilité, sa différence et son importance étant clairement formulées.

Cette nouvelle ère pour les marques, qui n'ont pas d'autre choix que de réagir et de répondre aux mutations globales, repose sur la clarté et l'honnêteté, les promesses et leur respect.

Les « vérités » du produit devront s'appuyer sur des fondations vraiment solides, les avantages de la marque devront être tangibles et véridiques. Les marques insipides finiront par se faner et périr, alors que celles qui s'engagent et s'obstinent à tenir leurs promesses verront que c'est pour elles l'occasion de gagner en puissance.

Pour les marques intelligentes et les cerveaux derrière elles, c'est clair comme le jour : la clarté fait tout.

Peter Knapp a exercé comme directeur de la création chez Landor pendant plus de 15 ans, se chargeant en 1996 des marchés européen et du Moyen-Orient après un temps passé dans les bureaux de Hong Kong. Il est spécialisé dans des programmes intégrés de branding et de design, dans lesquels sont combinés des designs graphiques et en trois dimensions pour offrir des expériences de marque absolues aux consommateurs.

BOOST MOBILE REBRAND

Evolving, Elevating, and Unifying to Appeal To a Broader (But Not Too Broad) Audience

By Ric Peralta, ATTIK

www.attik.com

Ric Peralta is the president of ATTIK, a hybrid creative agency based in Leeds and San Francisco that focuses on serving its clients' brands and their specific needs through non-traditional creative approaches. Their output includes advertising, branding, and interactive work, and their clients include Virgin, Nike, Coca-Cola, and the NFL.

Ric Peralta ist Präsident von ATTIK, einer hybriden Kreativagentur mit Sitz in Leeds und San Francisco, die sich darauf konzentriert, mittels unkonventioneller kreativer Ansätze den Marken ihrer Kunden und deren spezifischen Anforderungen gerecht zu werden. Die Agentur arbeitet in den Bereichen Werbung, Markenentwicklung und interaktive Auftritte, zu ihren Auftraggebern gehören Virgin, Nike, Coca-Cola und die National Football League (NFL).

Ric Peralta est le président d'ATTIK, une agence de création hybride installée à Leeds et à San Francisco qui s'attache à servir les marques de ses clients et répondre à leurs besoins spécifiques à l'aide d'approches non traditionnelles. La production inclut un travail de publicité, de branding et interactif, et l'agence compte Virgin, Nike, Coca-Cola et le NFL parmi ses clients.

Left
3D logos for broadcast
and interactive applications

Right
Grid for the primary logo

In 2002, Boost Mobile changed the face of prepaid wireless services – appealing to a new set of young mobile-phone users with an irreverent brand and deep ties to the worlds of sports, music, and entertainment. Year after year, Boost Mobile was one of the fastest growing wireless brands in the U.S., but this success had not gone unnoticed.

In a crowded market-place of new phones, confusing pricing plans, multiplying competitors, and younger and younger customers, the Boost Mobile brand was getting lost.

Boost realised that its emphasis on growth in multiple cultural niches had created confusion. They wanted to regain the brand of style, independence, and value that they once owned.

ATTIK worked with Boost leadership and creative teams to identify the brand vision and opportunities. ATTIK's concurrent youth research found that despite the number of phones marketed to the segment, no brand dominated: most wireless brands were perceived as being marketed to and made for "parents".

2002 verwandelte Boost Mobile das Gesicht der Prepaid Wireless Services: Mit einer respektlosen Marke und engen Bindungen an die Welt von Sport, Musik und Entertainment öffnete man sich einer neuen Gruppe von jungen Handynutzern. Jahr um Jahr gehörte Boost Mobile zu den am schnellsten wachsenden Funknetzmarken der USA. Doch dieser Erfolg blieb von der Konkurrenz nicht unbemerkt. In einem übersättigten Markt voller neuer Handys, verwirrender Preisgestaltung, immer mehr Konkurrenten und immer jüngerer Kundschaft ging die Marke Boost Mobile unter.

Boost erkannte, dass die bisherige Betonung des Wachstums in verschiedenen kulturellen Nischen zu Verwirrung und Chaos geführt hatte, und wollte wieder zu der Marke werden, die sie einmal war und die für Stil, Unabhängigkeit und bestimmte Werte stand.

ATTIK machte sich in Zusammenarbeit mit der Boost-Führung und mit kreativen Teams daran, die Vision für die Marke und ihre Möglichkeiten neu zu erschaffen. Durch parallele Recherchen von ATTIK unter Jugendlichen stellte sich heraus,

En 2002, Boost Mobile a bouleversé le monde des services sans fil prépayés en attirant un nouveau public de jeunes utilisateurs de téléphones portables grâce à une marque irrévérencieuse et à de solides associations avec le monde du sport, de la musique et des loisirs. Chaque année, Boost Mobile a été l'une des marques de sans fil à la croissance la plus rapide aux États-Unis. Ce succès n'est pas passé inaperçu.

Sur un marché saturé de nouveaux téléphones, de plans de tarification flous, de nouveaux concurrents et de consommateurs de plus en plus jeunes, la marque Boost Mobile était en train de se perdre.

Boost a compris que le fait d'avoir mis l'accent sur la croissance dans plusieurs niches culturelles avait porté à confusion. L'entreprise voulait retrouver le style, l'indépendance et la valeur qu'elle avait connus.

ATTIK a travaillé avec la direction de Boost et des équipes créatives pour identifier la vision et les perspectives de la marque. L'étude simultanée par ATTIK du public jeune a montré que malgré le nombre de téléphones dans ce segment,

19

Above
Model of store

Right
The type family "Boost
Neo Grotesk" developed
for the brand

For young people, mobile-phone relationships were paradoxical and full of compromises. This group never went anywhere without their phone yet felt limited because of long-term commitments and exorbitant coverage fees. And, although they considered the phone an extension of their personality, they called the phones in their price range "cheap" and "disposable".

ATTIK's new brand idea, "Life without limits", hit the open "no compromises" opportunity hard. An invitation to young people who were NOT tied down by previous generations' rules – and phone companies – and were open to expressing themselves in sports, music, entertainment or whatever they chose.

Creatively Boost and ATTIK aimed to capture this wider audience by creating a simple, distinguished, and dramatically different look from any other wireless brand.

The new identity was based on a simplification of the original Boost logo. The logo's recognisable elements and type were retooled to add a sense of

dass trotz der Vielzahl der in diesem Segment angebotenen Handys keine Marke dominierte: Die meisten Mobilfunkmarken wurden so wahrgenommen, dass sie sich in Produktion und Werbung eigentlich an die Eltern richteten.

Junge Menschen haben zu ihren Handys eine paradoxe Beziehung voller Kompromisse. Sie haben das Handy immer dabei, fühlen sich aber durch langfristige Verträge und hohe Gebühren eingeschränkt. Und obwohl sie das Handy als Erweiterung ihrer Persönlichkeit betrachten, bezeichnen sie die Geräte der für sie gedachten Preisklasse als „billig" und „Wegwerfartikel".

Die neue Markenidee von ATTIK, „Life without limits", kollidierte heftig mit der bisherigen „Keine-Kompromisse"-Philosphie der Firma, eine Einladung an junge Menschen, die sich nicht von den Regeln früherer Generationen – und von Telefonanbietern – fesseln ließen, sondern offen dafür waren, sich selbst über Sport, Musik, Entertainment oder andere, selbst gewählte Möglichkeiten auszudrücken.

aucune marque ne s'imposait : la plupart des marques sans fil étaient perçues comme conçues et faites pour « leurs parents ».

Pour les jeunes, la relation avec leur téléphone portable était paradoxale et pleine de compromis. Ils n'allaient jamais nulle part sans leur téléphone, mais se sentaient limités par les engagements à long terme et les forfaits exorbitants. Même si le téléphone leur semblait une extension de leur personnalité, ils qualifiaient ceux qu'ils pouvaient s'offrir de « basse qualité » et « jetables ».

La nouvelle marque imaginée par ATTIK, « Vivre sans limites », a totalement répondu au créneau « zéro compromis » : une invitation aux jeunes qui n'étaient PAS tenus par des règles de générations antérieures (et des compagnies de téléphone) et qui étaient disposés à s'exprimer dans les domaines du sport, de la musique, des loisirs ou autres de leur choix.

Boost et ATTIK ont donc tenté de capter ce public plus large en créant un look simple, distingué et complètement différent de toutes les autres marques sans fil.

BOOST
NEO
GROTESK
REGULAR

ABC123
ABCDEFGHIJKLMNO
PQRSTUVWXYZ

abcdefghijklmnopqrstuvwxyz
/1234567890

BOOST
NEO
GROTESK
BOLD

ABC123
ABCDEFGHIJKLMNO
PQRSTUVWXYZ

abcdefghijklmnopqrstuvwxyz
/1234567890

momentum while elevating the aesthetic value and strengthening the design sustainability. The result was an improved, recognisable identity that was more relevant to a discerning young audience.

Over the years Boost used celebrities from different backgrounds as its brand ambassadors; and though different, the values and attitudes among them were pervasive. ATTIK's goal was to create a system that would showcase these celebrities, but also seamlessly feature the consumer as hero in identical scenarios. The art direction for the Boost "hero" photography puts the focus on the uniqueness and creativity of the individual. For portraits, a studio environment shot on clean black backgrounds, with contrast mood-lighting schemes, puts the emphasis on the subject while allowing plenty of "active black space" for messaging, additional graphics, or products. The black fields give additional edge to the new visual language as well as leveraging a unique look to the category.

ATTIK developed a unique display typeface for use across all of Boost's

Mit dem Ziel, dieses breiter gefächerte Zielpublikum auf kreative Weise anzusprechen, schufen Boost und ATTIK einen simplen Look, der sich von anderen abhob und verglichen mit anderen Mobilfunkmarken verblüffend anders wirkte.

Die neue Identität basierte auf einer Vereinfachung des ursprünglichen Boost-Logos. Die wiedererkennbaren Elemente und die Schrift des Logos wurden überarbeitet, um das Gefühl von Dynamik einzubauen und gleichzeitig den ästhetischen Wert zu heben. Das führte zu einer klareren Identität mit hohem Wiedererkennungswert, was auf ein junges, anspruchsvolles Zielpublikum bedeutsamer wirkte.

In den vergangenen Jahre hat Boost bekannte Persönlichkeiten als Markenbotschafter eingesetzt; obwohl sie alle unterschiedliche Hintergründe hatten, teilten sie doch gemeinsame Werte und Einstellungen. ATTIK machte es sich zum Ziel, ein System zu schaffen, mit dem berühmte Persönlichkeiten einerseits angemessen in Szene gesetzt werden konnten, es den Kunden aber gleichzeitig ermöglichte, nahtlos in deren Rolle zu schlüpfen und als Helden

La nouvelle identité repose sur une simplification du logo d'origine de Boost. Les éléments distinctifs et les lettres du logo ont été retravaillés pour ajouter une touche de dynamisme, tout en améliorant son esthétique et en renforçant la durabilité du concept graphique. Le résultat est une identité reconnaissable et améliorée, plus pertinente pour un public jeune et exigeant.

Au fil des ans, Boost a fait appel à des célébrités de différents horizons pour représenter la marque. Malgré leur diversité, ces personnalités avaient en commun certaines valeurs et attitudes. L'objectif d'ATTIK était de créer un système pour mettre en valeur ces célébrités, tout en plaçant de façon naturelle le consommateur comme un héros dans des scénarios identiques. La direction artistique de la photo du « héros » de Boost souligne le caractère unique et la créativité de l'individu. Pour les portraits, les prises en studio sur fond noir, contrastant avec les éclairages d'ambiance, mettent l'accent sur le sujet tout en laissant un grand « espace noir actif » pour le message,

phones with benefits

no contracts / no credit checks
boost mobile pay as you go
boostmobile.com

boost
mobile

Left & below
Model of print advertising feel

Right
Pictures of the application manual

contact more,
contract less

no contracts / no credit checks
boost mobile pay as you go
boostmobile.com

boost
mobile

deal breaker

no contracts / no credit checks
boost mobile pay as you go
boostmobile.com

boost
mobile

contract
killer

no contracts / no credit checks
boost mobile pay as you go
boostmobile.com

boost
mobile

phones

icons

boost mobile®
master brand colors

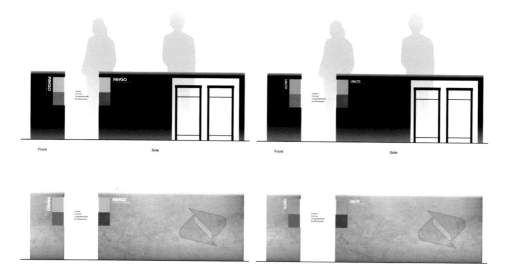

Above
Store bench examples
for PAYGO and UNLTD

consumer-facing communications.
The handcrafted letterforms capture
the aspects of momentum and fluidity
inherent in the new Boost mark. Built
from a geometric sanserif base, the
font needed to be legible for outdoor
use but easy to typeset by third-party
vendors. This new typeface, "Boost
Neo Grotesk", created a unique typo-
graphic tone claimed by no one else
in the category.

Colour definitions delineating the
Boost master-brand and distinguishing
it from other service and product
offerings further strengthen the system.
ATTIK leveraged orange for the master
brand from Boost's previous palette
and added additional colours, such as
electric green, for its PAYGO plan.
With black as a foundational colour
field this allowed flexibility for additional
colours to be used for new services,
events, or developments over time,
while maintaining the system's integrity.

In order for all the newly designed
elements to work in concert without
cancelling each other out, compositions

in identischen Szenarien zu erscheinen.
Die Art Direction für diese „Hero"-Fotoserie
konzentrierte sich auf die Einzigartigkeit
und Kreativität des Individuums. Die Port-
räts wurden im Studio vor einem einfarbig
schwarzen Hintergrund fotografiert. Beleuchtung und Einstellung schufen kontras-
tierende Stimmungen. Gleichzeitig bekam
man so ausreichend „aktiven schwarzen
Leerraum" für Werbebotschaften, weitere
Grafiken oder Produkte. Die schwarzen
Bereiche verleihen der neuen visuellen
Sprache zusätzlichen Schliff und einen in
diesem Segment unverwechselbaren Look.

ATTIK entwickelte eigens eine spezielle
Displayschrift, die in allen Kommunika-
tionskanälen eingesetzt wird, mit denen
die Kunden zu tun haben. Die von Hand
entwickelten Schriftzüge fangen Tempo,
Beschleunigung und fließende Bewegun-
gen ein – Aspekte, die für die Marke Boost
typisch sind. Der auf einer geometrischen,
serifenlosen Basis aufgebaute Font sollte auf
Außenwerbeflächen leicht lesbar sein, aber
auch gut von Drittanbietern gesetzt werden
können. Diese neue Schriftart namens
„Boost Neo Grotesk" schuf eine einzigartige

d'autres graphismes ou des produits.
Les zones noires donnent plus de tranchant
au nouveau langage visuel et confèrent
à la catégorie un style unique.

ATTIK a créé une police de caractères
unique pour l'ensemble des communications
de Boost destinées aux consommateurs. Les
formes des lettres soulignent le dynamisme
et la fluidité propres à la nouvelle marque de
Boost. Conçue à partir d'une base géométrique et sans empattement, la police devait
être lisible pour un emploi en extérieur, mais
aussi facile à composer par des fournisseurs
externes. Cette nouvelle police « Boost Neo
Grotesk » a donné jour à un style typographique unique qui se différencie de tous les
autres dans la catégorie.

Les définitions des couleurs, qui repré-
sentent la marque maîtresse de Boost et
la distinguent des autres offres de services
et de produits, renforcent encore davantage
le système. ATTIK a exploité la couleur
orange de la marque principale issue de
la palette antérieure de Boost et y a ajouté
d'autres couleurs, comme le vert électrique
pour le plan PAYGO. Le noir étant la couleur de base, il laisse beaucoup de marge

This page
Packaging, pre-paid cards, and brochure for PAYGO and UNLTD

needed to be clean and simple. These precise structures added the integrity needed to deliver on the promise of Boost's elevated offer, while embracing its already loyal customer base.

typographische Stimmung, die in diesem Marktsegment sonst niemand für sich in Anspruch nehmen konnte.

Darüber hinaus wird dieses System durch Farbdefinitionen gestärkt, die die Hauptmarke Boost näher beschreiben und sie von anderen Dienstleistungen und Produktangeboten abheben. ATTIK setzte für die Hauptmarke ein Orange aus der früheren Boost-Farbpalette ein und ergänzte für den PAYGO-Plan verschiedene weitere Farben wie z.B. Electric Green. Das Schwarz als grundlegendes Farbfeld bot genügend Flexibilität, um im Laufe der Zeit zusätzliche Farben für neue Services, Events oder Weiterentwicklungen aufnehmen zu können. Gleichzeitig blieb aber die Integrität des Systems erhalten.

Damit all die neu entworfenen Elemente gemeinsam funktionieren, ohne sich gegenseitig aufzuheben, mussten die Kompositionen klar, sauber und einfach sein. Diese präzisen Strukturen ergänzten die Integrität, die man benötigte, um das Versprechen der gehobenen Palette von Boost einzulösen und gleichzeitig auch die treuen Stammkunden zufriedenzustellen.

pour d'autres couleurs devant intervenir pour de nouveaux services, événements ou développements, tout en conservant l'intégrité du système.

Pour que tous les éléments récemment créés fonctionnent de concert sans s'annuler mutuellement, les compositions devaient être propres et simples. Ces structures précises ont apporté l'intégrité requise pour tenir la promesse d'offre supérieure de Boost, tout en englobant sa base de clients déjà fidèles.

COCOON CLUB

The Visual Experience of a Night Club

By 3deluxe

www.3deluxe.com

3deluxe Transdisciplinary Design is a German agency with offices in Wiesbaden, Hamburg, and Berlin. Their creative output ranges from architecture to brand identity, and from motion graphics to artworks. The company was formed in 1992 and today numbers over 40 professionals in its four main divisions: graphics, in/exterior, motion, and biorhythm.

3deluxe Transdisciplinary Design ist eine deutsche Agentur mit Büros in Wiesbaden, Hamburg und Berlin. Ihre kreativen Arbeiten umfassen Architektur und Markenidentität, sie reichen von Motion Graphics bis zu Artwork. Die Firma wurde 1992 gegründet und beschäftigt heute über 40 Mitarbeiter in ihren vier Hauptabteilungen Graphics, In-/Exterior, Motion und Biorhythm.

3deluxe Transdisciplinary Design est une agence allemande avec des bureaux à Wiesbaden, Hambourg et Berlin. La production créative va de l'architecture à l'identité de marque et des animations aux illustrations. L'entreprise a été créée en 1992 et rassemble aujourd'hui plus de 40 professionnels dans ses quatre principaux secteurs : graphisme, in/extérieur, animation et biorythme.

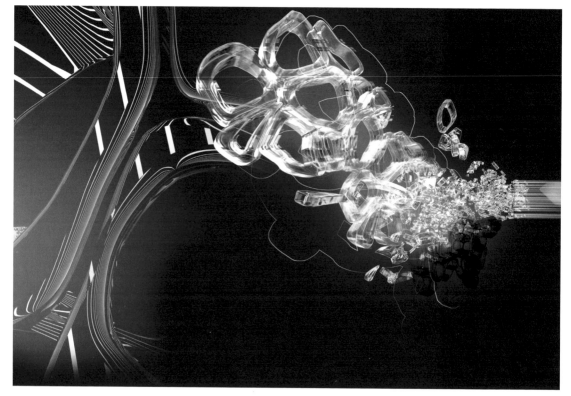

Below
Key visual for
the corporate identity

Right
"Membran" printed pane

The CocoonClub was conceived as an avant-garde field of experimentation where space and perception can be transformed. In its semi-virtual ambience diverse sensations can be experienced simultaneously. The highly complex multimedia staging submerges the space into constantly changing atmospheres; ever new virtual layers overlay the real space and generate an enhanced, concentrated reality.

In an interdisciplinary process we designed all elements to form a holistic space in which architecture, a graphic programme as well as media and web design influenced each other reciprocally.

Membran: The ornamentally printed panes of the three Cocoons that are closed off on both sides allow the gaze to fall directly on to the DJ booth. The so-called VIP Cocoons can be reserved exclusively for one night; they are modern loges, providing privacy for "cocooning" in the midst of a semi-public environment.

InBetween: The InBetween connects the main floor to the two restaurants, a lounge, and the entrance area as an atmospheric mood zone. A cherry blossom motif covers

Der CocoonClub wurde als Experimentierfeld für die Transformation von Raum und Wahrnehmung konzipiert. In seinem semivirtuell gestalteten Ambiente werden verschiedenartige Sinneseindrücke simultan erlebbar. Die hochkomplexe multimediale Inszenierung taucht den Raum in sich konstant wandelnde Atmosphären; immer neue, virtuelle Schichten überlagern den Realraum und bringen so eine erweiterte, verdichtete Wirklichkeit hervor – die Wahrnehmung der Besucher wird für die Dauer ihres Aufenthalts im CocoonClub verändert.

In dem für uns charakteristischen interdisziplinären Prozess haben wir alle Elemente zu einem ganzheitlichen Raum gestaltet, in dem sich Architektur, grafisches Programm sowie Medien- und Webdesign wechselseitig beeinflussen.

Membran: Durch die ornamental bedruckten Scheiben der drei beidseitig geschlossenen Cocoons blickt man direkt auf die DJ-Kanzel. Die so genannten VipCocoons können exklusiv für einen Abend gemietet werden; als moderne Logen erlauben sie den privaten Zustand des „cocooning" inmitten eines halböffentlichen Umfeldes.

Le CocoonClub a été créé comme une zone d'expérimentation d'avant-garde permettant de transformer l'espace et la perception. Dans son atmosphère semi-virtuelle, diverses sensations peuvent être éprouvées à la fois. Une mise en scène multimédia des plus complexes submerge l'espace dans des ambiances en perpétuelle évolution : de nouvelles couches virtuelles recouvrent l'espace réel et créent une réalité à la fois dense et étendue.

Au cours d'un processus interdisciplinaire, nous avons conçu tous les éléments de façon à créer un espace holistique dans lequel l'architecture, un programme de graphisme et le design Web et multimédia se sont mutuellement influencés.

Membrane : grâce aux panneaux aux motifs ornementaux des trois Cocoons fermés de chaque côté, le regard se pose directement sur la cabine du DJ. Les fameux Cocoons VIP peuvent être réservés en exclusivité pour une nuit : ces salons modernes permettent un « cocooning » en toute intimité au milieu d'un environnement semi-public.

Left
Visual for the toilets

Below
Main logo

Right
Interior design for
the lounge area InBetween

the walls and floors as well as the furniture in the lounge: a photograph of Japanese cherry blossoms in different stages of blooming was converted to eight colours digitally, to be painted by hand and then transferred back into an analogue medium.

Toilets: The reduced design in the sanitary facilities creates a counterpoint to the opulence in the club interior. Only the pinkish-violet toilet partitions stand out in colour and design against the anthracite grey and rough texture of the wall tiles that lend the space an almost archaic feel – they are printed with a pattern of mirrored pine branches that create a kaleidoscope-like impression.

Key Visual for MainFloor: For the club as well as both of the incorporated restaurants a key visual was designed as an interpretation of the architectonic key elements in order to make the atmosphere of each room tangible in terms of graphic design. The pore-like structure of the membrane wall forms the basis for the key visual of the club area.

Invitation: Invitations enclosed in an envelope of SoftTouch material with special tactile appeal were distributed in the course

InBetween: Das InBetween verbindet als eine atmosphärische Zwischenzone den MainFloor mit den beiden Restaurants, einer Lounge und dem Eingangsbereich. Ein Kirschblütenmotiv überzieht Wand- und Bodenflächen der Lounge: Eine Fotografie japanischer Zierkirschen in unterschiedlichen Phasen des Aufblühens wurde zunächst digital in acht Farben umgesetzt, um sodann von Hand gemalt und somit wieder in ein analoges Medium übertragen zu werden.

Toiletten: Das reduzierte Design der Sanitärräume bildet einen Ausgleich zum opulent inszenierten Clubbereich. Einziger farblicher und grafischer Akzent in dem durch die anthrazitgraue Farbe und die raue Textur der gefliesten Wände nahezu archaisch wirkenden Raum sind die pink-violetten Toilettentrennwände – sie sind mit einem unendlichen Muster aus mehrfach gespiegelten Kiefernzweigen bedruckt, die einen kaleidoskophaften Eindruck erzeugen.

Key-Visual MainFloor: Für den Club sowie die beiden dazugehörigen Restaurants *Micro* und *Silk* wurde jeweils ein Key-Visual gestaltet, das als Interpretation architektonischer Schlüsselelemente die

InBetween : InBetween relie l'étage principal aux deux restaurants, à un salon et à la zone d'entrée sous forme d'espace d'ambiance. Un motif de cerisier orne les murs, le sol et le mobilier du salon. Une photographie de cerisiers japonais à différents stades de floraison a été convertie de façon numérique en huit couleurs en vue d'être peinte à la main, avant d'être repassée sur un support analogique.

Toilettes : le design minimaliste des toilettes crée un contrepoint à l'opulence de l'intérieur du club. Seules les divisions violet rosé tranchent par leur couleur et leur design sur le gris anthracite et la texture rugueuse des carreaux au mur, ce qui donne à l'espace un air presque archaïque. Elles sont décorées d'un motif de branches de pin qui se reflète et crée une impression de kaléidoscope.

Image clé pour l'étage principal : pour le club et les deux restaurants à l'intérieur, l'image clé a été pensée comme l'interprétation des principaux éléments architectoniques, afin de rendre tangible l'ambiance de chaque salle en matière de design

of the opening of the CocoonClub on July 16, 2004. The slipcase with perforations for opening contained 24 individually designed inlay cards that showed computer visualisations of the club or graphic artworks.

Brochure: The brochure for the invitation of sponsors shows all areas as 3D-visualisations in the context of their corporate design. To emphasise the multi-faceted layout with a material aesthetic, special papers with several layers of colour were used.

The ornamental patterns on the inside of the cover and on the front are derived from natural motifs which were mirrored and arranged in sequences. They appear in different areas of the club.

Each section is introduced with the respective key visual and the word and design mark. A pictogram allows for the spatial integration of the presented area into the constructional whole.

In the chapter "Silk", a transparent leaf printed with the pink key visual was added.

Web Visual: The elaborate website also integrates the key visuals as graphic realisations of the architectural elements into its design concept. On the content level, differ-

Raumatmosphäre im Grafikdesign erfahrbar macht. Die Basis für das Key-Visual des Clubbereichs bildet die porenartige Lochstruktur der Membranwand.

Einladungen: Anlässlich der Eröffnung des CocoonClub am 16. Juli 2004 wurden Einladungen in einem Umschlag aus haptisch reizvollem SoftTouch-Material versandt. Der gestanzte Schuber enthielt 24 individuell gelayoutete Einlegekarten, die Computervisualisierungen des Clubs oder Grafik-Artworks und visuelle Experimente zeigten.

Broschüre: Die Broschüre zur Sponsorenakquise präsentiert sämtliche Räumlichkeiten im Rahmen ihres Corporate Designs als 3D-Visualisierungen. Um das vielschichtige Layout durch eine materielle Ästhetik zu unterstreichen, wurden Spezialpapiere mit mehreren Farbschichten verwendet.

Die Ornamentmuster auf Umschlaginnenseite und Titel sind durch Spiegelung und Aneinanderreihung naturentlehnter Motive entstanden. Sie finden sich in verschiedenen Bereichen des Clubs wieder.

graphique. La structure évoquant des pores des murs de la membrane sert de base à l'image clé de la zone du club.

Invitation : les invitations glissées dans une enveloppe douce et agréable au toucher ont été distribuées lors de l'ouverture du CocoonClub le 16 juillet 2004. L'étui, doté de perforations pour l'ouverture, contenait 24 cartes avec incrustations et au design unique, présentant des vues générées par ordinateur du club et des illustrations.

Brochure : la brochure pour inviter les sponsors montre tous les espaces sous forme de représentations en 3D dans le contexte du design. Pour mettre en valeur la composition variée avec une esthétique matérielle, des papiers spéciaux de plusieurs couches de couleur ont été employés.

Les motifs ornementaux à l'intérieur de la couverture et au devant proviennent de formes naturelles qui ont été copiées et composées en séquences. Ils se retrouvent à différents endroits dans le club.

Chaque section est introduite avec l'image clé, la marque et le design correspondants. Un pictogramme permet de

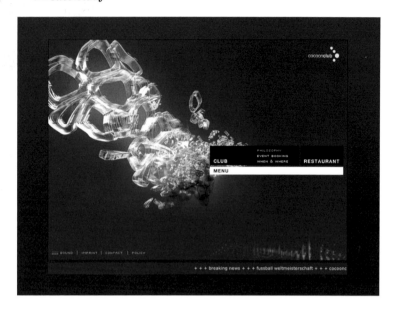

Left
Website for CocoonClub
www.cocoonclub.net

Right
Web visual

ent categories are associated with one of the spatial sections of the club. The atmosphere of each space is transferred into the Internet presence in the form of flash animations and extended by subtly placed interactive elements. Once again, the design disciplines – interior, media, and graphic as well as web design – interpenetrate each other.

Micro: The ClubRestaurant *Micro* is visually connected to the MainFloor by means of a glass front; at the interface, an atmospheric transition zone is created where reflections of the two formally divergent sections are overlaid. The effect of atmospheric concentration through overlaying infuses almost all elements of the restaurant design.

By means of its austere geometrical language of forms, the ClubRestaurant *Micro* contrasts effectively with the club area and its organic design. At the glass front which visually connects the *Micro* to the MainFloor an atmospheric interspace is created in which design elements of both sections overlap.

Jedes Kapitel wird mit dem entsprechenden Key-Visual und der Wort-Bild-Marke eingeleitet. Ein Piktogramm ermöglicht die räumliche Einordnung des dargestellten Bereichs in das bauliche Gesamtgefüge.

In das Kapitel „Silk" wurde eine mit dem pinkfarbenen Key-Visual bedruckte Transparentfolie als Zwischenblatt eingefügt.

Webvisual: Auch die aufwändig gestaltete Website bezieht die Key-Visuals als grafische Umsetzung architektonischer Elemente des Clubdesigns konzeptionell in die Gestaltung mit ein. Auf der inhaltlichen Ebene sind unterschiedliche Rubriken jeweils einem räumlichen Abschnitt des Clubs zugeordnet. Die Raumatmosphäre jedes einzelnen Bereichs wird durch Flashanimationen in den Internetauftritt transferiert und durch subtil platzierte interaktive Elemente erweitert. Erneut durchdringen sich so die einzelnen Gestaltungsdisziplinen Interior, Medien- und Grafik- sowie Webdesign.

Mirco: Das Clubrestaurant *Micro* steht über eine Glasfront in direkter visueller Beziehung zum MainFloor; an dieser Schnittstelle entsteht eine Übergangszone, an der sich die beiden formal divergenten

placer la zone présentée dans l'ensemble de la construction.

Au chapitre « Silk », une feuille transparente imprimée avec l'image clé en rose a été ajoutée.

Image Web : le site Web recherché inclut aussi dans son design les images clés sous forme de représentations graphiques des éléments d'architecture. Au niveau du contenu, diverses catégories sont associées à l'un des espaces du club. L'ambiance de chaque espace se retrouve sur Internet sous forme d'animations Flash ; elle est prolongée à l'aide d'éléments interactifs placés de façon subtile. Là encore, les disciplines de design (d'intérieur, multimédia et graphique, ainsi que Web) sont interdépendantes.

Micro : le ClubRestaurant *Micro* est visuellement connecté à l'étage principal grâce à une devanture vitrée. À la rencontre des deux espaces se trouve une zone de transition d'ambiance, où se superposent les reflets des deux sections divergentes. L'effet de cette ambiance obtenue par superposition inspire quasiment tous les aspects de design du restaurant.

Above
Interior design for
the BedRestaurant *Silk*

Right
CD packaging for the
compilation "silk pearls"

Below
Logo for the BedRestaurant *Silk*

micro

Above
Logo for the ClubRestaurant *Micro*

Right
Drinks and meals menus in
the formats of sound carriers:
12" LP, 10" record, 7" Single,
and 5" CD

Below
Interior design of
the ClubRestaurant *Micro*

Graphic Micro: The *Micro* key visual results from computer-simulated projections overlaid on to the string matrix. During the interdisciplinary design process the graphic once again became part of the real space as a photo print wallpaper.

The design of the drinks and meals menus refers to the formats of sound carriers: 12" LP, 10" record, 7" Single and 5" CD.

Silk: In BedRestaurant *Silk*, eating and drinking is elevated to the level of an artistic ceremony based on Asian and ancient eating habits. Soft materials, soft pulsing light, and bright colours define the atmosphere that, as on the MainFloor and in *Micro*, is defined by the overlaying of real and virtual design elements.

Graphic Silk: The key visual quotes the lightness of the gauze curtains and the changing light colours on their surfaces. Silky, flowing forms refer to the name of the restaurant. The cover artwork for the digipack of the compilation "silk pearls" released in 2006 is composed of the key visual and a grid of silver printed circular decorations. The labels of the two CDs

Bereiche durch Einspiegelung überlagern. Der Effekt der atmosphärischen Verdichtung durch Überlagerung durchzieht nahezu alle Elemente des Restaurantdesigns.

Graphic Micro: Das Key-Visual des *Micro* resultiert aus computersimulierten Projektionen in der Fadenmatrix. Im Verlauf des interdisziplinären Entwurfsprozesses wurde die Grafik als Fotoprint-Tapete wieder Teil des Realraums. Das Design der Speise- und Getränkekarten spielt mit den Formaten von Tonträgern: 12"-LP, 10"-Ten Inch, 7"-Single und 5"-CD.

Silk: Im BedRestaurant *Silk* wird Essen und Trinken zu einer kunstvoll inszenierten Zeremonie erhoben, die in Anlehnung an asiatische, aber auch an antike Esskulturen konzipiert wurde. Weiche Materialien, sanft pulsierendes Licht und helle Farben bestimmen die Atmosphäre, die wie im CocoonClub und dem *Micro* durch die Überlagerung realer und virtueller Gestaltungselemente geprägt ist.

Graphic Silk: Das Key-Visual des *Silk* zitiert die Leichtigkeit der Gazevorhänge und die in ihnen changierenden Lichtfarben. Seidig fließende Formen verweisen

Grâce au langage géométrique austère des formes, le ClubRestaurant *Micro* contraste de façon réussie avec la zone du club et son design organique. À l'avant vitré, qui connecte visuellement le *Micro* et l'étage principal, se trouve un espace d'ambiance dans lequel les éléments de design des deux sections se chevauchent.

Graphisme Micro : l'image clé du *Micro* est obtenue par des projections simulées par ordinateur qui se superposent à la matrice. Lors du processus de design interdisciplinaire, l'aspect graphique a une fois de plus été intégré à l'espace réel avec un papier peint à partir d'une photo.

Le design des menus de boissons et de plats fait référence aux formats des ondes porteuses de sons : 33 tours 12", 45 tours 10", single 7" et CD 5".

Silk : dans BedRestaurant *Silk*, la restauration est élevée au niveau d'une cérémonie artistique basée sur des traditions asiatiques et anciennes. Des matériaux délicats, une lumière douce à impulsions et des couleurs vives créent l'ambiance qui, comme à l'étage

Left
Invitation: 24 individually
designed inlay cards enclosed
in an envelope

Right
Promotional material

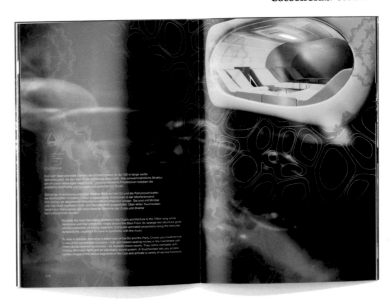

were also printed with the decorative grid
which is raised like a relief from the pink
cover layer.

auf den Namen des Restaurants. Das
Cover-Artwork für das Digipack der 2006
veröffentlichten Compilation „silk pearls"
setzt sich aus dem Key-Visual und einem
Raster aus silberfarben unterdruckten
Kreisornamenten zusammen. Das Label
der beiden CDs wurde ebenfalls mit dem
Ornamentraster unterdruckt, das unter der
pinkfarbenen Deckfarbschicht reliefartig
hervortritt.

principal et dans le *Micro*, se caractérise
par la superposition d'éléments de design
réels et virtuels.

Graphisme Silk : l'image clé transmet la
légèreté des rideaux de gaze et les couleurs
de lumière changeante de leur surface. Des
formes soyeuses et flottantes renvoient au
nom du restaurant. L'illustration en couverture pour le digipack de la compilation
« silk pearls » publiée en 2006 se com-
pose de l'image clé et d'une grille de déco-
rations circulaires argentées. Les étiquettes
des deux CD ont aussi été imprimées avec
la grille décorative, qui se détache comme
un relief de la couverture rose.

ECO BRANDING

How Branding and Design Are Going Hand in Hand To Shape the Future of Entire Companies

By Frederico Gelli, Tátil Design

www.tatil.com.br

Frederico Gelli is the leading name in branding and sustainable design in his native Brazil, working today for clients around the world such as Nokia, Coca-Cola, Procter & Gamble, among many others. His consultancy firm, Tátil, has over 20 years of successful history and has been awarded projects linking brands to coherent environmental policies.

Frederico Gelli ist in seinem Heimatland Brasilien der führende Name im Hinblick auf Markenbildung und nachhaltiges Design. Heute arbeitet er für Kunden in der ganzen Welt, wie Nokia, Coca-Cola, Procter & Gamble u. v. a. m. Sein Beratungsunternehmen Tátil blickt auf eine über zwanzigjährige Erfolgsgeschichte zurück und wurde für Projekte ausgezeichnet, die Marken mit einer schlüssigen Umweltpolitik verknüpfen.

Frederico Gelli est la figure de marque du branding et du design durable de son Brésil natal ; il travaille aujourd'hui pour des clients du monde entier comme Nokia, Coca-Cola et Procter & Gamble, entre autres. Au fil de ses 20 ans de réussite, sa société de conseil Tátil s'est vu attribuer des projets associant des marques à des stratégies environnementales cohérentes.

Left & right
Laser-printed real leaves with
computerised images

For some time now our planet has been sending messages that the effects of 20th-Century excesses are becoming unworkable and demand a profound transformation in our relationship with consumption and, accordingly, with brands.

This new reality brings an enormous challenge to the creativity of capitalism. The logic of profit at any price and the economic model of win – lose, where 10 percent of the population enjoys the profits of the system, and 90 percent lives in adverse conditions, is a philosophy of numbered days.

Essentially, brand survival will depend on their ability to occupy a new place in society and in the hearts and minds of people. At the market level, this will define "sustainability" in its truest sense.

We must separate the concept of *sustainable* from the traditional, small-scale, and alternative and establish a fusion between ECOLOGY and TECHNOLOGY. After all, becoming sustainable does not imply a return to the Stone Age.

More than just being about environmental issues, the new business logic will have to account for a contract of interdependence

Schon seit einiger Zeit sendet unser Planet Warnsignale aus, dass die Auswirkungen der Exzesse des 20. Jahrhunderts nicht mehr zu bewältigen sind und wir unser Verhältnis zum Konsum sowie auch unseren Umgang mit Marken grundlegend werden ändern müssen.

Diese neue Realität stellt die Kreativität des Kapitalismus vor eine enorme Herausforderung. Die Logik des Profits um jeden Preis und des ökonomischen Gewinner-Verlierer-Modells, bei dem 10 Prozent der Erdbevölkerung Nutznießer des Systems sind, während 90 Prozent unter nachteiligen Bedingungen leben, ist eine Philosophie, deren Tage gezählt sind.

Im Wesentlichen wird das Überleben von Marken davon abhängen, inwieweit sie fähig sein werden, einen neuen Platz in der Gesellschaft und im Bewusstsein der Menschen einzunehmen. Dies wird den Begriff „Nachhaltigkeit" im wahrsten Sinne des Wortes definieren.

Das *Konzept der Nachhaltigkeit* ist nicht mit der traditionellen alternativen Lebensweise im kleinen Maßstab gleich-

Depuis quelque temps, notre planète envoie des messages pour dire que les conséquences des excès du XXᵉ siècle deviennent insoutenables : elles demandent une profonde transformation de nos relations en matière de consommation, et donc avec les marques.

Cette nouvelle réalité suppose un défi de taille pour la créativité du capitalisme. La logique du profit à tout prix et le modèle économique de gagnant-perdant, où 10 % de la population tire parti du système et 90 % vit dans des conditions défavorables, symbolisent une philosophie aux jours comptés.

La survie des marques dépendra essentiellement de la capacité d'occuper une nouvelle place dans la société et dans le cœur et l'esprit des gens. Au niveau du marché, il faudra un « développement durable » dans son sens le plus littéral.

Nous devons distinguer le concept de *durable* de celui de traditionnel, à petite échelle et alternatif, et trouver la fusion entre ÉCOLOGIE et TECHNOLOGIE. Après tout, devenir durable ne demande pas forcément de revenir à l'âge de la pierre.

among all stakeholders. Companies will no longer be able to prosper without considering their socio-environmental impact. They will have to take responsibility for their entire performance chain and invest a considerable part of their expertise and energy so that, ultimately, their existence as part of this ecosystem is relevant and contributes to the well-being of everyone.

This is why we believe that branding and design tools can help – and in a big way. For such a process of profound change to take place positively, this new entrepreneurial approach must be constructed on the basis of real brand vocations. There will be no set formula for making brands and companies "sustainable". Each brand within each company will have to find its own way.

I believe in Branding Version 3.0, with its broadened outlook and freedom from hackneyed, constraining practices. Branding that throws itself unconditionally into the world of the brand, the market, and most of all, the world of people who interact with the brand on all levels, and who, ultimately, ensure its existence. These are

zusetzen; vielmehr geht es um eine Fusion von *Ökologie* und *Technologie*; dennoch impliziert es nicht die Rückkehr in die Steinzeit.

Es geht nicht nur um Umweltfragen. In dieser neuen Geschäfts-Ethik muss ein Unternehmen für einen Kontrakt der gegenseitigen Abhängigkeit unter allen Anteilseignern sorgen. Unternehmen können nicht weiter erfolgreich sein, ohne die eigenen sozio-ökonomischen Auswirkungen auf die Umwelt in Betracht zu ziehen. Sie werden die Verantwortung für die gesamte Produktions- und Leistungskette übernehmen und Kompetenz und Energie investieren müssen, damit ihre Existenz als Teil dieses Ökosystems bedeutungsvoll und relevant bleibt und zum Wohlergehen aller beiträgt.

Wir sind daher der Ansicht, dass Branding- und Design-Instrumente hilfreich sein können. Damit ein solcher Prozess des Wandels auf positive Weise stattfindet, muss dieser neue unternehmerische Ansatz auf Basis einer echten Selbstverpflichtung durch die Marken geschaffen werden. Es wird keine vorgegebene Formel geben,

Au-delà des questions concernant l'environnement, la nouvelle logique commerciale devra constituer un contrat d'interdépendance entre toutes les parties prenantes. Les entreprises ne pourront plus prospérer sans tenir compte de leur impact socio-environnemental. Elles devront assumer la responsabilité de l'ensemble de leur chaîne logistique et investir une partie considérable de leur savoir et énergie pour que leur présence au sein de l'écosystème soit au final pertinente et contribue au bien-être de tous.

C'est pourquoi nous pensons que les outils de branding et de design peuvent être utiles, et ce dans une large mesure. Pour qu'un changement si profond se déroule de façon positive, cette nouvelle approche des entreprises doit reposer sur la base de véritables vocations de marque. Il n'y a pas de formule établie pour rendre les marques et les entreprises « durables ». Chaque marque de chaque entreprise devra trouver sa propre voie.

Je crois au branding version 3.0, avec une perspective plus large et libéré des pratiques contraignantes et rebattues. Un branding qui se lance inconditionnellement

Left
Seat produced with recycled material

Right
Tátil's bamboo pen-drive

the people who soon will no longer accept the reductionist nickname of "consumers", and who will help brands find a new direction.

New requirements... new desires... new expectations. The "buy now" era of cheap persuasion, built on the tyranny of brand economic power where products are imposed on consumers under savage market forces, is finished. Conscious consumption, which is already a reality in many niche markets, will demand much more from companies and their marketing partners.

The nature of this partnership is already undergoing a profound transformation. Traditional publicity agencies and their accompanying fanfare are losing ground, setting the stage for more strategic partners who will abandon the superficial brand level and aim at the brand essence, their real and sustainable relationship with society. Brands that think of the business as a whole, considering the magnitude of the innovation more than the extent of marketing, not just helping to sell more of "anything", but to construct

um Marken und Firmen „nachhaltig" zu machen. Jede Marke eines Unternehmens wird ihren eigenen Weg finden müssen.

Ich glaube an das Branding Version 3.0 mit seiner Perspektive, die frei ist von einschränkenden Praktiken. Ein Branding, das sich bedingungslos in die Welt der Marken, des Marktes und der Menschen begibt, die mit der Marke interagieren und letzten Endes deren Existenz sicherstellen. Das sind die Leute, die nicht mehr länger darauf reduziert werden möchten, „Konsumenten" zu sein, und dabei helfen, dass Marken eine neue Ausrichtung bekommen.

Neue Anforderungen ... neue Begehrlichkeiten ... neue Erwartungen. Nun ist sie vorbei, die billige Konsumentenbeeinflussung der „Kaufen Sie jetzt"-Ära, die auf der Tyrannei ökonomischer Markenmacht beruht und die den Verbrauchern Produkte aufzwingt. Bewusster Konsum, in vielen Nischenmärkten bereits Realität, wird Unternehmen und ihren Marketing-Partnern deutlich mehr abverlangen als bisher.

Bereits die Natur dieser Partnerschaft muss sich einem grundlegenden Wandel unterziehen. Die traditionellen Werbe-

dans le monde de la marque, le marché et surtout l'univers des personnes qui interagissent avec la marque à tous les niveaux et qui en assurent en fin de compte l'existence. Ces personnes n'accepteront bientôt plus le qualificatif réductionniste de « consommateurs » et aideront les marques à prendre la bonne direction.

Nouvelles exigences... nouveaux désirs... nouvelles attentes. L'ère de « l'achat immédiat », de persuasion au rabais, basée sur la tyrannie du pouvoir économique des marques, où les produits sont imposés aux consommateurs par des forces commerciales sauvages, cette ère est bien révolue. La consommation consciente, qui est déjà une réalité dans de nombreux créneaux, exigera beaucoup plus aux entreprises et à leurs partenaires de marketing.

La nature de ce partenariat est déjà l'objet d'une profonde transformation. Les agences de publicité traditionnelles et la fanfare qui les accompagne perdent du terrain, laissant place à des partenaires plus stratégiques qui abandonneront le niveau superficiel de la marque pour en prendre l'essence comme objectif, la relation véritable

41

a new vision of what to sell, to whom, and in compensation for the system as a whole. We are duty-bound to undertake this deep re-examination of our ecosystem.

Once the direction is established, and with the "branding compass" showing us the way, design can take centre stage, with its multidisciplinary inclination, integrating and assimilating diverse areas of expertise and information: from anthropology to engineering, from psychology to the research of new materials. The design DNA is manifold and boundary-crossing. It will make a profound contribution to a landscape where economic and technological innovations will have to pay close attention to new requirements and innovative practices.

We are facing the enormous challenge of scrutinising our ideas of well-being and development, and we will need to have intelligent and attractive alternatives, with solutions that are ECOEDUCATIONAL and no longer ECOBORING. This is about pursuing ideas of low environmental but high sensory impact.

agenturen und ihre Lobeshymnen werden an Boden verlieren und die Bühne strategischen Partnern überlassen, die auf die Essenz einer Marke und auf deren nachhaltige Beziehung mit der Gesellschaft, abzielen. Sie berücksichtigen das Ausmaß der Innovation mehr als den Umfang des Marketings. Sie helfen nicht einfach nur dabei, dass „mehr" von allem verkauft werden kann, sondern konstruieren eine neue Vision dessen, was an wen und als Kompensation für das System als Ganzes verkauft werden soll. Wir sind dazu verpflichtet, diese tief greifende Neuuntersuchung unseres Ökosystems vorzunehmen.

Wenn die Richtung erst einmal festgelegt ist und der „Branding-Kompass" uns den Weg zeigt, kann Design mit multidisziplinären Ausrichtungen und der Integration und Assimilation unterschiedlicher Kompetenz- und Informationsbereiche in den Mittelpunkt rücken: Das reicht von der Anthropologie zum Ingenieurswesen und von der Psychologie zur Forschung nach neuen Materialien. Es wird einen grundlegenden Beitrag zu einer neuen Landschaft leisten, in der ökonomische und

et durable avec la société. Des marques qui ont une approche commerciale globale et prennent davantage en compte l'ampleur de l'innovation que l'étendue du marketing, en tentant non pas de vendre plus de « rien » mais de construire une nouvelle vision de ce qu'il faut vendre, à qui et en compensation du système dans son ensemble. Nous sommes tenus d'entreprendre ce nouvel examen approfondi de notre écosystème.

Une fois la direction décidée, avec la « boussole du branding » marquant le chemin, le design peut occuper une place centrale grâce à sa propension multidisciplinaire, en intégrant et en rapprochant plusieurs domaines de savoir-faire et d'information : de l'anthropologie à l'ingénierie, de la psychologie à la recherche de nouveaux matériaux. L'ADN du design est infini et traverse les frontières. Il sera d'une aide précieuse pour un paysage où les innovations économiques et technologiques devront prêter attention aux nouvelles exigences et pratiques innovantes.

Nous sommes confrontés au défi de taille d'examiner à la loupe nos idées de bien-être et de développement, et nous

Left & right
Package design for Natura
with recycled materials

The idea that "sustainable development" would create a world of self-denial with regard to comfort, resources, and pleasures is a myth created by the superficiality of supposed green solutions that have saturated the world with tasteless, meaningless, and unattractive *ecokitsch*, in the name of marketing that is vacuous and actually very unsustainable.

It is clear that we are talking about a paradigm shift, about a new relationship with the physical and material world. Brands will occupy new spaces: they will have more cultural relevance, a social role, and much more environmental responsibility. Their strength with respect to business will derive from the integration of these three aspects. New consumers… new brands … new ways of communication. Products and services designed in partnership with this new consumer, who might gain new status in a society evolving from one that consumes to one that uses, with an enormous range of products transformed into services and following a trend without regressing from economic dematerialisation.

technologische Innovationen aufmerksam im Hinblick auf neue Anforderungen und innovative Praktiken entwickelt werden.

Wir stehen vor der enormen Herausforderung, alle unsere Vorstellungen von Wohlergehen und Entwicklung eingehend unter die Lupe nehmen zu müssen. Wir werden intelligente Alternativen brauchen, und dafür benötigen wir Lösungen, die das ökologische Bewusstsein bilden und sich nicht in billigen, langweiligen Öko-Slogans erschöpfen. Es geht um Konzepte, die die Umwelt möglichst wenig belasten und die dennoch möglichst sinnlich wirken können.

Die Vorstellung, dass „nachhaltige Entwicklung" zu einer Welt der Selbstverleugnung ohne Komfort, Ressourcen und die angenehmen Seiten des Lebens führen würde, ist ein Mythos. Er wurde aus oberflächlichen Lösungen geboren, die die Welt im Namen eines geistlosen Marketings mit geschmacklosem und bedeutungslosem Ökokitsch überschwemmt haben.

Klar ist, dass wir hier von einem Paradigmenwechsel sprechen. Marken werden neue Räume einnehmen: Sie werden über eine größere kulturelle Relevanz verfügen,

aurons besoin de solutions intelligentes et attirantes, ÉCOÉDUCATIONNELLES et non plus ÉCOENNUYEUSES. Il faut exploiter les idées d'un impact faible sur l'environnement mais hautement sensoriel.

L'idée que le « développement durable » pourrait déboucher un jour sur un monde d'abnégation en matière de confort, de ressources et de plaisirs est un mythe créé par la superficialité des solutions soidisant vertes : elles ont saturé le monde d'un *écokitsch* insipide, dénué de sens et peu séduisant, au nom du marketing vide et en rien durable.

Il est évident que se joue un changement de paradigme, une nouvelle relation avec le monde physique et matériel. Les marques occuperont de nouveaux espaces : elles revêtiront une plus grande importance culturelle, joueront un rôle social et endosseront une responsabilité accrue envers l'environnement. Leur force sur le plan commercial tiendra à l'intégration de ces trois aspects. Nouveaux consommateurs… nouvelles marques… nouveaux modes de communication. Des produits et des services conçus en collaboration avec ce

Above & right
Gift set for Natura

Below
Herbal-based cosmetic
line for Natura

Right
Nokia Button in use

Below
The Nokia Button

Bottom
Detail of the plastic base

From consumer to beneficiary

The importance is not in possessing, but enjoying. Putting aside the myth of possession in return for enjoyment may be the greatest behavioural challenge for this new consumer.

Of course, marketing has a fundamental role in the construction of this new scenario: it will have to help sell the idea that rather than owning one under-utilised SUV in the garage, with all the costs and effects that come with having such a "benefit", it is far better to enjoy many different models of cars suitable for various occasions, rented from new auto rental/sharing companies. Or even the idea that it's much *cooler* to use a super-cellphone with all bells and whistles for five years, with virtual upgrades, than it is to replace a device every six months just for the sake of following a fashion fad.

The vanguard brands, those looking for new solutions to these challenges, will create reference points for the rest, and, with the onus and bonus that go with being a pioneer, will inaugurate a new business world model, allowing beneficiaries

über eine soziale Rolle und ein größeres Verantwortungsbewusstsein gegenüber der Umwelt. Ihre geschäftliche Stärke wird sich aus der Integration dieser drei Aspekte herleiten: neue Konsumenten, neue Verbraucher, neue Kommunikationswege. Produkte und Dienste, die in Partnerschaft mit diesen neuen Konsumenten entworfen werden, könnten in einer Gesellschaft, die nicht konsum- sondern verwendungsorientiert ist, einen neuen Status erringen. Dazu steht eine enorme Bandbreite von Produkten zur Verfügung, die einem Trend folgen, ohne sich zurückzuentwickeln zu einer ökonomischen Entmaterialisierung.

Vom Konsumenten zum Berechtigten

Wirklich wichtig ist nicht der Besitz von Dingen, sondern ihr Genuss. Dass er den Mythos des Besitzens ablegt und dafür in den Genuss von etwas kommt, könnte für den neuen Konsumenten die größte Herausforderung in seiner Entwicklung werden.

Natürlich spielt das Marketing eine fundamentale Rolle in diesem neuen Szenario. Es wird dabei helfen müssen zu vermitteln,

nouveau consommateur, qui peut conquérir un nouveau statut dans une société passant de la consommation à l'utilisation, avec une très large gamme de produits devenus services et suivant une tendance n'allant pas au-delà de la dématérialisation économique.

De consommateur à bénéficiaire

L'important n'est pas de posséder, mais de profiter. Mettre de côté le mythe de la possession en échange du plaisir peut s'avérer être pour ce nouveau consommateur le défi le plus difficile en matière de comportement.

Le marketing joue évidemment un rôle clé dans l'élaboration de ce nouveau scénario : il devra aider à vendre l'idée qu'au lieu d'avoir une voiture de sport rarement utilisée au garage, avec les frais et les conséquences d'un tel « privilège », mieux vaut profiter de différents modèles de voitures adaptés à chaque occasion, à louer auprès de nouvelles agences de location/partage de véhicules. Ou encore l'idée qu'il est nettement plus *cool* d'utiliser pendant cinq

Left & right
Presentation of the Nokia Button

to be connected with their products, services, and communication in a balanced, fair, and sustainable way.

Cases:

<u>Nokia</u>: Nokia and Tátil have already been working together for eight years, developing solutions that are compatible with nature and the environment *(nature-friendly)* for points of sale worldwide. The Nokia Button is a central part of Nokia's merchandising portfolio. Its compact yet durable design and striking shape enable devices, accessories, and communication items to be displayed in multiple forms, positions, and combinations, conveying the concepts of innovation and high technology in a friendlier and more human environment.

<u>Natura</u>: Natura by name reflects the company's concern with sustainability. The Brazilian cosmetics company has made innovations in the sector by opting for simpler but no less attractive packaging, which uses recycled materials and creates low environmental impact in the production process. The company itself

dass einem lieber mehrere verschiedene Autos zur Verfügung stehen, die zu den jeweiligen Gelegenheiten passen und von Verleih- oder Car-Sharing-Unternehmen vermietet werden, als dass man einen wenig genutzten tollen Geländewagen in der Garage stehen hat – mit allen Kosten. Oder die Idee, dass es cooler ist, die nächsten fünf Jahre ein Handy mit allem Drum und Dran über virtuelle Upgrades zu nutzen, als das Gerät jedes halbe Jahr auszutauschen, bloß um einem Modetrend Genüge zu tun.

Markenpioniere werden für die restliche Welt Referenzpunkte schaffen. Mit aller Last und allen Vorteilen, die dem Pionierdasein eigen sind, werden sie ein neues Geschäftsmodell einführen, das den Berechtigten erlaubt, mit ihren Produkten, Dienstleistungen und Kommunikationsformen in einer fairen und nachhaltigen Weise verbunden zu sein.

Falldarstellungen

<u>Nokia</u>: Nokia und Tátil arbeiten schon seit acht Jahren zusammen und entwickeln für die weltweiten Points of Sale Lösungen, die mit Natur und Umwelt kompatibel

ans un formidable téléphone portable avec toutes les sonneries et tonalités intégrées et d'éventuelles mises à jour, que de changer d'appareil tous les six mois juste pour suivre une mode.

Les marques d'avant-garde, en quête de nouvelles solutions pour ces défis, créeront des points de référence pour les autres et, avec les obligations et les avantages propres des pionniers, inaugureront un nouveau modèle commercial, ce qui permettra aux bénéficiaires d'entretenir avec leurs produits, leur services et leur communication une relation équilibrée, juste et durable.

Cas :

<u>Nokia</u> : Nokia et Tátil travaillent ensemble depuis huit ans déjà et développent des solutions respectant la nature et l'environnement pour les points de vente à travers le monde. Le bouton Nokia représente une pièce clé dans le merchandising de Nokia. Grâce à son design à la fois compact et résistant et à sa forme étonnante, les appareils, accessoires et outils de communication peuvent se décliner sous divers aspects, positions et combinaisons, véhiculant les

Pixel-art made from bottle caps

PET bottle hangers

T-shirt stock

Floor made from smashed cans

YESTERDAY I WAS A PLASTIC BOTTLE TODAY I'M A T-SHIRT.

A smile in every sip
LIVE POSITIVELY Coca-Cola
www.livepositively.com

uses LCA (Life Cycle Assessment), which assesses the total environmental impact of the manufacture of each product, from the fuel used to transport raw materials to the way in which the product or packaging is thrown away by the consumer. A partner with Tátil Design for 10 years, Natura still invests in products made with raw materials of national biodiversity and genuinely values Brazilian traditions and expressions.

Coca-Cola: *"Live Positively"* is Coca-Cola's new way of facing the world: the company's pledge to making a positive difference for the world, redesigning how we work and live, where sustainability is part of everything the company does: forever. This global alignment is a new business strategy that starts within Coca-Cola itself, since the company believes it can't ask everyone to "live positively" without understanding what that means on a personal level. Taking that as a starting point, Coca-Cola is inviting everyone to act positively, showing that we can increase our pleasure, happiness, and passion, while maintaining awareness of the future of the world and human relations. The primary objective

sind. Der Nokia-Button ist ein wesentlicher Teil des Merchandising-Portfolios von Nokia. Durch sein kompaktes, haltbares Design und seine bestechende Form können Geräte und Accessoires in verschiedenster Weise und Kombination ausgestellt werden, was die Konzepte von Innovation und Hochtechnologie in einer freundlicheren und menschlicheren Umwelt vermittelt.

Natura: Schon der Name Natura reflektiert, dass diese Firma sich der Nachhaltigkeit verschrieben hat. Die brasilianische Kosmetikfirma hat in dieser Sparte für Innovationen gesorgt, indem sie sich für einfachere, aber dennoch attraktive Verpackungen entschieden hat, bei denen recycelte Materialien genutzt werden und während der Produktion auf eine möglichst geringe Umweltbelastung geachtet wird. Die Firma selbst arbeitet mit einer Ökobilanz (Life Cycle Assessment), die die gesamte Umweltbelastung bei der Herstellung jedes Produktes beurteilt: vom Treibstoff für den Transport von Rohmaterialien, bis zu der Art der Entsorgung durch den Verbraucher. Natura arbeitet seit 10 Jahren mit Tátil Design und investiert

concepts d'innovation et de haute technologie dans un environnement plus convivial et plus humain.

Natura : Le nom même de Natura dénote l'intérêt de l'entreprise pour le développement durable. Cette société brésilienne de produits de cosmétique a innové dans le secteur, en optant pour des emballages plus simples mais non moins attirants à base de matériaux recyclés et avec un faible impact sur l'environnement lors du processus de production. L'entreprise a recours à l'analyse du cycle de vie, qui évalue l'impact global sur l'environnement de la fabrication de chaque produit, depuis le carburant employé pour transporter les matières premières à la façon dont le produit ou l'emballage est jeté par le consommateur. Partenaire de Tátil Design depuis 10 ans, Natura ne cesse d'investir dans des produits fabriqués à partir des matières premières de la biodiversité du pays et met vraiment en valeur les traditions et les expressions du Brésil.

Coca-Cola : « *Live Positively* » est a nouvelle approche du monde par Coca-Cola : l'engagement de l'entreprise de changer le monde de façon positive en repensant

Left
Live Positively retail
promotional material

Right
Coca-Cola campaign posters

is to do more of what we love, using less of what we need. This strategy is being implemented in all sectors of the company, with Tátil being in charge of developing the guidelines for Latin America.

weiterhin in Produkte aus heimischen Materialien, die brasilianische Traditionen und Ausdrucksformen aufrichtig wertschätzen.

Coca-Cola: „Live Positively" ist der neue Weg von Coca-Cola, die Welt zu betrachten: das Gelöbnis des Unternehmens, einen positiven Unterschied für die Welt zu bewirken und die Art und Weise, wie wir arbeiten und leben, neu zu gestalten, wobei Nachhaltigkeit zu allem gehört, was die Firma anpackt. Diese Ausrichtung ist eine Strategie, die bei Coca-Cola selbst beginnt, weil das Unternehmen der Ansicht ist, man könne nicht alle auffordern, „positiv zu leben", ohne dass sie begreifen, was das auf der persönlichen Ebene bedeutet. Coca-Cola lädt alle Menschen ein, sich positiv zu verhalten und zu zeigen, dass wir unseren Genuss und unsere Leidenschaften steigern können und uns gleichzeitig der Zukunft der Welt bewusst sein können. Vorrangiges Ziel ist es, mehr von dem zu tun, was wir lieben, und dabei weniger von dem zu verbrauchen, was wir benötigen. Diese Strategie wird in allen Sektoren des Unternehmens eingeführt, wobei Tátil für die Entwicklung der Richtlinien in Lateinamerika verantwortlich ist.

notre façon de travailler et de vivre, où le développement durable est intégré à toutes les activités de la firme, et ce pour toujours. Cet alignement mondial est une nouvelle stratégie commerciale partant en interne et qui pense motiver tout le monde à « vivre de façon positive » sans comprendre ce que cela signifie au niveau personnel. Avec cet aspect comme point de départ, Coca-Cola nous invite tous à agir positivement, en montrant que nous pouvons avoir plus de plaisir, de bonheur et de passion sans perdre de vue l'avenir du monde et des relations humaines. L'objectif principal est de faire davantage ce que nous aimons avec moins de ce dont nous avons besoin. Cette stratégie est appliquée à tous les secteurs de l'entreprise, Tátil se chargeant de développer les instructions pour l'Amérique latine.

MAD: MUSEUM WITH SPIRIT

A Typographic Brand Work for the Museum of Arts and Design in New York

By Michael Bierut, Pentagram

www.pentagram.com

Michael Bierut was born in Cleveland, Ohio, and was vice-president of graphic design at Vignelli Associates before joining Pentagram as a partner in 1990. He has won hundreds of design awards and his work is represented in several permanent collections including MoMA, the Library of Congress, and the Museum für Gestaltung in Zürich.

Michael Bierut wurde in Cleveland, Ohio, geboren und war Vice President of Graphic Design bei Vignelli Associates, bevor er 1990 Partner bei Pentagram wurde. Er hat Hunderte von Designauszeichnungen gewonnen, und seine Arbeiten sind Bestandteil verschiedener Sammlungen, z.B. des MoMA, der Library of Congress und des Museums für Gestaltung in Zürich.

Michael Bierut est né à Cleveland, en Ohio et a été vice-président pour le design graphique chez Vignelli Associates, avant de rejoindre Pentagram comme partenaire en 1990. Il a remporté des centaines de prix de design et son travail est présent dans plusieurs collections permanentes, dont celles du MoMA, de la Library of Congress et du Museum für Gestaltung de Zurich.

Left
Print material

Right
Wooden game with the MAD type

In September 2008, the Museum of Arts and Design moved to an impressive new home on New York's Columbus Circle, a dramatic location where Broadway intersects with the southern and western boundaries of Central Park. Brad Cloepfil of Allied Works Architecture was commissioned to renovate a building by MoMA architect Edward Durrell Stone that had stood on the site since 1964. Prior to 2002, the Museum of Arts and Design was called the American Craft Museum; it changed its name to accommodate the growing scope of its collection. But there were doubts at the Museum that the new name had caught on. The move to Columbus Circle represented a great chance to reintroduce the institution to the public. Pentagram was commissioned to create a signage program, interactive graphics, and a new identity.

Discussions of what is craft and what is art and design aside, the Museum's acronym – MAD – is a great asset. It's short, pronounceable, and memorable. But it's also in some ways overly familiar. For example, there already is a well-known

Im September 2008 bekam das Museum of Arts and Design in New York eine beeindruckende neue Heimat am Columbus Circle, einem imposanten Standort, wo der Broadway den südlichen und westlichen Rand des Central Park berührt. Brad Cloepfil von Allied Works Architecture bekam den Auftrag, das Gebäude des MoMA-Architekten Edward Durrel Stone zu sanieren und zu renovieren, das dort seit 1964 stand. Vor 2002 trug das Museum of Arts and Design den Namen American Craft Museum. Es wurde umgetauft, um der wachsenden Bandbreite seiner Sammlung Rechnung zu tragen. Doch im Museum waren Stimmen zu hören, die bezweifelten, dass der neue Name Anklang gefunden hatte. Der Umzug an den Columbus Circle stellte eine ausgezeichnete Möglichkeit dar, der Öffentlichkeit diese Institution erneut vorzustellen. Pentagram wurde beauftragt, Beschilderungssysteme, interaktive Grafiken und eine neue Identität zu entwickeln.

Lässt man einmal die Diskussion beiseite, wie man Kunst und Design vom Kunsthandwerk abgrenzen kann, so verfügt das Museum über einen ausgezeichneten

En septembre 2008, le Museum of Arts and Design s'est installé dans un bâtiment impressionnant au Columbus Circle de New York, un emplacement spectaculaire où Broadway est à la jonction des limites sud et ouest de Central Park. Brad Cloepfil, d'Allied Works Architecture, a été chargé de renouveler le bâtiment de l'architecte du MoMA, Edward Durrell Stone, construit en 1964. Avant 2002, le Museum of Arts and Design s'appelait American Craft Museum (musée des arts appliqués américains) : son nom a changé pour s'adapter à la portée croissante de sa collection. Les responsables du musée n'étaient toutefois pas convaincus que le nouveau nom marchait. L'installation au Columbus Circle a été l'occasion rêvée de présenter à nouveau l'institution au public. Pentagram a été chargé de créer un programme de signalisation, des graphismes interactifs et une nouvelle identité.

En marge des discussions sur ce que sont les arts appliqués ainsi que l'art et le design, l'acronyme même du musée (MAD, « fou » en anglais) est un grand atout. Il est court, facile à prononcer et à

museum of arts and design

This page
Logo and the initial sketches

Right
Posters series

MAD logo, which appears on the cover of a much-loved American humor magazine. So part of our design problem was to make it surprising, less familiar, and proprietary – to come up with a MAD that could only be the Museum.

We also wanted a way of writing the name that could embody the values of the Museum, something that seemed inventive and surprising, and that could appear in different ways on different occasions. The Museum, after all, is dedicated to artists who take typical forms – say vessels, or chairs – and transform them over and over again. Our goal as we began the work was to discover some simple forms in the new logo which would permit just that kind of transformation. In short, we were looking for a very specific combination of uniqueness and flexibility.

We tried a lot of different things along the way, including changing the acronym altogether. At one point we developed an interesting linear version that echoed the ingenious system of connected light slots that Cloepfil designed in the walls, floors, and ceilings of the gallery spaces. In the

Aktivposten: Sein Akronym MAD (etwa: *verrückt, irre*) ist kurz, einprägsam und leicht auszusprechen. Doch in gewisser Hinsicht ist es auch allzu bekannt. Es gibt beispielsweise das bekannte MAD-Logo, das auf dem Cover einer in den USA beliebten und auch in Deutschland erscheinenden Satirezeitschrift prangt. Unsere Aufgabe bestand also darin, das Design u. a. überraschend, weniger vertraut und charakteristisch für das Museum zu gestalten – kurz gesagt, wir mussten uns ein MAD einfallen lassen, das nur das Museum meinen konnte.

In der Art der Namensschreibung sollten auch die Werte des Museums zum Ausdruck gebracht werden – etwas, das erfindungsreich und außergewöhnlich ist, und das zu verschiedenen Gelegenheiten auch auf unterschiedliche Weise in Erscheinung treten kann. Das Museum widmet seine Arbeit immerhin Künstlern, die bekannte Formen wie z. B. Gefäße oder Stühle in ihren Entwürfen umgestalten und immer wieder neu anpassen. Als wir mit der Arbeit begannen, hatten wir uns zum Ziel gesetzt, für das neue Logo einige

mémoriser, mais il est aussi d'une certaine façon trop familier. Par exemple, il existe déjà un célèbre logo MAD, qui apparaît sur la couverture d'une BD humoristique américaine très populaire. En partie, la difficulté du design était qu'il soit surprenant, moins familier et surtout exclusif (un MAD qui n'évoque que le musée).

Nous cherchions également une façon d'écrire un nom pouvant incarner les valeurs du musée, quelque chose qui serait à la fois inventif et surprenant, capable d'apparaître sous plusieurs formes et dans des situations diverses. Après tout, le musée est consacré à des artistes qui partent de formes typiques (par exemple des navires ou des chaises) et les transforment à volonté. Au départ, notre objectif était de trouver pour le nouveau logo des formes simples qui permettraient ce genre de transformation. Bref, nous cherchions une combinaison bien déterminée d'exclusivité et de flexibilité.

Nous avons fait de multiples essais, et avons même tenté de modifier l'acronyme lui-même. Nous sommes parvenus à un moment donné à une version linéaire inté-

end we decided to start with MAD's physical location: a more or less square building that sits on the most prominent circle in Manhattan. By combining squares and circles we came up with an alphabet that rendered a unique MAD monogram. Some people who see it are reminded as well of Edward Durrell Stone's famous – or infamous "lollipop" columns, which Cloepfil and his team retained as "ghosts" visible from outside the building.

We then designed an entire alphabet and numbers based on the basic MAD combination and again, made out of squares and circles. It's fun and distinctive but, as one can imagine, not the easiest thing to read, which precluded its use on fire exit signs, for instance. But it definitely reflects the inventive spirit of MAD, and we use it in advertising, on gift-shop products and souvenirs, and on special occasions. A more conventional typeface, Futura, is used in print applications and signage. Like the logo, it is also based on geometry, with a perfectly round letter "o".

We also created a program of dynamic digital media for the Museum that includes

einfache Formen zu entdecken, die genau diese Art der Umgestaltung erlaubten. Mit anderen Worten: Wir suchten nach einer sehr speziellen Kombination aus Einzigartigkeit und Flexibilität.

Im Laufe der Zeit probierten wir sehr viele verschiedene Varianten aus und änderten beispielsweise auch einmal das Akronym komplett. Ein anderes Mal entwickelten wir eine interessante, schnörkellose Version, die das ausgeklügelte System der miteinander verbundenen Lichtschlitze aufgriff, die Cloepfil in den Wänden, Fluren und Decken der Galerieräume gestaltet hatte. Schließlich beschlossen wir, mit dem Standort des MAD zu beginnen: Es ist ein mehr oder weniger quadratisches Gebäude, das an dem bekanntesten Kreisverkehr Manhattans steht. Indem wir Quadrate und Kreise miteinander kombinierten, erfanden wir ein Alphabet, mit dem man ein unverwechselbares MAD-Monogramm darstellen konnte. Manche Leute fühlten sich dadurch auch an die berühmten (oder berüchtigten) „Lollipop"-Säulen erinnert, die Cloepfil und sein Team als von außen sichtbare „Geister" in der Architektur bewahrt hatten.

ressante qui évoquait l'ingénieux réseau de fentes que Cloepfil avait ouvertes dans les murs, les sols et les plafonds des galeries. Finalement, nous avons décidé de partir de l'emplacement du MAD, un bâtiment plus ou moins carré reposant sur le cercle le plus en vue de Manhattan. La combinaison de carrés et de cercles nous a conduits à un alphabet qui donnait un monogramme MAD unique. Pour certaines personnes, c'est aussi un rappel des célèbres (ou infâmes) colonnes « lollipop » d'Edward Durrell Stone, que Cloepfil et son équipe ont conservées telles des « fantômes » visibles de l'extérieur du bâtiment.

Nous avons ensuite créé un alphabet entier et des chiffres selon la combinaison MAD de base, là encore à partir de carrés et de cercles. L'ensemble est à la fois amusant et différent mais, évidemment, aussi difficile à lire, ce qui en a par exemple empêché l'utilisation pour les panneaux des sorties de secours. Il reflète pourtant absolument l'esprit inventif du MAD : nous l'utilisons donc pour la publicité, la boutique de cadeaux et de souvenirs, ainsi que pour les occasions spéciales. Une police de

Above
Gift wrapping

Right
Gift shop packaging

Below
Shopping bag

Right
Gift boxes of the museum shop

Below
Membership card

Bottom
Information leaflet

Left
Museum information desk

Right
Identity applied to tourist tour bus

animated totems that will serve as directories to the various floors of the Museum, screens facing the sidewalk that will let passers-by know what's happening inside, and interpretive kiosks with interactive databases that will let visitors explore the collection. Pattern is a major element of the identity, as it is for the art, and the Museum's media installations present shifting patterns of objects from the collection. This pattern in turn appears on print materials like the cover of the catalog of the Museum's permanent collection.

The museum's new graphic identity can be seen throughout the city, on the sides of buses, on street banners, in print ads, and in the subways. Its impact is out of scale with its modest size and certainly with its budget. By combining a simple, bold identity with a system that permits an almost infinite range of variations, we gave MAD the tools to create and maintain a competitive profile in an ever more crowded cultural market-place.

Anschließend schufen wir ein vollständiges Alphabet mit Buchstaben und Zahlen, das auf der grundlegenden MAD-Kombination beruhte und somit natürlich aus Quadraten und Kreisen bestand. Es ist lustig und sehr charakteristisch, aber wie man sich vorstellen kann, ist es nicht gerade einfach zu lesen, und somit war es ausgeschlossen, diese Schrift z. B. bei Notausgängen zu verwenden. Aber sie reflektiert eindeutig den Erfindergeist, für den das MAD steht, und wir nutzten es für die Werbung, für im Museums-Shop angebotene Produkte und Souvenirs und für Sonderaktionen. Die konventionellere Schriftart Futura wird bei Druckerzeugnissen und dem Beschilderungssystem verwendet. Wie das Logo basiert auch diese Schriftfamilie auf geometrischen Formen und einem vollkommen runden „o".

Für das Museum erfanden wir auch dynamische digitale Medien. Dazu gehören animierte Stelen, die als Wegweiser zu den verschiedenen Ebenen des Museums dienen, vom Gehweg aus sichtbare Monitore, aus denen die Vorübergehenden erfahren, was im Gebäude stattfindet, sowie Ter-

caractères plus conventionnelle (Futura) est employée pour les supports imprimés et la signalisation. Comme le logo, elle repose sur la géométrie, avec une lettre « o » parfaitement ronde.

Nous avons par ailleurs créé un ensemble de supports numériques dynamiques pour le musée : totems animés faisant office de guides pour les différents étages, écrans face au trottoir pour informer les passants de ce qu'il se passe à l'intérieur, kiosques d'interprétation avec des bases de données interactives permettant aux visiteurs d'explorer la collection. Comme pour l'art, le motif est un élément clé de l'identité, et les installations multimédias du musée présentent des motifs changeants d'objets de la collection. Ce motif apparaît aussi sur les documents imprimés, comme la couverture du catalogue de la collection permanente du musée.

La nouvelle identité graphique du musée est visible dans toute la ville, sur les bus, sur des affiches dans les rues, dans des publicités dans la presse et dans le métro. Son impact est démesuré comparé à sa taille modeste et à son budget. En mariant

minals mit interaktiven Datenbanken, an
denen Besucher die Sammlung erschließen
können. Muster sind ein Hauptelement
von Identität und auch von Kunst, und
die Medieninstallationen des Museums
präsentieren veränderliche Muster mit
Objekten aus der Sammlung. Diese Muster
tauchen wiederum auf Druckmaterialien
wie dem Cover des Katalogs für die Dauer-
ausstellung des Museums auf.

Die neue visuelle Identität des Museums
erscheint in der ganzen Stadt, auf Bussen,
auf Straßenplakaten, in Zeitungsanzeigen
und in der U-Bahn. Ihre Wirkung steht in
keinem Verhältnis zu der bescheidenen
Größe des Museums und sicherlich auch
nicht zu seinem Budget. Durch Kombination einer einfachen, gewagten Identität
mit einem System, das eine beinahe unendliche Bandbreite an Variationen ermöglicht,
gaben wir dem MAD die Instrumente an
die Hand, um auf einem immer gedräng-
teren Kulturmarkt ein konkurrenzfähiges
Profil zu schaffen und zu pflegen.

une identité simple et audacieuse à un
système permettant une gamme presque
infinie de déclinaisons, nous avons donné
au MAD les outils pour afficher et conser-
ver un profil concurrentiel sur un marché
culturel de plus en plus saturé.

A VISUAL EXPLORATION

The Explora Way to Travel in the Remote Regions of Patagonia, Atacama, and Easter Island

By Nevenka Marcic, Pozo Marcic Ensamble

www.ensamble.cl

Nevenka Marcic is a founding member and creative director of Pozo Marcic Ensamble together with Patricio Pozo. Marcic was born in Viña del Mar in Chile, and later moved to Valparaíso to study, before starting her branding consultancy in the capital, Santiago. Her office has managed many of the leading brands in the country and the wider region.

Nevenka Marcic ist Gründungsmitglied und gemeinsam mit Patricio Pozo Creative Director von Pozo Marcic Ensamble. Marcic stammt aus dem chilenischen Viña del Mar und zog später zum Studium nach Valparaíso, bevor sie ihr Markenberatungsunternehmen in der Hauptstadt Santiago de Chile gründete. Ihre Agentur betreut viele der führenden Marken Chiles und der umliegenden Länder.

Avec Patricio Pozo, **Nevenka Marcic** est membre fondateur et la directrice de la création de Pozo Marcic Ensamble. Marcic est née à Viña del Mar (Chili), avant d'aller étudier à Valparaíso et de monter sa société de conseil en branding à la capitale, Santiago. Son agence a géré de nombreuses marques phares du pays et alentours.

Left
Logo application on a car
in the Atacama Desert

Right
Natural landscape in Patagonia,
base of one of the hotels

South America is one of the least well known and perhaps least explored parts of the world. Travelling to some of its more remote areas promises to be a great and unforgettable experience, with large expanses, very few inhabitants, and lots of unique places to explore. Its vast, remote lands are centred on the Andes mountain range, the South Pacific, and Patagonia, where ancient cultures originated and remain to this day. South America is a land that fires the imagination and challenges the explorer with its volcanoes, salt flats, ancient forests, lakes, and rivers. But it is also a land of history with great archaeological treasures, and vibrant towns and villages that bear witness to the past and guard the traditions of its people.

Explora is a company that promotes travel to these remote South American destinations, making its hotels the focus, and exploration the philosophy of its holidays, with programmes in Patagonia in the south, in the Atacama Desert in the north of Chile, and on Easter Island. The programmes are aimed at enthusiastic travellers who are in search of remote

In Südamerika gibt es die am wenigsten bekannten und vielleicht auch am wenigsten erforschten Regionen der Welt. Die Reise in einige der abgelegenen Gegenden verspricht, eine großartige und unvergessliche Erfahrung zu werden: weiträumige Landschaften, eine sehr dünne Besiedlung und viele einzigartige Orte, die es zu entdecken gilt. Diese riesigen, abgeschiedenen Areale konzentrieren sich um den Gebirgszug der Anden, den Südpazifik und um Patagonien, wo uralte Kulturen entstanden und bis zum heutigen Tag erhalten sind. Südamerika ist ein Kontinent, der die Fantasie anregt und mit seinen Vulkanen, Salzebenen, uralten Wäldern, Seen und Flüssen die Forscher herausfordert. Doch es ist auch eine sehr geschichtsträchtige Landmasse mit großartigen archäologischen Schätzen, pulsierenden Städten und lebendigen Dörfern – Zeugen und Bewahrer der Traditionen ihrer Völker.

Explora ist ein Unternehmen, das für Entdeckungsreisen in diese abgelegenen südamerikanischen Ziele wirbt. Es legt den Schwerpunkt auf die Hotels und macht das Erforschen zur Philosophie seiner

L'Amérique du Sud est l'une des régions les plus méconnues au monde, et sans doute la moins explorée. La visite de ces contrées lointaines promet une expérience inoubliable : de grandes étendues, très peu d'habitants et des endroits uniques à explorer. Ses territoires vastes et reculés se centrent sur la cordillère des Andes, le Pacifique Sud et la Patagonie, et ont vu naître des cultures millénaires qui existent aujourd'hui encore. L'Amérique du Sud est un territoire ouvert à notre imagination et un défi pour l'exploration : volcans, déserts de sel, forêts millénaires, lacs, rivières. Mais elle représente aussi un voyage à travers l'histoire, avec une grande richesse archéologique et la vitalité de ses villes et villages, témoins du passé et gardiens des traditions.

Explora est une entreprise faisant la promotion de voyages à ces destinations lointaines d'Amérique du Sud, les hôtels étant des points phares et l'exploration la philosophie de voyage, avec des itinéraires en Patagonie au sud, dans le désert d'Atacama au nord du Chili et sur l'Île de Pâques. Ces parcours s'adressent

places and unique experiences. A pioneer in this approach to travel in the Americas, Explora has become a global landmark in tourism and is recognised by experts and the specialist media as one of the most outstanding wilderness tour operators in the world.

Accordingly, Explora attaches particular importance to architecture and design. Its hotels are in carefully selected locations: in the ancient town of San Pedro de Atacama, facing Lake Pehoé in the Torres del Paine National Park, and on the outskirts of Hanga Roa on Easter Island. The architecture of all these hotels is integrated into and interacts with the surroundings in contemporary fashion.

The design had to rise to the challenge of conceptualising, planning, and creating exclusive pieces that reflect and support the concepts that sum up the "Explora philosophy" – which we call "the art of travel" – by integrating the extreme nature and cultural richness of the American continent. Everything from the visual branding, marketing, goods, publications, packaging, and amenities, right through

Urlaubsreisen. Dazu bietet Explora Reisen nach Patagonien im Süden Lateinamerikas, in die Atacamawüste im Norden Chiles und auf die Osterinseln an. Die Programme richten sich an begeisterte Reisende, die abgeschiedene Orte und einzigartige Erfahrungen suchen. Explora hat für diese Art, in Südamerika zu reisen, Pionierarbeit geleistet und wurde zu einem globalen Wahrzeichen des Tourismus. Von Experten und von der Fachpresse wird Explora als eine herausragende Organisation für Wildnis- und Abenteuerreisen weltweit betrachtet.

Entsprechend achtet Explora besonders auf Architektur und Design. Die Hotels befinden sich an sorgfältig ausgewählten Standorten: in der alten Stadt San Pedro de Atacama mit Blick auf den Lake Pehoé (Nationalpark Torres del Paine) und in den Randgebieten von Hanga Roa auf den Osterinseln. Die Architektur dieser Hotels ist auf zeitgemäße Weise in die Umgebung integriert und steht mit ihr in enger Wechselbeziehung.

Beim Design lag die Herausforderung darin, exklusive Bestandteile zu konzipieren, zu planen und umzusetzen, die die Ideen

à des voyageurs enthousiastes en quête de contrées reculées et d'expériences uniques. Pionnier dans cette approche de voyage en Amérique, Explora est devenue une référence mondiale du tourisme et est reconnue comme l'un des tour opérateurs de destinations lointaines les plus exceptionnels au monde par les experts et les médias spécialisés.

Explora accorde une importance toute particulière à l'architecture et au design. Ses hôtels se trouvent dans des lieux choisis avec soin : dans le village millénaire de San Pedro de Atacama, face au lac Pehoe dans le parc national Torres del Paine et aux alentours d'Hanga Roa, sur l'Île de Pâques. Dans chacun d'eux, l'architecture s'intègre à son environnement et dialogue avec lui de façon contemporaine.

Côté design, le défi consistait à conceptualiser, à planifier et à créer des pièces exclusives reflétant et renforçant les concepts qui résument la « philosophie Explora », que nous qualifions d' « art du voyage », en y intégrant la nature extrême et la richesse culturelle du territoire américain. Tous les éléments, du branding visuel

Left
Sign design at the hotel

Right
Room amenities of the Explora hotel

to the signage on the hotels, is part of a vast visual identity programme.

For this we are developing a design in which the formats and materials are in continuous dialogue with each individual location: recycled paper, wood, leather, and items that evoke the nature and cultures of South America in contemporary style and which, at the same time, create a simple, sophisticated tone and visual texture. The images use curves, diagonals, and combinations of textures directly associated with the architecture of the hotels and their interaction with the landscape.

In the case of the brochures, we designed a series of five packages showing two of the destinations: Patagonia and the Atacama Desert. Each package is an invitation, through images and textures, to experience a slice of these remote and extreme natural environments: stones next to a glacier in Patagonia, tree trunks in ancient forests, rocks sculpted by the wind in the Atacama Desert, and so forth. Individually they represent a living sample of the land, and shown as a series they describe the huge diversity of this landscape.

der „Explora-Philosophie" (von uns als „Kunst des Reisens" bezeichnet) zusammenfassen, spiegeln und unterstützen, indem die außergewöhnlichen Natur- und Kulturschätze des südamerikanischen Kontinents integriert werden. Alles, von der visuellen Markenbildung über das Marketing, die verfügbaren Waren und Produkte, die Publikationen, Verpackungen und Freizeitanlagen bis hin zur Beschilderung in den Hotels, gehört zu dem umfassenden, weitreichenden Progamm der visuellen Identität.

Dafür entwickelten wir Designlösungen, bei denen sich die Formate und Materialien in einem fortwährenden Dialog mit jedem einzelnen Standort befinden. Wir arbeiten mit recyceltem Papier, Holz, Leder und Elementen, die, zeitgemäß modifiziert, den Reichtum der südamerikanischen Natur und Kultur wachrufen und gleichzeitig ein schlichtes, aber anspruchsvolles Niveau sowie eine visuelle Textur zum Ausdruck bringen. In den Illustrationen und Bildern werden Kurven, Diagonalen und Kombinationen aus Texturen verwendet, die direkt mit der Architektur der Hotels und ihrer Wechselwirkung mit der Landschaft verknüpft sind.

à la signalétique propre aux hôtels, en passant par le marketing, les produits, les publications, le packaging et les équipements, forment un vaste programme d'identité visuelle.

Nous avons pour cela mis au point un design dans lequel les formats et les matériaux dialoguent en permanence avec chaque lieu : papier recyclé, bois, cuirs et éléments qui évoquent la nature et les cultures de l'Amérique du Sud sous une forme contemporaine, tout en procurant une touche simple et sophistiquée et une texture visuelle. Les images utilisent des courbes, des diagonales et des combinaisons de textures directement associées à l'architecture des hôtels et au dialogue avec le paysage.

Pour les catalogues, nous avons conçu cinq packs présentant deux des destinations : la Patagonie et le désert d'Atacama. Chaque pack permet par le biais d'images et de textures de découvrir un extrait de cette nature lointaine et extrême : des pierres à côté d'un glacier en Patagonie, des troncs d'arbres millénaires, des roches sculptées par le vent dans le désert

This page
Package and brochure
for Explora at Rapa Nui

the fascinating
Rapa Nui culture

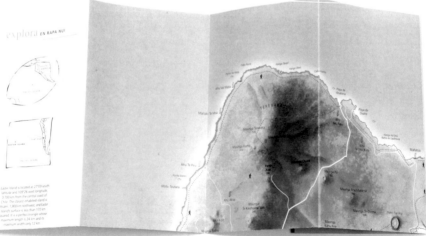

**a hotel
for adventure
and leisure:
Hotel Salto Chico**

The architecture of our hotels
makes it possible to revel in far
regions. The design creates an aura
of mystery, while showcasing the
unfathomable beauty of the natural
environment.

Strategically set on the shore of
Lake Pehoé, **explora**'s Hotel Salto
Chico was conceived as an
exploration base site. It features
refined comfort for total relaxation
and the best gear ideally suited for
exploring Patagonia.

travesías explora

travesia in Patagonia

This page
Book set design for Explora:
Patagonia and Atacama Desert

Left & right
The information pack for guests

This technique of using elements of nature as if they were tangible is present in one way or another in all the pieces developed by Explora. For example, each bathroom in the hotels contains natural products made from local grasses, and each of the labels shows a type of grass and stones against the backdrop of a wild meadow.

To introduce its new destination on Easter Island, Explora Rapa Nui, a package was designed containing the promotional brochure and a series of items designed to evoke the island by appealing to the senses: flowered paper, a CD with pictures, another with local *rapanui* music, and a traditional handmade island greeting necklace.

The design brief was extended to include the production of exclusive publications for the clients, in the style of old travel journals. A set of three books was designed – *Stories*, *Landscapes and Nature*, and *Travel Log* – and presented in a pack with a slide-out tab, which serves as a welcome gift for travellers visiting Patagonia. Unlike the usual kind of promotional material, this publication was designed

Für die Broschüren haben wir eine aus fünf Komponenten bestehende Reihe gestaltet, die zwei der Reiseziele vorstellt: Patagonien und die Atacamawüste. Jede dieser Broschüren lädt schon durch die Abbildungen und ihre Beschaffenheit ein, einen Ausschnitt dieser abgelegenen und außergewöhnlichen Natur zu erfahren: Steine neben einem Gletscher in Patagonien, Baumstämme in uralten Wäldern, vom Wind geformte Felsen in der Atacamawüste usw. Jede Broschüre repräsentiert einen lebendigen Ausschnitt aus dem jeweiligen Land, und in ihrer Gesamtheit beschreibt die Reihe die unglaubliche Vielfalt der vorgestellten Landschaften.

Diese Technik, Elemente der Natur zu verwenden, als wären sie greifbar, ist auf die eine oder andere Weise bei allen von Explora entwickelten Gegenständen gegenwärtig. So finden sich beispielsweise in jedem Bad der Hotels natürliche Produkte, die aus einheimischen Gräsern hergestellt wurden; die Etiketten zeigen eine Grassorte und Steine vor dem Hintergrund einer Wiese.

Um die neue Destination „Explora Rapa Nui" auf den Osterinseln vorzustellen, wurde

d'Atacama, etc. De façon individuelle, elles apportent une preuve vivante du territoire ; dans cette série, elles montrent la grande diversité du paysage.

Cette manière d'utiliser des éléments de la nature comme s'ils étaient tangibles se retrouve sous une forme ou une autre dans toutes les pièces créées par Explora. À titre d'exemple, les produits de toilette offerts dans les hôtels contiennent des produits naturels fabriqués à base d'herbes de la région, et chaque étiquette illustre un type d'herbe et de pierre sur fond de prairie.

Pour promouvoir sa nouvelle destination à l'Île de Pâques, Explora Rapa Nui, nous avons conçu une pochette contenant le dépliant et une série d'éléments pensés pour faire découvrir l'île à travers les sens : du papier floral, un CD avec des images, un autre de musique locale *rapanui* et un collier de bienvenue traditionnel fait à la main.

Le brief de design a été étendu pour inclure la production de publications exclusives pour les clients, à l'image des anciens carnets de voyage, avec une collection

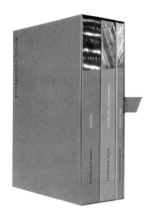

This page
The set of three volumes *Patagonia Book:
"Stories", "Landscapes and Nature",
and "Travel Log"*

Right
Promotional material

to bring to mind the field guides and travel
diaries used by legendary explorers and
pioneers, making it a collector's piece and
a cultural legacy.

The information pack left for guests
in their hotel rooms was designed as an
introduction to exploration, welcoming
them and preparing them for the adventure ahead and the lands to be discovered.
Made entirely from paper, it has pockets
and folds to hold all the necessary documentation and stationery, and includes a
natural wood pencil that serves as a hinge
when the pack is opened.

The use of natural materials native to
each location is central to the development
of the packaging and hotel signage. For the
packaging we opted for 100 percent recycled Kraft paperboard fastened with leather
cords or straps. In the case of Atacama,
for example, there are organic objects from
the north of Chile, worked in natural woods
and fixed to walls and fences with leather
straps, linking with the organic forms of
the decor.

ein Set entworfen, das die Werbebroschüre
und einige andere Elemente enthält. Es
wurde so gestaltet, dass die Insel geradezu
sinnlich fassbar wird: In geblümtem
Papier finden sich z.B. eine Foto-CD, eine
Audio-CD mit einheimischer *rapanui*-Musik
und eine traditionelle, handgemachte
Begrüßungskette der Insel.

Das Design-Briefing wurde erweitert,
um für die Kunden exklusive Publikationen
im Stile alter Reisejournale produzieren zu
können. Ein dreiteiliges Buchset mit den
Titeln *Stories, Landscapes and Nature*
und *Travel Log* wurde entworfen und in
einem Schuber mit ausziehbarer Lasche
umgesetzt. Es dient als Willkommensge-
schenk für Reisende in Patagonien. Anders
als übliche Werbematerialien wurde diese
Publikation so gestaltet, dass sie an die
von legendären Forschern und Pionieren
benutzten Naturführer und Reisetagebücher
erinnert; das machte sie zu einem Sammler-
stück und einem kulturellen Erbe.

Das Informationspaket, das den Gästen
zur Begrüßung ins Hotelzimmer gelegt wird,
dient der Einführung und soll auf das bevor-
stehende Abenteuer und das zu entdeckende

de trois livres : *Stories, Landscapes and
Nature* et *Travel Log*, glissés dans une
pochette avec une bande coulissante. Cette
édition sert de cadeau de bienvenue pour
les explorateurs qui se rendent en Patagonie.
Contrairement au support habituel de promotion, cette publication a été pensée pour
évoquer les guides de terrain et les carnets
de voyage utilisés par les explorateurs et
les pionniers de légende, afin d'en faire une
pièce de collection et un héritage culturel.

Le dossier d'information à disposition
des voyageurs dans les chambres des hôtels
a été pensé comme une introduction à
l'exploration : il leur donne la bienvenue et
les prépare pour l'aventure et les territoires
à découvrir. Il est entièrement fait en papier,
avec des pochettes et des plis pour accueillir
toute la documentation nécessaire, et
inclut un crayon en bois naturel qui sert
de charnière.

L'emploi de matériaux naturels et
originaux de chaque lieu est primordial
dans le packaging et le système de signalisation des hôtels. Dans le premier cas,
nous avons choisi un carton kraft 100 %
recyclé, avec des cordons ou des liens en

Land einstimmen. Es ist ganz aus Papier hergestellt und so gefaltet und mit Taschen versehen, dass es alle erforderlichen Unterlagen und das Briefpapier aufnehmen kann. Auch ein Bleistift aus Naturholz ist darin enthalten, der beim Öffnen der Verpackung als Scharnier dient.

Die Verwendung von heimischen Materialien direkt aus der Natur vor Ort ist für die Entwicklung der Verpackungen und der Beschilderung in den Hotels ganz wesentlich. Bei den Verpackungen haben wir uns für 100 Prozent recycelte Pappe von Kraft entschieden; Lederbänder oder -riemen dienen als Verschluss beziehungsweise zur Befestigung. Am Standort Atacama gibt es beispielsweise organische Objekte aus dem Norden Chiles, die in Naturholz eingearbeitet wurden und mit Lederriemen an Wänden und Einfriedungen befestigt sind. Auf diese Weise passen sie sich den organischen Formen des Dekors an.

cuir pour la fermeture. Dans le second cas, comme à Atacama, des objets organiques du nord du Chili, travaillés dans des bois naturels et fixés aux murs et aux clôtures à l'aide d'attaches en cuir, font le lien avec les formes organiques du décor.

ILLUSTRATED EVENT

How Illustrative Built an International Brand Around Coloured Pencils

By Roman Bittner, Apfel Zet

www.apfelzet.de

Roman Bittner was founder of the Berlin-based graphic design studio Apfel Zet in 1996 along with his university colleague Matthias Ernstberger. Their creative production has garnered international recognition for the highly illustrated and colourful works which range from T-shirts and wallpaper to corporate identities and book designs.

Roman Bittner gründete zusammen mit seinem Kommilitonen Matthias Ernstberger 1996 das in Berlin ansässige Grafikdesignstudio Apfel Zet. Ihre kreativen Produktionen erlangten internationale Anerkennung wegen ihrer höchst vielfältig illustrierten und farbenprächtigen Arbeiten, die von T-Shirts und Tapeten bis zu Corporate Identities und Buchgestaltungen reichen.

En 1996, **Roman Bittner** a fondé à Berlin le studio de design graphique Apfel Zet avec son camarade d'université Matthias Ernstberger. Leur production créative a obtenu une reconnaissance internationale pour leurs travaux riches en illustrations et en couleurs, allant de T-shirts et de papiers muraux à des identités d'entreprises et des designs de livres.

Illustrative
07 Berlin

EINTRITTSKARTE

INTERNATIONAL
ILLUSTRATION
FORUM

01.09.-16.09.2007

Villa Elisabeth
Invalidenstr. 3
10115 Berlin

Left
Tickets for the event in Berlin 2007

Right
Poster for the event in Berlin 2006

I can still clearly remember the first time Pascal Johanssen mentioned his plan for an illustrators' exhibition; he was in our office at the time. Jens Bonnke – an illustrator and a neighbour – had suggested the idea to him, probably not entirely for altruistic reasons. At this time Galerie Johanssen was still a thoroughly conventional kind of gallery. Initially I was involved only as a potential exhibiting graphic artist. Yet after a few weeks suddenly the event had a catchy name and a logo had to be found for it. Unfortunately I can't remember my alternative designs, and I no longer have the old files, but in any case the coloured pencil logo was my clear favourite. I was thinking of Stapelberg & Fritz's corporate design, which used stylised felt tips, and I wanted to try something similar with geometrically drawn pencils, because it suited the theme. After trying some combinations in the office I myself was surprised at how effectively three pencils could be fitted together, producing an attractive "cockade" design which is vaguely reminiscent of the Adidas trefoil logo, while at the same time radiating the irresistible retro-chic of an

Ich erinnere mich noch genau, wie Pascal Johanssen bei uns im Büro zum ersten Mal über das Projekt einer Illustratoren-Ausstellung sprach. Der Illustrator und Nachbar Jens Bonnke hatte ihn wohl nicht ganz uneigennützig auf diese Idee gebracht. Zu diesem Zeitpunkt war die Galerie Johanssen noch eine Galerie im ganz konventionellen Sinne. Vorerst war ich nur als möglicher ausstellender Grafiker eingeplant. Doch nach wenigen Wochen gab es mit einem Mal einen einprägsamen Namen, für den ein Logo gefunden werden wollte. Leider habe ich weder eine Erinnerung an meine Alternativentwürfe noch die alten Dateien, aber das Buntstift-Logo war auf jeden Fall mein uneingeschränkter Favorit. Ich hatte ein Erscheinungsbild von Stapelberg & Fritz im Kopf, die mit schematisierten Magic-Markern gearbeitet hatten, und wollte, passend zum Thema, etwas Ähnliches mit geometrisierten Buntstiften ausprobieren. Im Büro war ich nach wenigen Kombinationen selber überrascht, wie gut drei Stifte sich zusammenfügen ließen und eine stimmige Kokarde ergaben, die entfernt an das Adidas-Dreiblatt erin-

Je me souviens encore parfaitement de la première fois que Pascal Johanssen a expliqué son idée pour une exposition d'illustrateurs : il travaillait alors chez nous à l'époque. Jens Bonnke, illustrateur et voisin, lui avait suggéré cette idée, certainement pas uniquement à des fins altruistes. À cette époque, la galerie Johanssen était encore grandement conventionnelle. Au départ, j'intervenais seulement comme artiste graphique avec un potentiel d'exposition. Au bout de quelques semaines cependant, l'événement avait un nom accrocheur et il fallait lui trouver un logo. J'ai malheureusement oublié le reste des mes designs et je n'ai plus les anciens fichiers, mais le logo à base de crayons de couleur était sans conteste mon préféré. J'avais en tête le design de Stapelberg & Fritz à base de feutres stylisés et je voulais essayer quelque chose de semblable avec des crayons dessinés de façon géométrique, appropriés pour le sujet. Après l'essai de plusieurs combinaisons au bureau, j'ai été surpris de voir à quel point trois crayons peuvent donner ensemble un résultat intéressant, avec un design attirant de type « cocarde »

Illustrative
07 Berlin

Illustrative
2007

31. August -
16. Oktober
Villa Elisabeth
Berlin

Forum für
zeitgenössische
Illustration

Left
Poster for the event in Berlin 2007

Right
Poster for the event in Paris 2007
and the pattern they create when
fitted together

East Berlin youth sports festival. For the
colours I imagined a contrast to our usual
palette of brown/beige/dark red: something
fresher and cleaner, and I used the three
main colours of additive colour mixing –
magenta, yellow, and cyan – to give the
logo the cheerful, hard brightness of a major chord. At this point all the key features
of the identity were effectively in place.
Initially I didn't recognise this fact myself,
though, and it took more than a year to
get through the final trial phase. As in
The Sorcerer's Apprentice, in the end the
logo was smarter than its designer and
defeated many opposing design ideas.

The same process was repeated when
the logo was combined with the name.
I can still remember how relieved I was
when Pascal's opinion concurred with mine,
after I'd shown him the alternatives in the
café opposite our office. "Illustrative" and
the coloured-pencil logo complemented
each other in a distinctive way and soon
took on a momentum of their own. Initially
the exhibition was too big for the gallery;
soon the gallery was no longer an art gallery that sometimes staged an illustrators'

nert, aber ebenso den unwiderstehlichen
Retro-Schick einer Ostberliner Jugend-
spartakiade versprühte. Bei den Farben
schwebte mir im Gegensatz zu unserer üblichen Braun-Beige-Dunkelrot-Palette etwas
Frischeres, Reineres vor, und ich stimmte
anhand der drei Grundfarben der additiven
Farbmischung Magenta-Gelb-Cyan das
Zeichen auf die fröhliche Härte eines Dur-
Akkords. Damit war das Erscheinungsbild
eigentlich schon in all seinen Komponenten angelegt. Allerdings durchschaute ich
das vorerst selber noch gar nicht, und es
dauerte mehr als ein Jahr, bis das letzte
Versuchsstadium durchlaufen war. Wie
beim „Zauberlehrling" war das Logo im
Grunde schlauer als sein eigener Entwerfer
und setzte sich gegen viele ihm zuwider-
laufende Gestaltungsideen durch.

In Kombination mit dem Namen
wiederholte sich das dann noch einmal.
Ich weiß noch genau, wie erleichtert ich
war, dass Pascal derselben Meinung war
wie ich, nachdem ich ihm die Varianten im
Café gegenüber von unserem Büro gezeigt
habe. „Illustrative" und „Buntstift"-Logo
ergänzten sich auf eine eigentümliche Art

rappelant vaguement le logo en feuille de
trèfle d'Adidas, tout en suggérant le rétro-
chic irrésistible d'une rencontre sportive
pour la jeunesse de Berlin Est. Pour les
couleurs, j'ai voulu trancher avec notre
palette habituelle de marron//beige/rouge
foncé, quelque chose de plus frais et net.
J'ai donc pris les trois couleurs soustractives
principales pour les mélanges (magenta,
jaune et cyan) afin de donner plus de présence. À ce stade, tous les éléments clés
de l'identité étaient bien définis, mais je ne
m'en suis pas aperçu et plus d'un an s'est
écoulé avant de conclure la phase finale.
Comme dans *L'apprenti sorcier*, le logo
était à la fin plus intelligent que son auteur
et il est venu à bout de beaucoup d'idées
adverses de design.

La même procédure a été suivie au
moment de composer le logo et le nom.
Je me souviens encore à quel point j'ai
été soulagé en voyant que Pascal était du
même avis que moi, après lui avoir montré
les options possibles au café en face du
bureau. Le mot « Illustrative » et le logo
de crayons de couleur se complémentaient
mutuellement d'une façon originale et se

exhibition, but an illustrators' gallery which primarily organised "Illustrative," and by the third year the media were already calling it the "world's biggest" illustration forum. I think we were all of us more than surprised by this development.

Really we're not an office that specialises in corporate identities and when it comes down to it we don't have the knowledge or the discipline for tough briefs – jobs to which we would have to subordinate ourselves as designers. From the beginning the process was about designing and discarding, and then at some stage coming into line with the most practical and effective principles. For us the next poster, the next leaflet is always in the foreground, and needs to work effectively on its own account. This is why the Illustrative identity lacks the usual adaptations of colours, grids, and typefaces to all the various printed materials, instead prioritising posters and catalogue covers. Even these, as mentioned above, only followed in a clear line to a certain degree at first. For the first event, Illustrative 06, the colours were already in place but the

und entwickelten bald eine ganz eigene Dynamik. Zuerst war die Ausstellung zu groß für die Galerie, bald war die Galerie gar keine Kunstgalerie mehr, die auch mal eine Illustratoren-Ausstellung machte, sondern eine Illustratoren-Galerie, die hauptsächlich die Illustrative organisierte, und bereits im dritten Jahr sprach man in den Medien schon vom „weltgrößten" Illustrations-Forum. Eine Entwicklung, die, so glaube ich, jeden von uns mehr als überraschte.

Wir sind eigentlich kein Büro, das auf Corporate Identities spezialisiert ist, und im Grunde haben wir auch weder die Einsicht noch die Disziplin für harte Vorgaben, denen wir uns als Entwerfer unterordnen müssten. Es blieb von Anfang an ein Entwerfen und Verwerfen im Prozess, um sich irgendwann den praktischsten und wirkungsvollsten Richtlinien anzunähern. Im Vordergund steht für uns immer nur das nächste Plakat, der nächste Flyer, der vor allem für sich alleine überzeugen soll. In diesem Sinne fehlt beim Illustrative-Erscheinungsbild auch das übliche Durchdeklinieren von Farben, Rastern und Schriften auf allen möglichen

sont rapidement imposés. L'exposition était au départ trop grande pour la galerie ; cette galerie d'art qui accueillait parfois l'œuvre d'illustrateurs est toutefois devenue une galerie d'illustrateurs qui organisait essentiellement l'exposition « Illustrative ». Dès la troisième année, les médias l'ont qualifiée de forum de l'illustration « le plus important au monde ». Je pense que tous étions plus que surpris par une telle évolution.

Nous ne sommes en rien un bureau spécialisé en identité d'entreprise et lorsqu'il est question d'en créer une, nous n'avons pas les connaissances ou la discipline nécessaires pour des briefs poussés, tâches auxquelles nous devrions nous subordonner en tant que designers. Dès le début, le processus a impliqué un effort de design et de sélection, et à un certain stade le respect des principes les plus pratiques et efficaces. Pour nous, la prochaine affiche, le prochain dépliant est toujours au premier plan et doit fonctionner à lui seul. C'est pourquoi l'identité d'Illustrative est dénuée de l'adaptation habituelle des couleurs, des grilles et de

coloured pencils weren't re-used in the poster design. Instead I was still playing with the idea of designing a new logo each time, as is always the case with the Baseball World Series final, for example. For the second session, Illustrative 07, I even wanted to drop the colours altogether in favour of a black and grey design which would alternate with the coloured version in different years, emphasising the graphic, "ink and pencil" aspect of illustration. As a result the logo consisted of a highly ornamented calligraphic design emerging from an ink pot. From the start I realised that I would have problems with Pascal here so this design was overturned – bit by bit, and then at some stage entirely. What remained was a leaflet and a logo for the "Neue Talente" ("New Talents") competition which was held for the first time in that year. Right at the last moment before printing, a new design was produced which was to prove definitive for all that followed. Now for the first time all the elements of the Corporate Identity came together in an effective way: colours, logo, coloured pencils, and a pared-down

Drucksachen zugunsten von Postern und Katalogcovern. Die, wie erwähnt, vorerst auch nur bedingt einer klaren Linie folgten. Bei der ersten „Illustrative 06" standen zwar die Farben schon fest, aber die Buntstifte wurden nicht erneut beim Postermotiv verwendet. Stattdessen spielte ich noch mit der Idee jedes Mal einen neuen Titelsatz zu entwerfen, wie dies z.B. beim Baseball World Series Finale stets der Fall ist. Bei der zweiten „Illustrative 07" wollte ich die Farben sogar ganz fallen lassen zugunsten eines schwarz-grauen Auftritts, der sich mit der bunten Variante im Jahresrhythmus hätte abwechseln sollen und den grafischen Tinten- und Bleistift-Aspekt der Illustration betont hätte. Der Schriftzug bestand dementsprechend aus einer verzierungsreichen Kalligrafie, die aus einem Tintenfass gelaufen war. Ich merkte sofort, dass ich hier mit Pascal Schwierigkeiten bekommen würde, und so wurde dieser Entwurf Stück für Stück und dann ganz und gar gekippt. Übrig blieb ein Flyer und ein Schriftzug für den „Neue Talente"-Wettbewerb, der in diesem Jahr zum ersten Mal ausgetragen wurde. Kurz vor Drucklegung entstand ein

typographies pour les publications et donne la priorité aux affiches et aux couvertures des catalogues. Même ces derniers, comme expliqué plus haut, n'ont suivi un chemin précis que dans un premier temps. Pour le premier événement, Illustrative'06, les couleurs étaient déjà là mais les crayons n'ont pas été retenus dans le design de l'affiche. À la place, j'ai continué avec l'idée d'un nouveau logo à chaque fois, comme c'est par exemple le cas pour la finale du mondial de basket. Pour la deuxième édition, Illustrative'07, j'ai même envisagé d'éliminer les couleurs en faveur d'un design noir et gris qui contrasterait avec la version en couleur plusieurs années de suite et mettrait en valeur l'aspect graphique « encre et crayon » de l'illustration. Résultat : le logo s'est composé d'un design calligraphique très riche sortant d'un pot d'encre. J'ai compris dès le début que j'allais avoir des problèmes avec Pascal ; le design a donc été modifié, d'abord en partie, puis entièrement. Il en est resté une brochure et un logo pour la compétition « Neue Talente » (« Nouveaux talents ») qui se tenait pour la première fois cette année-

Left
Poster variants for the
event in Berlin 2007

Right
Poster for the event in
Zurich 2008

design echoing Josef Müller-Brockmann's uncompromising clarity. Nonetheless here too there was another variant for a while, featuring a circle with the title made up of assorted characters, but this disappeared again in the very final stages. Now the basic design elements had been established for the two first international exhibitions in Paris and Zurich. For the Paris printed material, the coloured pencils wound their way beyond the borders of the format, allowing individual posters to be part of a larger pattern. In Zurich by contrast I felt almost compelled to re-work the pencils into the irresistible Swiss cross. It's a design inspired by Swiss poster designer Niklaus Troxler.

For Illustrative 08 in Zurich the "Junge Talente" ("Young Talents") competition was renamed the Young Illustrators Award, or YIA for short, and the pencil logo had to be expanded into a small family of logos because new applications had to be devised for the subcategories Book Art, Animation and Illustration. However, because of the word lengths and in order to avoid confusion with the main exhibition, it seemed

neuer Entwurf, der für alle weiteren ausschlaggebend war. Zum ersten Mal trafen nun die Elemente des CIs zusammen: Farben, Logo, Buntstifte und eine an Josef Müller-Brockmanns bedingungslose Klarheit angelehnte Reduziertheit. Allerdings gab es hier kurzfristig auch noch eine Variante, die, wie im vorangegangenen Jahr, einen Kreis mit einem neuen Titelsatz aus bunt gemixten Buchstaben vorsah, der erst im allerletzten Stadium wieder verschwand. Für die beiden ersten Internationalen Ausstellungen in Paris und Zürich war nun der stilistische Weg gefunden. Auf den Pariser Drucksachen schlängelten sich die Buntstifte über die Grenzen des Formats hinweg, ließen das einzelne Poster zum Rapport in einem größeren Muster werden. In Zürich empfand ich es dagegen schon fast als Zwang, die Buntstifte in das unwiderstehliche Schweizer Kreuz umzuinterpretieren. Für diesen Entwurf stand sicherlich auch Niklaus Troxler, der Schweizer Plakatdesigner, Pate.

Für die „Illustrative 08" in Zürich wurde der „Junge Talente"-Wettbewerb in „Young Illustrators Award", kurz „YIA", umbenannt,

là. Au tout dernier moment avant impression, un nouveau design a été créé et s'est avéré définitif. Dès lors, tous les éléments s'assemblaient pour la première fois de façon efficace : couleurs, logo, crayons de couleur et un design réduit faisant écho à la clarté absolue du designer graphique Josef Müller-Brockmann. Néanmoins, il y a eu là encore pendant un temps une autre variante présentant un cercle avec le titre composé de différents caractères, mais elle a finalement disparu. Les éléments du design de base existaient alors pour les deux premières expositions internationales à Paris et Zurich. Dans les publications pour Paris, les crayons de couleur dépassaient les marges, ce qui a permis d'obtenir une image plus grande à cheval sur plusieurs affiches. À Zurich en revanche, je me suis presque senti obligé de transformer les crayons en irrésistible croix suisse. Ce design a été inspiré du designer graphique suisse Niklaus Troxler.

Pour Illustrative'08 à Zurich, la compétition « Junge Talente » (« Jeunes talents ») a été rebaptisée Young Illustrators Award (YIA) et le logo de crayons a dû être décliné en

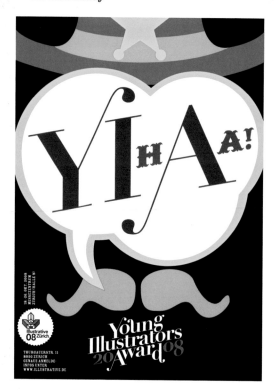

Left & right
Posters for the event Young Illustrators
Award 2008 in Zurich

impossible to remain very close to the original logo and so we did what we like best: in the end we opted for an entirely new design. This event-within-an-event had its own poster, with its affiliation signalled primarily by the colours. Zurich was the first time that a strict Corporate Identity style guide had to be set up: an external designer was producing part of the identity. Comic animation artist Kathi Käppel was asked to produce a short teaser film and it turned out that the prescribed colours and the coloured pencils provided freedom and definition in exactly the right proportions to ensure that the resulting work was artistically autonomous while at the same time supporting the visual identity as a whole.

und das Buntstift-Zeichen musste zu einer kleinen Logo-Familie erweitert werden, da zusätzlich auch noch für die Unterkategorien „bookart", „Animation" und „Illustration" Anwendungen gefunden werden musste. Es schien allerdings auf Grund der Wortlängen und um Verwechslungen mit der Hauptausstellung zu vermeiden unmöglich, ganz nah am Ursprungslogo zu bleiben, und so taten wir das, was wir am liebsten machen: wir entschieden uns letztlich für einen gänzlich neuen Auftritt. Auch für diese Teilveranstaltung gab es eigene Poster, die vor allem über die Farben Zugehörigkeit signalisierten.

Für Zürich trat auch erstmals der Fall ein, dass ein strikter CI-Styleguide angelegt werden musste. Ein außenstehender Grafiker sollte einen Teil des Auftritts realisieren. Die Trickfilmerin Kathi Käppel wurde aufgefordert einen kleinen Teaserfilm zu animieren, und es zeigte sich, dass die vorgegebenen Farben und die Buntstifte gerade das richtige Maß von Einschränkung und Freiheit halten, um eine eigenständige Arbeit zu gewährleisten, die trotzdem das Gesamterscheinungsbild unterstützt.

une petite famille de petites images, car de nouvelles applications devaient être pensées pour les sous-catégories Book Art, Animation et Illustration. Toutefois, en raison de la longueur des mots et pour éviter toute confusion avec l'exposition principale, il était impossible de coller au logo original. Nous avons donc fait ce que nous aimons le plus : nous avons finalement opté pour un design complètement nouveau. Cet « événement dans un autre » a eu sa propre affiche, avec une relation surtout marquée par les couleurs.

À Zurich, un guide de style devait être conçu pour la première fois par un designer externe, qui se chargeait d'une partie de l'identité. L'artiste en animations Kathi Käppel a été sollicitée pour produire une petite bande-annonce : les couleurs choisies et les crayons de couleur ont offert la liberté et la définition nécessaires pour que le travail soit autonome sur le plan artistique, tout en assurant l'identité visuelle dans son ensemble.

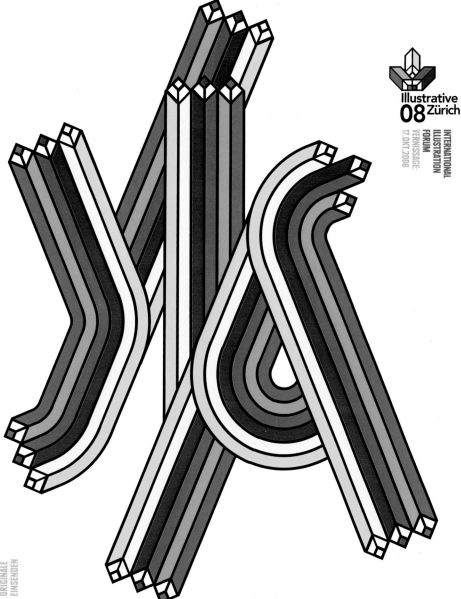

Illustrative
08 Zürich

INTERNATIONAL
ILLUSTRATION
FORUM
VERNISSAGE:
17. OKT. 2008

ANMELDESCHLUSS:
22. SEPT. 2008
BITTE KEINE
ORIGINALE
EINSENDEN

**18.-26. OKT. 2008
MESSEZENTRUM
ZÜRICH (HALLE 9)**

THURGAUERSTR. 11
8050 ZÜRICH
GENAUE ANMELDE-
INFOS UNTER
WWW.ILLUSTRATIVE.DE

Young
Illustrators
20 Award 08

WOMEN IN MIND

How Preem and Landor Worked Together To Create a New Brand Concept

By Landor Associates

www.landor.com

Landor Design is part of the WPP Group and is one of the world's leading design and branding consultancies, with 24 offices around the globe and over 800 professionals. Founded over six decades ago by Walter Landor, the company has helped shape the way branding is used as a decisive form to improve products and services in all industries.

Landor Design gehört zur WPP Group und ist mit international 24 Niederlassungen und über 800 Mitarbeitern eine der weltweit führenden Design- und Branding-Agenturen. Vor mehr als sechs Jahrzehnten von Walter Landor gegründet, hat das Unternehmen dazu beigetragen, Markenbildung branchenübergreifend als maßgebliches Instrument zur Verbesserung von Produkten und Dienstleistungen zu etablieren.

Landor Design appartient au groupe WPP et s'inscrit parmi les sociétés de conseil en design et branding leaders au monde, avec 24 bureaux à travers la planète et plus de 800 professionnels à son service. Fondée il y a plus six décennies par Walter Landor, l'entreprise a permis de forger la façon dont le branding est utilisé sous une forme décisive pour améliorer des produits et des services dans tous les secteurs.

Left
The new petrol station

Right
The old identity

Preem is a major Swedish petroleum company with retail petrol and convenience-store offers. Ongoing petroleum price wars had eroded petrol sales profits to almost nothing, and with increased competition, their c-store operations were facing price pressures, failing to realise significant profit margins, and struggling to meet customers' needs. Preem looked to the example of other successful petroleum companies' retail offerings, and saw its future salvation and only hope of retail profitability in its c-stores.

Landor was brought in to execute and drive Preem's transformation. The team's brief was an extensive one: to review Preem's retail offer, reposition the brand, create a distinct look and feel based on the existing identity, and redesign the forecourt and c-store environments. Furthermore, Landor needed to act as brand guardians to ensure the brand promise was integrated throughout the customer experience, from the pumps to the checkout.

Landor put together a team of experts to transform Preem's vision into a reality. Having analysed the market, the consumers,

Preem ist ein großes Mineralölunternehmen in Schweden mit Tankstellen und angegliederten Geschäften. Andauernde Preiskämpfe auf dem Treibstoffmarkt ließen die Gewinne schrumpfen, und aufgrund der wachsenden Konkurrenz waren die Geschäfte einem hohen Preisdruck ausgesetzt und hatten sehr damit zu kämpfen, den Kundenwünschen gerecht zu werden. Preem nahm sich die Einzelhandelsangebote anderer erfolgreicher Mineralölunternehmen zum Vorbild und sah in der Profitabilität der den Tankstellen angegliederten Geschäfte die Rettung für die Zukunft und seine einzige Hoffnung.

Landor kam ins Spiel, um die Umwandlung von Preem durchzusetzen. Das Briefing für das Team war sehr umfassend: Das Einzelhandelsangebot von Preem sollte überprüft und die Marke neu positioniert werden. Überdies galt es, ein charakteristisches Erscheinungsbild zu schaffen, das auf der vorhandenen Identität beruhte. Die Tankstellenvorplätze sowie die Einrichtung der Läden sollten neu gestaltet werden. Darüber hinaus musste Landor auch als Markenwächter fungieren, um das

Preem est une grande compagnie pétrolière suédoise qui possède des stations essence avec des boutiques. Les guerres en cours sur le prix du pétrole ont quasiment réduit à néant les bénéfices et avec le durcissement de la concurrence, l'activité des boutiques était soumise à des pressions de baisse des prix, ne dégageait pas une marge bénéficiaire suffisante et avait du mal à répondre aux besoins des clients. Preem a analysé les offres de vente en boutique d'autres compagnies pétrolières prospères et a compris que son salut et unique espoir de rentabilité passaient par ses boutiques.

Landor a été chargé d'exécuter et de mener la transformation de Preem. La mission de l'équipe était vaste : analyser l'offre en boutique de Preem, repositionner la marque, créer une image différente à partir de l'identité existante et repenser le devant et les alentours des boutiques. Landor devait par ailleurs agir en gardien de la marque, afin que la promesse de celle-ci soit présente tout au long de l'expérience des clients, de la pompe à la caisse.

and the brand's position, research indicated that Preem could attract more female customers and was perceived to be more caring and friendly than its competitors.

Landor's recommendation was to reposition Preem as a retailer with a petrol offer rather than a petrol station with a retail offer and the team came up with a radical and audacious segmented proposition – instead of trying to grab a larger part of the total consumer cake, Preem should focus on attracting and appealing specifically to women – a hitherto untapped consumer segment. The new brand concept and ensuing design did not mean that men's needs were to be ignored, but rather that by delivering what women wanted, Preem would be raising the bar for all its customers.

Refurbishments on a retail outlet like a petrol station are traditionally done from the canopy signage downwards. Landor took a more radical approach – to focus on the most potent points of interface, the areas where customers would really notice a difference and those that would reflect the radical market segmentation of women.

Markenversprechen in jeglicher Form des Kundenkontakts – von den Zapfsäulen bis zur Kasse – zu integrieren.

Landor stellte ein Expertenteam zusammen, um die Vision von Preem in die Realität umzusetzen. Nachdem Markt, Kunden und die Position der Marke analysiert worden waren, einigte man sich, dass Preem mehr weibliche Kunden gewinnen sollte und dass es als sozial engagierter und freundlicher wahrgenommen werden sollte als die Konkurrenten.

Landor empfahl, Preem anstelle einer Tankstelle mit Warenangebot als Einzelhändler mit einem Tankangebot zu positionieren. Dazu ließ sich das Team ein radikales und kühnes Vorhaben einfallen: Anstatt zu versuchen, einen größeren Teil der gesamten Kundschaft zu bekommen, sollte sich Preem darauf konzentrieren, speziell für Frauen (ein bis dato unerschlossenes Segment der Konsumenten) attraktiv und einladend zu werden. Das neue Markenkonzept und das darauf aufbauende Design bedeutete nicht, dass die Bedürfnisse der männlichen Kundschaft ignoriert werden sollten. Indem sich das

Landor a formé une équipe d'experts pour faire de la vision de Preem une réalité. Après avoir analysé le marché, les consommateurs et la position de la marque, l'étude a montré que Preem pouvait attirer plus de femmes et transmettait une image plus attentionnée et conviviale que ses concurrents.

La recommandation de Landor consistait à repositionner Preem comme une boutique vendant du carburant, plutôt qu'une station essence dotée d'une boutique. L'équipe a formulé une proposition segmentée à la fois radicale et audacieuse : au lieu de tenter de gagner une plus grosse part du gâteau de la clientèle totale, Preem devait s'attacher à attirer et convaincre les femmes, un segment de consommateurs jusqu'ici inexploité. Le nouveau concept de marque et le design en découlant n'impliquaient pas que les hommes étaient ignorés, mais en offrant ce que les femmes souhaitaient, Preem allait élever le niveau pour l'ensemble de sa clientèle.

La rénovation d'un magasin de détail comme une boutique de station essence se base sur la signalisation

Left
Remodelled fuel pumps

Right
Remodelled toilets at
the petrol station

The number one most potent point of interface for women had to be the toilets. It was essential that these were done to the highest standards – they were an emblematic manifestation of Preem's whole approach, and needed to be akin to those in a restaurant or department store in order to deliver the new positioning and to exceed traditional expectations.

Landor's work with Preem covered everything from the brand strategy to the design concept, and the product offer was created with women in mind. The solution separates "carbohydrates from hydrocarbons" through the use of colour and transforms the experiences most important to women – the petrol station forecourts and c-stores.

In a country with such long winters it was vital that Preem petrol stations felt like a safe environment for all its customers and in particular women. The utilitarian and stark forecourt design was replaced by softened, curvaceous architectural features, and brighter lights were added to facilitate a safer, more user-friendly environment. A glass fascia invites customers

Angebot mehr an Frauen ausrichtete, würde Preem vielmehr die Messlatte für alle seine Kunden höher setzen.

Die Modernisierung einer Verkaufsstelle wie einer Tankstelle wird traditionell von der Baldachin-Beschilderung abwärts vorgenommen. Landor griff einen radikaleren Ansatz auf: Man konzentrierte sich auf die potentesten Kontaktpunkte, in denen die Kundschaft wirklich einen Unterschied bemerken würde, und auf jene, die die radikale Ausrichtung des Marktsegments auf Frauen am besten reflektieren würden.

An oberster Stelle bei den wichtigsten Kontaktpunkten für Frauen lagen die Sanitäranlagen. Diese mussten unbedingt den höchsten Standards genügen – sie sollten denen in einem Restaurant oder einem Kaufhaus ähneln, um die neue Positionierung der Marke auch wirklich einzulösen.

Die Arbeit von Landor deckte alles ab, von der Markenstrategie bis hin zum Designkonzept und zum Produktangebot. Die Lösung trennt anhand des gezielten Einsatzes von Farben sozusagen die „Kohlehydrate von den Kohlenwasserstoffen" und verändert jene Erfahrungen, die für Frauen

de l'auvent, et le reste suit. L'approche de Landor a été plus radicale : travailler sur les points d'interface les plus significatifs, les zones dans lesquelles les clients allaient réellement apprécier une différence et celles qui reflèteraient la claire segmentation de marché des femmes.

En tête de liste des points d'interface clés pour les femmes arrivaient forcément les toilettes. Celles-ci devaient à tout prix répondre aux meilleurs standards, car elles étaient une manifestation symbolique de l'approche globale de Preem. Elles devaient s'apparenter à celles d'un restaurant ou d'un grand magasin afin d'indiquer le nouveau positionnement et dépasser les attentes traditionnelles.

Le travail de Landor avec Preem a tout couvert, de la stratégie de marque au concept graphique, et l'offre de produit a été pensée en gardant les femmes à l'esprit. La solution sépare les « hydrates de carbone des hydrocarbures » grâce à l'emploi de la couleur et transforme les expériences les plus importantes pour les femmes : le devant des stations et les boutiques.

Pages 80–81
Development sketches

Left
Key visuals for the brand

Right
Interior design of
the convenience shop

into a new coffee-bar area, a cool place to hang out and a destination in its own right, where the food is fresher and healthier, and toilet facilities were redesigned to be the best petrol station toilets, bar none.

In fact, Preem's toilets have become a talking point, a genuine point of differentiation and something for women to tell their friends about. Featuring full-length mirrors, baby-changing facilities, and softened lighting, they have transformed consumer ideas about what a petrol station toilet facility looks and feels like.

Initially implemented in two pilot sites, the female-focused strategy has paid off and virtually all of Preem's five-year objectives have now either been reached or surpassed. There's been a 30 percent increase in overall revenue and a 20 percent increase in customer numbers, and Preem's market share on petrol became its highest in four years. Buoyed up by these results, Preem launched another five sites and has an ambitious plan to extend the offering.

Following the work with Preem, Landor's brand strategy and design solutions are now filtering through to every decision

am wichtigsten sind: die der Tankstellen-vorplätze und der Geschäfte.

In einem Land mit einem so langen Winter sollten sich Preem-Tankstellen für alle Kunden und vor allem für Frauen als sichere Umgebung darbieten. Die nüchterne Vorplatzgestaltung wurde durch architektonische Features mit weichen, geschwungenen Kurven ersetzt. Überall wurde die Beleuchtung verbessert, um eine sichere, kundenfreundliche Umgebung zu schaffen. Eine Glasfront lädt die Kunden in einen neuen Coffeebar-Bereich ein, der sich als cooler Platz zum Entspannen anbietet und an sich schon ein Ziel ist, wo die Lebensmittel frischer und gesünder sind. Auch die Sanitäreinrichtungen wurden neu gestaltet, damit sie zu den besten Toiletten an Tankstellen überhaupt werden konnten.

Und tatsächlich sind die Preem-Toiletten zu einem Gesprächsthema geworden. Sie sind etwas, wovon Frauen ihren Freundinnen erzählen. Mit großen Wandspiegeln, Wickeltischen und einer dezenten Beleuchtung haben sie die Vorstellung der Kundschaft darüber, wie Tankstellentoiletten aussehen, nachdrücklich verändert.

Dans un pays où les hivers sont si longs, il était essentiel que les stations Preem évoquent un environnement sûr pour tous les clients, notamment les femmes. L'aspect utilitaire et austère du devant a été remplacé par des éléments architecturaux plus doux et curvilignes, et un éclairage plus vif a été ajouté pour contribuer à la sensation d'environnement sûr et convivial. Un panneau en verre invite les clients à une nouvelle zone de cafétéria-bar, un endroit agréable où s'installer et une destination en soi, où la nourriture est plus fraîche et saine, et où les toilettes ont été remodelées pour être indiscutablement les meilleures toilettes de station essence.

De fait, les toilettes de Preem sont devenues un sujet de discussion, une authentique marque de distinction et quelque chose dont les femmes parlent autour d'elles. Grâce à des miroirs sur toute la longueur, des tables à langer et un éclairage plus doux, elles ont changé l'idée que les clients se font des toilettes de station essence.

D'abord appliquée sur deux sites pilotes, la stratégie centrée sur les femmes a porté ses fruits et quasiment tous les

Preem petrol stations makes about its business, from actions to behaviours to communications. A holistic approach to brand repositioning, it has been wholeheartedly embraced by both the customer and the client. The old petrol station mantra for women of "rush in, rush out" has been replaced by "browse, buy, and bond," and it has become a destination that women drive towards as opposed to drive by.

Zu Anfang wurde diese auf Frauen fokussierte Strategie bei zwei Anlagen testweise implementiert. Das hat sich nun ausgezahlt, und Preem hat mittlerweile seine Fünf-Jahres-Ziele erreicht oder übertroffen. Der Gesamtumsatz stieg um 30 Prozent, die Anzahl der Kunden um 20 Prozent, und beim Treibstoff konnte Preem den höchsten Marktanteil seit vier Jahren verzeichnen. Preem erhielt durch diese Ergebnisse beachtlichen Auftrieb und eröffnete fünf weitere Verkaufsstellen und plant, das Angebot noch weiter auszubauen.

Auf Grundlage dieser Arbeit werden von den Abläufen bis hin zur Kommunikation alle von den Preem-Tankstellen getroffenen Geschäftsentscheidungen durch die Strategie- und Designlösungen von Landor gefiltert. Dieser holistische Ansatz wurde sowohl von den Verbrauchern als auch dem Auftraggeber begeistert begrüßt. Das alte Frauenmotto für Tankstellen „Reinhetzen, raushetzen" wurde nun durch ein „Schauen, Shoppen und Wiederkommen" ersetzt, und die Tankstellen sind zu einem Ort geworden, auf den Frauen sich freuen, anstatt ihn möglichst schnell wieder verlassen zu wollen.

objectifs sur cinq ans de Preem ont été atteints ou dépassés. Les recettes globales ont connu une hausse de 30 %, et le nombre de clients de 20 %, faisant passer la part de marché de Preem à son niveau le plus élevé en quatre ans. Encouragée par ces résultats, Preem a lancé cinq autres sites et a élaboré un plan ambitieux pour étendre l'offre.

Après ce travail avec Preem, la stratégie de marque et les solutions de design de Landor servent à présent de filtres pour toutes les décisions prises par les stations essence de la marque concernant l'activité (actions, comportements et communications). Cette approche globale du repositionnement de la marque a été complètement adoptée par les consommateurs et par le client. L'ancien mantra des femmes pour les stations essence, « vite entrer, vite sortir », est devenu « visiter, acheter et rester fidèle ». C'est maintenant une destination, et non plus un lieu de passage obligé.

THE OFFICIAL CAMPAIGN

Obama '08 Election Campaign Identity
From the Logo to Desktop Backgrounds

By Sol Sender

http://senderllc.com

Sol Sender From being founder and principal of Sender LLC, Sol Sender now works as a strategist with VSA Partners. He works across a range of disciplines with some of the world's most valuable businesses and brands. His work as both a designer and a strategist has been recognized by the Webby Awards, The International Web Awards, and Communication Arts, among many others.

Sol Sender, der Gründer und Leiter von Sender LLC, arbeitet heute als Werbestratege bei VSA Partners. Er ist interdisziplinär für einige der weltweit größten und finanzkräftigsten Branchen und Marken tätig. Seine Leistung als Designer und Stratege wurde unter anderem durch die Webby Awards, The International Web Awards und Communication Arts anerkannt.

D'abord fondateur et membre principal de Sender LLC, **Sol Sender** exerce à présent comme stratégiste pour VSA Partners. Il touche à une série de disciplines pour certaines des entreprises et marques les plus prisées au monde. Son travail comme designer et stratégiste a été récompensé par les Webby Awards, les International Web Awards et Communication Arts, entre autres.

Left & right
Desktop backgrounds
available for download
on the website:
www.barackobama.com

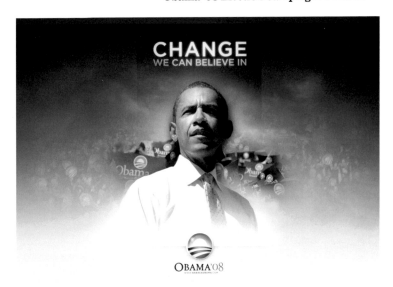

Though the development of a successful identity can be a long and painstaking journey, there are three criteria that I often use as guideposts.

<u>First</u>: Does the logo tell a clear and appropriate story? Does it capture the essence of the message? Is it capable of being comfortably told by the company's key constituents?

<u>Then</u>, <u>style</u>: Does the style of the logo resonate with contemporary sensibilities – but with a long shelf-life, a timeless potential? And is it ownable?

<u>Finally</u>, <u>execution</u>: Is the craftsmanship precise and deliberate, balanced, simple but nuanced?

The story is especially crucial, so before we begin sketching, we look to certain value propositions – as platforms that form the basis of our explorations. For the Obama 2008 campaign, these included:

– A candidate profoundly new and different; a new day; new possibilities; change

– The end of red states and blue states; one country coming together

– A groundswell of enthusiasm and hope; infinite possibilities.

Obwohl die Entwicklung einer erfolgreichen Identität eine lange und mühsame Reise sein kann, gibt es drei Kriterien, die ich oft als Wegweiser nutze.

<u>Erstens</u> – <u>das Logo</u>: Erzählt es eine klare und angemessene Geschichte? Fängt es das Wesentliche der Botschaft ein? Kann es problemlos von den wesentlichen Schlüsselelementen des Unternehmens vermittelt werden?

<u>Zweitens</u> – <u>der Stil</u>: Stimmt das Logo mit dem Zeitgeist überein, ist aber gleichzeitig auch langlebig und verfügt über ein zeitloses Potenzial? Ist es zwingend und unverwechselbar mit dem Produkt oder der Dienstleistung verbunden?

<u>Drittens</u> – <u>die Ausführung</u>: Ist die Umsetzung präzise und wohldurchdacht, ausgewogen und einfach, aber dennoch nuanciert?

Vor allem die Story ist ausschlaggebend. Bevor wir uns also ans Entwerfen machen, sollten wir uns mit bestimmten Aussagen beschäftigen – sie dienen als Plattformen, auf denen wir unsere Entwürfe entwickeln können. Bei der Kampagne für Barack Obama im Jahr 2008 waren das u. a.:

Même si le développement d'une identité réussie peut être une aventure longue et laborieuse, je me sers souvent de trois critères comme repères.

<u>Un</u> : le logo raconte-t-il une histoire claire et appropriée ? Capte-t-il l'essence du message ? Est-il capable d'être aisément utilisé par les composants clés de l'entreprise ?

<u>Deux</u>, <u>le style</u> : le style du logo fait-il écho aux sensibilités contemporaines mais avec une longue durée de vie, un potentiel infini ? Est-il distinctif ?

<u>Trois</u>, <u>l'exécution</u> : le travail est-il précis et réfléchi, équilibré, simple mais aussi nuancé ?

L'histoire est particulièrement importante ; avant de commencer des ébauches, nous prenons donc en compte plusieurs propositions de valeur, comme les plateformes servant de base à nos explorations. Pour la campagne Obama 2008, il s'agissait de ce qui suit :

– Un candidat profondément nouveau et différent ; un nouveau jour ; de nouvelles possibilités ; un changement

– La fin des états bleus et rouges ; un pays uni

Left
Campaign's key identity

Right
Official campaign poster

As our sketches develop, we seek the most immediate expression of each idea. For Obama '08, we began to assess the style through applications: pins, T-shirts, billboards, bumper stickers. This helped us and the campaign team envision each identity as a potential centerpiece for the campaign's visual expression. Many of us were immediately drawn to the powerful message of the sun on the horizon – a rising star across the American landscape. But we had other strong options – identity systems that were further "out of the box", that more naturally lent themselves to a broad visual palette.

This we knew: The candidate was young and, some would say, inexperienced. His father's family was Muslim. He could be the first African American nominee of a major party. For much of America, he might be seen as different, even threatening. For these reasons, we felt strongly about balancing a message of "profoundly new and different" with the traditional (and reassuring) vernacular of American campaign graphics: red, white, blue, stars and stripes. We wanted the identity to say "yes,

– Ein Kandidat, der völlig neu und ganz anders war, ein neuer Tag, neue Möglichkeiten, Veränderung („Change")

– Das Ende der „red states and blue states" (die Aufteilung der Bundesstaaten nach Republikanern und Demokraten), ein Land, das zusammenfindet

– Eine Grundströmung der Begeisterung und Hoffnung, unendliche Möglichkeiten.

Je mehr sich unsere Skizzen entwickeln, desto intensiver suchen wir nach einem möglichst unmittelbaren Ausdruck für jede Idee. Für *Obama '08* begannen wir damit, den Stil durch verschiedene Umsetzungen einzuschätzen: in Form von Anstecknadeln, T-Shirts, Werbetafeln, Autoaufkleber. Das half uns dabei, uns die jeweilige Identität als potenzielles Kernstück für den visuellen Ausdruck der Kampagne auszumalen. Viele von uns waren sofort begeistert von der kraftvollen Botschaft einer Sonne am Horizont – ein aufgehender Stern über einer amerikanischen Landschaft. Doch wir hatten auch andere Optionen – Identitätssysteme, die einsatzbereit waren und sich auf natürliche Weise eher für eine breite visuelle Palette eigneten.

– Un vague d'enthousiasme et d'espoir ; des possibilités infinies

Au fil de nos esquisses, nous cherchons l'expression la plus directe de chaque idée. Pour Obama '08, nous avons d'abord évalué le style à travers des applications : pins, T-shirts, panneaux d'affichage, autocollants pour véhicules. Grâce à cela, nous avons pu, ainsi que l'équipe de la campagne, imaginer chaque identité comme un élément central possible pour l'expression visuelle de la campagne. Beaucoup d'entre nous ont été immédiatement attirés par le message puissant du soleil à l'horizon, une étoile qui se lève sur le paysage américain. Nous avions aussi d'autres options de poids, des systèmes d'identité davantage « clé en main » et qui se prêtaient plus naturellement à une large palette visuelle.

Nous le savions : le candidat était jeune et, pour certains, il manquait d'expérience. La famille de son père était musulmane. Il pouvait être le premier candidat afroaméricain d'un grand parti. Pour un grand nombre d'Américains, il pouvait être vu comme différent, comme une menace même. C'est pourquoi nous avons insisté

OBAMA'08

YES WE CAN

WWW.**BARACKOBAMA**.COM

 PAID FOR BY OBAMA FOR AMERICA

CALIFORNIA

NEW YORK

MISSISSIPPI

ALABAMA

KENTUCKY

TENNESSEE

ILLINOIS

FLORIDA

MICHIGAN

Above
Identity adapted to names of states

Right
Various followers' badges

this is a breakthrough candidate unlike any other, but this is also a man who believes – and stands for – the most fundamental principles of our constitution and country." With this in mind, we recommended the sun rising across a blue sky, shining on a red and white striped landscape. It held a potent, resonant story, real visual power and it struck the right balance of innovation and tradition. It was also strong enough to be used independent of the candidate's name: it was a real symbol – on some level capable of standing for something even broader.

Within weeks of identity finalization, however, we began to see poor applications of the mark. On the podium at the candidate's formal announcement, the center of the logo was knocked out and the story severely compromised: it became a dark star rising on the American landscape. Though we hurried to develop clearer guidelines for usage, it was only when the campaign brought in a talented team of in-house designers, led by Scott Thomas and John Slabyk, that we began to see real consistency. I had worked with my team

Folgendes war uns bekannt: Der Kandidat war jung und – wie manche sagen würden – unerfahren. Die Familie seines Vaters war muslimisch. Er könnte der erste afroamerikanische Kandidat einer großen Partei sein. Für viele Amerikaner könnte er als andersartig oder gar bedrohlich erscheinen. Aus diesen Gründen hatten wir den Eindruck, dass wir eine ausgewogene Botschaft brauchten. Diese sollte das „ganz Neue und Andere" mit der traditionellen Bildgebung amerikanischer Kampagnengestaltung ausbalancieren: rot, weiß, blau, Stars and Stripes. Wir wollten, dass die Identität besagt: „Hier haben wir den Durchbruch eines Kandidaten, der wie kein anderer ist, aber gleichzeitig jemand, der an die grundlegenden Prinzipien unserer Verfassung und unseres Landes glaubt und dafür einsteht". Darum haben wir empfohlen, die vor einem blauen Himmel aufgehende Sonne zu nehmen, die auf eine Landschaft mit blauen und weißen Streifen scheint. Sie besaß eine kraftvolle Story, echte visuelle Ausdruckskraft und wahrte genau die richtige Balance zwischen Innovation und Tradition. Sie war auch stark

pour équilibrer le message de « profondément nouveau et différent » avec le jargon traditionnel (et rassurant) du graphisme de campagne aux États-Unis : rouge, blanc, bleu, des étoiles et des bandes. Nous voulions que l'identité dise : « oui, c'est un candidat révolutionnaire comme aucun autre, et c'est aussi un homme qui croit et défend les principes les plus essentiels à notre Constitution et à notre pays ». Avec cette idée en tête, nous avons conseillé un soleil levant dans un ciel bleu, brillant sur un paysage fait de bandes blanches et rouges. Il évoquait une histoire forte et résonante, possédait un véritable pouvoir visuel et apportait l'équilibre parfait entre innovation et tradition. Il avait aussi la force suffisante pour être utilisé indépendamment du nom du candidat et être un véritable symbole, capable dans une certaine mesure d'illustrer un concept encore plus large.

Lors des semaines de finalisation de l'identité, des applications médiocres de la marque ont commencé à apparaître. Sur l'estrade lors de l'annonce officielle du candidat, le centre du logo était taché et

– Amanda Gentry, Andy Keene, and Steve Juras at mo/de – to launch the identity. Now it was up to the campaign – and millions of supporters – to infuse it with the energy that the candidate inspired.

For any brand, consistency and rules are essential: color, clear space, typography, formal integrity, voice. With this in mind, the campaign team expanded upon our guidelines and developed a system that informed a broader brand language and an evolution of the mark. They identified three categories of expression: campaign, instant vintage, and timelessness. These shaped the design of everything from the website to posters, bumper stickers, reproductions of speeches, and a fantastic array of logo variations.

But a successful political campaign is unlike a commercial brand. It is not selling a product to be consumed; it is seeking a more authentic connection. And though the campaign's official use of the logo and further development of the brand language was extraordinary, it was the grassroots expression of support that would make Obama's candidacy a movement. With this

genug, um sie unabhängig vom Namen des Kandidaten einzusetzen: Es war ein echtes Symbol – in gewisser Weise fähig, für etwas zu stehen, das noch breiter angelegt war.

Ein paar Wochen vor Abschluss der Identitätsfindung begegnete uns allerdings eine negative Umdeutung des Symbols. Die Mitte des Logos war entfernt worden, was seine Story böse kompromittiert: Das Symbol wurde zu einem dunklen Stern, der über der amerikanischen Landschaft aufsteigt. Obwohl wir uns beeilten, eindeutige Richtlinien für die Verwendung zu entwickeln, erzielten wir erst dann eine geschlossene Umsetzung, als sich die Kampagne die Unterstützung eines talentierten Designteams holte, das von Scott Thomas und John Slabyk geleitet wurde. Ich hatte mit meinem Team Amanda Gentry, Andy Keene und Steve Juras bei mo/de daran gearbeitet, die Identität anzustoßen, nun war es Sache der Kampagne und deren millionenfacher Unterstützer, ihr die Energie einzuflößen, mit der der Kandidat die Menschen inspirieren sollte.

Für jede Marke sind Konsistenz und Regeln unverzichtbar: Farbe, klarer Raum,

l'histoire sérieusement compromise : une étoile noire s'élevait au-dessus du paysage américain. Nous nous sommes empressés de donner des instructions plus claires pour les applications, mais c'est seulement lorsque la campagne a recruté une équipe compétente de designers en interne dirigée par Scott Thomas et John Slabyk que la cohérence a pu s'apprécier. J'avais travaillé avec mon équipe (Amanda Gentry, Andy Keene et Steve Juras chez mo/de) pour lancer l'identité. Il revenait désormais à la campagne et aux millions de partisans de l'insuffler avec l'énergie que le candidat inspirait.

Pour n'importe quelle marque, la cohérence et les règles sont cruciales : couleur, espace libre, typographie, intégrité de forme, voix. Avec ces aspects en tête, l'équipe de la campagne a développé nos instructions et mis au point un système qui donnait un langage de marque plus large et une évolution de la marque. Ils ont identifié trois catégories d'expression : campagne, référence immédiate et éternité. Ces catégories ont conditionné l'ensemble du design, du site Web aux affiches, auto-

 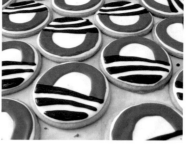 

in mind, a fourth, "open-source" category of expression emerged: the expression of supporters. Yes, there were pre-packaged tools to utilize, but the logo was also made available for download – to use as anyone saw fit. These expressions – the brand in the hands of supporters (and non-supporters, for that matter) everywhere – went totally un-policed. They were imprecise. They broke rules. They were rough and sometimes poorly executed. They were extraordinary.

At its most powerful then, the logo was utilized by thousands, perhaps millions – as an expression of their belief in the candidate. Cookies and muffins, hand-made signs, carved pumpkins, babies' bibs, tattoos: Here was a brand identity unlike any other – not because it was revolutionary in form, but because it was revolutionary in usage; because it helped people make the candidate's message their own; because it was simple and flexible enough to contain and express the depth of feeling of an electorate that made Barack Obama the 44th President of the United States.

Typografie, formale Integrität, Stimme. Dahingehend entwickelte das Team der Kampagne ein System, das eine breitere Markensprache und eine Weiterentwicklung des Symbols ermöglichte. Sie identifizierten drei Kategorien des Markenausdrucks: Kampagne, „Instant Vintage" (etwa: „sofort ein guter Jahrgang") und Zeitlosigkeit. Anhand dieser Kategorien wurde das Design auf alles Mögliche übertragen – von der Website über Plakate, die Wiedergabe der Reden bis hin zu einem fantastischen Arrangement von Logovariationen.

Doch eine politische Kampagne funktioniert anders als eine Kampagne für eine kommerzielle Marke. Sie verkauft kein Produkt für den Konsum, sondern strebt eine authentischere Verbindung an. Und obwohl die offizielle Verwendung des Logos außergewöhnlich war, war es die Art, in der die Freiwilligen an der Basis ihre Unterstützung bekundeten, die aus der Kandidatur von Obama eine regelrechte Bewegung machte. Vor diesem Hintergrund entstand eine vierte Kategorie der Brand Expression, quasi „Open Source" und ohne Copyright: das waren die Ausdrucksmöglichkeiten derjeni-

collants, reproductions de discours et une incroyable série de déclinaisons du logo.

Une campagne politique réussie n'a rien d'une marque commerciale. Elle ne vend pas un produit à consommer, mais recherche une connexion plus authentique. Même si l'usage officiel du logo par la campagne et le développement ultérieur du langage de marque ont été extraordinaires, ils n'ont été que l'expression de base du soutien qui allait faire de la candidature d'Obama un mouvement. En prenant cela en compte, une quatrième catégorie « libre » d'expression s'est présentée : celle des partisans. Des outils prédéfinis existaient bien, mais le logo pouvait aussi être téléchargé pour que chacun l'utilise comme bon lui semble. Ces expressions (la marque partout, dans les mains des partisans et aussi des détracteurs) sont devenues totalement hors contrôle. Elles étaient inexactes. Elles ne respectaient pas les règles. Elles étaient approximatives et parfois mal appliquées. Elles étaient extraordinaires.

À son apogée, le logo a été utilisé par des milliers de personnes, des millions

Left & right
User-generated applications
with the original logo

Photography:
"House" by Mary Basu
"Cookies" by Megan Paonessa
"Stadium" by Sarah Parker
"Posters" by Richard Rodriguez
"Pride" by Arvind Chahal
"Pumpkin" by Sol Sender
"Baby" by Ahmie Yeung

gen, die Obama freiwillig unterstützten. Das Logo wurde zum Download bereitgestellt, damit jeder es nach Belieben verwenden konnte. Diese Formen des Ausdrucks, bei denen die Marke überall in die Hände von Anhängern (aber auch von Gegnern) kam, verliefen völlig unkontrolliert: Sie waren unpräzise. Sie brachen die Regeln. Sie waren außergewöhnlich.

Am kraftvollsten kam dies in der Art und Weise zum Ausdruck, mit der das Logo bei Tausenden, vielleicht Millionen von Menschen als Bekundung ihres Vertrauens in den Kandidaten umgesetzt wurde. Kekse und Muffins, handgemalte Schilder, Babylätzchen, Tätowierungen: Hier bekamen wir es mit einer Markenidentität zu tun wie nie zuvor – nicht weil sie der Form nach, sondern weil sie in der Nutzung revolutionär war. Weil sie den Menschen dabei half, sich die Botschaft des Kandidaten anzueignen. Weil sie einfach und flexibel genug war, um die Gefühle der Wählerschaft in sich aufzunehmen und auszudrücken – jene Wähler, die Barack Obama zum 44. Präsidenten der USA gemacht haben.

peut-être, comme expression de leur confiance dans le candidat. Cookies, muffins, panneaux faits à la main, citrouilles creusées, biberons, tatouages : c'était une identité de marque comme aucune autre, non pas car elle était en soi révolutionnaire, mais parce que son utilisation était elle révolutionnaire, car elle permettait aux gens de s'approprier le message du candidat, car elle était suffisamment simple et adaptable pour intégrer et exprimer la profondeur des sentiments d'un électorat qui a fait de Barack Obama le 44e Président des États-Unis.

THE RELEASE CHARITY

A Simple Brand Transformed to Communicate Effectively About Serious Issues

By Sasha Vidakovic, SViDesign

www.svidesign.com

Sasha Vidakovic was born in Yugoslavia and studied at the Academy of Fine Arts in Sarajevo before moving to work for companies such as Enterprise IG, Interbrand, Landor, and the Conran Design Group. In 2006 he opened his branding and design consultancy in London, SVIDesign, where he works for small to big European companies.

Sasha Vidakovic wurde im früheren Jugoslawien geboren und studierte an der Akademie der Schönen Künste in Sarajewo, bevor er für Unternehmen wie Enterprise IG, Interbrand, Landor und die Conran Design Group arbeitete. 2006 eröffnete er seine Design- und Branding-Agentur SViDesign in London, wo er für kleine und große europäische Firmen tätig ist.

Sasha Vidakovic est né en Yougoslavie et a étudié à l'Academy of Fine Arts de Sarajevo, avant d'être engagé par des entreprises comme Enterprise IG, Interbrand, Landor et le Conran Design Group. En 2006, il a ouvert sa propre société de conseil en branding et design à Londres, SVIDesign, où il travail pour des entreprises européennes de toute taille.

Release
Drugs, The Law & Human Rights

HELPLINE 0845 4500 215

HOME
ABOUT US
SERVICES
CAMPAIGNS
INFORMATION
SHOP
DONATE

 GO

In 1967 Release established the first ever national drugs help line. Maintaining its pivotal role in the drugs and legal advice field, it now operates a number of specialist services.

Newsletter
Keep in touch with our latest news and campaigns

Donate
Your generosity helps us provide our free services

Membership
Join Release and support our work

Log In
Existing members log in here

Latest News
Our latest publication 'Drugs and the Law'
Release's latest publication which covers all aspects of drugs related law.

• Preview 'Drugs and the Law' online
• See other booklets that are available
• See our other publications

Conference 2009
Book your ticket for the conference online.

Latest Campaigns
Changes in UK drug policy
This year Release has chosen to campaign on 4 areas of drug policy that contradict principles of human rights.

• Medical Cannabis
• Hepatitis C (HCV)
• Drug Paraphernalia
• Women in prison

Left
New website design

Right
Old website design

Branding is often associated with big budgets and mega-advertising campaigns, the remit of big corporations. And yet branding is, at core, about intelligent communication: helping define what you are and what you stand for, supported by a distinctive and clear visual language. That means any company, product, or idea is amenable to branding. In fact, one could argue that effective branding is all the more relevant to resource-scarce organisations such as charities. Our recent work with UK-based drugs and drugs law charity Release provides a telling case in point.

Founded in the 1960s as a helpline advising callers on drugs law, Release had by 2007 substantially grown in stature and ambit. Its activities encompassed an array of legal and drugs services for the public and professionals, as well as an active engagement in the national and international drug policy arena. Well recognised and respected, the brand nevertheless suffered from an over-reliance on its original, counter-culture image; its more sophisticated, contemporary interventions, adapted to the UK's evolved legal, cultural and

Branding wird oft im Kontext üppiger Budgets und riesiger Werbekampagnen wahrgenommen, bei denen große Unternehmen Unmengen Geld investieren. Und doch geht es bei der Markenentwicklung im Grunde um intelligente Kommunikation: Sie hilft zu definieren, wer man ist und wofür man steht, und das wird von einer charakteristischen und klaren visuellen Sprache unterstützt. Also ist im Prinzip jedes Unternehmen, jedes Produkt und jede Idee für ein Branding geeignet. Tatsächlich ist effektives Branding für Wohltätigkeits- oder nicht-kommerzielle Organisationen noch viel wichtiger. Unsere jüngste Arbeit mit Release, einer in Großbritannien beheimateten Initiative, die sich in den Bereichen Drogenhilfe und Drogengesetzgebung engagiert, vermittelt dies sehr anschaulich.

Release wurde in den 1960er-Jahren als Telefondienst gegründet, bei dem Anrufer über Drogengesetze beraten wurden, doch schon 2007 war Release in Format und Anspruch deutlich gewachsen. Die Aktivitäten umfassten verschiedene Dienste zur rechtlichen Beratung und Drogenhilfe. Außerdem war Release sowohl national als

Le branding se voit souvent associé à de gros budgets et à des macrocampagnes publicitaires, domaine des grandes entreprises. Pourtant, le branding relève au fond d'une communication intelligente : il s'agit d'aider à définir qui vous êtes et ce que vous représentez à l'aide d'un langage visuel clair et pertinent. N'importe quelle entreprise, produit ou idée peut donc faire l'objet du branding. On pourrait même alléguer que le branding est d'autant plus important pour les organisations qui manquent de ressources, comme les institutions caritatives. Notre récent travail avec Release, une fondation britannique qui agit dans le domaine de la toxicomanie et de la législation relative aux drogues, offre un exemple éloquent en la matière.

Fondée dans les années 1960 comme un service d'assistance téléphonique pour informer sur les lois relatives aux drogues, en 2007 Release avait pris une ampleur considérable, tant en envergure qu'en compétences. Ses activités englobaient un ensemble de services juridiques et liés aux drogues, pour le public comme pour les professionnels, ainsi qu'un engagement

political context, tended to be overlooked. With a 40-year anniversary looming, the brand needed reinvigorating.

The new "look and feel" had to entice a younger public to Release, transmit the organisation's evolved functions, while reaffirming its commitment to challenging authorities in relation to their stance on drug use. For Sebastian Saville, Director of Release, "we needed to reflect the seriousness of what we do without losing our well-established 'on the street' credentials." The new visual language would have to talk to a highly diverse audience, and be easily applicable to a variety of media (web, publications, conferences, etc.). Moreover, strict financial constraints and the requirement of in-house management of the brand called for cost-effective, clear, consistent, and flexible solutions.

To translate visually this brand (re) positioning, a first step entailed revamping the basic identity elements: logo, colours, and typeface. Release's original mark was a bold logotype with an enmeshed dove symbolising escape. Relevant to the '60s and '70s when drug users were

auch international in der Drogenpolitik engagiert. Die Marke war zwar allgemein bekannt und respektiert, litt jedoch darunter, dass sie sich auf ihr ursprünglich aus der Gegenkultur stammendes Image verließ. Durch ihre anspruchsvollen, zeitgemäßen Aktivitäten hatte sich die Organisation dem juristischen, kulturellen und politischen Kontext in Großbritannien angepasst. Als das 40. Jubiläum näher rückte, benötigte die Marke eine deutliche Auffrischung.

Das neue Erscheinungsbild sollte ein jüngeres Publikum zu Release locken und vermitteln, welche Funktionen die Organisation weiterentwickelt hatte. Doch man fühlte sich weiterhin dem Anspruch verpflichtet, Behörden und Autoritäten in Bezug auf Drogen kritisch herauszufordern. Sebastian Saville, dem Direktor von Release, zufolge „mussten wir die Seriosität dessen reflektieren, was wir tun, ohne die alte Glaubwürdigkeit auf der Straße einzubüßen". Die neue visuelle Sprache musste sich einer vielschichtigen Zielgruppe vermitteln lassen und in verschiedenen Medienkontexte (z. B. Internet, Konferenzen etc.) umsetzbar sein. Überdies verlangten strenge Bud-

actif dans le domaine politique tant au niveau national qu'international. Bien que reconnue et respectée, la marque a été victime d'une confiance excessive en son image originale et à contre-courant. Ses interventions plus modernes et sophistiquées, adaptées à l'évolution du contexte juridique, culturel et politique du Royaume-Uni, avaient tendance à passer inaperçues. À l'approche de son 40ᵉ anniversaire, la marque devait se revitaliser.

Le nouveau « look » devait attirer un public plus jeune, transmettre les nouvelles fonctions de l'organisation, tout en réaffirmant son engagement à défier les autorités sur leur position envers la consommation de drogues. Selon Sebastian Saville, directeur de Release, « nous avions besoin de refléter le caractère sérieux de nos activités sans perdre notre solide réputation de proximité avec la rue ». Le nouveau langage visuel devait s'adresser à un public des plus divers et s'appliquer facilement à une multitude de supports (Web, publications, conférences, etc.). De plus, les contraintes strictement financières et la demande d'une gestion

insufficiently represented and supported, the symbol had lost its pertinence in an evolved legal environment. We therefore felt that the logo would be more relevant and confident in its message, stripped of symbolic representation. However, to emphasise continuity with the previous logo we retained a bold and confident typeface which additionally reflected the organisation's authority and professionalism. Finally, we chose orange as primary colour (along with black and white) to convey new energy and, at the same time, ensure that the brand would stand out in a charity environment overburdened with the colour red.

If designing the brand's basic elements proved an evolutionary process, designing Release's "house style" or broader visual language brought about a mini revolution: the organisation had simply never had any such consistency and its web or print output was highly disparate. Yet we were confident that a clearly set-out and applied "house style", linking all points of the brand expression tightly, was the key to flexible, efficient, and especially

getgrenzen und die Anforderung, dass die Marke im eigenen Haus verwaltet werden sollte, kosteneffektive, klare, konsistente und flexible Lösungen.

Für diese (Neu-)Positionierung der Marke wurden in einem ersten Schritt die grundlegenden Identitätselemente Logo, Farben und Schriften erneuert. Das ursprüngliche Logo war ein Schriftzug mit einer Taube, die Entkommen und Ausbruch symbolisieren sollte. Das mochte in den 60er- und 70er-Jahren bedeutsam gewesen sein, als die Drogenkonsumenten nur wenig repräsentiert und unterstützt wurden. Da sich der rechtliche Rahmen jedoch weiterentwickelt hatte, war dieses Symbol belanglos geworden. Das Logo könnte relevanter und seine Botschaft überzeugender sein, wenn es von seinem symbolischen Repräsentanten befreit würde. Um die Kontinuität mit dem vorherigen Logo zu wahren, wählten wir eine Schrift mit gefetteten Buchstaben, die außerdem der Autorität und der Professionalität der Organisation entsprach. Schließlich entschieden wir uns neben Schwarz und Weiß für Orange als Hauptfarbe, um die

en interne de la marque imposaient des solutions rentables, claires, cohérentes et flexibles.

Pour traduire visuellement ce (re)positionnement de marque, la première étape a supposé la refonte des éléments d'identité de base : logo, couleurs et police de caractères. La marque d'origine de Release était un logo en gras, avec une colombe captive, symbole de fuite. Justifié dans les années 1960 et 1970, lorsque les toxicomanes ne bénéficiaient pas d'une représentation et d'un soutien suffisants, le symbole avait perdu sa pertinence dans le nouvel environnement juridique. Nous avons donc pensé que le logo serait plus approprié et véhiculerait un message plus confiant s'il était dénué de représentation symbolique. Pour souligner toutefois la continuité avec le logo antérieur, nous avons conservé une solide typographie en gras, qui reflétait en outre l'expertise et le professionnalisme de l'organisation. Enfin, nous avons opté pour l'orange comme couleur de base (avec le noir et le blanc) pour transmettre une nouvelle énergie et garantir en parallèle que la marque se

This page
Series of old leaflets and print material

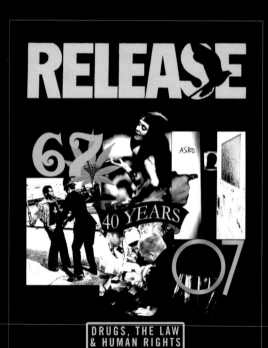

Release
Drugs, The Law & Human Rights

**DRUGS
AND
THE
LAW**

HELPLINE 0845 4500 215

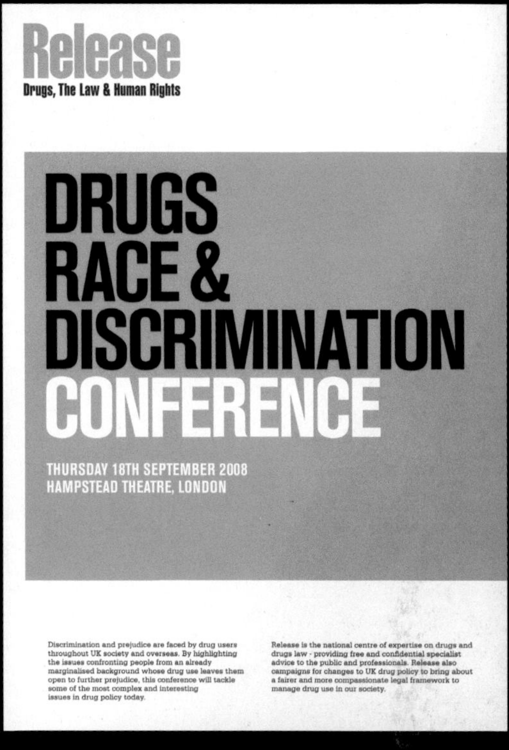

Release
Drugs, The Law & Human Rights

**DRUGS
RACE &
DISCRIMINATION
CONFERENCE**

THURSDAY 18TH SEPTEMBER 2008
HAMPSTEAD THEATRE, LONDON

Discrimination and prejudice are faced by drug users throughout UK society and overseas. By highlighting the issues confronting people from an already marginalised background whose drug use leaves them open to further prejudice, this conference will tackle some of the most complex and interesting issues in drug policy today.

Release is the national centre of expertise on drugs and drugs law - providing free and confidential specialist advice to the public and professionals. Release also campaigns for changes to UK drug policy to bring about a fairer and more compassionate legal framework to manage drug use in our society.

Release
Drugs, The Law & Human Rights

**RELEASE
OUR
WORK**

HELPLINE 0845 4500 215

www.release.org.uk

This page
Print material with the new identity

Left
Poster at bus shelter

Right
T-shirt and eco-bag for the charity

cost-effective communication. We therefore introduced a simple secondary graphic element: a rectangular form that bleeds on one side of any given format (book or leaflet cover, website, etc.). Conceptually, this would translate the idea of "a way out" in a more subtle manner than the earlier dove symbol; functionally, the block would provide the backdrop to text or illustration. The simplicity of the secondary element and the combination of colours (orange, black, and white) would allow great flexibility through permutation, as well as facilitate the development of a consistent and easily recognisable image. Playing a much more prominent role, typography was kept strikingly simple with a strong, condensed typeface for headlines and titles, echoing the personality of the logo.

The end result of this re-branding exercise has so far been particularly successful. Staff at Release welcomed the change and have embraced the new image with enthusiasm and vigour. Energised by the new colour, they have appreciated the ease and flexibility of the house style and feel it has contributed to brand recognition in a

neue Energie zu verdeutlichen und gleich-zeitig zu gewährleisten, dass die Marke im Kontext von Wohltätigkeitsorganisationen, die von der Farbe Rot dominiert sind, hervorsticht.

Das neue Design des „Hausstils" von Release war eine Minirevolution: Bei dieser Organisation war einfach noch nie etwas so konsistent durchgezogen worden, und ihre Erscheinungsformen in Print oder Web waren grundverschieden. Dennoch vertrauten wir darauf, dass ein klar und eindeutig umgesetzter „Stil des Hauses", bei dem alle Punkte, an denen die Marke ihren Ausdruck findet, eng miteinander verknüpft werden, der zentrale Schlüssel zu einer flexiblen, effizienten und vor allem kostenwirksamen Kommunikation ist. Von daher führten wir ein zweites grafisches Element ein: eine schlichtes Rechteck, das in allen vorgegebenen Formaten (Buch, Flyer, Website etc.) nach einer Seite hin verblasst. Vom Konzept her sollte damit die Vorstellung eines „Auswegs" auf subtilere Weise vermittelt werden als mit dem alten Symbol der Taube; von seiner Funktion her sollte dieser Block den Hintergrund für Text

distinguerait dans le paysage surchargé de rouge des institutions caritatives.

Si la conception des éléments de base de la marque s'est révélée être un processus d'évolution, celle du « style maison » ou du langage visuel à plus grande échelle de Release a quant à elle supposé une petite révolution : l'organisation n'avait tout sim-plement jamais connu une telle cohérence et son site Web et ses documents imprimés étaient très disparates. Nous étions toutefois certains qu'un « style maison » clairement défini et appliqué, créant des liens forts entre tous les modes d'expression de la marque, était la clé pour une communica-tion flexible, efficace et en particulier rentable. Nous avons donc introduit un élément graphique secondaire simple : une forme rectangulaire qui se retrouve sur un côté de chaque page pour tous les formats (couverture de livre ou de brochure, site Web, etc.). Sur le plan conceptuel, il traduit l'idée d'une « voie de sortie » plus subtilement que l'ancien symbole de la colombe ; sur le plan fonctionnel, le bloc offre une toile de fond pour du texte et des illustrations. La simplicité de cet élément

positive manner. Possibly more gratifying still has been the immediate approving reaction from Release's audience nationally and internationally.

oder Illustrationen bilden. Die Einfachheit dieses sekundären Elements in Kombination mit den Farben Orange, Schwarz und Weiß erlaubte durch Vertauschung und Umstellung eine größere Flexibilität und erleichterte überdies die Entwicklung eines konsistenten Logos von hohem Wiedererkennungswert. Weil die Typografie eine deutlich wichtigere Rolle spielt, wurde sie bestechend einfach gehalten. Dabei wird eine gestauchte Fettschrift für Überschriften und Titel eingesetzt, die sozusagen ein Echo der Persönlichkeit des Logos bildet.

Das Endergebnis dieser Re-Branding-Aufgabe war bisher außergewöhnlich erfolgreich. Die Mitarbeiter von Release begrüßten die Überarbeitung und waren von dem aktualisierten Image begeistert. Die neue Farbe wurde als sehr energetisch empfunden und die Leichtigkeit und Flexibilität des Hausstils gewürdigt. Man spürte, dass sie sich auf die Erkennbarkeit der Marke sehr positiv ausgewirkt hat. Noch erfreulicher ist vielleicht die unmittelbare Anerkennung, mit der das nationale und internationale Zielpublikum von Release reagierte.

secondaire et la combinaison des couleurs (orange, noir et blanc) permettent une plus grande flexibilité par permutation, et simplifient la création d'une image cohérente et facilement reconnaissable. Jouant un rôle plus en vue, la typographie est restée remarquablement simple, avec une police de caractères solide et condensée pour les titres, à l'image de la personnalité du logo.

Le résultat final de cet exercice de re-branding s'est pour l'instant avéré être un véritable succès. Le personnel de Release a bien accueilli le changement et a adopté la nouvelle image avec enthousiasme et motivation. Les collaborateurs, stimulés par la nouvelle couleur, ont apprécié la simplicité et la flexibilité du style maison et l'ont perçu comme un élément positif pour la reconnaissance de la marque. L'approbation immédiate du public de Release, au niveau national et international, a peut-être été plus gratifiante encore.

THE CITY OF SHEFFIELD

No Logo and No Spin
The Soul of a City Brought Out by Its Own People

By Lars Hemming Jorgensen

www.storyworldwide.com

Lars Hemming Jorgensen is chief creative officer of Story Worldwide, a post-advertising and media-neutral agency as he himself has described it. Hemming was a founding member of Large Design before the merge with Story Worldwide, which has offices in both the USA and the UK. He has already managed brands such as Agent Provocateur, Lexus, and the city of Sheffield.

Lars Hemming Jorgensen ist Chief Creative Officer bei Story Worldwide, einer „Post-Advertising und medienneutralen Agentur", wie er selbst es einmal beschrieben hat. Er war Gründungsmitglied von Large Design, bevor man mit Story Worldwide fusionierte, das Niederlassungen in den USA und Großbritannien führt. Er hat bereits Marken wie Agent Provocateur, Lexus und die Stadt Sheffield betreut.

Lars Hemming Jorgensen est le responsable en chef de la création de Story Worldwide, une agence post-publicitaire et neutre en matière de média, comme il la décrit lui-même. Hemming a été un membre fondateur de Large Design avant la fusion avec Story Worldwide, avec des bureaux aux États-Unis et au Royaume-Uni. Il a déjà géré des marques comme Agent Provocateur, Lexus et la ville de Sheffield.

Left
Projection on a building with
questions to the inhabitants

Right
Website developed to collect
information for the project

After countless international branding assignments it was refreshing, and a touch terrifying, to take on the branding of the city of Sheffield. The city has two great universities; human capital in droves; a national park at its footsteps; and a location right in the middle of England – and yet most companies fail to add Sheffield to their consideration list when setting up offices or relocating. The city doesn't even feature on the BBC weather map! Imagine the insult.

The project should've been simple. Go through our proven brand process, get all the fantastic Sheffield facts down to a shortlist, create an iconic logo, run campaigns in the UK and abroad, and then wait for companies to set their sights on Sheffield. It soon became clear, however, that there were two big problems with this scenario.

First, moving is a highly emotional decision. All the great rational points for relocating go out of the window if the decision makers and staff just don't want to live there. That's not the biggest challenge, though – as we all know, great marketing

Nach zahllosen Aufträgen zur Markenentwicklung von Produkten aus aller Welt war es erfrischend anders, aber auch ein wenig Angst einflößend, das Branding für die Stadt Sheffield zu übernehmen. Die Stadt hat zwei Universitäten, viel menschliches Kapital, einen Nationalpark und liegt direkt in der Mitte Englands – und doch fällt den meisten Unternehmen nicht Sheffield ein, wenn eine neue Zweigstelle eingerichtet werden soll oder ein neuer Hauptsitz gesucht wird. Die Stadt ist nicht einmal auf der Wetterkarte der BBC!

Das Projekt sollte recht simpel sein. Wir wollten unseren bewährten Prozess der Markenbildung durchlaufen, all die fantastischen Fakten von Sheffield auflisten, ein kultiges Logo schaffen, in ganz Großbritannien und im Ausland Kampagnen starten und abwarten, bis die Firmen Sheffield in den Blick bekommen. Es wurde allerdings recht bald klar, dass es dabei zwei große Probleme gab.

Erstens ist ein Umzug eine höchst emotionale Entscheidung. Alle rationalen Aspekte für eine Umsiedlung gehen den Bach runter, wenn die Entscheidungsträger

Après d'innombrables projets internationaux de branding, il était agréable (et quelque peu angoissant) de se charger du branding de la ville de Sheffield. Elle possède deux universités importantes, un capital humain abondant, un parc national à ses pieds et une situation en plein cœur de l'Angleterre. Pourtant, la plupart des entreprises qui mettent en place de nouveaux locaux ne pensent pas à Sheffield comme une option possible. La ville n'apparaît même pas sur la carte météo de la BBC ! Imaginez l'insulte.

Le projet devait être simple : suivre notre processus maintes fois éprouvé de création de marque, dresser la liste des fantastiques attraits de Sheffield à retenir, créer un logo emblématique, mener des campagnes au Royaume-Uni et à l'étranger, puis attendre que des entreprises posent leur regard sur Sheffield. Il est néanmoins très vite apparu que ce scénario comportait deux problèmes de taille.

En premier lieu, tout déménagement suppose une décision chargée d'émotions. Tous les grands points rationnels d'une relocalisation s'effondrent si les décisionnaires

can help change minds. No, the real issue was an extension of the classic brand identity issue: the need for stakeholder buy-in. On the basis that, ultimately, buy-in is more important than choosing the right colour or font, we've always looked to include the stakeholders in the discussions – consulting them, asking for ideas, getting them to become champions, etc.

Now initially we had ten stakeholders on the Sheffield project, all smart and influential representatives of the city's academic, cultural, institutional, and commercial sectors. We went through our usual approach of workshops and sparring sessions, seemingly making good progress. But there was something nagging at us: every time we were happy with an identity and creative route, we didn't feel as strongly about it the next day. The problem was pointed out to us by a team member with a journalist background: "The people of Sheffield haven't bought into this."

He was right. From an image point of view it was straightforward to communicate all of Sheffield's great advantages and represent the values at the heart of the

und das Personal dort einfach nicht leben wollen. Das andere Problem war die Notwendigkeit, dass die Stakeholder die Entscheidung ebenfalls akzeptieren. Diese Akzeptanz ist letzten Endes wichtiger als die Wahl der richtigen Farbe oder Schriftart, darum war uns immer daran gelegen, die Stakeholder in die Diskussionen einzubinden.

Nun hatten wir beim Sheffield-Projekt zehn Stakeholder, allesamt kluge und einflussreiche Repräsentanten aus kulturellen, institutionellen und kommerziellen Bereichen der Stadt. Wir durchliefen unseren üblichen Ansatz mit Workshops und kontroversem Gedankenaustausch, wobei wir gute Fortschritte machten. Aber es gab etwas, was uns störte: Immer wenn wir mit einer Identität und einer kreativen Richtung zufrieden waren, war dieses Gefühl am nächsten Tag wie weggeblasen, und wir fühlten uns gar nicht mehr so sicher. Das Problem wurde von jemanden aus dem Team auf den Punkt gebracht, der einen journalistischen Hintergrund hatte: „Die Leute aus Sheffield glauben einfach nicht daran."

et le personnel sont contre l'idée de vivre à cet endroit. Ce n'est pas en soi le plus grand défi, car nous savons tous qu'un bon marketing peut faire changer d'avis. Non, la véritable difficulté était le prolongement d'un problème classique dans l'identité de marque : le besoin de l'adhésion des intéressés. Partant du principe que cette adhésion est finalement plus importante que le choix de la bonne couleur ou police de caractères, nous avons toujours tenté d'impliquer les partenaires aux discussions en les consultant, en leur demandant des idées, en les motivant à défendre le projet, etc.

Nous avions au départ dix partenaires pour le projet de Sheffield, tous représentants éminents et influents des domaines universitaire, culturel, institutionnel et commercial de la ville. Nous avons suivi notre approche habituelle, au rythme d'ateliers et de séances de discussion, avec une progression apparemment bonne. Une chose pourtant nous travaillait : chaque fois que nous étions satisfaits d'une d'identité et d'un chemin créatif, le lendemain nous n'étions plus aussi convaincus. Un membre de l'équipe, doté d'une expérience

Left
Mobile screen with sample
SMS, and the same message
displayed in public

Right
Bus shelter panel adapted
to receive and display SMS

city. However, without getting the people of Sheffield onboard, foreign investors would never get an experience in person that lived up to the marketing that had got them there in the first place.

Sheffield isn't the only brand facing this challenge. With the Internet providing a free flow of information, brand consultancies like ours can't simply make your companies or cities pretty if there is no substance behind it – a simple Google search can bring a brand façade crashing down. The only sensible response is to do what people like the brand managers of Unilever are doing. Where once the objective was winning a larger share of voice, we now see businesses investing in better products that can deliver what they promised and that actually warrant talking about.

So what did we create for Sheffield? We decided that the stakeholders were really the entire population of Sheffield – all 500,000+ of them. It's probably a record of some kind and certainly a challenge when it comes to presenting design work.

At every stage of the process, we're now trying to explain our work and, crucially,

Er hatte recht. Unter dem Aspekt „Image" war es konsequent, Sheffields Vorzüge zu vermitteln und die Werte der Stadt zu repräsentieren. Doch ohne die Menschen zu überzeugen, die in Sheffield leben, würden ausländische Investoren niemals die Erfahrung machen können, die ihnen das Marketing versprochen hatte und derentwegen sie überhaupt in die Stadt kämen.

Sheffield ist nicht die einzige Marke, die sich dieser Herausforderung stellen muss. Weil durch das Internet Informationen frei verfügbar sind, können Markenberater wie wir nicht einfach ein Unternehmen oder eine Stadt schön reden, ohne dass dies begründet ist – durch eine einfache Google-Suche kann man eine Marke zum Einsturz bringen. Die einzige vernünftige Reaktion darauf ist, das zu machen, was die Brand Manager von Unilever machen. Wo einst das Ziel lautete, einen größeren Share of Voice (also den Anteil einer Marke an den Kontakten eines Gesamtmarktes) zu gewinnen, können wir heute feststellen, dass Branchen in bessere Produkte investieren, die ihre Werbeversprechen auch einlösen können.

en journalisme, nous a montré le problème du doigt : « Les habitants de Sheffield n'y croient pas ».

Il avait raison. Du point de vue de l'image, il était facile de transmettre tous les grands avantages de Sheffield et de représenter les valeurs essentielles de la ville. Mais si ses habitants n'étaient pas convaincus, les investisseurs étrangers ne vivraient jamais une expérience à la hauteur du marketing qui les avait attirés en premier lieu.

Sheffield n'est pas la seule marque confrontée à ce problème. Avec le flux gratuit d'informations disponibles sur Internet, les experts en marque comme nous ne peuvent pas rendre vos entreprises ou villes plus attirantes qu'elles ne le sont en réalité, car une simple recherche sur Google peut démolir la façade d'une marque creuse. La seule réponse sensée est donc de suivre l'exemple de gens comme les directeurs de marque d'Unilever. Alors que l'objectif était auparavant de conquérir une part de voix plus grande, nous voyons maintenant des entreprises qui investissent dans de meilleurs produits leur permettant

Left & above
Sample pages of the book
created for the campaign
to rebrand the city

Left
City wall painted with
a campaign theme

Right
Poster celebrating features
special to Sheffield

ground everything in the real stories of Sheffield. So, for example, we're running a series of workshops to help people in Sheffield produce and broadcast their content. This means that, long after the project's media budget is used up, people will be creating media to be consumed across the globe. This will be their Sheffield, their pride, their stories – told through correctly tagged images, newly published blogs, music made available for sharing.

In other words, we're creating for Sheffield an identity that lives and breathes… just like the city itself.

Was haben wir also nun für Sheffield geschaffen? Wir beschlossen, dass zu den Stakeholdern die gesamte Bevölkerung von Sheffield zählen müsse – jeder, der mehr als 500.000 Einwohner. Vermutlich ist das irgendein Rekord, ganz sicher aber eine Herausforderung, wenn es um die Präsentation der Designarbeiten geht.

Wir versuchen, in jeder Phase des Prozesses unsere Arbeit zu erläutern, aber wichtig ist, alles in den echten Stories von Sheffield gründen zu lassen. Wir führen beispielsweise Workshops durch, um den Leuten aus Sheffield zu helfen, ihre Inhalte zu produzieren und zu veröffentlichen. Das bedeutet, dass sich die Menschen, wenn das Medienbudget des Projekts verbraucht ist, immer noch über die selbst erstellten Medien ausdrücken können, die dann weltweit konsumiert werden. Das wird ihr Sheffield sein, ihr Stolz, ihre Geschichte – erzählt durch korrekt getaggte Bilder, neu installierte Blogs oder auch durch zur freien Weitergabe produzierte Musik.

Anders ausgedrückt: Wir schaffen für Sheffield eine Identität, die lebt und atmet … genau wie die Stadt selbst.

d'honorer leurs promesses et dont il est légitime de parler.

Alors, qu'avons-nous créé pour Sheffield ? Nous avons décidé que nos partenaires étaient en fait toute la population de Sheffield, les plus de 500 000 habitants que la ville compte. C'est probablement un record du genre et sans aucun doute un défi pour la présentation d'un projet de design.

À chaque étape du processus, nous tentons d'expliquer notre travail et, point crucial, de tout lier à ce qui se passe réellement à Sheffield. Par exemple, nous organisons une série d'ateliers pour aider des habitants à produire et à diffuser des contenus. De cette façon, bien après que le budget médias du projet ait été épuisé, les gens continueront à générer des informations qui seront utilisées aux quatre coins du globe. Ce sera leur Sheffield, leur fierté, leurs histoires, racontées par le biais d'images correctement balisées, de blogs publiés, de musique mise en partage.

En d'autres termes, nous créons pour Sheffield une identité qui vit et qui respire… comme la ville elle-même.

WE CREATE

PLASTIC DRESSES

THAT DISSOLVE ON CONTACT WITH WATER

WE'VE GOT NO ROCKET SCIENTISTS, BUT LOTS OF

BRAINSURGEONS

OUR GREENPCs ARE CHANGING THE WAY THE COMPUTING INDUSTRY WORKS

WE PRODUCED

MORE STEEL

LAST YEAR THAN AT ANY TIME IN THE CITY'S HISTORY

WE'RE REPLACING BLOOD TRANSFUSIONS

WITH PLASTIC BLOOD

WE EAT A

SAUCE

THE REST OF THE COUNTRY'S NEVER HEARD OF

WE'VE GOT

ROCKY

ON SPEED-DIAL

Sheffield stories
— *Rebuilding our city's reputation and prosperity*

City Hall, Sheffield
— *June 19th 2008*

THE CO-OPERATIVE

Making the Truth Visible

By Harry Pearce, Pentagram

www.pentagram.com

Harry Pearce founded consultancy Lippa Pearce together with Domenic Lippa in 1990 before joining Pentagram in London in 2006. A designer and human rights activist, he created all the design material for Witness in New York City, a charity founded by the musician and also activist Peter Gabriel, and on whose advisory board Pearce also sits.

Harry Pearce gründete gemeinsam mit Domenic Lippa 1990 die Agentur Lippa Pearce, bevor er 2006 nach London zu Pentagram kam. Als Designer und Menschenrechtsaktivist und hat er das gesamte Design für Witness in New York City gestaltet, eine Wohltätigkeitsorganisation, die von dem Musiker und Mitaktivisten Peter Gabriel gegründet wurde, dessen beratendem Gremium Pearce ebenfalls angehört.

En 1990, **Harry Pearce** a fondé la société de conseil Lippa Pearce avec Domenic Lippa, avant de rejoindre Pentagram à Londres en 2006. Designer et activiste en matière de droits de l'homme, il a créé tout le matériel de design pour Witness in New York City, une fondation créée par le musicien et également activiste Peter Gabriel, et au conseil consultatif de laquelle Pearce participe.

Left
Series of shopping bags

Right
Package designs for flour

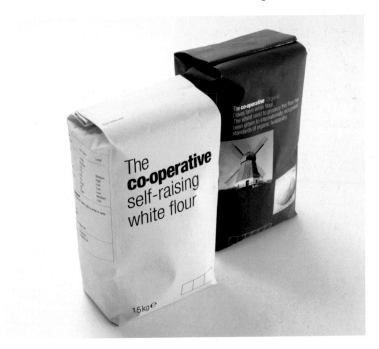

I have always thought that great design is about revealing a distinctive truth to the world. Brand identity design is no different. This Co-operative Group case study is a clear demonstration of how brand identity can reconnect a business with its distinctive truth, creating a renewed sense of unity internally and driving commercial success externally.

Background

The Co-operative Group is Britain's largest consumer co-operative with an £8 billion turnover and 65,000 employees. It operates across multiple sectors with high-street offers in food, travel, banking, pharmacy, and funerals.

The co-operative movement began in 1844 as a response to the inequality caused by the industrial revolution, forming numerous co-operative societies in retail, agriculture, and housing. Each society was owned and run by its members and worked for the benefit of its local community. The Co-operative Group was formed from the merger of many independent retail societies.

Ich war stets der Ansicht, dass es bei erstklassigem Design darum geht, der Welt eine unverwechselbare Wahrheit zu enthüllen. Beim Design einer Markenidentität ist das nicht anders. Das Fallbeispiel der *Co-operative Group* ist ein Beweis dafür, wie eine Firma mittels Markenidentität mit ihrer ureigenen, unverwechselbaren Wahrheit verbunden werden kann, wenn diese intern ein Gefühl von Einheit erzeugt und extern den kommerziellen Erfolg vorantreibt.

Hintergrund

Die *Co-operative Group* ist mit 65.000 Mitarbeitern und einem Umsatz von £8 Milliarden die größte Verbraucherkooperative Großbritanniens. Sie operiert in verschiedenen Branchen und bietet pharmazeutische Produkte, Lebensmittel sowie Reisen an. Außerdem ist sie im Finanzsektor und im Bereich Bestattungen tätig.

Die Kooperativenbewegung entstand 1844 als Reaktion auf die von der industriellen Revolution verursachte Ungleichheit. Damals wurden im Einzelhandel, in der Landwirtschaft und im Wohnungswesen zahlreiche kooperative Gemeinschaften

J'ai toujours pensé qu'un bon design consiste à révéler une certaine vérité au monde. Il en va de même pour la création d'identité de marque. Cette étude de cas du groupe The Co-operative démontre clairement comment l'identité de marque peut réconcilier une entreprise avec sa propre vérité, en créant un sentiment nouveau d'unité en interne et en guidant en externe la réussite commerciale.

Contexte

Le groupe The Co-operative est la plus grande coopérative d'Angleterre, avec un chiffre d'affaires de 8 milliards de livres sterling et 65 000 employés. Il est présent dans de nombreux secteurs, dans des établissements d'alimentation, de voyage, bancaires, des pharmacies et des pompes funèbres.

Le mouvement coopératif s'est constitué en 1844, en réponse aux inégalités causées par la révolution industrielle, ce qui a donné le jour à de nombreuses coopératives de vente au détail, d'agriculture et de logement. Chaque société coopérative était détenue et gérée par ses membres et

109

Left
Fruit packaging

Right
Image of shop front

But by 2000 its survival was under threat. Its share of the grocery market had shrunk as giants like Tesco and Sainsbury's pioneered new levels of value, service, and choice. The Co-operative's patchwork high-street presence was divisive and incoherent. The "Co-op" brand name had become synonymous with low quality products and dated retail. The brand's key point of difference – that of responsible commerce through member ownership and control – had become all but invisible.

The idea driving the design

The new brand identity would reconnect the business with the fundamental principles of fairness, responsibility, and community ownership that were so central to its origination. These values were more relevant than ever. They had the power to unite a fragmented organisation and motivate staff. And they were motivating to customers, who were becoming increasingly concerned with the power of "big retail", the homogenisation of the high street and the ethical issues of production and consumption.

gegründet. Jede Gesellschaft war im Besitz ihrer Mitglieder, die sie auch leiteten und zum Wohle der Gemeinschaft vor Ort arbeiteten. Die *Co-operative Group* entstand aus dem Zusammenschluss vieler unabhängiger Handelsgesellschaften.

Doch im Jahr 2000 stand ihr Überleben unter schlechten Vorzeichen: Der Marktanteil in der Lebensmittelbranche war geschrumpft, seit solche Riesen wie Tesco und Sainsbury's Wertschöpfung, Dienstleistung und Produktauswahl zu neuen Höhen getrieben haben. Die Präsenz der *Co-operative Group* im Einzelhandel war zersplittert und ohne Zusammenhang. Der Markenname „Co-op" stand für Produkte von geringer Qualität und für ein veraltetes Einzelhandelswesen. Der zentrale Punkt, der die Marke von anderen unterschied, nämlich der verantwortungsvolle Handel im Besitz und unter der Leitung der Mitglieder, war nahezu unsichtbar geworden.

Die Idee treibt das Design voran

Die neue Markenidentität sollte die Firma wieder mit den fundamentalen Prinzipien

fonctionnait dans l'intérêt de la communauté locale. Le groupe The Co-operative s'est formé à partir de la fusion d'un grand nombre de sociétés indépendantes de vente au détail.

En 2000 pourtant, sa survie était menacée. Sa part du marché de l'alimentation s'était réduite depuis que des géants comme Tesco et Sainsbury's s'étaient mis à proposer des niveaux inédits de valeur, de service et de choix. La présence inégale des enseignes de The Co-operative donnait une image divisée et incohérente. La marque « Co-op » était devenue synonyme de produits de basse qualité et de commerce de détail démodé. La caractéristique essentielle de la marque, un commerce responsable grâce à la propriété et le contrôle de ses membres, était devenue totalement invisible.

L'idée derrière le design

La nouvelle identité de marque devait réconcilier l'activité avec les principes de base d'équité, de responsabilité et de communauté, si présents au moment de sa création. Ces valeurs s'imposaient plus que jamais. Elles avaient le pouvoir

The **co-operative**
we were the first
supermarket to
change all of
our own coffee
to Fairtrade.

The **co-operative**
uses the UK's first
degradable bread bag.

The **co-oper**
does not tes
Household p
on animals.

We realised that if the Co-operative Group could communicate these values more confidently and consistently audiences would begin to trust the brand again.

So, at the centre of the new identity was a pragmatic, confident, and straightforward logotype that had an innate honesty and openness, just like the business it represented. We changed the name back to "The Co-operative". This name felt like a straightforward and authoritative statement of fact and reconnected the business with the roots that were so central to its ethos.

Delivering the identity

We created an identity system that could be delivered across the whole Co-operative experience, from store environments to adverts, packaging, and the website. By delivering consistency and quality across the total experience, we would reinforce the fact that The Co-operative had really changed whilst building a welcoming, pleasing, and rewarding customer experience. We started this process of change with an internal initiative called "Together" which rallied employees behind one common business vision.

von Fairness, Verantwortlichkeit und gemeinschaftlichem Eigentum verbinden. Diese Werte waren relevanter als je zuvor. Sie bargen das Potenzial, eine zersplitterte Organisation zu vereinen und deren Mitarbeiter zu motivieren. Das wiederum würde auch die Kunden motivieren, die der Macht der Branchenriesen, dem Einheitsbrei des Einzelhandels und den ethischen Problemen im Hinblick auf Produktion und Verbrauch zunehmend skeptisch gegenüberstehen.

Wir erkannten, dass die Marke für das Zielpublikum wieder vertrauenswürdig werden kann, wenn die *Co-operative Group* wieder selbstbewusst und konsequent für diese Werte einstehen würde. Somit bildete ein überzeugender und geradliniger Firmenschriftzug den Kern der neuen Identität. Genau wie das Unternehmen, das er repräsentiert, besitzt er eine ganz eigene Aufrichtigkeit und Offenheit. Außerdem kehrten wir zum ursprünglichen Namen „The Co-operative" zurück. Er vermittelt eine geradlinige und verbindliche, faktenbezogene Aussage und stellt die Verbindung des Unternehmens zu seinen Wurzeln her, die für die Firmenethik so zentral ist.

d'unir une organisation fragmentée et d'en motiver le personnel. Elles motivaient aussi les clients, de plus en plus inquiets de la puissance de la grande distribution, de l'homogénéisation des magasins et des problèmes éthiques liés à la production et à la consommation.

Nous avons compris que si le groupe The Co-operative pouvait transmettre ces valeurs avec plus d'assurance et de cohérence, le public accorderait à nouveau sa confiance à la marque.

Au cœur de la nouvelle identité, un logo pragmatique, solide et simple exprimait une honnêteté et une ouverture intrinsèques, tout comme l'entreprise qu'il représentait. Nous sommes revenus à « The Co-operative ». Ce nom évoquait une déclaration de fait simple et officielle et réconciliait l'entreprise avec les racines de sa philosophie.

Présenter l'identité

Nous avons créé un système d'identité qui pouvait fonctionner à travers toute l'expérience de The Co-operative, des points de vente aux publicités, aux emballages et

Left
Print material

Our solution would unite all the Co-operative Group businesses under one brand. All business lines, from grocery to travel and funeral care, had a single brand essence, represented by the consistent presence of the "The Co-operative" name locked up to a descriptive business-line name (such as "The Co-operative Travel"). This straightforward way of structuring the businesses would make sense to customers and was a very visual reminder that they were one family of businesses.

We continually reinforced the central role of "The Co-operative" right across the customer experience by leading all communication, whether on-pack, in-store or ATL, with this name. This removed the need for any sub-brands and endowed all products with the authority and ethos of "The Co-operative".

The one exception to this rule was the creation of a sub-brand for "The Co-operative Membership". The membership scheme is the lifeblood of the brand. It links all the businesses and draws customers into a deeper relationship. Only here did we allow the creation of a modest

Identität kommunizieren

Wir schufen ein Identitätssystem, das sich dem Verbraucher in allen Begegnungen mit dem Unternehmen *Co-operative* vermittelt – von der Ladeneinrichtungen über die Werbung bis hin zu Verpackung und Website. Durch Einheitlichkeit und Qualität wollten wir die Tatsache bekräftigen, dass *The Co-operative* sich wirklich gewandelt hat, und gleichzeitig ein einladendes, angenehmes und lohnendes Kauferlebnis schaffen. Wir begannen diesen Veränderungsprozess mit einer internen Initiative namens „Together" (*Gemeinsam*), die bewirken sollte, dass sich die Mitarbeiter hinter eine gemeinsame Unternehmensvision stellten.

Unsere Lösung versammelte alle zur *Co-operative Group* gehörenden Unternehmen unter dem Schirm einer einzigen Marke. Jeder Firmenzweig vom Lebensmittelsektor bis hin zu Reisen und Bestattungen erhielt eine eigene Kernaussage, wobei der übergeordnete Name „The Co-operative" durchgängig zum Ausdruck kam und mit dem beschreibenden Namensbestandteils des jeweiligen Geschäftszweigs verknüpft

au site Web. En affichant une cohérence et une qualité dans l'intégralité de l'expérience, nous renforcions le fait que The Co-operative avait vraiment changé, tout en permettant une expérience accueillante, agréable et gratifiante pour les clients. Nous avons lancé ce processus de changement avec une initiative en interne appelée « Together » (Ensemble), qui rassemblait les employés derrière une même vision.

Notre solution allait regrouper toutes les activités du groupe The Co-operative sous une même marque. Tous les secteurs d'activité, de l'alimentation aux voyages en passant par les pompes funèbres, allaient partager une même essence, symbolisée par la présence continue du nom « The Co-operative » associé à un nom de secteur d'activité descriptif (par exemple, « The Co-operative Voyage »). Cette façon simple de structurer les activités serait compréhensible pour les clients et rappelait visuellement que toutes les activités forment une seule et même famille.

Nous avons continuellement renforcé le rôle central de « The Co-operative » à travers toute l'expérience des clients, en

The **co-operative**
little book of facts

Left, below and right
Co-operative manual of conduct

Bottom
Covers and spreads for
the different manual sections

We are
Britain's
most
ethical
brand.*

Why?
We'll let
the facts
speak for
themselves.

Some businesses seem to be
big on claims but short on facts.
The Co-operative Group is different.

We are owned by our members.
That means we are not controlled
by shareholders or financial investors,
but by our customers, colleagues
and people in our local communities.
Each of our members has an equal
say in how the business is run, and
help us to achieve our social goals.

We've been championing this
approach to business for decades,
quietly doing good and delivering
promises that have made us the
UK's most ethical brand.

* The GfK NOP Ethics Brands survey was conducted in US, UK, France, Germany and Spain, covering a total of 5,000 respondents between January and February 2007

The **co-operative**

Left
Series of own-brand
olive oil bottles

Right
Series of own-brand
wine bottles

Above
The main logo

symbol – a little bee. It would symbolise the communal co-operative spirit and the rewards enjoyed by members.

Results

Within one year of the relaunch The Co-operative Group had rebranded over 1,800 outlets, attracted more than 1,000,000 new members and had completed a £1.5 billion acquisition of a rival grocery retailer.

In late 2007, spurred on by the evidence of dramatic improvements in sales and rapid growth in membership numbers, The Co-operative Group announced an accelerated programme of store refits backed by a £200 million investment package.

Pentagram was awarded a DBA Design Effectiveness Award in 2007 in recognition of the outstanding effectiveness of our design solution.

In this age of uncertainty, truth and straightforwardness hold sway.

wurde (bei Reisen z.B. „The Co-operative Travel"). Diese gradlinige Neustrukturierung der Unternehmen war für die Kunden sinnvoll und nachvollziehbar. Auch rein optisch wurden sie stets daran erinnert, dass es sich um Geschäftszweige einer Unternehmensgruppe handelte.

Wir bekräftigten fortwährend die zentrale Rolle von „The Co-operative" in der gesamten Kontaktsphäre des Kunden, indem die ganze Kommunikation unter diesem Namen geführt wurde, seien es Rabattcoupons, die Gestaltung der Ladeneinrichtung oder die klassischen Werbemedien. Somit entfiel der Bedarf an irgendwelchen Untermarken, und alle Produkte waren mit der Kompetenz und dem Ethos von „The Co-operative" ausgestattet.

Die eine Ausnahme zu dieser Regel bestand in der Schaffung einer Untermarke für die Mitgliedschaft: „The Co-operative membership". Das Mitgliedsmodell ist der Lebensnerv der Marke. Es verknüpft alle Unternehmen untereinander und bindet die Kunden enger an die Marke. Nur hier erlaubten wir die Schaffung eines bescheidenen Symbols: eine kleine Biene. Sie sollte

réalisant toutes les communications (sur les emballages, en magasin ou dans les médias) avec ce nom. Cela rendait les sous-marques superflues, et conférait à tous les produits le sceau officiel et la philosophie de « The Co-operative ».

L'unique exception à cette règle a été la création d'une sous-marque pour « The Co-operative Membership ». Le concept de membres est l'âme de la marque. Il fait la liaison entre toutes les activités et établit des relations plus profondes avec les clients. Pour ce seul aspect, nous avons permis la création d'un symbole modeste, une petite abeille, à l'image de l'esprit coopératif communautaire et des récompenses dont profitent les membres.

Résultats

Un an après le lancement, le groupe The Co-operative avait remodelé plus de 1 800 points de vente, attiré plus d'1 million de nouveaux membres et acheté un concurrent dans le secteur de l'alimentation pour 1,5 milliard de livres sterling.

Fin 2007, encouragé par la hausse considérable des ventes et la croissance

den gemeinschaftlichen Geist von „The Co-operative" und die Vorteile, die deren Mitglieder genießen, symbolisieren.

Resultate

Nach dem Relaunch hat die *Co-operative Group* innerhalb eines Jahres 1.800 Geschäfte umfirmiert, mehr als eine Million neue Mitglieder gewonnen und die Marktanteile eines konkurrierenden Lebensmittelhändlers im Werte von £ 1,5 Milliarden übernommen. Ende 2007 kündigte die *Co-operative Group* – angespornt von nachweislich drastischen Umsatzverbesserungen und einem rasanten Zuwachs bei den Mitgliederzahlen – ein Programm an, das die Renovierung der Läden beschleunigen sollte und dem ein Investmentpaket im Werte von £ 200 Millionen zugrunde lag.

Der Agentur Pentagram wurde 2007 in Anerkennung der hervorragenden Effektivität unserer Designlösung der *DBA Design Effectiveness Award* verliehen.

Das beweist: In unserem Zeitalter der Ungewissheit können sich Wahrheit und Aufrichtigkeit durchsetzen.

rapide du nombre d'adhésions, le groupe The Co-operative a annoncé un programme accéléré de remodelage de ses magasins, avec un investissement de 200 millions de livres sterling.

Pentagram a reçu le prix DBA Design Effectiveness 2007 pour l'efficacité exceptionnelle de sa solution de design.

Dans cette ère d'incertitude, la vérité et la simplicité l'emportent.

VAJA QUALITY PRODUCTS

An International Challenge for an Argentinian Company Selling Leather Products

By Ricardo Drab, RDYA

www.rdya.com

Ricardo Drab is a designer and brand strategist from Buenos Aires where he runs his consultancy firm RDYA Design Group and works for some of the leading companies in Argentina. Founded in 1996, the company works almost as a full service agency, working on advertising, interactive, print design, and motion graphics.

Ricardo Drab ist Designer und Markenstratege aus Buenos Aires. Dort leitet er ein eigenes Beratungsunternehmen, die RDYA Design Group, und arbeitet für einige der führenden Unternehmen Argentiniens. Das 1996 gegründete Unternehmen kommt einer Full-Service-Agentur nahe und arbeitet in den Bereichen Werbung, interaktive Kommunikation, Printdesign und Motion Graphics.

Ricardo Drab est un designer et un stratégiste de marque de Buenos Aires, où il gère sa société de conseil RDYA Design Group et travaille pour certaines entreprises phares d'Argentine. Fondée en 1996, l'entreprise fonctionne quasiment comme une agence multiservice : publicité, projets interactifs, graphisme et animations.

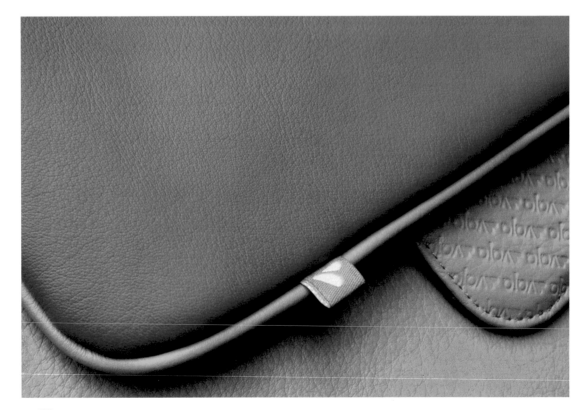

Left
Example of logo applied
to final product

Right
Patterns for textiles
and leather

Phase I:
New Brand Concept

Vaja's story begins with the dream of a group of young professionals who shared an interest in creating better products to protect all kinds of technological items. An Argentinian-funded company based in Buenos Aires, Vaja is dedicated to the design and manufacture of bags and cases made from the best leather for mobiles, laptops, and technological products in general. With their main markets in the United States and Europe, Vaja is recognised as a premium brand, known for the exclusive design of its high-quality leather cases for protecting advanced technology products.

In 2001 Vaja chose RDYA (Ricardo Drab y Asociados) design studio to resolve a number of marketing problems it was experiencing. Vaja had some design conflicts: its brand architecture was not consistent with the quality of the product; it needed new packaging; and its logo concept was difficult to grasp.

RDYA took care of developing the concept, the packaging, and the new brand architecture, based on the idea that Vaja's

Phase I:
Ein neues Markenkonzept

Die Geschichte von Vaja beginnt mit dem Traum einer Gruppe von Berufseinsteigern, die alle von dem Interesse beseelt waren, bessere Produkte zum Schutz technischer Geräte zu schaffen. Als argentinisches Unternehmen mit Hauptsitz in Buenos Aires widmet sich Vaja dem Design und der Herstellung von Taschen und Etuis aus bestem Leder für Handys, Laptops und anderen technologischen Produkten. Der Hauptmarkt von Vaja liegt in den USA und Europa. Das Unternehmen wird als Premium-Marke betrachtet und ist bekannt für das exklusive Design seiner qualitativ besonders hochwertigen Ledertaschen zum Schutz spitzentechnologischer Produkte.

Im Jahr 2001 entschied sich Vaja für das Designstudio RDYA (Ricardo Drab y Asociados), um für die Firma einige Marketingprobleme zu lösen. Vaja befand sich in Bezug auf Design im Zwiespalt: Die Architektur der Marke passte nicht konsistent zur Qualität des Produkts, eine neue Verpackungslinie war gefragt und das Konzept des Logos war nicht eingängig.

Première étape :
nouveau concept de marque

L'histoire de Vaja commence par le rêve d'un groupe de jeunes professionnels qui partageaient l'envie de créer de meilleurs produits pour des articles technologiques. Spécialisée dans le design et la fabrication avec le meilleur cuir argentin de sacs et d'étuis pour téléphones portables, ordinateurs et appareils technologiques en général, Vaja est une entreprise de capital argentin installée à Buenos Aires et dont les principaux marchés sont les États-Unis et l'Europe. Vaja est connue pour être une marque *premium*, en raison du design exclusif de ses housses en cuir de grande qualité pour protéger des produits high tech.

En 2001, Vaja a fait appel à RDYA (Ricardo Drab y Asociados) comme studio de design pour ses problèmes de marketing. Vaja connaissait en effet certains conflits en matière de design. D'une part, l'architecture de sa marque était peu cohérente avec la qualité des produits. D'autre part, l'entreprise avait besoin d'un nouveau packaging et son logo ne se comprenait pas facilement.

Above
Colour scheme of products

Right
Colour palette

cases not only protect the product but also enhance it and give it personality. So the concept changed from "Vaja cases" to "Vaja, clothes for technology. A garment that suits your mobile or your laptop."

The intelligent design of Vaja products is in keeping with their functionality and use. These are not just protective cases; they also enhance your device. In this way, the cases increase the potential of the products inside, giving them a style all their own and differentiating them from other products. Vaja also developed and patented a new technological process, the precursor of thermoforming, which enables the leather to be shaped to fit each product. The leather is designed according to the product it is going to "clothe". The wide palette of colours available also sets it apart from the competition.

Phase II: Customisation

Nowadays new technology is a commodity. Anyone can buy the latest products on the market in just a few months. Faced with this reality, Vaja decided to add something extra to its products. It was proving

RDYA nahm sich der Entwicklung des Konzepts, der Verpackung und der neuen Architektur der Marke an und legte dabei den Gedanken zugrunde, dass die Hüllen und Taschen von Vaja ein Produkt nicht nur schützen, sondern es aufwerten und ihm Persönlichkeit verleihen. Also veränderte sich das Konzept von „Vaja-Taschen" zu „Vaja – Ummantelungen für Technologie. Das passende Kleidungsstück für Ihr Handy und Ihr Laptop".

Das Design der Vaja-Produkte steht im Einklang mit ihrer Funktionalität und Verwendung, und die Geräte werden durch die Schutzhüllen aufgewertet. Auf diese Weise steigern die Taschen das Potenzial der geschützten Geräte, verleihen ihnen einen ganz eigenen Stil und heben sie von anderen Produkten ab. Vaja entwickelte außerdem einen neuen technologischen Prozess und ließ ihn patentieren. Das war der Vorläufer des Thermoformings: Dabei wird das Leder so geformt, dass es jedem Produkt wie angegossen passt. Das Leder wird dem Produkt entsprechend gestaltet, das es „bekleiden" soll. Die breite Palette der verfügbaren Farben hebt Vaja ebenfalls von der Konkurrenz ab.

RDYA s'est chargé de développer le concept, le packaging et la nouvelle architecture de marque, en partant de l'idée que les étuis de Vaja, au-delà de protéger, habillent et confèrent une personnalité aux appareils. Le concept est alors passé de « Étuis Vaja » à « Vaja, des habits pour la technologie. Un vêtement adapté à votre téléphone portable, à votre ordinateur ».

Le design intelligent des produits Vaja s'adapte à la fonctionnalité et à l'usage. Il ne s'agit pas de simples étuis de protection, ils habillent les appareils. De cette façon, ils augmentent le potentiel du produit qu'ils enveloppent et le dotent d'un style propre qui le distingue des autres. Vaja a en outre conçu et breveté un nouveau procédé technologique précurseur dans le domaine du thermoformage, qui permet de donner au cuir la forme de chaque produit. Le cuir est conçu selon le produit qu'il va habiller. Il est par ailleurs décliné dans une large palette de couleurs qui le démarque de la concurrence.

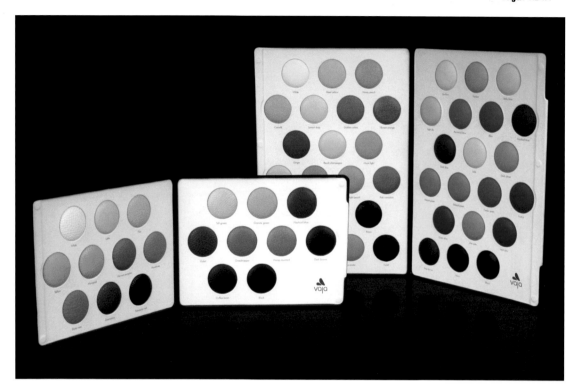

difficult to stand out from the crowd, so in 2007 Vaja once more got together with RDYA to do some rebranding. They worked on the development of the overall identity, including, among other things, the brand concept, brand guide, brand style, packaging, web design, advertising campaign, and product concept.

In this new phase, RDYA decided to use different props with which to convey the brand's message:

Personality: This is concerned with a person's thoughts, feelings and behaviour. Communicating from this standpoint implies associating the personality of the customer with something that the brand is offering or a challenge it sets. The emphasis is on a message that motivates in a positive way.

Customisation: The customer participates in the production process and has an influence on the end result of the product he is going to buy. This enables emphasis to be placed on the product and the act of choosing, a very common trend nowadays.

Freedom: This word refers to the power to decide or carry out a particular action according to the will or intelligence of each

Phase II: Maßanfertigung

Digitale Medien sind heutzutage normale Gebrauchsgegenstände. Jeder kann die neuesten Produkte innerhalb weniger Monate auf dem Markt kaufen. Vor diesem Hintergrund beschloss Vaja, seinen Produkten das gewisse Etwas zu verleihen, obwohl es nicht so einfach ist, sich von der üblichen Massenware abzuheben. Also setzte sich Vaja 2007 erneut mit RDYA zusammen, um die Marke neu zu positionieren. Man arbeitete an der Entwicklung einer übergreifenden Markenidentität, die unter anderem das Markenkonzept, die -richtlinien, den Stil der Marke sowie Verpackung, Webdesign, Werbekampagnen und das Produktkonzept einschloss.

In dieser neuen Phase beschloss RDYA, die Botschaft der Marke anhand verschiedener Konzepte zu vermitteln:

Persönlichkeit: Sie hat mit Gedanken, Gefühlen und dem Verhalten einer Person zu tun. Daher impliziert Kommunikation, dass die Persönlichkeit des Kunden mit etwas assoziiert wird, das die Marke anbietet oder vorstellt. Die Betonung liegt auf einer Botschaft, die auf positive Weise motiviert.

Seconde étape : personnalisation

À l'heure actuelle, la nouvelle technologie est un produit de base. En quelques mois, il est possible d'acheter les dernières nouveautés disponibles sur le marché. Face à cette réalité, Vaja a décidé de rajouter un plus à ses produits, qui n'arrivaient plus à se distinguer des autres. En 2007, l'entreprise a de nouveau fait appel à RDYA pour travailler ensemble sur le nouveau branding de la marque. L'effort a porté sur le développement de l'identité globale incluant, entre autres, le concept de marque, le guide de marque, le style de marque, le packaging, le site Web, la campagne de publicité et le concept de produit.

Pour cette nouvelle étape, RDYA a décidé de s'appuyer sur plusieurs bases à partir desquelles communiquer la marque :

Personnalité : parle des réflexions, des sentiments et des attitudes d'une personne. Communiquer depuis cet aspect suppose associer la personnalité du client à une proposition ou un défi que propose la marque. L'accent est mis sur un message qui motive de façon positive.

individual. Developing the marketing from this angle means the brand can be linked with an image that goes much further than the product itself. It is a question of linking the brand to a way of life.

Colour: Colour, with its various meanings, is a valuable method of conveying sensations and an effective way of expressing a character or personality. Associating the brand communication with the use of colours creates a simple, memorable brand image.

The central idea is that each customer can express their personality and individuality through the uniqueness of the product, and thus create synergy with the brand. This particular brand is defined by a very strong product, which is why it was decided to leave the product to speak for itself.

The product and its visual aesthetics were to create that connection with the senses that is closer to the "Vaja Experience". The senses of smell, touch, and sight are aroused through the scent and texture of the leather and the broad palette of colours. The experience is summed up by the signature "by Vaja", in which the

Maßanfertigung: Der Kunde nimmt am Produktionsprozess teil und kann das Endresultat beeinflussen, das er kaufen will. Somit kann die Betonung auf das Produkt und den Akt des Kaufens gelegt werden – heutzutage eine verbreitete Entwicklung.

Freiheit: Dieser Begriff bezieht sich auf die Fähigkeit, dem Willen oder der Intelligenz eines Individuums folgend eine bestimmte Handlung auszuführen. Die Entwicklung des Marketings aus dieser Perspektive heraus bedeutet, dass die Marke mit einem Bild verknüpft werden kann, das viel weiter reicht als das Produkt selbst. Es ist eine Frage der Verknüpfung der Marke mit einem bestimmten Lebensstil.

Farbe: Farbe ist mit ihren verschiedenen Bedeutungen eine wertvolle Methode, um Gefühle und Erlebnisse zu vermitteln, und eine effektive Möglichkeit, Charakter oder Persönlichkeit auszudrücken. Wenn die Kommunikation der Marke mit der Verwendung von Farben verknüpft wird, wird ein einprägsames Markenimage geschaffen.

Hinter all dem verbirgt sich der zentrale Gedanke, dass jeder Kunde seine Persön-

Personnalisation : le client participe au processus de production et influence le résultat final du produit qu'il va acheter. Le produit est ainsi mis en valeur, tout comme l'action de sélection, tendance très courante dans le contexte actuel.

Liberté : ce terme désigne la capacité de décider ou de mener une action déterminée en fonction de l'intelligence ou de la volonté de chaque individu. Élaborer le marketing à partir de ce concept permet de mettre en relation la marque et un imaginaire dépassant le produit. Il s'agit d'associer la marque à un mode de vie.

Couleur : la couleur (et ses différentes significations) est un moyen précieux pour transmettre des sensations et une façon efficace d'exprimer un caractère ou une personnalité. Associer la communication de la marque et l'emploi de couleurs donne une image simple et marquante.

L'idée centrale est que chaque client peut exprimer sa personnalité et son individualité à travers le caractère unique de son produit, et ainsi créer la synergie de la marque. Cette marque est symbolisée par un produit très fort ; un espace a donc

Left
Manual with logo variations

Right
Stationery

idea of playing with the senses speaks for itself and brand identity is created.

Vaja offers a canvas, a place to express your personal creativity by playing with colour choice and customising designs. That makes it yours. That makes it unique. Whether it's a telephone or a computer, Vaja adds to it the best of you, the user. This led to the strapline "Make it yours", which instils in the user a sense of belonging and personality. This claim encompasses the four key concepts: freedom, colour, customisation, and personality.

"By Vaja" talks about the product and the brand: quality, design, and style.

"Make it yours" adds to this the emotional connection with the person, their interaction with the product and the brand.

Two product lines were developed in this second phase: the i-volution line and the Classic line, both with a great variety of colours. Using a new brand language, the different lifestyles within each of the brand's product lines were defined. The pixel was taken as the starting point, reinforcing the concept of technology on which the brand is based, and from this

lichkeit und seine Individualität durch die Einzigartigkeit des Produktes ausdrücken und somit eine Synergie mit der Marke schaffen kann. In diesem speziellen Fall wird die Marke durch ein sehr starkes Produkt definiert, daher wurde beschlossen, das Produkt für sich selbst sprechen zu lassen.

Das Produkt und seine visuelle Ästhetik sollten eine Verbindung zu den Sinnen herstellen, die der „Vaja-Erfahrung" nahe kommen. Die Wahrnehmung über den Geruchs-, Tast- und Sehsinn wird durch den Duft und die Beschaffenheit des Leders sowie eine breite Farbpalette angeregt. Diese Erfahrung summiert sich in der Signatur „by Vaja", die mit den Sinnen spielt, für sich selbst spricht und eine Markenidentität schafft.

Vaja bietet eine Projektionsfläche, auf der jeder seine persönliche Kreativität ausdrücken kann, indem er mit der Farbauswahl und den Designs spielt. Auf diese Weise macht er sich das Produkt zueigen, es wird einzigartig. Egal, ob es sich um ein Telefon oder einen Computer handelt – vom Benutzer nimmt Vaja das Beste und gibt es dem Produkt mit. Das führte zum Werbe-

été laissé pour que ce produit parle de lui-même.

Avec son esthétique visuelle, le produit crée cette connexion avec les sens, plus proche de l' « Expérience Vaja ». Il y a un jeu avec l'odorat, le toucher et la vue grâce à l'odeur du cuir, ses textures et la large palette de couleurs. L'expérience se résume dans la signature « by Vaja », où le jeu avec les sens parle de lui-même et où l'identité de marque prend forme.

Par ailleurs, Vaja offre un canevas, un lieu d'expression de la créativité personnelle en jouant avec les couleurs et les designs de personnalisation. Le produit est à vous. Le produit est unique. Qu'il s'agisse d'un téléphone ou d'un ordinateur, Vaja lui rajoute le meilleur de vous-même, l'usager, d'où le message « Make it yours », qui confère le sentiment d'appartenance et de personnalité. Cette affirmation englobe les quatre concepts clés : liberté, couleur, personnalisation et personnalité.

« By Vaja » parle du produit et de la marque : qualité, design et style.

« Make it yours » rajoute la connexion émotionnelle avec la personne, l'interaction

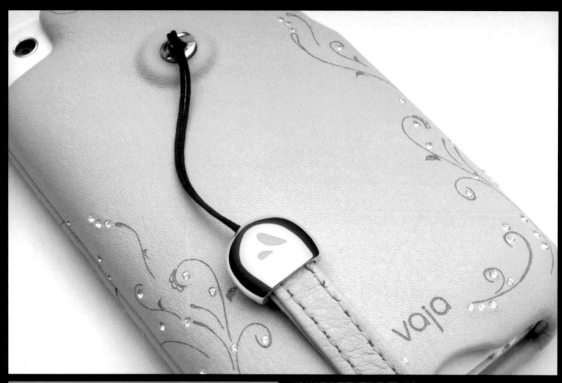

This page
Main logo, mobile case, and bag details

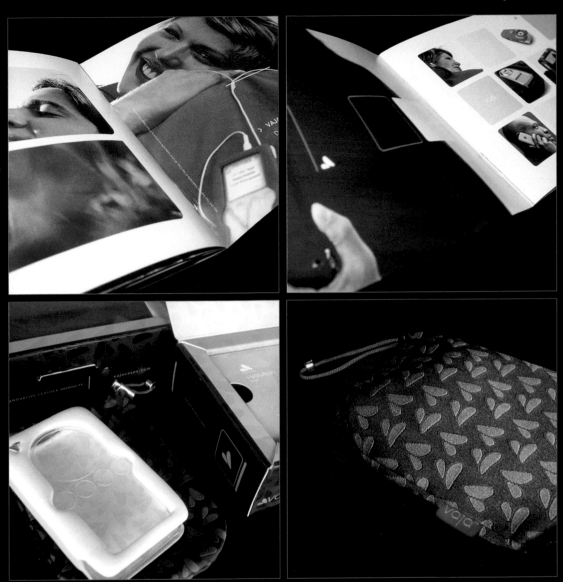

Top
Printed promotional material

Above
Package and its bag

Left
Catalogue spreads

Right
Packaging

point various different scenarios reinforcing the idea of individuality and diversity were formed. The use of colour as a basis for communication offers a world with more than a million possibilities.

Reinforcing the idea of uniqueness, some unusual limited editions have been created using exclusive leathers, often in co-branding deals with other international brands.

Vaja's objective is to become the products' second skin and to be able to customise these skins according to personal taste. To achieve this, users have a wide range of colours, original designs, premium quality, and the world's best leathers. This combination of design, functionality, and quality makes it a unique product.

Vaja's brand strategy suggests being ourselves, playing, and expressing ourselves freely. Cases are linked to what each individual uses, to their desires and state of mind. The case is an accessory related to your wardrobe – a garment rather than an item of furniture – something you choose.

The year 2009 will see the implementation of the new language, and with that

slogan „Make it yours", der dem Käufer das Gefühl der Zugehörigkeit und Persönlichkeit vermittelt. Diese Werbebotschaft umfasst die vier zentralen Konzepte Freiheit, Farbe, Maßanfertigung und Persönlichkeit.

Die Signatur „by Vaja" sagt etwas über das Produkt und die Marke aus: Qualität, Design und Stil. Der Slogan „Make it yours" fügt eine emotionale Verbindung zum Kunden und seiner Interaktion mit dem Produkt und der Marke hinzu.

In dieser zweiten Phase wurden zwei Produktlinien entwickelt: i-volution und Classic, die beide über eine große Farbpalette verfügen. Mit dem Pixel als Ausgangspunkt wurde das Konzept der Technologie unterstrichen, auf dem die Marke basiert. Die Nutzung von Farben als Basis der Kommunikation eröffnet eine Welt mit mehr als einer Million Möglichkeiten.

Um die Idee der Einzigartigartigkeit zu verstärken, wurden – häufig im Kontext von Co-Brandings mit anderen internationalen Marken – einige ungewöhnliche *Limited Editions* geschaffen, bei denen exklusive Ledersorten verwendet wurden.

de celle-ci avec le produit et la marque.

Lors de cette seconde phase ont été développées deux lignes de produit : i-volution et Classic, avec une grande variété de couleurs. Via un nouveau langage de marque ont été définis les différents modes de vie correspondant à chaque ligne. Le pixel a servi de point de départ pour renforcer le concept de technologie sur lequel repose la marque ; à partir de là, divers scénarios sont apparus et ont renforcé l'idée d'individualité et de diversité. L'emploi de la couleur comme base pour la communication offre un monde avec plus d'un million de possibilités.

Pour souligner le caractère unique, il existe actuellement des éditions limitées créées dans des cuirs exclusifs, souvent en co-branding avec d'autres marques de niveau international.

L'objectif de Vaja est de devenir la seconde peau des produits et de pouvoir les personnaliser en fonction des goûts personnels. Pour cela, les usagers disposent d'une large palette de couleurs, de designs nouveaux, d'une qualité *premium*

the rebranding process will be complete – a process that recategorised the brand and turned Vaja into a unique personal product.

Vaja möchte zur zweiten Haut des Produktes werden und diese dem persönlichen Geschmack des Besitzers anpassen können. Um das zu erreichen, können die Kunden aus einer großen Bandbreite an Farben, Originaldesigns, Premium-Qualitäten und weltbesten Ledersorten auswählen. Aus dieser Kombination von Design, Funktionalität und Qualität entsteht ein einzigartiges Produkt.

Die Strategie für die Marke Vaja suggeriert Individualität, Verspieltheit und freien Ausdruck. Die Schutzummantelung ist mit dem, was jeder Einzelne nutzt, mit seinen Wünschen und seiner inneren Haltung verbunden. Die Ummantelung ist ein Accessoire, das zu Ihrer Garderobe passt – es gehört mehr in den Bereich Bekleidung als in den Bereich Ausstattung und ist etwas, das man selbst wählt.

Im Jahr 2009 wird diese neue Markensprache eingeführt, und damit wird der Rebranding-Prozess abgeschlossen sein. Im Laufe dieses Prozesses wurde die Marke neu positioniert und Vaja zu einem einzigartigen, individuellen Produkt umgewandelt.

et des meilleurs cuirs du monde. Cette combinaison de design, fonctionnalité et qualité en font un produit unique.

La stratégie de marque de Vaja implique qu'il faut être soi-même, jouer et s'exprimer librement. Les housses sont liées à ce que chacun utilise, aux envies et à l'état d'esprit. Elles sont des accessoires en accord avec la garde-robe, comme des vêtements de plus dans le placard, quelque chose que l'on choisit.

En 2009 sera mis en œuvre un nouveau langage, ce qui mettra fin au processus de re-branding ayant permis de recatégoriser la marque et de faire de Vaja un produit personnel et unique.

DESIGN IS BRANDING

Telling Stories Through Images
The Designer and His Work with Big Brands

By Gui Borchert

www.guiborchert.com

Gui Borchert is a New York-based art director who has worked with many big international brands. His career started in Rio de Janeiro, Brazil, where he studied graphic design, soon shifting his work to motion and interactive design, as well as print. In the USA, Borchert has worked for R/GA, Mother, and most recently Syrup New York.

Gui Borchert ist ein in New York ansässiger Art Director, der für viele große internationale Marken gearbeitet hat. Seine Karriere begann in Brasilien: In Rio de Janeiro studierte er Grafikdesign, wechselte in seiner Arbeit aber bald zum Motion und interaktiven Design sowie zu den Printmedien. In den USA hat Borchert für R/GA, Mother und kürzlich für Syrup New York gearbeitet.

Gui Borchert est un directeur artistique installé à New York et qui a travaillé avec de nombreuses grandes marques internationales. Sa carrière a débuté à Rio de Janeiro (Brésil), où il a étudié le design graphique, avant de diriger rapidement son travail vers l'animation et le design interactif, ainsi que le graphisme. Aux États-Unis, Borchert a travaillé pour R/GA, Mother et, plus récemment, Syrup New York.

Left & right
Campaign for Puma
Women's Professional Soccer
http://wps.pumafootball.com/tag/wps

All creative assignments or design projects have one thing in common: they are always about telling a story – communicating an idea, a thought, a narrative, or a concept to the audience. And those stories can be told in many ways. They can be told through a series of images, a film, or even a single logo. Every successful design says something. It communicates an idea to an audience. Makes them think. Engages them. And when someone looks at a logo, watches a commercial, stares at a print ad, glances at a poster, and even if for a quick moment stops to think, it means you've made that person think. And when that happens, an everlasting connection takes place. And that is why it is so important to create that moment. To create design with substance. That is why there is such an interesting parallel between art and design. Art usually communicates thoughts, feelings, or reactions to moments to a viewer. And so does good design.

A good story engages the audience, leaving us with something to think about. Obvious stories tend to get boring, just as a movie with an obvious plot usually won't

Allen kreativen Aufträgen oder Design-projekten ist eines gemeinsam: Sie erzählen stets eine Geschichte und vermitteln dem Publikum eine Idee, eine Erzählung oder ein Konzept. Diese Geschichten können auf vielerlei Weise kommuniziert werden: durch eine Bilderreihe, einen Film oder nur durch ein einziges Logo. Jedes erfolgreiche Design trifft eine Aussage. Es vermittelt dem Publikum eine Idee, regt zum Nach-denken an und bindet es ein. Wenn jemand ein Logo sieht, einen Werbefilm anschaut, eine Zeitungsanzeige anstarrt, einen Blick auf ein Plakat wirft und dann – wenn auch nur für einen kurzen Moment – innehält, um darüber nachzudenken, wurde diese Person zum Nachdenken gebracht. Sobald das geschieht, wird eine dauerhafte Verbindung aufgebaut. Und genau deshalb ist es wichtig, einen solchen Moment zu kreieren: um ein Design mit Substanz zu schaffen. Das ist die interessante Parallele zwischen Kunst und Design: Kunst kommuniziert über Gedanken, Gefühle oder Reaktionen mit dem Betrachter. Das Gleiche gilt auch für gutes Design.

Tous les projets créatifs et de design ont un point commun : ils demandent toujours de raconter une histoire, qu'il s'agisse de transmettre une idée, une pensée, un récit ou un concept au public. Et toutes ces histoires peuvent être racontées de bien des manières, à travers une série d'images, un film, voire un simple logo. Tous les designs qui marchent transmettent quelque chose. Ils communiquent une idée à un public. Le font réfléchir. L'impliquent. Lorsque quelqu'un observe un logo, voit un spot publicitaire, regarde une publicité dans un magazine ou fixe une affiche et s'arrête ne serait-ce qu'un instant pour penser, vous avez fait réfléchir cette personne. Lorsque cela se produit, une connexion éternelle s'établit. C'est pourquoi il est tellement im-portant de provoquer ce moment. De créer un design qui a de l'étoffe. C'est pourquoi il existe aussi un parallèle intéressant entre l'art et le design. En général l'art com-munique au spectateur des pensées, des sentiments ou des réactions à des situa-tions. Un bon design en fait autant.

Une bonne histoire implique le public et lui laisse des éléments sur lesquels

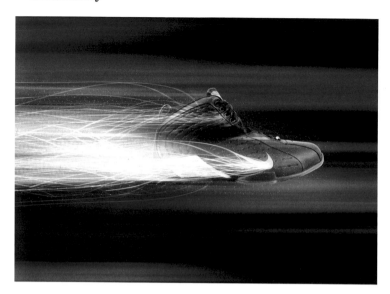

Left & right
Campaign for Nike Vapor Series, Nikelab

captivate viewers. That is why it's really important to choose carefully how much of the idea is explicitly explained and what is left out. It's so important to leave a piece of the puzzle out intentionally. Meet the audience in the middle. If you spell out everything to a viewer, it's like assuming they can't think for themselves. It's like if we needed a sign on every car out there that read "automobile" because otherwise we wouldn't know what we were looking at. It sounds like a stretch but in a way it's true. Assuming someone won't get it is simply settling for a safe, uninteresting piece that will, at its very best, provide information that will most likely be quickly forgotten. A good, captivating design will have the audience thinking about it, imprinted in their subconscious, and we are then rewarded for believing our audience is smarter than what statistics, charts, and research would tell us is normally the case. That is why there is a vast amount of the classic see-and-say ads and average design work out there, usually shaped by focus groups and marketing requirements that tell us nothing but the obvious. That kind

Eine gute Geschichte bindet das Publikum ein und schenkt ihm etwas zum Nachdenken. Wenn die Geschichte zu offensichtlich ist, wird sie schnell langweilig. Darum ist es auch so entscheidend, sorgfältig auszuwählen, wie viel von der Idee explizit erklärt werden soll und was man weglassen sollte. Es ist sehr wichtig, absichtlich einen Teil des Puzzles auszulassen. Wenn Sie dem Zuschauer alles erklären, ist es, als gingen Sie davon aus, dass er nicht selbst denken kann. Setzt man voraus, dass jemand etwas nicht versteht, setzt man auf uninteressante Fakten, die bestenfalls Informationen vermitteln, die wahrscheinlich schnell wieder vergessen sind. Ein gutes, fesselndes Design bringt das Publikum ins Nachdenken und prägt sich ins Unterbewusstsein ein. Und wir werden dafür belohnt, dass wir unser Publikum für schlauer halten als das, was uns Statistiken, Diagramme und Recherchen als normal verkaufen wollen. Deretwegen ist die Welt voll von Beispielen für geistlose Werbung und durchschnittliches Design, die uns, meist von Fokusgruppen und Marketinganforderungen geformt,

réfléchir. Les histoires trop évidentes tendent à être ennuyeuses, tout comme un film à l'intrigue facile ne tient pas les spectateurs en haleine. C'est pourquoi il est si important de décider avec soin dans quelle mesure l'idée est exposée de façon explicite, et ce qui est laissé dans l'ombre. Il est essentiel de volontairement omettre une partie du puzzle. De ne révéler que la moitié de l'histoire au public. Si vous dévoilez tout au spectateur, vous supposez qu'il n'est pas capable de penser par lui-même. C'est comme si nous avions besoin de mettre sur chaque voiture un panneau « véhicule » pour savoir ce que nous regardons. Tout cela semble tiré par les cheveux, mais c'est pourtant vrai. Le fait de supposer que les gens ne comprendront pas donne un résultat trop prudent et inintéressant qui apportera, au mieux, des informations risquant d'être rapidement oubliées. Un design de qualité et séduisant fera réfléchir le public à son sujet, ce qui le gravera dans son subconscient, et nous serons récompensés d'avoir cru que notre public est plus intelligent que ce que les statistiques, les graphiques et les

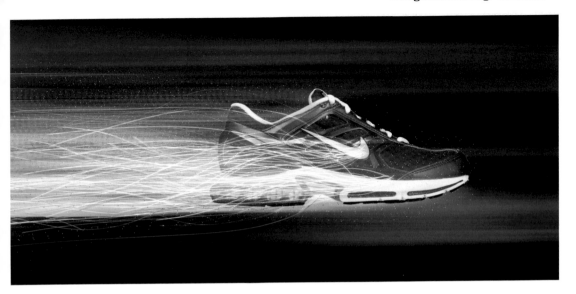

of work is usually a checklist of information spelled out and already digested for the audience, and is usually forgotten a lot quicker than the focus groups and research results would indicate. On the other hand, work that dares to challenge its audience and assume the best in them, stands out and does wonders for the brave clients who choose to trust not only their creatives but also their target audience, and believe it is a good idea. That is why if you look back at the best creative and design work from the past, you will find that the common thread among most, if not all, is that they were interesting and daring ideas that made us think, even if for just a second.

The moment I get briefed on a project I start looking for an interesting angle and a good story to tell. Doesn't matter if it's a simple logo or a long video. Every image tells us something and I start looking for what this one will tell. And sometimes that story comes from its own limitations. It is good to have restriction. If I am handed a pen and a piece of paper and asked to draw anything I want, chances are I will spend hours trying to figure out what I want

nichts anderes als das Offensichtliche erzählen. Solche Arbeiten sind häufig reine Sammlungen von Informationen, die dem Zielpublikum haarklein buchstabiert präsentiert werden. Sie werden meist schneller vergessen, als man es aufgrund der Recherchen denken sollte. Arbeiten hingegen, die ihr Publikum herauszufordern wagen und das Beste in ihm sehen, wirken Wunder für die mutigen Auftraggeber, die solche Werke für eine gute Idee halten und die sich dafür entschieden haben, nicht nur ihren kreativen Köpfen zu vertrauen, sondern auch ihrem Zielpublikum. Wer sich die besten Kreativ- und Designarbeiten der Vergangenheit anschaut, wird daher schnell bemerken, dass die meisten, wenn nicht gar alle, einen gemeinsamen Nenner haben: Sie enthalten interessante und wagemutige Ideen, die uns zum Nachdenken bringen, auch wenn es nur für ein paar Sekunden ist.

Sobald ich für ein Projekt gebrieft werde, fange ich an, einen interessanten Ansatzpunkt zu suchen, um eine gute Geschichte erzählen zu können. Dabei ist es egal, ob es sich um ein einfaches Logo oder ein

études veulent nous faire croire. Il existe ainsi une foule de publicités très premier degré et de designs médiocres, en général l'œuvre de groupes de discussion et le fruit d'exigences marketing, qui se contentent d'exprimer ce qui est évident. Ce type de travail se réduit normalement à une liste d'informations énoncées et déjà digérées par le public, qui les oublie bien plus vite que ce qu'indiquent les résultats des groupes de discussion ou des enquêtes. À l'opposé, un projet qui ose lancer un défi à son public et le considère capable de le relever se distingue du lot et fait des merveilles pour les clients courageux qui ont décidé de faire confiance non seulement à leurs créatifs, mais aussi à leur public cible, et de croire que l'idée était bonne. C'est pourquoi, si vous observez les meilleurs projets de création et de design du passé, vous trouverez que le fil conducteur dans la plupart des cas, pour ne pas dire tous, est qu'ils exploitaient des idées intéressantes et audacieuses qui font réfléchir, ne serait-ce qu'une seconde.

Dès que l'on m'explique la mission d'un projet, je cherche un angle intéressant et

to do and end up with the same blank canvas until I decide what I want to say. On the other hand, if instead of anything I am asked to draw something extremely specific, the creative juices start flowing right away with the challenge. The NYC2012 logos are a good example. The brief had a requirement. The logo had to be a running Statue of Liberty. It's a pretty constraining requirement, since it right away states what you have to create. But in a way it opened up an interesting door for me. If I could have chosen anything, I would have spent a lot of time thinking about where to start – which would have been fun too, don't get me wrong – but in a way since I had to use the Statue, it felt like all my creativity then went into looking for a way to make it interesting. Using the actual color of the Statue, for instance, was a common solution in all of my directions. It fascinated me how iconic that otherwise dull color became and how much meaning it added to each logo. Right away it made even the initial sketches feel right, in a subtle way. I then identified the other elements I had to include in order to

längeres Video handelt. Jedes Bild hat etwas zu berichten, und ich mache mich auf die Suche nach dem, was mir das Bild gerade erzählen will. Manchmal entspringt die Geschichte gar aus ihren eigenen Beschränkungen. Es ist gut, Einschränkungen zu haben. Wenn man mir einen Stift und ein Blatt Papier gibt und sagt, ich dürfe alles zeichnen, was ich wolle, dann würde ich wahrscheinlich stundenlang damit zubringen herauszufinden, was ich eigentlich machen will. Schließlich lande ich dann wieder vor dem leeren Blatt, ehe ich mich entschieden habe, was ich eigentlich sagen will. Wenn ich andererseits nicht irgendetwas Beliebiges, sondern etwas höchst Spezielles malen soll, beginnen die kreativen Energien durch diese Herausforderung zu strömen. Die NYC2012-Logos sind dafür ein gutes Beispiel. Das Briefing enthielt die Auflage: Das Logo sollte eine laufende Freiheitsstatue zeigen. Diese Anforderung ist ganz schön streng, weil sie direkt festlegt, was man kreieren soll. Doch in gewisser Weise öffnete sie mir eine interessante Tür. Wenn ich die freie Wahl gehabt hätte, hätte ich wahrscheinlich viel Zeit damit

une bonne histoire à raconter. Peu importe qu'il s'agisse d'un logo tout simple ou d'une longue vidéo. Chaque image raconte quelque chose, et je commence tout de suite à m'interroger sur ce que cette image va raconter. Parfois, l'histoire vient de ses propres limitations. Il est bon d'avoir des limites. Si j'ai un papier et un stylo en main et qu'on me demande de dessiner ce que je veux, je risque de passer des heures à chercher ce que je veux faire et de rester avec la même feuille blanche tant que je n'ai pas trouvé ce que je veux dire. Si on me demande plutôt de dessiner quelque chose de très spécifique, l'énergie créatrice commence à circuler pour relever le défi. Les logos NYC2012 en sont un bon exemple. La mission posait une condition. Le logo devait inclure la statue de la Liberté, condition plutôt contraignante puisqu'elle dicte immédiatement ce que vous devez créer. D'un autre côté, elle m'a ouvert une porte intéressante. Si mon choix avait été libre, j'aurais passé beaucoup de temps à chercher par où commencer (ce qui aurait aussi été agréable, ne m'interprétez pas mal), mais puisque je devais utiliser la

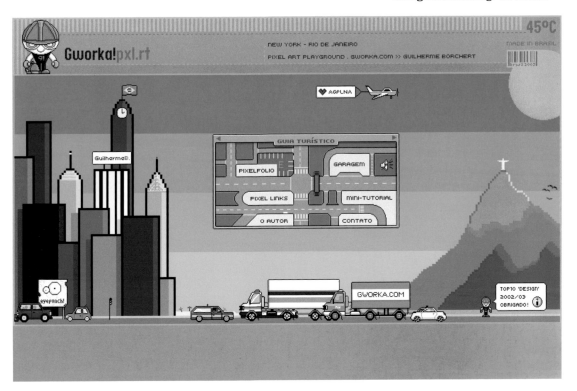

communicate what the image was, without losing it or going too far into the obvious. Then, for each solution I created that same iconic shape but through the lenses of different elements of New York City: graffiti, art, typography, geography, etc., as well as one direction that felt a bit more like what the Olympics graphic language felt like to me over the years.

As a kid, I remember spending hours drawing scenes that had very small elements in them, usually a city or a road, with lots of cars, people, buildings, and things happening. I would spend so much time on them and in the end they didn't look like much, just a lot of very small bits and pieces on the paper. I remember my dad would tease me about how tiny everything was. But I could spend hours explaining everything that had happened and what represented what. Years later I remember creating a pixel art website that was pretty much one of my drawings but in color and moving – which I didn't realize until years later. When Nike redesigned one of their most iconic shoes, with new materials and technologies, based on the

zugebracht, mir auszudenken, wo ich anfangen sollte (nicht, dass Sie mich falsch verstehen: das hätte wahrscheinlich auch Spaß gemacht). Aber weil ich mit der Freiheitsstatue arbeiten musste, fühlte es sich in gewisser Weise so an, als würde meine ganze Kreativität nun dort einfließen, um nach einer Möglichkeit zu suchen, wie man sie interessant machen konnte. Mit der echten Farbe der Statue zu arbeiten, war eine Lösung bei allen meinen Versuchen. Es faszinierte mich, wie ikonisch diese ansonsten so langweilige Farbe wurde und wie aussagekräftig sie jedes Logo gemacht hat. Sofort sorgte sie dafür, dass sich schon die ersten Skizzen auf subtile Weise richtig angefühlt haben. Dann identifizierte ich die anderen Elemente, die ich einbauen musste, um vermitteln zu können, um was es bei dem Bild geht, ohne es zu verlieren oder zu offensichtlich zu werden. Anschließend schuf ich für jede Lösung die gleiche bildhafte Form, betrachtete sie aber zum einen unter verschiedenen für die Stadt New York charakteristischen Aspekten wie Graffiti, Kunst, Typografie, Geografie etc., zum anderen gab ich ihnen eine Anmutung,

statue, toute ma créativité s'est portée sur la façon de rendre le résultat intéressant. L'emploi de la couleur de la statue a par exemple été une solution commune appliquée dans toutes les directions que j'ai suivies. J'étais fasciné par le caractère emblématique que cette couleur terne avait acquis et par la signification supplémentaire qu'elle conférait à chaque logo. Grâce à elle, les premiers croquis ont été, d'une façon subtile, tout de suite satisfaisants. J'ai ensuite trouvé les autres éléments à inclure pour transmettre ce que représentait l'image, sans perdre le nord et sans pousser trop loin l'évidence. Pour chaque solution, j'ai ensuite créé cette même forme emblématique, mais à travers différents éléments de New York : graffitis, art, typographie, géographie, etc. J'ai aussi suivi une direction correspondant davantage à ce que le langage graphique des Jeux olympiques m'avait transmis au fil des années.

Je me souviens, enfant, avoir passé des heures à dessiner des scènes composées d'éléments minuscules, en général une ville ou une route avec une foule de voitu-

Left
Poster for the "Restoration"
campaign for Nike

Right
Website for the "Restoration"
campaign for Nike

same original idea, they named the project Restoration. Without me even noticing it I would have the opportunity to have as much fun on a real project as I had drawing as a kid. The first part of the brief was to create a poster for the project. The second part was an interactive experience to showcase the process and the product. It was the first cross trainer shoe ever designed and that sneaker set the standards and created an entire successful segment with influence across multiple brands. The idea of the poster was then to feature that very iconic nature of the sneaker. To make it feel grand, the restoration process was depicted as an architectural process. In the center we have the shoe in mid-restoration and parts of both the old sneaker as well as the new one can be seen. Around it was an array of characters and elements that you would see on a construction site. Everything represents something, and you can spend a lot of time watching the poster and imagining what each character is doing or thinking. That became even more true when the actual interactive experience became the exact poster brought to life,

die an die Bildsprache der Olympischen Spiele erinnerte, wie ich sie im Laufe der Jahre wahrgenommen habe.

Ich weiß noch, wie ich als Kind stundenlang sehr kleinteilige Szenen gezeichnet habe, meist eine Stadt oder eine Straße mit vielen Autos, Menschen, Gebäuden und Ereignissen, die sich darin zutrugen. Ich verbrachte viel Zeit damit, aber am Ende sahen die Bilder nach kaum etwas aus, einfach nur nach einer Ansammlung vieler kleiner Elemente auf dem Papier. Mein Vater hat mich immer damit aufgezogen, wie winzig alles war. Doch ich konnte stundenlang erklären, was da alles passiert war und welche Elemente was darstellen sollten. Jahre später habe ich dann eine Website mit Pixelkunst erstellt, die ziemlich genau wie meine Zeichnungen, aber farbig und bewegt war. Als Nike einen der wichtigsten Kult-Schuhe mit neuen Materialien und Technologien, aber auf der ursprünglichen Idee beruhend neu gestalten wollte, bekam das Projekt den Namen „Restoration" (Restaurierung). Da bekam ich die Gelegenheit, mit einem echten Projekt soviel Spaß zu haben wie

res, de gens, de bâtiments et de choses qui s'y passent. J'y passais beaucoup de temps et à la fin, ce n'était pas grand-chose, juste une série de petits éléments sur le papier. Je me souviens que mon père me taquinait sur la taille minuscule de tout ce que je dessinais. Je pouvais pourtant expliquer pendant des heures ce qu'il s'y passait et ce que chaque chose représentait. Des années plus tard, je me souviens avoir créé un site Web de pixel art qui ressemblait beaucoup à l'un de mes dessins, mais en couleur et animé, ce que j'ai mis des années à comprendre. Lorsque Nike a remodelé le design de l'une de ses chaussures les plus célèbres, en changeant les matériaux et les technologies mais en reprenant la même idée d'origine, ils ont intitulé le projet « Restoration ». Sans même m'en apercevoir, j'allais avoir la chance de passer autant de bon temps sur ce projet tout à fait réel que lorsque je dessinais enfant. La première partie de ma mission consistait à créer une affiche pour le projet. La seconde était une expérience interactive pour présenter le processus et le produit. Il s'agissait de la première

where everything moved and clicking on each person displayed a bit of information and content about the project. Through time-lapse animation users could go back in time to see the original sneaker or advance into the future to see the completed product.

With time, the saying that an image is worth a thousand words has become increasingly more meaningful to me. And in the poster I created for the Barack Obama campaign it came to life, literally. As part of the Artists for Obama initiative, nine artists were commissioned by the Campaign to create and donate a poster to be sold as a limited run on the online store. I was very honored to be one of the artists. I wanted to create a portrait based on his ideals and beliefs. I wanted it to be iconic as well as typographically beautiful. So I created a portrait made up entirely of words. The campaign sent me speeches and words they had previously used. I went through them and selected nine words I felt were inspiring and moving. Each word was carefully placed one at a time in succession to create the image,

beim Zeichnen in Kindertagen. Der erste Teil des Briefings bestand darin, ein Plakat für das Projekt zu entwerfen. Beim zweiten Teil ging es um eine interaktive Website, auf der der Prozess und das Produkt vorgestellt werden sollten. Es handelte sich um den ersten Crosstraining-Schuh, der jemals gestaltet wurde. Dieser Sneaker setzte einen Standard und begründete ein ganzes erfolgreiches Segment, das markenübergreifend beeinflussend war. Als Idee für das Plakat sollte genau dieser Kultcharakter herausgestellt werden. Um das Gefühl von etwas Großartigem zu erzeugen, wurde der Restaurierungsvorgang als architektonischer Prozess dargestellt: In der Mitte sehen wir den Schuh mitten in der Restaurierung, Teile sowohl des alten als auch des neuen Sneakers sind erkennbar. Der Schuh ist von verschiedenen Elementen umgeben, die auch auf Baustellen zu finden sind. Jedes Teil repräsentiert etwas, und man kann das Plakat sehr lange anschauen und sich vorstellen, was jede Figur gerade macht und denkt. Das traf sogar noch mehr auf die interaktive Website zu, die das Plakat regelrecht zum Leben erweckte: Mit jedem

chaussure de cross-training jamais conçue. Elle a établi la norme et ouvert tout un segment prospère qui a influencé de nombreuses marques. L'idée de l'affiche était donc de montrer sa nature très emblématique. Pour lui donner de l'envergure, la « restauration » a été décrite comme un processus architectural. Au centre se trouve la chaussure en cours de restauration, avec des parties visibles de l'ancienne version et de la nouvelle. Autour gravite un ensemble de personnages et d'éléments caractéristiques d'un chantier de construction. Tout a une signification et vous pouvez passer un bon moment à observer l'affiche et à imaginer ce que chaque personnage fait ou pense. Tout ceci s'est d'autant plus vérifié lorsque l'expérience interactive a donné vie à cette même affiche : tous les éléments étaient animés et le fait de cliquer sur chaque personnage affichait des informations et des contenus multimédias sur le projet. Via une animation accélérée, les utilisateurs pouvaient reculer dans le temps pour voir la basket d'origine, ou bien se projeter dans le futur et observer le produit achevé.

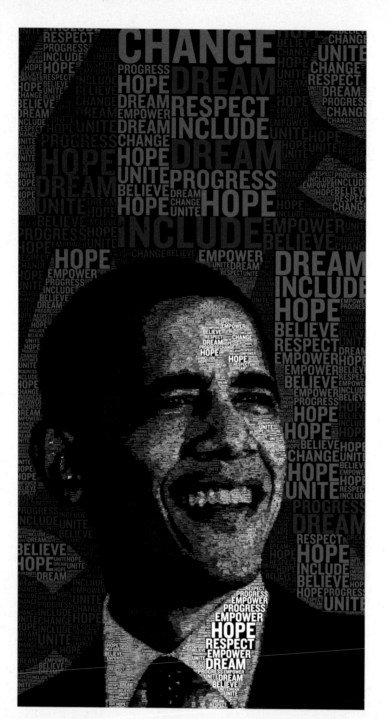

PAID FOR BY OBAMA FOR AMERICA · WWW.BARACKOBAMA.COM

Left
Poster commissioned
by the Obama Election
Campaign 2008

Right
Key visual for the campaign
Nike Design by Nature

and about twenty thousand words later, the idea became a reality. Cropped in the background the words "Yes we can" created an interesting type-on-type backdrop for the image. In the foreground Barack Obama stands represented by the very words he believes in. Within a week all five thousand posters were sold out and I couldn't be happier with the result.

At the end of the day what I strive for are images that don't just sit there telling you everything you need to know. I would much rather give the audience just enough to figure things out on their own. It's a much more rewarding process. For the Nike Design by Nature poster and interactive experience, I wanted to create something that merged nature and technology in an original way and thus told a story about evolution and bionics, without taking the obvious route. The poster was inspired by the Golden Section, a beautiful geometrical relationship found in nature. The parts of the shoe were positioned to create the Fibonacci Spiral, rising out of plants. In the experience, shoe parts, plants, flowers, and products were placed together in harmony,

Klick auf eine Person wurden Informationen und Inhalte des Projekts dargestellt. Durch Zeitrafferanimationen konnten die User in der Zeit zurückgehen, um einen Blick auf den ursprünglichen Sneaker zu werfen, oder in die Zukunft springen, um das vollendete Produkt anzuschauen.

Im Laufe der Zeit ist das Sprichwort „Ein Bild sagt mehr wert als tausend Worte" für mich immer bedeutungsvoller geworden. Und bei dem Plakat, das ich für die Wahlkampagne von Barack Obama kreiert habe, wurde es buchstäblich lebendig. Als Teil der Initiative „Künstler für Obama" wurden neun Künstler beauftragt, ein Plakat als Spende zu entwerfen, das als limitierte Auflage im Online-Shop verkauft werden sollte. Ich fühlte mich geehrt, zu diesen Künstlern zu gehören. Ich wollte ein Porträt schaffen, das auf Obamas Idealen und Überzeugungen basierte. Es sollte bildlich ebenso ansprechend sein wie typografisch. Also schuf ich ein Porträt, das vollständig aus Wörtern bestand. Von der Kampagne bekam ich Reden und Zitate von Obama. Ich ging sie alle durch und wählte neun Wörter aus, die meines Erachtens inspirie-

Avec le temps, l'expression « une image vaut mieux que de longs discours » prend une signification de plus en plus riche et importante à mes yeux. Dans l'affiche que j'ai créée pour la campagne de Barack Obama, tout ceci se matérialise. Dans le cadre de l'initiative « Artists for Obama », neuf artistes ont été chargés par les organisateurs de la campagne de créer et céder une affiche qui serait vendue à tirage limité sur la boutique en ligne. J'ai été très fier de faire partie de ces artistes. Je voulais créer un portrait reposant sur les idéaux et les convictions d'Obama. Je souhaitais que le résultat soit emblématique et très esthétique sur le plan typographique. J'ai donc réalisé un portrait exclusivement composé de mots. L'organisation de la campagne m'a envoyé des discours et les termes qu'ils avaient déjà utilisés. Je les ai parcourus et ai retenu neuf mots que je trouvais inspirants et émouvants. Je les ai placés un à un avec soin, en une séquence qui se répète pour créer l'image, et quelque vingt mille mots plus tard, l'idée s'est concrétisée. Les mots « Yes we can » se détachent à l'arrière-plan et donnent

Left & right
Nike posters for the campaign
Nike Design by Nature

in different scenarios that combined nature and technology, and each told a different part of the product story. Hidden elements throughout rewarded curious users with fun facts and details about the project and about nature itself.

Good design and good ideas should always go hand in hand. Of course there will always be room for beautiful art just for esthetic purposes, especially when experimenting visually, but even then we might not realize that something is being communicated, especially if it's so subjective that we ourselves do not notice. It is still there, however. All the same, a great idea needs a great execution. And the same can be said the other way round as well.

rend und bewegend waren. Jedes Wort wurde sorgfältig eines nach dem anderen platziert, woraus das Bild entstand, und etwa 20.000 Wörter später war die Idee Wirklichkeit geworden. Die in den Hintergrund eingebetteten Worte „Yes we can" schufen die Schriftkulisse für das Bild. Im Vordergrund steht Barack Obama und wird von genau jenen Wörtern repräsentiert, an die er glaubt. Innerhalb einer Woche waren alle 5.000 Plakate verkauft, und ich hätte mit dem Ergebnis nicht glücklicher sein können.

Letzten Endes lege ich es auf Bilder an, die einem nicht förmlich ins Gesicht springen und die einem nicht schon alles sagen, was man wissen soll. Ich bevorzuge es, den Betrachtern gerade eben genug an die Hand zu geben, um es selbst herauszufinden. Das ist ein weitaus lohnenderer Prozess. Bei dem Plakat und der Website „Design by Nature" von Nike wollte ich etwas schaffen, bei dem Natur und Technologie auf originelle Weise verschmelzen und somit eine Geschichte über Evolution und Bionik erzählen, ohne einen offensichtlichen Weg einzuschlagen. Das Plakat war vom Goldenen

une toile de fond intéressante à l'image en superposant deux couches typographiques. Au premier plan, Barack Obama pose, représenté par les mots auxquels il croit. Les cinq mille affiches se sont vendues en une semaine ; je ne pouvais pas être plus satisfait du résultat.

En fin de compte, je cherche des images qui ne se contentent pas d'exister et d'exprimer tout ce qu'il y a à savoir. Je préfère donner au public juste ce qu'il lui faut pour comprendre de lui-même, car l'approche est nettement plus gratifiante. Pour l'affiche et l'expérience interactive Design by Nature de Nike, je voulais créer quelque chose qui fusionnerait la nature et la technologie avec originalité, et donc raconter une histoire sur l'évolution et la bionique, sans emprunter la voie la plus évidente. L'affiche s'est inspirée du nombre d'or, un rapport géométrique superbe qui existe dans la nature. Les éléments de la chaussure étaient placés de façon à créer une spirale de Fibonacci s'élevant au milieu de plantes. Les éléments de la chaussure, les plantes, les fleurs et les produits étaient arrangés en toute harmonie,

Schnitt inspiriert (einer schönen, geometrischen Beziehung, die man in der Natur vorfindet). Die Teile des Schuhs wurden so positioniert, dass sie die Form der Fibonacci-Spirale annehmen, wie Pflanzen sie in ihrem Bauplan aufweisen. Auf der Website wurden Schuhteile, Pflanzen, Blumen und Produkte harmonisch nebeneinander platziert, und zwar in verschiedenen Szenarien, die Natur und Technologie kombinieren. Alle erzählen einen anderen Teil der Story für dieses Produkt. Überall belohnen versteckte Elemente neugierige Besucher mit spannenden Fakten und Details über das Projekt und auch über die Natur selbst.

Gutes Design und gute Ideen sollten immer Hand in Hand gehen. Gerade wenn man visuell experimentiert, wird es natürlich immer Raum für schöne, rein ästhetisch motivierte Kunst geben. Doch selbst dann erkennen wir vielleicht nicht, dass etwas vermittelt werden soll, vor allem, wenn es so subjektiv ist, dass wir selbst es einfach nicht bemerken. Trotzdem ist es da! Wie auch immer: Eine großartige Idee braucht eine großartige Ausführung. Und das Gleiche gilt auch umgekehrt!

dans différents scénarios associant nature et technologie, chacun expliquant un passage de l'histoire du produit. Des éléments dissimulés un peu partout récompensaient les utilisateurs curieux par des informations amusantes et des détails sur le projet et sur la nature.

Un bon design doit toujours aller de pair avec une bonne idée. Il y aura toujours de la place pour l'art purement esthétique, notamment dans le cadre de l'expérimentation visuelle. Mais même dans ce cas, nous pouvons ne pas réaliser la présence d'un message, surtout s'il est tellement subjectif que nous ne le remarquons pas. Il est pourtant bien là. Il n'empêche qu'à grande idée, grande exécution. Et l'inverse aussi est vrai.

MIGRANTAS INITIATIVE

Hieroglyphics for Democracy
From Personal Experience to Social Message

By Professor Enrique Longinotti, University of Buenos Aires

www.migrantas.org

Migrantas is a Berlin-based collective formed by Argentineans Marula Di Como, Florencia Young, Estela Schindel, Alejandra López, and German-born Irma Leinauer, who have focused their work on the identity of foreign migrants.

Enrique Longinotti is an Argentinean architect and Professor of graphic design at the University of Buenos Aires.

Migrantas ist ein Kollektiv in Berlin, das sich aus den Argentinierinnen Marula Di Como, Florencia Young, Estela Schindel und Alejandra López sowie der in Deutschland geborenen Irma Leinauer zusammensetzt. Im Mittelpunkt der Arbeiten steht die Identität von Menschen mit Migrationshintergrund.

Enrique Longinotti ist Architekt aus Argentinien und lehrt als Professor für Grafikdesign an der Universität von Buenos Aires.

Migrantas est un collectif installé à Berlin et composé des Argentines Marula Di Como, Florencia Young, Estela Schindel et Alejandra López, ainsi que de l'Allemande Irma Leinauer. Elles ont centré leur travail sur l'identité d'immigrants étrangers.

Enrique Longinotti est un architecte argentin, professeur de design graphique à l'université de Buenos Aires.

Left
Migrantas bag with the pictogram
"I am Berlin too", Berlin 2006

Right
Street outdoor with the pictogram
"Why and what for?", Buenos Aires 2004

The Migrantas project has been evolving for a number of years. It is particularly notable as a visual initiative inserted into a complex social territory whose content is built up from participating community initiatives.

It started off as the Ausländer project, developed by two Argentinian women, both immigrants, who met in Berlin in 2002: the artist Marula Di Como, who since 2000 had been using pictograms as part of the language of her work, and the graphic designer Florencia Young. Between December 2003 and January 2004, an initial series of pictograms was shown on advertising hoardings in the center of Buenos Aires, Argentina, drawing attention, in the public arena, to an unpalatable fact of life in the city: looking at the problems of immigrants as if through a mirror and recognizing the anxiety of those who have been forced to emigrate, as has happened to thousands of Argentinians since the crisis of 2001.

The communicative effect of the project was such that its creators decided to invite the sociologist Estela Schindel to broaden her personal perception to encom-

Das Migrantas-Projekt hat sich über mehrere Jahre entwickelt und ist insbesondere deswegen bemerkenswert, weil es sich um eine visuelle Initiative handelt, die in einen komplexen sozialen Bereich eingefügt ist und deren Inhalte von Gemeinschaftsinitiativen gestaltet werden.

Migrantas begann als „Projekt Ausländer", das von zwei argentinischen Immigrantinnen 2002 in Berlin initiiert wurde: von der Künstlerin Marula Di Como, die seit 2000 Piktogramme als Teil der Bildsprache verwendet, und von der Grafikdesignerin Florencia Young. Zwischen Dezember 2003 und Januar 2004 wurde auf Werbetafeln in Buenos Aires eine erste Serie von Piktogrammen gezeigt. Sie machten auf eine der unbequemen Wahrheiten des Lebens in der Stadt aufmerksam: Wie mit einem Spiegel wurde der Blick auf die Probleme der Immigranten gerichtet und die Unruhe derer anerkannt, die zur Emigration gezwungen werden, wie es Tausenden von Argentiniern seit der Krise im Jahr 2001 geschehen ist.

Die kommunikative Wirkung des Projekts war entscheidend für die Künstlerinnen, so dass sie die Soziologin Estela

Migrantas est un projet qui évolue depuis plusieurs années et se caractérise par une initiative visuelle prenant place dans un territoire social complexe ; les contenus sont élaborés à partir d'actions participatives de la communauté.

Tout a commencé avec le projet Ausländer, créé par deux immigrantes d'origine argentine qui s'étaient retrouvées en 2002 à Berlin : l'artiste Marula Di Como, qui utilisait depuis l'an 2000 des pictogrammes comme éléments de langage dans son œuvre, et la designer graphique Florencia Young. Entre décembre 2003 et janvier 2004, une première série de pictogrammes a été présentée sur des panneaux publicitaires dans le centre de Buenos Aires (Argentine), révélant au public une vérité gênante pour cette ville : observer les problèmes des immigrants comme dans un miroir et vivre d'une certaine façon l'angoisse de ces personnes qui ont dû émigrer, cas de milliers d'Argentins depuis la crise de 2001.

L'impact de communication du projet a été tel que les auteurs ont décidé d'inviter la sociologue Estela Schindel pour élargir sa perception personnelle et englober

Left
Workshop participants, Hamburg 2007

Right
Development from drawing to pictogram:
"Where will it belong?"

pass the entire immigration phenomenon in Berlin, and extend the invitation to hundreds of women from different cultures and origins. By 2005, Migrantas had begun to take shape. The working method was defined in workshops where groups of immigrant women, after exchanging viewpoints and discussing personal experiences, draw and comment on the results of this form of expression.

In the offices of this group, which currently includes the Argentinian journalist Alejandra López and the German town planner Irma Leinauer in addition to Di Como and Young, the results from the workshops are analyzed and selected and then translated into pictograms which are to be the main feature of the urban initiatives.

The project breaks down many barriers, above all in terms of type. On the one hand, the "graphic design" becomes a professional system that is different from the normal style created as a result of client – designer dialectics. Here an atypical invitation and dialogue occur. It is interesting to detect the role of design in this process. Above all, it is a place of lis-

Schindel einluden, um mit ihr das Projekt auf das Phänomen der Immigration in Berlin auszudehnen. Seit 2005 hat das Projekt Form angenommen: Frauen verschiedenster Kulturen und Herkunft werden in Workshops eingeladen, tauschen ihre Standpunkte und Erfahrungen aus, zeichnen und diskutieren die entstandenen Entwürfe.

Im Atelier der Gruppe, zu der aktuell neben Di Como und Young auch die argentinische Journalistin Alejandra López und die deutsche Stadtplanerin Irma Leinauer gehören, werden die Resultate aus den Workshops analysiert, ausgewählt und in Piktogramme übersetzt, die zum Hauptmerkmal der Initiative werden sollten.

Das Projekt überschreitet zahlreiche Grenzen, vor allem die von Genres. Auf der einen Seite wird das „Grafikdesign" zu einem professionellen System, das sich von der üblichen Dialektik Auftraggeber-Designer unterscheidet. Bei Migrantas kommt es zu einem besonderen Dialog. Es ist interessant, in diesem Prozess die Rolle des Designs zu erkennen. Vor allem ist dieser Dialog ein Ort des Zuhörens und der Teilnahme. Das Design führt hier keinen

l'ensemble du phénomène d'immigration à Berlin, ainsi qu'ouvrir la participation à des centaines de femmes de cultures et origines distinctes. Depuis 2005, Migrantas a commencé à prendre forme. La méthode de travail a été définie lors d'ateliers où des groupes de femmes immigrantes, après avoir échangé des points de vue et exposé des expériences personnelles, explorent et commentent les résultats de cette forme d'expression.

Dans les bureaux de ce collectif, qui inclut aussi actuellement la journaliste argentine Alejandra López et la chargée de planification urbaine allemande Irma Leinauer, en plus de Di Como et Young, les résultats des ateliers ont été analysés et sélectionnés, puis traduits en pictogrammes qui allaient devenir les protagonistes des actions urbaines.

Le projet est truffé de transgressions, notamment en matière de genre. D'un côté, le « design graphique » devient un processus différent du style habituel créé par la dialectique client-designer. Chez Migrantas, le dialogue est atypique. Il est intéressant d'identifier la place occupée par le design

Where will it belong?

tening and invitation, an act that opens up a space for others. Design does not hold a discourse of its own, based on class, but interprets – in the musical sense – the notes that someone else leaves on a piece of paper, with its graphics rich in subjective social content. On the other hand, it is about women giving voice to other women, and this point of view should not go unnoticed. The project crosses more than one boundary and more than one social prejudice with each step it takes into the urban space.

Pictograms or Ideograms

Sifting through the history of visual communication we find, almost from the beginning, pictographic practices in which the person at whom they are aimed, when they understand the sense in which an image is used, accesses the communicative intention of the person who devised it. In this sense, every pictogram conceals an *ideographic* condition.

I think, therefore, that the term *ideogram* is the most apposite to refer to the Migrantas project and its own

eigenen Diskurs, der einer bestimmten Klasse zugehört, sondern interpretiert eher die Bilderwelten, voller subjektiver Inhalte, in einem musikalischen Sinn, wie „Noten". Andererseits, und das ist keineswegs unwichtig, sind es Frauen, die anderen Frauen eine Stimme geben. Das Projekt überschreitet mit jedem Schritt, den es in den urbanen Raum macht, mehr als nur eine Grenze und mehr als nur ein soziales Vorurteil.

Piktogramme / Ideogramme

Wenn man die Geschichte der visuellen Kommunikation durchstöbert, findet man fast schon von Anbeginn an piktografische Praktiken. Wenn der Adressat den Sinn versteht, in dem ein Bild verwendet wird, kann diese Person auf die kommunikative Absicht der Person zugreifen, die es erfunden hat. In diesem Sinne birgt jedes Piktogramm eine ideografische Bedingung.

Ich glaube daher, dass der Begriff Ideogramm der treffendste ist, wenn man vom Migrantas-Projekt und seiner eigenen visuellen Grammatik spricht. Wir haben es hier mit Zeichen und ihren hochverdichteten Konnotationen zu tun, bei denen die

dans ce processus : elle est avant tout un espace d'écoute et d'invitation, une attitude qui laisse une place pour tous. En soi, le design n'apporte pas un discours basé sur la classe : il interprète (dans le sens musical du terme) les notes qu'autrui marque sur un papier, avec des graphismes riches en contenu social subjectif. D'un autre côté, des femmes parlent aux femmes, un point de vue qui ne doit pas passer inaperçu. Ce projet franchit plus d'une frontière et plus d'un préjugé social à chaque pas effectué dans l'espace urbain.

Pictogrammes ou idéogrammes

En analysant l'histoire de la communication visuelle, on découvre dès le début quasiment des pratiques pictographiques dans lesquelles leur destinataire, s'il comprend la signification d'une image, capte l'intention de communication de la personne à l'origine. Tout pictogramme cache dans ce sens une condition *idéographique*.

Je crois par conséquent que le terme *idéogramme* est le plus adéquat pour faire référence au projet Migrantas et à sa

141

Us?

Left & right
Pictograms as a result of workshops
in Berlin, Hamburg, and Cologne

particular visual grammar. We are talking about signs with multiple connotations, in which the concepts are distilled into images from the moment the immigrant women produce their drawings charged with ideas and emotions, and in which the denotative strokes are carefully selected and arranged so that they fulfil their communicative intention.

To decipher true social hieroglyphics is to access what we all, not just a few of us, should know: that there are others and that they feel, speak, and express themselves. When we understand them, we understand that the others exist, and in so doing we include them and include ourselves. In this project, the ideographic language of the modern world displays a true visual democracy that sidesteps the language barriers that conceal practically all the strategies of discrimination. Here, design reclaims its noble tradition of universality: that of equal opportunities of perception and not homogeneity of consumption.

Through conceptual images, the design of these graphic pieces reinterprets the drawings that hundreds of women make

Konzepte von Anfang an in Bilder destilliert werden, wenn die Immigrantinnen ihre Zeichnungen produzieren, die mit Ideen und Emotionen aufgeladen sind und bei denen die denotativen Eigenschaften sorgfältig ausgewählt und arrangiert werden, um ihre kommunikative Intention zu erfüllen.

Es handelt sich also um soziale Hieroglyphen, bei deren Entzifferung man auf das zugreift, was wir alle wissen sollten: dass es andere gibt und dass sie fühlende, sprechende Wesen sind, die sich selbst ausdrücken. Indem wir sie verstehen, erkennen wir ihr Existenz; in diesen Akt beziehen wir sie ein und beziehen uns zugleich auf uns selbst. Dabei bildet die ideografische Sprache eine visuelle Demokratie, die jene Sprachbarrieren umgeht, die praktisch alle Strategien der Diskriminierung kaschieren. Hier erobert das Design seine Tradition der Universalität zurück: die der gleichberechtigten Möglichkeiten der Wahrnehmung, und nicht die der Homogenität des Konsums.

Durch konzeptuelle Bilder reinterpretiert das Design die Zeichnungen, die Hunderte von Frauen aus ihren Emotionen und Gedanken heraus geschaffen haben.

grammaire visuelle particulière. Il s'agit de signes fortement connotés, dans lesquels les concepts se distillent dès le départ en images, depuis l'instant où les femmes immigrantes font des dessins riches en idées et en émotions et dans lesquels les traits identificateurs sont choisis et placés avec soin pour respecter leur intention communicative.

Véritables hiéroglyphes sociaux, les déchiffrer signifie accéder à ce que tout le monde, et non une minorité, devrait savoir : que l'autre existe et qu'il a des sentiments, qu'il parle et qu'il s'exprime. En comprenant autrui, on assimile son existence et par là même on l'intègre et on s'intègre. Le langage idéographique moderne révèle dans ce projet une véritable démocratie visuelle qui échappe aux barrières idiomatiques dans lesquelles se trament presque toutes les stratégies de discrimination. Ici, le design retrouve sa belle tradition d'universalité, d'égalité des chances de perception, au lieu de l'homogénéité de consommation.

À travers des images conceptuelles, le design de ces œuvres graphiques réin-

Am I allowed to stay?

Different?

Residence permit

Here and there

My country

Migrant's job

based on their own emotions, anxieties, and thoughts. Certainly, Migrantas is not "designing emotions," since doing so would be programming only consumers, in this case in a kind of "emotional consumerism". It is the messages that count or, rather, the signs, the writing of these messages. The message really happens in the consciousness of those who discover it, understand it, and make it present.

From Brand to Sign

A few interesting questions arise in this respect. Is it possible to identify without branding? Is there room for an act of design that does not fetishize what it refers to in terms of merchandise? In this sense, the challenge that Migrantas offers to society through its urban initiatives is that of making the presence of the Other, his situation and emotion, clear and precise. The global language of its pictograms has the courage to assert that the foreigner's problem can be read, understood, and communicated. The combination of objectivity and subjectivity is what turns these signs into true discourses of integration.

Natürlich macht sich Migrantas nicht daran, Gefühle zu gestalten, weil das nur dazu führen würde, Konsumenten oder einen Gefühlskonsum zu programmieren. Es sind die Botschaften, die zählen, oder vielmehr die Zeichen, also die Handschrift dieser Botschaften. Die Botschaft entsteht im Bewusstsein derjenigen, die sie entdecken, verstehen und präsent machen.

Von der Marke zum Zeichen

In dieser Hinsicht tauchen spannende Fragen auf: Kann man etwas identifizieren, ohne ihm eine Marke zu verleihen? Gibt es Raum für einen Akt der Gestaltung, der nicht das zum Fetisch macht, worauf er sich in kommerzieller Hinsicht bezieht? In diesem Sinne besteht die Herausforderung darin, die Präsenz der Anderen, ihre Situationen und Emotionen, klar und präzise vorzustellen. Die globale Sprache ihrer Piktogramme besteht darauf, dass die Probleme der Ausländer gelesen, verstanden und kommuniziert werden können. Die Kombination aus Objektivität und Subjektivität ist es, was diese Zeichen in einen echten Diskurs der Integration verwandelt.

terprète donc les dessins de centaines de femmes basés sur leurs propres émotions, inquiétudes et réflexions. Il est clair que Migrantas ne cherche pas à « créer des émotions », car il s'agirait dans ce cas de programmer des consommateurs, pour une sorte de « consommation émotionnelle ». Les messages sont ce qui compte vraiment, ou plutôt les signes, l'écriture de ces messages. Ils se produisent réellement dans la conscience des personnes qui les découvrent, les comprennent et les rendent présents.

De la marque au signe

Plusieurs questions intéressantes se posent. Peut-on identifier sans marquer ? Y a-t-il un espace pour un design sans fétichisme de l'objet en question, en termes de marchandise ? Le défi que Migrantas propose à la société à travers ses actions urbaines est dans ce cas de clarifier et préciser la présence de l'autre, sa situation et ses émotions. Le langage global des pictogrammes a l'audace d'affirmer que le problème de l'étranger peut être lu, compris et communiqué. Le mélange d'objecti-

Much closer to the *archetype* than the *logotype*, it is not a question of branding consumption or an identity but of reinstating a critical way of thinking. The austerity of the Migrantas language shows the intention of being pure content, a minimal medium for a message that belongs to everyone. The significance in this case coincides point by point with the signifier. Not one stroke too many but neither one too few, to be precise.

Like an ideological minimum, we are not talking here about the apology of silence but an appeal to the subjectivity of the social, the act of stating, using a visual voice, what those who cannot fully make their own statement think, that of language and customs. We are talking about a neutrality that does not want to be identified with anything other than the message itself, issued by the group of migrants who communicate their view in this way. So Migrantas is not a branding of the foreign but a set of signs to better understand the diverse global society in which we live, full of opportunities to put ourselves in the place of others, with others.

Viel näher am Archetyp als am Logotyp, geht es hier nicht um Markenkonsum, sondern um eine kritische Denkweise. Die Sparsamkeit der Sprache von Migrantas zeigt die Absicht, reiner Inhalt zu sein, ein minimales Medium für eine Botschaft, die jedem gehört. Das Signifikat deckt sich in diesem Fall Punkt für Punkt mit dem Signifikant, dem Bedeuteten: ganz präzise, nicht ein Strich zu viel, aber auch keiner zu wenig.

Wie ein ideologisches Minimum geht es hier nicht um eine Apologie des Schweigens, sondern um einen Appell an die Subjektivität des Sozialen; eine Aussage darüber, was jene denken, die ihre eigenen Aussagen nicht vollständig zum Ausdruck bringen können. Wir sprechen von einer Neutralität, die über nichts anderes identifiziert werden will als über ihre eigene Botschaft. Somit haben wir es bei Migrantas nicht mit der Entwicklung einer Marke für „das Ausländische" zu tun, sondern mit einer Gruppe von Zeichen, um die vielfältige globale Gesellschaft, in der wir leben, besser verstehen zu können: Sie bietet uns zahlreiche Möglichkeiten, selbst einmal den Platz anderer einzunehmen – gemeinsam mit den anderen.

vité et de subjectivité transforme ces signes en véritables discours d'intégration.

Beaucoup plus proche de *l'archétype* que du logo, il n'est pas question de marquer une consommation ou une identité, mais de restaurer une réflexion critique. L'austérité du langage de Migrantas démontre l'intention d'offrir un contenu pur, un support minimal pour un message universel. La signification équivaut dans ce cas point par point au signifiant. Pas un trait de plus, mais pas un de moins non plus.

Comme un minimum idéologique, l'idée n'est pas ici de faire l'apologie du silence, mais d'en appeler à la subjectivité sur le plan social, de déclarer avec une voix visuelle ce que pensent ceux qui ne peuvent faire entendre la leur, leur langue et leurs coutumes. Il s'agit d'une neutralité qui veut seulement être identifiée au message lui-même, dont l'émetteur est l'ensemble des immigrants qui montrent ainsi leur regard. Migrantas n'est donc pas un branding de l'étranger, mais un ensemble de signes pour mieux comprendre la société mondiale, pleine de diversité et d'occasions de nous mettre à la place de l'autre, avec l'autre.

PROJECTS

Project
Cesar and Evo series
North Kiteboarding
collection 2008/2009

Client
North Kiteboarding

Area
Sports equipment

Year
2008

Design
3deluxe

Country
Germany

Project
Vegas and Young Blood series
North Kiteboarding
collection 2008/2009

Year
2008

Country
Germany

Client
North Kiteboarding

Area
Sports equipment

Design
3deluxe

Project
Rotterdam City of Architecture

Country
The Netherlands

Area
City branding

Year
2007

Client
Rotterdam Marketing

Design
75B

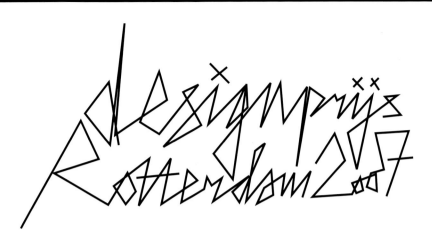

Project
Rotterdam Design
Prize 2007

Year
2007

Country
The Netherlands

Client
Stichting Designprijs
Rotterdam

Area
Design competition

Design
75B

uitnodiging

invitation

Het bestuur van de Stichting Designprijs Rotterdam en de
directeur van Museum Boijmans Van Beuningen nodigen
u uit voor de feestelijke opening van de tentoonstelling
'Designprijs Rotterdam 2007' op 25 mei om 17.00 uur in
Museum Boijmans Van Beuningen.

The committee of the Rotterdam Design Prize and the director of Museum Boijmans Van Beuningen invite you to
the festive opening of the exhibition 'Rotterdam Design
Prize 2007' on 25 May at 5 pm in Museum Boijmans
Van Beuningen.

vernieuwde editie
De inschrijving is gestart!

Designprijs Rotterdam toont de belang-
rijkste creatieve visies van de afgelopen
twee jaar. Vanaf 26 mei 2007 te zien in
Museum Boijmans Van Beuningen.

www.designprijs.nl

codarts

Project
Codarts, University for the Arts
Rotterdam Conservatoire
Rotterdam Dance Academy

Year
2005

Country
The Netherlands

Client
Codarts, University for the Arts

Area
Education

Design
75B

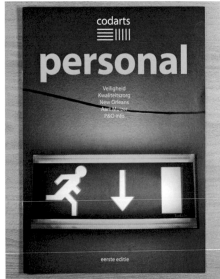

codarts

rotterdams conservatorium

rotterdamse dansacademie

codarts
hogeschool voor de kunsten

Codarts
Symphony
Orchestra

Hans Leenders, dirigent
Myrthe Helder, solist

Zondag 18 maart 2007
St. Franciscus Xaveriuskerk, Amersfoort
15.00 uur, € 10,-
Maandag 19 maart 2007
de Doelen, Rotterdam
20.15 uur, € 15,- / € 5,-
Dinsdag 20 maart 2007
De Singel, Antwerpen
20.00 uur, € 20,-

Strauss
Till Eulenspiegels lustige Streiche
Bruch
Schotse Fantasie voor viool en orkest
Tsjaikovski
Symfonie nr. 4

www.codarts.nl

rotterdams conservatorium

codarts magazine
hogeschool voor de kunsten

Milou Nuyens
Lilian Vieira
Sven Janssens
Daniel Costa
Celine Wadier
Chicago
Brasilectro

Juni / June 2005

rotterdams conservatorium   rotterdamse dansacademie

Project
Raw Sushi & Grill

Year
2005

Country
Sweden

Client
Raw Sushi & Grill

Area
Food outlet

Design
802

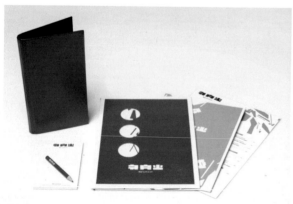

わたしの英会話

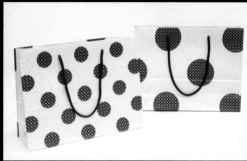

Project
b

Client
byZOO Corporation

Year
2006

Area
English school for women

Country
Japan

Design
A.C.O.

Project
Airplot

Year
2009

Country
UK

Client
Greenpeace

Area
Environmental
activist group

Design
Airside

Home
Blog
About Greenpeace
What we do
What you can do
Donate now
Media centre

Login | Register

Search

[ ] Go

GP Worldwide ▼

RSS | What is RSS?

Some rights reserved

Home > Blogs > tracy's blog

Join the plot to stop airport expansion

Posted by tracy on 12 January 2009.

TV impressionist Alistair McGowan has bought a piece of the Heathrow third runway site along with Emma Thompson, Zac Goldsmith and Greenpeace.

It started like most good ideas around here, with a conversation down at the pub. And there have been many times over the last few months when I wasn't sure we were going to pull it off, but we're now the proud owners of a small piece of land within the site of the proposed third runway at Heathrow.

We're expecting the government will announce that they're going ahead with expansion at Heathrow this week and we now need you to join us. Sign up now to get your own piece of the plot. It's not a financial thing, but you will be included as an owner on the legal deed of trust.

Sign up to get your piece of the plot and updates about the campaign to stop airport expansion.

Email*
[ ]

First name*
[ ]

Last name*
[ ]

Postcode
[ ]

Country

TAKE ACTION

We've bought a plot of land at the third runway site. Join us now to stop Heathrow expansion.

- Visit EfficienCity, a clean energy town
- Call for a green energy revolution
- Weblog: climate change

Recent entries

- What's Greenpeace doing at the Sundance Film Festival?
- The impacts of Amazon soya are shown on the map
- Hello from the new guy
- Season may have ended early for damaged whaling ship
- Sign the 'no third runway' petition on Number 10's website
- Flashmob Heathrow tomorrow
- Video: John Sauven tells it like it is on Heathrow
- Video: Emma gets mad while MP gets suspended over Heathrow
- Government gives

GREENPEACE UK   Donate   Take action   Sign up for e-updates   email   GO›

Home
Blog
About Greenpeace
What we do
▼ Climate change
  The problems
  The solutions
  What we are doing
  What you can do
  Videos
  Related links
▶ Forests
▶ Oceans
▶ Nuclear power
▶ Peace
▶ GM food
▶ Toxic chemicals
What you can do
Donate now

Home

The plot to stop airport expansion begins here

We've bought a piece of land slap bang in the middle of the proposed third runway site at Heathrow. We're not going to let the runway get built and we need your help. The government plans to go ahead with airport expansion across the country even though this means we'll have no hope of meeting our climate emission targets. Tackling climate change means stopping airport expansion and we need you to join the plot.

We've bought the land with Oscar winning actress Emma Thompson, comedian Alistair McGowan and prospective Tory parliamentary candidate Zac Goldsmith. Sign up now to get your own piece of the plot. It's not a financial thing, but you will be included as an owner on the legal deed of trust. **more »**

Find out more about Airplot »
Invite your friends to join »
Download an Airplot banner for your

Sign up to get your piece of the plot and updates about the campaign to stop airport expansion.

Email*
[ ]

First name*
[ ]

Last name*
[ ]

Postcode

TAKE ACTION

We've bought a plot of land at the third runway site. Join us now to stop Heathrow expansion.

- Visit EfficienCity, a clean energy town
- Call for a green energy revolution
- Weblog: climate change

Climate news

- Sign the 'no third

tierra chigüire

Project
Tierra Chigüire

Year
2000

Country
Venezuela

Client
Tierra Chigüire

Area
Educational and
ecological products

Design
Annella Armas

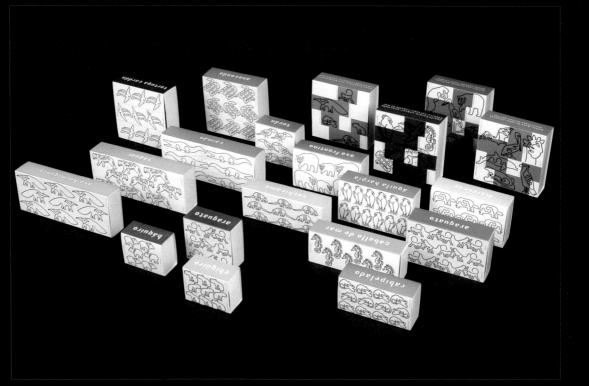

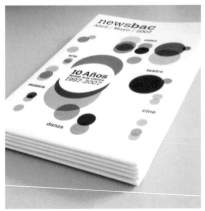

Project
10 Years
British Arts Centre
1997–2007

Year
2007

Country
Argentina

Client
British Arts Centre
Buenos Aires

Area
Cultural centre

Design
Bernardo + Celis

Project
Grupo FAAP

Client
Grupo FAAP

Year
2006

Area
Real state developer

Country
Argentina

Design
Bernardo+Celis

Project
Madonna
The Confessions Tour
CD, DVD, and book

Year
2006

Country
USA

Client
Madonna

Area
Music

Design
Giovanni Bianco
Studio 65

DSQUARED²

Project
Dsquared2 and
Dsquared2 Perfumes

Year
1998

Country
Italy

Client
Dsquared2

Area
Fashion

Design
Giovanni Bianco
Studio 65

Project
Tierra Atacama

Year
2006

Country
Chile

Client
Hotel Tierra Atacama

Area
Hotel and spa

Design
Blanco Diseño

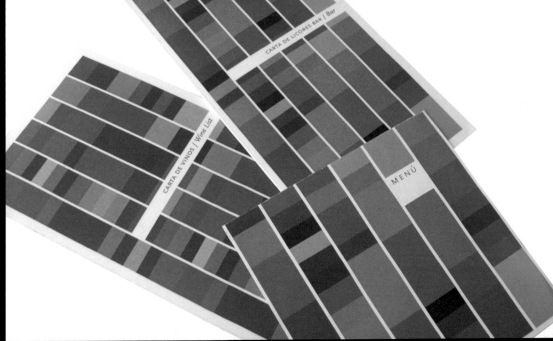

Project
Valbona

Year
2007

Country
Argentina

Client
Bodega Augusto Pulenta

Area
Winery

Design
Boldrini & Ficcardi

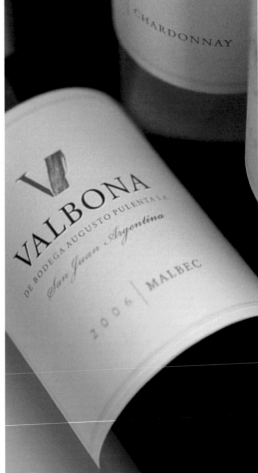

Project
Kura Selections

Country
USA

Area
Sake import/export

Year
2008

Client
Matt Hedges

Design
Boldrini & Ficcardi

Maginus

Project
Maginus

Client
Maginus

Year
2007

Area
Software developer

Country
UK

Design
Brahm

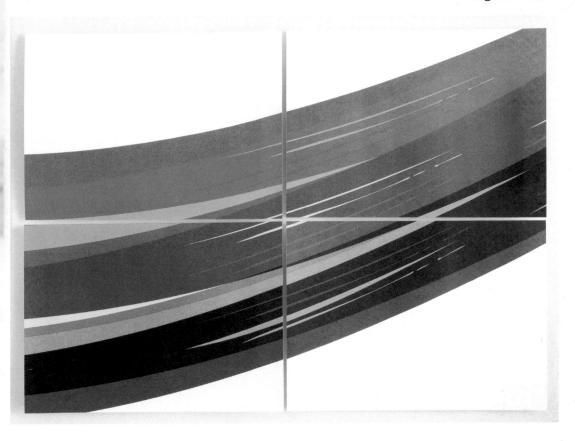

Project
The Cornish Mill + Bakehouse

Year
2007

Country
UK

Client
The Cornish Mill + Bakehouse

Area
Working farm, mill and bakery

Design
Buddy

TEA HOUSE . RESTAURANT . BAR

Project
Oojam

Client
Oojam Ltd

Year
2008

Area
Food outlet

Country
UK

Design
Buddy

Project
Design Museum Shop

Country
UK

Area
Design shop and online store

Year
2007

Client
Design Museum

Design
Build

Q Design Store

Project
Q Design Store

Client
Q Design Store

Year
2007

Area
Retailer

Country
Colombia

Design
Cuartopiso

Project
Popular Workshop

Year
2007

Country
UK

Client
Popular Workshop/
Toughlove Records

Area
Record label

Design
Chris Clarke

Project
La Ferme du Biereau

Year
2008

Country
Belgium

Client
La Ferme du Biereau

Area
Concert hall

Design
Coast

Cava/Concrete Design Communications Inc.

Project
Cava

Year
2007

Country
Canada

Client
Cava

Area
Restaurant

Design
Concrete Design
Communications Inc.

1560 YONGE STREET
TORONTO ONTARIO M4T 2S9

416 979 9918
CAVARESTAURANT.CA

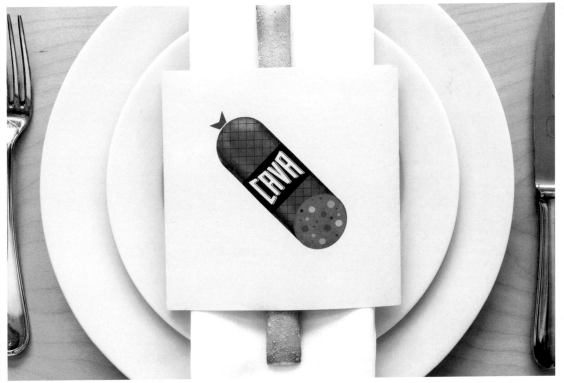

KEILHAUER

Keilhauer
1450 Birchmount Road
Toronto, Ontario
Canada M1P 2E3
www.keilhauer.com

Barry Moore
Vice President,
Finance & Administration

416 701 4101
877 701 4101
barry.moore@keilhauer.com

KEILHAUER

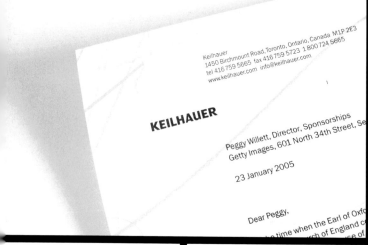

Keilhauer
1450 Birchmount Road, Toronto, Ontario, Canada, M1P 2E3
tel 416 759 5665 fax 416 759 5723 1 800 724 5665
www.keilhauer.com info@keilhauer.com

KEILHAUER

Peggy Willett, Director, Sponsorships
Getty Images, 601 North 34th Street, Se

23 January 2005

Dear Peggy,

Project
Keilhauer

Year
2005

Country
Canada

Client
Keilhauer Inc.

Area
Office seating manufacturer

Design
Concrete Design
Communications Inc.

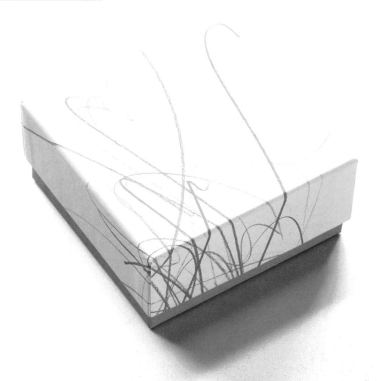

Masterfile

Project
Masterfile

Country
Canada

Area
Stock photo agency

Year
2004

Client
Masterfile

Design
Concrete Design
Communications Inc.

A PERIODIC FOLIO OF IMAGES, STORIES AND OTHER DIVERSIONS
MASTERFILE.COM / YOU AFRAID? / TALKING ABOUT LANGUAGE
CHARLIE FISH'S "DEATH BY SCRABBLE" / ARTIST ANITA CLARK

Masterfile

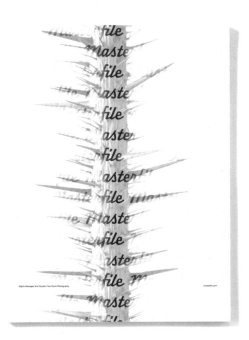

Perricone MD

Perricone MD

Year
2009

Country
Canada

Client
Perricone MD

Area
Skin care products

Design
Concrete Design
Communications Inc.

Perricone MD

SHOPPING BAG
18 items $4123.45

1-888-823-7873

Bestsellers   Prescriptions   Skin Care   Supplements   Patented Science   Dr. Perricone   Perricone Lifestyle

INTRODUCING:

High Potency Eye Lift
Lifts, Tones, Tightens, Brightens

*This instant lift for your eyes is the perfect complement
to your existing eye care regimen.*

Ships free in the US.

BUY NOW

Celebrate Our Launch: **Free Shipping** – US orders over $75, Canadian orders over $150, international orders over $250. **No promo code needed.**

RX Replenishment has many Rewards!
10% off all replenishment orders
and free shipping.
No promo code needed!

Learn More

RX Collections
Repair aging skin
with RX3.

Learn more

Spend $250:
Get free international
shipping, anywhere!

CAREERS
PERRICONE MD PROFESSIONALS
FIND A STORE

CONTACT US
FAQs
INTERNATIONAL

RETURN POLICY
TERMS OF USE
SITE MAP

RSS FEEDS & SUBSCRIPTIONS
REPLENISHMENT PROGRAM

©2008 PERRICONE MD

SIGN-UP FOR NEWSLETTERS
Sign-up

Perricone MD
NUTRICEUTICALS

Perricone
Super Antioxidant
Dietary Supplement
*Customized to provide superior
antioxidant protection.*
60 caplets

Perricone MD
NUTRICEUTICALS

Super Berry with Acai
Dietary Supplement Powder
Provides antioxidant protection.
30 packets. Net wt. 4.76 oz /135 g

Perricone MD
NUTRICEUTICALS

PEP – Polysaccharide Peptide Blend
Dietary Supplement Powder
Enhances health and vitality.
30 packets. Net wt. 5.3 oz / 150 g

Perricone MD
NUTRICEUTICALS

Omega 3
Dietary Supplement
Supports normal cardiovascular health.
270 softgels

Perricone MD
NUTRICEUTICALS

Health & Weight Management
Dietary Supplements
Promotes healthy weight maintenance.
Contains 90 packets. Each packet contains: 3 softgels, 4 capsules and 1 caplet.

Project
Pizza Nova

Year
2007

Country
Canada

Client
Pizza Nova

Area
Food outlet

Design
Concrete Design
Communications Inc.

Project
Sguig

Year
2006

Country
Canada

Client
Keilhauer Inc.

Area
Office seating manufacturer

Design
Concrete Design
Communications Inc.

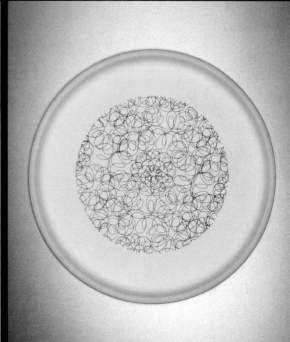

SUNEEVA

Project
Suneeva

Year
2007

Country
Canada

Client
Suneeva

Area
Film production company

Design
Concrete Design
Communications Inc.

MADE IN SUNEEVA   MADE IN SUNEEVA

MADE IN SUNEEVA   MADE IN SUNEEVA

MADE IN SUNEEVA   MADE IN SUNEEVA

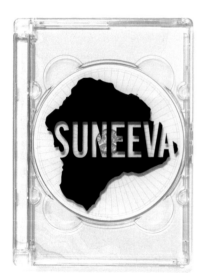

Project
Umbra

Client
Umbra

Year
1998

Area
Homeware design
and manufacture

Country
Canada

Design
Concrete Design
Communications Inc.

Project
Xococava

Year
2008

Country
Canada

Client
Xococava

Area
Chocolate and ice-cream shop

Design
Concrete Design
Communications Inc.

SPANISH	SPANISH	SPANISH	SPANISH	SPANISH
XO	XC	XA	XV	XX
CHORIZO	BLACK OLIVE	SEVILLE ORANGE	PEDRO XIMÉNEZ	SPANISH COFFEE
SAVORY	**SAVORY**	**SAVORY**	**SAVORY**	**SAVORY**
OX	OC	OA	OV	OO
ROSEMARY & HONEY	BLACK TRUMPET MUSHROOM	MALDON SALTED CARAMEL	OLIVE OIL	PRESERVED LEMON
WILD	**WILD**	**WILD**	**WILD**	**WILD**
CX	CO	CA	CV	CC
CEDAR DARK	WILD ROSE	MOUNTAIN CRANBERRY JELLY	BIRCH SYRUP	SUMAC JELLY
EXOTIC	**EXOTIC**	**EXOTIC**	**EXOTIC**	**EXOTIC**
AX	AO	AC	AV	AA
SZECHWAN PEPPERCORN	MASALA CHAI	CAJETA	FENNEL POLLEN	GRAPPA CHERRY
CLASSIC	**CLASSIC**	**CLASSIC**	**CLASSIC**	**CLASSIC**
VX	VO	VC	VA	VV
AMEDEI PLAIN	GIANDUJA	MARZIPAN	RASPBERRY	MINT

ICE CREAM

S $4.00 **M** $5.00 **L** $6.00

TAKE AWAY ICE CREAM (1/2 LITRE) $7.50 + TAX

MILKSHAKES

VANILLA XOCOLATA ESPRESSO $7.00

COFFEE / ESPRESSO

SINGLE $2.25	LATTE/ CAPPUCINO $3.50	EXTRA SHOT $1.00

HOT XOCOLATA

SHORT SHOT $3.75	ALLONGÉ $5.25

BEVERAGES

MINERAL WATER	$1.50
SPARKLING WATER, STILL	$1.75
ORANGINA	$1.75

PASTRIES

CHURROS	$0.50	CATALAN BISCOTTI	$1.00
XOCOLATA DIPPED HAZELNUT BISCOTTI	$1.75	CROISSANT	$2.00
XOCOLATA-WALNUT MACAROONS	$2.50	BROWNIE ROULADE	$2.50
PAIN AU XOCOLATA	$2.50	CHUCHOS	$2.70
XOCOLATE CHUNK COOKIES	$3.00	CAVA CORN	$3.00

CANDY

PEANUT CROQUANT AND JELLY DISKS	$1.50	XOCOLATA DISKS WITH PINE NUTS AND CURRANTS	$1.50
SPICED XOCOLATE SHORTBREAD	$1.50	MARSHMALLOWS	$3.00
SPONGE TOFFEE	$3.00	HANDMADE XOCOLATA BAR	$3.25

XOXOXOXOXOXOXOXOXOXOXOXOXOXOXOXOXOXOXOXOX

XOCO CAVA XOCO CAVA

Project
Clover New York

Year
2008

Country
The Netherlands

Client
Clover New York

Area
Kids clothing company

Design
DAY Creative
Business Partners

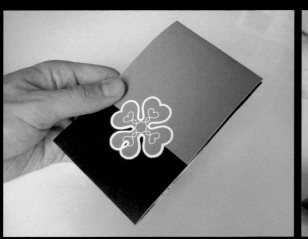
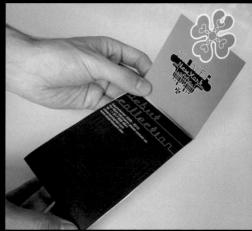

Project
Dream Amsterdam

Country
The Netherlands

Area
Foundation for art exhibitions

Year
2007

Client
Dream Amsterdam

Design
DAY Creative
Business Partners

Project
YouSee

Year
2008

Country
Denmark

Client
YouSee

Area
Telecommunications

Design
Designit

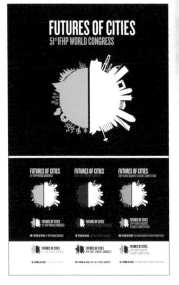

Project
IFHP

Year
2007

Country
Denmark

Client
International Federation
of Housing and Planning

Area
Sustainable Urban
Development

Design
Designit

Project
MAC de Niterói

Year
2006

Country
Brazil

Client
Museu de Arte
Contemporânea de Niterói

Area
Contemporary art museum

Design
Dupla Design

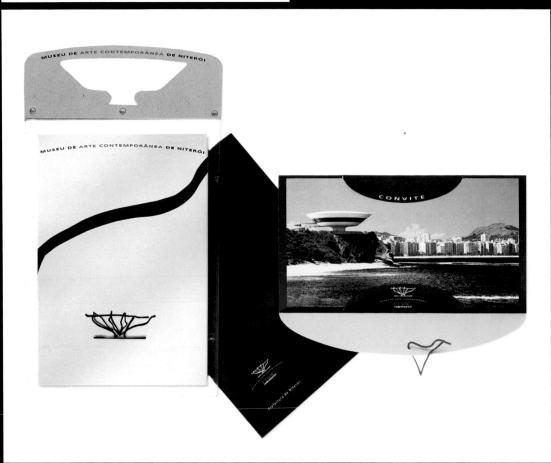

Project
Parapan Rio 2007

Client
Brazilian Olympic Committee

Year
2007

Area
Pan-American
Paralympic Games

Country
Brazil

Design
Dupla Design

Project
Mercado Infantil

Country
Brazil

Area
Children's boutique

Year
1998

Client
Mercado Infantil

Design
eg.design

Project
Caminho das Águas

Year
2007

Country
Brazil

Client
Fundação Roberto Marinho

Area
Education

Design
eg.design

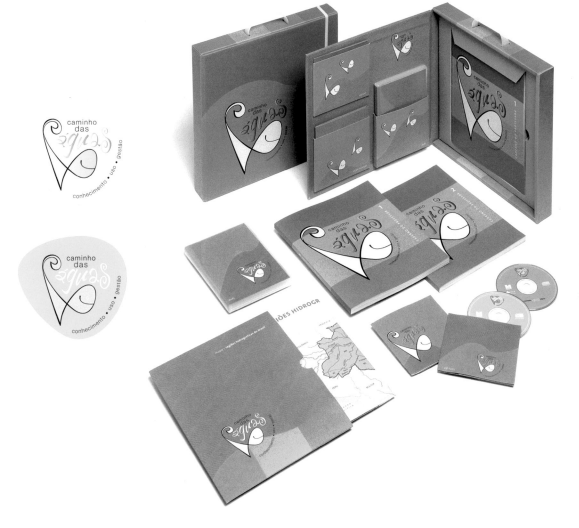

Project
Light

Year
1998

Country
Brazil

Client
Light S.A.

Area
Energy company

Design
eg.design

Project
Vitaminica

Year
2003

Country
Mexico

Client
Pisa Laboratories

Area
Pharmaceuticals supplier

Design
Paco Estrella

bedigital

Project
bedigital

Year
2007

Country
Spain

Client
bedigital

Area
Digital printing equipment

Design
espluga+associates

chic&basic®

Project
chic&basic

Year
2006

Country
Spain

Client
chic&basic

Area
Hotel

Design
espluga + associates

El Plan de
chic&basic
para Conquistar
el Mundo:

abrimos un hotel muy cool en barcelona. la gente nos adora y llena nuestras habitaciones de amor y esperanza. el buen rollo se extiende. primero por la ciudad. luego españa, europa, el mundo. todos nos volvemos + chic + basic. frescura, mestizaje y simplicidad se convierten en palabras importantes. la fusión sale de la cocina para vivir en el mundo real. después de esto, quién sabe... tal vez gobernar un país y redecorar los edificios gubernamentales con muebles ikea y colores vivos. o tal vez forrarnos vendiendo libros que cuenten esta maravillosa historia que comenzó la noche del 20 de julio, cuando el chic&basic born finalmente ha abierto sus puertas con una fiesta para amigos y gente que quede bien en la fiesta.

chic&basic Born abre sus puertas. y como eres amigo o quedarás bien en la fiesta, estás invitado inauguración. esta noche cambiará el mundo (al menos el nuestro). ven! será divertido.

20 julio de 2006
cena cocktail
21:00 a 1:00 h
chic&basic Born
Princesa, 50. 08003.
Barcelona.

amazing quality
shower gel
rarely found
as hotel amenity.

Gel de ducha nutrivo / Champú
Nourishing shower gel / Shampoo

chic&basic®

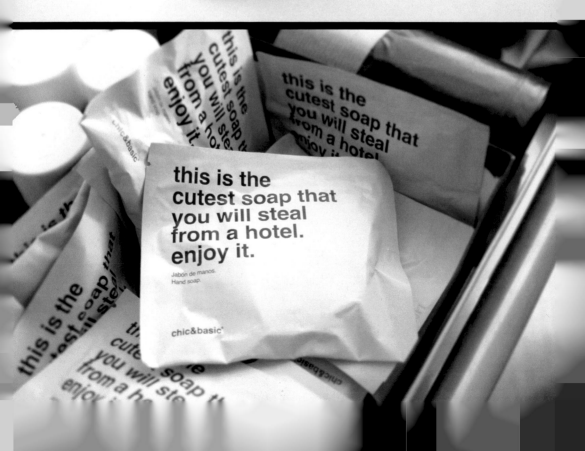

this is the
cutest soap that
you will steal
from a hotel.
enjoy it.

Jabón de manos.
Hand soap.

chic&basic®

BOUQUET

RESTAURANT

Project
Bouquet

Year
2007

Country
Spain

Client
Hesperia

Area
Restaurant

Design
espluga+associates

BOUQUET

BAR

COCKTAILS

Project
Foundation Ruimtevaart

Year
2007

Country
The Netherlands

Client
Foundation Ruimtevaart

Area
Artist initiative

Design
Faydherbe & De Vringer

MUSEON

Project
Museon

Client
Museon

Year
2008

Area
Natural history and science
museum for children

Country
The Netherlands

Design
Faydherbe & De Vringer

 MUSEON

De directie, medewerkers en de
leden van de Raad van Toezicht
wensen u **een voorspoedig en
gelukkig 2004** toe.

MUSEON

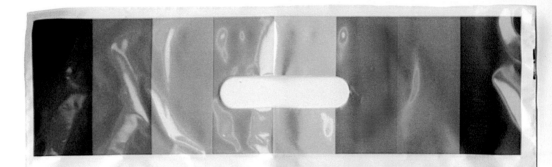

MUSEON

STADHOUDERSLAAN 37 DEN HAAG WWW.MUSEON.NL

100 JAAR
100 GEZICHTEN
100 KEUZES
UIT DE
COLLECTIE

26-03 T/M 31-10

met onder andere:

Ezgi Akin
Raymond Atteveld
Sjaak Bral
Bart Chabot
Chuck Deely
Wim Deetman
Floortje Dessing
Winston Gerschtanowitz
Thom Hoffman

Yvonne Keuls
Fajah Lourens
Ferry Mingelen
Fabian Paagman
Erica Terpstra
Paul van Vliet
John Williams
Jan Wolkers
Cesar Zuiderwijk

ONTWERP: WOUT DE VRINGER (FAXIMEDIE); DE VRINGER; DRUK: ALBANI DRUKKERS BV

MUSEON

STADHOUDERSLAAN 37 DEN HAAG WWW.MUSEON.NL

DE **HAAGSE**
HOGESCHOOL

THE **HAGUE**
UNIVERSITY
OF PROFESSIONAL EDUCATION

Project
The Hague University

Year
2007

Country
The Netherlands

Client
The Hague University
De Haagse Hogeschool

Area
Education

Design
Faydherbe & De Vringer

AGENDA
2007 2006

DE HAAGSE
HOGESCHOOL

D1QUE

Project
Dique 1

Country
Argentina

Area
Real estate

Year
2007

Client
GNV Group

Design
Fileni Fileni Design

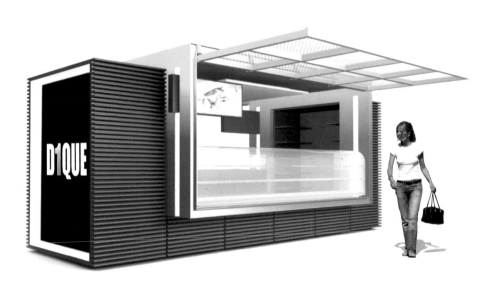

Project
300 Years of San Isidro

Year
2005

Country
Argentina

Client
Buenos Aires municipality

Area
City branding

Design
Fileni Fileni Design

Belinda Café & Deli

Project	**Client**
Belinda Café & Deli	Vizora
Year	**Area**
2008	Coffee shop
Country	**Design**
Argentina	Fileni Fileni Design

Project
An Outlet

Year
2008

Country
UK

Client
An Outlet

Area
Food outlet

Design
Four 23

An Outlet

An Outlet

CARVER'S WAREHOUSE
77 DALE STREET
MANCHESTER
M1 2HG
UK

COFFEE
TEA
CONVERSATION
WINE
BEER
SOUP
MUSIC
SALADS
GROCERIES

anoutlet.net
T +44 (0) 161 236 3043

An Outlet

AN INDEPENDENT LICENSED COFFEEHOUSE

Project
Plattform08

Year
2008

Country
Switzerland

Client
Kunstwollen Association

Area
Art exhibition

Design
Ronnie Fueglister
& Martin Stoecklin

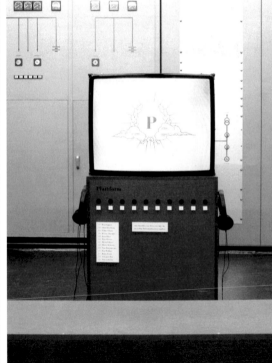

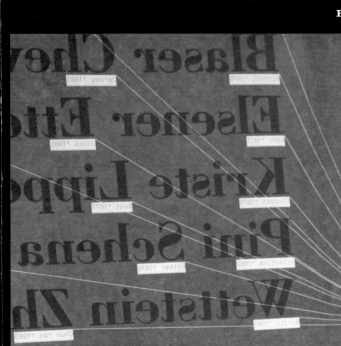

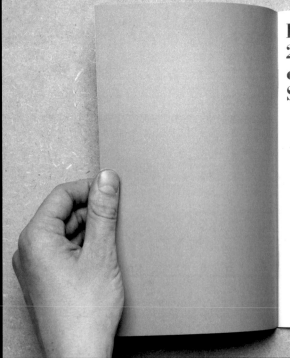

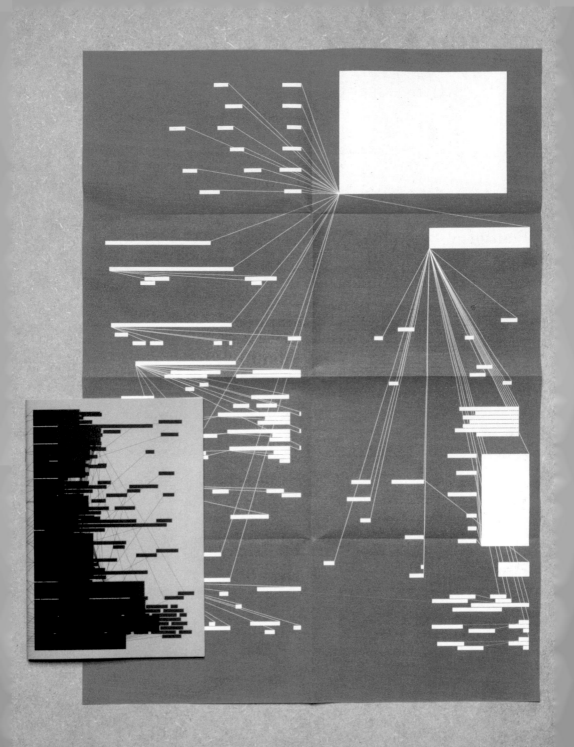

Project
bFelix

Country
France

Area
Furniture manufacturer

Year
2008

Client
bFelix

Design
gardens&co.

More Club Chairs,
www.bfelix.com

More Coffee & Side Table,
www.bfelix.com

bFelix
French

bFelix French brings the most authentic classic French designs available on the market. Sourcing natural materials and applying traditional techniques, our pieces are made to last and stay with you for a lifetime.

The fabrics used, mostly velvets, are made by Europe's finest weavers.

bFelix French布艺沙发系列为家具市场带来最经典的古典法式设计。全采用天然质配套传统制作技术令bFelix French终生受用。

以诚信为言的一系列家材全部来自欧洲最优秀的布料生产商。

bFelix - Main Office
Rm 1902, Hua Fu Commercial Bld,
111 Queen's Road West,
Central, Hong Kong

T +852 2987 1025
F +852 2987 2611

www.bfelix.com

---

bFelix
Deco

bFelix DECO brings a range of art deco inspired pieces with a modern twist. Sourcing natural materials and applying traditional techniques, our pieces are made to last and stay with you for a lifetime.

bFelix DECO chairs are upholstered with natural materials only, making DECO truly ECO.

充满艺术味道的 bFelix DECO 沙发系列极具时代气息，选用全天然物料，配合传统的制作手法，带来最经得起考验的产品。

透用天然材料的 bFelix DECO 沙发系列成为百分百的环保家具系列。

bFelix - Main Office
Rm 1902, Hua Fu Commercial Bld,
111 Queen's Road West,
Central, Hong Kong

T +852 2987 1025
F +852 2987 2611

www.bfelix.com

zoe

Project
Zoe

Year
2008

Country
Ecuador

Client
Zoe Restaurant Café Bar

Area
Food outlet

Design
Helou Design

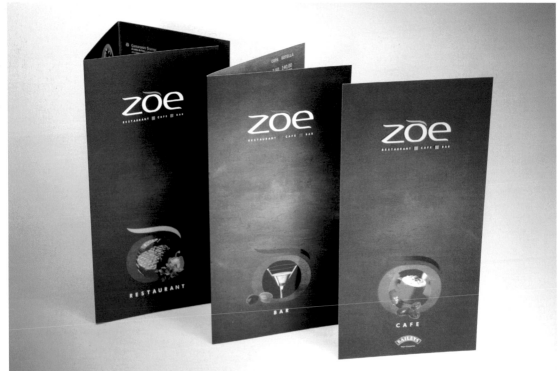

City Hopper
Airports Group

Project
City Hopper Airports Group

Year
2006

Country
UK

Client
City Hopper Airports Group

Area
Airports

Design
ICG

Blackpool
International Airport

Wolverhampton
Airport

Biella Milano / Torino
Nord Ovest Italia Airport

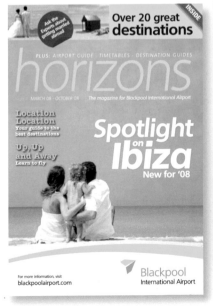

Project	**Client**
League Football Education	League Football Education
Year	**Area**
2007	Football apprenticeships
Country	**Design**
UK	ICG

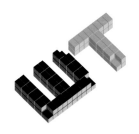 

Project
W.T. SeaAir

Year
2008

Country
UK

Client
W.T. SeaAir

Area
Logistics

Design
CG

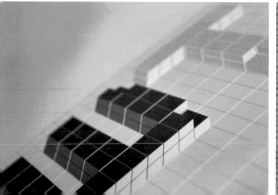

W.T. AirCargo

 W.T. Shipping

 W.T. Duty Management

 W.T. Couriers

 W.T. Logistics

 W.T. ERMEC

Project
Dolphin Square

Year
2006

Country
UK

Client
Mantilla Limited

Area
Property

Design
ico design

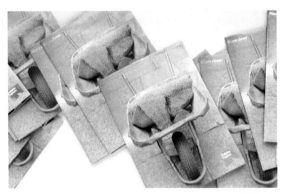

Project	Client
SNOG	SNOG
Year	**Area**
2008	Food outlet
Country	**Design**
UK	ico design

Project
Lácteos Piamonte

Country
Peru

Area
Dairy producer

Year
2008

Client
Lácteos Piamonte

Design
Ideo Comunicadores

DISFRUTA
DE LA MEJOR
CALIDAD

LÁCTEOS
PIAMONTE
DESDE 1900

Elaborado por Lácteos Piamonte S.A.C.
Av. Quilca 541 Callao. Producto Peruano
Pedidos 572-1876 • 572-242   4 9822 4909

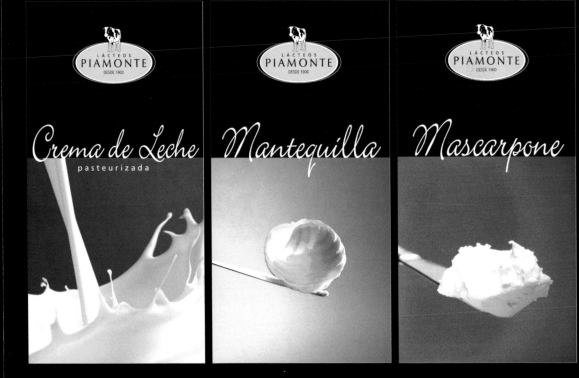

dog poo
bags

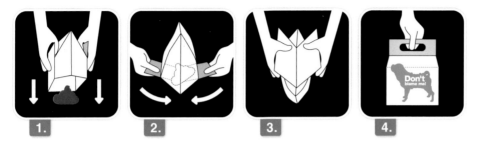

Project
dog poo bags

Year
2008

Country
Germany

Client
jungeschachtel

Area
Product and communication
design agency
promotional piece

Design
jungeschachtel

jungeschachtel

martyn bal

Project
Martyn Bal

Client
Martyn Bal

Year
2007

Area
Fashion label

Country
France

Design
Kasia Korczak

pantera

Project	**Client**	
pantera	pantera	
Year	**Area**	
2007	Accessories manufacturer	
Country	**Design**	
Mexico	La fe ciega studio	

pantera

SPRING
SUMMER COLLECTION
2008

SPRING / SUMMER 2008

pantera

SPRING SUMMER 2008

pantera

FE
M
N
NE

FEMININE

PRIVATE SALE

ALEJANDRA Y LAURA LAVIADA
TE INVITAN A CONOCER SU
NUEVA COLECCIÓN DE BOLSAS
Y CINTURONES PANTERA

28 Y 29 DE NOVIEMBRE
10:00 AM A 8:00 PM
SIERRA MADRE 525
LOMAS DE CHAPULTEPEC

pantera

AGGRE
SSIVELY
FEMIN
INE

pantera

PRIVATE SALE

28 Y 29 DE NOVIEMBRE
10:00 AM A 8:00 PM
SIERRA MADRE 525
LOMAS DE CHAPULTEPEC

ALEJANDRA Y LAURA LAVIADA
TE INVITAN A CONOCER SU
NUEVA COLECCIÓN DE BOLSAS
Y CINTURONES PANTERA

CINEMANÍA

Project
Cinemanía

Year
2008

Country
Mexico

Client
Editorial Televisa

Area
Film magazine

Design
La fe ciega studio

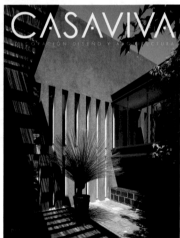

Project
Casaviva

Year
2007

Country
Mexico

Client
Editorial Televisa

Area
Architecture magazine

Design
La fe ciega studio

Project
F1-X

Year
2008

Country
Dubai, UAE

Client
F1-X Theme Park Dubai

Area
Theme park

Design
Landor Associates

1800Rpm
55Bpm
4DDARKRIDE
Admit One

Areyouready?

2.3km
3.10min
18000rpm
345kph

0
to
100

km/h

Pulse Rate
55bpm

1800rpm

in 2.0
seconds

10-13
January
2008

PADDOCK

PADDOCKRACERSHOW
Admit One

320KMH3G

MOTORHOME
TOUR THIS WEEK

SEEINSIDE

Be amazed at the detail in every part of the F1 car

TESTYOURSKILLS

The ultimate speed and driving experi...

EXCLUSIVE SIGNING
For the ride of your life?

Welcome to the F1-X Theme Park.

Are you ready for an adventure?

Project
Traidcraft

Year
2006

Country
UK

Client
Traidcraft

Area
Fair-trade label

Design
Landor Associates

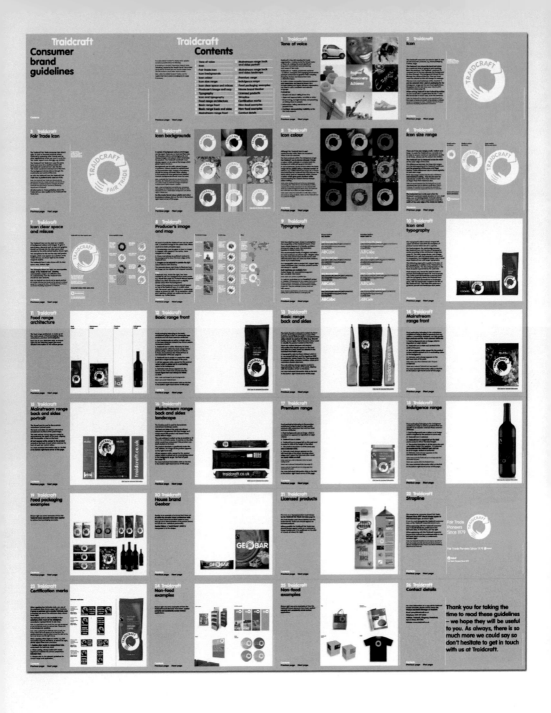

Fair Trade
Pioneers
Since 1979

**Transforming trade.
Transforming lives.**

On her small farm in India Siji Jose carefully grows fair trade tea. "I am proud that people are enjoying my tea. Now I am getting a good price – before it was very poor."

This product is
handmade using
traditional craft
techniques and
minor variations in
size and colour
may occur.

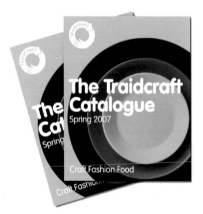

The Traidcraft
Catalogue
Spring 2007

Craft. Fashion. Food.

Project
Al Dente

Year
2008

Country
Mexico

Client
Al Dente

Area
Restaurant

Design
Henriquez Lara Estudio

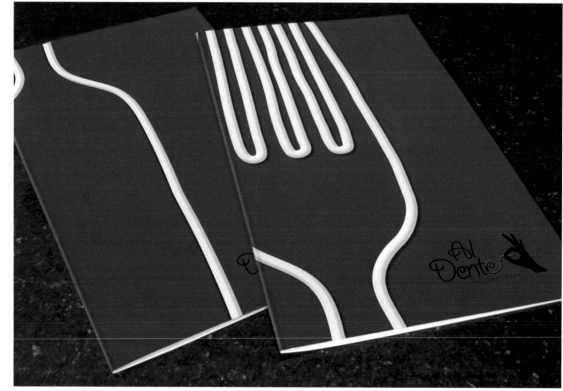

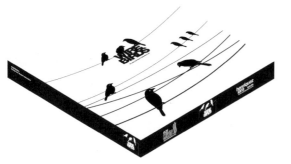

Project
Wire Birds

Year
2007

Country
Mexico

Client
Henriquez Lara Estudio

Area
Decorative and interior lighting

Design
Henriquez Lara Estudio

café color sabor

Project
BLVD

Year
2007

Country
Ecuador

Client
BLVD

Area
Food outlet

Design
Latinbrand

Project
Teatro Nacional Sucre

Year
2007

Country
Ecuador

Client
Teatro Nacional Sucre

Area
Theatre

Design
Latinbrand

Project
Combo Street Denim
ComboBELLA Street Denim

Year
2005

Country
Italy

Client
Combo Street Denim

Area
Fashion

Design
Longe Design

COMBO
strong work & devotion since '95

ComboBELLA
strong work & devotion for ladies

COMBO

ComboBELLA

Project
CH4

Country
Brazil

Area
Natural gas station

Year
2003

Client
CH4 Fuel Company

Design
M.Quatro Design

Gás natural
com pressão total

Posto Universidade

Gás Natural

Conveniência

24 Horas

Gás Natural

Gás natural com pressão total.

INTERVINOS

Project
Intervinos

Year
2008

Country
Brazil

Client
Intervinos Vinhos & Bistro

Area
Food outlet

Design
M.Quatro Design

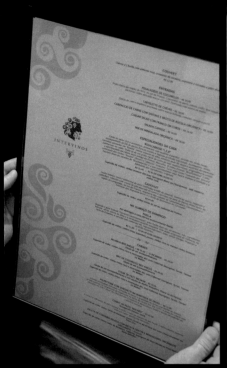

Project
Arquimia

Country
Argentina

Area
Architecture

Year
2008

Client
Arquimia Architecture

Design
martino

www.arquimiaweb.com.ar
SADONIO / SCHWANDER ARQUITECTURA

Project
Fixie – Betty Leeds series

Client
Fixie Inc.

Year
2007

Area
Bicycle manufacturer

Country
Germany

Design
MAGMA Brand Design

Project
A-Glow-Glow

Year
2008

Country
Hong Kong

Client
Microwave

Area
New media arts exhibition

Design
milkxhake

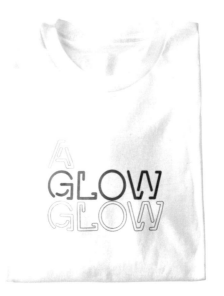

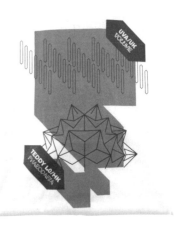

microwave

Project	**Client**
microwave	microwave
Year	**Area**
2006	New media arts organization
Country	**Design**
Hong Kong	milkxhake

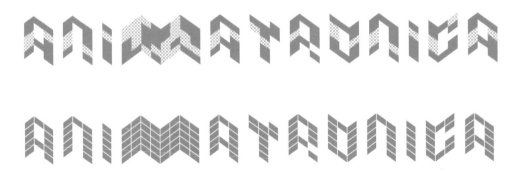

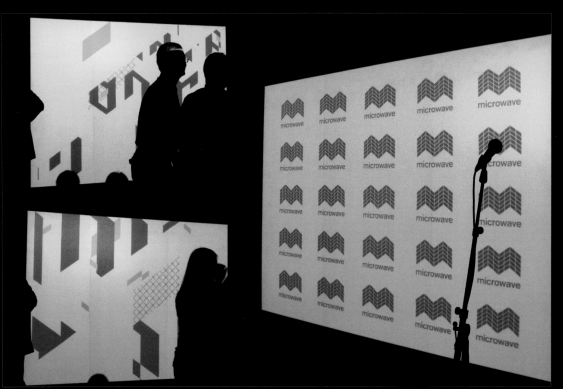

October
Contemporary
拾月當代

Project
October Contemporary

Client
October Contemporary

Year
2007

Area
Contemporary arts festival

Country
Hong Kong

Design
milkxhake

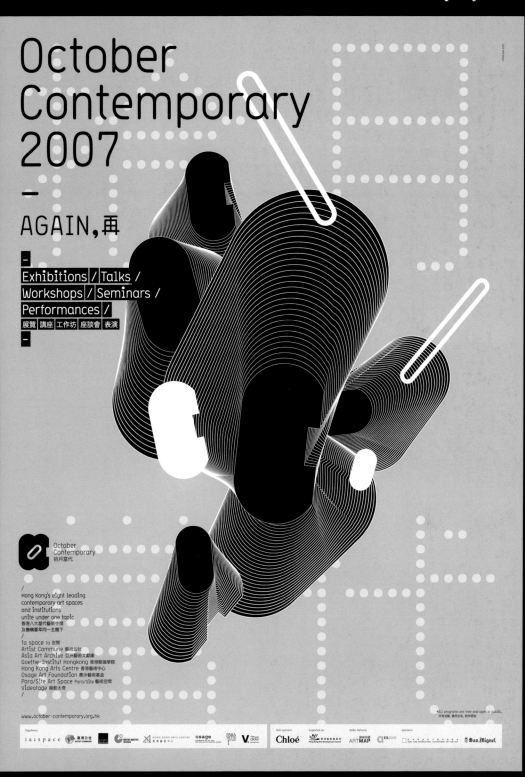

October Contemporary 2007

—

AGAIN, 再

—

Exhibitions / Talks /
Workshops / Seminars /
Performances /
展覽 講座 工作坊 座談會 表演
—

October
Contemporary
拾月當代

/
Hong Kong's eight leading
contemporary art spaces
and institutions
unite under one topic
香港八大當代藝術空間
及機構薈萃同一主題下
/
1a space 1a 空間
Artist Commune 藝術公社
Asia Art Archive 亞洲藝術文獻庫
Goethe-Institut Hongkong 香港歌德學院
Hong Kong Arts Centre 香港藝術中心
Osage Art Foundation 奧沙藝術基金
Para/Site Art Space Para/Site 藝術空間
Videotage 錄影太奇
/

www.october-contemporary.org.hk

*All programs are free and open to public.
所有活動，費用全免，對外開放

Organisers:
1a1space   ARTIST COMMUNE   asia art archive   Goethe-Institut   HONG KONG ARTS CENTRE   osage   PARA/SITE   V.

Main sponsors: Chloé
Supported by: Hong Kong Arts Development Council
Media Partners: ARTMAP   am post
Sponsors: San Miguel

Alter
Ego

V/M

Project
Alter Ego

Year
2007

Country
The Netherlands

Client
Alter Ego

Area
Recruitment consultant

Design
MrBowlegs
G2k Designers

PATAGONIA AGRESTE

Project	**Client**
Patagonia Agreste	Patagonia Agreste
Year	**Area**
2006	Food manufacturer
Country	**Design**
Argentina	NNSS Design

Project
Garrick

Client
Emanuel Zadua

Year
2006

Area
Personal entertainer

Country
Argentina

Design
NNSS Design

DAMIEN MERCIER
CHOCOLATIER BELGE

Project
Damien Mercier

Client
Damien Mercier

Year
2008

Area
Food retailer

Country
Chile

Design
Pozo Marcic Ensamble

Project
100% design

Client
100% design

Year
2007

Area
Architecture and design event

Country
UK

Design
Pentagram

Project
Bertazzoni

Client
Bertazzoni Spa

Year
2007

Area
Cooker manufacturer

Country
Italy

Design
Pentagram

Project
Dorchester Collection

Client
The Dorchester

Year
2006

Area
Hotel

Country
UK

Design
Pentagram

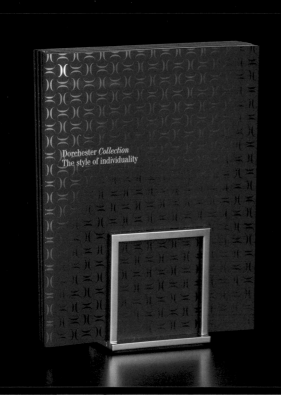

HEAL'S

Project
Heal's

Year
2005

Country
UK

Client
Heal's

Area
Homeware store

Design
Pentagram

LSA International
Vases and Glassware

HEAL'S

Panton Chair 1967
Herman Miller | Vitra

The Panton Chair is a furniture design classic. Verner Panton created it back in 1960, and with the assistance of Vitra developed a version ready for production in 1967. It was the first fully plastic chair made from a single section.

ilā

Project	**Client**
Ila	Ila
Year	**Area**
2007	Spa products
Country	**Design**
UK	Pentagram

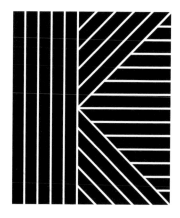

Project
Kanuhura

Year
2008

Country
UK

Client
Sun Resorts

Area
Resort

Design
Pentagram

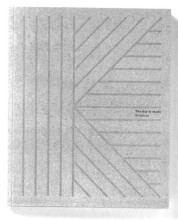

Kanuhura
Lhaviyani Atoll
Maldives

T +960 662 00 44
F +960 662 00 33
www.kanuhura.com

Kanuhura
Lhaviyani Atoll
Maldives

T +960 662 00 44
F +960 662 00 33
www.kanuhura.com

A member of
The Leading Small Hotels of the World

Alessandro Schenone
General Manager

Kanuhura Lhaviyani Atoll Maldives
T +960 662 00 44 **F** +960 662 00 33
Alessandro.Schenone@kanuhura.com.mv
www.kanuhura.com

A member of
The Leading Small Hotels of the World

A member of
The Leading Small Hotels of the World

Project
Launchpad

Year
2008

Country
UK

Client
The Science Museum

Area
Museum

Design
Pentagram

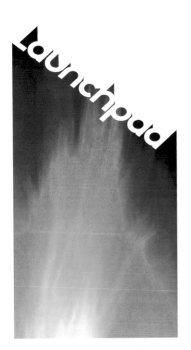

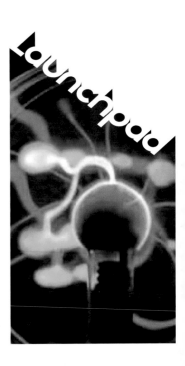

Project
Le Touessrok

Client
Sun Resorts

Year
2007

Area
Resort

Country
Mauritius

Design
Pentagram

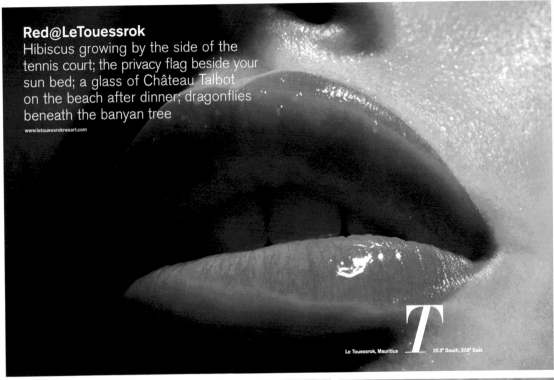

Red@LeTouessrok
Hibiscus growing by the side of the
tennis court; the privacy flag beside your
sun bed; a glass of Château Talbot
on the beach after dinner; dragonflies
beneath the banyan tree

www.letouessrokresort.com

Le Touessrok, Mauritius   20.3° South, 57.8° East

Colours of the day
Le Touessrok

Project
Matter

Year
2008

Country
UK

Client
Fabric

Area
Nightclub

Design
Pentagram

Project
Romeo

Client
Romeo Group

Year
2008

Area
Hotel

Country
Italy

Design
Pentagram

Romeo, Naples
Art of contrasts

Project
Skincare

Year
2005

Country
UK

Client
Sainsbury's

Area
Cosmetics

Design
Pentagram

Grant Thornton

Project
Grant Thornton

Year
2007

Country
UK

Client
Grant Thornton

Area
Financial and business advisor

Design
Pentagram

Project
The Criterion Collection

Client
The Criterion Collection

Year
2007

Area
Film distributor

Country
USA

Design
Pentagram

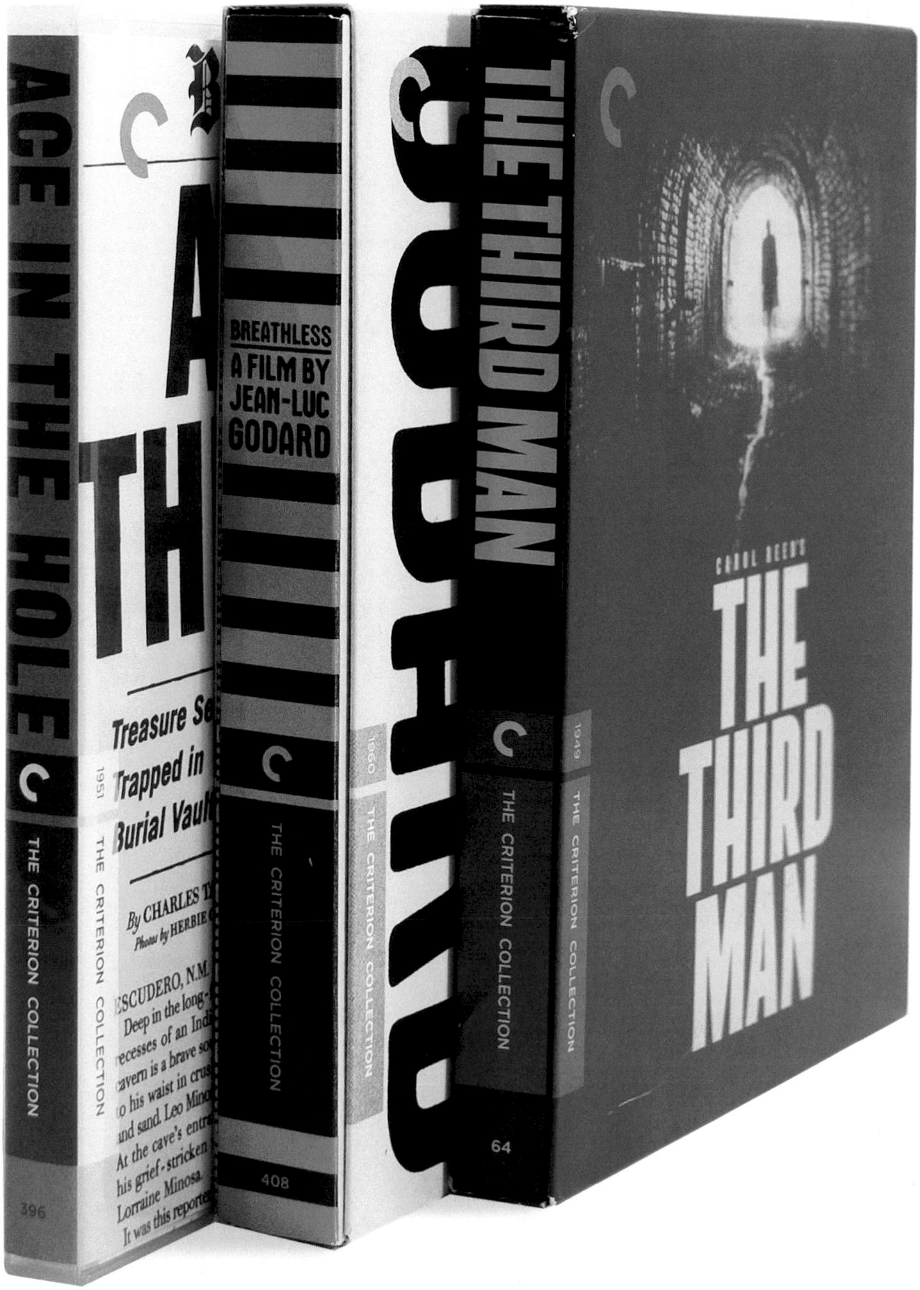

ACE IN THE HOLE

Treasure Se...
Trapped in...
Burial Vaul...

By CHARLES T...
Photos by HERBIE ...

...SCUDERO, N.M.
Deep in the long...
recesses of an Ind...
cavern is a brave so...
to his waist in crus...
and sand. Leo Mino...
At the cave's entr...
his grief-stricken...
Lorraine Minosa...
It was this reporte...

1951

THE CRITERION COLLECTION

396

BREATHLESS
A FILM BY
JEAN-LUC
GODARD

THE CRITERION COLLECTION

408

THE THIRD MAN

1960

THE CRITERION COLLECTION

CAROL REED'S
THE
THIRD
MAN

1949

THE CRITERION COLLECTION

64

Research
Centre
for Fashion
the Body
& Material
Cultures

Research
Centre
for Fashion
the Body
& Material
Cultures

Research
Centre
for Fashion
the Body
& Material
Cultures

Project
Research Centre for Fashion
the Body & Material Cultures

Year
2008

Country
UK

Client
University of the Arts London

Area
Cultural institution

Design
Praline

Project
1ERE HEURE

Year
2008

Country
France

Client
1ERE HEURE

Area
Production company

Design
Praline

Project
Buenos Aires
Festival de Diseño

Year
2006

Country
Argentina

Client
Buenos Aires
Festival de Diseño

Area
Creative conference

Design
RDYA

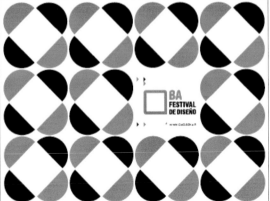

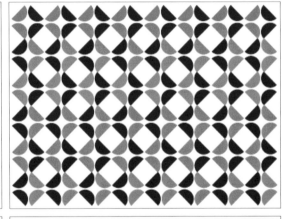

F:06

12 AL 29
DE OCTUBRE
2006

PRIMER FESTIVAL
DE DISEÑO DE BUENOS AIRES

→

INSTALACIONES
EXPOSICIONES
MUESTRAS
PRESENTACIONES

SEMINARIOS
CONFERENCIAS
WORKSHOPS
EVENTOS INTERDISCIPLINARIOS

+ INFO: WWW.CMD.GOV.AR

Sede principal

Predio El Dorrego
Zapiola y Dorrego

info@cmd.rg.ar

mD
CENTRO
METROPOLITANO
DE DISEÑO

BA
FESTIVAL
DE DISEÑO

gobBsAs

a+BA
actitudBsAs

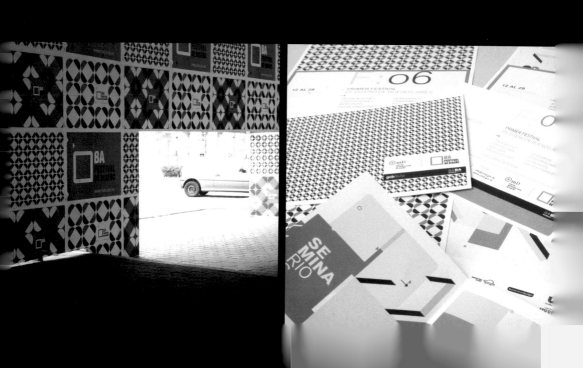

DIARIO DE
ARQUITECTURA

Project
Diario de Arquitectura

Client
Clarín

Year
2007

Area
Newspaper supplement

Country
Argentina

Design
RDYA

Project
Tinta Fresca

Client
Tinta Fresca

Year
2006

Area
Printing company

Country
Argentina

Design
RDYA

Project
Hacienda

Year
2006

Country
Denmark

Client
Hacienda

Area
Food outlet

Design
re-public

PRINT
DIVISION

Project
Printdivision

Year
2006

Country
Denmark

Client
Printdivision

Area
Printing company

Design
re-public

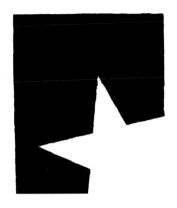

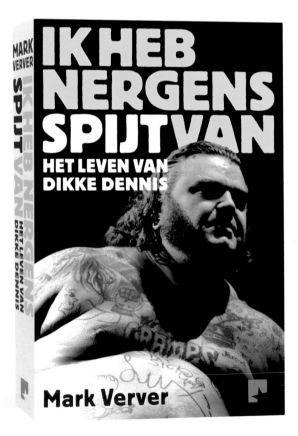

Project	**Client**
Donker en Donker	Donker en Donker
Year	**Area**
2008	Publishing house
Country	**Design**
The Netherlands	Riesenkind

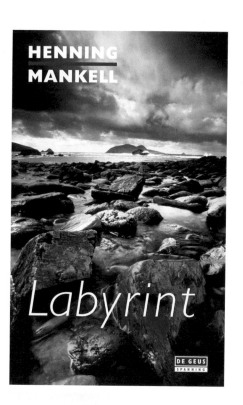

Project
Henning Mankell

Year
2008

Country
The Netherlands

Client
De Geus

Area
Publishing house

Design
Riesenkind in co-operation
with Robert Nix

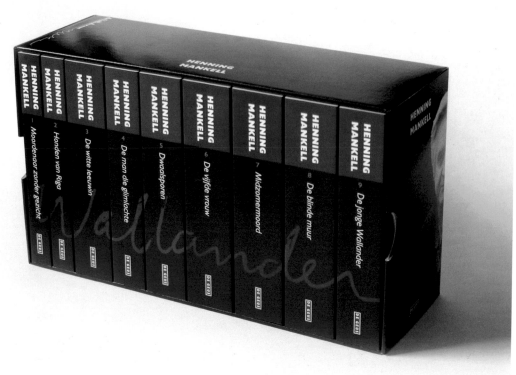

Project
Be Events

Year
2007

Country
UK

Client
Be Events

Area
Music event management

Design
Sawdust

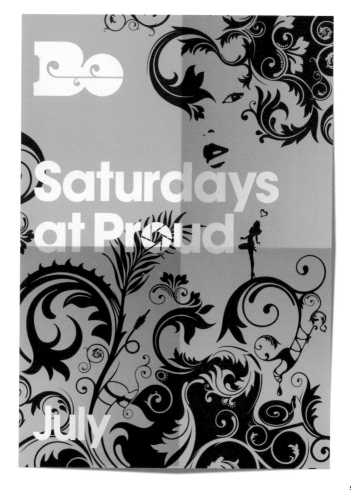

Luigi Bosca

Project
Luigi Bosca

Year
2007

Country
Argentina

Client
Bodegas Leoncio Arizu

Area
Wine label

Design
Shakespear Design

Project
Banco Galicia

Client
Banco Galicia

Year
2007

Area
Banking

Country
Argentina

Design
Shakespear Design

atomium

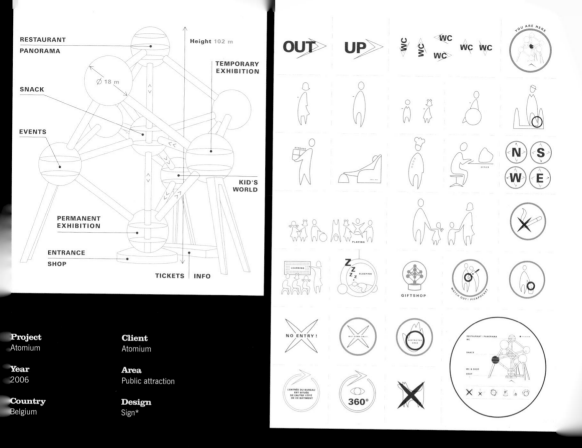

Project
Atomium

Year
2006

Country
Belgium

Client
Atomium

Area
Public attraction

Design
Sign*

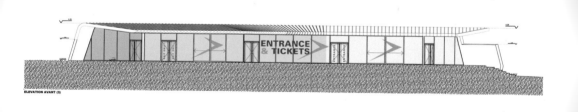

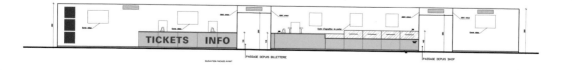

Project
Atomium 1958–2008

Year
2008

Country
Belgium

Client
Atomium

Area
Public attraction

Design
Sign*

Project
Tohi

Client
Dolfin

Year
2008

Area
Chocolate manufacturer

Country
Belgium

Design
Sign*

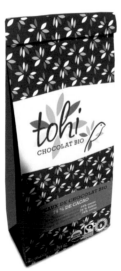

Project
Sugarcoat

Year
2008

Country
USA

Client
Sugarcoat Designer
Vinyl Decals

Area
Designer decals for cars

Design
Spunk Design Machine

sugarcoat

go stick it!

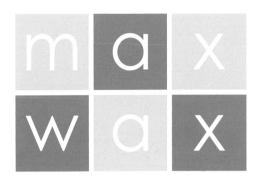

Project
Maxwax

Year
2003

Country
USA

Client
Maxwax

Area
Waxing salon

Design
Anke Stohlmann Design

Project
The Chipper

Year
2002

Country
USA

Client
The Chipper

Area
Food outlet

Design
Anke Stohlmann Design

Project
DWP
Digital Water Pavilion

Year
2008

Country
Spain

Client
Zaragoza municipality

Area
City offices

Design
studio FM milano

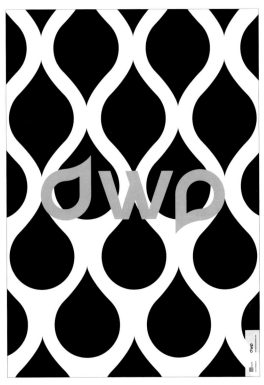

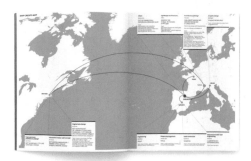

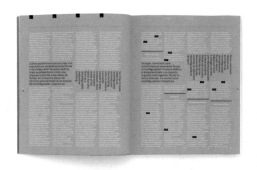

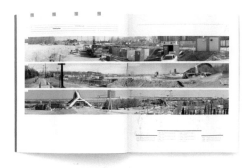

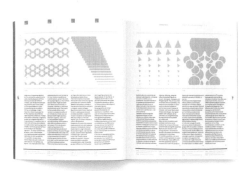

Riders

Project
Riders Magazine

Year
2007

Country
Italy

Client
Hachette Rusconi Publisher

Area
Publishing house

Design
studio FM milano

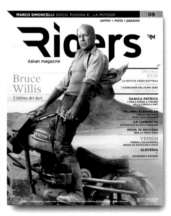

Beachdown
Festival

Project	**Country**	**Area**
Beachdown Festival	UK	Festival
Year	**Client**	**Design**
2008	Beachdown Festival	Studio Makgill

Finish:

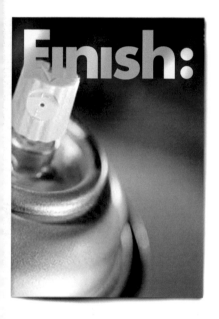

Project Finish	**Client** Finish Creative Ltd
Year 2008	**Area** Print and production company
Country UK	**Design** SViDesign

OPERO

Project
Opero

Client
Opero Bearings

Year
2006

Area
Manufacturer

Country
Sweden

Design
SViDesign

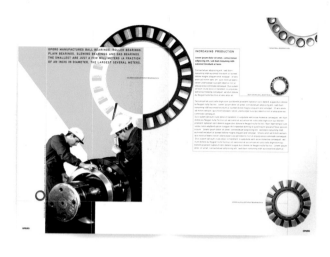

RED
PHOTOGRAPHIC

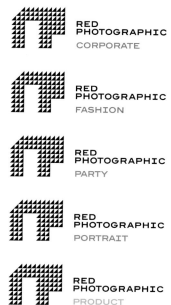

Project	**Country**	**Area**
Red Photographic	UK	Photographic services

Year	**Client**	**Design**
2007	Red Group Ltd	SViDesign

Project
Anita Schwartz Galeria de Arte

Country
Brazil

Area
Art gallery

Year
2008

Client
Anita Schwartz Galeria de Arte

Design
Felipe Taborda Design

Anita Schwartz convida para a abertura da exposição

NUINO
RAIMOS

MAR MOR TO

quarta | 18 março | 19h

anitaschwartz
GALERIA DE ARTE

19 março a 16 maio 2009
segunda a sexta | 10h às 20h
sábado | 11h às 17h

Rua José Roberto Macedo Soares 30 | Gávea
22470-100 Rio de Janeiro RJ | Brasil
+(55-21) 2540 6446 / 2274 3873
galeria@anitaschwartz.com.br
www.anitaschwartz.com.br

Project
Tamawa

Country
Belgium

Area
Jewellery

Year
2008

Client
Tamawa

Design
Tamawa

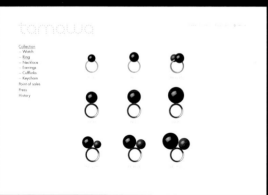

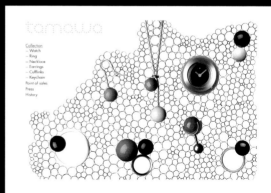

FEDERICO
AUBELE
PANAMERICANA

Project
Federico Aubele
Panamericana

Year
2007

Country
USA

Client
Federico Aubele
ESL Music

Area
Music

Design
Tea Time Studio

ĕcacahuetes co.

CINEMATOGRAPHIC OPERATIONS ®

Project
Cacahuetes Co.

Country
Spain

Area
Film production

Year
2006

Client
Cacahuetes Co.

Design
Tea Time Studio

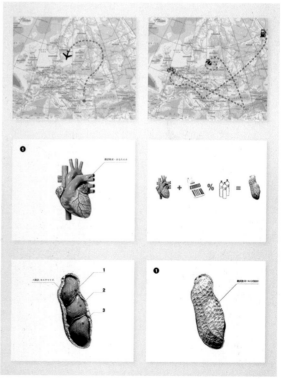

weetu ®

Project
Weetu

Year
2007

Country
USA

Client
Weetu

Area
Architecture and
design studio

Design
"NOP™ DESIGN

Project
britspotting 7

Country
Germany

Area
Film festival

Year
2006

Client
britspotting film festival

Design
upstruct berlin oslo

S V E R R E   S Æ T R E

O S L O

Project
Sverre Sætre

Year
2007

Country
Norway

Client
Sverre Sætre

Area
Food manufacturer

Design
upstruct berlin oslo

INDEX/ BRANDS

INDEX/ DESIGN

After finishing *Logo Design Volume 2*, I realised that there was a need for a book dedicated to the next logical step in brand awareness – the strategic application of logos and imagery created specifically for a company, person or institution. After the creation of a logo there are many factors that come together to create a brand identity. These are often as important as the logos themselves and can range from stationary to packaging, from vehicles to glasses, from store signage to billboards, just to mention a few examples.

To make this publication a really exciting reference for all of our readers working in design, marketing, communication and branding, we collaborated with top-notch experts who do this kind of thing everyday. As such you will notice that we have included case studies of projects from around the world and that despite this being a book on design about 40% of it is text.

We are honoured to have collaborated on these texts with the following group of dedicated individuals: John Rushworth and Peter Knapp for the introductions, Ric Peralta from ATTIK for Boost Mobile, 3deluxe for CocoonClub, Frederico Gelli from Tátil Design for *Eco Branding*, Michael Bierut from Pentagram for Museum of Arts and Design, Nevenka Marcic from Pozo Marcic Ensamble for Explora, Roman Bittner from Apfel Zet for Illustrative, Landor for Preem, Sol Sender for Obama '08 Election Campaign, Sasha Vidakovic from SViDesign for Release, Lars Hemming Jorgensen from Story Worldwide for The City of Sheffield, Harry Pearce from Pentagram for The Co-operative, Ricardo Drab from RDYA for Vaja, Gui Borchert for *Design is Branding*, Migrantas and Prof. Enrique Longinotti for the Migrantas initiative. I would like to extend my heartfelt thanks to all of them for their commitment to this project and for the high quality of their contributions.

I would also like to thank the design studios and branding agencies that submitted their incredible work, including those whose work was ultimately not included in the book. We look forward to working with all of you in the future!

On the editorial and production side of this project, I must once more extend a special thanks to my right-hand man, Daniel Siciliano Bretas. This book would not have been possible without him. As always, his hard work and commitment, particularly in the design and layout of the book, has made all the difference. Thank you also to Jutta Hendricks, whose unstinting attention to detail has contributed immensely to the quality of this book and to others I have edited. Finally, thank you to Stefan Klatte in production. It has been a pleasure to work with him once again. The team in Germany has done an amazing job!

I am sure that you will find many stories here to interest and inspire you.
Happy reading!

Julius Wiedemann

Imprint

© 2009 TASCHEN GmbH
Hohenzollernring 53, D-50672 Köln
www.taschen.com

To stay informed about upcoming TASCHEN titles, please
request our magazine at www.taschen.com/magazine or write to
TASCHEN, Hohenzollernring 53, D-50672 Cologne, Germany,
contact@taschen.com, Fax: +49-221-254919. We will be happy
to send you a free copy of our magazine which is filled with
information about all of our books.

Design & Layout
Daniel Siciliano Bretas
Cover Design
Gui Borchert, Daniel Siciliano Bretas and Andy Disl
Production
Stefan Klatte

Editor
Julius Wiedemann
Editorial Coordination
Daniel Siciliano Bretas and Jutta Hendricks

English Revision
Chris Allen
German Translation
Jürgen Dubau
French Translation
Valérie Lavoyer (Equipo de Edición)

Printed in China
ISBN: 978–3–8365–1584–9

TASCHEN is not responsible when web addresses cannot be reached,
if they are offline or can be viewed just with plug-ins.